ALL ABOUT AVENUE

The Definitive BRADFORD PARK AVENUE AFC

A complete record

Malcolm Hartley and Tim Clapham

Volume 21 in a series of club histories
A *SoccerData* Publication from Tony Brown

Published in Great Britain by Tony Brown,
4 Adrian Close, Beeston, Nottingham NG9 6FL.
Telephone 0115 973 6086. E-mail soccer@innotts.co.uk
First published 2004

Other volumes in this series are:

Rochdale
Northampton Town
Chesterfield
Portsmouth
Barnsley
Queen's Park Rangers
Scunthorpe United
Aldershot
Torquay United
Luton Town
Reading
Hartlepool United
Hull City
Barrow
Darlington
Newton Heath
Cardiff City
Bournemouth
West Ham United
Gillingham

Please write to the publisher for news of future volumes.

ISBN 1 899468 21 8

Printed by 4edge Limited, Hockley. www.4edge.co.uk

CONTENTS

AUTHORS' INTRODUCTION

When in 1987 we compiled *The Avenue, a pictorial history and record of Bradford Park Avenue AFC,* we were gratified by the acclaim it received. In the seventeen years since then, we have accumulated more material about the club, uncovered more facts, spoken to former players and come by additional photographs. With the help of Tony Brown we now offer a companion volume to our first book.

Information has been analysed, updated and presented in a fresh format for at-a-glance reference. But this is more than an assembly of facts and figures. While all the facts about the club and its records are between these pages, there are profiles and stories of more than forty players, some of whom look back on their days at the club.

Did you know Bobby Ham might have become a manager?
What's the most Bradford-born players fielded by the club?
Can you remember when the red, amber and black hoops were replaced with green and white?
Which Avenue player became the owner of a Rolls Royce?
What were the perils of playing with Scoular?
What's been happening between 1974 when the old club disbanded and 2004 when the new Avenue find themselves in the Conference North?

You will find the answers among the wealth of detail and stories set out from A to Z. We hope that all followers of Bradford football past and present will find our second book both informative and entertaining.

We are indebted to the Telegraph & Argus, Bradford, and editor Perry Austin-Clarke for permission to reproduce several photographs taken by T&A staff.

We wish to acknowledge the co-operation of Johnny Downie, the late Jock Buchanan, Bobby Ham, Gerry Lightowler, Barry Smith and Jeff Suddards.

Thanks also for various forms of help to Douglas Lamming, Tom Icke, Michael Braham, George Hudson and Paul Harrison.

Malcolm Hartley and Tim Clapham
Bradford, November 2004

THE AVENUE STORY IN "SIGHTBITES"

BRADFORD BULLS

Pardon? You thought this was a book on Bradford Park Avenue Football Club? Well, yes, it is. But it's odd how there's a rugby fringe to the story. The Avenue ground was originally the home of Bradford Rugby Club but the room-filling personality of Harry Briggs influenced members to switch to soccer in 1907.

Fast-forward to the 1990s and it was a chap with the same name as a former Avenue player – Peter Deakin – who was announcing that Bradford Northern RLFC would in future be known as the Bulls. Many thought it would never catch on. But it did. And it marked the start of great success at Odsal.

Here we are in 2004, the re-formed Avenue without a ground of their own. What's the best case scenario? A ground at the planned Odsal Village development, which would take them into the shadow of the rugby ground.

Park Avenue in days of yore

IN THE PREMIERSHIP

Jimmy Bauchop

We can't really claim Avenue were members of the Premiership - but only because the Premiership did not exist at the time when Bradford were numbered among the country's top 22 clubs. That was the three seasons 1914-15, 1919-20 and 1920-1.

In the first of these campaigns they hit their high water mark, finishing ninth. They earned more points than Manchester United, Chelsea, Liverpool, Newcastle United and Spurs. So no one can say Bradford did not have a proud history. Spurs and Manchester United were both BauCHOPPED for five at Avenue - Jimmy Bauchop, star top scorer with 28, collected three in both games.

ROLLER-COASTER

A big slide sucked the club from the First Division, through the Second and into the Third in 1922 as they became the first to be relegated in successive seasons. But they were not down-and-outs. Their first experience of the basement saw them runners-up (only one team promoted), then fifth for two years in a row, runners-up again in 1925-6, then third and then champions.

GOALS GALORE

No other team scored exactly 101 goals in each of three consecutive seasons as Avenue did in the heady days of the Twenties. The crowd hero was Ken McDonald, a centre-forward who accounted for 111 of those goals. The team had a run of 25 consecutive home wins.

NEAR MISSES

There was never any thought of "consolidation" in the Second Division. The aim was to reverse their successive relegations and catch the lift to the top section. At the beginning of April 1929 the leading positions were (1) Grimsby played 36 for 47 points; (2) Middlesbrough 37-46; (3) Notts County 37-44; (4) Southampton 37-42; (5) Stoke 37-41, on goal average from Avenue who also had 41 points but from only 36 games. If they won their match in hand they would be fourth, three points behind the second promotion place with five fixtures left. Avenue won three of them, including a lone goal victory over Grimsby, who finished second and went up, leaving Bradford third.

In New Year 1930 Bradford were in the top four and more or less stayed there the rest of the season. In 1933-4 promotion beckoned when by March 24 the second, third and fourth teams all had 40 points from 34 games, Bradford had 38 from 33. This was the team driven from wing-half by Jim McClelland and with ex-Bolton cup finalist Harold Blackmore hitting 27 goals. In the end they were only fifth. They never finished as high again.

BETTER THAN ENSA

Len Shackleton, whilst at Carlton High School

One of Avenue's best and most entertaining sides thrilled spectators during the 1939-45 war. Providing uncommon dexterity, cheek, the unexpected and many memorable moments of characteristic individuality was Len Shackleton, who went on to national fame via Newcastle, Sunderland and England. In a quieter but thoroughly competent vein there was Jimmy Stephen, a thoughtful full-back who, unlike so many of his contemporaries, did not kick the way he happened to be facing and did not kick opponents. He was rewarded with the captaincy of Scotland before he left Bradford for First Division champions Portsmouth.

MAKING MANAGERS

Several of the immediate post-war Second Division players went on to managerial posts, including Ron Greenwood who was England leader 1977-82 (see 'Managers' later in the book). There were exciting cup-ties, notably victory at Highbury over runaway First Division leaders Arsenal, at Newcastle and a three-game ding-dong with Manchester United watched by huge crowds.

THE DAYDREAM

Relegation back to the Third North in 1950 was a big disappointment but once Barrow had been blown away 5-0 in the opening match of the new season (four goals for future international Billy Elliott, one for recent international Jack Haines), the supporters' confidence came surging: "We'll be straight back. Bet on it." Modest Rochdale crossed the Pennines for the next match. A crowd of 19,058 turned up to enjoy the slaughter. Dale scored the only goal. Daydreams dented. At the season's end we were sixth.

NEVER AGAIN

In 1955-6 Bradford sank to a new low point in their history when they were forced to apply for re-election. They conceded 122 goals and I wrote to a friend: "Never again will a team wearing the famous red, amber and black shirts be allowed to disgrace themselves like this. In future they will wear green and white shirts!" (See 'Colours', next section).

THE LAST HURRAH

After two seasons of struggle the club were revitalised by the arrival of Walter Galbraith as boss and his valuable contacts in Scotland began to supply players who in 1960 made a promising bid for promotion. Rumbustious Jimmy Scoular stepped in to crack the whip from midfield and complete the drive from Division Four to Division Three.

SOME TALK OF HECTOR....

Avenue were unlucky to be relegated in 1963, first season of goal-hungry Kevin Hector. In 1965-6 he struck 44 goals in 46 league games but when he was sold to Derby County it was the beginning of the end for Bradford.

INTO THE DOLDRUMS

Despite the gallant efforts of the Supporters' Club under George Hudson, financial alarm bells were jangling and after three successive re-election applications had been accepted the fourth wasn't and Bradford gave way to Cambridge United in 1970.

In and among these journeys up and down the League were plenty of highlights, like George Henson's six goals in a match, cup surprises, clashes with foreign teams, odd incidents and much more, which is set out in the next part of this book.

PHOENIX

Bradford dropped into non-League circles and then folded. An indoor cricket school was built on the old pitch. But the publication in 1987 of our hardback Avenue pictorial history and record fired the enthusiasm of a group of devotees to reinvent the club. Despite many difficulties "new" Avenue have since made admirable progress through a number of leagues until they are now in the new Conference North.

Malcolm Hartley

THE A-Z OF BRADFORD PARK AVENUE AFC

ABANDONED MATCHES

On February 13 1915, Bradford held a 3-0 lead when the First Division match at Park Avenue with Everton was abandoned after 35 minutes. The referee called a halt when several Everton players, who had faced a blinding snowstorm, went down with exhaustion. Everton won the replayed match 2-1.

Bradford played a Second Division match at Notts County's Meadow Lane ground on March 10 1934, which began in spring-like weather, but was held up after ten minutes by a violent storm and torrential rain. After a halt of ten minutes the game was restarted, but after it had gone on for seven minutes, play was curtailed because the playing area was under water.

On December 12 1941 the home game with Huddersfield Town was abandoned and replayed on Christmas Day afternoon following a home meeting with York City that morning!

The shortest match in which Bradford played lasted for just eight minutes. The Division Three clash with Southend United at Park Avenue on December 16 1961 was abandoned due to thick fog.

Tragedy struck the West Riding County Cup semi-final match between Farsley Celtic and Bradford on March 6 1996 when the referee, Ian Billingham, collapsed. Due to the serious illness the match was abandoned. Sadly, the official died in hospital later that evening.

ADVERSE WEATHER

Like most other clubs Bradford were hit hard by the severe weather in early 1963. After completing a match on January 4, the team ended their long spell of inactivity when the away meeting with Bristol City beat the weather on February 16.

AGE

Albert Geldard became the youngest debutant in the Football League when he turned out for Bradford against Millwall in an away match on September 16 1929, aged 15 years 158 days. By strange coincidence Wrexham's Ken Roberts, who later became assistant manager at Park Avenue, made his debut against Bradford on September 1 1951 in a Third Division (North) match at the age of 15 years 158 days! Roberts, a ground staff boy at the time, came with the Wrexham team to Park Avenue which arrived late and had to change in the coach on the way after they had waited in vain for inside-right Wootton in Manchester.

Barnsley-born Sid Storey was the oldest player to make his Football League debut for Bradford. He was just two months away from his 40th birthday when turning out at Chester on October 3 1959.

On October 3 1942 Bradford manager David Steele turned out at centre-forward against Sheffield Wednesday at Park Avenue at the age of 48.

When Albert Geldard (15) and Walter Millership (19) played together as Bradford's right wing against Millwall on September 16 1929 they created a League record, their combined ages being only 34 years.

Bradford manager Trevor Storton rolled back the years and pulled on his boots again to help his club through an injury crisis at Workington on November 1 1997. And his 23-minute appearance in the UniBond League First Division match made the 47-year-old former Tranmere, Liverpool and Chester defender the oldest player to turn out for the club in peace-time.

AIR TRAVEL

Bradford's first domestic flight to an away match was on September 30 1961 to Torquay United.

ALDERSHOT

Aldershot's Recreation Ground was the venue for Bradford's last match in the Football League. On April 20 1970 the team lost 4-2 and so extended their run of away games without a win to 56 in the Fourth Division.

JOHN ALLAN

Apart from the prolific Ken McDonald, John Allan had the best ratio of goals to games for Bradford during his short stay from 1959 to 1961. Born at Falkirk, he first showed promise with Aberdeen before joining Third Lanark and ending top scorer with 30 as they gained promotion to the First Division in 1956-7. He led their list again with 26 from 33 outings the following season before Wally Galbraith brought him south of the border. He scored Avenue's only goal in a 1-1 draw against Watford on his debut in February 1959 and was the club's crack marksman in the next campaign with 26 in 33 appearances. This sharp goalscorer had netted 17 times in 27 matches of the 1960-1 promotion season and was joint leading scorer with Buchanan when on February 24 manager Scoular signed Tommy Spratt from Manchester United and Allan was the man who had to make way. His Avenue total was 57 in 79 senior appearances when he left for Halifax Town and obscurity in March 1961. Allan came from Scotland from a club that became defunct (Third Lanark) to join Bradford (who became defunct) and then Halifax Town (who lost League status).

Charlie Currie and Charlie Heffron left Ireland and Belfast Celtic (defunct) to join Bradford. George Beattie left Wales and Newport County (who became defunct) to sign for Bradford. Also, a number of players came from Accrington Stanley, another English club that went to the wall besides Avenue.

ALL-ENGLISH

The Bradford team beaten by Nottingham Forest at Park Avenue on February 1 1936 was the only one in the Football League played by the club to December 10 1949 that did not contain a Scot, the all-English eleven being Tewkesbury; Ward, Lloyd; Strange, Danskin, Harrison; Doran, Meek, Nolan, Wesley, Lewis.

The club almost fielded an all-Scottish team on February 24 1912, when nine Scots were in the F.A. Cup side against Bradford City. City were the Cup holders and won 1-0 with a goal from O'Rourke.

ALL-TICKET

The first all-ticket match at Park Avenue was for a third round F.A. Cup tie against Manchester United on January 11 1947. The club sold 26,900 tickets, but the crowd was 24,370 (receipts £2,935). This was also the first all-ticket match in Bradford football history.

AMATEURS

Jack Gibbons

The most famous amateur to play for the club was A.H. ('Jack') Gibbons. A pre-war amateur international with Spurs, he also played for the full England side against Wales in 1942. Bradford secured his amateur registration in 1945 after he had appeared as a guest player during wartime. He turned professional in May 1946 and was captain the following year before departing for Brentford as player-manager in February 1949. Midway through 1940-1 he turned out for Spurs against Orient four times in 22 days and scored a hat-trick in all four games!

Other notable amateurs with the club were: W.G. McConnell, an Irish amateur full-back, who was part of the squad which won promotion to the First Division in 1914; Albert Geldard, who had made several first team appearances before signing professional forms on his 17th birthday in April 1931; and Harry McIlvenny, who joined his home club in 1946 and featured in the historic F.A. Cup ties with Newcastle United and Manchester United in 1949. He unfortunately broke a leg in the home replay with Manchester United. McIlvenny was in England's 1948 Olympic Games team which came fourth. His father Jimmy played for Bradford City.

Harry McIlvenny

ANNUAL TRIP

The first annual trip made by the club's supporters as an association organisation was to Queens Park Rangers for a Southern League match on February 22 1908.

APPEARANCES

The top ten players with the most Football League appearances are:

Charlie Atkinson	339	1956-7 to 1963-4
Harold Taylor	334	1921-2 to 1931-2
Tommy Lloyd	328	1927-8 to 1936-7
Jeff Suddards	327	1949-50 to 1958-9
David Howie	306	1911-12 to 1924-5
Don McCalman	297	1959-60 to 1965-6
Tommy (Chick) Farr	294	1934-5 to 1949-50
Bill Deplidge	274	1946-7 to 1955-6
Ernald Scattergood	268	1914-15 to 1924-5
John Hardie	265	1963-4 to 1969-70

It is worth noting that with the addition of wartime and F.A. Cup matches, Farr made 542 appearances and Bob Danskin reached 506.

Most F.A Cup appearances: Taylor 25 (21 in succession), Howie 23, Lloyd 22, Jack Scott, Sam Blackham and Farr 21, Scattergood 20.

Consecutive League appearances: Kevin Hector made 166 consecutive League appearances for Bradford from December 15 1962 to September 6 1966. The record-breaking sequence was ended when he was transferred to Derby County. Hector's club record beat the previous best by eleven matches, both Jack Scott (April 6 1912 to April 6 1920) and Don McCalman (February 27 1960 to August 26 1963) having made 155 consecutive appearances.

Jack Scott

Ever-presents: Five players share the distinction of having played three successive full seasons of League fixtures: Jack Scott, Jack Clough, Tommy Farr, Don McCalman and Kevin Hector. The most ever-present in a single season of League football is four in 1925-6 and 1961-2.

Odds and ends: Jeff Suddards (1950-9) made 343 Football League and F.A. Cup appearances without scoring a goal. This was a record for an outfield player.

The record for the shortest first-team career belongs to Garry Halliday who was limited to 76 minutes as substitute against Swansea Town in March 1969.

On December 16 1950, Alec Horsfield scored for Bradford in eight minutes at Barrow when making his Football League debut four days after being secured from Arsenal, with whom he had had no first team chance in over four years.

Bradford captain Wayne Benn (1995-2004) broke Charlie Atkinson's peace-time record for the most appearances when he turned out for the 364th time on December 28 2002 in a League match at Stalybridge Celtic. His 406th and final appearance took place in an F.A. Trophy tie at Hucknall Town on January 10 2004.

CHARLIE ATKINSON

Charlie Atkinson was Bradford's "Mr Consistency" which is reflected in his record 339 League selections for the club between 1956 and 1964.

Basically a right-sided midfielder, he was versatile enough to fill seven positions as occasion dictated. When the Avenue board decided not to retain him at the end of 1963-4 there was a public outcry. "He is the most consistently reliable player on the staff and he has always given of his absolute best" wrote one fan. "In his role of captain he has always marshalled both defence and attack with great effect and enthusiasm." Another said: "In positional play, distribution, ball control, verve and stamina, Atkinson was outstanding to a point when, on many occasions this last season. he shamed other first-teamers"

It transpired that Atkinson had been working in a betting shop in Bradford, apparently unaware that this was contrary to F.A. regulations. He was signed by Bradford City and made 16 appearances in five positions in 1964-5 before leaving the professional game and starting ten years in local minor soccer while becoming a bookmaker.

Charlie was a Hull man who was signed from Hull City after Avenue's disastrous 1955-6 season when they conceded 122 goals and had to ask for re-election for the first time. Full-back Arthur Perry, a Tigers reserve, came with him and both straight away became regulars.

There was no more re-election while Charlie was at Avenue and he missed only one match when the team won promotion in 1960-1. His son Paul played for Oldham Athletic and Watford, for whom he stepped on to the Wembley turf as substitute in the 1984 F.A. Cup final against Everton.

Charlie is President of the "new" Avenue club.

ATTENDANCES

Bradford set a unique record of attracting their biggest attendance during wartime football. On April 8 1944, a crowd of 32,810 turned up to watch a League North Cup quarter-final tie between Bradford and Blackpool.

Six attendances at Park Avenue topped 30,000:
32,810 v Blackpool (League North Cup) April 8 1944
32,429 v Leeds United (Second Division) Dec 25 1931
32,184 v Leeds United (Second Division) Jan 17 1914
31,347 v Stoke City (F.A. Cup, 4th round) Jan 22 1938
30,362 v Bradford City (Second Division) Sep 14 1929
30,303 v Huddersfield Town (F.A. Cup, 2nd round) January 29 1921

The highest aggregate attendance was set up in 1928-9 when 372,519 passed through the Park Avenue turnstiles (average 17,739). When Bradford won the Third North championship in 1927-8 they enjoyed the highest average attendance for that section (14,172) for the fourth successive season. The highest post-war average was 17,687 in 1947-8. The lowest aggregate attendance was 72,156 (3,137) in 1969-70. Bradford's lowest-ever Football League attendance was 1,572 for the visit of Port Vale in 1968-9.

In non-League football, Bradford's highest attendance stands at 18,000 (receipts £428) against Plymouth Argyle in 1907-8 for a Southern League match.

On January 29 1949, Bradford played in front of a crowd of 82,771 (£7,070) at Maine Road. The attendance for the F.A. Cup match with Manchester United was the biggest before which any Bradford association team ever played. It also remains Manchester United's highest home attendance in any competition.

The biggest League "gate" in their history was 54,905 at White Hart Lane on October 1 1949 when Spurs won 5-0.

BENEFITS

Striker Tommy Little took the first benefit awarded to a Bradford player in a game against Glossop North End at Park Avenue on February 7 1914. That season the club won promotion to the First Division and Tommy received a cheque for £470 at the end of term celebrations held at the Midland Hotel.

On April 25 1927 a joint benefit match was staged for Gerald Fell, Harold Taylor and George McLean. Scottish club Clyde provided the opposition. The following April West Ham United came to Park Avenue for a benefit match for the late George Turnbull, who had been killed in a motor cycle accident.

Popular clubmen Tommy Lloyd and Ralph Ward both earned benefits in the 1930s. Lloyd took his in a Second Division match on February 11 1933 against Charlton, while Ward's was a friendly between Bradford and Heart of Midlothian on April 24,1935.

In February 1948 Bradford launched a public testimonial fund for stalwart defender Bob Danskin who had been with the club since arriving from Leeds United in 1932. The target set was 20,000 shillings (£1,000).

In March 1951, Bill Deplidge was awarded a maximum benefit of £750. Les Horsman and Billy Elliott had had a similar grant.

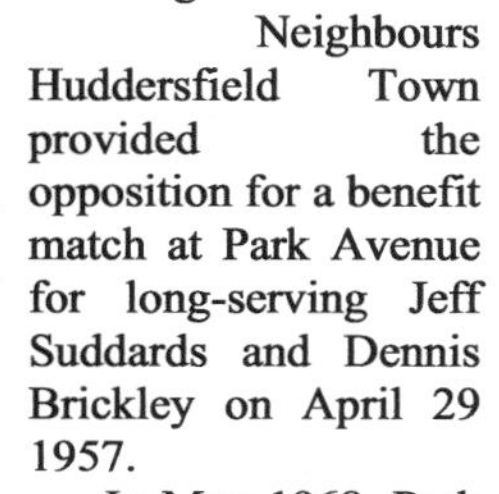
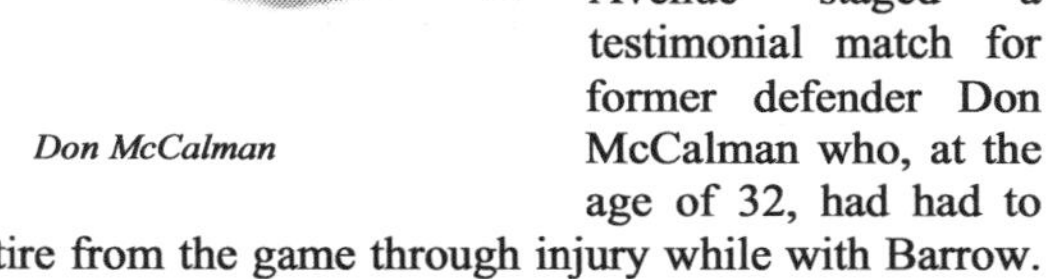

Don McCalman

Neighbours Huddersfield Town provided the opposition for a benefit match at Park Avenue for long-serving Jeff Suddards and Dennis Brickley on April 29 1957.

In May 1968, Park Avenue staged a testimonial match for former defender Don McCalman who, at the age of 32, had had to retire from the game through injury while with Barrow. He was to return to Park Avenue a few years later as manager.

BLACK SEPTEMBER

During the month of September 1955, Bradford played seven League matches, losing five and drawing two. In the process only two goals were scored but 23 were conceded. The defeat by 7-0 at Accrington Stanley was their joint-heaviest in the League, equalling that at Barnsley in 1911.

BOLTON WANDERERS

Bolton Wanderers were the first Football League club to be seen in Bradford. On September 24 1895, a Bradford amateur team were defeated 7-2 by the Wanderers in an exhibition match at Park Avenue watched by a crowd of 5,000.

BRADFORD CHAMPIONSHIP

This was a competition involving Bradford City and Bradford Park Avenue which ran for three seasons. Money generated from the matches went towards players' benefits. Played over two legs, the first "championship" was won by Bradford City 4-1 on aggregate during 1961-2, but Avenue won the other two by aggregate scores of 6-1 (1962-3) and 6-5 (1963-4).

Spring 1962:	City 1 Avenue 0 (VP)
	Avenue 2 City 3 (PA)
May 1963:	City 1 Avenue 5 (VP)
	Avenue 1 City 0 (PA)
April 1964:	City 2 Avenue 4 (VP)
	Avenue 2 City 3 (PA)

BRADFORD CITY

Avenue met Bradford City in 52 Football League matches. The overall won/drawn/lost record will be found on a later page.

Leading Avenue scorers are: 5 - Crosbie, Ham and Hector; 3 - Little, McDonald and McLean (G); 2 - Brickley, Harwood, Lewis, McLaren, McPhee, Rhodes, Robertson (J), Suggett, Turner.

Leading Avenue appearances 1914-39: 15 - Lloyd; 7 - Dickinson, Lewis, Taylor; 6 - Blackham, Clough, Crozier, Danskin, Davis, Howie, McCandless (J), McClelland, Parris, Scattergood, Scott.

Leading Avenue appearances 1946-69: 11 - Suddards; 10 - Hardie; 9 - Deplidge; 8 - Hindle; 7 - Brickley, Gould, Hector, Lightowler; 6 - Atkinson, Ham, McCalman

Leading Avenue appearances 1915-19: 15 - Crozier; 14 - Bauchop; 13 - Howling; 10 - Blackham; 9 - Dickinson; 8 - Howie, Scott; 7 - Carr (G). Top scorer - Bauchop (7)

Leading Avenue appearances 1939-45: 21 - Danskin, Farr; 19 - Stabb; 17 - Shackleton; 16 - Stephen; 15 - Farrell; 10 - Carr, Walker. Top scorers - Shackleton (18), Carr (7).

In addition the clubs met several times in the West Riding Senior Cup and the unofficial Bradford championship.

Information about the war-time meetings is included because they were heady days for Avenue followers. There was a 10-0 triumph at Valley Parade on December 19 1942 for instance. (City: Teasdale; Moore, Gregory; Westlake, Richardson, Lewin; Alldis, Isaac, Stone, Hinsley, Adams. Avenue: Farr; Hirst, Farrell; Stabb, Danskin, Green; Flatley, Shackleton, McGarry, Johnson (Everton), Walker. Goals from McGarry 2, Johnson 3, Shackleton 2, Flatley, Walker and Green).

For those who missed the fun, Avenue came close to repeating the dose twelve months later with an eight-goal whitewash at home (Avenue: Farr; Stephen, Compton; Elliott, Danskin, Farrell; Smith, Shackleton, Ainsley, Carr, Walker. City: Teasdale; Westlake, Lewin; Lindley, Tyrell, Page; lsaac, Harvey, Rodgers, McGinn, Woffinden. Shack ran riot with five and George Ainsley added three).

City goalkeeper Jock Ewart figured in all the first eight derby matches. After the 1939-45 war City's David Gray was an ever-present for the first twelve. Avenue's Jeff Suddards appeared in eleven in succession - twelve if an F.A. Cup-tie is included.

Dick Conroy

Dick Conroy was the first player to represent both clubs in a peacetime meeting (December 1953).

The biggest derby attendance was 38,442 at Valley Parade on September 17 1927. Best at Avenue: 30,362, September 14 1929.

The first derby of all was a First Division fixture that drew 29,802 to Valley Parade in October 1914.

Avenue full-back Tommy Lloyd took part in the most Football League derbies (15). City's Charlie Moore filled six different positions against Avenue.

Avenue's best wins: 5-0 (January 1928), 5-1 (April 1966), 4-0 (October 1930 at Valley Parade), 4-0 (August 1953). Worst defeat 0-5 (April 1956).

The 1928 team was - Jack Clough; Bert Manderson, Tommy Lloyd;. Harold Taylor, Bob Matthews, Donald Duckett; Bert Davis, George McLean, Ken McDonald, Arthur "Tricky" Hawes, Alf Quantrill.

1966: John Hardie; Don McCalman, Gerry Lightowler; Peter Flynn, Ken Taylor, Mick McGrath; Geoff Gould, Kevin Hector, Bobby Ham, Albert Broadbent, Jim Gilpin.

1930: Jack Clough; Sam Cookson, Ralph Ward; Harold Taylor, Jimmy Elwood, John Smith; Davis, McLean, Trevor Rhodes, Steve Kilcar, Syd Dickinson.

Donald Duckett

1953: Mitch Downie, Jeff Suddards, Jim Milburn; Alec Wright, Frank Hindle, Bill Deplidge; Dennis Brickley, George Beattie, Bob Crosbie, Willie Dunlop, Colin Whitaker.

Avenue's last "double" in the Football League was against City in 1966-7.

Donald Duckett, Rod Green and Gerry Hudson all played for Avenue, City and Halifax Town.

BRIBE

Bradford were the innocent party in a football "fix" on April 20 1963, when 6,794 at Park Avenue saw Bristol Rovers goalkeeper Esmond Million make two "mistakes" from which Kevin Hector scored the home goals in a 2-2 draw. The following week The People alleged that Million had accepted a £300 bribe to allow Bradford to win and quoted him as saying he had deliberately fumbled a back pass and missed punching away a cross. Rovers, who had paid Middlesbrough £4,000 for Million, suspended him and in July he was one of three players to plead guilty at Doncaster magistrates' court under the Prevention of Corruption Act and was fined £100. Million was then permanently suspended from football by the F.A. and he became a bus driver in Middlesbrough. Rovers inside-forward Keith Williams was also involved in the bribery transactions and fined £50 and subsequently suspended from the game. Million and Williams never received their £300 of course because the deal was that Avenue should win. At the end of the season Bradford were relegated from Division Three and Rovers escaped by a point.

ARTHUR HARRY BRIGGS

Harry Briggs masterminded the changeover from rugby to association football at Park Avenue in 1907. A very wealthy mill owner, Briggs thought this would improve the club's prospects. He believed that the potentially expensive change to association football would generate the profits that rugby could not. This move created much enmity among the old guard, some of it unsettling, but Briggs steered a path through the opposition to his plans. He served as chairman until his death at the age of 57 in March 1920. His death deprived the club of financial support and a sense of direction. He left £243,000, a huge fortune in the 1920s.

JOCK BUCHANAN

Jock Buchanan, who played in Avenue's last Football League promotion team and then managed the club for a spell, had a trial with Glasgow Rangers but started his professional football career with Clyde. He was outside-right in one of their finest-ever attacks (Buchanan, Archie Robertson, Billy McPhail, Sammy Baird and Tommy Ring) which rattled the net 100 times in winning the 16-club Scottish "B" Division championship in 1951-2, when they also carried off the Glasgow Charity Cup, the Glasgow Cup (by beating Celtic) and the Supplementary Cup. Jock played for Scotland "B" against France in Toulouse in November 1952: "Behind me at right-half was Tommy Docherty and my room mate was Willie Ormond who became the Scottish team manager in 1973." While with Clyde he played in an early floodlit Meadow Lane game which was a testimonial for Notts County's former Clyde full-back Tommy Deans. His direct opponent that night was Leon Leuty who had not long left Avenue. "Buchanan was in riproaring form" said the Daily Express. He scored the first and the second was a Robertson penalty after Jock had beaten Leuty and been tripped.

Papers linked him with Aston Villa but it was Derby County that became his destination. A bad leg injury slowed him - "I'd been a real flyer before that" - and he started to play at inside-right and centre-forward.

Jock arrived in Bradford in November 1957. He was top scorer in the 1960-1 promotion season with 21. He recalled the match at Accrington on Christmas Eve when he was fouled by Lord, the opposing left-back, who broke his leg in the incident and so not only conceded a free-kick but was stretchered off into the bargain. Accrington missed a penalty and Jock scored the winner near the end.

Under his management, Avenue were close to promotion in 1964-5. Two seasons later they won their first three matches and Jock felt promotion was again a realistic possibility. Then the board sold Hector and terminal decline set in quickly. After leaving Park Avenue Jock spent some 20 years at A. E. Auto Parts and held a supervisory post. He then lived at Low Moor in retirement with Grace, the wife he met at Shawfield where she worked on the greyhound tote at the ground. Their sons David and Gordon have been connected with local football.

"One strange thing" recalled Jock, "is that the only time I played against Bradford City was as a Derby County player (September 10 1955). I was once approached to be manager at Valley Parade but turned it down". Jock Buchanan died in December 2000.

EDDIE CARR

Eddie Carr never appeared in the Football League for Bradford yet any player who can bulge the net of that lot over Manningham way six times in one match and five in another must surely be numbered among Avenue heroes? Especially when he scored his five at Valley Parade for Avenue in a League North match on January 29 1944. Two months earlier he had been guesting for Newcastle United when he hit six against City at St .James's Park.

Carr, a pre-war Arsenal forward, was in Avenue's team 88 times between 1940-44 and netted 52 goals. In July 1945 he signed for Huddersfield Town and appeared in two of their first three First Division matches on the resumption of League football, but soon afterwards joined Division Two Newport County (October 1946). In 1949 he returned to West Yorkshire like an avenger, scoring goals in cup knock-out shocks against Leeds United and Huddersfield Town. Later that year Bradford City put him on their payroll and he scored 49 times in 94 appearances.

GRAHAM CARR

Graham Carr was the only ex-Avenue player who received a cup as the winning skipper at Wembley. It happened when he captained Telford to victory in the F.A. Trophy against Hillingdon Borough in 1971. He was at Wembley again three years later with Dartford but they fell to Morecambe. Born in Newcastle, he was an England youth international who turned pro at Northampton in 1962 and played 27 times in the club's only First Division season. Avenue signed him from York City in July 1969 and he was a mainstay of the team in their final League season, missing only four games. Going into non-League management, he led Nuneaton to the Southern League championship and then guided Northampton to the Division Four title in 1987. On the downside he had short and unsuccessful spells in the hot seat at Blackpool and Maidstone United while they were in the Fourth Division.

CENTRAL MIDLANDS LEAGUE

Bradford made a successful application to join the Central Midlands League in 1989 following their resignation from the West Riding County Amateur League. The change of league also entailed a relocation of the club where facilities were of the required standard. A move to Bramley's Rugby League ground at McLaren Field took place in the summer of 1989 where a ground-sharing agreement was hammered out with the Leeds-based club. Bradford were members of the Central Midlands League Supreme Division for one season before a further move was made to the North West Counties League.

City again! Player manager Mick Hall makes a successful tackle during a pre-season friendly in 1989 against the old foe.

CHAIRMEN

Originally Bradford FC, the club played in the Southern League during 1907-8 and in the Second Division of the Football League the season after. In August 1909 the Bradford (Park Avenue) Association Football Club Limited was established.

Chairmen:

A.H. Briggs	1909-20
C.L. Arnold	1920-24
R. Ingham	1924-26
S. Waddilove	1926-30
W.E. Collins	1930-32
C.H. Turner	1932-35
E. Waddilove	1935-37
S. Waddilove	1937-55
R. Kellett	1955-60
W. Hirst	1960-62
G. Butler	1962-63
C.F.H. Phillips	1963-64
J. Murphy	1964-67
J.L. Evans	1967-68
C.R. Ambler	1968-69
H. Metcalfe	1969-70
G. Sutcliffe	1970-74
T. Steele	1988-90
J. Russell	1990-92
R. Robinson	1992-94
M. Firth	1994-99
F. Thornton	1999

CHAMPIONSHIP

Despite winning promotion on several occasions, Bradford's only championship success as a Football League side was in 1927-8 when they won the Third Division (Northern Section) title. They finished eight points clear of Lincoln City.

CLAPTON ORIENT

On September 22 1928, Bradford made their eighth and last Football League appearance at Clapton Orient's ground up to the outbreak of the 1939-45 war and did not secure a point or score a goal in any of them, six being lost 1-0 and two 2-0.

COLOURS

Bradford's original colours of red, amber and black hooped shirts, unique in the Football League, were a continuation of the strip sported by the rugby club. In 1911, when Tom Maley took charge as secretary-manager, the shirts were changed to green and white hoops. After Maley departed in 1924 the old colours returned. Following a disastrous season in 1955-6, when the club was forced to apply for re-election for the first time, a green and white strip was reintroduced. This remained until 1967, albeit in varying styles, when a combination of (predominantly) red and white saw the club through to 1974. Following the club's re-formation in 1988 the colours have been green and white.

1907 Red, amber and black hooped shirts, white shorts

1911 Green and white hooped shirts, white shorts

1924 Broad red, amber and black hooped shirts with white collars, black shorts, black and red socks with amber turnovers

1932 As before but vertically striped shirts

1937 White shirts with 4 inch hoop on chest (red, amber and black), shorts and socks as before

1949 Broad red, amber and black hooped shirts with amber collars, White shorts, red, amber and black hooped socks

Over the next six years the configuration of the hoops and collars varied but the basic strip remained the same.

1956 Green shirts with narrow white stripes and "v" neck, white shorts with green stripe, hooped socks

1959 White shirts with green "v" neck, black shorts, white socks with green tops

1960 All white shirts with green and white rings at crew neck and cuffs, white shorts, white socks with green band

1962 Shirts as before but with BPA on left breast, white shorts, all white socks

1967 White shirts with single red and single amber hoop, white shorts, white socks with red and amber rings on turnovers

1968 Shirts and socks as before, black shorts

1969 White shirts with amber crew neck and cuffs, red shorts, white socks

1970 All red shirts, white shorts, then amber later in season 1970-71, amber socks

1971 All white

1972 Red shirts with white sleeves and collars, white shorts with black stripes, red socks

1973 Shirts and shorts as before, black socks with red and white turnovers

CONFERENCE NORTH

The UniBond League were allocated 14 places in the newly-created Conference North for the 2004-5 season with the top 13 clubs in the Premier Division receiving automatic promotion.

Despite finishing 17th in the Premier Division, Bradford claimed the final place after successfully negotiating the UniBond League play-offs where they defeated Burscough by 2-0 after extra time in the final at Horsfall Stadium.

SAM COOKSON

In Sam Cookson's four seasons with Avenue the club never finished lower than sixth in the Second Division. He was signed from Manchester City to strengthen the side after they had gained promotion. He was born in Bradford - but not in Yorkshire: just as the city of Bradford has a suburb called Bolton, so Manchester has a suburb called Bradford and it was there that Sam first saw the light of day.

When signed by Manchester City he was paid 15s a week (75p) but it was not long before he was in the first team and on the maximum wage of £5. His debut was against Bradford City on January 1 1920 and he went on to play in the Cup Final against Bolton Wanderers in 1926. He represented Manchester City 306 times in league and cup, turned out in 146 games for Avenue and then retired to take a pub. But after two years he returned to the game with Barnsley and at the age of 38 won a Third Division championship medal. His total of League appearances was 463.

Contemporary descriptions spoke of his "tireless energy and hearty use of shoulders. His clearances are clean and hefty with a full-back's proper aptitude to place to either wing, though he sometimes indulges in brilliant dainty movements." A stocky 12st at 5ft 8in in height, he was the elder brother of scoring phenomenon Jimmy Cookson who was second quickest in football history to notch 100 goals (he required only 89 matches for Chesterfield and WBA) and averaged more than one a match through his first five seasons. (George Camsell scored his first 100 goals in only 80 games).

CORINTHIANS

A team representing Bradford took on the famous amateur club at Park Avenue during their Christmas tour of 1897. The Corinthians had already beaten Derby County, Preston North End and Leicester Fosse so the Bradford side was given little hope. The amateurs didn't disappoint and ran out 6-1 winners. Bradford team: Harker; Clegg, Norman Thorne; Healey, Gates, Duncan Menzies; Matthews, David Menzies, E.W. Moore, Potts, Collinson. Corinthians: W. Campbell (Cambridge); W.J. Oakley (Oxford & England), W.U. Timmis (Oxford & England); C.B. Ward (Cambridge), G.O.S. Hatton (Cambridge), H. Vickers (Cambridge); C.D. Hewitt (Oxford), G.C.Vassall (Oxford), M.M. Morgan-Owen (Oxford & Wales), A.J.B. Dunn (Cambridge), C.J. Burnup (Cambridge, Kent & England). C. Wreford~Brown and the famous Forster brothers, of Worcestershire & England cricket fame, were selected for the game but stood down for Hatton, Hewitt and Dunn.

Winters as they used to be; Avenue v Barnsley, January 12 1946.

YOU • SHOULD • JOIN • THE
5
BRADFORD • PARK • AVENUE
SUPPORTERS' CLUB
WHIST DRIVES DANCES SOCIALS
JUNIOR SECTION MEMBERSHIP 1/-
JOIN at the TEA ROOM After the Match

JACK CRAYSTON

Two of Avenue's most famous players are linked with Grange-over-Sands. Jack Crayston was born there – the town's first professional footballer - and Len Shackleton lived there in retirement. Bradford landed Crayston from Barrow for a fee of only £750 in 1930 and though he started at centre-half it was not long before he was moved around the team. A Bradford programme noted: "You might put Crayston in almost any position and be certain he would play well. His raking strides devour space, he tackles well and is at all times scrupulously fair." He also had a long throw-in at a time when such things were few and far between.

A Yorkshire Sports comment of April 1933: "If I name Crayston as the brightest star it is because of his exceptional physique, an attribute which enabled him to reach the ball when none other could, command and dribble it with remarkable speed for a big man and to throw in an amazing distance. With the aid of the wind he was throwing the ball into the goal area at Millwall with the result that a surprised and confused defence scarcely knew how to position itself."

He broke a wrist at Nottingham in September 1933 and then a bone in his ankle at Oldham on December 30 and never again wore the boots he had used in those games, leaving them behind at Park Avenue on his departure to Arsenal in May 1934.

He scored on his debut in an 8-1 slaughter of Liverpool on September 9 1934 but afterwards revealed. "I may tell you I didn't get many congratulations. The chief point brought home to me was that I was out of position and should never have been in a position to have scored. I was too much inclined to play the attacking game to which I had been accustomed at Bradford." But Crayston was so talented that it was not long before he was allowed the flexibility to indulge his attacking flair and Arsenal were often grateful, as 20 goals in 208 senior games may suggest. He would probably have been Arsenal's Player of the Year in 1935-6 had such awards then been invented. He was selected for the Football League in the autumn, his first cap soon followed - against Germany at White Hart Lane - and he held his place for the remaining four internationals of the season. He wound up the campaign with a cup-winner's medal when the Gunners beat Sheffield United at Wembley. Crayston sent the England shirt he wore against Germany to Avenue manager Claude Ingram with a note: "I hope you will accept it with my best wishes and appreciation of the valuable help and advice given to me at Bradford towards realising my ambition."

He collected League championship medals in 1935 and 1938. He earned three more England appearances in 1937-8, and during the season C.B.Fry wrote: "Crayston is the sort of fellow those National Fitness campaigners should engage as an instructor and games master. The example of his build, appearance and manner would be good for our youth".

Crayston was a giant with brains - fast, constructive, brilliant in the air, a strong tackler, cool tempered. More than one observer described him as "the complete half-back."

"For all-round competence, perhaps the greatest wing-half ever to play for Arsenal" wrote Brian Glanville. "The elegant gentleman of the football field," was how trainer Tom Whittaker described him. Topical Times said he played "with much charm" and the Daily Express described a display against Charlton in 1937 as "polished almost without a flaw."

Jack was good at tennis, played golf and roomed with his Arsenal wing-half colleague Wilf Copping; and learnt how to write in old English lettering.

He was an RAF officer during the 1939-45 war, married a WAAF officer in 1944, returned to Highbury as assistant manager and became manager in 1956. He resigned in May 1958 and managed Doncaster Rovers before leaving football. He ran a store at Streetly, near Birmingham, and retired there. He was made an honorary life vice president of Barrow FC in 1957. Jack died on December 26 1992.

Playing record:

			FL app	*Fl gls*	*F.A.C app*	*Fac gls*
1928-9	Barrow	D3	35	1	2	0
1929-30	Barrow	D3	42	0	2	0
1930-1	Bradford	D2	21	9	0	0
1931/2	Bradford		24	5	3	0
1932-3	Bradford		33	1	2	0
1933-4	Bradford		19	0	0	0
1934-5	Arsenal	D1	37	3	3	0
1935-6	Arsenal		36	5	7	0
1936-7	Arsenal		30	1	2	1
1937-8	Arsenal		31	4	3	0
1938-9	Arsenal		34	3	1	0
Totals			*342*	*32*	*25*	*1*

CRICKETERS

Henry Horton

Henry Horton, Avenue wing-half of 1954-5 who also played for Blackburn and Southampton, was a Hampshire batsman (1953~67) who scored 21,536 runs at an average of 33.49 and helped the county to their first-ever championship in 1961.

Goalkeeper Willis Walker was a member of the Nottinghamshire 1929 championship team. He scored 1,000 runs in a season ten times and 31 centuries - one fewer than Horton. His team-mates included George Gunn, Harold Larwood and Bill Voce. In the Bradford League he turned out for Keighley where he built a sports outfitters' business (still operating in Cavendish Street) and remained a resident until he died at the ripe old age of 99 in 1991. As a goalkeeper he also played for South Shields, Leeds City (signed by Herbert Chapman), Sheffield United, Doncaster Rovers and Stockport County.

Centre-half Ken Taylor played for England in three Test matches and scored 12,864 runs for Yorkshire (1953-68) at an average of 26.80. In February 1957 he scored four goals from centre-forward for Huddersfield Town against West Ham.

Barry Wood played ten times plus once as a substitute in Avenue's first Northern Premier League season. As a Lancashire and Derbyshire cricketer he played in 12 Tests, scored 17,453 runs at an average of 33.82 and had a testimonial in 1979 which realised £62,429.

Denis Compton's brother Les, who guested for Avenue from Arsenal during the war, was a Middlesex player (1938-56) who was a right-hand bat, bowled and kept wicket.

Another guest during the 1939-45 war was Alec Coxon who played once at centre-forward and once at right-back! He was a key Yorkshire bowler who in 1950 took 131 wickets at 18.60 and in all first-class matches had career figures of 464 at 20.31. He played in the Lord's Test against Australia in 1948.

Fred Bracey represented Derbyshire(1906-14) in 77 matches as a slow left-arm bowler whose best performance was 6-36.

Avenue's Frank Lowson (inside-left with 12 appearances 1921-3) was father of the Yorkshire and England cricketer of the same name.

Among Avenue players who figured in Bradford League cricket were Pete Brannan, Peter Dinsdale, Albert Geldard (who was secretary of Bradford CC in 1931 and 1932), Bobby Ham, Irvine Harwood, Les Horsman, Geoff Kay, Brian Redfearn, Wilson Rose, Ernie Suggett, Harold Taylor and more recently, James Stansfield.

On April 17 1939 Bradford Park Avenue footballers played Yorkshire's cricketers (who went on to win the championship for the seventh time in nine years) first at football, then at cricket. At soccer Avenue beat "The Crackerjacks" 4-0 (McGarry 2, Martin pen, Hallard). The referee was Bill Bowes and the cricketers fielded (not in order) Waddington, Barber, Robinson, Mitchell, Yardley, Hutton, Wood, Leyland, Sellers, Gibb and Johnson. When they changed into flannels Yorkshire scored 69 (Hutton 25 including successive strokes off Danskin for 4-4-6-4-4) and the footballers 53. The Bradford team was Johnstone, Danskin, Farr (who naturally kept wicket), Peel, Lindley, Hallard, Smith, Fairbairn, Gilbert and Foster (from Bradford Northern). There were 6,000 spectators and the event raised £51 3s 6d plus a collection of £10 9s 4d for Yorkshire wicketkeeper Arthur Wood's benefit.

BOB CROSBIE

Bob Crosbie was a Glaswegian centre-forward who scored 72 goals in five seasons at Avenue - and missed another hatful. He was adept at finding the right position but not always adept at hitting the target.

Bury were pleased to accept Bradford's cheque for £11,000 for him in May 1949 when he was deputy to Dave Massart and playing most of his football in the Central League. The transfer record at that time stood at £24,000 (paid by Derby County to Manchester United for Johnny Morris). Crosbie repaid manager Fred Emery's confidence in him by scoring more goals for his new club than all but four others. He moved on to Hull City in October 1953 (£4,000) and hit his peak in 1955-6 with 35 goals in 42 appearances to lead Grimsby Town to the championship of Division Three North. He scored in both matches against his old club Avenue at Christmas and notched four in a 6-1 home victory over Chester. The team were captained by Allenby Chilton, previously Manchester United's centre-half. Bob signed for Queen of the South in the Scottish First Division in August 1957 when he was 31.

CROWD TROUBLE

On June 23 1921 an F.A. Commission at Sheffield suspended centre-forward David McLean from the following August 27 to November 1 and outside-right Bob Turnbull from August 27 to October 1 and also prohibited Bradford from admitting boys to Park Avenue before October 1. These decisions were a sequel to events during a match against Manchester City on the previous April 30 when McLean was ordered off and stones were alleged to have been thrown at the referee.

Bradford were ordered to post warning notices and to ban a spectator from attending Park Avenue for a year on January 9 1951. This was a result of an incident in an F.A. Cup replay with Millwall on December 13 when a spectator had thrown a small whisky bottle at the referee, George Iliffe, whose leg had been cut.

BOB DANSKIN

"If they get past Bob, we're in trouble," Avenue supporters used to say. It was a tribute to Bob Danskin, who match after consistent match was the main bulwark of the defence, keeping opposition forwards well away from the whites of Chick Farr's eyes.

Danskin never forgot his League debut - for Leeds United against Derby County in the last game of 1930-1. United had to win to have a chance of avoiding relegation from the First Division. They did so (3-1) but Backpool, the team they were hoping to overtake, gained a draw which gave them safety. It was the last match for 1929 cup final referee Arnold Josephs, who asked all the players to autograph a new football for him. – "I was trembling with excitement and just couldn't sign my name!" Bob recalled.

Bradford landed him in December 1932. The cup-tie which stood out for him was a three-game battle with West Brom, the previous season's finalists, in 1936, when Avenue finally won 2-0 at Old Trafford. The centre-forward he had most difficulty with was burly Jock Dodds (Blackpool) who scored twice when Danskin was chosen for a Football League XI against an All-British XI at Avenue on March 2 1940. Peter

Doherty scored two as well while Willie Hall (Spurs) twice, Stanley Matthews and Tommy Sale (Stoke City) were on the mark for the league selection.

Some of his hardest moments, said Bob, were leading the team out for a big match: "Everyone is naturally keyed up and looking to the skipper to be a calm example. It's the hardest job on earth pretending that you're not as nervous as they are!"

Danskin liked his pipe, an occasional round of golf and a Sunday morning visit to his local Methodist chapel. While a professional he worked on the land during the summer and when he retired from football he worked for a couple of years at Horton Park adjacent to the ground and then in 1952 took the 26-acre Standage Farm at Shelf (Frank Worthington's village) where he bred pigs and had a small dairy herd.

Bob was born at Scotswood in the North-east and died at Newcastle in September 1985.

Playing record:

		FL app	*FAC app*
1931-2	Leeds Utd	4	1
1932-3	Bradford	23	
1933-4	Bradford	34	
1934-5	Bradford	40	1
1935-6	Bradford	33	6
1936-7	Bradford	37	1
1937-8	Bradford	40	4
1938-9	Bradford	34	
Wartime	Bradford	227	6
1946-7	Bradford	18	1
1947-8	Bradford	1	

DIXIE DEAN

When Bradford lost 4-2 at Goodison Park on April 4 1931, Everton's Dixie Dean scored his 200th goal.

DEATH

George Turnbull, Bradford left-back, who had played in an away Midland League match against Hull City on the previous day, died in the city's Royal Infirmary on March 25 1928, after suffering a fractured skull when falling off a motorcycle between Oakenshaw and Cleckheaton earlier in the day. His untimely death cast a shadow over the team's promotion push.

At the time of his death in 1958 former Bradford chairman Lt. Col. Ernest Waddilove was the club's largest guarantor.

The death of chairman Herbert Metcalfe on October 24 1970, less than six months after the club had lost its place in the Football League, rocked Park Avenue. He had been pumping into the ailing club large sums of money and following his death the directors had no option but to adopt a "sell to survive" policy. Although the club played on for a further four years, his passing was undoubtedly a major contributory factor of the club's demise.

DEBUTS

The most striking debut was that of Bob Turnbull who scored five times from inside-left against Barnsley in a wartime match at Park Avenue on January 5 1918. His introduction to the highest grade of football had been an accident. On January 1 Bradford manager Tom Maley had taken a team to Middlesbrough to play a benefit match for Cook and McLeod, two Tees-side players, and being a man short, Turnbull was asked to play. He did so well that the Bradford manager invited him for a trial at Park Avenue where he made his sensational debut. So rapid was his rise that by October 1919 he had been capped by England and played against Ireland. He departed for Leeds United in May 1925 after scoring 49 league and cup goals in 223 appearances.

Peter O'Rourke junior made his debut at the time his father was manager of the club. As Bradford's inside-left against Durham City on October 4 1924, he scored twice in the first six minutes of the match.

Tom Tomlinson went into the Bradford record book as the only player to score a hat-trick on his debut in peacetime soccer when he grabbed three against Grimsby Town in a 6-1 home win in the Second Division on February 8 1910.

Fred Field (1933-4) and Jack Padgett (1938-9) both made just one appearance for the club in the Football League and both scored a goal.

The last player to make his Football League debut for the club was Eric Fitzsimmons at Chesterfield on April 17 1970.

The most debuts in a season was 34 in 1908-9, the club's first campaign in the Football League. The fewest debuts were made in 1964-5 when just three new players pulled on an Avenue shirt.

DEFEATS

Individual games

Bradford's record Football League defeat stands at 7-0. This scoreline was recorded twice, both on travel (1910-11 at Barnsley and at Accrington Stanley in 1955-6).

The biggest defeat looking at goals conceded was 8-2 at Port Vale during 1930-1.

Oldham Athletic inflicted Bradford's biggest home league defeat during 1909-10 when they won 6-1.

In the F.A. Cup Bradford's biggest defeat stands at 6-0. In 1928-9 West Brom won by that score at The Hawthorns in a fifth round tie; then Birmingham City defeated Bradford by the same score at St. Andrews in a sixth round second leg game during 1945-6. Taking the home tie into account the aggregate score was 8-2 to City.

Bradford's biggest Football League Cup defeat was 5-0 at Halifax Town in the first round of the 1967-8 competition.

In non-League soccer Bradford's biggest defeat stands at 7-1. This was recorded at Valley Parade in 1973-4 when Stafford Rangers visited for a Northern Premier League match. Worksop Town repeated the feat at home to Bradford during 2002-3.

In a season:

The fewest Football League defeats in a season were six in the club's 1927-8 championship campaign. The most Football League defeats in a season were 31 in 1968-9 when Bradford lost 21 of their 23 away engagements.

In non-League soccer the fewest number of defeats is currently five. This excellent record enabled the club to gain promotion to the North West Counties League's First Division in 1990-1. The most defeats in a season in non-League soccer stands at 22 during the club's stay at Valley Parade in 1973-4.

DERBY COUNTY

Leon Leuty

When centre-half Leon Leuty signed for Bradford in March 1950 for £24,500 the fee paid to Derby County was the second highest in the history of the game. Only Eddie Quigley's transfer from Sheffield Wednesday to Preston North End for £26,000 had been higher. The Leuty signing exceeded by £8,000 the previous biggest fee any club had paid for a centre-half.

Early in season 1966-7 Bradford received the biggest transfer fee in their history when Derby County paid £34,000 for Kevin Hector.

DIRECTORS

When Bradford (Park Avenue) AFC was established in 1909 the first Board of Directors were A.H. Briggs (chairman), J. Brunt, H.J. Coates, H. Geldard, F. Lister, T.H. Marshall, A. Shepherd. Prior to the forming of a limited liability the club had been run by a committee.

Several directors gave long service to the club. These include:

W.E. Collins	28 years
S. Waddilove	28 years
Ald. J.W. Turner	21 years
Coun. H.J. White	19 years
J. Canning	17 years

The Bradford FC committee in 1907-8 had 13 members looking after the club's affairs, while between 1964 and 1966 there were just three directors: J. Murphy (chairman), L.N.B. Jackson (vice-chairman) and A. Pickles.

DISCIPLINE

For misconduct in a reserve match at Halifax Town George McLean began a suspension on April 8 1926, which lasted until the end of the season and from the last Saturday in August to September 30.

On December 29 1950, Bradford announced that they had suspended left-back Arthur Farrell for a fortnight because of his refusal to play at right-back against Rotherham United at Millmoor on Boxing Day.

Bradford suspended Arthur Adey on December 30 1954, after the centre-forward had twice arrived late at the ground for home matches. His suspension lasted for 14 days.

On January 15 1964, Bradford player-manager Jimmy Scoular was suspended for 28 days and fined 20 guineas after being sent off in a home game against Gillingham on December 14 1963.

George Halley became the first Bradford player to receive marching orders in a Football League match at Bristol City on Easter Monday 1912.

Bradford did not have a player sent off in League football from September 13 1924 until February 4 1939, a time span of almost 15 years. On that February afternoon Bradford travelled to Sheffield Wednesday and Bill Hallard and George Stabb were both ordered off.

Football League history was created on January 8 1955, when four players – Henry Horton and Alex Wright (Bradford) and Les Samuels and Jimmy McGuigan (Crewe) – were all ordered off by Sam Bostock (Manchester) in the second half of a Third Division (Northern Section) game at Crewe.

When George Beattie kicked a Darlington player on September 5 1953, he became the first player to be ordered off at Park Avenue in a Football League game since David McLean "walked" against Manchester City on April 30 1921.

Ronnie Bird was sent off during a home Football League Cup-tie against Huddersfield Town on September 26 1962. However no action was taken by the League, a decision that suggested that his dismissal was scarcely necessary. Bradford won 3-1, Bird having opened the scoring after just 30 seconds.

Bradford player-manager Jimmy Scoular picked up an unwanted record on December 14 1963, when he became the only Avenue player to be sent off twice in the Football League. His dismissal in a home game with Gillingham followed a similar indiscretion at Halifax Town on April 13 1963 when he was sent off with Town's Alex South during a rousing tussle which ended 4-4.

The most unusual sending off took place at Altrincham in the Northern Premier League on August 23 1971, after Bradford goalkeeper Alan Aubrey and Altrincham's Dick Young had clashed as the players left the field. Referee Gale (Blackpool) and his two linesmen were already off the field but a St. John Ambulance Brigade worker reported the incident to the referee, who went to see Aubrey, cautioned him, and is reported to have told the 6ft 3ins goalkeeper: "Although you are off the field you can take it that you have been sent off for striking an opponent." Earlier Young and Aubrey had been involved in a collision which resulted in Altrincham gaining a match-winning penalty.

Bradford's McLean (left) and McDonald in action against Halifax Town, 1927-8 season.

TERRY DOLAN

Although Terry Dolan started his playing career in the Football League with Avenue, he is best remembered in the city as the manager who took Bradford City within a whisker of the First Division (now the Premiership) in 1987-8. They finished one point behind an automatic promotion place but fell in the play-offs to Middlesbrough. City's side, in which Stuart McCall and John Hendrie stood out, was generally reckoned to be two men short of a successful outfit but the board were hesitant about letting Terry have the necessary backing.

After a spell in charge of Rochdale he became Hull City manager in January 1991 and achieved a minor miracle in 1994-5 by taking them to a final position of eighth in Division Two when they had been tipped for relegation before the start. His tenure ended in July 1997. He then joined Huddersfield Town's coaching staff and was later manager of York City.

As a player he made his Football League debut for Avenue at centre-half on March 8 1969 and totalled 46 appearances during the club's last two seasons as a senior club, wearing numbers 2, 4, 5, 6, 9 and 10. He stayed at the start of their NPL days but Huddersfield Town, then in the First Division, paid £2,000 for him in October 1970 and he made his debut as substitute goalkeeper when Terry Poole was injured in a cup match at Birmingham. He clocked up 446 League games with Town, Bradford City and Rochdale, including at least one on every League ground.

DOUBLE DESCENT

Bradford created Football League history in 1922 when they became the first club to be relegated two seasons running. After dropping out of the First Division at the end of 1920-1, the club started the 1922-3 season as members of the Third Division (Northern Section). Bristol City (1980-1-2) and Wolves (1984-5-6) suffered even worse misfortune in being relegated for three successive seasons.

JOHNNY DOWNIE

When Johnny Downie says: "I have had three love affairs in my life and I have enjoyed them all," the listener pricks up his ears expectantly. Then the let-down: "Football, my wife and golf." He married Sheila in 1949. She lived in Horton Grange Road and Johnny was in digs at nearby Horton Green Farm and they have lived in Bradford most of their married life despite the fact that Johnny's unquenchable enthusiasm for football took him round twelve clubs before at long reluctant last he gave up after turning out for Halifax Town reserves.

He came to Bradford from Lanark during the war aged 16 and developed with East Bierley, winning WR County Amateur League and cup honours. His first appearances for Avenue (1942-3) were on the right wing and in October 1944 he actually played three times for Bradford City (guest players were a prime feature of war-time soccer) before being called on at centre-forward for Avenue and scoring twice in a 5-3 victory at home to York City. He soon moved to inside-left but because he was naturally right-footed he was able to fill either the No. 8 or No. 10 shirt with equal facility.

He played in Bradford's post-war cup triumphs at Highbury and St. James's Park and in three epic matches against Manchester United in 1949. In the first tie, at Avenue, he missed a sitter in the last seconds and recalls that after the whistle, manager Fred Emery shook hands with every player as they came off. "I should have scored," Johnny said to him with pent up frustration; but Fred smiled broadly. A draw meant a money-spinning replay for the club and he was well pleased with that.

Despite that miss Johnny made a hit with United's hierarchy and when Johnny Morris left Old Trafford for Derby County they paid Avenue £18,000 for Downie - then their biggest fee - as the inside-right replacement.

He earned a First Division championship medal in 1952 and says: "When people look back they always recall the great 1948 cup-winning team and then the

Busby Babes but they never mention the side which won the championship for them for the first time for 41 years."

He toured the United States and has a shield as his memento of the 1952 Charity Shield match in which United beat Newcastle 4-3. He also played twice at Hampden Park in the 1953 Coronation Cup tournament in which United knocked out Rangers but fell to Celtic in the semi-final. At this time he would collect his £12 weekly pay in a wage packet. Today's glamour boys of Old Trafford would not know what a wage packet was!

His Manchester United wing partners were Jimmy Delaney, Charlie Mitten, Harry McShane (father of "Lovejoy" Ian) and the long forgotten Ernie Bond; then Johnny Berry and David Pegg.

When Second Division Luton signed him he made an instant impact with a hat-trick against Oldham but the club let him down over a housing agreement and he decided to leave at the end of the season no matter what happened and return to live in Bradford. "Dally Duncan was the manager but the team was really run by Sid Owen" he recalls. (Owen was centre-half and captain and later a key figure in Leeds United's leadership set-up).

One of his funniest recollections is of his time at Darlington, where he played with another former Avenue forward Brian Redfearn. "We played a practice game, first-team forwards against first-team defence," remembers Johnny. "The manager said to me, 'I'm going to get this big blankety-blank to run like hell down the wing so whenever you get the ball, just aim it towards the corner flag.' When I did this for the third time, the right-back, who was Jimmy Dunn, had twigged what was going on and was waiting for it. So the next time I got the ball I played it square to Brian. The manager was refereeing and immediately blew the whistle and shouted: 'I thought I'd told you - down into the corner!' You wouldn't believe it, would you, but it's true."

Johnny bought a newsagents at Lidget Green which gave him a large measure of independence and enabled him to indulge his love of the game with minor clubs, such as Hyde United. Then he turned to golf and these days is a 13-handicap member of West Bradford. He and Sheila have one son (John Andrew) and four girls - "marvellous family who always help each other." Now retired, he goes to watch Rugby League but still enjoys soccer on TV and Sunday League games.

He marvelled at the skill of Shackleton; regards Chick Farr as the greatest goalkeeper entertainer he has ever seen - "he used to go dribbling up the wing;" remains grateful for the care and concern that Bob Danskin, George Stabb and others showed him when he was a youngster; and remembers Jimmy Stephen (later with Portsmouth) as a gentleman and Gerry Henry (also of Leeds) as an intimidating character who it was better to be playing with than against.

Lanark lad's League life

	Apps	*Goals*
Bradford 1946-8	86	34
Manchester Utd. 1948-52	110	36
Luton Town 1953-4	26	12
Hull City 1954-5	28	5
Mansfield Town 1958-9	19	4
Darlington 1959-60	15	2
Totals:	*274*	*92*

DEREK DRAPER

Derek ("Didi") Draper, one of the more skilled players among Avenue's hapless re-election sides of 1967-8-9, gained Welsh under-23 international honours in November 1964 against an England team which included Alan Ball and Norman Hunter. Among his team-mates were Gary Sprake, the Leeds United goalkeeper, and Mike England (Blackburn Rovers) - England was captain against England!

Earlier that year Derek, born in Swansea and a Welsh youth international, had the excitement of helping his home town team, then in the Second Division, to reach the semi-finals of the F.A. Cup with a staggering 2-1 victory at Anfield against Lawrence; Byrne, Moran; Milne, Yeats, Stevenson; Callaghan, Hunt, St.John, Arrowsmith and Thompson. At Villa Park they led Preston North End by the only first-half goal but succumbed 2-1; at Wembley Preston lost in injury time to West Ham.

Another Villa Park disappointment lay in store for Draper. In 1974-5 he was an ever-present in Chester's remarkable League Cup run, during which they shocked a full-strength Leeds United 3-0, but it ended with a 3-2 defeat by Aston Villa in the semi-final second leg, the crucial goal coming from Brian Little, later manager at Villa and Tranmere.

DRAWS

Bradford's highest scoring draw in league football was a 5-5 goal feast against New Brompton on December 14 1907 during the club's first season when they played in the Southern League. At one stage Bradford held a 5-1 lead in this Park Avenue clash.

The most drawn games in a season stands at 17 in 1964-5 and 1972-3 while the fewest was one in 1988-9. It should be noted that the latter season was in the WR County Amateur League when just 24 league matches were played.

Most home draws were 10 in 1959-60 and 1995-6; most on travel were 11 during 1972-3.

BILLY ELLIOTT

Billy Elliott, who won five England caps after leaving Bradford for Burnley, was hard as nails and took the field with an uncompromising approach born of his earlier days as a wing-half and advice given him by Bob Danskin, who said: "There are 22 players in a match and all have a share in the ball - but when you go into a tackle, forget about fair shares and come out with the ball all to yourself."

He wrote himself into the list of Avenue legends by scoring the goal at Highbury which knocked out champions-elect Arsenal in the third round of the 1948 F.A. Cup. It was a real "local lad makes good" story as

Bill had lived in Bradford all his life and represented Bradford and Yorkshire Boys.

He was a happy man that Saturday evening as he made his way back to his digs in Upper Rushton Road. In the first match after Bradford's relegation to the Third Division (Northern Section) he scored four from the wing at home to Barrow, but a year later he crossed the Pennines to Burnley (£23,000).

April 25 1952 was one of the most memorable days of his life. It started when his house caught fire and the fire brigade were called. While he was surveying the resultant mess there was a knock at the door. It was Burnley manager Frank Hill to tell him he had been chosen for the England party to make an end-of-season tour of the Continent. Elliott played against Italy, Austria and Switzerland and kept his place for the first two home internationals of 1952-3 against Ireland and Wales. He scored in Belfast (along with Nat Lofthouse) in a 2-2 draw. Incidentally it was after the match against Austria that Lofthouse became known as "the lion of Vienna" because of his indomitable display and two goals in a 3-2 triumph.

Elliott was also in the Football League team in which Lofthouse scored a record six against the Irish in September 1952 and both of them scored in Elliott's fourth appearance for the Football League (also against the Irish) at Anfield in October 1954. In the summer of 1953 he linked up with his former Bradford war-time team-mate Len Shackleton at Sunderland and stayed at Roker for six years. After that he coached extensively abroad and had managerial experience at Darlington. He still lives in the Sunderland area.

ELM PARK

Bradford's first senior outing in league football was in the Southern League at Reading on September 7 1907. Avenue made a winning start by 3-1.

EXCHANGING PLACES

Bradford, in a home victory against Millwall on April 24 1961, won promotion to Division Three while neighbours Bradford City, though winning at Colchester United, were relegated on the same evening to Division Four.

Jimmy Robertson

The two Bradford clubs made their first player exchange in 1938 when Jack Gallon came to Avenue and Jimmy Robertson left for Valley Parade. Both were inside-forwards.

EYESIGHT

One of the first players in the Football League to wear contact lenses was Avenue's David Reid, who came from Rochdale in 1950.

Goalkeeper Ken Tewkesbury, who played for Avenue during 1935-6, turned out wearing glasses. He was one of five goalkeepers known to have worn spectacles in senior football before the 1939-45 war.

JOE FAGAN

Joe Fagan's short stop at Bradford on the road through his football life was not a success. He had been a Manchester City regular 1947-50, dropped into non-League circles, but spent 1953-4 with Avenue when he was 32.

After he had made his debut at centre-half in a 2-0 defeat at Port Vale on September 7, the local paper used the journalistic euphemism for moderate newcomers - "made a useful first appearance." It was so useful that he was immediately dropped; and when he returned at home to Workington in February he "did not always find it easy to hold the dashing Dailey" - the Workington leader scored his side's only goal after beating Fagan - while at Tranmere Fagan and the rest of the defence "compared unfavourably" with Rovers' Bell, Lamont and Steele.

Joe went on to earn his place in football's fame frame as manager of the 1984 Liverpool team who won the League Cup, First Division championship and European Cup. And we believe he was the oldest man at 62 to secure his first managerial appointment. There have been older managers but all had had previous experience.

An attractive programme cover design from 1935

CHICK FARR

Chick Farr was the Bruce Grobbelaar of his day - an entertainer, a goalkeeper as mad as goalkeepers are supposed to be. He sometimes took throw-ins, was known to dribble a long way forward down the touchline and always provoked plenty of comment - by no means all of it complimentary! - "Get back into your goal you stupid ...." bawled his detractors.

I think he would have nodded approvingly of the modern day appearances in the opposition penalty area in the dying minutes of Schmeichel, Jimmy Glass and others. That was something not even Farr dared to do. Not that he was remotely short of courage. Oblivious to the prospects of a serious injury he flung himself head first among the boots to smother the ball in goalmouth scrambles and three or four times was carried off on a stretcher unconscious as a result.

On his best day this green-jerseyed hero made inspired saves and his daredevil antics made him one of the more popular visitors on opponents' grounds. Writing in the F.A. News in 1965, Jack Braithwaite said: "The crowd at Barnsley were especially fond of baiting goalkeepers. The only two they unanimously admired were the incomparable Frank Swift and a chunky character called Chick Farr who played for Bradford PA. Both these men were liked because they shared the crowd's irreverent humour for the game. Swift the genial clown, and Farr, the zaniest of goalkeepers who specialised in swinging on crossbars and galloping deep into his opponents' half of the field or dribbling like a winger."

A Scot who came to Bradford in 1934 at the age of 20, Farr married a Bradford girl three years later and settled in the city. He, Arthur Farrell and Billy Elliott were all Avenue lads who married in the morning and turned out for the club the same afternoon. In May 1947 Chick was able to claim he had not missed a single Football League match in the last ten years! The sequence began on February 20 1937 at Bury. He played in the last 12 matches of the season and was an ever-present the next two; then, of course, the war distorted the "record" (though even then he wasn't missing often) and he had played in all the first 36 post-war League fixtures. Then one of his inimitable dives into Manchester City feet left him with a broken arm and put him out of the last six games (the season did not end until June 14). No other goalkeeper ever equalled Farr's 17 years' first-team service for the club. He was later a chauffeur and died at Wibsey in 1980 aged 66.

Playing record:

	FL apps	*F.A.C Apps*
1934-5	29	1
1935-6	19	
1936-7	30	
1937-8	42	4
1928-9	42	1
1945-6		8
1946-7	36	1
1947-8	28	2
1948-9	42	4
1949-50	26	
	294	21
Wartime		
1939-40	11	
1940-1	28	
1941-2	36	
1942-3	35	
1943-4	38	
1944-5	37	
1945-6	42	
Total	*227*	

FESTIVAL OF BRITAIN

Bradford received Partizan of Yugoslavia to celebrate the Festival of Britain in 1951. A crowd of 14,338 saw Bob Crosbic and Jack Haines give Avenue a 2-0 verdict on May 14. Partizan were Yugoslav league champions in 1946-7 and 1948-9 and also cup winners in 1948-9.

FILMED

On August 25 1956, Bradford arranged for their Third Division (Northern Section) match with Derby County to be filmed. In a great second half rally Avenue overturned a 2-0 half-time deficit into a 3-2 win.

FLOODLIGHTS

Floodlights were erected at Park Avenue in 1961. Installed by Simplex Electric Company, the four standard towers generated enough power to provide domestic lighting for an estate of 500 houses, or main road illumination from Bradford to Manchester. To mark the inauguration of the new lights the club played host to Czechoslovakia's international team that included seven players who were to help them to the 1962 World Cup Final. The visitors won 3-2 in front of a bumper crowd of 17,422. All tickets for the match had been sold out within a few hours of going on sale.

Gale-force winds brought down the floodlight pylons on February 11 1962 after just three first-team games had been played under them. The four pylons were replaced by angular steel constructions dug deep into reinforced foundations during May 1962. These pylons were 120 feet tall and carried 36 lights each. Repairs were also carried out on part of the main stand, which had been damaged when one of the pylons crashed into it.

FOOTBALL ASSOCIATION CHALLENGE CUP

Bradford entered the F.A. Cup competition with a bang. Their first game was in the first qualifying round on October 3 1908 and they crushed South Kirkby 8-1. To accommodate the match they had to postpone their Second Division fixture with Birmingham to a Tuesday so when the second qualifying round match away to Denby Dale clashed with a League match at home to Grimsby, Bradford put out two teams the same afternoon. The seniors went down 2-0 at Park Avenue but the other team recorded the club's biggest-ever victory by 11-0.

The Yorkshire Daily Observer said: "Over 20 men have played for the first team this season and it is a little difficult to say which is the recognised league side." The F.A. didn't find it difficult at all: they fined Bradford £50 for not fielding their strongest team in the cup-tie - a high penalty at that time.

Avenue made a bigger impact in 1912-13 when as a Second Division side they knocked out Sheffield Wednesday (who finished third in the First Division) to reach the quarter-finals before losing to Aston Villa (championship runners-up); and in 1919-20 when they reached the same stage while in the First Division, this time going out to Chelsea.

There was a notable replay victory in 1930 over Derby County (runners-up in the First Division that year) with 29,738 watching. Walter Millership and Bert Davis scored in a 2-1 success.

In January 1936 George Henson netted four in a 7-4 scoring riot against Newport County and then Stoke City and Stan Matthews drew 31,347 to Park Avenue in the fourth round. Frank Soo put the visitors ahead by charging Chick Farr over the line as he caught the ball but Bradford's man of the match, Jack Wesley, equalised. Then Avenue shocked their First Division opponents 2-1 in the replay (Stabb, Henson). An unkind fifth round draw sent them to take on the holders, Sunderland. Bob Danskin and Chick Farr performed heroics in a strong wind but they fell to a goal by Len Duns on the hour.

Soo charges Farr over the line

The late 1940s saw Bradford's greatest cup exploits of all. First the two-leg rounds of 1945-6. After taking care of Port Vale (2-1 at home, 1-1 away) Avenue were beaten 3-1 at home by Manchester City and that appeared to end their interest in the competition. But on Wednesday January 30 they staggered the football world by going to Maine Road and netting eight past England goalkeeper Frank Swift. Many declined to believe the 8-2 result when they first heard it!

Shack scored the only goal at Barnsley in the next round and the second leg was watched by 29,341. Gibbons scored in a 1-1 draw which put Bradford into the quarter-finals for the third and last time. They came out of the hat against Birmingham at home and could only draw 2-2 before a surprisingly low crowd of 19,732, thought to have been affected by a wireless commentary on the match and forecast of a full house. Birmingham had won every home match and demonstrated their dominance in the second leg 6-0. Nuff said!

But in 1948 Avenue hit the national headlines again. This time they went to Highbury, home of First Division champions-elect Arsenal, and Billy Elliott scored the only goal. Skipper Ron Greenwood was outstanding in the centre of the defence. What did Kipling say about triumph and disaster? After that wonderful win Bradford had to visit Colchester United, then a leading Southern League club, who had just knocked out First Division Huddersfield Town and were said to be fortified by oysters. And Colchester took another West Yorkshire scalp by 3-2. A year later, however, Bradford did it again, going up to Newcastle (fourth in the First Division that season) and winning 2-0 through Downie and the amateur Harry McIlvenny. Les Horsman was the defensive hero, while "Downie stood out as the supreme schemer of the game." That earned a money-spinning ding-dong against Manchester United (who were to be First Division runners-up). Bradford drew 1-1 in Manchester (82,771 at Maine Road, used because Old Trafford was still being rebuilt after bomb damage), repeated the result at home (29,092) and sank 5-0 in the second replay at Maine Road (70,434) where Chick Farr saved them from total humiliation.

Les Horsman clears a West Ham attack at Upton Park, 1948-9

When, in 1949-50, Avenue drew Third South Bournemouth at home and after outplaying the visitors lost by the only goal eight minutes from the end, there was a real feeling of anti-climax among supporters after four years of technicoloured tilts against the big names.

The only other F.A. Cup competition to create major interest was that of 1951-2 when Bradford were drawn against Yorkshire opposition four rounds running. They needed two replays to dispose of York City but then knocked out Bradford City (Phil Turner two, Terry Lyons) before 24,430 and Sheffield Wednesday (who went on to the Second Division championship) 2-1, 28,449 cheering Turner as he turned in another brace. The run came to an end at Leeds but the attendance was 50,645.

Phil Turner

The re-formed club hit the national headlines in 2003-4 when they won through to the First Round Proper and earned a plum home tie against Second Division Bristol City. An all-ticket crowd of 2,045 saw the Nationwide side win by 5-2.

FOOTBALL ASSOCIATION CHALLENGE TROPHY

Bradford first entered the F.A. Challenge Trophy in 1970-1 after losing Football League status. As members of the Northern Premier League they competed in the competition for four seasons until going out of business in 1974. Following the re-formed club's promotion to the Northern Premier (UniBond) League in 1995, Bradford again earned the right to compete in the F.A. Trophy after an absence of 21 years.

Their best score in the competition is 7-0. They beat Alfreton Town by this score at Park Avenue in 1972-3 in the third qualifying round, then repeated it the following season at the same stage at Valley Parade against Kimberley Town. Mick Fleming had the distinction of grabbing a hat-trick in both cup-ties.

Although the club have not enjoyed much success in the competition they have reached the last 32 on three occasions. In 1972-3, with hopes of a possible trip to Wembley running high, a visit to Northern Premier League rivals Morecambe ended in a disappointing 3-1 defeat.

Morecambe, then in the Conference, came to Horsfall in 1996-7 for a second round tie and UniBond First Division Avenue won many friends despite a 1-0 defeat.

In 1998-9 the club faced UniBond Premier Division Colwyn Bay and their higher ranked opponents proved too strong, winning 3-1 in North Wales.

FOOTBALL ASSOCIATION CHALLENGE VASE

The F.A. Challenge Vase was introduced in 1974 as a replacement for the F.A. Amateur Cup. Bradford were admitted to the competition for the first time in 1991-2 when they were handed an away tie at Winterton Rangers. The club made a poor start, losing 4-1. Bradford's last season in the Vase was 1994-5 when they reached the second round before bowing out by 3-1 at Eastwood Hanley. Earlier that season Avenue had recorded their best-ever result, beating South Normanton Athletic 6-4 at Mount Pleasant.

FOOTBALL LEAGUE CUP

Bradford competed in the Football League Cup from its inaugural season in 1960-1 until their final season in the Football League, 1969-70. They did not meet with much success and only reached the third round on two occasions, 1962-3 and 1963-4. The most successful season was 1963-4. In the first round Avenue recorded their best score when they defeated neighbours Bradford City 7-3 at Park Avenue. With the competition still in its infancy it was perhaps not surprising that only 6,593 turned up for the derby clash. In the second round, Fourth Division Avenue held Second Division Middlesbrough 2-2 at Park Avenue and then travelled to Ayresome Park and beat Boro' 3-2 before 11,991, the biggest Football League Cup crowd they played in front of. In the third round they went out 3-2 to Third Division Notts County at Meadow Lane.

FRIENDLIES

Before the 1960s clubs played many friendly matches, but following the introduction of the Football League Cup and various other competitions the number dropped. Nowadays most clubs face a congested programme and any friendly matches tend to be pre-season affairs. Bradford have played as many friendly matches as most clubs over the years and below is a selection.

The very first association fixture ever played at Park Avenue was on September 14 1895 between a Bradford team and Moss Side (Manchester). The Bradford team won 4-1 before a crowd of 3,000. The match would have been a bit of a novelty at the time with rugby football the main sport in the city.

On September 15 1908 Bradford played Nottingham Forest at Park Avenue. The match was in recognition of Charles Craig's long service to the Midlands club before his transfer to Park Avenue. Bradford, who had played their first-ever match in the Football League a few weeks earlier, lost 2-1.

Without a First Division fixture on February 27 1915, Bradford received Northampton Town from the Southern League and ran out 5-2 winners.

On October 15 1934, a combined Bradford/Bradford City team played a team made up from players of Leeds United and Huddersfield Town at Valley Parade in a match for the Gresford Colliery Disaster Fund. The Bradford team won 3-2 and the attendance of 3,193 raised receipts of £200.

Bradford had to switch their friendly with Swiss side F.C. Lugano to Valley Parade when the Park Avenue ground was damaged by gale force winds over the weekend of February 10 and 11 1962. The match attracted 6,044, with Avenue winning 2-0.

Following Kevin Hector's record transfer to Derby County in September 1966, the Midlands club came to Park Avenue with a full-strength side to play Bradford in a friendly on October 25. The Rams won 2-0 with 3,254 turning out to have one last look at their departed hero.

One of the highest scoring friendlies seen at Park Avenue was a match between Bradford and Shrewsbury Town on August 10 1967 when the visitors won 5-4.

When Bradford met Bohemians (Prague) on March 3 1969, Terry Dolan made his debut. The Czechs, who were on a three-match tour, went down 2-1 before a disappointing crowd of just 2,034.

On August 1 1990, Bradford took the opportunity to play what was then a rare match in the city when they met former Football League rivals Accrington Stanley at Horsfall Playing Fields. Some pre-match publicity on local television and a fine evening drew a crowd of 400. NW Counties League Avenue lost narrowly to their Northern Premier League visitors 2-1.

FULHAM

Bradford's first-ever win in London as a Football League side was at Craven Cottage on February 21 1914. Their previous 15 visits to the capital had all ended in defeat.

WALLY GALBRAITH

Wally Galbraith was a smooth-talking charmer who as manager rejuvenated the club in 1958-60 by making full use of his valuable string of contacts in Scotland. He liked to keep tip-offs to himself and would disappear on scouting expeditions north of the border and then startle his chairman with a phone call to say he had signed another new player. Many of them cost no fee.

As a Scot from Glasgow, he was a firm believer in the tartan touch and put out a Bradford team in April 1960 containing eight Scots, all but one his own signings: - Jimmy Walker (from Aberdeen), Wattie Dick (Accrington Stanley), Don Brims (Motherwell), Don McCalman (Hibs), Ian Gibson (Accrington), John Allan (Third Lanark), Felix Reilly (Portsmouth) and Jock Buchanan, who was already at the club when Walter arrived. The three Englishmen were Harry Hough (goal), Charlie Atkinson (left-half) and Ray Byrom (outside-left).

This was the basis of the 1961 promotion team which clinched success after Galbraith had left in January to take over at Tranmere. He was later manager of Hibernian, general manager of Avenue (1965-7) and manager of Stockport County.

His playing career began at Queen's Park in 1945 in the same team as Ronnie Simpson (Celtic's goalkeeper when they became the first British club to win the European Cup in 1967) and Ian McColl who went on to fame with Rangers and Scotland. Wally was then a full-back with New Brighton, Grimsby Town and Accrington Stanley (who under his management finished 15th, 2nd, 3rd, 3rd and 2nd in the Third North). While he was at Accrington, Galbraith once called off a floodlit friendly an hour before the kick-off because the visitors, First Division Bolton Wanderers, brought only three members of the first team and he felt it was unfair that home fans should pay to see largely reserves. Wally died in Glasgow in November 1995, aged 77.

GATE RECEIPTS

As a Football League club, top receipts from a home game were £3,388 for a third round F.A. Cup match against Manchester City on January 9 1954. Although undisclosed, the receipts for the visit of Bristol City in the F.A. Cup first round of 2003-4 created a new record.

Here are a selection of special matches and the receipts taken:

First-ever home fixture in Southern League v Watford September 14 1907: £311

First-ever home fixture in Football League v Hull City September 1 1908: £240

First-ever home fixture in First Division v Blackburn Rovers September 5 1914: £680

All First Division F.A. Cup second round derby v Huddersfield Town January 29 1921: £2,000

First all-ticket match at Park Avenue v Manchester United January 11 1947: £2,935

Second all-ticket match at Park Avenue v Manchester United February 5 1949: £3,200

An F.A. Cup first round tie at Park Avenue on January 1 1913 against Barrow ended 1-1. A crowd of 7,000 paid receipts of £248 of which the Lancashire Combination outfit received £110. Bradford then persuaded the Holker Street club to relinquish their right to home advantage in the replay for £650. Bradford duly won the replay 1-0 before 10,000 spectators who paid receipts of £314.

The biggest crowd Bradford ever played before was at Maine Road on January 29 1949, when the F.A. Cup fourth round tie with Manchester United drew in 82,771. Receipts were £7,070.

ALBERT GELDARD

That old cliche "meteoric rise to fame" might have been coined for Albert Geldard. He knew what fame was even as a schoolboy because he scored 125 goals in one season and was chosen successively for Bradford Boys, Yorkshire and England. (He also captained Bradford Boys at cricket and won the 220 yards at the Yorkshire boys' athletic championships). At 14 he first played for Avenue reserves and he created a Football League record when he appeared in the first team at Millwall aged 15 and 158 days (later equalled precisely by Ken Roberts of Wrexham in a match at Park Avenue).

At 18 he brought a new record Bradford fee of £4,000 from Everton, scored in each of his first two matches in the First Division, gained a cup-winner's medal a fortnight after his 19th birthday and was promptly chosen for England matches against Italy and Switzerland.

His style around the time of his departure from Avenue was described like this: "The first thing you notice is his remarkably long stride; the second is his trick of going past the ball and dragging it up from behind with a clutching foot just as the defender is deluding himself that Geldard has over-run it."

At home to Villa (March 1933): "Geldard sprinted beyond Simpson at a pace likened to that of Kellsborough Jack." K.J. won the Grand National that year.

Geldard played a major part in one of the great football matches of all time, the 1935 F.A. Cup replay in which Everton beat Sunderland 6-4 after extra time. Six of the ten goals were scored by the wingers, Geldard's brace coming after 26 and 29 minutes of extra time. Another outstanding cup replay was at Tottenham in 1937 where Everton led 3-1 after 66 minutes. Morrison soon made it 3-2 and there the score stayed until four minutes from the end when Spurs sent their crowd into ecstasies by scoring twice through ex-Avenue forward Joe Meek and Morrison again. The Daily Mail said. "Geldard was one of the men of the match. Time and time again he evaded tackles with insouciant ease. His long loping stride gave pace without apparent effort and his centres made the first two goals."

Albert had become an accomplished conjuror and member of the Liverpool Mahatma Circle of Magicians and gave professional performances.

October 1937 was a stand-out month. On the 2nd the Blues won 2-1 at Anfield (only 12 fouls were noted) and "Geldard was Everton's best player, now right back to the form that won him honours so early in his career."

Four days later he really went to town for the Football League against the Irish League. Charles Buchan wrote: "Geldard and Hall were the outstanding wing on the field. The Everton wingman, yards faster than the opposition, made good use of his speed, beating his man and centreing precisely from any angle."

Next on the Geldard engagement list came an international trial (October 13) followed by another cap against Ireland. England won 5-1 and Buchan described the forward line as the best since the (1914-18) war. But to Albert's great disappointment he was superseded by Stanley Matthews for England's next match. Chelsea came to Goodison and the Sunday Express reported: "It was a real I'll-show-the-selectors display of brilliant dribbling, grand tactics and combination with Cunliffe and terrific speed - all the attributes which go to take up a star footballer. The Bradford boy dazzled Barber and was the star of a five-barrelled attack which never gave Chelsea a moment's respite."

Geldard was transferred to Bolton in the 1938 close season and received a letter from an Everton supporter which said: "When you are on form there is none better, but good or bad you are always what the Liverpool Echo calls you, a most gentlemanly player, and many spectators will remember and admire you for that as much as your ability."

After the war Albert became a journalist for a while and saved up for a Jaguar - he always had been interested in cars. He then developed a chain of dry cleaning and laundering businesses. He died at 75 in October 1989 at Bury.

Playing record:

			FL apps	*Fl gls*	*FAC apps*	*FAC gls*
1929-30	Bradford	D2	4			
1930-1	Bradford	D2	2	1		
1931-2	Bradford	D2	17	3	1	
1932-3	Bradford	D2	11	2		
	Everton	D1	26	5	4	
1933-4	Everton	D1	24	5		
1934-5	Everton	D1	31	5	5	5
1935-6	Everton	D1	39	7	1	1
1936-7	Everton	D1	13	3	1	
1937-8	Everton	D1	34	6	1	
1938-9	Bolton Wan	D1	20	1	1	
1946-7	Bolton Wan	D1	9		1	1
Totals			*230*	*38*	*15*	*7*

IAN GIBSON

Ian Gibson won four Scottish schoolboy caps, one of them at Wembley with Billy Bremner a team-mate and Terry Venables among the opposition. He left his native Newton Stewart for Accrington Stanley at the age of only 15 and before his next birthday turned out in nine Football League matches (1958-9), occupying four different positions. He later said: "It was a lucky break that my debut was against Norwich City, a fine football side who allowed others to try to play their game." After his manager Walter Galbraith had moved to Bradford he came back for Gibbo, who played 15 games at outside-right in 1959-60 and was absent only four times the following season when Avenue gained promotion.

He became an inside forward in February and stayed there, attracting the attention of a number of bigger clubs. Middlesbrough landed him in March 1962 for £20,000 and while with them he was capped twice for Scotland at under 23 level in 1963-4. Gibson joined Jimmy Hill's Coventry City in July 1966 (£57,500) and helped them to the Second Division championship the following season. He was later with Cardiff City (managed by former Avenue chief Jimmy Scoular) where he became penalty taker, and Bournemouth (1972-3). His career total was 461 League appearances plus seven as substitute.

GOALKEEPERS

The first ex-international to sign for Bradford was goalkeeper Tom Baddeley who made his debut at Reading in the club's first-ever fixture in the Southern League. Baddeley made 28 successive appearances up to missing the away match at Swindon on March 7 1908. On that occasion Baddeley, who had been on holiday, missed his train at Birmingham, and in the emergency Fred Halliday, Bradford's team manager, deputised in goal. Swindon won 4-0.

Bob Mason (1909-14) at 5ft. 6in. was Bradford's smallest goalkeeper.

Hugh McDonald (1911-12) weighing in at 15st. 6lb was the club's heaviest goalkeeper. He was also one of the tallest at 6ft. 1½in.

Jack Clough (1926-32) saved seven out of nine penalties awarded against Bradford during their 1927-8 promotion campaign. All the saves had a bearing on the result of each match.

Chick Farr made more appearances for Bradford than any other player in the club's history - 542 including wartime matches.

During Avenue's 1994-5 promotion-winning campaign goalkeeper Lee Williams did not concede a League goal in seven successive games. When Neil Ottley scored for visitors Clitheroe in the 9th minute of the NW Counties clash on December 3, it brought to an end the record-breaking run which had lasted for 706 minutes.

Bob Ward, in his last five appearances for Bradford (November/December 1908) conceded none v Bolton, one v Wolves, two v Orient, three v Barnsley and four v Oldham in successive matches. At that rate, it was as well he was discarded!

GOALS

Avenue's biggest win in the Football League was 8-0 at home to Walsall on September 14 1925. All the forwards but Quantrill netted twice each. Only one up at half-time, Bradford hit seven attacking the Horton Park end.

Jimmy Quantrill

The club's first two F.A. Cup matches in October 1908 resulted in victories of 8-1 v South Kirkby at home and 11-0 at Denby Dale (accomplished by the reserves - see F.A. Cup). Another crushing cup conquest was 8-0 at home to Bishop Auckland in January 1910.

From March 26 to September 5 1927, Avenue scored at least four goals in each of seven consecutive home matches, a feat exceeded by only three clubs. The results were 4-1 v Hartlepools, 6-2 v Southport, 5-0 v Wrexham, 5-3 v Tranmere, 6-1 v Accrington, 4-0 v Durham City and 5-3 v Southport.

The most sustained productive period for goals in the club's history was the ten seasons 1924-5 to 1933-4 when they rattled up 898 in 420 matches. This included the unparalleled achievement of totalling exactly 101 goals in each of three consecutive seasons 1925-6 to 1927-8.

In 1965-6 however a new club highpoint was reached when Kevin Hector (44) and Bobby Ham (24) led the way to a total of 102. No other Park Avenue pair ever contributed so many to a season's haul. Jim Fryatt (11 goals), Albert Broadbent (10) and Geoff Gould (6) were the other regular members of the attack which accounted for all but seven of the 102. As the defence conceded 92 that same season, anyone who watched all 46 Bradford matches saw 194 goals.

But 1967-8 was the most shot-shy season when Bradford scored only 30 in 46 League fixtures, never managed three in one match and failed to score 22 times. No player was able to score more than once in a match.

Despite scoring difficulties in their last three seasons of League life Avenue never went as many as five successive games without a goal as they did at the start of 1912-13 (0-0 away to Bristol City, 0-0 at home to Birmingham, 0-2 at Huddersfield, 0-1 at home to Leeds City and 0-3 at Grimsby). But they found the net 60 times after that.

Matches at Avenue crammed with goals were against Doncaster Rovers (7-3, Christmas Day, 1926), Chesterfield (4-5, February 1937), Newport County (7-4 in the cup, January 1938), Accrington Stanley (6-4 October 31 1953), Tranmere Rovers (4-5, April 1956), Bradford City (7-3 in the League Cup, September 4 1963).

Bradford were never a club to concentrate on defence. Their best-ever goals-against figure was 38 in 42 Third North matches in 1922-3 in the days of Ernie Scattergood, Tom Brandon and Andy McCluggage. The home record was only ten concessions in 1925-6.

Although Bradford conceded 106 in their penultimate League season, it was not the club's worst defensive record. That occurred in 1955-6 when unfortunate goalkeepers Brian Taylor and Dennis Ward saw 122 go behind them. That was also the season the directors decided they could do without a manager.

But don't these results look good through modern eyes - 5-1 v Wolves (April 1913), 6-1 v Aston Villa (September 1919), 6-2 v Forest (February 1934), 6-1 v Manchester United (October 1933), 7-1 v Blackburn Rovers (January 1938) and 8-2 away to Manchester City (F.A. Cup, 1946)

In non-League soccer (to the end of 2003-4) Andy Hayward leads the way with 88 goals in 183 appearances (2000-04). Other players to reach the half-century of goals are Jason Maxwell (87, 1998-04), Darren Wardman (85, 1989-93) and Rohan Eli (50, 1989-94). The quickest goal was scored by Rohan Eli after 30 seconds in a home North West Counties League match with Burscough in September 1994.

Rohan Eli (right) in action against. Accrington Stanley, September 26 1992

FOOTBALL LEAGUE
Most home goals: 74 in 1926-7 (21 matches, the only season in which Bradford were unbeaten at Park Avenue)
Most away goals: 44 in 1950-1 (23 matches)
Fewest home goals scored: 18 in 1967-8 (23 matches)
Fewest away goals scored: 9 in 1910-11 (19 matches)
Fewest conceded at home: 10 in 1925-6 (21 matches)
Fewest conceded away: 23 in 1922-3 and 1927-8 (21 matches)
Most conceded at home: 41 in 1957-8 (23 matches)
Most conceded away: 84 in 1955-6 (23 matches)

NON-LEAGUE
Most home goals: 50 in 1994-5 (21 matches)
Most away goals: 54 in 1988-9 (12 matches)
Fewest home goals scored: 22 in 1973-4 (23 matches)
Fewest away goals scored: 17 in 1993-4 (21 matches)
Fewest conceded at home: 18 in 1988-9 (12 matches)
Fewest conceded away: 19 in 1990-1 (17 matches)
Most conceded at home: 38 in 1973-4 (23 matches) and 1989-90 (19 matches)
Most conceded away: 46 in 1971-2 and 1973-4 (23 matches)

Avenue's Jim Fryatt entered the record books on April 25 1964, when he was credited with the fastest Football League goal - in only four seconds, according to referee Bob Simons of Carlisle. Fryatt kicked off against Tranmere towards the Canterbury Avenue end. Atkinson fed Lawrie at outside-right, he slipped it inside and Hector played the ball down the middle for Fryatt to shoot past John Heath. Most people were adamant that such a move must have taken more than four seconds but the referee said he had timed it. In December 1980 Barrow's centre-forward touched the ball sideways from the kick-off and Colin Cowperthwaite shot into the Kettering net from 55 yards. F.I.F.A. referee Alf Grey timed that goal in 3.55 seconds. Peter Flynn (v Darlington) and Sam Lawrie (v Southport) also scored inside the first minute that same season.

Bradford's previous quickest goals were said to be 12 seconds by Archie McHard (Southport again the victims) on Boxing Day 1959, and 15 seconds by Harry McIlvenny (v Cardiff, September 24 1949). Peter Saville scored in 12 seconds at Peterborough on August 16 1969.

Bradford's highest goalscorers are George McLean (136 FL, plus 3 F.A.C), Ken McDonald (135 FL plus 3 F.A.C) and Kevin Hector (113 FL plus 8 F.A.C/FLC).

On three occasions Bradford's top scorer has exceeded 30 in a season. That is a total Manchester United, Leeds United and Preston North End (among others) can only equal, while clubs including West Ham, Forest and Norwich - to say nothing of Bradford City (Bronco Layne) - have never had more than one player who scored so many as 30 in one season. The three are Ken McDonald (43 in 1925-6 and 39 in 1926-7) and Kevin Hector (44, 1965-6).

HAT-TRICKS
Forty-four players scored 93 hat-tricks for Bradford in Football League matches. Ken McDonald led the way with 11, followed by George McLean (7), Jimmy Bauchop, Barry Smith and Kevin Hector (6), and Tommy Little (5).

Three players called Smith are in the list. Albert, an outside-left, scored the first-ever, away to Hull City on Christmas Day 1908. Fred scored hat-tricks in successive home matches against West Brom and Norwich in December 1938 and Barry notched three in each of two consecutive matches also in December (1956) at Tranmere and at home to Crewe.

A third player to score successive hat-tricks was Jimmy Bauchop. His were in January 1915. Jimmy also registered three in a match against two former clubs, Spurs and Derby County.

On January 31 1930, outside-right Syd Dickinson scored three at home to Burnley - two of them direct from corners - and in the following match the other winger, Bert Davis, contributed the three goals which gave Avenue a 3-2 victory at Southampton.

Bob Crosbie netted a trio at Crewe on December 2 1950 and on his visit to the same ground the following season he did it again.

Two who scored a hat-trick for Bradford but were on the losing side are George Beattie (3-4 at Accrington, March 1955) and Barry Smith (4-5 at home to Tranmere, April 1956).

Most hat-tricks in a season – six during the Division Three championship campaign of 1927-8.

Hat-tricks in the F.A. Cup:
October 1908 George Reid v South Kirkby; Alec Fraser and John Manning v Denby Dale; November 1908 Bob Grierson v Mexborough; January 1910 Frank Newton v Bishop Auckland; January 1914 Jimmy Bauchop v Reading; January 1938 George Henson 4 v Newport County; January 1946 Jack Gibbons 4 v Manchester City; November 1959 Jock Buchanan 4 v Scarborough; November 1970 Allan Ham v Washington; October 1973 Mick Walker v Mexborough Town.

Four or more in a match by one player:
Football League
Jimmy McClarence v Glossop NE H 26.12.10 6-0
Jimmy Bauchop v Rotherham County H 24.9.21 4-2
Bob Wilson v Ashington H 17.12.24 7-1
George Henson (6) v Blackburn Rov. H 29.1.38 7-1
Jack Gibbons v Coventry City H 15.3.47 5-1
Billy Elliott v Barrow H 19.8.50 5-0
Len Pickard v Accrington Stanley H 31.10.53 6-4
Kenny Booth v Gateshead A 6.9.58 4-1
Jock Buchanan v Crystal Palace H 7.2.59 5-0
Kevin Hector (5) v Barnsley H 20.11.65 7-2
Bobby Ham v Newport County H 12.2.66 6-1

F.A. Cup
George Henson v Newport County H 8.1.38 7-4
Jack Gibbons v Manchester City A 30.1.46 8-2
Jock Buchanan v Scarborough H 14.11.59 6-1

1914-18 War
Jimmy Bauchop v Lincoln City H 11.9.15 4-0
Billy McLeod (5) v Grimsby Town H 18.11.16 9-0
Bob Turnbull (5) v Barnsley H 5.1.18 8-0
Jimmy Bauchop v Lincoln City H 23.11.18 6-1

1939-45 War
Len Shackleton v Leeds United H 11.10.41 6-0
Len Shackleton (5) v York City A 5.12.42 6-3
Len Shackleton (5) v Bradford City H 18.12.43 8-0
Eddie Carr (5) v Bradford City A 29.1.44 5-1
George Ainsley v Manchester City H 29.4.44 5-0
Len Shackleton (5) v Hull City H 23.12.44 6-1
Len Shackleton v Preston North End H 2.4.45 6-1
Jack Gibbons v Leeds United H 16.3.46 9-4

Top Marksmen
How Avenue followers must have enjoyed reading the Daily Express on August 5 1932. It gave a list of current players who had hit the most League goals and there right at the top, ahead of such notables as Dixie Dean and David Jack, was an Avenue player – Harry Bedford, just signed from Derby County the previous May.

The leading marksmen of the day were: Bedford (Bradford) 281, Dean (Everton) 275, Dave Morris (Swindon) 271, Tom Keetley (Notts County) 265, Arthur Chandler (Leicester City) 256, D.B.N. Jack (Arsenal) 244. In 30th place was George McLean (Huddersfield Town and formerly of Avenue) and 39th a second newly-signed Avenue forward in Joe Robson with 144.

Bedford the travelling goal machine had earned the cheers of crowds at Nottingham Forest, Blackpool, Derby County, Newcastle and Sunderland. Tom Keetley's first four Football League seasons (five goals in 21 appearances) were spent at Park Avenue. Bedford scored 15 in 33 Second Division matches in his only season for Bradford, the list being led by Avenue's third new forward, Ernie Suggett from Barrow, with 22.

Robson, who had a fruitful six years with Grimsby Town before joining Huddersfield Town, was on the fade and found the net only four times in 15 matches. He then dropped into non-League circles. He died in Bradford in 1969.

NON-LEAGUE HAT-TRICKS

1907-8	George Reid v Bristol Rovers
1970-1	Bernard Rafferty v Matlock Town
	Tommy Henderson v Runcorn
1971-2	Les Massie v Goole Town
1972-3	Tommy Henderson v Matlock Town
	Mick Fleming v Alfreton Town (FAT)
1973-4	Mick Fleming v Kimberley T (FAT)
1988-9	Chris McDonald v Crag Road United
	Steve Jansen v Hall Green United
	Paul Armitage v Hall Green United
	Dean Benn v Eccleshill United
	Dean Benn (4) v Trinity Athletic
1989-90	Darren Wardman v Priory
1990-1	Darren Wardman v Ashton Town
	Darren Wardman v Castleton Gabriels
1991-2	Rohan Eli v Clitheroe
1992-3	Rohan Eli v Penrith
1993-4	Steve Daykin (4) v Castleton Gab. (LC)
1994-5	Peter Mumby v Skelmersdale United
	Tony Marshall v Skelmersdale United
	Dave Morgan v South Normanton Ath (F.A.V)
1998-9	Martin McClennon v Whitley Bay (LC)
1999-0	John Francis v Harrogate Town
	Stephen Ball v Lincoln United
	Martin Pemberton v Netherfield Kendal
2000-1	Jason Maxwell v Matlock Town
2001-2	Jason Maxwell v Colwyn Bay
	Andy Hayward (4) v Ossett Albion (CC)
	Andy Hayward (4) v Blyth Spartans (LC)
	Dean Calcutt v Whitby Town (LC)
2003-4	Stephen Oleksewycz v Liversedge (CC)

Another goal for Darren Wardman

GOING TO THE DOGS

During the big freeze of 1963, Bradford fixed up a private friendly match with Leeds United which was played at the Elland Road Greyhound Stadium. The game ended in a 2-2 draw.

GREAT HARWOOD

Bradford's last match in the Northern Premier League before the club went into voluntary liquidation in 1974 was against Great Harwood at Valley Parade on May 2. Coincidentally it had been a home game against the same opponents that had brought League play to a close at the Park Avenue ground on April 21 1973.

RON GREENWOOD

Ron Greenwood, later manager of West Ham United and England, played in 59 Football League matches for Bradford immediately after the 1939-45 war and as a boy (born at Worsthorne, near Burnley) went to Turf Moor and watched among others Andy McCluggage who had been an Avenue personality of the 1920s.

His father took the family to London when Ron was ten and he became an apprentice signwriter whose firm had the Wembley contract. Ron did signs for the dressing rooms and many more when the Olympic Games were held at the stadium in 1948.

As a Chelsea player he enlisted in the RAF and was eventually posted to Yorkshire. He guested for Avenue in 1945-6, signed for them afterwards and took part in the F.A. Cup away triumphs against Manchester City and Arsenal - he captained the team at Highbury.

Ron was a thoughtful and scrupulously sporting player, a centre-half who often reached the ball before his opponents through intelligent anticipation. His former Bradford team-mate Jack Gibbons became Brentford manager and signed Greenwood in 1949. He went on to captain England "B", win a First Division championship medal with Chelsea and wound up his playing career at Fulham.

JACK HAINES

When England swamped Switzerland 6-0 at Highbury in December 1948 they gave first caps to two inside-forwards both of whom found their way subsequently to Park Avenue. Inside-left Jack Haines (West Bromwich Albion) headed the first goal in the fifth minute and gave a repeat performance before half an hour had past. After 55 minutes inside-right Jack Rowley (Manchester United and later Bradford manager) scored the most spectacular goal of the six - a blockbuster from 30 yards.

Another England debutant that day was Alf Ramsey (Southampton), who became the architect of our 1966 World Cup triumph.

Despite scoring twice, Haines never played for England again. He helped West Brom earn promotion to the First Division in 1948-9 but after losing his place the following October asked for a transfer. Avenue eventually found £15,000, then their highest fee, to bring him to Bradford. Haines thus had the rare experience of being in a team promoted to the First Division one season and in another relegated to the Third the next. In 1946-7 he had been with Swansea when they suffered relegation from the Second Division.

Jack, lean and wiry, stayed four years at Avenue and later served Rochdale, Chester and non-League clubs including Evesham Town two miles from the village of Wickhamford where he was born. He died in that area in March 1987 aged 66.

BOBBY HAM

Football lovers of middle age and beyond will identify with Bobby Ham when he says: "A genuine love of the game seems to have been supplanted by interest in how much they can earn. Even before I was a pro I used to go to the Avenue-City derbies and listen to the banter. You would go home side by side taking the mickey out of each other but all in a matey spirit. I was born at Little Horton in Bailey Wells Avenue and Avenue were always my first love as I was on that side of town At that time clubs owned houses occupied by the players and they were all near me - Chick Farr lived next door to my granddad. Even in the school holidays I used to go down to the ground and volunteer to do any odd jobs. I lived and slept and dreamt football."

At Grange school he teamed up with Bruce Stowell - later a cultured captain of Bradford City - and while only 11 was chosen for the school under 13s. "My first cup game was away to St.Bede's and we got beat 10-1. I said to Bruce, 'We can still win yet' after the ninth went in, I was that enthusiastic. That was the only time I wore a Grange shirt and was on the losing side in a cup match. We won everything." In goal was Dave ("George") Batty, who became better known as a Bradford Cricket League bowler; there was Alan Peel, a table tennis player of some note; and Bruce Bannister came along behind.

After trials for Bradford Boys Bobby was usually told he was too small but one year he scored a semi-final hat-trick against Belle Vue whose attack was led by big Dave Beanland and probably on the strength of that performance he represented Bradford against Glasgow at Park Avenue. From school he went straight on to the Avenue ground staff and played in the intermediate league and for the "A" team but soon, on his father's advice, he took a job in the wool trade. He became a close friend of Brian Kelly of Bradford City and that was why he first went to Valley Parade. He recalls: "We had a great run in the F.A. Youth Cup and reached the fourth round for the first time. We were drawn at Liverpool and were leading 2-1 with 15 minutes left when a lad called Ian Callaghan scored a hat-trick. The following Saturday he was playing for Liverpool's first team and he never looked back."

Bobby's first love was still Avenue and he returned there when Jimmy Scoular was manager. He was given his debut against a Crystal Palace side which included Johnny Byrne (later of England) and he scored in a 3-1 victory. After playing the last 17 matches of 1961-2 at outside-right he felt that at 18 he had established a first-team place but the following campaign he was back in the reserves and when his chance came again he was soon injured and needed to undergo an operation. Bradford did not know whether it was going to be a success and gave him a free transfer.

He resumed his career with Gainsborough Trinity and in one match they knocked Grimsby Town out of the Lincolnshire Cup, which prompted the Mariners' manager, Tom Johnston, to sign him. His debut was at Elland Road against the Leeds United side which that season won the Second Division championship but Bobby scored the visitors' goal - with a header! - in a 3-1 defeat. In the next match they were beaten at home by Preston, who went on to the cup final.

He was offered full-time terms but part-time money and his wool trade work brought in more so he declined and was therefore given another free transfer. Jock Buchanan brought the pocket rocket back to Avenue and it led to that fruitful 1965-6 season when Hector hit 44 and Ham 24 for the club. On February 10 1968, they were at Valley Parade and Alec Smith who was marking him said: "Don't try too hard because you'll be playing for us next week." Bobby thought it was just a wind-up and played as hard as ever, scoring the first goal in what turned out to be Bradford's last-ever away victory in the Football League. A day or two later chairman Leonard Evans told him City had made an offer for him and advised him to accept it because the club were in such a poor state.

He helped City win promotion in 1968-9 with 18 goals and the following season they were second in the Third Division when Tony Leighton was injured at Luton and they slumped into mid-table.

In 1970-1 Bob asked for another fiver on his pay which had not been improved and when it was refused he asked for a move and signed for Preston. North End paid £8,000 for him as replacement for Archie Gemmill who had left for Derby County and fame and he experienced a tremendous 18 months at Deepdale under Alan Ball senior as they clinched the Third Division championship to bring Bobby a much cherished medal. He hit it off with Clive ("Chippy") Clark of WBA and QPR fame and Gerry Ingram who have remained good friends.

After a spell at Rotherham when they missed promotion by a place, Bobby returned to City for his third spell in the summer of 1973, retiring two years later at the age of 33 having formed a business with his brother Allan which is now the thriving Ham Construction (Bradford) Ltd.

For some years they ran Odsal speedway with an enterprise that brought the first-ever trophy successes on the track. Bobby was a wicket-keeper-batsman with Bankfoot juniors, Cleckheaton, Blackley, Brighouse and Addingham; and played Bradford League table tennis for Deighton Brothers. He says: "I have enjoyed every minute of my sporting life and would do it again for the same money or even less."

What-might-have-beens

After Kevin Hector had left Avenue for Derby County he told Bobby that Rams manager Tim Ward had tried to sign him to re-establish the scoring partnership at Derby. But Bradford's directors had been so heavily criticised over the Hector sale that they dared not let him go.

While he was at City (1968-70) Jimmy Sirrel tried to sign him for Notts County but he said no matter what the terms, as a Bradford lad he was happy to stay with his home town team.

And when he retired he was offered the post of player-manager of Scunthorpe United.

HARD HITTING

One of the hardest shots Bradford ever had was Harold Blackmore, an F.A. Cup winner with Bolton Wanderers in 1929. He became a Bradford player in 1933 and in his first season scored 27 in 42 Second Division games. Between the wars other players with powerful shots were Harry Bedford, brothers David and George McLean and Tommy Lewis.

Alvan Williams

Alvan Williams (1957-60) was a dreadnought centre-half who specialised in taking penalty kicks. He blasted them in hard and rarely missed. Off the pitch he was a soft spoken chap in contrast to his "iron man" playing image.

HARTLEPOOL UNITED

Bradford's last-ever victory in the Football League was against Hartlepool on March 31 1970. The 3-0 win at Park Avenue in the Fourth Division came courtesy of two goals from former England-centre-forward Ray Charnley and one from Trevor Atkinson. Bradford's team that day was: Hickman; Dolan, Brodie; Atkinson, Campbell, Wright; Woolmer, Tewley, Charnley, Brannan, Thom.

KEVIN HECTOR

Kevin Hector was the lethal hit man who always got away. His prolific goalscoring progress was almost free from injury, which enabled him to turn out in more matches for Derby County than any other player and score more goals for them in all competitions than anyone except the legendary Steve Bloomer. Blessed with pace and balance, he seemed able to ride tackles with deceptive ease and then accelerate away from the defender so that not even the European hatchet men of the 1970s committed much damage on him.

And as Avenue fans will remember he had a rare appetite for goals and supreme belief in his ability to score them from either flank.

Talk to his contemporary professionals and one thing they all mention about his natural attributes is his balance. He had skill, composure, pace in possession and never indulged in an extravagant display of histrionics after scoring.

Two appraisals from the early 1970s. Phil Beal (Spurs): "He has the ability to turn quickly with the ball even in a crowded penalty area - he is very sharp in the box." Bob McNab (Arsenal): "It baffles me that he has never played for England. He has the ability to lose his marker and he is a great finisher." Well he did play for England - but his only two appearances were both as a substitute.

Instinct took Hector into scoring positions and the two he scored for Derby against Spartak Trnava in the 1973 European Cup quarter-final were testimony to his talent. The second, a volleyed drive from 20 yards, was spectacular but it was the first, tucked between goalkeeper and post, which emphasised another threat to defences - the way he could steal into a crucial position to convert, say, a centre to the near post. Roy McFarland (manager of Chesterfield and Bradford City boss May 1981 to November 1982) says: "The supporters worshipped him at Derby. Week in, week out, he was hardly ever missing and in all that time he was a regular scorer." Hector and McFarland both hit goals at Wembley when Derby won the Charity Shield in 1975 against West Ham United.

Hector was born in Leeds but it was Bradford who gave him his professional chance after Leeds United had been to have a look. In four seasons he collected 113 League goals including a club record 44 in Division Four in 1965-6 during which he reached a personal peak with five at home to Barnsley on November 20. After he had left early in 1966-7 Avenue sank to the first of four consecutive re~election appeals.

At Derby he became known as Zak and The King, won a Second Division and two First Division championship medals and had the distinction of topping a century of goals for his second club as well. In each of his first seven Football League seasons he was his club's top scorer and only two Yorkshireman have ever been credited with more League goals: Harry Johnson and Ernest Hine.

His manner on and off the field was above reproach and he remained unaffected by his success. He was also deft with needle and cotton and enjoyed golf, tennis, swimming, roast beef, Morecambe and Wise and Frank Sinatra. Like Johnny Downie he loved football so much he found it hard to stop playing and turned out for Vancouver Whitecaps, Boston United, Burton Albion, Gresley Rovers, Shepshed Charterhouse, Belper Town, Eastwood Town and Heanor Town. King Kevin will never be forgotten by the Avenue faithful.

Kevin's career

		Apps	*Gls*
1962-3	Bradford	34	19*
1963-4	Bradford	46	17*
1964-5	Bradford	46	29*
1965-6	Bradford	46	44*
1966-7	Bradford	4	4
	Derby Co.	30	16*
1967-8	Derby Co.	41	21*
1968-9	Derby Co.	41	16*
1969-70	Derby Co.	41	12
1970-1	Derby Co.	42	11
1971-2	Derby Co.	42	12
1972-3	Derby Co.	41	14*
1973-4	Derby Co.	42	19*
1974-5	Derby Co.	38	13
1975-6	Derby Co.	29(3)	9
1976-7	Derby Co.	28(1)	3
1977-8	Derby Co.	11	1
1980-1	Derby Co.	25	3
1981-2	Derby Co.	27(4)	5
Totals		658(8)	268

* *top scorer*

1967-8., Back; Hughes, Peel, Barnes, Hardy, Turner, I'Anson. Centre; McBride, Burgen, Hibbitt, Clancy, Ham. Front; Gould, Robinson, Lloyd.

KENNY HIBBITT

Kenny Hibbitt became the first Bradfordian to score in a Wembley cup final when he hit one of the two goals which enabled Wolves to beat Manchester City 2-1 and lift the League Cup in 1974. He earned another League Cup winner's memento in 1980 when Wolves defeated Nottingham Forest through a goal by Andy Gray, now a big name in satellite TV sport.

Kenny, brother of Terry (Leeds United, Newcastle and Birmingham), was Avenue's last player of any value and fetched £5,000 from the Molineux coffers in November 1966. But before that he almost gave up before he started. As a 17-year-old apprentice at Park Avenue he had to roll and mark the pitch and clean the boots. During his 8.30 - 6.30 day he had no time for training and was ready to quit when Ken Roberts arrived as assistant manager to Jack Rowley. They started a youth policy which brought in other young players and Roberts spent a lot of time helping Kenny to work on his game.

A match at Molineux in February 1973 threw up the unprecedented instance of brothers scoring the only goals for either side in a draw against Newcastle, Kenny's opener for Wolves being equalised by Terry.

In March 1974 Kenny became the player who booked himself. The referee of a match at Maine Road stopped the game when Hibbitt tripped Mick Horswill but had difficulty with his name and gave his little black book to Kenny with the instruction: "Write it in yourself."

In the third match of 1974-5 Kenny hit four goals against Newcastle (who included Terry) at Molineux. In April 1983 he scored direct from a corner at Rotherham.

Kenny always maintained a high work rate and had a deep reservoir of enthusiasm and commitment which took him through more than 550 games for Wolves and earned one England U.23 appearance. Only Derek Parkin (ex-Huddersfield) made more senior appearances for the club. And no Bradfordian ever exceeded his total of 481 appearances (21 as sub) in the Football League.

He was coach under Gerry Francis for two successful seasons with Bristol Rovers, which led to the manager's seat at Walsall (1990-4) and Cardiff City (1995-6).

The tragedy in the family's life was the early death of brother Terry in August 1994 at the age of 47.

HULL CITY

On September 1 1908 Bradford recorded their first-ever victory in the Football League with a 1-0 home success against Hull City in the Second Division. Alec Fraser got the goal.

CLAUDE INGRAM

Claude Ingram was arguably the most successful Bradford-born manager of all time. He was Bradford City's secretary for 17 years before he "crossed the road" to become manager at Park Avenue in 1925. The regime lasted for nine years. Three years after it began Bradford ran away with the Third North championship, and in the next three seasons they almost became a First Division club by finishing third, fourth and sixth in the Second Division. It was one of the most strikingly successful appointments in Park Avenue history. Yet Ingram was the only man among the long list of managers the club had after the 1914-18 war who never played the game at any level.

INJURIES

Careers of many Bradford players have been affected by injuries. Below is a selection of the most notable casualties down the years.

Bradford's ambition to reach the First Division was achieved in 1913-4, though it was a near thing. They were going well when half-back David Howie broke his collar bone against Lincoln City on December 13, and the next three matches were lost. However a victory on the last day of the season at home to Blackpool clinched second place and promotion.

Albert Bradley, who had scored nine goals in 18 appearances in his debut season, broke a leg in the match with Rochdale at Park Avenue on March 24 1923. Harold Hodgson was not so lucky on October 10 1925. The Bradford left-back broke his right leg in a collision with Tranmere's centre-forward Johnson at Park Avenue and never played again.

Another player's career was seriously affected on December 24 1927 when a severe knee injury to outside-right Phil Cartwright at New Brighton put him out of the game for a long spell.

During 1933-4 Bradford suffered badly through injuries. On September 23 half-back Jack Crayston broke a wrist at Nottingham Forest, then on December 30 he fractured his left ankle at Oldham. In between inside-right Jimmy Robertson suffered a cracked fibula at Lincoln on November 18.

On September 28 1935, left-back Tommy Lloyd suffered concussion when struck on the head during a Second Division match against Nottingham Forest at Park Avenue. He played on, and after the game he did not remember what had happened and did not know what the result was.

A player with a most unusual forename was Urbon Lindley. The Bradford right-back fractured a leg at Hillsborough on February 5 1938.

Goalkeeper Chick Farr broke his right forearm against Manchester City at Park Avenue on May 14 1947. This injury ended his run of 135 consecutive appearances in the Second Division, the sequence having started on February 20 1937.

During an F.A. Cup fourth round replay at Park Avenue on February 5 1949, Bradford's centre-forward, Harry McIlvenny, was stretchered off with a broken leg shortly after the start of extra-time but the game still finished level.

Bradford outside-left Ray Byrom's Football League career was ended on August 22 1960, when he broke a leg in the second minute of the second match of the season at home to Chester.

Bradford left-back John March, who had missed just one of the club's League matches in 1961-2, suffered a badly broken leg on October 27 1962, at Park Avenue against Queens Park Rangers. He later retired from the game.

The quick reactions of Avenue physio Ray Killick almost certainly saved the life of German goalkeeper Lutz Pfannensteil on Boxing Day 2002. Knocked unconscious in the 29th minute of the home UniBond League derby with Harrogate Town, the player was given mouth-to-mouth resuscitation after he stopped breathing three times.

INTERNATIONAL MATCH

A feature of Bradford's first Football League season was the allocation of their only international match to Park Avenue - England 4 Ireland 0, on February 13. The teams were - England: Sam Hardy (Liverpool); Bob Crompton (Blackburn Rovers), Joe Cottle (Bristol City); Ben Warren (Chelsea), Fatty Wedlock (Bristol City), Evelyn Lintott (Bradford City); Arthur Berry (Oxford University), Viv Woodward (Spurs), George Hilsdon (Chelsea), Jimmy Windridge (Chelsea), Arthur Bridgett (Sunderland). Ireland: Billy Scott (Everton); Balfe (Shelbourne), McCartney (Glentoran); Harris (Everton), McConnell (Sheffield Wednesday), McClure (Distillery); Hunter (Belfast Celtic), Lacey (Everton), Grier (Queen's Park Rangers), O'Hagan (Aberdeen), Young (Airdrie).

Skipper Woodward scored twice and so did Hilsdon, one of them a penalty. Ireland were skippered by Charles O'Hagan. The attendance was more than 25,000 and the programme, printed on 16 unusual fawn-coloured pages, cost one penny. It contained full-length caricatures of Woodward, Crompton, Windridge, Wedlock, Hilsdon and Lintott and the advertisers included the Alexandra Hotel, Knutton's outfitters, Silver Grill restaurant and Oxo.

INTERNATIONAL PLAYERS

England
Tom Baddeley (5) Feb 1903 - Apr 1904
Harry Bedford (2) May 1923 - Oct 1924
Ray Charnley (1) Oct 1962
Jack Crayston (8) Dec 1935 - Dec 1938
Billy Elliott (5) May 1952 - Nov 1952
Albert Geldard (4) May 1933 - Oct 1937
Harold Gough (1) Apr 1921
Jack Haines (1) Dec 1948
Kevin Hector (2) Oct, Nov 1973
Derek Kevan (14) Apr 1957 - May 1961 & four U23
Alf Quantrill (4) Mar 1920 - Mar 1921
Ernie Scattergood (1) Mar 1913
Len Shackleton (5) Sep 1948 - Dec 1954 plus victory international Apr 1946 and England "B" v Holland Feb 1950
Alf Strange (20) Apr 1930 - Dec 1933
Bob Turnbull (1) Oct 1919 plus three victory internationals
Peter O'Dowd (Chelsea), capped three times Apr 1922 - May 1923 and was on Bradford's books as an amateur.

England "B" team
Ron Greenwood v Holland Mar 1952
Leon Leuty v Holland May 1949 and Feb 1950
Jack Taylor v Holland Mar 1952

England U23
Kenny Hibbitt v Wales Dec 1970 (substitute for Mick Channon, 35m.)

England Amateurs
A.H. Gibbons (3) Jan - May 1939 plus war-time 'full' international Oct 1942
H.J. McIlvenny (7) 1948
K.C. Tewkesbury (6) Nov 1930- Mar 1932

Scottish Internationals
David McLean (1) Mar 1912
Charlie Pringle (1) Feb 1921
Jimmy Scoular (9) May 1951 - Nov 1952
Finlay Speedie (3) Mar & Apr 1903
Jimmy Stephen (2) Oct 1946 - Nov 1947 (plus five wartime Feb 1944 - Apr 1945)

Scottish U23
Ian Gibson (2) Dec 1963, May 1964

Irish Internationals
Sam Burnison (8) Feb 1908 - Jan 1913 (first to be capped while at Bradford)
Jimmy Elwood (2) Feb & Oct 1929
Jack McCandless (5) Apr 1912 - Oct 1920
Andy McCluggage (12) Oct 1923 - Apr 1931
Bill McConnell (6) Apr 1912 - Mar 1914
Bert Manderson (5) Feb 1920 - Feb 1926

Republic of Ireland International
Mick McGrath (22) May 1958 – Feb 1967

Welsh Internationals
Mel Hopkins (34) Apr 1956 - Apr 1963
Bill Matthews (3) Apr 1921 - Feb 1926
Eddie Parris (1) Dec 1931

Welsh U.23 International
Derek Draper (1) Nov 1964

F.A. XI tours of South Africa
Bob Turnbull 1920 & 1927
George Ainsley 1939
Jack Gibbons 1939

England Schools/Youth
Ronnie Bird 1 (1958), Dennis Brickley 2 (1948), Walter Buckley 2 (1920), Graham Carr 4 (1962)
Chuck Drury 1 (1955), Albert Geldard 3 (1927 & 1928), Albert Ross 2 (1931), Len Shackleton 3 (1936), Tommy Spratt 6 (1959), Ralph Ward 2 (1925).

Scottish Schoolboy
Ian Gibson (4)

IPSWICH TOWN

When Bradford dropped out of the Football League in 1970 they had met every other club then in the League apart from Ipswich Town.

GEORGE JOBEY

George Jobey played against Bradford City in the Cup final of 1911 as Newcastle United's inside-right. He joined Woolwich Arsenal in 1913 in time for the opening of Highbury and scored the first goal there for Arsenal on September 6; an equaliser against Leicester Fosse. On the last day of the season it was Avenue or Arsenal for promotion to the First Division behind Notts County. Arsenal beat Glossop 2-0 but Avenue saw off Blackpool 4-1 and pipped Arsenal on goal average to join the elite.

Then they signed Jobey for themselves and in 14 First Division outings the following campaign he filled five different positions as right-half, centre-half, inside-right, centre-forward and inside-left. He had collected a First Division championship medal with Newcastle United in 1909. After Avenue came a short spell with Hamilton Academical and he was manager-coach of Wolves when they took the Third North title in 1924. He made his reputation as a strict, shrewd and successful manager of Derby County, taking them to promotion from the Second Division in his first season of 1925-6 and building one of the best teams in the country in the 1930s, though they could do no better than the First Division runners-up spot in 1930 and 1936.

Over the years there was quite a connection between Park Avenue and the Baseball Ground. Goalkeeper Ernie Scattergood came to Bradford from Derby (his son Ken also played for the Rams in the 1930s) and Harry Bedford, one of the most prolific scorers in Football League history, turned out for both clubs. In the late 1930s Avenue half-back Les Bailey made the 80-mile move to the north Midlands and was seen 20 times in the First Division during 1938-9 when

Derby had a five-point lead at the turn of the year. After the war Leon Leuty took the reverse route when someone saw him as the man to save Bradford from relegation. Johnny Hannigan and Jock Buchanan, leading lights at Avenue in the 1960s, both came from the Baseball Ground and the most famous transfer between the two clubs then took Kevin Hector in the opposite direction. Lastly Derek (Didi) Draper arrived at Avenue from the Rams. Other men to serve both clubs were Tom Dilly, Jimmy Bauchop and Ted Garry who were members of the Avenue team promoted to the First Division.

JUBILEE TRUST FUND

To mark the 50th anniversary of the Football League, local derby matches were arranged as pre-season friendlies with the proceeds going to the Fund. Bradford met neighbours Bradford City at Valley Parade on August 20 1938 and the teams lined up again on August 19 1939 at Park Avenue. Avenue won each time, beating City 4-1 away (goals from McCall, Henson, Wesley, Lewis, attendance 6,159) and 3-2 at home (Hallard, Wesley, Martin, 4,843).

PADDY KENNY

Paddy was discovered by Avenue manager Trevor Storton in the West Riding County Amateur League playing with Ovenden WR and brought to Park Avenue in the summer of 1997. He was an ever-present during 1997-8. His talents had not gone unnoticed and following a trial at Birmingham City, Bury's Neil Warnock came in with an offer which saw the Halifax-born goalkeeper move to Gigg Lane in August 1998. The Bradford club received a reported £10,000 and a sell-on clause was attached to the deal.

With Irish international Dean Kiely the number one at Gigg Lane, Kenny's chances were limited. But his elevation to the first team came in May 1999 when Kiely was transferred to Charlton Athletic for £1 million. He soon became a crowd favourite and went on to appear 139 times for the Shakers. In August 2002 Kenny moved to Sheffield United to team up once more with former boss Warnock who had earlier left Bury for Bramall Lane.

There were mixed emotions for Kenny during 2003-4. Although there was disappointment in the team's failure to reach the Premiership, he received a call-up into the Republic of Ireland squad in March and came on as a substitute against the Czech Republic. The Yorkshireman qualified for selection through his Irish parents. His joy was completed three months later when he made his first full international appearance against Jamaica.

DEREK KEVAN

Derek Kevan was the only Avenue product to appear in the World Cup finals - he was England's centre-forward in all their four matches in Sweden in 1958 along with such players as Don Howe, Billy Wright and Johnny Haynes. A big blond bomber who relied on power and determination, he made quick impacts. He scored five on his debut for Avenue's Northern Intermediate League side against Bradford City at Valley Parade; he reached the first team after the club's worst-ever start of only two wins in 11 matches (1952-3) and they were unbeaten in the next nine; he scored two on his debut for West Brom (August 1955); and one on his debut for England (v Scotland at Wembley, April 1957).

He spent only one season as Bradford's teenage leader before following manager Vic Buckingham to West Bromwich where he enjoyed his best days, winning 14 caps. After a spell with Chelsea he set up a Manchester City post-war scoring record with 30 in 1963-4 and went on to serve Crystal Palace, Peterborborough, Luton, Stockport, Macclesfield and Boston United. He was born at Ripon and his middle name is Tennyson.

KICK-OFF

Bradford Junior Supporters' Club and then the senior supporters' club brought out a small magazine in 1946 and 1947 called The Kick-Off. It was edited by Muriel Curtis and designed by "Dixie" Dean. The first issue included "The Supporters ABC" which started "A is for Avenue and for Attack, what's lacked in the front rank, you'll find in the back." And ended "Z is the zeal we supporters display, in following our team when they play far away!"

The publication also contained pieces of comment, a player profile and a message from the Chairman (Harold Waite), a football crossword or quiz, a flashback series, letters and so on. A supporters club magazine was also published in 1967.

In 1993 a new Bradford Park Avenue fanzine appeared on the scene called "The Wings of a Sparrow" which was well–received in soccer circles. Edited by supporter Paul Hirst, the fanzine donated almost £400 to the football club by way of sponsorships.

BILL LAYTON

Bill Layton was a tall and constructive Midlander in midfield who packed a terrific low shot. At the time of his transfer to Bradford from Reading in January 1947 he commanded the club's highest fee and completed a half-back line signed from clubs in the South (Roy White from Spurs, Ron Greenwood from Chelsea). Before the month was out they also had George Wilkins (from Brentford) and Jack Gibbons (Spurs) in the attack.

And Avenue never lost in the capital that season - beating Millwall and Fulham and gaining a point from Spurs and West Ham.

In March, Dick Williamson wrote in Yorkshire Sports: "There has been no more skilled aggression from any Bradford wing-half I have seen since the war than has come from Layton in the last two matches. In addition he carries a left-foot shot of such force as has been an urgent need up front."

Layton had once scored four for Reading in a 7-1 League South victory against Brentford (February 1943) and helped the Elm Parkers win the London War Cup in 1941 with former Avenue centre-forward Tony McPhee the captain. They received 7s 6d (37p) National Savings certificates as their reward.

Bill represented the RAF in company with stars like Stan Matthews, George Hardwick, Raich Carter and Neil Franklin; toured Belgium with an F.A. XI in 1945-6; and was reserve for England v Wales at Cardiff in 1945.

Only two players were sent off in the Second Division throughout the whole of 1948-9. Layton was one of them. Put on the transfer list at £4,000, he went non-League with Colchester United in 1949 and when they were admitted to the Football League a year later Avenue accepted £800 for Layton, who was then 35.

Bill enjoyed a considerable coaching success when he guided the little known Harwich and Parkeston side to the F.A. Amateur Cup final at Wembley in 1953 when they were beaten by Pegasus.

GERRY LIGHTOWLER

Avenue were the sort of club that engendered camaraderie, says Gerry Lightowler, right-back in the 1961 promotion team. "I had a really deep affection for the club. I had followed them since the age of eight and when I was made captain it was the highlight of my life. I remember shaking hands with Ron Atkinson when he was skipper of Oxford United."

Two matches Gerry specially recalls were away from his beloved Park Avenue. One was at Northampton in the promotion season when they were third and Avenue fourth: "They murdered us but Bert Gebbie played the game of his life in goal and Johnny Allan snatched the only goal."

Move on two seasons and a visit to Swindon Town, challenging for the championship of Division Three with players like Mike Summerbee, Ernie Hunt and Don Rogers; Avenue, under Scoular, struggling to retain their status. Swindon won 2-1 and afterwards the Mayor of Swindon looked into the Avenue dressing room with well meaning words of consolation – "Hard luck, lads - you gave us a good game." Gerry says "We had to hold Jimmy Scoular back! I think he fancied strangling him with his chain of office!"

Gerry goes on: "Playing behind Scoular was not easy. He loved this crossfield pass to the left-wing and was exceptionally good at it but it meant he played a lot in space so his right-back had two men to mark. He was a good player, though. He was not easy to get on with but he was good for Avenue; and he used to buy all the players fish and chips out of his own pocket."

But Jack Rowley, who followed him, was poor on tactics and communication. Apart from George Stabb - "a real gentleman" - the biggest influence on Gerry during his time with the club was Billy Neil, who ran the juniors at East Bierley: "There were no shirts outside shorts or socks around the ankles," recalls Gerry. "He used to say, 'Go out there and LOOK as if you can play football.' He always insisted we conduct ourselves properly on the field too and not get involved in anything unseemly."

Lightowler was born in Bradford, attended St.Ann's and St.Bede's schools and played for St.Bede's Old Boys. He completed his apprenticeship as an engineer but did not return to that trade after a decade in pro football. He left Avenue when Ray Wood, the Manchester United goalkeeper, was gathering a team to play in the North American Soccer League as Los Angeles Wolves based at the Pasadena Rose Bowl and he spent a very enjoyable six months travelling round the States and Canada. After a season with Bradford City he moved into the retail trade with Asda and was a store manager at Halifax, opened a new outlet at Grimsby and managed another new store at Rochdale. He had a short spell with a building firm, took a pub near Goole and then the Commercial in Cleckheaton. Latterly he has been with the textile firm of Heydemann Shaw Ltd.

He has three daughters and three grandchildren; sits on a couple of committees at Gomersal Cricket Club; and plays golf off 17, having at one time enjoyed single handicap while a member at Ogden.

LINCOLN CITY

On March 31 1934, Bradford played their 12th and last Football League game against Lincoln City up to the start of the 1939-45 war. The series started in 1910-11 and Avenue won every match outright with a goals record of 45-5.

TOMMY LLOYD

Tommy Lloyd, who appeared in more peace-time derby matches against City than any other player, was given a free transfer by Sunderland in May 1927 and snapped up by Avenue just five days later.

Described in the programme as "a muscular clean-limbed, fearless and fine-kicking full-back," he made 328 League appearances for the club, a total exceeded only by Charlie Atkinson and Harold Taylor. He was impetuous at first but learned from his first-season partner, Irish international Bert Manderson (signed from Glasgow Rangers), to develop cooler and more calculating ways.

After leaving football, Tommy was a masseur and then opened a grocer's shop at Great Horton. He and his wife Ida celebrated their golden wedding anniversary in 1978.

1927-8; A McDonald header for Bradford v Wigan Borough.

LOCALS

A total of 522 players appeared for Bradford in the Football League from 1908 until 1970. Of these 45 were Bradford natives. Out of the 522, nearly half were Yorkshiremen (136) or Scots (122).

On February 17 1923 five locals - Harold Hodgson, Harold Taylor, Hugh Hubbert, Albert Bradley and Harold Peel - were in the team for the first time in a match against Darlington at Park Avenue, this being a joint record for a peace-time Football League game for either Bradford club. The following season Bradford twice fielded teams containing five locals.

Bill Deplidge

On March 22 1924, Bradford played their ninth local of the season in a home match against Durham City. Bradley joined Alfred Laycock, Robert Walker, Hodgson, Taylor, Hubbert, Hiram Tasker, Peel and George Kennie in having turned out in a League match that season - a club record.

Bradford played more locals than in any other peace-time League match in the club's history on January 29 1955, six natives of the city - Jeff Suddards, Dick Conroy, Dennis Brickley, Bill Deplidge, Reg Worsman and Brian Redfearn - being in the team against Crewe Alexandra.

On February 3 1951 seven players born within 12 miles of Bradford Town Hall were in the team that beat Tranmere Rovers 4-1 at Park Avenue.

Another famous 'local': Len Shackleton

LOCKED OUT

When Bradford met Barnsley on February 13 1946 in an F.A. Cup fifth round second leg tie at Park Avenue fans began to queue outside the ground at 11am, many having made the trip from South Yorkshire. By 2.05pm the gates were closed with 29,341 inside and many hundreds locked out. Bradford were held to a draw but progressed, having won the first leg 1-0.

LONG SERVICE

George Brigg

When Bradford secretary George Brigg retired in 1973 he ended a marathon spell at the club which had started on March 28 1934. When Bradford lost their Football League status in 1970 he was the longest-serving secretary in the League. In all he served 39 years.

George Stabb was recruited as a player from Port Vale in 1936 and went on to make in excess of 300 appearances for Bradford until he retired in 1948. After that, apart from a short spell at Halifax Town, he remained at Park Avenue as a trainer until he was given the sack in 1970 in a cost cutting exercise

George Stabb

Directors W.E. "Willie" Collins and Stanley Waddilove both served on the board for 28 years.

Other players giving lengthy service were Bob Danskin (1932-1949), Chick Farr (1934-1950) and Bill Deplidge (1946-1956). Trainer Fred Chadwick, who joined the club in 1908, remained in the post for 14 years until he moved to Stockport County in 1922.

JIMMY McALLISTER

Among Avenue players Kenny Hibbitt went on to play in 17 European club matches (for Wolves) but another who tasted European fare was the much less known inside forward Jimmy McAllister.

A regular in 1959-60, he made 11 appearances in Bradford's promotion team of the following season, then joined Rhyl and was with Bangor City when they won the Welsh Cup to qualify for the European Cup-winners' Cup and drew Italian giants Naples. McAllister was partnered on the wing by Reg Hunter, a former Busby babe who scored in both legs of the F.A. Youth Cup final of 1957 in which Manchester United defeated West Ham. But he never lived up to his potential and left Old Trafford with one solitary First Division appearance to his name. Bangor surprised Naples 2-0 in North Wales. The Italians drew level on aggregate in the return before McAllister scored in the 70th minute from Hunter's pass across the goalmouth but Naples sealed it 3-1 six minutes from the end. If the away goals rule had been in force the Welsh club would have gone through but there was a play-off instead. This took place at Highbury and although Bangor lost 2-1 it was McAllister again who scored their goal.

McAllister came from Barrhead near Paisley and was signed by Avenue from Morton. He had gained some previous Football League experience with Millwall (1954-6).

JIMMY McCLELLAND

Driven on by the inspiring captaincy of six-foot Scot Jimmy McClelland at right-half, Avenue made their last genuine bid to regain First Division status in 1933-4.

McClelland, signed from Blackpool at the age of 31, began at inside-right and the team's start was unexceptional; but once he dropped back into the half-back line on New Year's Day the points began to flow. In February Claude Ingram would have won the Second Division manager of the month award had there been one as his side thrashed Nottingham Forest 6-2, won at West Ham, panned Plymouth 4-1 and then went to Old Trafford and vanquished Manchester United 4-0 (attendance 13,389). They entered Easter with the leading positions like this:

	P	*W*	*D*	*L*	*F*	*A*	*Pts*
Grimsby T	34	22	4	8	83	49	48
Preston NE	34	17	6	11	60	44	40
Brentford	34	17	6	11	69	74	40
Bolton Wan.	34	18	4	12	65	50	40
Bradford	33	18	2	13	69	59	38
Port Vale	34	16	6	12	49	47	38

No one in the section had scored more goals at home and provided Avenue won their match in hand they had every chance of runners-up spot and promotion with eight fixtures left. Alas, defeats at Burnley, Bury and Notts County proved costly and 11 points out of the last 18 was not enough. They finished fifth, three points behind Preston in second place. Nevertheless they continued to rattle in the goals at Park Avenue and their final haul of 63 was more than any of their rivals managed at home. Much of this goal-happy aura was down to Harold Blackmore, a crackshot of a centre-forward, signed from Bolton and top scorer with 27. Harold came from a little Devon village called Silverton where he would suspend a cider barrel horizontally with top and bottom knocked out and practise shooting a football through it. Building on such early dedication, he went on to receive a cup-winner's medal from the Prince of Wales at Wembley in 1929, scoring Bolton's second goal in their 2-0 triumph over Portsmouth.

AFTER THIS AN AVENUE ENTHUSIAST BEGAN EXERCISING HIS VOCAL CORDS,— WITH EARS WELL BACK AND DINNER AND TEA WELL FORWARD HE BESEECHED BLACKMORE FOR "JUST ANOTHER"
SO BLACKMORE OBLIGED WITH A "HAT TRICK"

McClelland, his inside-right in that match, was approaching the end of an eight-club career when he came to Bradford. Born in Dysart adjoining Kirkcaldy, he first signed, not surprisingly, for the local club, Raith Rovers, where he was a 1922-3 contemporary of Alex James. He was Southend's leading marksman in 1924-5 and hit a club record 32 for Middlesbrough from centre-forward the following season, during which he enjoyed the red letter day of his career. He scored all Middlesbrough's goals in a 5-1 F.A. Cup spectacular against Leeds United and was chaired off by his team-mates. To crown a memorable occasion his son Charles was born the same day.

An injury in September that year let in George Camsell, who proceeded to surpass McClelland's efforts by setting up a 59-goal Football League record (which Everton's Dixie Dean pushed up by one the following season). Jim earned his cup medal with Bolton, moved on to Preston and then to Blackpool who saw him as the man to save their First Division status. But down they went and McClelland joined Bradford. He finished up with a brief spell at Manchester United and settled in the city.

The babe Charlie grew up to play for Blackburn Rovers and Exeter and another son, John - who was born in Bradford - was with Portsmouth and Newport County in the 1960s and married sprinter Heather Armitage. Oddly both were left-footed players whereas father Jim was more accomplished with his right.

Avenue skipper Jimmy McClelland (left) shakes hands with Tommy Glidden (WBA) before a cup tie in 1936. The referee is Reg Rudd.

KEN McDONALD

Why Bradford put centre-forward Ken McDonald on the transfer list after he had scored 135 goals in five seasons remains an unsolved mystery. Look at his record for the club:

Season	*Apps*	*Goals*	*Position*
1923-4	28	17 (top)	5th
1924-5	12	7	5th
1925-6	39	43 (top)	2nd
1926-7	33	39 (top)	3rd
1927-8	33	29 (top)	1st

Those 43 goals in 1925-6 were only one fewer than the new Football League record set up the same season by Jimmy Cookson (Chesterfield) - that was the figure improved upon by George Camsell (59) the following year and then Dixie Dean who pushed the record up to 60 the year after that. And McDonald's 43 remained a Bradford record until Kevin Hector went one better in 1965-6.

Ken gained an early honour when as a Cardiff City player he represented the Welsh League against the Southern League at Portsmouth in November 1922. Three months later he joined Manchester United and in 1923-4 he scored two minutes after the start of the season away to Bristol City. But in October Avenue manager Tom Maley made a shrewd investment of £1,500 for Ken and inside-forward Joe Myerscough.

Writing in "Yorkshire Sports" not long after the war McDonald said: "My unhappiest moment was when Bradford put me on the transfer list for no reason whatever so far as I know. I had had no row with the manager or directors but perhaps they thought I was not getting enough goals for them!" McDonald, aged 30, joined Hull City and continued his scoring form with 23 in 32 matches. He became a house and ship's painter in Newcastle where he worked on every class of ship from landing barges through a luxury liner to battleships.

He wrote in the 1940s: "Len Shackleton's moves are a delight to watch and sometimes I've wished he had been playing at Bradford when I was there. With his passes down the middle I could have scored three a match!" One far-sighted idea Ken advocated was to ban all transfers during a season. Ken played football in all four home countries, turning out in Scotland for Highland Leaguers Clachnacuddin, and at the end of his career in Ireland for Coleraine.

MICK McGRATH

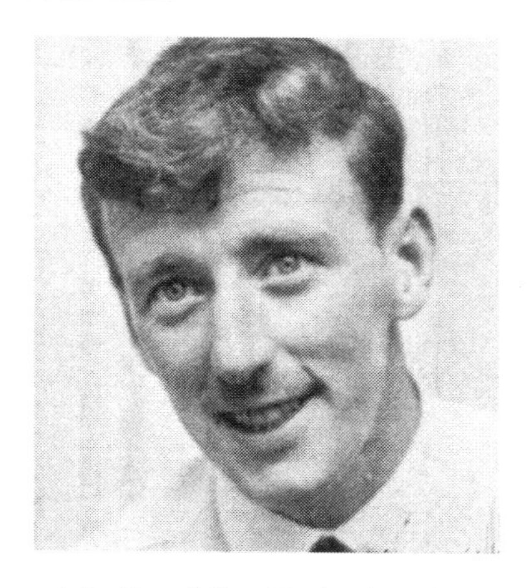

Represented the Republic of Ireland 22 times and when he was selected for the match against West Germany in May 1966 he was the last player to be capped while with Bradford - the first was Sam Burnison (Northern Ireland) in 1908.

McGrath figured in the 1960 F.A. Cup final for Blackburn Rovers and enjoyed the rare distinction for an Irishman of representing the Football League *against* the League of Ireland at Dalymount Park in September 1960, playing behind Jimmy Greaves.

Mick made 268 League appearances for Rovers and another 50 for Avenue after joining them in March 1966. Captain in 1966-7, he left to become manager of Bangor City (in the Cheshire League).

GEORGE McLEAN

George McLean scored more goals for Bradford than any other player - 136 during the 1920s. Though only 5ft 8in tall he was stocky and tough and was a sharpshooter of rare power. On the club's return to the Second Division in 1928 he succeeded Ken McDonald at centre-forward and led the marksmen's list for the next two seasons with 28 and 20. He then drew a useful transfer fee from Huddersfield Town even though he was 33 and was twice their top scorer before suffering a broken leg in a match against Manchester City (March 31 1934) when he collided with Sam Cowan (later with Bradford City) which ended his Football League career.

Town were leading the First Division at the time and the fact that they finished only as runners-up three points behind Arsenal was attributed by their followers to George's misfortune for he had been their outstanding player that season. He went back to his native Forfar and made a sufficiently good recovery to take up football again with Forfar Athletic until he was 42.

In 1921-2, George's first season at Bradford, he played twice alongside his elder brother David who had been signed in 1919 when he was 32. David, during a multi-club career, was capped once for Scotland against England at Hampden in 1912. He had been with Forfar Athletic, Celtic, Preston and Sheffield Wednesday before Avenue, with whom he stayed for two years. George scored 23 from inside-right in Avenue's 1927-8 Division Three championship season.

TOM MALEY

Tom Maley was described as one of the most charismatic managers of the early years of the century during which he guided Manchester City to the Second Division championship (1903) and F.A. Cup victory over Bolton the following season with a team featuring the legendary Billy Meredith on the right wing. But he was then caught up in an illegal payments inquiry which resulted in his being suspended sine die by the F.A. Maley said he could not deny making illegal payments; they were an accepted part of the way the club was run when he joined City, and most other First Division clubs also broke the rules.

He returned to his native Scotland and became a headmaster but in 1908 his ban was lifted, which enabled Bradford to tempt him back into the game on February 25 1911. Maley signed David Howie who went on to play 306 Football League games and George Halley who later found fame with Burnley: the Halley-Boyle-Watson half-back line was the backbone of the team which in 1920-1 went a record 30 matches without defeat on their way to the First Division championship.

On February 24 1912 Maley fielded a Bradford side containing nine Scots. He was in charge through Bradford's most eminent period, taking them into the First Division in 1914. Bradford won only eight matches in 1920-1 and lost their place in the top flight (Sheffield United survived though they won only six!) and the following season they became the first club to suffer relegation in successive seasons.

Avenue almost came back in 1922-3, finishing runners-up to Nelson in the Third North, but when it became clear they were not going to be promoted in the next campaign Maley left the club at the end of February 1924. But he left one rich legacy - he had signed Ken McDonald who became top scorer in four seasons out of five.

Tom, whose brothers Willie and Alex were also managers, had been an outside-left, mainly in Scotland, in the 1880s.

MANAGERS

Bradford's managers since 1907 have been as follows:

Fred Halliday	May 1907 - May 1908
George Gillies	May 1908 - Feb 1911
Tom Maley	Feb 1911 - Feb 1924
Charles Parker	Mar 1924 - Mar 1924
Peter O'Rourke	Apr 1924 - Feb 1925
David Howie	Feb 1925 - Aug 1925
Claude Ingram	Aug 1925 - May 1934
Billy Hardy	May 1934 - Apr 1936
David Steele	May 1936 - Sep 1943
Fred Emery	Oct 1943 - Jun 1951
Vic Buckingham	Jun 1951 - Jan 1953
Norman Kirkman	Mar 1953 - Jan 1955
Jack Breedon	Jan 1955 - Oct1955
Vacant*	Oct 1955 - May 1956
Bill Corkhill	May 1956 - Nov 1957
Alf Young	Dec 1957 - Nov 1959
Walter Galbraith	Nov 1958 - Jan 1961
Jimmy Scoular	Jan 1961 - May 1964
Jock Buchanan	May 1964 - Mar 1967
Jack Rowley	Mar 1967 - Sep 1968
Don McCalman	Oct 1968 - Dec 1968
Laurie Brown	Dec 1968 - Oct 1969
Don McCalman	Oct 1969 - Feb 1970
Frank Tomlinson	Feb 1970 - Dec 1970
Tony Leighton	Dec 1970 - Oct 1973
Roy Ambler	Nov 1973 - May 1974
Bob Wood	Aug 1988 - Oct 1988
Mick Hall	Oct 1988 - Nov 1989
Jim Mackay	Nov 1989 - Oct 1993
Gordon Rayner	Oct 1993 - Aug 1996
Trevor Storton	Sep 1996 - Mar 2004
Carl Shutt	Mar 2004

** Club chairman acted as hon .manager.*

The following Avenue players went on to become managers of other Football League clubs: George Ainsley (Workington), Bill Anderson (Lincoln City - he was an Avenue reserve), Graham Carr (Northampton, Blackpool, Maidstone), Jack Crayston (Arsenal, Doncaster Rovers), Terry Dolan (Bradford City, Rochdale, Hull City, York City), Billy Elliott (Darlington), Joe Fagan (Liverpool), Bert Flatley (Workington), Jack Gibbons (Brentford), Ron Greenwood (West Ham), Vince Hayes (Rochdale, Preston), Gerry Henry (Halifax Town), Kenny Hibbitt (Walsall, Cardiff), Geoff (known as Gerry at Avenue) Hudson (Southend), George Jobey (Wolves, Derby,

Gerry Hudson stretches to try to block a cross by Gateshead's Johnny Ingram

Mansfield), Jimmy Logan (Raith Rovers, Wrexham), David McLean (East Fife, Bristol Rovers), Tony McPhee (Walsall), Peter Madden (Darlington, Rochdale), Fred Mavin (Exeter, Palace, Gillingham), Jimmy Sirrel (Notts County, Sheffield United), Ralph Ward (Crewe Alexandra) and Alvan Williams (Hartlepool, Southend, Wrexham).

Bradford players who later managed the club were David Howie, Jock Buchanan, Don McCalman and Jim Mackay.

The most extraordinary appointment of all was that of Charles Parker, who accepted the post on March 13 1924 - on condition he could negotiate a satisfactory departure from his job as manager of the Poultry Fanciers Utility Association of Preston! It transpired that he couldn't, and withdrew his acceptance on March 29.

Tom Maley actually stayed with the club until April 5, Peter O'Rourke taking over the following week.

Vic Buckingham, who came as manager in 1951, was born on October 23 1915, the day W.G. Grace died. "Buck" used to joke: "One great man coming in as another went out!" He was in charge at West Brom when they won the F.A. Cup in 1954 and finished First Division runners-up and later he managed Ajax, Sheffield Wednesday, Fulham, Ethnikos, Barcelona and Seville.

Only a dozen or so pairs of brothers have each been managers of FL clubs, but Avenue provide three of them - David Howie (Jimmy, Middlesbrough 1920-3), Tom Maley (Alex, Crystal Palace 1925-7) and Jack Rowley (Arthur, Shrewsbury, Sheffield Utd and Southend between 1958 and 1976).

MARATHON TOUR

On December 20 1907, Bradford began probably the longest inland tour in the history of either local club. They stayed Friday night and also Saturday, Sunday and Monday in London after having met Millwall in the Southern League on the Saturday (21st). They travelled to Bristol on the Tuesday to meet Rovers on the Wednesday (Christmas Day) returned to London in the evening for a Boxing Day match with Leyton on the Thursday, and came back to Bradford on the Friday.

MARKSMEN

During a six-month period Bradford used four players who shared an aggregate of 743 Football League goals. During the year 1933, covering the latter part of 1932-3 and the start of 1933-4, the club had the services of Harry Bedford (298), Joe Robson (148), Harold Blackmore (170) and Jimmy McClelland (127).

MASCOTS

No, not the tots who hang around at pre-match warm-ups hoping to get a kick but personalities whose arrival on the first-team scene coincided with an invincible spell which suggested "mascot" properties. Donald Barker, for instance, a 20-year-old inside-left who made his debut on February 3 1934, and began with a goal within four minutes against Forest. He helped Avenue to a run of six wins and a draw. In the last of those matches he scored the only goal at Millwall, who later signed him.

Eddie Carr, a war-time guest inside-left, had an even greater effect on Arsenal. He made his debut in a 2-1 win at Maine Road on February 16 1938, and although he missed four of the season's remaining 14 matches the side never lost when he was in it and they wound up as First Division champions.

In 1952-3 Bradford were unbeaten in centre-forward Derek Kevan's first nine outings for the club.

Manager Norman Kirkman had a happy start because after taking over in March 1953 he saw the team go 12 matches without defeat until they slipped up in the final fixture at Stockport.

From the arrival of Felix Reilly in March 1960 Bradford went nine matches without defeat. As a point of interest, note that Barker, Carr and Reilly all played at inside-left.

When Tony Marshall made his debut for Bradford in an away match against Clitheroe on March 11 1995, he came on for the last 20 minutes and scored Avenue's only goal in a 2-1 defeat. That result left Avenue 17 points behind leaders Clitheroe, but Marshall was present in the following 13 matches, all of which were won in an unprecedented run-in and the club lifted the NW Counties League championship with four points to spare. Marshall's contribution was nine League goals in 14 appearances.

HERBERT METCALFE

When club chairman Herbert Metcalfe died in a Glasgow hotel on October 24 1970, the future of the football club looked far from rosy.

A Manchester businessman living in Cheshire, he had been continually pumping large amounts of money into the ailing club believed to have been up to £500 a week. His sudden death ended an association with Park Avenue which had begun on the pavement outside Stockport County's ground in November 1968 - the day Avenue were dumped out of that year's F.A. Cup competition. He joined the board that day after meeting directors George Sutcliffe and Jim Burkinshaw and soon became the club's largest shareholder with a stake believed to have been almost £100,000.

He took over as chairman during October 1969, fired manager Laurie Brown and took charge of the club in a welter of publicity when he began picking the team.

When Bradford lost their Football League status in 1970 he was still at the helm. It will always be something of a mystery why a Manchester businessman with no previous Bradford connections should have chosen to devote so much time and money to Avenue.

Shortly before his death his doctors had told him to take things easy because of heart trouble. He did so for a time but then there came the urge to try to put right one of the things he believed passionately in - Park

Avenue. There seems little doubt that it cost him his life in the end.

Two days before he died he told Avenue supporter Tony Rawnsley in a letter that Avenue had tried to sign Alex Dawson, the former Manchester United centre-forward, but Brighton's asking fee of £7,000 was too high.

MIDLAND LEAGUE

For several seasons Bradford's reserves were one of the most powerful units in the Midland League and the club's emphasis on attacking football, mentioned elsewhere, yielded goals by the hatful.

Only once did they capture the championship, however. This was in 1931-2 when they netted no fewer than 189 goals in 46 matches yet still found themselves in a tie for top spot with Grimsby Town. This had happened the previous season when the Mariners had won a play-off 3-0 against Bradford City to take the title. In the 1932 play-off, Bradford beat Grimsby by 2-1. The leading scorer, Steve Kilcar, had netted only 35 but he did well enough to attract a successful bid from Coventry City.

Top three:

Bradford	46	36	3	7	189	63	75
Grimsby T	46	36	3	7	178	60	75
Nottm Forest	46	30	7	9	117	62	67

Here is an outline of the Reserves' record around that period:
1929-30: third, top scorers with 163 in 50 games
1930-1: third, 138 in 46
1931-2: first, top scorers with 189 in 46
1932-3: third, 146 in 44
1933-4: third, 90 in 32
1934-5: fourth, 94 in 38
1935-6: runners-up to Barnsley; 107 in 40
1936-7: runners-up to Barnsley, top scorers with 124 in 42
1937-8: 14th
1938-9: 16th
1945-6: 15th
1946-7: third, second top scorers with 131 in 42 1947-8: fourth, top scorers with 138 in 42
1948-9: runners-up to Gainsborough Trinity, top scorers with 117 in 42

WALTER MILLERSHIP

Walter Millership was an attacking inside-forward with Avenue who made his first three appearances in the 1927-8 Third Division championship side and became a regular in 1929-30. He scored five goals for Avenue reserves on November 17 1928 when they trounced Methley Perseverance 20-1 in the Yorkshire League. Centre-forward Hart bagged six, Little five, Cartwright three and Parris one. As inside-left against Sheffield Wednesday in a cup match (February 1930) he must have impressed his opponents even though Bradford were well beaten and the following month they took him to Hillsborough for £3,000.

Converted to centre-half, he won an F.A. Cup winner's medal against West Brom in 1935, played for England against Scotland in a jubilee international the following August and captained The Rest against England in an international trial.

When he deputised at centre-forward in 1936-7 a keen supporter gave him a golf ball for every goal he scored (he collected eight). He was a member of the Wednesday team beaten in the 1943 League North Cup final by Blackpool and received three savings certificates as his reward. As a centre-half he was not slow to use his weight and became known as "Battleship."

MONEYBAGS

When Avenue were relegated from the Second Division in 1950 the board took an optimistic view and retained a Second Division infrastructure. In fact they became the "moneybags" club of the Third North. They started the 1950-1 season with the most expensive team ever seen up to then in that division. Never had such a costly centre-half as Leon Leuty (£24,500) been seen in either of the lower sections and the line-up cost a total of about £50,000. Leuty did not stay long - after the first nine matches he left for Notts County (£24,000)

Mitch Downie

There were no fewer than five professional goalkeepers - Mitch Downie, Chick Farr, Jim Nicholls, Charlie Heffron and Andy Pirrie. That was lavish economics for a club of their standing; especially as Downie played in every first-team match. So too was the fact that they continued to pay a manager, secretary, coach, three trainers and two full-time scouts.

In 1951-2 they had two strikers, both Scots, each of whom had cost a five-figure fee. Bob Crosbie lost form so they forked out £12,000 to buy Alex Wright from Spurs. The transfer record at that time was £34,000 paid by Sheffield Wednesday to Notts County for Jackie Sewell.

Alex Wright

Bradford coined in an estimated £60,000 in the 1940s for five players who cost them nothing - Len Shackleton (to Newcastle United), Geoff Walker (Middlesbrough), Johnny Downie (Manchester United), Jack Gibbons (Brentford) and Jimmy Stephen (Portsmouth).

In their vain effort to avoid relegation from the Second Division (now called the FL Championship) in 1950 Bradford paid out in transfer fees as much as that season's F.A. Cup finalists combined! Arsenal's side cost £35,000 and Liverpool's £30,000. Six of the Highbury men and seven at Anfield had been recruited for nothing. In the Arsenal camp were ex-Avenue wartime guest Les Compton, former Bradford City full-back Laurie Scott and Jack Crayston, the assistant manager and former Avenue wing-half.

NEUTRAL GROUNDS

Bradford have been forced to resolve an F.A. Cup-tie on a neutral ground on three occasions. In a first round second replay on December 7 1925 they beat Lincoln City 2-1 at Bramall Lane where the crowd was a meagre 5,500.

On February 10 1936 a third meeting was necessary to settle a tie against West Brom. The fourth round second replay was staged at Old Trafford where the 11,635 crowd was swelled by 1,230 Tykes who had crossed the Pennines by special train. Again it was third time lucky and Avenue won 2-0 to earn a plum fifth round tie with Spurs.

On December 3 1952, after two draws against York City in the first round, the clubs met for the third time at Elland Road where a 10,000 crowd saw Avenue run out emphatic winners by 4-0.

Following gale damage at Park Avenue a friendly match with Swiss side F.C. Lugano was switched to neighbouring Valley Parade on February 13 1962. Bradford won 2-0.

Several of Avenue's WR Senior Cup ties have been played on neutral grounds and, in more recent times, pitch problems at Bramley RLFC's McLaren Field and Batley RLFC's Mount Pleasant resulted in Bradford switching home fixtures to other local non-League grounds.

NORTH EASTERN LEAGUE

When Bradford turned to association football in 1907 the club put out a reserve side in the North Eastern League which had been formed a year earlier. Bradford finished third in their second season, 1908-9, and then resigned. The following season the reserves competed in the much stronger Midland League.

Although Bradford's first-ever senior match in League football was at Reading in the Southern League on September 7 1907, the first-ever league match played by the club was at Newcastle five days earlier where the second string beat United 2-1 in the NE League.

NORTH WEST COUNTIES LEAGUE

Bradford were elected to the North West Counties League in 1990 after resigning from the Central Midlands League which, at the time, was not a feeder league to the football "pyramid." Bradford's stay in the league lasted five seasons. They won promotion from Division Two in their first season, but almost dropped back to the lower division a year later after finishing next-to-bottom. They won the Division One championship in 1994-5 and earned the right to a place in the Northern Premier League.

NORTHERN PREMIER LEAGUE

Just seven years after the club had been re-formed Bradford gained a promotion to the Northern Premier League as a result of winning the N.W. Counties League championship. Initially the club were refused promotion by the NPL, but an F.A. appeal hearing in Sheffield overturned the League's decision not to promote Bradford after a misunderstanding about the choice of ground for 1995-6 had been cleared up. So the club returned to the league that they had resigned from in 1974 after getting into serious financial difficulties.

When Bradford lost their Football League place in 1970 the directors voted to carry on and an application was made for membership of the NPL. One of seven clubs seeking membership, Bradford, together with Chorley, Goole Town, Matlock Town, Lancaster City and Kirkby Town were elected at the League's A.G.M. in Leeds.

Bradford survived just four seasons in the league the last of which was spent sharing with neighbours Bradford City following the 1973 sale of Park Avenue. At the end of 1973-4 dwindling attendances and large debts forced the directors into closing the club.

NOTTS COUNTY

Bradford met Notts County on three successive Saturdays February 7, 14 and 21 1920 – and each time the visiting team won! Avenue succeeded 2-0 in the First Division at Meadow Lane, lost at home 1-0 and then returned to Nottingham for a 4-3 third round F.A. cup success.

OVERSEAS OPPOSITION

Bradford played host to overseas touring sides on six occasions from 1935 until 1969. Results of these matches were as follows:

December 4 1935 v F.C. Wien (Austria) 3-1 (Lewis, McGrath,Wesley)
May 14 1951 v Partizan (Yugoslavia) Festival of Britain 2-0 (Crosbie, Haines)
October 3 1961 v Czechoslovakia (Inauguration of floodlights) 2-3 (Gibson, own goal)
February 13 1962 v F.C. Lugano (Switzerland) 2-0 (Bleanch, Ashworth)
December 3 1965 v Slovan Bratislava (Czech) 1-3 (Gould)
March 3 1969 v Prague Bohemians (Czech) 2-1 (Andrews, Henderson)

Billy Martin

The match against F.C. Lugano was played at Valley Parade due to storm damage at Park Avenue.

During the summer of 1938 Bradford toured Denmark and played two friendly matches:

June 7 v Copenhagen 2-2 (Martin, Lewis)
June 9 v Nykobing 1-0 (Martin)

OWN GOALS

In Football League matches from 1908 until 1970 Bradford recorded 3,516 goals of which 54 were scored by a player in the opposing team. An unusual scoring feat came in 1927-8, the club's championship-winning campaign. On Christmas Eve Bradford beat New Brighton 2-1 at Sandheys Park with home defender John McDonald putting through his own goal. In the return clash at Park Avenue on the last Saturday of the season, May 5, Bradford completed a Third North double with a 2-1 victory. Again New Brighton's McDonald helped by scoring another own goal!

PARK AVENUE

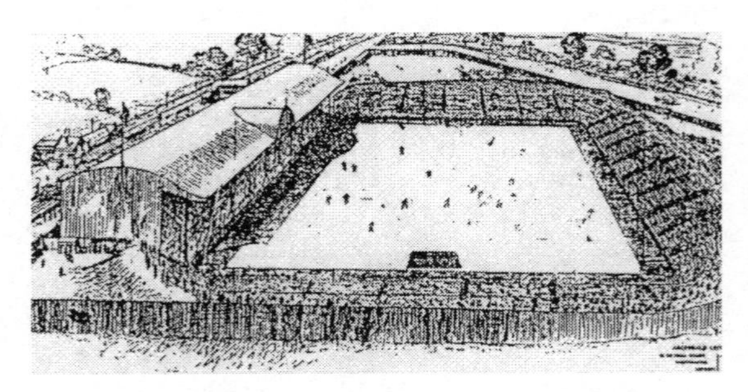

Noted grounds architect Archibald Leitch proposed this early plan for Park Avenue.

During 1879 talks took place between Bradford Cricket Club and Bradford Rugby Club, which at the time was playing rugby several miles away at Apperley Bridge. The cricket club had been forced to vacate their ground in Great Horton as it was required for building and a short move was planned to a site adjacent to a station that had been opened in 1878 by the Bradford and Thornton Railway. As a result of talks between the two clubs an amalgamation was agreed and the combined body became Bradford Cricket Athletic and Football Club.

The new ground at Park Avenue was soon made ready and on July 21 1880 it was officially opened by the mayor, Alderman A. Holden. The eight-acre site boasted two grand pavilions, the lower of which had frontages on to both the cricket and football grounds.

The rugby club brought Park Avenue into great prominence by winning the Yorkshire Cup in 1884. Thereafter the ground became a battlefield for giants in the carrying game.

Following the "Great Split" as it was commonly known, in 1895 the rugby club continued to bring success as a member of the Northern Union. Despite the club's excellent record there was sufficient evidence to show that the dribbling game, which had caught on in a big way with the emergence of Bradford City (1903) and Leeds City (1904) would eventually absorb the public interest. As a pointer to this the club formed an association team and on September 14 1895, they defeated Moss Side (Manchester) in front of a 3,000 crowd.

Things finally came to a head in 1907 and through the efforts of club chairman Harry Briggs the changeover to association football took place and the rugby fraternity left for pastures new.

Extensive alterations were carried out at Park Avenue and the club committee secured the advice of architect Archibald Leitch who had designed the stands at Fulham, Chelsea and Hampden Park. On completion of the work the ground was capable of holding 37,000 although such an attendance was never achieved.

On June 14 1947 the club completed the purchase of Park Avenue football ground as a result of funds raised on the security of the club's properties.

Not long after Football League status was lost in 1970 a rapid decline set in and by mid-l972 the financial situation was very grave indeed. The local council offered to buy the ground for £80,000 in February 1973 but this was turned down by the board, the offer being described as derisory. Chairman George Sutcliffe said: "As it is a fully-equipped stadium we think the ground is worth much more than the Corporation have offered." By the end of March the board had received approval to sell Park Avenue for any offer in excess of £80,000 which was regarded as "fair and reasonable in all the circumstances of the case." This decision had been made by shareholders at an extraordinary general meeting. Within a month a Leeds-based development company, Titan Properties, had bought the ground

without planning permission for a sum in excess of that offered by the council, but not over £100,000. The sale of Park Avenue enabled Bradford to clear their debts and move across the city to share facilities with neighbours Bradford City for the 1973-4 season. In November 1973 the council tried to buy the ground from Titan Properties and in February 1974 agreed terms, believed to be £110,000. This gave the property company a quick profit and left the football club with the feeling that they had been badly treated by the council. Despite various grandiose schemes being put forward nothing was done with the ground and it gradually fell into rack and ruin.

In May 1988 any hopes of soccer returning to Park Avenue were ended when a cricket centre was built on part of the land next to Canterbury Avenue. Ironically the firm which won the contract to build the centre was Ham Construction (Bradford) Ltd., a company run by two former Avenue players, Bobby and Allan Ham!

EDDIE PARRIS

Long before dark-skinned folk from Pakistan formed a significant portion of Bradford's population, Avenue supplied the first coloured footballer to appear in the home internationals. This was Eddie Parris, who was born near Chepstow of Jamaican parents on January 31 1911. Signed on trial in August 1928 at 17, he made his first-team debut in the cup the following January and scored the goal at Hull which brought the Tigers back for a replay. Parris had the creditable scoring record for a winger of 38 goals in 133 League matches and in 1931-2 he was the club's leading marksman with 14. That season he was capped by Wales against Ireland in Belfast. He later joined Bournemouth (summer 1934), Luton (February 1937) and Northampton (November 1937). During the war he turned out for Bath City, Northampton and Cheltenham Town.

The first coloured player in League football was Arthur Wharton, a Ghanaian, who appeared in goal for Sheffield United in 1894.

PENALTIES

On March 8 1924 Bradford's goalkeeper faced four penalties in five minutes during a Third North match at Crewe. It all started when Andy McCluggage handled and Alf Laycock saved the penalty taken by Jack Doran. Avenue's Bob Turnbull was adjudged to have handled a few minutes later and Crewe were awarded another penalty. This time Doran shot wide. However because Turnbull had been prancing about, a retake was ordered and William Goodwin struck the crossbar. Alas Turnbull had moved again and another retake took place and this time Doran scored!

During 1927-8 Bradford goalkeeper Jack Clough saved seven out of nine penalties awarded against his team.

Arthur Farrell scored against West Brom in a home match on November 20 1948 and in one against Barnsley on February 25 1950 Jack Haines shot wide. Between those two Second Division fixtures Bradford played 53 others without receiving a penalty award.

Bradford once went 57 Second Division matches without conceding a penalty. That was between penalties taken by Manchester United's Bryant at Old Trafford on the last day of the 1935-6 season and Fulham's Woodward at Craven Cottage on October 2 1937.

On August 23 1948 Bradford had three penalties – one missed and two converted – given against them at Blackburn, but won the Second Division match 3-2.

Ronnie Bird (1961-5) was the undisputed Bradford penalty king. He converted 14 spot kicks in League football - a club record.

One of the hardest shots the club ever had when it came to taking penalties was Alvan Williams (1957-60). From October 1957 to March 1959 he was successful ten times.

PLAYER OF THE YEAR

Football League
1966 Kevin Hector
1967 John Hardie
1968 John Hardie
1969 Glen Andrews
1970 Graham Carr

John Hardie is congratulated by Gillian Simpson, Miss Park Avenue 1968

Non League
1971 Tony Leighton
1972 Les Massie
1973 Wilson Rose
1974 Alan Myers
1990 Billy Payton
1991 Darren Wardman
1992 Rohan Eli
1993 Graham Jones
1994 Karl Goddard
1995 Lee Williams
1996 Mark Price
1997 Tony Brown
1998 Phil Sharpe
1999 Wayne Benn
2000 Jason Maxwell
2001 Jason Maxwell
2002 James Stansfield
2003 Andy Quinn
2004 Andy Quinn

POINTS

Football League:	
Most in a season:	63 (1927-8)
Fewest in a season	20 (1968-9)
Most at home	39 (1926-7)
Fewest at home	13 (1967-8)
Most on travel	25 (1927-8)
Fewest on travel	2 (1968-9)
Non-league:	
Most in a season	94 (1994-5)
Fewest in a season	33 (1973-4)
Most at home	50 (1994-5, 1999-00)
Fewest at home	15 (2003-4)
Most on travel	45 (2000-1)
Fewest on travel	11 (1973-4)

PROMOTION

The club's first promotion season came in 1913-14 when in finishing as runners-up to Notts County a place was earned in the First Division.

In 1927-8 Bradford won their first championship in taking the Third North title.

Under player-manager Jimmy Scoular, Bradford gained a third promotion in 1961 when, in finishing fourth in Division Four, the club was elevated to Division Three.

The next promotion was achieved in 1988-9 by the re-formed club when they were runners-up in the West Riding County Amateur League Division Three.

The club gained promotion again in 1990-1 when, as members of the North West Counties League, third place in Division Two took them into Division One.

Bradford won the second championship in their history and their first-ever in non-League football in 1994-5 when they finished top of the North West Counties League. A third came in 2000-1 when they won the UniBond First Division by ten clear points.

QUEEN

The Queen and Duke of Edinburgh visited Park Avenue on October 28 1954. Admittedly they went to the "wrong" part - the cricket field instead of the football ground - but at least they saw the main stand which served soccer on the northern side and county cricket on the other. It was part of a longer visit to the city and about 20,000 schoolchildren greeted them by singing the National Anthem, a hymn, and On Ilkla Moor Baht 'At.

Bradford played in front of Royalty on November 1 1919, when the King of Spain was a guest at Stamford Bridge to see Chelsea beat their visitors 4-0 in the First Division.

RADIO

On March 2 1946 Bradford's F.A. Cup quarter-final with Birmingham City at Park Avenue was broadcast on B.B.C. Radio. Only 19,732 attended, partly because a record crowd had been forecast and with memories of the gates being closed against Barnsley in the previous round many felt there would be no room. Also, the second half was the featured radio commentary, and it was a very cold day so many stayed at home to keep warm and listen in.

One of the most popular quiz shows ever broadcast was "Have a Go." It travelled England with Wilfred Pickles in charge and "Mabel at the table." The first show was broadcast from Southgate Hall in Yorkshire on March 4 1946. On June 2 1948, the 100th show was transmitted from Rochdale. One of these early shows actually came from Park Avenue when on November 15 1947, Wilfred asked several contestants his favourite question: "What was yer most embarrassin' moment, loov?" One shudders to think what the replies were on that occasion!

In more recent times several of Bradford's non-League matches have been featured by B.B.C. Radio Leeds on their Saturday afternoon sports programme.

GORDON RAYNER

Gordon Rayner, one of Yorkshire's most successful non-League managers, arrived at Mount Pleasant to take charge of the club in October 1993 following the departure of Jim Mackay.

He had previously spent a highly successful period at Guiseley, leading them to an F.A. Vase triumph in 1991. They also won the Northern Counties East League Premier Division championship that season and promotion to the Northern Premier League. Rayner led Guiseley to the F.A. Vase final at Wembley for the second time in 1992, but they were beaten by Wimborne. In the same season they reached the F.A. Cup first round for the first time.

After steering Bradford away from the relegation zone in 1993-4, he and assistant Dave Heeley masterminded the club's 1994-5 championship-winning campaign so he became the first manager to pilot a club to both the Northern Counties East and North West Counties League championships. Bradford's record-breaking 1994-5 season earned Rayner the NW Counties League's manager of the season award.

Following a series of poor results in the second half of the 1995-6 season and a disappointing start to the 1996-7 campaign he was given the sack.

RE-ELECTION

A dreadful 1955-6 season saw Bradford concede a club record 122 League goals and, in finishing next-to-bottom of the Third North, they were obliged to apply for re-election for the first time. The club did not have to go "cap in hand" to the Football League again until 1967. This application turned out to be the first of four in succession and at the AGM in London during June 1970 the club was voted out of membership.

Re-election voting

1956 Bradford 47
Crewe Alexandra 45
Crystal Palace 44
Swindon Town 42

1967	Lincoln City 43
	Bradford 42
	Wrexham 40
	Rochdale 36
1968	York City 46
	Bradford 44
	Chester 44
	Workington 38
1969	Grimsby Town 47
	York City 45
	Bradford 38
	Newport County 27
	Cambridge United 16
	Wigan Athletic 11
1970	Darlington 47
	Hartlepool 42
	Newport County 31
	Cambridge United 31
	Wigan Athletic 18
	Bradford 17

Despite their poor playing record many felt that Bradford would be saved in 1970 and that if any club was going to be axed it would be Newport County. The Welsh club had applied with Avenue in 1969 and had received fewer votes. In the final analysis, what really caused the club's slide from 38 votes in 1969 to just 17 in 1970 and Cambridge and Newport drastically to improve on their figures of the previous annual meeting? There was plenty of unofficial speculation after the meeting and it appears most club delegates were of the opinion that the chopping and changes at the club over the previous couple of years in directors, managers and players had caused many clubs to put their votes elsewhere.

RE-FORMED CLUB

1988/89. Back; Edmondson, Rohan Eli, Saunders, Allen, Mackay, Watmuff, Kershaw (capt.). Front; Byrne, Wardman, McDonald, Payton, Henry, Hudson.

Our first book, The Avenue, triggered off a resurgence of interest in the club in 1987. Bob Robinson, a Bradford man who was then vice-chairman of Belper Town, organised a meeting at the Central Library which became the launch pad of revival. The club was re-formed, played at Manningham Mills' ground in Division Three of the WR County Amateur League in 1988-9 and earned promotion as runners-up.

With mounting ambition they joined the Central Midlands League and moved to Bramley RLFC (McLaren Field) as a better ground was a prerequisite for their new status. A year later they went into the NW Counties League so as to get a "toe-hold" on the non-League pyramid system and won promotion as well as the county cup. In 1993-4 their home became Batley RLFC's Mount Pleasant and in 1994-5 with an irresistible late surge of 13 wins off the reel they overtook Clitheroe to take the championship and earn promotion back to the Northern Premier League, now known as the UniBond League.

It took six years to climb out of the First Division, but season 2000-01 saw them take the championship by ten clear points.

The club appeared to have stalled in 2003-4 when, in finishing 17th, they failed to secure an automatic place in the newly-formed Conference North. However, three victories in six days in the play-offs earned them the right to join the top 13 sides who had automatically qualified for the new League.

Bradford players celebrate victory over Burscough in the 2004 play-off final (photo Roy Sims)

RELATIVES

Alf Quantrill

A modern-day Avenue-Bradford City link is that ex-Valley Parade striker Ian Ormondroyd is married to Debbie who is the granddaughter of former Bradford skipper Bob Danskin.

Alf Quantrill, Avenue winger 1924-30 who had been capped four times for England while with Derby County, married the daughter of legendary international hotshot Steve Bloomer.

And the father-in-law of Charlie Pringle, Bradford left-half 1929-31, was Welsh wing wizard Billy Meredith. Pringle, who went prematurely grey, captained Avenue and had won a Second Division championship medal with Manchester City in 1927-8.

During the 1990s brothers Roger, Rohan and Rupert Eli made 303 appearances between them with Rohan completing a half-century of goals.

Father and son Bob and Geoff Walker rank to this day as the only family pair who both played in the Football League for both their home-town clubs. Bob first of all was a City centre-forward and later Avenue back; outside-left Geoff reversed the process in playing first at Park Avenue and afterwards at Valley Parade.

RELEGATION

When normal football resumed after the 1914-18 war, Bradford enjoyed a successful season in the First Division and, in averaging a point a match during 1919-20, they finished as top Yorkshire team. Then followed one of the darkest periods in the club's history. Many of the players on the books had begun to find the pace too hot, some long-serving squad members having reached the veteran stage. Another blow was the loss of the chairman, Harry Briggs, who had always supported the club most generously. At the end of season 1920-1 they were relegated to the Second Division and the following season fared even worse with a drop into the Third North. Bradford created Football League history in being the first club to be relegated twice in successive seasons.

As in the Thirties so in the late Forties Bradford declined following the transfer of some of their most prominent players and relegation to the Third North, which had threatened for some time, became a reality in 1949-50 when a bad run in the second half of the season sealed their fate. Promotion to Division Three in 1961 lifted the gloom for a short time, but the club suffered a fourth relegation in 1963. Although never fully out of danger they were in the bottom four only on two occasions before May, but four defeats (three against fellow strugglers) in the last six outings left them 19th, their programme completed. Barnsley and Bristol Rovers each won a match in hand to climb past them and Avenue were the last team down - on goal average - with a haul of 40 points, and no other team had ever been demoted with such a record (Southend were equally unlucky in 1988-9, relegated with 54 under the 3 points-for-a-win system).

Although it was not strictly a relegation, Bradford became founder members of the newly-created Division Four in 1958 after finishing 1957-8 in the bottom half of the Third North. The new division also took the clubs which had finished in the bottom half of the Third South.

REPRESENTATIVE MATCHES

Two star-studded matches were played at Avenue during the 1939-45 war. The first, on March 2 1940, featured eight goals as a Football League XI drew 4-4 with an All British XI.

Matt Busby, Frank Swift and Joe Mercer, here pictured at Hampden Park, all took part in the 1944 game at Avenue

League: Sagar (Everton); Craig (Newcastle U), Catlin (Sheffield Wednesday); Kaye (Liverpool), Danskin (Bradford), Taylor (Bolton Wanderers); Matthews (Stoke City), Hall (Spurs), Sale (Stoke City), Willingham and Beasley (both Huddersfield Town).
British XI: Hesford; Hayes (both Huddersfield Town), Beattie (PNE); Busby (Liverpool), Harper (Barnsley), Buck (Grimsby Town); Cochrane (Leeds United), Mannion (Middlesbrough), Dodds (Blackpool), Doherty (Manchester City), O'Donnell (Blackpool).
Scorers: Matthews, Ball (2), Sale; Dodds (2), Doherty (2). Attendance: 14,575.

The second, on December 9 1944, was also drawn.
F.A. XI: Williams (Walsall); Mountford (Huddersfield Town), Hardwick (Middles-brough); Franklin (Stoke City), Brown (Hud-dersfield Town), Foss (Chelsea); Broome (Aston Villa), Shackleton (Bradford), Price (Huddersfield), Mortensen (Blackpool), Smith (Brentford).
Army: Swift; Sproston (both Manchester City), Barnes (Arsenal); Busby (Liverpool), Smith (Charlton Athletic), Mercer (Everton); Elliott (WBA), Macaulay (West Ham), Welsh (Charlton Athletic), Edelston (Reading), Deakin (St Mirren).
Scorers: Broome, Macaulay. Attendance: 12,638.

RUGBY

Park Avenue was the only Football League ground to have housed the Rugby League Challenge Cup for 12 months. This happened because Bradford Rugby Club played at Avenue and were the last team to win the Challenge Cup (in 1906) with a 15-man team. They beat Salford 5-0 at Headingley in the final. The following June the annual meeting of the Northern Rugby Union voted to have 13 players to a team. The Challenge Cup was made in 1897 by Fattorini's, the Bradford silversmiths who also made the F.A. Cup. As the rugby team was known at that time simply as "Bradford" it could be claimed that this is the only Football League club to have had their name on the RL Challenge Cup!

JIMMY SCOULAR

When Wally Galbraith left Avenue to take an apparently better post at Tranmere the board were bold and decisive in engaging Jimmy Scoular as player-manager. The team stood fourth in their quest for promotion from Division Four and were playing the most constructive football a lot of followers had ever seen from a Bradford team. Sometimes they would be barged out of their stride by a clogger or two but no clogger could intimidate Scoular, a man hewn from oak and a belligerent leader. He added longer passes to the style and the team forged forward into Division Three.

Scoular made his name at Portsmouth straight after the war and was quickly in the record books for playing for two clubs in the same F.A. Cup competition (Gosport and Portsmouth through special dispensation in 1946). He helped Pompey win the First Division championship in successive seasons and there was a vivid contrast between two outstanding wing-halves - Scoular the hard man who dished it out but could take it and was ill-tempered when anyone couldn't; and the impeccably behaved Jimmy Dickinson, who played 48 times for England. In 1951 Scoular was sent off by Halifax referee Arthur Ellis in the first match of a summer tour to South America. A Fluminense player had been digging his elbows into Jimmy - an unwise approach - and Ellis, knowing Scoular's nature, warned him about taking reprisals. But eventually Scoular was unwilling to tolerate any more niggling, floored his opponent and straight away said, "All right, Arthur, I'm off" as he made for the dressing rooms. Portsmouth's officials were annoyed and sent him home.

Scoular gained nine Scottish caps and many times played for Pompey in front of former Avenue full-back and fellow Scottish international Jimmy Stephen (1951-3) before Newcastle United paid a club record £22,500 for his services in the close season of 1953. Jimmy received the F.A. Cup from the Queen in 1955 after driving the Geordies to victory against Manchester City with his "bishop's move" - piercing diagonal passes to the brilliant outside-left Bobby Mitchell.

Frank Swift, the year before he was killed in the Munich air crash, wrote: "Jimmy can be depended on to fight hardest when the odds are stacked against him. And if his tactics are sometimes a bit over-zealous for squeamish sections of the soccer public they are entirely due to his unbounded enthusiasm for the game. While he is unlikely to be voted First Gentleman of Soccer, he certainly does not deserve the dirty player label hung on him in some quarters. To Jimmy Scoular football is a man's game. 'There's no lying down for every wee knock,' he told me as he soothed a collection of ugly bruises in a Blackpool brine bath. They were his battle scars from the cup replay at Maine Road but I can't remember the trainer coming on for him. He is as rugged as his native Scots granite. The fans thrill to his powerhouse drive or they scream for his blood. But they can never ignore his presence on the field."

Scoular was 35 when he arrived at Bradford and as age began to catch up with him on the field he became increasingly petulant and was twice sent off. In his career he was suspended seven times. But he played in 108 League games for Bradford to bring his total to 602.

Sacked in May 1964, he became manager of Cardiff City and built a team which came closer than any since to regaining the First Division place they lost in 1962: in mid-March 1969 they stood second but finished fifth; and in 1971 they came third after he had signed Ian Gibson who had been at Avenue with him.

In 1968 he guided Cardiff to the semi-final of the European Cup-winners' Cup where they lost 4-3 on aggregate to Hamburg with an attack which included John Toshack. Scoular later had a short spell as manager of Newport County and completed his South Wales club hat-trick by scouting for Swansea. He survived a heart attack before retiring to Portsmouth, where he died in March 1998, aged 73.

Career record:

			FL apps	*FL gls*	*FAC apps*
1946-7	Portsmouth	D1	24		2
1947-8	Portsmouth	D1	40	1	1
1948-9	Portsmouth	D1	42		5
1949-50	Portsmouth	D1	36		5
1950-1	Portsmouth	D1	38	2	1
1951-2	Portsmouth	D1	28	2	4
1952-3	Portsmouth	D1	39	3	2
1953-4	Newcastle U	D1	27	1	5
1954-5	Newcastle U	D1	42	1	10
1955-6	Newcastle U	D1	31	1	1
1956-7	Newcastle U	D1	33	3	3
1957-8	Newcastle U	D1	41		2
1958-9	Newcastle U	D1	32		1
1959-60	Newcastle U	D1	32		2
1960-1	Newcastle U	D1	9		
	Bradford	D4	18	2	
1961-2	Bradford	D3	33		1
1962-3	Bradford	D3	37	3	1
1963-4	Bradford	D4	20		2
Totals			*602*	*19*	*48*

SECRETARIES

Nowadays clubs employ both a secretary and a manager, but in the early days of football it was common for one man to combine both jobs. Bradford did not follow this line until 1913 when secretary Ernest Hoyle left the club.

Bradford Secretaries

E.R. Hoyle (secretary)	1907-13
T.E. Maley (secretary-manager)	1913-24
P. O'Rourke (secretary-manager)	1924-5
C. Ingram (secretary then secretary-manager)	1925-34
G.H. Brigg (secretary)	1934-73
J. Burkinshaw (hon. secretary)	1973-4
R. Wood (secretary)	1988-9
M. Worthy (secretary)	1989-90
R. Griffiths (secretary)	1990-2
A.M. Sutcliffe (secretary)	1992-6
A. Hirst (secretary)	1996-2001
S. Burnett (secretary)	2001

When Bradford moved to Valley Parade for 1973 director Jim Burkinshaw acted as honorary secretary following the retirement of long-serving George Brigg.

LEN SHACKLETON

Outside Ninian Park before a Wales v Scotland match in 1952 a man identified himself as a Sunderland supporter. "Who is the greatest inside forward in the world?" I asked him. The reply was given without hesitation – "Len Shackleton." I was glad to find that Shack had made as big an impact at Roker Park as he did on me during his days at Park Avenue. Shack was pure magic. OK, so there was some guy called Pele who wasn't so bad at No. 10 but who is there in the whole wide world today to compare with either? Admittedly the game has changed and in Shack's time there was scope for the individual to indulge his skills to the delight of spectators who went home sated with glorious entertainment. I saw Pele at Hillsborough and after a while you wanted him to get the ball all the time: the other 21 were an irrelevance. Shack had much the same magnetism. Years after he had left Avenue I went to see him at Leeds in a testimonial for Brian Close, thinking that maybe in the rosy glow of nostalgia I had over-estimated his abilities. He was brilliant! Doubts expelled for ever. One of the ways he entertained was by taking a corner with a drop kick! Shack had an individual style, a beautiful body swerve, a cracking shot, a football brain. If you're beginning to think I'm totally biased, read some evidence from others. John Graydon (World Sports): "Shack is one of British soccer's greatest characters and stands out on the field like a lighthouse on a dark and stormy winter night. He is the footballer with the chuckle in his boots, a smile on his lean face and the ability to tear open an opposing defence with a shrug of a shoulder." Colin Bell (Manchester City): "He was a magician with the ball at his feet and could make opponents look foolish with his tantalising tricks. I used to watch him as a youngster and what he could do with a ball was nobody's business. Shack always set out to make football what it should be - an entertainment. More than anybody it was Shack who gave me the urge to become a professional." Don Revie: "Shackleton was capable of quite extraordinary tricks with the ball. He was an entertainer rather than a great professional and that is why he seldom achieved the success his ability deserved." Former Scottish international Jimmy Carabine, writing about Scottish Select 5 Sunderland 0: "The Scots were superior in all departments except inside-left where Len Shackleton, the complete artist, gave an exhibition of juggling seldom seen on this side of the border. He flicked and passed the ball when and where he pleased." Daily Mail report of the match for Norwich City's floodlight switch-on (October 1956): "Len Shackleton was in his most impish entertaining mood. Shackleton the artist, using the wide-open left-wing spaces as a stage, flicked and fooled his way through perhaps the most colourful individual show ever seen at Carrow Road." Sunday Express (1949): "Shackleton was so fast he reminded me of a burglar making off with a sable wrap. To these dazzled eyes he combined dribbling on a hairpin with the trickery of a cardsharp on the spree. No words I can conjure can begin to describe the shifting, swerving wizardry of this stupendous Sunderland star."

Tommy Docherty: "I have seen some ball artists in different parts of the world. I have watched the Continental and South American ball jugglers going through their party pieces. Believe me, not one of them could hold a candle to Len Shackleton. The ball not only talked for him, it sang an aria from Faust! I first met him when I was a lad of 19 playing for Celtic against Sunderland in a testimonial match. He put on an inside-forward display that was fabulous. Despite his activity he still found time to direct me, an opponent, through my game. Constantly he was shouting at me telling me when to hold the ball, when and where to release it. You can imagine how much such advice meant to me at that age, coming from such a player. Not many stars would spend their time helping a raw boy who probably they would never see again. But then, not many stars possess the generosity of Len Shackleton."

Stan Mortensen (Blackpool) in 1953: "Unlike most of the ultra-clever chaps Shack can also get goals, as witness his 22 in the First Division last season."

Top journalist Alan Hoby: "Len Shackleton was born in the wrong country. He is not understood over here and his quixotic moves and the remarkable screw and curve he can put on a football are considered clever but eccentric. If he had been a Hungarian or an Austrian or a Brazilian his genius, I am sure, would not have been wasted."

Shack scored 166 goals for Bradford during the war (and one F.A. Cup goal in 1946) and no player ever put the ball into the net so many times for the club. He was transferred to Newcastle for £13,000 and captivated Tyneside from day one by scoring six on his debut against Newport County.

He moved to Sunderland in February 1948 for a record £20,050. His rich talent was not recognised often at top level - five full caps and a victory International and three goals in two outings for the Football League. Shack was a strong-minded personality with views as individual as his game and no reservations about expressing them, which did nothing for his popularity with the establishment. Some would also argue that he didn't worry about tackling back (taking the view that he was not going to chance breaking a leg for the then maximum wage); point to his fondness for what some regard an over-elaboration and others called entertainment. Yet after his last England match when he scored a brilliant goal in a 3-1 triumph over West Germany the Daily Mail said: "The millions watching either at Wembley or on TV saw Matthews and Shackleton put on a two-man show which should be the next variety command performance."

Shack retired at the start of 1957-8 through injury. And without him Sunderland were relegated for the first time since they entered the Football League in 1890. He lived in retirement at Grange-over-Sands and had a flat in Tenerife for the winter. When he died on November 27 2000, aged 78, national newspapers devoted many columns of newsprint in tribute.

Career record:

	War time		*Apps*	*Gls*	*FAC app*	*FAC gls*
1939-40	Bradford		2	1		
1940-1	Bradford		33	19*		
1941-2	Bradford		34	24*		
1942-3	Bradford		36	36*		
1943-4	Bradford		28	34*		
1944-5	Bradford		39	40*		
1945-6	Bradford		30	12**	8	1
Totals			*202*	*166*	*8*	*1*

	Post War		*FL app*	*FL gls*	*FAC app*	*FAC gls*
1946-7	Bradford	D2	7	4		
	Newcastle U	D2	32	19	6	3
1947-8	Newcastle U	D2	25	7	1	
	Sunderland	D1	14	4		
1948-9	Sunderland	D1	39	8	2	
1949-50	Sunderland	D1	40	14	2	2
1950-1	Sunderland	D1	30	7	4	
1951-2	Sunderland	D1	41	22**	2	
1952-3	Sunderland	D1	31	6	3	
1953-4	Sunderland	D1	38	14	1	
1954-5	Sunderland	D1	32	8	6	1
1955-6	Sunderland	D1	28	7	6	
1956-7	Sunderland	D1	26	8	2	
1957-8	Sunderland	D1	1			
Totals			*384*	*128*	*35*	*6*

** top scorer ** joint top scorer*

BILL SHANKLY

When Bradford's board were choosing a successor to Vic Buckingham as manager early in 1953 they wound up with a short list of two, one of whom was Bill Shankly, then in charge of Grimsby Town, also in the Third North. Instead they chose the little-known Norman Kirkman, player-manager of Exeter City. It sounds like one of soccer's all-time howlers; but the directors were not willing to hand over 100 per cent control and it is possible that in these circumstances Shankly might have withdrawn. We don't know.

By the end of the season the board were probably patting themselves on the back because under Kirkman the team went 12 matches unbeaten to finish seventh (two points behind Shankly's Grimsby).

SHORT TIME

In an away League match at Halifax Town on September 5 1925, the referee played short time in the first half and had to recall both teams for four minutes, during which time Halifax scored. Bradford won 2-1.

CARL SHUTT

The former Sheffield Wednesday, Leeds United and Bradford City player was appointed manager following the departure of Trevor Storton in March 2004. His arrival at Avenue sparked an astonishing revival that saw his team climb out of the bottom three and eventually win a place in the newly-formed Conference North.

Shutt began his long playing career in non-League football before being taken to Hillsborough by Howard Wilkinson in 1985. He later moved to Bristol City, but in 1989 Wilkinson signed him for a second time as Leeds United boss. His most memorable appearance came in 1992 when he scored the winning goal against Stuttgart at the Nou Camp in a replayed European Cup tie. He was with Bradford City when the Paraders climbed out of Division Two in May 1996 after defeating Notts County in the play-offs. In 1999 his Football League career ended at Darlington where he was player-coach.

Shutt then turned his hand to management and in 2002 he piloted Kettering Town into the Nationwide Conference. Unfortunately the crisis-torn club was relegated the following season and Shutt's contract was terminated.

JIMMY SIRREL

Jimmy Sirrel arrived at Avenue on a free transfer from Celtic in time for 1949-50 but managed only 12 appearances in two seasons. He later played for Brighton and Aldershot and gained valuable coaching experience in the South before making his name as manager of Notts County in the 1970s, taking them from the Fourth Division to the First.

Around the time he left Parkhead there was quite an exodus from Celtic to the south. Among others who came to England not long after the war were Jimmy Delaney (to Manchester United), Tommy Docherty and Willie Corbett (Preston North End), Roland Ugolini (Middlesbrough), Tommy Kiernan and Les Johnstone (Stoke City), Duncan McMillan (Grimsby Town) and George Paterson and Johnny Paton (Brentford).

BARRY SMITH

Barry Smith had only two seasons with Avenue but his scoring achievement in the second was notable. In a team which finished 20th in the Third North he was top scorer with 28 - and only three players ever scored more than that in one Bradford season. Avenue netted 25 in 23 away matches and Smith's share was 15, including three hat-tricks.

His first trio came at Darlington on September 22 and he recalls: "They had not won an away match for 18 months but we beat Darlington 5-0 and I got three of them. After the match Bill Corkhill said: 'Well we won but I've never seen a worse Darlington team.' I threw my boots at him. Well I was only on £12 a week so they could not have taken much off me. I was always at loggerheads with the management because the money was poor and we were treated like dirt and I wasn't having that. It was a smashing little club with a beautiful playing area but looking back there was poor management and there were poor directors.

"In the New Year I went up to sign for Sunderland but I had scored three at Gateshead and Avenue then wanted another £3,000 - from £12,000 to £15,000. They argued about it and the same week Sunderland's books were taken away for investigation and the transfer fell through. It is not easy playing centre-forward in a bad side but I could always score goals. Jock Buchanan was a clever player who could hold the ball and lay it off. If I had had someone like him up front with me I would have scored 50.

"Charlie Atkinson was a good player all the time I was there and a very nice fellow who gave 110 per cent but there were very few like him. If I'd been playing today I would have been making a fortune because the style of play would have suited me - up the middle with a twin striker. I could run fast. No one could catch me. I could do 100 yards in 11 seconds. I got a lot of individual goals at Avenue. It's so different now: defenders don't tackle in the modern game because they're frightened of giving away a penalty or a free kick within shooting distance. So they run alongside and try to nick the ball off the forward's toes.

"When I left Avenue I went to Wrexham. It was a bad move in a football sense but while I was there I met my wife Joan and that was the best thing that happened to me in my football career."

Barry made up for lack of success in football by working hard to achieve big success after leaving the game. A "failed plumber" by trade, he became a plumbing equipment rep with Rycroft's; realised it was better to work for a manufacturer and did so for Bert McGee - "a wonderful man who became chairman of Sheffield Wednesday." He wound up as northern area sales manager. Then he started his own firm, Industrial Equipment, at Dudley Hill, selling nuts and bolts in a big way. He retired after 42 years of work though he is still a consultant with the firm which he sold to the lads who were with him.

His business success at one time enabled him to indulge in running a Rolls Royce and he has a second home in Spain. He has been a single-figure handicap golfer for more than 24 years and despite a triple by-pass operation still runs two and a-half miles an-hour every morning. His best man was former Avenue colleague Bud Houghton, who died in 1995 from lung cancer at the age of 59.

SOUTHERN LEAGUE

On May 31 1907 Bradford applied for membership of the Football League, there being vacancies in the lower division. The Rev. James Leighton, affectionately known as the "Sporting Parson", put forward Bradford's case. Unfortunately they were unsuccessful. Someone then had an outrageous idea. It was to apply for membership of the Southern League! Fulham had gained admission to the Football League Second Division leaving a vacancy in the Southern League. This time Bradford were in luck. Their election was almost unanimous.

Voting 1907-8	
Bradford	36
Oldham Athletic	2
Croydon	2

Bradford stayed in the Southern League for just one season before successfully gaining admission to the Football League at the second attempt, in 1908.

JIMMY STEPHEN

Jimmy Stephen was the only player from either Bradford club who was chosen to captain his country while playing in the city. He first wore the dark blue jersey of Scotland in a war international at Wembley in February 1944, playing left-back against Stanley Matthews after the original selection, Jimmy Carabine (Third Lanark), was injured. He held his place for Scotland's next four games and then after a gap was given the captaincy against Wales at Wrexham in October 1946 - a strange decision as he had never previously skippered any team he'd played for! Walley Barnes (Arsenal) was another full-back whose first experience of captaincy was for his country (Wales) in 1948. He gained another full cap against Wales at Hampden in November 1947.

Stephen was transferred to Portsmouth in October 1949 for what was then a record for a full-back of £15,000 but made only one appearance in their First Division championship team of that season. After two years as a Pompey regular he was afflicted by injuries and was released in 1955.

He played in minor football until he was 45, worked as a representative for a firm of timber importers and still lives near Portsmouth. Small but sturdy, Stephen was a tenacious defender but unruffled in temperament.

TREVOR STORTON

Bradford's longest-serving manager since Fred Emery (1942-1951). He became the oldest player to turn out for Avenue in peace-time when appearing as a second half substitute in a Northern Premier League match at Workington in 1998.

Storton was appointed in September 1996. His teams were always hard to beat and in his first four seasons the club did not finish below tenth place in the UniBond League First Division. Ably assisted by former Frickley Athletic boss Ian Thompson, he guided Avenue into the Premier Division in 2001 after the team won the First Division title by ten clear points.

Top ten places were achieved in the following two campaigns. However he reserved his poorest league season for 2003-4, when all that was needed was a top 13 finish to qualify for automatic promotion to the newly-created Conference North. With the team struggling in the bottom three and looking unlikely to reach the play-offs and with it an outside chance of gaining promotion, Storton and the club parted company. His final season in charge had not been all gloom and doom. He steered the club into the First Round of the F.A. Cup for the first time since 1970 and a money-spinning home tie with Second Division Bristol City enabled supporters to forget league strife.

The Keighley-born defender came to prominence with Tranmere Rovers in the 1960s after joining the Prenton Park outfit as an apprentice at 16 years of age. He made his first team debut against Swindon Town and in the same season represented England Youth. In 1972 he was snapped up by Bill Shankly and spent two years at Anfield with the likes of Tommy Smith, Kevin Keegan, John Toshack and Emlyn Hughes. Although his time at Liverpool was short he says those years shaped his approach to the game. Due to limited chances he moved to Chester in 1974 and became their most expensive signing, at £25,000. In his first season they were promoted to Division Three and also reached the semi-finals of the Football League Cup. He was voted best defender by his fellow professionals, which was a great honour to him. He completed ten years at Sealand Road, during which time he made a record number of appearances before his League career came to an end. Moving into the non-League game, Storton joined Oswestry Town as player-coach and later manager. When the club folded he moved on to Telford United taking the position of player-coach. He led the club out twice at Wembley in F.A. Trophy finals against Enfield (1988) and Macclesfield Town (1989).

He gained his first managerial experience at Chorley in the early 1990s and before accepting the Bradford post had been scouting for various clubs.

ALF STRANGE

The only Avenue player to have captained England was Alf Strange, who led his country against Wales at Anfield in November 1931 (England won 3-1).

Strange, then of Sheffield Wednesday, was first capped against Scotland at Wembley in 1930 (5-2) and held the right-half position for the next 12 internationals, missed one against Wales and returned for the next seven. He was the wing-half behind Albert Geldard when he first represented England on the Continental tour of 1933.

His first league club was Portsmouth for whom he scored five from centre-forward against Gillingham in Division Three South in January 1923, a feat no Pompey man has ever bettered. Port Vale brought him nearer his Derbyshire home but it was Wednesday who converted him to a half-back and his reward was two First Division championship medals in 1929 and 1930. After breaking a bone in his foot at Liverpool in December 1933 he was visited in the dressing room by Lord Derby, who gave him his walking stick with a gold band, a keepsake Alf always treasured. He played only ten times for Avenue. In the summer of 1935 he was one of seven players of repute recruited by the club but they were mostly failures. Alf dropped out of the League to join Ripley Town and run a poultry farm.

SUBSTITUTES

Substitutes were first introduced in 1965-6 but in that initial season they were allowed to replace only injured players. Thereafter substitutes could be used for any reason. Bradford's first substitute to be used was Eric Burns who replaced Sam Lawrie at Luton on the opening Saturday. Burns was one of only 14 substitutes used in the Football League on that day. Phil Robinson was Bradford's first F.A. Cup substitute and he came on for Geoff Gould against Workington in a second-round tie on January 11 1967. Alan Turner became the club's first used substitute in the Football League Cup when he replaced Paul I'Anson at Halifax Town on August 23 1967 in a first-round tie.

JEFF SUDDARDS

Jeff Suddards was the most cultured full-back in the Third North during the 1950s and he says none of the seven managers he played for asked him to change his style.

A transfer was set up to Sheffield Wednesday during Norman Kirkman's reign but it fell through when Jeff was injured. At the time Kirkman said: "Given a chance in the First Division Jeff will soon be England class." The crowd in the low stand thought on similar lines: "Come on, Jeff, show them how it's done," they would shout. That bad injury to his knee was a complete accident and Jeff owed the rest of his career to the expertise of the surgeon, Mr. Wishart.

He went on to play 327 League matches, a figure exceeded for the club by only three others. When Alf Young was manager his influence took Jeff into the All Stars team who were an attraction at several grounds' floodlight opening and included personalities like Shankly, Hagan, Walley Barnes and Ivor Powell.

Jeff says: "The professional footballer needs to be alert and look round to see where everyone is. That way he knows what he wants to do with the ball before it comes to him. It doesn't matter how the ball comes, he should be able to control it and do something with it. I used to run up the wing with the ball in the days before such things were done. The trouble at Avenue was we had players who couldn't control the ball properly and because of the wage system which meant your money was halved if you were dropped into the reserves there were some who would 'hide' rather than risk going wrong.

"Park Avenue was a beautiful ground to play on and the crowds liked to go there. When I first came into the team in 1950 we would meet at the Victoria Hotel for a few games of snooker and lunch of chicken and toast and then we were taken to the ground in taxis. It took them quite a while because people used to walk up from town and spilled into the road The club started to go downhill when they got directors who were small men with little knowledge of the game and they would not pay for players of the quality we needed."

Suddards went to Tyersal School with Dick Conroy (who later played for both Bradford clubs) and took part in a schools cup final at Valley Parade. Given a free transfer by Galbraith in 1959 he joined Cambridge City who had a side good enough to win the Southern League in 1963. "It was a lovely ground and I excelled there," recalls Jeff, "because I was free to play as I liked. They paid me more than Avenue and found me a job besides." He was captain for part of his stay.

After football he became warehouse and distribution manager for ISA, a computer company he says are the biggest in Europe in their field. He is now retired and trying to get his golf handicap back into single figures.

SUNDAY

Bradford's first taste of Sunday football came in 1971-2. On February 20, Hyde United arrived at Park Avenue for a NW Floodlit League match, which ended 3-3. The match was originally scheduled for the following day but the ban on floodlighting as a result of a power dispute gave the club the opportunity to try a Sunday match. The following month the club played their first-ever league match on a Sunday when they travelled to Great Harwood on March 5. In 1973-4 there were four further Sunday engagements all in the Northern Premier League. One of these, on February 3, was at home to Wigan Athletic which drew a crowd of 1,322, Bradford's best home attendance of the season.

During March 1997 the team made the long trip to Workington for a Sunday UniBond League match, which ended goalless, after losing 0-5 at home to Droylsden just 24 hours earlier.

The re-formed club's second Sunday outing was certainly a memorable one. On November 9 2003, Nationwide Second Division pacesetters Bristol City came to Horsfall Stadium in the First Round of the F.A. Cup and gained a 5-2 victory.

SUPPORTERS' CLUB

The first meeting of the Supporters' Club, newly founded, was held at Bradford Mechanics Institute on April 11 1922. On January 8 1947, the supporters' club, "apprehensive of the gradual present decline," passed a unanimous no-confidence vote in the football club directorate.

George Hudson

Over the years the Avenue Supporters' Club has been responsible for raising thousands of pounds for the parent club. In the football club's 51st Annual Report, published on September 6 1960, the invaluable work done by the Supporters' Club was acknowledged: "Once again the directors owe a great debt of gratitude to the Auxiliary Committee, Supporters' Club and Sportsmen's Association for their wonderful help they have been in contributing during the year the sum of £14,540 to the funds of the club. The raising of so large a sum of money is a great credit to the members of those bodies and we thank them most sincerely for the time they have given and the work they have done so enthusiastically to make this possible." George Hudson, who still lives near Park Avenue, was elected to the Supporters' Club committee in 1948 and worked tirelessly to raise funds as secretary-treasurer for 20 years from 1954. During that period the Supporters handed over more than a quarter of a million pounds and among other things George remembers once paying the club's electricity bill.

Bradfordian George began watching Avenue in 1926 and the team that still trips off his tongue is Clough; Cookson, Lloyd; Taylor, Elwood, Dickinson; Davis, McLean, McDonald, Hawes and Quantrill (1928-9). Not that he lives in the past: he nominates Kevin Hector as his favourite player. For 47 years he was a Bradford Cricket League umpire. He officiated at the indoor cricket and football centre which was built on the former ground. He has fond memories of the 1940s team and of watching the F.A. Cup triumph at Newcastle in 1949 - "Les Horsman kept Jackie Milburn right in his pocket." The current supporters' club is a thriving organisation and over the past few years has handed over several thousands of pounds to the football club.

TELEVISION

On December 21 1968, Bradford were featured for the first and only time on ITV. Their Fourth Division clash with Doncaster Rovers was covered by Yorkshire Television (commentator Danny Blanchflower) and was transmitted on Sunday afternoon at 2.30pm.

When the club was re-formed in 1988, BBC Look North visited Manningham Mills football ground where Bradford played their home games during 1988-9 in the West Riding County Amateur League. Various officials were interviewed, as was supporter and former player George Stabb.

When Bradford were paired with Accrington Stanley in the F.A. Cup second qualifying round during the 1992-3 season, the match attracted a great deal of media attention and a short piece was included in the BBC's Nine O'Clock News programme that evening. Unfortunately Avenue lost 2-0 to their Northern Premier League opponents.

On Yorkshire Day, August 1 1990, Bradford played a friendly with Accrington Stanley at Horsfall Playing Fields in the city. The occasion was included in that evening's Yorkshire Television news programme "Calendar." The pre-match publicity boosted the attendance to 400.

Bradford's appearance in the F.A. Cup First Round on November 9 2003 brought plenty of media coverage. Following match previews from BBC "Look North" and ITV's "Calendar" the goals from the first half against Bristol City were shown on national TV, BBC's Sunday Grandstand cameras being present at Horsfall Stadium.

TENNIS

Four world stars of the sport battled it out in exhibition lawn tennis matches on a specially prepared court at Park Avenue football ground on June 10 1956. The display, sponsored by the Bradford Parks Amateur

Lawn Tennis Association, was watched by a crowd of 2,500. The personalities taking part were Althea Gibson, the then French champion, Thelma Long, a leading Australian player, Jaroslav Drobny, the 1954 Wimbledon winner, and Lew Hoad, who a few weeks later became Wimbledon champion.

TRANSFERS

Before the 1939-45 war clubs tended not to divulge players' transfer fees apart from on the odd occasion or when only a small fee was involved. Clubs would frequently describe a fee as being either "small", "substantial" or "a club record". Below is a list of Bradford's more notable transfers.

On September 3 1951, Bradford paid Burnley a fee in the region of £6,000 for outside-left Terry Lyons, a local lad to whom they had given two "A" team trials three years previously.

When Jimmy Stephen left for Portsmouth the fee Bradford received was the biggest-ever to that time for a back in the Football League.

When goalkeeper Bob Mason joined Bradford from Hamilton Academicals in December 1909, two fees had to be paid as he was jointly on the books of Hamilton and Clyde at the time.

Ernest Waddilove was chairman when Bradford, during the close season of 1935, spent not wisely but too well in signing players like Villa goalkeeper Ken Tewkesbury, Blackburn left-back Crawford Whyte, Sheffield Wednesday right-half Alf Strange, Villa centre-half Alec Talbot, Hearts outside-right (later full-back) Bobby Johnstone, Port Vale centre-forward Tommy Nolan and Hull City inside-left David Wright. Bradford spent about £12,000 on transfer fees which was more than any other Second Division club – contrasted to Bradford City who had spent nothing. The enterprise did not turn out nearly so happily as was envisaged and Bradford finished 16th. City were 12th.

ARRIVALS	
Jimmy Smith from Brighton, Nov 1912	£735
Jimmy Bauchop from Spurs, Dec 1913	£1,500*
George McMillan from Rangers, Dec 1930	*
Alec Talbot from Villa, Jun 1935	*
Ron Greenwood from Chelsea, Dec 1945	*
Bill Woods from Rochdale, Jan 1947	*
Bill Layton from Reading, Jan 1947	£6,000*
George Wilkins from Brentford, Feb 1947	£6,500*
Les Stevens from Spurs, Feb 1949	£7,000*
Bob Crosbie from Bury, May 1949	£10,000*
Jack Haines from west Brom, Dec 1949	£15,000*
Leon Leuty from Derby County, Mar 1950	£24,500*
Alec Wright from Spurs, Aug 1951	£12,000
Phil Turner from Carlisle U, Jun 1951	Substantial
DEPARTURES	
George Halley to Burnley, Mar 1913	£1,200
Harold Peel to Arsenal, Dec 1926	£1,750
Walter Millership to Sheff. Wednesday, Mar 1930	*
Tommy Lewis to Blackpool, Dec 1938	£5,000
Geoff Walker to Middlesbrough, May 1946	£6,000
Len Shackleton to Newcastle United, Oct 1946	£13,000*
Johnny Downie to Manchester United, Mar 1949	£18,000*
Jimmy Stephen to Portsmouth, Oct 1949	£15,000
Leon Leuty to Notts County, Sep 1950	£24,500*
Billy Elliott to Burnley, Aug 1951	£20,000
Ian Gibson to Middlesbrough, Mar 1962	£20,000
Kevin Hector to Derby County, Sep 1966	£34,000*

** club record*

When Jimmy Smith was transferred to Park Avenue the deal also included the departure of Bobby Simpson to Brighton. The signing of Bill Woods and Bill Layton took place on the same day, hence the club record payment for Woods was broken just hours later when Layton arrived.

TRANSPORT

At one time supporters came to Park Avenue by train, tram, car and on foot. Opposite the ground was Horton Park station and with private transport still fairly rare the trains were well filled. The station was closed in 1952, though on several occasions after that it was brought back into use for big events.

Pictured are the station's twin sports symbols depicting soccer and cricket, though they had known better days when the photograph was taken in 1954.

Manchester United and Hull City are other clubs to have had stations hard by the ground and Arsenal of course have an Underground station named after the club.

Due to a strike on the railways in October 1919, Bradford were forced to find alternative transport to convey the team to Aston Villa for a First Division fixture. The 250-mile round trip was eventually made using three vehicles, one of which was the chairman's chauffeur-driven limousine.

The Bradford Supporters' Club coach to Swansea on March 7 1970 left the city at 6.45am with 20 or so cheering fans. When the coach was 32 miles from London somebody asked the driver where he was going. He replied: "Isn't it to Wembley?" – the League Cup final was on that day. The Bradford supporters eventually arrived at Vetch Field ten minutes after the start of the match!

During 1949-50 Avenue winger Les Stevens continued to live in London and do his training there after signing from Spurs, making a round trip by rail of 400 miles for home matches.

UNDEFEATED

During the 1920s Bradford put together an incredible run at Park Avenue which saw the team go undefeated in the League for 38 matches. After losing to Grimsby Town on Boxing Day 1925, they did not lose again until November 19 1927, when again the visitors were Grimsby Town! Included in this sequence were 25 successive wins from October 9 1926, until that defeat by Grimsby. This remains the Football League record for consecutive home wins.

During 1964 Bradford did not lose a home match in the Fourth Division. After going down at home to Lincoln City on December 28 1963, the team remained invincible until Crewe Alexandra arrived on February 6 1965 and won 3-2 to inflict on Avenue their only home League defeat of 1964-5.

Bradford's best start to a League season was in 1964-5 when they went undefeated for 12 Fourth Division matches. Before the defeat at Wrexham on October 7, they held the distinction of being the only unbeaten team in the League. In 1947-8 they won all their opening six matches to lead the Second Division and some might argue that was an even better start!

There is an all-pervading optimism about a new season and Avenue always contrived to engender high hopes after the 1939-45 War, because they never lost their first home match for 17 years. Newport County spoilt the sequence by winning 5-2 in August 1963.

In non-League football Bradford's 1994-5 championship-winning season saw the team twice string together a run of 14 matches unbeaten in league and cup football. In the second run the team won their final 13 league matches to clinch the NW Counties League championship in spectacular fashion.

UNUSUAL SIGNINGS

Ernie Suggett

Outside-right Ernie Suggett was in Newcastle infirmary, where he was recovering from an injury, when he was transferred from Barrow to Bradford in May 1932.

Bradford manager Tom Maley signed Sheffield Wednesday centre-forward David McLean in a Sheffield picture house in October 1919.

Doncaster full-back Pat Carlin was signed by Bradford boss Norman Kirkman in the cookhouse at RAF Station Lindholme in 1953. The Bradford manager was apparently in tears at the time – the youngster, employed as a civilian cook, was peeling onions!

VICTORIA CROSS

Donald Simpson Bell was one of only two English footballers to earn the Victoria Cross. A full-back who had made just five appearances for Avenue, he was awarded the medal "for conspicuous bravery" on the Somme in 1916. On his own initiative he crept up on a communication trench, rushed across the open under fire and destroyed an enemy machine gun nest with revolver and grenades. He returned from his attack but was killed five days later while leading another assault.

Bell was a Second Lieutenant in the Green Howards and had been a schoolmaster at Harrogate. The P.F.A. and Green Howards have erected a 5ft Yorkstone cross on the spot where he fell, known locally as Bell's Redoubt. He turned professional with Avenue in 1912 and when the war broke out he became the first professional footballer to enlist.

Bell's headstone at the Gordon Dump Cemetery

The other English pro to receive the VC posthumously was Bernard Vann - a grammar schoolmaster who played three matches for Derby County in 1907. Lieutenant-Colonel William Angus, who had been on the books of Celtic, and James McIntosh, centre-forward of Highland Leaguers Buckie Thistle, were other players to be awarded the VC. Jack Clough, ever-present goalkeeper in Bradford's 1927-8 Third Division (North) championship team, earned the Military Medal and bar as a stretcher-bearer in the 1914-18 war.

VICTORIES

Individual Games

Bradford's record Football League victory stands at 8-0 on September 14 1925 against Walsall in a home Third North match.

Bradford set a Football League record by winning 25 consecutive home games between October 9 1926 and November 5 1927.

On travel the club's biggest victory came on February 21 1914 at Fulham where they won 6-1 to register their first-ever Football League success in the capital.

In the F.A. Cup the record victory was actually achieved by the reserve team on October 17 1908. Representing the first team, they won 11-0 at Denby Dale, while the seniors fulfilled a Second Division fixture at home to Grimsby Town - and lost 2-0. The club were then fined £50 by the Football Association for not fielding their strongest side in the cup-tie!

Bradford's biggest Football League cup victory was against neighbours Bradford City at Park Avenue where the visitors were crushed 7-3 on September 4 1963.

In non-League soccer Bradford's biggest victory stands at 7-0 which was the scoreline at Gateshead in the UniBond League Premier Division on April 3 2002.

In a season

The most Football League victories in a season came in 1927-8 when the club were Third North champions and won 27 of their 42 matches.

The fewest victories in a Football League season were four in 1967-8 when the club were obliged to make a third re-election application.

In non-League soccer the most victories in a season were 30 (in 42 matches) when the club won the NW Counties League championship in 1994-5.

The fewest victories in a non-League season stands at nine in the Northern Premier League campaigns of 1973-4 and 1995-6.

WADDILOVE FAMILY

Stanley Waddilove

After the death of Harry Briggs, who had been the club's chairman and benefactor since the association game had been adopted in 1907, there was a long period of constant change at board room level until the emergence of the Waddilove family.

In May 1935 the club was in a bad way and Ernest Waddilove, then a major shareholder and bank guarantor, requested an extraordinary meeting to consider the financial problems. The meeting eventually resolved that Ernest and his cousin Stanley Waddilove, who had been a director from 1923 to 1931, be co-opted to the board. There followed a major shake-up which saw seven board members resign. This left Coun. H.J. White and the two Waddiloves in control, though within a month four more directors were appointed.

Although Stanley Waddilove later took over as chairman, cousin Ernest remained an influential figure at Park Avenue until he resigned in 1955. At the time of his death in 1958, Ernest was still the club's largest guarantor.

The money behind Park Avenue during the Waddiloves' reign from 1935 to 1955 came from the family business, the Provident Clothing and Supply Company. The business was started in 1880 by Joshua Waddilove and it eventually became the world's biggest check-trading organisation. When Joshua died in 1920 he left an estate worth £1,250,000.

In February 1937 it was announced that Bradford had received an offer for the transfer of the entire club to London. The present club would go out of existence and the transferred club would become, maybe, London White City or London Wimbledon. Chairman Ernest Waddilove received the letter from a London syndicate with the offer to transfer their control for them to promote and operate in London. "The letter was placed on the files where it has remained ever since" said Mr. Waddilove.

Ernest and Stanley Waddilove resigned at Park Avenue on April 8 1955 "to enable the board to put into operation the details of a scheme outlined by the chairman of the financial committee."

A third member of the family, Gordon Waddilove, was a club director from 1926 to 1930.

GEOFF WALKER

Geoff Walker, tricky outside-left with a fierce shot, was the grandson of a Keighley Rugby League full-back and followed in his father's stud marks in turning out for both Bradford soccer clubs. Still savoured by those who saw it was a goal against Sheffield Wednesday in March 1944 when he corkscrewed round five men in a brilliant dribble before blasting the ball past a helpless Jack Curnow.

Though an Avenue teenage-regular from 1943-4 to 1946, which included three appearances in F.A. Cup ties, he never actually played in the Football League for them because he was transferred to First Division Middlesbrough for £6,000 before peace-time soccer was resumed. After scoring 50 in 240 League games for the Ayresome Park club, he had a spell with Second Division Doncaster Rovers before signing for Bradford City in June 1957 when he was 30.

He later played for Clacton Town and Chelmsford and was sports master at a public school. What is not generally known is that Geoff had two brothers who both also played at outside-left and that Jack was in Middlesbrough reserves while Geoff was in the first team. Dennis played for Avenue juniors. Geoff died at Chelmsford in March 1997.

WARTIME

How's this for an extraordinary fact of football life? During the 1914-18 war Avenue had one guest and during the 1939-45 conflict another, both of whom were defenders and both of whom went on to become the oldest players ever capped by England. First came Frank Hudspeth who made his Newcastle United debut against Bradford City in December 1910 and went on to make 472 appearances in league and cup football for the club, a total surpassed only by Jimmy Lawrence (1904-22). He became captain (1923-6) and when he made his full England debut against Ireland in Belfast in October 1925 he was 35 years six months and four days old. It should perhaps be added that he was not the selectors' first choice but injuries to others gave him his chance. He collected an F.A. Cup winners' medal and a League championship medal with Newcastle during the 1920s. He was Avenue's right-back in ten games during 1915-16 and scored from the spot against Bradford City and Huddersfield Town in April. At one time be held the record for a scoring full-back of 36 goals (1912-29).

Move on 23 years and at left-back in Avenue's League North encounters with City and Huddersfield was Leslie Compton who during the 1930s had become the outstanding reserve in all football as he understudied Arsenal's international full-back pairing of George Male and Eddie Hapgood. It was seldom he failed to impress on his rare first-team opportunities. One was against Preston (October 1938) and James Freeman wrote in the Daily Mail: "Everything came alike to the nonchalant-looking Leslie Compton whose magnificent play reminded me of Tommy Clay at his best. Perhaps as it was on the left flank I should have said Jesse Pennington." Partnering Hapgood against Stoke in December he drew this comment from the Daily Herald: "The men who prompted most of the Arsenal attacks were Hapgood and Compton who gave just about the most impudent exhibition of the attacking full-back game I have ever seen." And that was in the days when attacking full-backs had never been heard of. So many of them, as Bernard Joy once put it so deliciously, "kicked the way they happened to be facing."

Leslie Compton

Compton started 13 matches for Avenue in 1943-4 two of them at centre-forward, where he had made one war-time appearance for England. Afterwards he was a cup and championship winner with Arsenal from centre-half. Always calm and unflurried and almost unbeatable in the air, he was affectionately called "Good old big 'ead" by the Highbury disciples.

Compton was the oldest player at 38 years two months ever to make his England debut when he played against Wales at Roker Park on November 15 1950, and he held his place for the following international fixture a week later when Yugoslavia were the visitors to his own home ground of Highbury. Another Arsenal man who was a regular in Avenue's successful war-time attack was Eddie Carr.

Two outstanding footballers who made a single appearance for Bradford were Tommy Walker, "the Ace of Hearts" and Scotland regular, who played inside-right at Newcastle on the opening day of 1942-3 and scored in a 4-1 victory; and Ivor Broadis, then with Spurs, who also scored in an opening match triumph, this time in 1944 against Leeds United. Later he became the manager who transferred himself: as player-manager of Carlisle he was involved in his own transfer to Sunderland and pulled in a fee of £18,000 for the Cumbrians. A unique idea of his at Brunton Park had been to take out a mortgage on himself which could be spent on other players!

Ivor Broadis

In November 1941 Albert Geldard made his last appearance in red amber and black as a guest (from Bolton Wanderers) against Middlesbrough while Jack Haines made his first appearance in November 1943, guesting from Swansea Town. Haines returned as a big money international signing from West Brom in 1949.

Tommy Lewis was another ex-Avenue winger who came back to play four matches as a guest from Blackpool; while full-back Ralph Ward also made his farewell Bradford appearance as a guest.

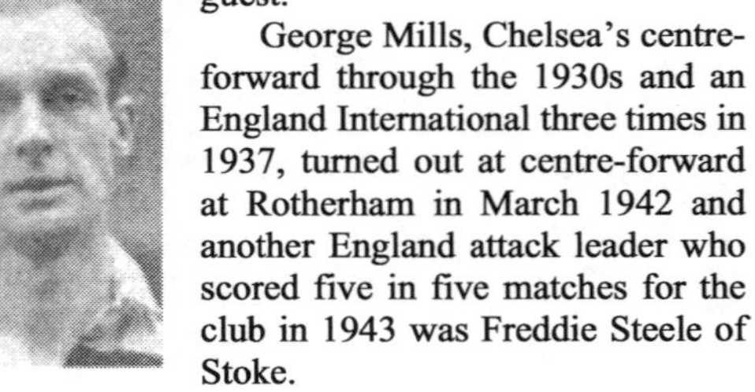

George Ainsley

George Mills, Chelsea's centre-forward through the 1930s and an England International three times in 1937, turned out at centre-forward at Rotherham in March 1942 and another England attack leader who scored five in five matches for the club in 1943 was Freddie Steele of Stoke.

Jack Gibbons and Roy White of Spurs first made themselves known to Avenue followers during the war and afterwards were signed by the club. So did big George Ainsley who arrived with his chunky Leeds United colleague Gerry Henry in 1947.

JACK WESLEY

On Saturday May 5 1934, Tom Postlethwaite turned out for Barrow when they secured their record Football League victory - 12-1 against Gateshead. The visitors' attack included Joe Meek and Jack Wesley. All three came to Bradford.

Wesley was one of the few professional footballers born at Cheltenham and was a Royal Navy regular for a time. He joined Gateshead in June 1932 and set up a club scoring record of 25 in 1933-4 which was never beaten. He arrived at Avenue in September 1934, played in more than 150 matches up to the war and is the only Bradford player to have been featured alone on the cover of a national magazine. Meek moved on to Spurs, Postlethwaite to Northampton Town.

WEST RIDING CHALLENGE CUP

Tommy Little

Bradford entered the WR Challenge Cup, also known as the West Yorkshire Cup, in 1907-8 and stayed in the competition until it was disbanded in 1910. In that first season Avenue reached the final but lost 2-1 to Bradford City at Park Avenue. In the last season of the cup, 1909-10, Avenue again reached the final where they met Huddersfield Town at Valley Parade. This time Avenue got their name on the trophy, winning 4-0 before a 10,000 crowd. Tommy Little grabbed all four goals.

WEST RIDING COUNTY AMATEUR LEAGUE

When Bradford re-formed in 1988 the club gained entry to the WR County Amateur League for 1988-9 playing home games at Manningham Mills football ground in the Heaton district of the city. Placed in Division Three, Avenue had a successful season, finishing as runners-up and gained promotion. However they resigned membership and joined the Central Midlands League the following season.

WEST RIDING COUNTY SENIOR CUP
(West Riding Senior Cup after 1939)

Bradford's name was inscribed on the WR County Senior Cup, which replaced the WR Challenge Cup, in its inaugural season, 1910-11, when they beat Leeds City 5-1 at Valley Parade in the final. The club won the trophy nine times having appeared in the final on 17 occasions.

Final successes:

1910-1	Leeds City	5-1
1912-3	Huddersfield Town	2-1 in a replay
1923-4	Leeds United	2-1
1926-7	Leeds United	3-2
1931-2	Bradford City	1-0
1935-6	Huddersfield Town	1-0
1950-1	Leeds United	4-0
1952-3	Bradford City	3-2
1962-3	Halifax Town	3-0

WEST RIDING COUNTY CUP

Bradford's reserve team got their name on the County Cup in the competition's fourth season, 1928-9. Before the 1939-45 war, Football League clubs entered their reserve teams in the cup, but when the competition was resumed in 1949 only junior sides took part. Following Bradford's loss of Football League status in 1970 the club re-entered the County cup for four seasons but never reached the final. Two years after re-forming, Bradford were back and they met with instant success, winning the trophy with a 5-1 victory against Pontefract Collieries at Valley Parade in 1990-1.

Bradford failed to put their name on the Cup for a second time in the 1990s when they lost 0-2 to Ossett Albion in the 1999 final at the West Riding F.A. County Ground, Woodlesford.

Cup winners: Avenue after their WR County Cup triumph in 1991. Second right at the front is Peter Edmondson, scorer of a vital equalizer. Front of pylon is manager Jim Mackay.

GEORGE WILKINS

On September 10 1947, Bradford dumped Doncaster 4-0 to set up a club record start of six straight wins in the Second Division. George Wilkins was captain and schemer of the side and the Yorkshire Sports said: "No single individual has wielded an influence more potent than that of Wilkins, whose tactical generalship has been rarely approached by any craftsman Bradford have had in modern times."

Wilkins was the father of the present Millwall assistant manager Ray and actually had four sons who all played in the Football League, the others being Graham, Dean and Steve.

George Wilkins

He joined Brentford in 1937-8 from the amateur club Hayes, spent the war in the Army and helped Brentford win the London War Cup at Wembley in 1942 against Portsmouth. Wilkins was inside-left in the Bees' terrific First Division start in 1946-7 when they won four of their first five - but at the end of the season were relegated. By then George had cost Avenue their record fee of approaching £7,000.

Despite his great September form they lost him to Nottingham Forest before the year was out, though they got their outlay back. George finished his League career by making three Second Division appearances for Leeds United in 1949; back in London he became coach of Hayes.

XMAS

On Christmas Day 1941 Bradford fulfilled two fixtures in the League North, playing York City at home in the morning and taking on Huddersfield Town at Leeds Road in the afternoon. Chick Farr and Jimmy Stephen turned out in both.

December 25 the previous year was a day fondly remembered by Len Shackleton, who signed as a professional, donned the Avenue jersey against Leeds United at Elland Road in the morning and then guested for Bradford City at Huddersfield scoring a rare headed goal. The prospect of Christmas seemed to sharpen Shack's appetite for goals because in three successive seasons he scored five in a match during December (1942-3-4). Incidentally, he was not the only player to figure in two games on Christmas Day 1940 - England centre-forward Tommy Lawton was involved in a Merseyside derby before lunch and then popped across the river to guest for Tranmere Rovers against Crewe.

Football on Christmas Day was a popular feature of fixture lists right up to the late 1950s – Avenue's last was in 1957 and although they lost to Southport the crowd at least saw eight goals (five for the visitors). Actually the club must have been quite pleased to see the end of Christmas Day activity; apart from a 1-0 win over Workington in 1956 Avenue never won a match on December 25 in post-war seasons. But it was on Christmas Day 1931 that Bradford enjoyed a record attendance of 32,429 against Leeds United, a figure exceeded in April 1944.

A Christmas Day baby grew up to figure prominently in Avenue history. This was George Henson, born in 1911 at Stoney Stratford in Bucks. His route to Park Avenue was via Northampton Town, Wolves and Swansea. In June 1937 he succeeded Tony McPhee as centre-forward and was poised for the most successful phase of his career. He established a club record of six goals in a match against Blackburn Rovers on January 29, having netted four times in a cup-tie against Newport County three weeks earlier, and wound up top scorer in the whole of the Second Division with 27. Known as "Humpy" in the dressing room because he was round-shouldered, George finished his League career with Sheffield United.

Sammy Lynn

Other Avenue players born on Christmas Day were Sammy Lynn (ex-Manchester United in the early 1950s), Sid Storey, who had been a clever York City inside-forward in more than 300 matches, and David Phillips, a Scottish centre-half whose solitary appearance was at Tranmere in 1939. Joe Hooley, a much-travelled pro, was a Boxing Day babe.

YORKSHIRE LEAGUE

Formed in 1920, the Yorkshire League was a competition for many miners' welfare and other works sides in addition to the reserve and "A" teams of several Football League clubs.

Bradford entered their reserves for the inaugural season, 1920-l, and met with immediate success, their 39 points from a 24-match programme being enough to clinch the title. The following year they finished runners-up to Houghton Main and in 1922-3 they regained the championship beating off the challenge of Halifax Town's reserves. A third and final championship arrived in 1928-9. Considering Bradford did not compete during the periods 1924-8 and 1929-36 they were undoubtedly the first successful club in the Yorkshire League.

By the 1950s most Football League clubs in the Yorkshire League were playing "A" teams and in 1958 most, including Bradford, had departed for the newly-formed North Regional League.

When Bradford joined the Northern Premier League in 1970 the club's reserve side rejoined the Yorkshire League, playing in the competition until 1973, when a move to Valley Parade ruled out the possibility of running a second team.

ZENITH

Jimmy Bauchop

Bradford recorded their highest-ever position in 1914-15 when they finished ninth in the First Division, having been promoted as runners-up to Notts County the previous season.

Three of their foremost personalities were forwards - Jimmy Bauchop (inside-right), dreadnought Jimmy Smith leading the attack and Willie Kivlichan who played at outside-right. Signed from Alloa, Bauchop filled the left-back, outside-left, centre-forward, inside-left and outside-right positions in Celtic's Scottish League championship team of 1906-7, though selected only eight times in 34 fixtures. He scored 11 in 22 outings for Norwich City when they were in the Southern League and had spells with Crystal Palace and Derby County (Second Division championship medal in 1912) before joining Spurs. After being dropped in November 1913 he asked for a transfer and came to Bradford for the club's then highest fee. He quickly felt at home and his dribbling and passing skills helped steer Avenue into the First Division. And in the top flight next season he was top scorer with 28 - including four hat-tricks, one of them against Spurs. He stayed nine years before ending his career with periods at Doncaster and Lincoln and then returned to live in Bradford and run a newsagent's shop in Lidget Green.

Kivlichan was another Scot who had been with Celtic and until at least recently was one of only three Catholics who played for both Celtic and Rangers - Mo Johnston was the third. Kivlichan appeared 14 times in Celtic's team of 1907-8 and won a championship medal in 1909-10. He added a Scottish Cup winner's medal the following season and was chosen three times to represent the Scottish League before being brought to Bradford by Tom Maley, who had also been a Celtic player. At Parkhead, Kivlichan filled every position except outside-left, an omission which was made good during his stay with Bradford, who used him primarily, however, on the other flank.

Willie Kivlichan

Kivlichan qualified as a doctor and became a Glasgow Police surgeon and doctor to the Scottish Boxing Board of Control.

Scottish skipper David Howie dropped back from the attack to take over the centre-half role where, as a classical player, he maintained his interest in going forward and distributing beautifully. On his left Jack Scott put some steel into the side and at inside-right thrustful Tommy Little, who though a ball player was not shy of using his shoulders, packed a cracking shot which brought him a hatful of goals. He was the first of only four players to net 100 for the club. After a stay of 12 years he left for Stoke.

Jimmy Smith, a swashbuckling centre-forward, was the crowd's hero, a Stafford man who had been top scorer with 25 in 29 appearances for Southern League Brighton in 1911-12. The fee to bring him to Avenue was £735 plus inside-forward Bobby Simpson. Tragically Smith was killed on the Western Front only weeks before the 1914-19 war ended.

Sam Blackham, a fixture at left-back, was burly and robust and the sparks flew when he opposed Dicky Bond in Avenue-City derbies, though it seemed each enjoyed the jousting. Remarkably, regular outside-left Jack McCandless was the nearest thing to a six-footer at 5ft 11in, so they must have been a footballing side.

Jack McCandless

Bob Mason, only 5ft 6in or 5ft 8in depending on which reference book you believe, was small of stature for a goalkeeper but he shared duties with Frank Drabble who stood 5ft 10in. Both were succeeded in the First Division by Ernie Scattergood (5ft 8in) who came from Derby County with one England cap and in 1921-2 became the team's penalty taker.

The Yorkshire Observer reported of a Boxing Day game against Clapton Orient: "After 18 minutes Peel being held on the ground by Bradby, the referee awarded a penalty. Scattergood hit it at Wood, from whom the ball went back to Scattergood. The same thing happened from the second shot; but with defenders crowding round him Scattergood completed the goal at the third attempt. It is an extraordinary thing for one player to have three chances of completing one penalty. After Orient had equalised in 61 minutes Bauchop was tripped when clean through and Avenue were awarded a second penalty. Scattergood had two kicks at this one, the first being taken again when players strayed beyond the penalty line."

Willis Walker

So the goalkeeper scored twice in one match. He added to his total at Nottingham Forest but his penalty-taking ended on Easter Saturday at South Shields when Willis Walker (later to keep goal for Bradford) saved Scattergood's shot and Ernie had to wheel and start a frantic, though successful, chase back to his own area to turn away a shot from England prospect Ernie Simms.

INTRODUCTION TO THE STATISTICS PAGES

The season-by-season grids show the results of games of the old and new clubs in all major competitions, including the Southern League, Football League, F.A. Cup, Football League Cup, UniBond League and other first-team competitions. The old club's records run from 1907/08 to 1973/74, the new club from 1988/89 to 2003/04.

Home games are identified by the opponents name in upper case, away games by the use of lower case. Bradford's score is always given first. Attendances for Football League games are taken from official Football League records from season 1925/26 onwards; for other seasons, attendances based on newspaper reports have been used.

A full player list is provided for every player who has made a Football League appearance for the old club. Date and place of birth are shown, where known, and the year of death. Players with the same surname and initials are given a (1) or (2) after their name to avoid confusion. The next two columns, "seasons played", act as an index to the season-by-season grids. The years shown are the "first year" of the season; for example, 1961 is season 1961/62. The two columns show the season in which the player made his first team debut; and the final season that he played. However, if he only played in one season, the second column is blank.

Note that some Football League players also made F.A. Cup appearances in 1945/46 and in Northern Premier League seasons 1970/71 to 1973/74. F.A. Cup appearances from these non-League seasons are included in the list. Previous and next clubs show where he was transferred from, and the club he moved to. Non-league club information is included when known. The appearance columns have separate totals for the League, F.A. Cup, Football League Cup and the other tournaments, which are the Southern League 1907/08 and the Northern Premier League 1970/71 to 1973/74. "Goals scored" are also shown under the four headings. If a player has had more than one spell at the club playing first team football, a consolidated set of appearance and goals are shown on the first line. Subsequent lines show the seasons involved on his return to the club, and his new pair of previous and next clubs.

A full record of meetings against all other League clubs (in the Football League) is included. Some clubs have played under different names, but the totals are consolidated under the present day name in this table. Final League tables are also included, either on the relevant page or in a special section later in the book.

The non-League seasons 1988/89 to 2003/04 contain results and line-ups for other first team competitions. 'L' denotes a league game; the other abbreviations are as follows:

FAC	F.A. Challenge Cup	DC	District Cup
FAT	F.A. Challenge Trophy	FC	Floodlit Cup
FAV	F.A. Challenge Vase	LPT	Lamot Pils Trophy
LC	League Cup	LCC	League Challenge Cup
CC	West Riding County Cup	LCT	League Challenge Trophy
PC	Presidents Cup	UC	Unifilla Cup
FDC	First Division Cup	PO	Play off

The rear of the Park Avenue football stand, used as a viewing gallery for the adjoining county cricket ground. Yorkshire CCC played there for more than a century, starting in 1881.

1907/08

13th in the Southern League Division One

						1	2	3	4	5	6	7	8	9	10	11	
1	Sep	7	Reading	3-1	7500	Baddeley	Craig	Christie	O'Rourke	Wood	Mair	Manning 1	McKie	Reid	Fisher 1	Carrick 1	
2		11	Watford	3-1		Baddeley	Craig	Christie	O'Rourke	Milnes	Mair	Manning 1	McKie	Reid 1	Fisher 1	Carrick	
3		14	WATFORD	3-2	15000	Baddeley	Craig	Christie	O'Rourke	Milnes	Mair	Manning 1	Ward	Reid 2	Fisher	Carrick	
4		21	Norwich City	0-2	10000	Baddeley	Craig	Christie	O'Rourke	Milnes	Mair	Manning	McKie	Reid	Spence	Carrick	
5		28	NORTHAMPTON T	1-1	12000	Baddeley	Craig	Christie	O'Rourke	Milnes	Mair	Manning	Blott 1	Reid	Spence	Carrick	
6	Oct	5	Southampton	1-2		Baddeley	Craig	Christie	O'Rourke	Milnes	Mair	Manning	Blott	Reid	Brown 1	Coles	
7		12	PLYMOUTH ARGYLE	0-0	18000	Baddeley	Craig	Christie	O'Rourke	Milnes	Mair	Manning	Fisher	McKie	Brown	Coles	
8		19	West Ham United	0-0	12000	Baddeley	Craig	Christie	O'Rourke	Wood	Mair	Ward	McKie	Reid	Brown	Coles	
9		26	QUEEN'S PARK RANGERS	2-2	12000	Baddeley	Craig	Christie	O'Rourke	Wood	Mair	Ward	McKie	Reid 1	Brown	Coles 1	
10	Nov	2	Tottenham Hotspur	0-0	20000	Baddeley	Walton	Struthers	O'Rourke	Wood	Mair	Manning	Spence	Reid	Brown	Coles	
11		9	SWINDON TOWN	2-2	9000	Baddeley	Walton	Struthers	O'Rourke	Milnes	Mair	Manning	Spence	Cox 1	Brown 1	Coles	
12		16	Crystal Palace	1-1		Baddeley	Walton	Craig	O'Rourke	Milnes	Mair	Manning	Spence	Cox	Brown 1	Coles	
13		23	LUTON TOWN	1-0	5000	Baddeley	Walton	Craig	O'Rourke	Milnes	Mair	Manning	Spence	Cox	Brown 1	Carrick	
14		30	Brighton & Hove Albion	1-1	5000	Baddeley	Walton	Craig	O'Rourke	Wood	Mair	Manning	Spence 1	Brown	Cox	Coles	
15	Dec	7	PORTSMOUTH	3-2	10000	Baddeley	Walton	Craig	O'Rourke	Wood	Mair	Manning	Cox	Reid 1	Brown	Coles 2	
16		14	NEW BROMPTON	5-5	7000	Baddeley	Craig	Christie	O'Rourke	Milnes	Richards	Manning	Cox 1	Reid	Brown 1	Coles 2	1og
17		21	Millwall	1-0		Baddeley	Walton	Struthers	O'Rourke	Milnes	Mair	Dunbavin	Spence	Reid	Cox 1	Coles	
18		25	Bristol Rovers	1-2	10000	Baddeley	Walton	Struthers	O'Rourke	Milnes	Mair	Dunbavin	Spence	Reid 1	Cox	Coles	
19		26	Leyton	3-0		Baddeley	Walton	Struthers	O'Rourke	Milnes	Mair	Dunbavin	McKie 1	Reid 2	Cox	Coles	
20		28	BRENTFORD	1-0	9000	Baddeley	Walton	Struthers	O'Rourke	Milnes	Mair	Manning	McKie	Reid	Cox 1	Coles	
21	Jan	1	LEYTON	4-0	6000	Baddeley	Walton	Craig	O'Rourke 2	Milnes 1	Mair	Manning	McKie	Reid	Cox 1	Coles	
22		4	READING	1-1	9000	Baddeley	Walton	Struthers	O'Rourke	Milnes	Mair	Manning	McKie	Reid 1	Carrick	Coles	
23		18	NORWICH CITY	1-1	12000	Baddeley	Walton	Craig	Richards	O'Rourke 1	Mair	Manning	McKie	Reid	Brown	Coles	
24		25	Northampton Town	1-1		Baddeley	Walton	Craig	Richards	O'Rourke	Mair	Manning 1	McKie	Reid	Brown	Coles	
25	Feb	8	Plymouth Argyle	1-2		Baddeley	Walton	Craig	O'Rourke	Milnes	Mair	Dunbavin	Cox	Reid	Brown	Coles 1	
26		15	WEST HAM UNITED	0-1	9000	Baddeley	Walton	Christie	O'Rourke	Craig	Wood	Manning	Reid	Ward	Brown	Coles	
27		22	Queen's Park Rangers	0-2		Baddeley	Craig	Christie	O'Rourke	Milnes	Mair	Manning	McKie	Reid	Cox	Coles	
28		29	TOTTENHAM HOTSPUR	1-2	8000	Baddeley	Craig	Christie	O'Rourke	Milnes	Mair	Manning	McKie	Reid 1	Cox	Coles	
29	Mar	7	Swindon Town	0-4		Halliday	Walton	Christie	O'Rourke	Milnes	Mair	Manning	Cox	Reid	Brown	Coles	
30		14	CRYSTAL PALACE	0-1	8000	Finch	Walton	Craig	O'Rourke	Milnes	Mair	Manning	Spence	Reid	Fisher	Coles	
31		21	Luton Town	0-1		Finch	Walton	Craig	O'Rourke	Milnes	Mair	Manning	Blott	Reid	Cox	Coles	
32		28	BRIGHTON & HOVE ALB.	0-2	10000	Finch	Walton	Craig	O'Rourke	Milnes	Richards	Manning	Blott	Reid	Brown	Coles	
33	Apr	4	Portsmouth	2-4		Lemoine	Walton	Craig	O'Rourke	Milnes	Mair	Manning	Blott	Reid 2	Fraser	Coles	
34		11	New Brompton	3-2	5000	Baddeley	Struthers	Craig	O'Rourke	Milnes 1	Mair	Manning	Blott 1	Reid	Fraser	Coles 1	
35		17	BRISTOL ROVERS	4-1	10000	Baddeley	Struthers	Craig	O'Rourke	Milnes	Mair	Manning 1	Blott	Reid 3	Fraser	Coles	
36		18	MILLWALL	0-1	7000	Baddeley	Struthers	Craig	O'Rourke	Milnes	Mair	Manning	Blott	Reid	Fraser	Coles	
37		25	Brentford	2-1	3000	Baddeley	Struthers	Craig	O'Rourke	Milnes	Mair	Manning	Blott	Ward 1	Fraser	Coles 1	
38		30	SOUTHAMPTON	1-3	1500	Baddeley	Walton	Craig	O'Rourke	Milnes	Mair	Blott 1	Reid	Ward	Fraser	Carrick	

		p	w	d	l	f	a	w	d	l	f	a	pts
1	Queen's Park Rangers	38	12	4	3	46	26	9	5	5	36	31	51
2	Plymouth Argyle	38	13	5	1	33	13	6	6	7	17	18	49
3	Millwall	38	11	5	3	25	9	8	3	8	24	23	46
4	Crystal Palace	38	10	4	5	35	28	7	6	6	19	23	44
5	Swindon Town	38	12	6	1	41	12	4	4	11	14	28	42
6	Bristol Rovers	38	11	5	3	36	19	5	5	9	23	37	42
7	Tottenham Hotspur	38	11	2	6	33	18	6	5	8	26	30	41
8	Northampton Town	38	9	5	5	30	17	6	6	7	20	24	41
9	Portsmouth	38	14	1	4	43	19	3	5	11	21	33	40
10	West Ham United	38	9	6	4	27	16	6	4	9	20	32	40
11	Southampton	38	11	5	3	32	21	5	1	13	19	39	38
12	Reading	38	12	1	6	38	18	3	5	11	17	32	36
13	BRADFORD	38	6	7	6	30	27	6	5	8	23	27	36
14	Watford	38	9	4	6	31	22	3	6	10	16	37	34
15	Norwich City	38	10	4	5	31	16	2	5	12	15	33	33
16	Brentford	38	13	3	3	38	15	1	2	16	11	38	33
17	Brighton & Hove Albion	38	9	6	4	29	19	3	2	14	17	40	32
18	Luton Town	38	9	4	6	21	17	3	2	14	12	39	30
19	Leyton	38	6	6	7	30	31	2	5	12	22	43	27
20	New Brompton	38	7	3	9	24	29	2	4	13	20	46	25

1908/09

16th in Division Two

	Date		Opponent	Score	Scorers	Att.	Baddeley T	Bolton H	Bracey FC	Dixon A	Donald DM	Donaldson JMcF	Fraser A	Freeborough J	Gordon D	Green WJ	Grierson RT	Hartwell AW	Little TSC	Manning JT	McClarence JP	McCulloch A	Milnes C	O'Donnell D	O'Rourke H	Parker J	Reid GT	Smith A	Speedie FB	Walton RW	Ward R	Ward W	Waterall T	Wolstenholme T
1	Sep	1	HULL CITY	1-0	Fraser	15000	1			3	11		10					5		7				8	4					2				6
2		5	CHESTERFIELD	1-0	Hartwell	13000	1			3	11		10					5		7				8	4					2				6
3		7	Birmingham	1-3	Fraser	10000	1			3	11		10					5						8	4					2		7		6
4		12	Glossop	1-1	O'Donnell	5000				3	11	4	10					5						8			9			2	1	7		6
5		19	STOCKPORT COUNTY	0-1		15000			8	3	11	4	10					5									9			2	1	7		6
6		26	West Bromwich Albion	0-1		12000	1		11	3			10					5						8	4		9					7		6
7	Oct	6	BIRMINGHAM	1-2	Hartwell	8000	1			3			10					5					4	8			9					7	11	6
8		10	Gainsborough Trinity	1-2	Little	5000	1			3			10					5	9				4	8								7	11	6
9		17	GRIMSBY TOWN	0-2		9000	1		10	3								5	9						4		8					7	11	6
10		24	Fulham	1-3	Ward	18000	1		11				10	4				5	9					8						2		7		6
11		31	BURNLEY	2-3	Little 2	14000	1		11				10	4			8	5	9	7										2				6
12	Nov	7	Bolton Wanderers	1-0	Fraser	8000			11	3			10	4	2		8	5	9												1	7		6
13		14	Wolverhampton Wan.	1-1	Fraser	10000			11	3			10	4	2						9	8	5								1	7		6
14		28	Clapton Orient	0-2						3				4	2				9		10	8				5		11			1	7		6
15	Dec	12	Barnsley	1-3	Fraser					3		6	10		2		9	5				8		4				11			1			
16		15	OLDHAM ATHLETIC	3-4	Smith, Donald, Little	7000					11	6		4	3			5	9			8						10		2	1	7		
17		19	TOTTENHAM HOTSPUR	0-2		9000					10	6		4	3	1		5	9			8						11				7		
18		25	Hull City	3-2	Smith 3	10000				3			10		2	1		5	9			8			4			11				7		6
19		26	GLOSSOP	1-0	McCulloch	20000				3			10		2	1		5			9	8			4			11				7		6
20		28	Derby County	1-3	McClarence	10000							10	2	3	1				7	9			8	4	5		11						6
21	Jan	1	BLACKPOOL	4-3	McClarence 2,Ward,Manning	12000		10						2	3	1				8	9				4	5		11				7		6
22		2	Chesterfield	1-2	McClarence	5000				2			10	4	3	1				8	9					5		11				7		6
23		23	Stockport County	1-0	McClarence	8000		10		2	7				3	1				8	9				4	5		11						6
24		30	WEST BROMWICH ALB.	0-0		16000		10		2	7				3	1				8	9				4	5		11						6
25	Feb	6	GAINSBOROUGH TRIN.	4-1	* see below	12000		10		2	7				3	1				8	9		4			5		11						6
26		20	Grimsby Town	1-1	Milnes	4000		10		2	7				3	1				8	9		4			5		11						6
27		27	FULHAM	1-1	McClarence	9000		10		2	7				3	1				8	9		4			5							11	6
28	Mar	13	BOLTON WANDERERS	1-2	Manning	10000		10		3	7				2	1				8	9		4			5		11						6
29		16	Burnley	3-3	Little, McClarence, Manning	3000		10		3					2	1		5	8	7	9		4			6		11						
30		20	WOLVERHAMPTON W.	4-1	Bolton 2, McClarence, Smith	12000		10		3					2	1		5	8	7	9		4			6		11						
31		27	Oldham Athletic	0-2		9000		10		3					2	1		5	8	7	9		4			6		11						
32		31	Blackpool	1-2	Grierson	2000		10							2	1	8	5		7	9		4					11						6
33	Apr	3	CLAPTON ORIENT	0-1		10000		10							2	1			9	8			4			6		11	5			7		
34		9	DERBY COUNTY	2-0	Smith, McClarence	12000		10		3					2	1				7	9		4			5		11	8					6
35		10	Leeds City	3-0	Speedie, McClarence, Smith	11000		10		3					2	1				7	9		4			5		11	8					6
36		17	BARNSLEY	3-2	McClarence, Bolton, Smith	10000		10		3					2	1				7	9		4			5		11	8					6
37		24	Tottenham Hotspur	0-3		25000		10		3		6			2	1				7	9		4			5		11	8					
38		27	LEEDS CITY	2-0	McClarence, Parker	6000		10		3	7				2	1				8	9		4			5		11						6
						Apps	9	17	7	30	14	6	17	10	27	22	4	21	13	22	21	7	17	10	11	19	5	24	5	8	7	18	4	30
						Goals		3			2		5				1	2	5	4	13	1	1	1		1		8	1			2		1

Scorers in game 25: Manning, McClarence, Wolstenholme, Donald

Played in one game: W Cawdry (17, at 2), T Dilly (3, at 9), AP Eccles (15, 7).

P Milson played at 9 in games 1 and 2

D Crosson played at 3 in games 32 and 33

CT Craig played in 6 games; 6 to 9 at 2, 10 and 11 at 3

F.A. Cup

	Date		Opponent	Score	Scorers	Att.	Baddeley T	Bolton H	Bracey FC	Dixon A	Donald DM	Donaldson JMcF	Fraser A	Freeborough J	Gordon D	Green WJ	Grierson RT	Hartwell AW	Little TSC	Manning JT	McClarence JP	McCulloch A	Milnes C	O'Donnell D	O'Rourke H	Parker J	Reid GT	Smith A	Speedie FB	Walton RW	Ward R	Ward W	Waterall T	Wolstenholme T
Q1	Oct	3	SOUTH KIRKBY COL.	8-1	* see below	6000	1		11				10	3				5					6		4		8			2		7	9	
Q2		17	Denby Dale	11-0	* see below	500						6	10	3						9			5	8						2	1			
Q3	Nov	7	Heckmondwike		(walkover)																													
Q4		21	MEXBOROUGH TOWN	6-0	* see below	4000				3			10	4	2		9						5	8							1	7	11	6
Q5	Dec	5	CROYDON COMMON	1-2	McClarence	4000				3	11				2			5			10	9		8	4						1	7		6

Scorers in Q1: Reid 3, Fraser 2, Bracey, Ward, Waterall

Scorers in Q2: Fraser 3, Manning 3, Cawdry, Eccles, O'Donnell 2, Milnes

Scorers in Q4: Grierson 3, Waterall, O'Donnell, Ward

Played in Q2: W Cawdry (at 4), T Dilly (11), AP Eccles (7)

David Donald

		P	W	D	L	F	A	W	D	L	F	A	Pts
1	Bolton Wanderers	38	14	3	2	37	8	10	1	8	22	20	52
2	Tottenham Hotspur	38	12	5	2	42	12	8	6	5	25	20	51
3	West Bromwich Albion	38	13	5	1	35	9	6	8	5	21	18	51
4	Hull City	38	14	2	3	44	15	5	4	10	19	24	44
5	Derby County	38	13	5	1	38	11	3	6	10	17	30	43
6	Oldham Athletic	38	14	4	1	39	9	3	2	14	16	34	40
7	Wolverhampton Wan.	38	10	6	3	32	12	4	5	10	24	36	39
8	Glossop	38	11	5	3	35	17	4	3	12	22	36	38
9	Gainsborough Trinity	38	12	3	4	30	20	3	5	11	19	50	38
10	Fulham	38	8	4	7	39	26	5	7	7	19	22	37
11	Birmingham	38	10	6	3	35	21	4	3	12	23	40	37
12	Leeds City	38	12	3	4	35	19	2	4	13	8	34	35
13	Grimsby Town	38	9	5	5	23	14	5	2	12	18	40	35
14	Burnley	38	8	4	7	33	28	5	3	11	18	30	33
15	Clapton Orient	38	7	7	5	25	19	5	2	12	12	30	33
16	BRADFORD	38	9	2	8	30	25	4	4	11	21	34	32
17	Barnsley	38	11	3	5	36	19	0	7	12	12	38	32
18	Stockport County	38	11	2	6	25	19	3	1	15	14	52	31
19	Chesterfield	38	10	3	6	30	28	1	5	13	7	39	30
20	Blackpool	38	9	6	4	30	22	0	5	14	16	46	29

1909/10

10th in Division Two

#	Month	Date	Opponent	Score	Scorers	Att.	Blackburn G	Bolton H	Clark DC	Crosson D	Dixon A	Donald DM	Gordon D	Green WJ	Handley TH	Little TSC	Logan JH	Manning JT	Mason R	McClarence JP	Milnes C	Morgan C	Newton LF	Noble WD	Parker J	Reeves G	Scott JMA	Smith A	Tomlinson T	Wolstenholme T
1	Sep	1	Grimsby Town	1-0	Bolton	5000		10	1		3	7	2		6		5	8		9	4							11		
2		4	West Bromwich Albion	0-1		10000		10	1		3	7	2		6		5	8		9	4							11		
3		11	LEICESTER FOSSE	1-3	McClarence	12000		10	1		3	7	2		6		5	8		9	4							11		
4		18	Oldham Athletic	1-1	McClarence	5000		8	1		3	11	2		6	10	5	7		9	4									
5		25	LINCOLN CITY	4-0	Maning 2, Little 2	10000		10	1		3	7	2		6	9	5	8			4							11		
6	Oct	2	Barnsley	0-4		6000		10	1		3	7	2		6	9	5	8			4							11		
7		9	CLAPTON ORIENT	3-1	Bolton 3	9000		10			3	7		1	6		2	8		9	4				5			11		
8		16	Fulham	1-3	Manning	10000		8		3	2	7		1	6	10		9			4				5			11		
9		23	BLACKPOOL	2-1	McClarence, Manning	7000		10			3	7	2	1			6	8		9	4				5			11		
10		30	Burnley	0-1		9000		10		3	2	7		1			6	8		9	4				5			11		
11	Nov	6	HULL CITY	0-1		14000		10		3	2	7		1			6	8		9	4				5			11		
12		13	Leeds City	3-2	Reeves, Blackburn 2	10000	7			3	2			1		10	6	8			4				5	9		11		
13		20	DERBY COUNTY	1-2	Newton	16000	7	10		3	2			1			6				4		9		5	8		11		
14		27	Wolverhampton Wan.	2-0	Little, Newton	6000	1			3		11	2	1		10	6				4		9		5	8				
15	Dec	4	STOCKPORT COUNTY	2-4	Blackburn, Milnes	8000	7			3			2	1		10	6				4		9		5	8		11		
16		11	Gainsborough Trinity	1-3	Smith	2000		7			3		2			10	6	8	1		4		9		5			11		
17		18	GLOSSOP	3-3	Blackburn 2, Newton	10000	7		1	3			2							10	4		9		5	8		11		6
18		25	MANCHESTER CITY	2-0	Reeves, Blackburn	25000	7			3			2						1	10	4		9		5	8		11		6
19		28	Birmingham	1-0	Reeves	10000	7			3			2						1	10	4		9		5	8		11		6
20	Jan	1	Manchester City	1-3	McClarence	23000				3			2					7	1	10		4	9		5	8		11		6
21		8	WEST BROMWICH ALB.	1-0	Newton	7980	7			3			2						1	10	4		9		5	8		11		6
22		22	Leicester Fosse	0-3		9000	7			3			2						1	10	4		9		5	8		11		6
23	Feb	8	GRIMSBY TOWN	6-1	Tomlinson 3, Milnes, Newton, Reeves	5000					3		2		5			7	1	10	4		9			8			11	6
24		12	BARNSLEY	2-0	Newton, Tomlinson	12000				3	2				5			7	1	10	4		9			8			11	6
25		19	Clapton Orient	0-1		0				3	2				5			7	1	10	4		9			8			11	6
26		26	FULHAM	3-0	Reeves, Newton 2	12000				3	2				5	10	6	7	1		4		9			8		11		
27	Mar	2	Lincoln City	1-1	Logan	3000				3	2				5	10	6	7	1		4		9			8		11		
28		5	Blackpool	0-0		4000				3	2				5	10	6	7	1		4		9			8		11		
29		8	OLDHAM ATHLETIC	1-6	Manning	10000				3	2	11			5	10	6	7	1		4		9			8				
30		12	BURNLEY	3-1	Smith, Newton, Reeves	10000					3		2			10	6	7	1		4		9		5	8		11		
31		19	Hull City	1-2	Little	9000	7				3		2			10	6		1		4		9		5	8		11		
32		26	LEEDS CITY	4-2	McClarence 2, Little 2	12000					3		2			8			1	10	4		9		5	7	6	11		
33		28	BIRMINGHAM	5-0	Reeves, Parker, McClarence, Little 2	8000	7				3		2			8			1	10	4				5	9	6	11		
34	Apr	2	Derby County	2-1	McClarence, Reeves	9000					3		2			8		7	1	10	4				5	9	6	11		
35		9	WOLVERHAMPTON W.	2-3	McClarence, Little	8000					3		2			8		7	1	10	4				5	9	6	11		
36		16	Stockport County	1-2	Newton	0					3					8			1	10	4		9	2	5	7	6		11	
37		23	GAINSBOROUGH TRIN.	2-0	Parker, Dixon	2000				3	2							7	1	10	4		9		5	8	6	11		
38		30	Glossop	1-3	Milnes	500				3					5	8			1	10	4		9	2		7	6	11		
						Apps	11	13	7	21	29	13	23	9	16	20	21	25	22	24	37	1	23	2	24	26	7	31	4	9
						Goals	6	4			1					9	1	5		9	3		10		2	8		2	4	

F.A. Cup

Rd	Month	Date	Opponent	Score	Scorers	Att.	Blackburn G	Bolton H	Clark DC	Crosson D	Dixon A	Donald DM	Gordon D	Green WJ	Handley TH	Little TSC	Logan JH	Manning JT	Mason R	McClarence JP	Milnes C	Morgan C	Newton LF	Noble WD	Parker J	Reeves G	Scott JMA	Smith A	Tomlinson T	Wolstenholme T
R1	Jan	15	BISHOP AUCKLAND	8-0	Newton 3, McClarence, Smith 2, Reeves 2	6000				3			2					7	1	10	4		9		5	8		11		6
R2	Feb	5	Sunderland	1-3	Reeves	18000				3	2				5			7	1	10	4		9			8			11	6

		P	W	D	L	F	A	W	D	L	F	A	Pts
1	Manchester City	38	15	2	2	51	17	8	6	5	30	23	54
2	Oldham Athletic	38	15	2	2	47	9	8	5	6	32	30	53
3	Hull City	38	13	4	2	52	19	10	3	6	28	27	53
4	Derby County	38	15	2	2	46	15	7	7	5	26	32	53
5	Leicester Fosse	38	15	2	2	60	20	5	2	12	19	38	44
6	Glossop	38	14	1	4	42	18	4	6	9	22	39	43
7	Fulham	38	9	7	3	28	13	5	6	8	23	30	41
8	Wolverhampton Wan.	38	14	3	2	51	22	3	3	13	13	41	40
9	Barnsley	38	15	3	1	48	15	1	4	14	14	44	39
10	BRADFORD	38	12	1	6	47	28	5	3	11	17	31	38
11	West Bromwich Albion	38	8	5	6	30	23	8	0	11	28	33	37
12	Blackpool	38	7	7	5	24	18	7	1	11	26	34	36
13	Stockport County	38	9	6	4	37	20	4	2	13	13	27	34
14	Burnley	38	12	2	5	43	21	2	4	13	19	40	34
15	Lincoln City	38	7	6	6	27	24	3	5	11	15	45	31
16	Clapton Orient	38	10	4	5	26	15	2	2	15	11	45	30
17	Leeds City	38	8	4	7	30	33	2	3	14	16	47	27
18	Gainsborough Trinity	38	8	3	8	22	21	2	3	14	11	54	26
19	Grimsby Town	38	8	3	8	31	19	1	3	15	19	58	24
20	Birmingham	38	7	4	8	28	26	1	3	15	14	52	23

1910/11

12th in Division Two

						Buchanan G	Burnison S	Dixon A	Gough HC	Handley TH	Hanson W	Hayes JV	Kenyon J	Little TSC	Logan JH	Mason R	McClarence JP	Milnes C	Munro D	Newton LF	Parker J	Reeves G	Scott JMA	Simpson RA	Thackeray J	Turnbull JMcL
1	Sep 1	Lincoln City	0-0		4000		2	3						10	6	1		4		9	5	7		8	11	
2	3	HUDDERSFIELD T	0-1		16000		2	3		5				10	6	1		4		9		7		8	11	
3	10	Birmingham	0-1		18000		2	3		5			7	10		1		4				9	6	8	11	
4	17	WEST BROMWICH ALB.	3-3	Little, Simpson, McClarence	12000		2	3		5				10		1	9	4				7	6	8	11	
5	24	Hull City	2-2	McClarence 2	10000		2	3		5				10		1	9	4				7	6	8	11	
6	Oct 1	FULHAM	1-0	Turnbull	20000		2	3		5				8		1	10	4				7	6		11	9
7	8	Bolton Wanderers	0-1		5000		2	3						10		1	9	4			5	7	6	8	11	
8	15	Burnley	1-1	Little	5000		2	3						8	4	1	9	5				7	6	10	11	
9	22	GAINSBOROUGH TRIN.	5-0	Little 3, Turnbull 2	10000		2	3						8	4	1		5				7	6	10	11	9
10	29	Leeds City	0-2		10000		2	3						8	4	1		5				7	6	10	11	9
11	Nov 5	STOCKPORT COUNTY	3-2	Turnbull 2, Thackeray	10000		2	3		6				8	4	1		5				7		10	11	9
12	12	Derby County	2-4	Little, Turnbull	10000		2	3						8	4	1		5	7				6	10	11	9
13	19	BARNSLEY	2-3	Turnbull, Reeves	12000		2	3						10	4	1			7		5	8	6		11	9
14	26	Leicester Fosse	0-2		3000			3				2		10	6	1		4	7	8	5				11	9
15	Dec 3	WOLVERHAMPTON W.	1-0	Little	10000			3				2		10	6	1		4	7	8	5				11	9
16	10	Chelsea	0-3		15000			3				2		10	6	1		4	7	8	5				11	9
17	17	CLAPTON ORIENT	3-0	Little, McClarence, Logan	9000			3				2		8	6	1	10	4	7	9	5				11	
18	24	Blackpool	1-4	Newton	3000			3				2		8	6	1	10	4	7	9	5				11	
19	26	GLOSSOP	6-0	McClarence 4, Reeves 2	20000			3				2		8	5	1	10	4	7			9	6		11	
20	31	Huddersfield Town	0-0		12000			3				2		8	5	1	10	4	7	9			6		11	
21	Jan 2	LINCOLN CITY	6-0	Thackeray, Little 3, Newton 2	7000			3				2		8	5	1	10	4	7	9			6		11	
22	7	BIRMINGHAM	2-2	Little, Thackeray	10000			3				2		8	5	1	10	4	7	9			6		11	
23	21	West Bromwich Albion	0-3		7000			3				2		8	4	1	10		7		5		6		11	9
24	28	HULL CITY	2-0	Munro, McClarence	15000			2			3			8	5	1	10	4	7				6		11	9
25	Feb 11	BOLTON WANDERERS	1-1	Little	8000			3	1	4		2		8	5				7				6	10	11	9
26	13	Fulham	0-4		5000		4	3	1	5		2			6		9		7			8		10	11	
27	18	BURNLEY	1-1	Dixon	9000			3	1			2		8	4		9		7		5	11	6	10		
28	25	Gainsborough Trinity	2-1	Simpson, Turnbull	4000			3				2		8	5	1			7		4	11	6	10		9
29	Mar 4	LEEDS CITY	0-2		12000			3				2		8	5	1			7		4		6	10	11	9
30	11	Stockport County	0-1		4000			3				2		8	5	1		4	7				6	10	11	9
31	18	DERBY COUNTY	2-1	Little, Turnbull	7000			3		6		2		8	5	1		4	7			11		10		9
32	25	Barnsley	0-7		4000		2	3		6				8	5	1		4	7			11		10		9
33	Apr 1	LEICESTER FOSSE	3-1	Turnbull, Little 2	10000			3				2		8	6	1	5	4	7					10	11	9
34	8	Wolverhampton Wan.	0-0		5000			3				2		8	6	1	5	4	7					10	11	9
35	14	Glossop	1-0	Little	3000			3				2		8	6	1	9	4	7		5			10	11	
36	15	CHELSEA	2-1	Little 2	15000			3				2		8	4	1			7		5		6	10	11	9
37	22	Clapton Orient	0-1		9000	11		3				2		8	4	1			7		5		6	10		9
38	29	BLACKPOOL	1-0	Buchanan	2000	9		3				2		8		1		4	7		5		6	10	11	
					Apps	2	15	38	3	10	1	23	1	37	32	35	18	29	27	10	16	18	24	25	33	21
					Goals	1		1						19	1		9		1	3		3		2	3	10

F.A. Cup

						Buchanan G	Burnison S	Dixon A	Gough HC	Handley TH	Hanson W	Hayes JV	Kenyon J	Little TSC	Logan JH	Mason R	McClarence JP	Milnes C	Munro D	Newton LF	Parker J	Reeves G	Scott JMA	Simpson RA	Thackeray J	Turnbull JMcL
R1	Jan 14	QUEEN'S PARK RANGERS	5-3	Turnbull 2, Little 2, Logan	20000			3				2		8	5	1	10	4	7				6		11	9
R2	Feb 4	Darlington	1-2	Thackeray	12000			2				3		4	5	1	10		7			8	6		11	9

Bobby Simpson

		P	*W*	*D*	*L*	*F*	*A*	*W*	*D*	*L*	*F*	*A*	*Pts*
1	West Bromwich Albion	38	14	2	3	40	18	8	7	4	27	23	53
2	Bolton Wanderers	38	17	2	0	53	12	4	7	8	16	28	51
3	Chelsea	38	17	2	0	48	7	3	7	9	23	28	49
4	Clapton Orient	38	14	4	1	28	7	5	3	11	16	28	45
5	Hull City	38	8	10	1	38	21	6	6	7	17	18	44
6	Derby County	38	11	5	3	48	24	6	3	10	25	28	42
7	Blackpool	38	10	5	4	29	15	6	5	8	20	23	42
8	Burnley	38	9	9	1	31	18	4	6	9	14	27	41
9	Wolverhampton Wan.	38	10	5	4	26	16	5	3	11	25	36	38
10	Fulham	38	12	3	4	35	15	3	4	12	17	33	37
11	Leeds City	38	11	4	4	35	18	4	3	12	23	38	37
12	BRADFORD	38	12	4	3	44	18	2	5	12	9	37	37
13	Huddersfield Town	38	10	4	5	35	21	3	4	12	22	37	34
14	Glossop	38	11	4	4	36	21	2	4	13	12	41	34
15	Leicester Fosse	38	12	3	4	37	19	2	2	15	15	43	33
16	Birmingham	38	10	4	5	23	18	2	4	13	19	46	32
17	Stockport County	38	10	4	5	27	26	1	4	14	20	53	30
18	Gainsborough Trinity	38	9	5	5	26	16	0	6	13	11	39	29
19	Barnsley	38	5	7	7	36	26	2	7	10	16	36	28
20	Lincoln City	38	5	7	7	16	23	2	3	14	12	49	24

1911/12

11th in Division Two

			Opponent	Score	Scorers	Att.	Blackham S	Buchanan G	Dainty HC	Dixon A	Halley G	Hayes JV	Howie D	Kivlichan WF	Little TSC	Logan JH	Mason R	McCandless J	McDonald HL	Munro D	Parker J	Reeves G	Scott JMA	Simpson RA	Turnbull JMcL	Wallace H	Watson A
1	Sep	2	Birmingham	3-2	Kivlichan, Turnbull, Simpson	20000		11	5	3	4	2	10	7		6	1							8	9		
2		9	HUDDERSFIELD T	3-1	Buchanan, Turnbull 2	16000		11	5	3	4	2	10	7	8	6	1								9		
3		16	Blackpool	4-0	Turnbull 2, Howie, Simpson	10000		11	5	3	4	2	10	7		6	1							8	9		
4		23	GLOSSOP	1-1	Simpson	17000		11	5	3	4	2	10	7		6	1							8	9		
5		30	Hull City	1-5	Logan	7000		11	5	3	4	2	10	7		6	1							8	9		
6	Oct	7	BARNSLEY	1-0	Little	20000	3	11	5	2	4		10	7	8		1						6		9		
7		14	BURNLEY	2-1	Halley, Little	23000	3	11			4		10	7	8		1				5		6		9		2
8		21	Fulham	0-2		20000	3	11			4		10	7	8		1				5		6		9		2
9		28	DERBY COUNTY	0-1		17000	3	11			4		10	7	8		1				5		6		9		2
10	Nov	4	Stockport County	0-1		7000	3	11			4		10	7			1				5		6	8	9		2
11		11	LEEDS CITY	1-1	Turnbull	25000		11		3	4		10	7			1				5		6	8	9		2
12		18	Wolverhampton Wan.	1-1	og	15000	3	11			4		10	7	8		1				5		6		9		2
13		25	LEICESTER FOSSE	1-1	Turnbull	12000	3	11	5		4		10	7	8		1						6		9		2
14	Dec	2	Grimsby Town	0-0		5000	3			2	4		10	7					1	11	5	9	6	8			
15		9	GRIMSBY TOWN	4-1	Reeves 2, Simpson, Howie	8000	3			2	4		10	7					1	11	5	9	6	8			
16		16	Nottingham Forest	1-2	Simpson	7000	3				4		10	7					1	11	5	9	6	8			2
17		23	CHELSEA	1-1	Turnbull	20000	3			2	4			7					1	11	5	10	6	8	9		
18		25	CLAPTON ORIENT	2-1	Buchanan, Kivlichan	30000	3	9			4			7	8				1	11	5		6	10			2
19		26	Clapton Orient	0-2		7000	3	9	5		4			7	8				1	11			6	10			2
20		30	BIRMINGHAM	3-0	Buchanan 2, Little	15000	3	9	5		4			7	8				1	11			6	10			2
21	Jan	6	Huddersfield Town	1-3	Little	3000	3	9			4			7	8				1	11	5		6	10			2
22		27	Glossop	0-0		1000	3	7			4		10						1	11	5		6	8	9		2
23	Feb	6	BLACKPOOL	0-0		3500	3	7	5		4								1	11		9	6	8	10		2
24		10	Barnsley	0-1		5000	3	7			4		10						1	11	5		6	8	9		2
25		17	Burnley	1-3	Howie	11000	3	7					10			4			1	11	5		6	8	9		2
26	Mar	2	Derby County	0-1		7000	3		5		4	2	10	7					1	11			6	8	9		
27		9	STOCKPORT COUNTY	1-0	Simpson	10000	3		5		4		10	7					1	11			6	8	9		2
28		16	Leeds City	2-1	Reeves, Munro	12000	3	7	5		4		10						1	11		9	6		8		2
29		20	HULL CITY	3-1	Turnbull, Dainty, Buchanan	3000	3	11	5		4				9				1			7	6	10	8		2
30		23	WOLVERHAMPTON W.	0-2		8000	3		5		4		10	7					1			9	6	11	8		2
31		27	FULHAM	0-2		4000	3				4		10	7					1		5	11	6	8	9		2
32		30	Leicester Fosse	0-3		10000	3		5		4		8	7				10	1	11			6		9		2
33	Apr	5	BRISTOL CITY	0-1		8000	3	11	5		4		6	7				10						8	9	1	2
34		6	GAINSBOROUGH TRIN.	5-0	Little 2, Kivlichan, Reeves 2	7000			5	3	4		10	7	8					11		9	6			1	2
35		8	Bristol City	0-1		9000			5	3	4		10	7	8					11		9	6			1	2
36		20	NOTTM. FOREST	2-1	McCandless, Kivlichan	6000	3		5		4		10	7	8			9		11			6			1	2
37		24	Gainsborough Trinity	0-0		1500	3		5		4		10		8			9	1	11			6		7		2
38		27	Chelsea	0-1		30000	3		5		4		10	7	8				1	11			6		9		2
						Apps	30	24	22	12	37	6	31	31	17	6	13	4	21	21	16	11	32	24	28	4	28
						Goals		5	1		1		3	4	6	1		1		1		5		6	9		

One own goal

F.A. Cup

			Opponent	Score	Scorers	Att.	Blackham S	Buchanan G	Dainty HC	Dixon A	Halley G	Hayes JV	Howie D	Kivlichan WF	Little TSC	Logan JH	Mason R	McCandless J	McDonald HL	Munro D	Parker J	Reeves G	Scott JMA	Simpson RA	Turnbull JMcL	Wallace H	Watson A
R1	Jan	13	Nottingham Forest	1-0	Reeves	12027	3	9	5		4		10						1	11		7	6	8			2
R2	Feb	3	PORTSMOUTH	2-0	Reeves, Simpson	8257	3	7	5		4		10						1	11		9	6	8			2
R3		24	BRADFORD CITY	0-1		24833	3		5		4		10	7					1	11			6	8	9		2

		P	*W*	*D*	*L*	*F*	*A*	*W*	*D*	*L*	*F*	*A*	*Pts*
1	Derby County	38	15	2	2	55	13	8	6	5	19	15	54
2	Chelsea	38	15	2	2	36	13	9	4	6	28	21	54
3	Burnley	38	14	5	0	50	14	8	3	8	27	27	52
4	Clapton Orient	38	16	0	3	44	14	5	3	11	17	30	45
5	Wolverhampton Wan.	38	12	3	4	41	10	4	7	8	16	23	42
6	Barnsley	38	10	5	4	28	19	5	7	7	17	23	42
7	Hull City	38	12	3	4	36	13	5	5	9	18	38	42
8	Fulham	38	10	3	6	42	24	6	4	9	24	34	39
9	Grimsby Town	38	9	6	4	24	18	6	3	10	24	37	39
10	Leicester Fosse	38	11	4	4	34	18	4	3	12	15	48	37
11	BRADFORD	38	10	5	4	30	16	3	4	12	14	29	35
12	Birmingham	38	11	3	5	44	29	3	3	13	11	30	34
13	Bristol City	38	11	4	4	27	17	3	2	14	14	43	34
14	Blackpool	38	12	4	3	24	12	1	4	14	8	40	34
15	Nottingham Forest	38	9	3	7	26	18	4	4	11	20	30	33
16	Stockport County	38	8	5	6	31	22	3	6	10	16	32	33
17	Huddersfield Town	38	8	5	6	30	22	5	1	13	20	42	32
18	Glossop	38	6	8	5	33	23	2	4	13	9	33	28
19	Leeds City	38	7	6	6	21	22	3	2	14	29	56	28
20	Gainsborough Trinity	38	4	6	9	17	22	1	7	11	13	42	23

1912/13

13th in Division Two

			Opponent	Score	Scorers	Att	Bell DS	Blackham S	Buchanan G	Dainty HC	Dixon A	Halley G	Howie D	Kivlichan WF	Little J	Little TSC	Mason R	McCandless J	McConnell WG	McDonald HL	Munro D	Parker J	Reeves G	Scott JMA	Shearer S	Simpson RA	Smith J	Thomson J	Watson A
1	Sep	4	Bristol City	0-0		10000		3	11	5			4	7		9		10		1				6		8			2
2		7	BIRMINGHAM	0-0		14000		3	11	5			4	7		9		10		1				6		8			2
3		14	Huddersfield Town	0-2		8000		3	11	5		4		7	9	8		10		1				6					2
4		21	LEEDS CITY	0-1		20000		3		5		4	8	7	9			10		1	11			6					2
5		28	Grimsby Town	0-3		4000		3	11	5		4	8	9				10		1	7			6					2
6	Oct	5	BURY	3-1	og, Scott, Halley	8000		3		5		4	8	7			1	9			11			6		10			2
7		12	Fulham	1-3	McCandless	10000		3		5		4	8	7			1	9			11			6		10			2
8		19	BARNSLEY	0-0		12000		3		5		4	8	7		10	1	9			11			6					2
9	Nov	2	Wolverhampton Wan.	0-0		14000		3	11	5		4	8		9		1	10			7			6					2
10		9	LEICESTER FOSSE	2-2	McCandless 2	11000		3		5		4	10	7		8	1	9			11			6					2
11		16	Stockport County	0-1		4000		3		5		4	8	7	9		1	10			11			6					2
12		23	PRESTON NORTH END	0-0		12000		3	11	5		4	10	7		8	1							6			9		2
13		27	Blackpool	2-0	Smith, T Little	2000		3	11	5		4	10			8	1						7	6			9		2
14		30	Burnley	1-5	T Little	12000		3	11	5		4	10			8	1						7	6			9		2
15	Dec	7	HULL CITY	2-0	Smith, T Little	10000		3	11	5		4	10			8	1				7			6			9		2
16		14	Preston North End	2-4	Halley, Smith			3	11	5		4	10			8	1				7			6			9		2
17		21	CLAPTON ORIENT	3-0	Smith. Munro, T Little	12000		3	11	5		4	10			8	1				7			6			9		2
18		25	Lincoln City	1-1	Smith	11000		3	11	5		4	10	7		8	1							6			9		2
19		26	LINCOLN CITY	3-0	og, Halley 2	18000		3				4	5	11		8	1	10			7			6			9		2
20		28	Birmingham	1-1	Halley	20000		3		5		4	10	11		8	1				7			6			9		2
21	Jan	1	BRISTOL CITY	4-1	T Little 2, Smith, Howie	10000		3		5		4	10	11		8	1				7			6			9		2
22		4	HUDDERSFIELD T	2-1	Halley, T Little	12000		3		5		4	10	11		8	1				7			6			9		2
23		18	Leeds City	0-2		10000		3		5		4	10	11	9	8	1				7			6					2
24		25	GRIMSBY TOWN	3-0	T Little, Smith 2	12000				5	3		4			8	1	10			7			6	11		9		2
25	Feb	4	Glossop	3-4	Reeves, T Little, Halley				11	5	3	4				8	1	10			7		9	6					2
26		8	Bury	0-2		7000		3	11		6	4		8			1	10			7			5			9		2
27		15	FULHAM	2-3	Howie, Smith	8000		3	11	5		4	10			8	1				7			6			9		2
28	Mar	1	BLACKPOOL	4-2	Howie, T Little, Buchanan, Smith	5000		3	11	5		4	10			8	1				7			6			9		2
29		15	Leicester Fosse	0-3				3	11	5			4			8	1	10			7			6			9		2
30		21	Nottingham Forest	2-1	Smith 2	10000		3	11	5			10			8	1				7	4		6			9		2
31		22	STOCKPORT COUNTY	4-2	Buchanan, Howie 2, Smith	7000		3	11	5			10			8	1				7	4		6			9		2
32		24	NOTTM. FOREST	3-1	T Little 3	12000			11	5	3		10			8	1				7	4		6			9		2
33	Apr	3	Barnsley	0-4		4000			11	5	3		10		9	8	1				7			4				6	2
34		5	BURNLEY	2-3	Buchanan, T Little	13000			11	5			10			8	1		3		7			4			9	6	2
35		12	Hull City	0-5		4000			11	5	3		10			8	1				7			4			9	6	2
36		16	WOLVERHAMPTON W.	5-1	Smith, Howie 2, T Little 2	8000	3		11				10			8	1				7	5		4			9	6	2
37		19	GLOSSOP	5-0	Smith 2, T Little, Parker, Howie	5000		3	11				10			8	1				7	5		4			9	6	2
38		26	Clapton Orient	0-1					11	5			10			8	1		3		7			4			9	6	2
						Apps	1	30	26	34	6	25	35	18	6	31	33	16	2	5	31	5	3	38	1	4	24	6	38
						Goals			3			7	8			17		3			1	1	1	1			16		

Two own goals

F.A. Cup

			Opponent	Score	Scorers	Att	Bell DS	Blackham S	Buchanan G	Dainty HC	Dixon A	Halley G	Howie D	Kivlichan WF	Little J	Little TSC	Mason R	McCandless J	McConnell WG	McDonald HL	Munro D	Parker J	Reeves G	Scott JMA	Shearer S	Simpson RA	Smith J	Thomson J	Watson A
R1	Jan	15	BARROW	1-1	Smith	7000		3		5		4	10	11		8	1				7			6			9		2
rep		22	BARROW	1-0	Smith	10000		3		5		4	10	11		8	1				7			6			9		2
R2	Feb	1	WOLVERHAMPTON WAN.	3-0	Smith 2, T Little	21000		3		5		4	10	11		8	1				7			6			9		2
R3	Feb	22	SHEFFIELD WEDNESDAY	2-1	Smith, Howie	24000		3		5		4	10	11		8	1				7			6			9		2
R4	Mar	8	ASTON VILLA	0-5		24000		3		5		4	10	11		8	1				7			6			9		2

		P	W	D	L	F	A	W	D	L	F	A	Pts
1	Preston North End	38	13	5	1	34	12	6	10	3	22	21	53
2	Burnley	38	13	4	2	58	23	8	4	7	30	30	50
3	Birmingham	38	11	6	2	39	18	7	4	8	20	26	46
4	Barnsley	38	15	3	1	46	18	4	4	11	11	29	45
5	Huddersfield Town	38	13	5	1	49	12	4	4	11	17	28	43
6	Leeds City	38	12	3	4	45	22	3	7	9	25	42	40
7	Grimsby Town	38	10	8	1	32	11	5	2	12	19	39	40
8	Lincoln City	38	10	6	3	31	16	5	4	10	19	36	40
9	Fulham	38	13	5	1	47	16	4	0	15	18	39	39
10	Wolverhampton Wan.	38	10	6	3	34	16	4	4	11	22	38	38
11	Bury	38	10	6	3	29	14	5	2	12	24	43	38
12	Hull City	38	12	2	5	42	18	3	4	12	18	37	36
13	BRADFORD	38	12	4	3	47	18	2	4	13	13	42	36
14	Clapton Orient	38	8	6	5	25	20	2	8	9	9	27	34
15	Leicester Fosse	38	12	2	5	34	20	1	5	13	15	45	33
16	Bristol City	38	7	9	3	32	25	2	6	11	14	47	33
17	Nottingham Forest	38	9	3	7	35	25	3	5	11	23	34	32
18	Glossop	38	11	2	6	34	26	1	6	12	15	42	32
19	Stockport County	38	8	4	7	32	23	0	6	13	24	55	26
20	Blackpool	38	8	4	7	22	22	1	4	14	17	47	26

1913/14

Second in Division Two: Promoted

							Bauchop JR	Bell DS	Blackham S	Dainty HC	Drabble F	Garry E	Howie D	Kivlichan WF	Leavey HJ	Little TSC	Mason R	Mavin F	McCandless J	McConnell WG	McLaughlin J	Munro D	Scott JMA	Smith J	Thomson J	Watson A
1	Sep	6	Birmingham	2-1	Little, Howie	20000			3	5	1	4	10		11	8						7	6	9		2
2		10	GRIMSBY TOWN	3-0	Smith 2, og	10000			3	5	1	4	10		11	8						7	6	9		2
3		13	BRISTOL CITY	4-3	Little 3, Smith	18000			3	5	1		10		11	8						7	6	9	4	2
4		20	Leeds City	1-5	Little	20000			3	5	1		10		11	8						7	6	9	4	2
5		27	CLAPTON ORIENT	1-0	Little	15000			3	5		4	10		11	8	1					7	6	9		2
6	Oct	4	Glossop	1-2	Smith	1500			3	5	1	4	10	7	11	8							6	9		2
7		11	STOCKPORT COUNTY	0-2		12000			3	5		4	10	7			1		11		8		6	9		2
8		18	FULHAM	1-0	Smith	12000		2				4	5	7		8	1		10			11	6	9		3
9		25	Notts County	3-2	Little, Smith, Leavey	10000		2				4	5	7	11	8	1		10				6	9		3
10	Nov	1	LEICESTER FOSSE	3-2	og, Smith 2	15000		2				4	5	7	11	8	1		10				6	9		3
11		8	Wolverhampton Wan.	0-1		5000		2				4	5	7	11	8	1		10				6	9		3
12		15	HULL CITY	2-0	Little 2	10000			3			4	5	7	11	8	1		10				6	9		2
13		22	Barnsley	2-1	Smith, McCandless	5000			3			4	5	7	11	8	1		10				6	9		2
14		29	BURY	3-1	Little 2, Smith	8000			3			4	5	7	11	8	1		10				6	9		2
15	Dec	6	Huddersfield Town	1-0	Kivlichan	12000			3			4	5	7	11	8	1		10				6	9		2
16		13	LINCOLN CITY	3-0	Bauchop 2, Little	6000	10		3			4	5	7	11	8	1						6	9		2
17		20	Blackpool	1-2	Smith	7000	10		3			4		7	11	8	1	5					6	9		2
18		25	WOOLWICH ARSENAL	2-3	Smith, Bauchop	22000	10		3			4		7		8	1	5	11				6	9		2
19		26	Woolwich Arsenal	0-2		30000	9		3			4		7	11	8	1	5	10				6			2
20		27	BIRMINGHAM	5-1	Mavin, Bauchop 2, Smith, Little	6000	10		3		1	4		7		8		5	11				6	9		2
21	Jan	3	Bristol City	0-2		10000			3		1	4		7	11	8		5	10				6	9		2
22		17	LEEDS CITY	3-1	Smith 2, Bauchop	32000	10		3		1	4		7		8		5	11				6	9		2
23		24	Clapton Orient	0-1		12000	10		3		1	4		7		8		5	11				6	9		2
24	Feb	7	GLOSSOP	2-1	Little, Smith	12000	10				1	4		7		8		5	11	2			6	9		3
25		14	Stockport County	1-3	Little	7000	10		3		1	4		7		8		5	11				6	9		2
26		21	Fulham	6-1	Smith 2, Little, McCandless 3	8000	10		3		1	4	5	7		8			11				6	9		2
27		24	Grimsby Town	0-0		0	10		3		1	4	5	7		8			11				6	9		2
28		28	NOTTS COUNTY	0-3		26000	10		3			4	5	7		8	1		11				6	9		2
29	Mar	7	Leicester Fosse	3-2	Little, Bauchop, Smith	0	10		3		1	4	5	7		8			11				6	9		2
30		14	WOLVERHAMPTON W.	1-0	Smith	8000	10		3		1	4		7	11	8		5					6	9		2
31		21	Hull City	3-1	Little 2, Bauchop	12000	10		3		1	4	5	7		8			11	2			6	9		
32		28	BARNSLEY	1-1	Bauchop	18000	10		3		1	4	5	7		8			11	2			6	9		
33	Apr	4	Bury	0-0		6000	10		3		1	4	5	7		8			11	2			6	9		
34		10	NOTTM. FOREST	4-0	Little 2, Bauchop, Smith	16000	10		3		1	4	5	7		8			11				6	9		2
35		11	HUDDERSFIELD T	2-1	Smith, Little	20000	10		3		1	4	5	7		8			11				6	9		2
36		13	Nottingham Forest	0-1		12000	10		3		1	4	5	7		8			11				6	9		2
37		18	Lincoln City	3-0	Smith, Bauchop, Little	9000	10		3		1	4	5	7		8			11				6	9		2
38		25	BLACKPOOL	4-1	Smith 2, McCandless, Little	28000			3		1	4	5	7	11	8			10				6	9		2
						Apps	21	4	33	7	23	36	28	33	19	37	15	10	29	4	1	6	38	37	2	35
						Goals	11						1	1	1	24		1	5					25		

Two own goals

F.A. Cup

R1	Jan	10	READING	5-1	Bauchop 3, Smith, McCandless	12000	10		3		1	4		7		8		5	11				6	9		2
R2		31	Sheffield United	1-3	Smith	51060	10		3		1	4		7	11	8		5					6	9		2

		P	W	D	L	F	A	W	D	L	F	A	Pts
1	Notts County	38	16	2	1	55	13	7	5	7	22	23	53
2	BRADFORD	38	15	1	3	44	20	8	2	9	27	27	49
3	Woolwich Arsenal	38	14	3	2	34	10	6	6	7	20	28	49
4	Leeds City	38	15	2	2	54	16	5	5	9	22	30	47
5	Barnsley	38	14	1	4	33	15	5	6	8	18	30	45
6	Clapton Orient	38	14	5	0	38	11	2	6	11	9	24	43
7	Hull City	38	9	5	5	29	13	7	4	8	24	24	41
8	Bristol City	38	12	5	2	32	10	4	4	11	20	40	41
9	Wolverhampton Wan.	38	14	1	4	33	16	4	4	11	18	36	41
10	Bury	38	12	6	1	30	14	3	4	12	9	26	40
11	Fulham	38	10	3	6	31	20	6	3	10	15	23	38
12	Stockport County	38	9	6	4	32	18	4	4	11	23	39	36
13	Huddersfield Town	38	8	4	7	28	22	5	4	10	19	31	34
14	Birmingham	38	10	4	5	31	18	2	6	11	17	42	34
15	Grimsby Town	38	10	4	5	24	15	3	4	12	18	43	34
16	Blackpool	38	6	10	3	24	19	3	4	12	9	25	32
17	Glossop	38	8	3	8	32	24	3	3	13	19	43	28
18	Leicester Fosse	38	7	2	10	29	28	4	2	13	16	33	26
19	Lincoln City	38	8	5	6	23	23	2	1	16	13	43	26
20	Nottingham Forest	38	7	7	5	27	23	0	2	17	10	53	23

1914/15

9th in Division One

			Opponent	Score	Scorers	Att	Bauchop JR	Blackham S	Crozier J	Dempsey M	Drabble F	Garry E	Howie D	Jobey G	Kirby F	Kivlichan WF	Little TSC	Mavin F	McCandless J	McConnell WG	Scattergood EO	Scott JMA	Smith J	Stirling J	Watson A
1	Sep	5	BLACKBURN ROVERS	1-2	Bauchop	22000	10	3			1	4	5				8		11			6	9	7	2
2		12	Notts County	2-1	Bauchop, Smith	10000	10	3			1	4					8	5	11			6	9	7	2
3		19	SUNDERLAND	2-1	Jobey, Little	22000	10	3			1	4		9			8	5	11			6		7	2
4		26	Sheffield Wednesday	0-6		15000	10	3			1	4		9			8	5	11			6		7	2
5	Oct	3	WEST BROMWICH ALB.	1-4	Smith	18000	10	3			1	4	5				8		11			6	9	7	2
6		7	BOLTON WANDERERS	1-2	Jobey	8000	10	3			1	4	5	8					11			6	9	7	2
7		10	Everton	1-4	Smith	20000		3			1	4	5	10			8		11			6	9	7	2
8		17	CHELSEA	3-0	Little 2, Jobey	20000		3	4				5	10			8		11	2	1	6	9	7	
9		24	Bradford City	2-3	og, Little	35000		3	4				5	10			8		11	2	1	6	9	7	
10		31	BURNLEY	2-2	Little, Smith	6000	10	3	4				5				8		11		1	6	9	7	2
11	Nov	7	Tottenham Hotspur	0-3		14000	10	3	4				5				8		11	2	1	6	9	7	
12		14	NEWCASTLE UNITED	1-0	Little	12000	10	3	4				5		9		8		11	2	1	6		7	
13		21	Middlesbrough	3-1	Bauchop, Smith, Kirby	10000	10	3	4				5		9		8		11		1	6	7		2
14		28	SHEFFIELD UNITED	2-0	Little, Bauchop	9000	10	3				4	5		9		8		11		1	6	7		2
15	Dec	5	Aston Villa	2-1	Kirby, Smith	10000	10	3					5	4	9		8		11		1	6	7		2
16		12	LIVERPOOL	1-0	McCandless	8000	10	3					5	4	9		8		11		1	6	7		2
17		19	Manchester City	3-2	Little 2, Bauchop	5000	10	3					5	4	9		8		11		1	6	7		2
18		25	OLDHAM ATHLETIC	1-1	Bauchop	25000	10	3	4				5				8		11		1	6	9	7	2
19		26	Oldham Athletic	2-6	Little, Kirby	12000	10	3					5	4	9		8		11		1	6		7	2
20	Jan	1	Manchester United	2-1	Stirling, Bauchop	12000	10	3	4				5	9			8		11		1	6		7	2
21		2	Blackburn Rovers	2-2	Bauchop, McCandless	8000	10	3	4				5		9		8		11		1	6		7	2
22		16	NOTTS COUNTY	3-1	Bauchop 3	9000	10	3	4				5				8		11		1	6	9	7	2
23		23	Sunderland	3-3	Bauchop 3	7000	10			3			5	4	9		8		11		1	6		7	2
24	Feb	6	West Bromwich Albion	0-1		8000	10	3	4				5		9		8		11		1	6		7	2
25	Mar	1	Chelsea	1-0	Stirling	5000	10	3	4				5				8		11		1	6	9	7	2
26		6	Burnley	0-2		10000	10	3	4				5				8		11		1	6	9	7	2
27		13	TOTTENHAM HOTSPUR	5-1	Bauchop 3, Smith, McCandless	9000	10	3	4				5				8		11		1	6	9	7	2
28		17	SHEFFIELD WEDNESDAY	1-1	Bauchop	7000	10	3	4				5			8			11		1	6	9	7	2
29		20	Newcastle United	1-1	Bauchop	10000	10	3	4				5			8			11		1	6	9	7	2
30		27	MIDDLESBROUGH	2-0	Smith, Scott	10000	10	3	4				5			8			11		1	6	9	7	2
31	Apr	2	Bolton Wanderers	2-3	Bauchop 2	15000	10	3	4				5			8			11		1	6	9	7	2
32		3	Sheffield United	2-3	Bauchop, Smith	10500	10	3	4					5		7	8		11		1	6	9		2
33		5	MANCHESTER UNITED	5-0	Smith, Bauchop 3, Little	15000	10	3	4		1		5				8		11			6	9	7	2
34		10	ASTON VILLA	2-2	Bauchop, Crozier	12000	10	3	4				5			7	8		11		1	6	9		2
35		14	EVERTON	1-2	Crozier	6000	10	3	4				5				8		11		1	6	9	7	2
36		17	Liverpool	1-2	Smith	20000	10	3	4		1		5				8		11			6	9	7	2
37		24	MANCHESTER CITY	3-1	Bauchop, Little 2	7000	10	3	4				5				8		11		1	6	9	7	2
38		28	BRADFORD CITY	3-0	Little 2, Bauchop	21011	10	3	4				5	9			8		11		1	6		7	2
						Apps	35	37	25	1	9	8	34	14	10	6	33	3	38	4	29	38	29	31	34
						Goals	28		2					3	3		15		3			1	11	2	

One own goal

F.A. Cup

			Opponent	Score	Scorers	Att	Bauchop JR	Blackham S	Crozier J	Dempsey M	Drabble F	Garry E	Howie D	Jobey G	Kirby F	Kivlichan WF	Little TSC	Mavin F	McCandless J	McConnell WG	Scattergood EO	Scott JMA	Smith J	Stirling J	Watson A
R1	Jan	9	PORTSMOUTH	1-0	Smith	14000	10	3	4				5				8		11		1	6	9	7	2
R2		30	Bury	1-0	Bauchop	11815	10	3					5	4			8		11		1	6	9	7	2
R3	Feb	20	Sheffield United	0-1	(aet)	25971	10	3	4				5				8		11		1	6	9	7	2

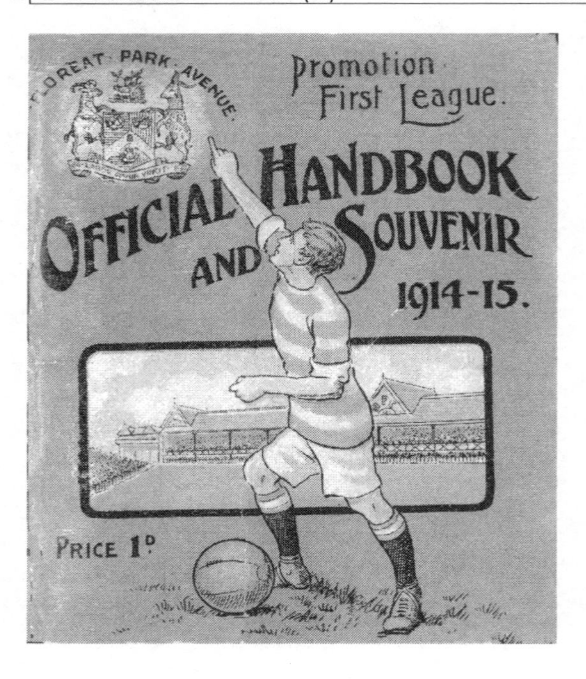

		P	W	D	L	F	A	W	D	L	F	A	Pts
1	Everton	38	8	5	6	44	29	11	3	5	32	18	46
2	Oldham Athletic	38	11	5	3	46	25	6	6	7	24	31	45
3	Blackburn Rovers	38	11	4	4	51	27	7	3	9	32	34	43
4	Burnley	38	12	1	6	38	18	6	6	7	23	29	43
5	Manchester City	38	9	7	3	29	15	6	6	7	20	24	43
6	Sheffield United	38	11	5	3	28	13	4	8	7	21	28	43
7	Sheffield Wednesday	38	10	7	2	43	23	5	6	8	18	31	43
8	Sunderland	38	11	3	5	46	30	7	2	10	35	42	41
9	BRADFORD	38	11	4	4	40	20	6	3	10	29	45	41
10	West Bromwich Albion	38	11	5	3	31	9	4	5	10	18	34	40
11	Bradford City	38	11	7	1	40	18	2	7	10	15	31	40
12	Middlesbrough	38	10	6	3	42	24	3	6	10	20	50	38
13	Liverpool	38	11	5	3	45	34	3	4	12	20	41	37
14	Aston Villa	38	10	5	4	39	32	3	6	10	23	40	37
15	Newcastle United	38	8	4	7	29	23	3	6	10	17	25	32
16	Notts County	38	8	7	4	28	18	1	6	12	13	39	31
17	Bolton Wanderers	38	8	5	6	35	27	3	3	13	33	57	30
18	Manchester United	38	8	6	5	27	19	1	6	12	19	43	30
19	Chelsea	38	8	6	5	32	25	0	7	12	19	40	29
20	Tottenham Hotspur	38	7	7	5	30	29	1	5	13	27	61	28

1915/16

Midland Section Tournament (games 1 to 25 and 33) and Northern Division Subsidiary Tournament (games 27 to 32 and 34 to 36)

	Month	Opponent	Score	Att	1	2	3	4	5	6	7	8	9	10	11	
1	Sep	4 Sheffield Wednesday	4-2	8000	Scattergood	Watson	Blackham	Crozier	Howie	Scott	Stirling	Jobey 1	Waite 3	Bauchop	Smith	
2		11 LINCOLN CITY	4-0	5000	Scattergood	Watson	Blackham	Crozier	Howie	Scott	Fawcett	Jobey	Waite	Bauchop 4	Smith	
3		18 LEEDS CITY	4-3	9000	Scattergood	Watson	Blackham	Crozier	Howie 1	Scott	Fawcett	Smith 1	Waite 1	Bauchop 1	Lawton	
4		25 Hull City	0-2	6000	Scattergood	Watson	Blackham	Crozier	Howie	Scott	Stirling	Briggs	Waite	Carr W	Smith	
5	Oct	2 NOTTM FOREST	1-0	6000	Scattergood	Mackrill	Blackham	Crozier	Howie	Scott	Stirling	Briggs	Waite	Bauchop	Smith 1	
6		9 Barnsley	2-5	2500	Scattergood	Watson	Blackham	Howard	Howie	Scott	Wilson	Briggs	Waite 1	Fearnley 1	Smith	
7		16 LEICESTER FOSSE	1-2	5000	Scattergood	Watson	Blackham	Crozier	Howie	Scott	Stirling	Briggs	Waite 1	Mavin	Smith	
8		23 Sheffield United	2-2	6000	Scattergood	Mackrill	Blackham	Crozier	Howie	Scott	Wilson	Allen	McLeod	Waite 2	Smith	
9		30 BRADFORD CITY	3-1	8500	Scattergood	Watson	Blackham	Crozier	Howie	Scott	Waite	Allen 1	McLeod 1	Bauchop 1	Smith	
10	Nov	6 Huddersfield T	1-2	3000	Scattergood	Watson	Blackham	Crozier	Howie	Scott	Wilson	Bauchop	Waite 1	McLeod	Briggs	
11		13 GRIMSBY TOWN	2-0	3000	Scattergood	Mackrill	Blackham	Howard	Howie 1	Scott	Stirling	Smith	Waite 1	McLeod	McCandless	
12		20 Notts County	0-3	5000	Scattergood	Watson	Blackham	Crozier	Howie	Scott	Wilson	Smith	Waite	McLeod	Bauchop	
13		27 DERBY COUNTY	2-3	3000	Scattergood	Watson	Blackham	Crozier	Howie	Scott	Wilson	McLeod 1	Waite	Bauchop 1	Smith	
14	Dec	4 SHEFFIELD WEDNESDAY	1-2	9000	Mutch	Watson	Lennon	Crozier	Howie	Scott	Smith	Allen	Waite	McLeod 1	McCandless	
15		11 Lincoln City	1-2	3000	Scattergood	Mackrill	Blackham	Lennon	Howie	Scott	Wilson 1	Waite	McLeod	Mavin	Briggs	
16		18 Leeds City	1-1	3000	Scattergood	Lennon	Blackham	Crozier	Howie	Scott	Wilson	McGuire 1	Waite	Bauchop	Briggs	
17		25 HULL CITY	1-2	10000	Hoffman	Watson	Blackham	Crozier	Howie	Scott	Smith	Carr J	Waite	McGuire	Bauchop 1	
18	Jan	1 Nottingham Forest	0-0	3000	Scattergood	Watson	Blackham	Crozier	Howie	Scott	Smith	McLeod	Waite	Bauchop	Bradbury	
19		8 BARNSLEY	6-0	5000	Howling	Watson	Blackham	Crozier	Howie	Scott	Bradbury	Waite 3	McLeod	Bauchop 2	Brown	1 og
20		15 Leicester Fosse	1-2	4000	Howling	Mackrill	Blackham	Crozier 1	Howie	Scott	Wilson	Waite	McLeod	Burrows	Briggs	
21		22 SHEFFIELD UNITED	0-1	4000	Howling	Lennon	Blackham	Crozier	Howie	Scott	Waite	Kennedy	McLeod	Bauchop	McCandless	
22		29 Bradford City	0-4	12000	Howling	Lennon	Blackham	Crozier	Howie	Scott	Wright	Kennedy	Waite	Barbour	Briggs	
23	Feb	5 HUDDERSFIELD T	3-0	5500	Howling	Mackrill	Blackham	Crozier 2	Howie	Scott	Cooper	McLeod	Waite 1	Bauchop	Wright	
24		12 Grimsby Town	1-1	3000	Howling	Mackrill	Blackham	Crozier	Howie	Scott	Wright	McLeod	Waite 1	Kemp	Ives	
25		19 NOTTS COUNTY	4-0	4000	Howling	Hudspeth 1	Blackham	Crozier	Howie	Scott	Cooper 1	Kemp	Waite 2	Bauchop	Ives	
26	Mar	4 BARNSLEY	4-1	3000	Howling	Hudspeth	Blackham	Crozier	Howie	Davidson	Cooper 1	McLeod 1	Waite 1	Bauchop 1	Ives	
27		11 Leeds City	2-3	3000	Howling	Hudspeth	Blackham	Crozier	Howie	Davidson	Cooper	McLeod	Waite	Bauchop 1	Ives	1 og
28		18 Rochdale	3-4	1000	Howling	Hudspeth	Blackham	Crozier	Howie	Davidson	Howard	McLeod	Waite 2	Kemp 1	Raybould	
29		25 HUDDERSFIELD T	2-0	3000	Howling	Hudspeth	Blackham	Crozier	Howie	Davidson	Cooper	McLeod	Waite	Kemp 2	Bauchop	
30	Apr	1 Bradford City	4-0	12000	Howling	Hudspeth	Blackham	Crozier	Howie	Davidson 1	Cooper 1	Little 1	Waite	McLeod	Bauchop 1	
31		8 Barnsley	0-3	2000	Howling	Hudspeth	Blackham	Crozier	Howie	Davidson	Cooper	Kemp	Waite	Box	McLeod	
32		15 LEEDS CITY	0-1	40000	Howling	Hudspeth	Blackham	Crozier	Howie	Scott	Cooper	McLeod	Waite	Robinson	Bauchop	
33		21 Derby County	1-6	7000	Palethorpe	Taylor	Blackham	Dexter	Mavin	Haynes	Brooks	Leigh	Waite	Davis	Harper	1 og
34		22 ROCHDALE	5-2	3000	Howling	Taylor	Blackham	Crozier	Howie 1	Scott	Shipway	McLeod 1	Waite 2	Kemp	Bauchop 1	
35		24 BRADFORD CITY	4-2	10000	Howling	Hudspeth 1	Blackham	Crozier	Howie	Scott	Cooper 1	McLeod	Waite 1	Kemp	Bauchop 1	
36		29 Huddersfield T	3-1	5000	Howling	Hudspeth 1	Scott	Crozier	Howie	Davidson	Cooper	McLeod 1	Waite	Kemp	Bauchop 1	

1916/17

Midland Section Principal Tournament (games 1 to 29 and 36) and Subsidiary Tournament (games 30 to 35)

#	Month	Date / Opponent	Score	Att												
1	Sep	2 LINCOLN CITY	1-0	3000	Howling	Hudspeth	Blackham	Crozier	Mavin	Scott	Cawdry	Kemp	McLeod	Howie 1	Bauchop	
2		9 Sheffield Wednesday	3-1	6000	Howling	Hudspeth	Taylor	Crozier	Howie	Scott	Cooper	Kemp	McLeod 1	Cawley 2	Bauchop	
3		16 Chesterfield	1-3	6000	Howling	Hudspeth	Taylor	Crozier	Howie	Cawdry	Cooper	Kemp 1	McLeod	Robinson S	Bauchop	
4		23 BIRMINGHAM	2-3	3500	Howling	Hudspeth	Taylor	Crozier 1	Howie 1	Walker	Cooper	Kemp	McLeod	Robinson S	Bauchop	
5		30 Hull City	1-1	5000	Howling	Hudspeth	Taylor	Crozier	Howie	Brown W	Robinson S	Kemp	Walker	McLeod 1	Bauchop	
6	Oct	7 NOTTM FOREST	1-0	1000	Howling	Hudspeth	Blackham	Crozier	Young	Scott	Robinson S	Kemp	Walker	McLeod 1	Bauchop	
7		14 Barnsley	0-3	2000	Howling	Marshall	Brooks	Crozier	Young	Brown W	Robinson S	Kemp	Walker	McLeod	Bauchop	
8		21 LEEDS CITY	1-3	8000	Howling	Hudspeth	Blackham	Crozier	Howie	Walker	Cooper 1	Carr W	McLeod	Robinson S	Bauchop	
9		28 Sheffield United	1-2	7000	Howling	Hudspeth	Taylor	Crozier	Brown W	Scott	Robinson S	Kemp	Walker	McLeod 1	Bauchop	
10	Nov	4 BRADFORD CITY	3-0	9000	Howling	Hudspeth	Taylor	Crozier	Howie	Scott	Cooper	Kemp	Walker	McLeod 2	Bauchop 1	
11		11 Leicester Fosse	2-0	6000	Howling	Scott	Taylor	Crozier	Howie	Brown W	Simonette	Kemp 2	Simpson	McLeod	Walker	
12		18 GRIMSBY TOWN	9-0	4000	Howling	Blackham	Taylor	Crozier	Carr G	Brown W	Carr W 1	Kemp 2	McLeod 5	Walker 1	Bauchop	
13		25 Notts County	1-2	3000	Howling	Hudspeth	Taylor	Crozier	Howie	Brown W	Robinson S	Kemp 1	McLeod	Scott	Walker	
14	Dec	2 ROTHERHAM COUNTY	3-1	2000	Howling	Hudspeth	Taylor	Crozier	Howie	Brown W	Robinson S	Walker 1	McLeod 1	Kemp 1	Bauchop	
15		9 Lincoln City	1-1	3000	Howling	Hudspeth	Potts	Crozier	Scott	Brown W	Cawdry	Walker	McLeod	Barraclough	Kemp	1 og
16		16 SHEFFIELD WEDNESDAY	3-1	2000	Howling	Hudspeth	Taylor	Crozier	Carr G	Scott	Barlow	Carr W 1	McLeod 1	Kemp	Bauchop 1	
17		25 HUDDERSFIELD T	1-2	3000	Howling	Hudspeth	Taylor	Crozier	Howie	Brown W	Walker 1	Scott	McLeod	Carr W	Bauchop	
18		26 Huddersfield Town	0-0	6000	Howling	Taylor	Gadsden	Crozier	Carr G	Scott	Barlow	Walker	Freeman	Carr W	Kemp	
19		30 Birmingham	2-1	14000	Howling	Hudspeth	Taylor	Crozier	Carr G	Brown W	Kemp	Walker	Freeman 1	Riley 1	Bauchop	
20	Jan	6 HULL CITY	4-0	2000	Howling	Hudspeth	Taylor	Crozier	Carr G	Walker	Carr W	Kemp	McLeod 3	Riley 1	Barlow	
21		13 Nottingham Forest	1-0	2000	Howling	Taylor	Gadsden	Crozier	Carr G	Brown W	Cawdry	Kemp 1	McLeod	Riley	Bauchop	
22		20 BARNSLEY	2-1	2000	Howling	Hudspeth	Taylor	Crozier	Carr G	Brown W	Cawdry	Little 1	McLeod 1	Kemp	Bauchop	
23		27 Leeds City	0-0	5000	Howling	Hudspeth	Taylor	Crozier	Carr G	Brown W	Cawdry	Little	Kemp	Riley	Bauchop	
24	Feb	3 SHEFFIELD UNITED	1-1	1500	Howling	Hudspeth	Taylor	Crozier	Carr G 1	Brown W	Carr W	Kemp	McLeod	Riley	Bauchop	
25		10 Bradford City	0-1	5000	Howling	Hudspeth	Taylor	Crozier	Carr G	Brown W	Robinson S	Kemp	McLeod	Walker	Bauchop	
26		17 LEICESTER FOSSE	0-1	1000	Howling	Hudspeth	Taylor	Crozier	Carr G	Brown W	Robinson S	Kemp	McLeod	Riley	Bauchop	
27		24 Grimsby Town	2-0	1800	Howling	Hudspeth	Taylor	Crozier	Carr G	Cheetham	Cawdry	Kemp	McLeod 2	Riley	Isherwood	
28	Mar	3 NOTTS COUNTY	1-1	2500	Howling	Hudspeth	Dickenson	Crozier	Carr G	Brown W	Brown T	Kemp	Elliott 1	Riley	Bauchop	
29		10 Rotherham County	1-2	2000	Howling	Mackrill	Blackham	Crozier	Carr G	Brown W	Cawdry	Dyson	Kemp	Robinson S 1	Butler	
30		17 LEEDS CITY	1-1	5000	Howling	Hudspeth	Dickenson	Crozier	Carr G	Cruise	Carr J	Kemp	Elliott 1	McLeod	Bauchop	
31		24 Bradford City	2-2	7000	Howling	Hudspeth	Blackham	Crozier	Carr G	Dickenson	Robinson J	Kemp	Elliott	Bauchop 1	Robinson S	1 og
32		31 HUDDERSFIELD T	2-0	3000	Howling	Hudspeth 1	Dickenson	Crozier	Carr G	Robinson J	Carr J	Kemp 1	Elliott	Brown (amat.)	Robinson S	
33	Apr	7 Leeds City	2-0	5000	Davies	Hudspeth	Blackham	Crozier	Howie	Carr J	Robinson J	Kemp 1	McLeod 1	Riley	Bauchop	
34		14 BRADFORD CITY	3-0	5000	Howling	Hudspeth	Dickenson	Robinson J	Crozier	Thorpe	Carr J	Carr G 1	Elliott 2	Riley	Bauchop	
35		21 Huddersfield Town	0-2	3000	Howling	Hudspeth	Blackham	Robinson J	Crozier	Brown W	Carr J	Carr G	Elliott	Riley	Robinson S	
36		28 CHESTERFIELD	3-1	2000	Sutcliffe	Hudspeth	Robinson J	Crozier	Brown D	Brown T	Carr G	Kemp	Elliott 2	Riley 1	Bauchop	

1917/18

Midland Section Principal Tournament (games 1 to 27 and 31) and Subsidiary Tournament (games 28 to 30 and 32 to 34)

1	Sep	1	Rotherham County	2-2	2000	Howling	Taylor	Dickenson	Crozier	Carr G	Brown	Carr J 1	Wild 1	Patefield	Kemp	Bauchop	
2		8	ROTHERHAM COUNTY	5-2	3500	Howling	Blackham	Dickenson	Crozier	Carr G	Brown	Carr J 1	Kemp 1	Elliott 2	Riley 1	Patefield	
3		15	Lincoln City	0-0	3000	Howling	Taylor	Dickenson	Crozier	Carr G	Brown	Isherwood	Kemp	Elliott	Riley	Bauchop	
4		22	LINCOLN CITY	1-0	4000	Howling	Blackham	Dickenson	Crozier	Carr G	Brown	Howard 1	Carr J	Patefield	Riley	Marshall	
5		29	Grimsby Town	2-1	5000	Howling	Taylor	Dickenson	Crozier	Carr G	Brown	Smith	Kemp 1	Bauchop 1	Elliott	Isherwood	
6	Oct	6	GRIMSBY TOWN	4-1	3000	Howling	Watson	Blackham	Crozier	Carr W	Scott	Cooper	Howie 1	Kemp 1	Riley	Carr G 2	
7		13	BIRMINGHAM	1-0	4000	Howling	Taylor	Dickenson	Crozier	Carr W	Brown	Barrett	Kemp 1	Carr G	Riley	Bauchop	
8		20	Birmingham	0-2	8000	Howling	Blackham	Dickenson	Crozier	Carr W	Brown	Barrett	Smart	Riley	Howie	Pollard	
9		27	NOTTS COUNTY	1-0	3000	Howling	Taylor	Dickenson	Crozier	Carr J	Brown	Barrett	Kemp	Bauchop 1	Riley	Patefield	
10	Nov	3	Notts County	1-0	2000	Howling	Blackham	Dickenson	Crozier	Carr G	Brown	Barrett	Kemp	Elliott 1	Smart	Griffin	
11		10	HUDDERSFIELD T	1-2	4000	Howling	Taylor	Dickenson	Crozier	Carr G	Brown	Robinson	Kemp	Elliott 1	Howie	Bauchop	
12		17	Huddersfield Town	0-1	4000	Howling	Blackham	Dickenson	Crozier	Carr G	Brown	Barrett	Robinson	Riley	Fearnley	Griffin	
13		24	SHEFFIELD WEDNESDAY	2-1	2000	Howling	Taylor	Dickenson	Crozier 1	Carr G	Brown	Barrett	Robinson	Riley	Kemp	Bauchop 1	
14	Dec	1	Sheffield Wednesday	1-3	3000	Howling	Taylor	Dickenson	Crozier	Carr G	Brown	Barrett	Robinson	Elliott	Kemp	Riley	*1 og*
15		8	SHEFFIELD UNITED	2-0	3000	Howling	Taylor	Dickenson	Crozier 1	Fox	Scott	Carr G 1	Kemp	Elliott	Howie	Bauchop	
16		15	Sheffield United	0-1	4000	Howling	Taylor	Dickenson	Crozier	Fox	Brown	Carr G	Kemp	Riley	Smart	Robinson	
17		22	LEICESTER FOSSE	1-0	2000	Howling	Blackham	Boocock	Crozier	Fox	Brown	Cooper	Kemp	Elliott 1	Bell	Bauchop	
18		25	Bradford City	2-1	10000	Howling	Blackham	Dickenson	Crozier 1	Carr G	Fox	Robinson	Riley	Fearnley	Bell	Bauchop 1	
19		26	BRADFORD CITY	0-1	8000	Howling	Blackham	Dickenson	Crozier	Carr G	Fox	Robinson	Riley	Elliott	Bell	Bauchop	
20		29	Leicester Fosse	0-2	2500	Howling	Watson	Dickenson	Crozier	Carr G	Fox	Gardner	Smart	Kemp	Bell	Bauchop	
21	Jan	5	BARNSLEY	8-0	3000	Howling	Fox	Dickenson	Crozier	Carr G	Brown	Smith	Bell 1	Kemp 1	Turnbull 5	Bauchop 1	
22		12	Barnsley	0-1	2000	Howling	Blackham	Dickenson	Crozier	Fox	Brown	Carr G	Bell	Riley	Turnbull	Robinson	
23		26	Nottingham Forest	0-0	3000	Howling	Blackham	Dickenson	Crozier	Fox	Scott	Carr G	Little	Kemp	Riley	Bell	
24	Feb	16	Leeds City	1-2	7000	Howling	Blackham	Dickenson	Crozier	Fox	Brown	Carr G	Bell	Riley	Turnbull	Bauchop 1	
25		23	LEEDS CITY	0-2	6000	Howling	Fox	Dickenson	Crozier	Carr G	Brown	Robinson	Turnbull	Riley	Howie	Bauchop	
26	Mar	2	Hull City	1-1	2000	Howling	Blackham	Dickenson	Fox	Carr G	Brown	Robinson	Bell	Priestley	Turnbull 1	Maley	
27		9	HULL CITY	1-3	3000	Howling	Fox	Dickenson	Crozier	Carr G	Brown	Bell	Turnbull	Priestley 1	Riley	Robinson	
28		16	Bradford City	1-1	5000	Howling	Fox	Blackham	Cawdry	Carr G	Brown	Robinson	Turnbull 1	Wellock	Riley	Bauchop	
29		23	BRADFORD CITY	3-1	6000	Howling	Fox	Dickenson	Crozier	Carr G	Brown	Bell	Turnbull 1	Priestley 1	Riley	Robinson 1	
30		30	Leeds City	1-3	3000	Howling	Blackham	Dickenson	Crozier	Carr G	Brown	Robinson 1	Bell	Turnbull	Riley	Bauchop	
31	Apr	2	NOTTM FOREST	3-0	2500	Turnbull	Chaplin	Dickenson	Wild	Duckett	Brown	McKenzie	Robinson	Buddery 1	Bell 1	Shearman 1	
32		6	LEEDS CITY	1-2	2000	Howling	Fox	Dickenson	Crozier 1	Carr G	Brown	Robinson	Riley	Fenwick	Turnbull	Bell	
33		13	HUDDERSFIELD T	1-2	3000	Howling	Blackham	Dickenson	Carr G	Fox	Brown	Robinson	Bell	Riley 1	Bauchop	Shearman	
34		20	Huddersfield Town	1-3	2000	Baker	Mackrill	Dickenson	Hay	Wilson	Brown	Robinson	Jarvis 1	Chapman	Bell	Hibbert	

1918/19

Midland Section Principal Tournament (games 1 to 29 and 34) and Subsidiary Tournament (games 30 to 33 and 35, 36)

1	Sep	7	SHEFFIELD WEDNESDAY	4-3	5000	Howling	Mackrill	Dickenson	Crozier	Fox	Brown	Carr	Turnbull 1	Elliott 2	Bell	Kay 1	
2		14	Sheffield Wednesday	3-2	6000	Howling	Howie	Dickenson	Crozier	Fox	Brown	Carr	Bell	Chapman 1	Turnbull 1	Kay 1	
3		21	HUDDERSFIELD T	2-2	3500	Howling	Watson	Dickenson	Crozier	Fox	Brown	Carr	Bell	Chapman 1	Turnbull 1	Kay	
4		28	Huddersfield Town	0-0	3000	Howling	Fox	Dickenson	Crozier	Carr	Brown	Wilson	Bell	Chapman	Turnbull	Kay	
5	Oct	5	NOTTS COUNTY	0-0	3000	Howling	Watson	Dickenson	Crozier	Fox	Brown	Carr	Chapman	Elliott	Turnbull	Kay	
6		12	Notts County	1-4	7000	Howling	Fox	Dickenson	Crozier	Carr	Brown	Sheldon	Bell	Chapman	Turnbull	Kay	1 og
7		19	Birmingham	0-2	7000	Howling	Blackham	Dickenson	Carr	Fox	Brown	Osborn	Bell	Chapman	Turnbull	Kay	
8		26	BIRMINGHAM	1-1	5500	Howling	Hudspeth 1	Dickenson	Crozier	Fox	McKenzie	Stansfield	Bell	Bauchop	Turnbull	Kay	
9	Nov	2	Rotherham County	1-1	3000	Howling	Hudspeth	Dickenson	Fox	Carr	Crozier	Stansfield	Bell	Chapman	Turnbull 1	Kay	
10		9	ROTHERHAM COUNTY	2-1	5000	Howling	Hudspeth	Dickenson	Crozier	Fox	Brown	Stansfield 1	Bell	Chapman 1	Turnbull	Kay	
11		16	Lincoln City	1-1	2000	Howling	Dickenson	Lawson	Crozier	Fox	Brown	Carr	Bell	Elliott 1	Howie	Turnbull	
12		23	LINCOLN CITY	6-1	3000	Watson	Lawson	Dickenson	Crozier	Fox	Brown	Carr 2	Kay	Chapman	Bauchop 4	Turnbull	
13		30	Grimsby Town	0-4	2000	Howling	Fox	Dickenson	Crozier	Brown	Graham	Carr	Kay	Chapman	Bell	Turnbull	
14	Dec	7	GRIMSBY TOWN	5-0	2000	Howling	Blackham	Dickenson	Crozier	Fox	Brown	Carr 1	Bell 1	Elliott 1	Bauchop 2	Turnbull	
15		14	Sheffield United	0-2	9000	Howling	Watson	Dickenson	Crozier	Cook	Brown	Chapman	Bell	Bird	Kay	Turnbull	
16		21	SHEFFIELD UNITED	3-0	4000	Howling	Watson	Dickenson	Crozier	Howie	Fox	Stansfield	Bell	Taylor 2	Bauchop	Turnbull 1	
17		25	BRADFORD CITY	2-1	8000	Howling	Watson	Dickenson	Crozier	Howie	Scott	Stansfield	Little 1	Taylor 1	Bauchop	Turnbull	
18		26	Bradford City	3-2	7000	Howling	Watson	Dickenson	Crozier	Howie 2	Scott	Stansfield	Fox	Taylor	Bauchop	Turnbull 1	
19		28	Leicester Fosse	2-1	5000	Howling	Watson	Dickenson	Crozier	Fox	Scott	Stansfield	Howie	Taylor 1	Bauchop 1	Turnbull	
20	Jan	11	Hull City	2-0	6000	Howling	Watson	Dickenson	Crozier	Howie	Brown	Bell	Whalley	Blackham	Bauchop 1	Turnbull 1	
21		18	HULL CITY	0-1	9000	Howling	Watson	Dickenson	Crozier	Fox	Brown	Stirling	Little	Bauchop	Bell	Turnbull	
22		25	Nottingham Forest	0-3	8000	Howling	Watson	Blackham	Crozier	Scott	Brown	Evans	Little	Taylor	Birch	Turnbull	
23	Feb	1	NOTTM FOREST	2-0	8000	Scattergood	Watson	Blackham	Crozier	Howie	Scott	Donald	Crowther	Taylor 1	Bauchop 1	Turnbull	
24		8	COVENTY CITY	0-0	7000	Scattergood	Watson	Dickenson	Crozier	Howie	Scott	Donald	Crowther	Taylor	Bauchop	Turnbull	
25		15	Coventry City	1-2	10000	Scattergood	Watson	Dickenson	Crozier	Howie 1	Scott	Stansfield	Crowther	Taylor	Bauchop	Turnbull	
26		22	LEEDS CITY	1-3	5000	Scattergood	Watson	Dickenson	Crozier	Howie	Scott	Crowther	Little	Taylor 1	Bauchop	Turnbull	
27	Mar	1	Leeds City	5-2	10000	Howling	Watson	Dickenson	Brown	Crozier	Scott	Turnbull 1	Howie	Taylor 2	Crowther 2	Bauchop	
28		8	BARNSLEY	3-1	9000	Howling	Watson	Dickenson	Brown	Crozier	Scott	Turnbull 1	Howie	Taylor 1	Crowther 1	Bauchop	
29		15	Barnsley	1-0	4000	Scattergood	Watson	Blackham	Brown	Crozier	Scott	Turnbull 1	Howie	Taylor	Crowther	Bauchop	
30		29	Bradford City	4-1	10000	Scattergood	Blackham	Dickenson	Brown	Crozier 1	Scott	Turnbull	Howie	Taylor 1	Crowther 1	Bauchop 1	
31	Apr	5	LEEDS CITY	5-0	12000	Scattergood	Blackham	Dickenson	Brown	Crozier	Scott	Turnbull 2	Howie	Taylor 1	Crowther 2	Bauchop	
32		12	Leeds City	1-3	8000	Scattergood	Blackham	Dickenson	Brown	Crozier	Scott	Turnbull	Howie 1	Taylor	Crowther	Bauchop	
33		19	Huddersfield Town	0-0	6000	Scattergood	Howie	Blackham	Brown	Crozier	Scott	Waite	Little	Taylor	Crowther	Bauchop	
34		21	LEICESTER FOSSE	2-1	20000	Scattergood	Hawley	Dickenson	Brown	Crozier	Scott	Waite	Little 1	Crowther 1	McLaughlin	Bauchop	
35		22	BRADFORD CITY	2-1	10000	Scattergood	Blackham	Dickenson	Brown	Crozier	Scott	Turnbull	Little	Taylor 1	Crowther 1	Bauchop	
36		26	HUDDERSFIELD T	1-1	5000	Scattergood	Blackham	Chaplin	Brown	Crozier	Scott	Waite	McLaughlin	Taylor	Crowther 1	McCandless	

FINAL TABLES 1915/16 TO 1918/19

1915-16 Midland Section - Principal Tournament

		p	w	d	l	f	a	pts
1	Nottingham Forest	26	15	5	6	48	25	35
2	Sheffield United	26	12	7	7	51	36	31
3	Huddersfield Town	26	12	5	9	43	36	29
4	Bradford City	26	12	4	10	52	32	28
5	Barnsley	26	12	4	10	46	55	28
6	Leicester Fosse	26	11	6	9	42	34	28
7	Sheffield Wednesday	26	11	5	10	46	43	27
8	Notts County	26	10	6	10	39	36	26
9	Lincoln City	26	12	2	12	54	54	26
10	Leeds City	26	10	5	11	39	43	25
11	Hull City	26	10	3	13	42	58	23
12	BRADFORD	26	9	4	13	46	46	22
13	Grimsby Town	26	7	6	13	31	46	20
14	Derby County	26	7	2	17	39	74	16

1915-16 Northern Division - Subsidiary Tournament

		p	w	d	l	f	a	pts
1	Leeds City	10	7	1	2	21	13	15
2	BRADFORD	10	6	0	4	27	17	12
3	Huddersfield Town	10	4	3	3	19	15	11
4	Bradford City	10	4	1	5	18	20	9
5	Rochdale	10	4	1	5	15	21	9
6	Barnsley	10	2	0	8	13	27	4

1916-17 Midland Section - Principal Tournament

		p	w	d	l	f	a	pts
1	Leeds City	30	18	10	2	68	29	46
2	Barnsley	30	15	8	7	65	41	38
3	Birmingham	30	14	9	7	56	38	37
4	Huddersfield Town	30	15	6	9	41	31	36
5	BRADFORD	30	14	6	10	51	32	34
6	Nottingham Forest	30	14	5	11	57	39	33
7	Notts County	30	13	6	11	47	52	32
8	Bradford City	30	12	7	11	41	41	31
9	Rotherham County	30	12	6	12	53	52	30
10	Sheffield United	30	11	7	12	43	47	29
11	Hull City	30	10	7	13	36	57	27
12	Chesterfield Town	30	11	4	15	59	62	26
13	Sheffield Wednesday	30	9	6	15	36	48	24
14	Grimsby Town	30	8	6	16	38	71	22
15	Leicester Fosse	30	6	7	17	29	53	19
16	Lincoln City	30	5	6	19	38	65	16

1916-17 Midland Section - Subsidiary Tournament

		p	w	d	l	f	a	pts
1	BRADFORD	6	3	2	1	10	5	8
2	Sheffield United	6	4	0	2	12	7	8
3	Birmingham	6	3	2	1	17	12	8
5	Chesterfield Town	6	4	0	2	12	12	8
5	Leicester Fosse	6	4	0	2	15	16	8
6	Huddersfield Town	6	3	1	2	6	4	7
7	Leeds City	6	2	2	2	8	7	6
8	Grimsby Town	6	2	2	2	12	11	6
9	Hull City	6	2	2	2	13	12	6
10	Sheffield Wednesday	6	2	2	2	12	12	6
11	Barnsley	6	1	3	2	8	9	5
12	Rotherham County	6	2	1	3	9	13	5
13	Lincoln City	6	1	2	3	11	12	4
14	Nottingham Forest	6	1	2	3	12	14	4
15	Notts County	6	1	2	3	9	12	4
16	Bradford City	6	0	3	3	5	13	3

1917-18 Midland Section - Principal Tournament

		p	w	d	l	f	a	pts
1	Leeds City	28	23	1	4	75	23	47
2	Sheffield United	28	20	1	7	66	27	41
3	Birmingham	28	14	6	8	59	38	34
4	Hull City	28	15	4	9	67	50	34
5	Nottingham Forest	28	13	4	11	41	28	30
6	BRADFORD	28	13	4	11	40	29	30
7	Leicester Fosse	28	13	3	12	52	43	29
8	Huddersfield Town	28	12	2	14	49	46	26
9	Rotherham County	28	8	9	11	42	52	25
10	Notts County	28	7	9	12	43	54	23
11	Sheffield Wednesday	28	9	5	14	45	59	23
12	Grimsby Town	28	5	11	12	24	62	21
13	Bradford City	28	8	4	16	34	55	20
14	Lincoln City	28	7	5	16	25	62	19
15	Barnsley	28	8	2	18	40	74	18

1917-18 Midland Section - Subsidiary Tournament

		p	w	d	l	f	a	pts
1	Grimsby Town	6	4	1	1	13	3	9
2	Notts County	6	4	0	2	19	9	8
3	Sheffield Wednesday	6	3	2	1	15	8	8
4	Hull City	6	3	2	1	12	9	8
5	Leeds City	6	3	2	1	8	6	8
6	Lincoln City	6	3	1	2	11	8	7
7	Huddersfield Town	6	3	1	2	13	11	7
8	Barnsley	6	3	1	2	14	12	7
9	Bradford City	6	1	4	1	8	8	6
10	Birmingham	6	2	2	2	6	9	6
11	Sheffield United	6	2	1	3	9	12	5
12	Leicester Fosse	6	2	1	3	6	10	5
13	Nottingham Forest	6	2	1	3	4	7	5
14	Rotherham County	6	1	2	3	4	10	4
15	BRADFORD	6	1	1	4	8	12	3
16	Gainsborough Trinity	6	0	0	6	3	19	0

1918-19 Midland Section - Principal Tournament

		p	w	d	l	f	a	pts
1	Nottingham Forest	30	18	6	6	59	31	42
2	Birmingham	30	20	1	9	72	36	41
3	Notts County	30	16	9	5	65	38	41
4	Leeds City	30	17	4	9	53	38	38
5	BRADFORD	30	15	7	8	53	41	37
6	Huddersfield Town	30	13	8	9	45	45	34
7	Hull City	30	12	7	11	48	42	31
8	Sheffield United	30	12	6	12	56	47	30
9	Coventry City	30	13	4	13	55	59	30
10	Leicester Fosse	30	13	3	14	53	53	29
11	Sheffield Wednesday	30	11	6	13	49	49	28
12	Lincoln City	30	10	4	16	38	59	24
13	Bradford City	30	9	4	17	48	56	22
14	Barnsley	30	9	3	18	45	79	21
15	Grimsby Town	30	7	6	17	40	69	20
16	Rotherham County	30	2	8	20	23	60	12

1918-19 Midland Section - Subsidiary Tournament Section C

		p	w	d	l	f	a	pts
1	BRADFORD	6	3	2	1	13	6	8
2	Huddersfield Town	6	2	3	1	7	4	7
3	Leeds City	6	3	0	3	10	9	6
4	Brdford City	6	1	1	4	4	15	3

NOTTM. FOREST F.C.

OFFICIAL CARD OF THE MATCH.

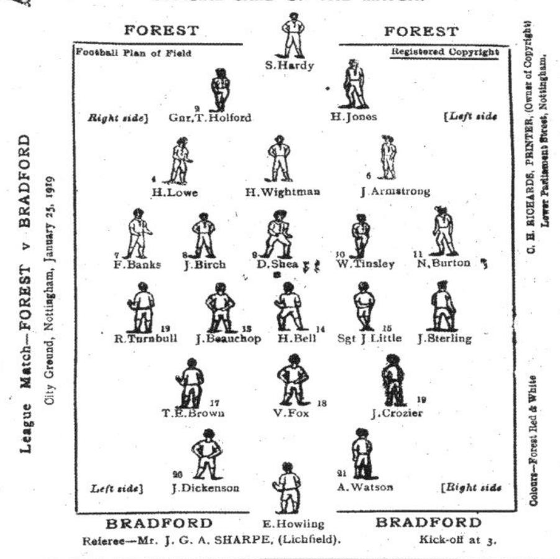

The card of the match for Nottingham Forest v Bradford, January 25 1919

1919/20

11th in Division One

							Bauchop JR	Blackham S	Boyle O	Brown TE	Crowther GL	Crozier J	Dickenson W	Howie D	Howling E	Keetley T	Little TSC	Loughran T	McCandless J	McLean DP	Scattergood EO	Scott JMA	Smith CF	Turnbull RJ	Waite GH	Watson A
1	Aug	30	Bolton Wanderers	2-1	Little, Bauchop	17540	11	3		4	10	5					8				1	6		7	9	2
2	Sep	3	EVERTON	0-2		10000	11				10	4	3	5			8				1	6		7	9	2
3		6	BOLTON WANDERERS	2-0	Loughran, Bauchop	15000	11	3		4		5	2	8				10			1	6		7	9	
4		8	Everton	0-2		20000	10	2		4	9	5	3	8					11		1	6		7		
5		13	OLDHAM ATHLETIC	2-0	Turnbull, McCandless	11000	10	2		4		5	3	8			9		11		1	6		7		
6		20	Oldham Athletic	2-2	Bauchop, Smith	8000	10	2		4		5	3	8					11		1	6	9	7		
7		27	ASTON VILLA	6-1	McCandless 2, Little 3, Turnbull	15000	10	2		4			3	5			8		11		1	6	9	7		
8	Oct	4	Aston Villa	0-1		30000	10	2		4			3	5			8		11		1	6	9		7	
9		11	NEWCASTLE UNITED	0-1		20000	10	2		4			3	5			9	8	11		1	6		7		
10		18	Newcastle United	0-4		30000	11	2	4				3	5			8	10	7		1	6			9	
11		25	CHELSEA	1-0	McLean	18000	11	2				4	3	5			8	10	7	9	1	6				
12	Nov	1	Chelsea	0-4		40000	10	3				4		5			8		11	9	1	6		7		2
13		8	LIVERPOOL	1-2	Bauchop	13000	10	3				4		5			8		11	9	1	6		7		2
14		15	Liverpool	3-3	Turnbull, Crozier, McLean	15000	10	2				4	3	5			8		11	9	1	6		7		
15		22	Burnley	6-2	* see below	15000	10	2				4	3	5			8	7	11	9	1	6				
16		29	BURNLEY	0-1		16000	10	2				4	3	5			8	7	11	9	1	6				
17	Dec	6	Preston North End	3-0	McLean 2, Bauchop	12000	10	2				4	3	5			8		11	9	1	6		7		
18		13	PRESTON NORTH END	3-3	McLean 3	15000	10	2				4	3	5			8		11	9	1	6		7		
19		20	Middlesbrough	2-1	McLean, Turnbull	15000	10	2				4	3	5			8		11	9	1	6		7		
20		25	Sheffield United	2-2	Little, McLean	25000	10	2				4	3	5			8		11	9	1	6		7		
21		26	SHEFFIELD UNITED	1-0	Bauchop	25000	10	2				4	3	5			8		11	9	1	6		7		
22		27	MIDDLESBROUGH	1-1	Turnbull	18000	11	2			10	4	3	5			8	7			1	6		9		
23	Jan	3	Bradford City	0-0		35000	10	2				4	3	5			8		11	9	1	6		7		
24		24	Blackburn Rovers	3-3	McLean 2, Bauchop	16000	10	2				4	3	5			8		11	9	1	6		7		
25	Feb	7	Notts County	2-0	Bauchop, Little	20000	8	2				6	3	5			10		7	9	1	4		11		
26		11	BRADFORD CITY	0-0		15000	10	2				4	3	5				8	11	9	1	6		7		
27		14	NOTTS COUNTY	0-1		20000	11	3			10	4		5				8		9	1	6		7		2
28		23	BLACKBURN ROVERS	5-2	Bauchop, McLean 3, Little	10000	10	3				4		5			8		11	9	1	6		7		2
29		28	SHEFFIELD WEDNESDAY	3-0	McLean 2, Little	17000	10	3				4		5	1		8		11	9		6		7		2
30	Mar	13	Manchester City	1-4	Little	10000	10					4	3	5			8	7		9	1	6		11		2
31		20	DERBY COUNTY	1-1	McCandless	15000	10					4	3	5			8	7	11	9	1	6				2
32		22	MANCHESTER CITY	2-1	Little, McLean	10000	10					4	3	5			8		11	9	1	6		7		2
33		27	Derby County	0-0		15000	10					4	3	5			8		11	9	1	6		7		2
34	Apr	2	Manchester United	1-0	Loughran	35000	10				9	4	3	5				8	11		1	6		7		2
35		3	WEST BROMWICH ALB.	0-4		15000	10				9	4	3	5				8	11		1	6		7		2
36		6	MANCHESTER UNITED	1-4	Keetley	12000	10	2			8	4	3	5		9			11		1	6		7		
37		10	West Bromwich Albion	1-3	Keetley	10000	10	2		6	8	4	3	5		9			11		1			7		
38		17	SUNDERLAND	2-2	Keetley 2	15000	10	2				4	3	5		9	8		11		1	6		7		
39		19	Sheffield Wednesday	1-0	Bauchop	5000	10					4	3	5			8		11		1	6		7	9	2
40		24	Sunderland	0-2		18000	10	2				4	3	5		8			11	9	1	6		7		
41		28	ARSENAL	0-0		6000	10					4	3	5		9	8		11		1	6		7		2
42	May	1	Arsenal	0-3		25000	10					4	3	5		9	8		11		1	6		7		2

Scorers in game 15: One og, McLean, Loughran, McCandless,Bauchop, Little

	Bauchop JR	Blackham S	Boyle O	Brown TE	Crowther GL	Crozier J	Dickenson W	Howie D	Howling E	Keetley T	Little TSC	Loughran T	McCandless J	McLean DP	Scattergood EO	Scott JMA	Smith CF	Turnbull RJ	Waite GH	Watson A
Apps	42	32	1	9	9	38	36	41	1	6	32	13	36	23	41	41	3	36	6	16
Goals	11					1				4	11	3	5	18			1	5		

One own goal

F.A. Cup

							Bauchop JR	Blackham S	Boyle O	Brown TE	Crowther GL	Crozier J	Dickenson W	Howie D	Howling E	Keetley T	Little TSC	Loughran T	McCandless J	McLean DP	Scattergood EO	Scott JMA	Smith CF	Turnbull RJ	Waite GH	Watson A
R1	Jan	10	NOTTM. FOREST	3-0	McLean, Bauchop, Turnbull	7000	10	2				4	3	5			8		11	9	1	6		7		
R2		31	CASTLEFORD TOWN	3-2	McLean 2, Little	10630	10	2				4	3	5			8		11	9	1	6		7		
R3	Feb	21	Notts County	4-3	McLean 2, McCandless, Bauchop	36246	10	3				4		5			8		11	9	1	6		7		2
R4	Mar	6	Chelsea	1-4	Little	61223	10	2				4	3	5			8		11	9	1	6		7		

		P	W	D	L	F	A	W	D	L	F	A	Pts
1	West Bromwich Albion	42	17	1	3	65	21	11	3	7	39	26	60
2	Burnley	42	13	5	3	43	27	8	4	9	22	32	51
3	Chelsea	42	15	3	3	33	10	7	2	12	23	41	49
4	Liverpool	42	12	5	4	35	18	7	5	9	24	26	48
5	Sunderland	42	17	2	2	45	16	5	2	14	27	43	48
6	Bolton Wanderers	42	11	3	7	35	29	8	6	7	37	36	47
7	Manchester City	42	14	5	2	52	27	4	4	13	19	35	45
8	Newcastle United	42	11	5	5	31	13	6	4	11	13	26	43
9	Aston Villa	42	11	3	7	49	36	7	3	11	26	37	42
10	Arsenal	42	11	5	5	32	21	4	7	10	24	37	42
11	BRADFORD	42	8	6	7	31	26	7	6	8	29	37	42
12	Manchester United	42	6	8	7	20	17	7	6	8	34	33	40
13	Middlesbrough	42	10	5	6	35	23	5	5	11	26	42	40
14	Sheffield United	42	14	5	2	43	20	2	3	16	16	49	40
15	Bradford City	42	10	6	5	36	25	4	5	12	18	38	39
16	Everton	42	8	6	7	42	29	4	8	9	27	39	38
17	Oldham Athletic	42	12	4	5	33	19	3	4	14	16	33	38
18	Derby County	42	12	5	4	36	18	1	7	13	11	39	38
19	Preston North End	42	9	6	6	35	27	5	4	12	22	46	38
20	Blackburn Rovers	42	11	4	6	48	30	2	7	12	16	47	37
21	Notts County	42	9	8	4	39	25	3	4	14	17	49	36
22	Sheffield Wednesday	42	6	4	11	14	23	1	5	15	14	41	23

1920/21

Bottom of Division One: Relegated

#	Month	Day	Opponent	Score	Scorers	Att.	Barrett LH	Batten J	Bauchop JR	Bingham S	Blackham S	Brown TE	Burkinshaw JDL	Crozier J	Curtis T	Dickenson W	Hartles W	Howie D	Howling E	Keetley T	Little TSC	Loughran T	McCandless J	McLean DP	Nicholson H	Peel HB	Scattergood EO	Scott JMA	Turnbull RJ
1	Aug	28	EVERTON	3-3	Burkinshaw, McLean 2	15000			10				8	4	2	3		5					11	9			1	6	7
2	Sep	1	Sunderland	1-5	McLean	35000			10					4	2	3		5			8		11	9			1	6	7
3		4	Everton	1-1	McLean	45000			10					4	2	3		5			8		11	9			1	6	7
4		8	SUNDERLAND	1-1	Scott	12000			10			6		5	2	3					8		11	9			1	4	7
5		11	SHEFFIELD UNITED	2-0	McLean 2	15000			10			6		5	2	3					8		11	9			1	4	7
6		18	Sheffield United	0-2		26000	4		10			6			2	3		5			8		11	9			1		7
7		25	BRADFORD CITY	1-2	Turnbull	30000	6		10		3			4		2		5			8		11	9			1		7
8	Oct	2	Bradford City	1-2	McCandless	28000	6		10		3			4		2		5			8		11	9			1		7
9		9	BURNLEY	1-3	Hartles	12000	6		10		3		8	4		2	11	5						9			1		7
10		16	Burnley	0-1		30000			10		3			4		2		5			8		11	9			1	6	7
11		23	Newcastle United	1-2	McLean	45000			10		2			4		3		5			8	11		9			1	6	7
12		30	NEWCASTLE UNITED	0-2		20000			10		2			4		3		5			8		11	9			1	6	7
13	Nov	6	Liverpool	1-0	McLean	30000	6		10		2			5		3				8			11	9			1	4	7
14		13	LIVERPOOL	1-3	McLean	17000			10		2			4		3		5			8		11	9			1	6	7
15		20	Aston Villa	1-4	McCandless	30000			10		2		4	5		3		8					11	9			1	6	7
16		27	ASTON VILLA	4-0	McLean, Turnbull 3	15000					2		8	4		3		10					11	9	5		1	6	7
17	Dec	4	Manchester United	1-5	Keetley	16000	6				2		8			3		10		9			11		5		1	4	7
18		11	MANCHESTER UNITED	2-4	Howie, Burkinshaw	12000					2		8	4		3		10					11	9	5		1	6	7
19		18	Chelsea	1-4	McLean	25000		8	11				4	5	2	3		10	1				7	9				6	
20		25	Oldham Athletic	0-1		20000					2		4	5		3		10		8			11	9			1	6	7
21		27	OLDHAM ATHLETIC	2-1	Bauchop, McLean	25000		8	10		2			4		3		5					11	9			1	6	7
22	Jan	1	CHELSEA	0-2		25000		8	10		2		4			3		5					11	9			1	6	7
23		15	HUDDERSFIELD TOWN	1-1	McLean	20000		10		7			4		2	3		5		8			11	9			1	6	
24		22	Huddersfield Town	0-0		16000	4		11	7	2		8			3		5						9			1	6	10
25	Feb	3	Tottenham Hotspur	0-2		22000			11	7	2		4	5		3		10		8				9			1	6	
26		5	TOTTENHAM HOTSPUR	1-1	McLean	20000	6	8	10	7				4		3		5					11	9			1	2	
27		12	MIDDLESBROUGH	3-0	Bauchop, Batten 2	15000		8	11	7	2		4	5		3		10						9			1	6	
28		19	Middlesbrough	1-2	McLean	25000		8	10	7	2		4			3		5					11	9			1	6	
29		26	BLACKBURN ROVERS	1-1	McLean	17000	6		10		2		4	5		3		8					11	9			1		7
30	Mar	5	Blackburn Rovers	0-1		25000	6	8	10		2		4			3		5					11	9			1		7
31		12	DERBY COUNTY	2-1	McLean, Bauchop	20000			10		2		4	6		3		5		8			11	9			1		7
32		19	Derby County	0-1		17000	6	10			2			4		3		5				7	11	9			1		8
33		25	Preston North End	3-3	Batten, McLean 2	20000		10	11		2		4			3		5				6	7	9			1		8
34		26	Bolton Wanderers	0-2		24808	6	10	11		2		4			3		5					7	9			1		8
35		28	PRESTON NORTH END	1-3	McLean	10000	6	10	11		2		4			3		5					7	9			1		8
36	Apr	2	BOLTON WANDERERS	2-1	McLean, Batten	15000		10			2			4		3	11	5		8				9			1	6	7
37		9	Arsenal	1-2	Bauchop	25000		10	11		2			4		3		5						9		8	1	6	7
38		16	ARSENAL	0-1		15000		10	11		2			4		3		5						9		8	1	6	7
39		23	Manchester City	0-1		18000	6		10		2		8	4		3		5					11	9			1		7
40		30	MANCHESTER CITY	1-2	Batten	12000	6	8	10		2			4		3		5					11	9			1		7
41	May	2	West Bromwich Albion	1-0	McLean	15000	6	8	10		2		4			3		5					11	9			1		7
42		7	WEST BROMWICH ALB.	0-3		8000	6	8	10	7			4		3	2		5		9			11				1		
						Apps	17	18	35	7	32	3	23	30	9	42	2	39	1	8	11	3	34	40	3	2	41	27	35
						Goals		5	4				2				1	1		1			2	22				1	4

F.A. Cup

Rd	Month	Day	Opponent	Score	Scorers	Att.	Barrett LH	Batten J	Bauchop JR	Bingham S	Blackham S	Brown TE	Burkinshaw JDL	Crozier J	Curtis T	Dickenson W	Hartles W	Howie D	Howling E	Keetley T	Little TSC	Loughran T	McCandless J	McLean DP	Nicholson H	Peel HB	Scattergood EO	Scott JMA	Turnbull RJ
R1	Jan	8	CLAPTON ORIENT	1-0	Burkinshaw	14000		8	10		2		4			3		5					11	9			1	6	7
R2		29	HUDDERSFIELD T	0-1		28000			7		3		6	5		2		8		10				9			1	4	11

		P	W	D	L	F	A	W	D	L	F	A	Pts
1	Burnley	42	17	3	1	56	16	6	10	5	23	20	59
2	Manchester City	42	19	2	0	50	13	5	4	12	20	37	54
3	Bolton Wanderers	42	15	6	0	53	17	4	8	9	24	36	52
4	Liverpool	42	11	7	3	41	17	7	8	6	22	18	51
5	Newcastle United	42	14	3	4	43	18	6	7	8	23	27	50
6	Tottenham Hotspur	42	15	2	4	46	16	4	7	10	24	32	47
7	Everton	42	9	8	4	40	26	8	5	8	26	29	47
8	Middlesbrough	42	10	6	5	29	21	7	6	8	24	32	46
9	Arsenal	42	9	8	4	31	25	6	6	9	28	38	44
10	Aston Villa	42	11	4	6	39	21	7	3	11	24	49	43
11	Blackburn Rovers	42	7	9	5	36	27	6	6	9	21	32	41
12	Sunderland	42	11	4	6	34	19	3	9	9	23	41	41
13	Manchester United	42	9	4	8	34	26	6	6	9	30	42	40
14	West Bromwich Albion	42	8	7	6	31	23	5	7	9	23	35	40
15	Bradford City	42	7	9	5	38	28	5	6	10	23	35	39
16	Preston North End	42	10	4	7	38	25	5	5	11	23	40	39
17	Huddersfield Town	42	11	4	6	26	16	4	5	12	16	33	39
18	Chelsea	42	9	7	5	35	24	4	6	11	13	34	39
19	Oldham Athletic	42	6	9	6	23	26	3	6	12	26	60	33
20	Sheffield United	42	5	11	5	22	19	1	7	13	20	49	30
21	Derby County	42	3	12	6	21	23	2	4	15	11	35	26
22	BRADFORD	42	6	5	10	29	35	2	3	16	14	41	24

1921/22

21st in Division Two: Relegated

#	Date		Opponent	Score	Scorers	Att.	Barnett LH	Batten J	Bauchop JR	Blackham S	Brown TE	Crozier J	Dickenson W	Donaghy J	Fell G	Howie D	Humphrey D	Keetley T	Kennie G	Kirkland A	Laycock A	Loughran T	Lowson F	McCandless J	McDonald DR	McGloughlin FJ	McLean DP	McLean G	Nicholson H	Peel HB	Scattergood EO	Taylor HW	Turnbull RJ
1	Aug	27	LEICESTER CITY	0-1		14000	6	8		2		4	3	11		10		9						7	5						1		
2		29	West Ham United	0-1		20000	6		9	2		4	3	11		10		7							5					8	1		
3	Sep	3	Leicester City	1-2	Bauchop	16000	6		9	2		4	3	11								8	10	7	5						1		
4		5	WEST HAM UNITED	2-0	Bauchop, Lowson	7000	6	8	9	2		4	3	11									10	7					5		1		
5		10	BURY	1-1	Crozier	8000	6	8	9	2		4	3	11				7					10						5		1		
6		17	Bury	2-2	Bauchop 2	12000		8	9	2			3	11		6							10	7	5				4		1		
7		24	ROTHERHAM COUNTY	4-2	Bauchop 4	8000			9	2			3	11		6							10	7	5				4	8	1		
8	Oct	1	Rotherham County	0-2		20000				2			3	11		6							10	7	5			9	4	8	1		
9		8	Stoke	1-0	McCandless	13000	6			2			3			10								11	5			9	4	8	1		7
10		15	STOKE	2-4	Lowson, Howie	12000	6		9	2			3			8							10	11	5				4		1		7
11		22	Sheffield Wednesday	1-2	Bauchop	10000			10	2		4	3			8								11	5			9	6		1		7
12		29	SHEFFIELD WEDNESDAY	2-1	Howie, G McLean	8000			11	2		4	3			8								7	5			9	6		1		10
13	Nov	5	Leeds United	0-3		15000			11	2		4	3			8							10		5		9		6		1		7
14		12	LEEDS UNITED	0-1		22000		8		2	4		3			5	11										9		6	10	1		7
15		19	FULHAM	1-2	D McLean	9000		8		2	4		3			5	11										9		6	10	1		7
16		26	Fulham	1-2	Peel	19000		8		2	6		3			5	11							7			9		4	10	1		
17	Dec	3	Hull City	0-3		16000		8		2	6		3			5	11							7			9		4	10	1		
18		10	HULL CITY	1-1	Humphrey	14000					6		3			5	11			8	1					2	9			10		4	7
19		17	Blackpool	1-1	Bauchop	10000			9				3			5	11			8					6	2				10	1	4	7
20		24	BLACKPOOL	0-0		12000			9			4	3							8			10	11	6	2			5		1		7
21		26	CLAPTON ORIENT	3-1	Scattergood 2, McCandless	20000		8	9		6	4	3											11	5	2				10	1		7
22		27	Clapton Orient	0-1		20000		8	9		6		3			5	11							7		2				10	1	4	
23		31	Notts County	0-3		12000			9			4	3			5				8				11	6	2				10	1		7
24	Jan	21	DERBY COUNTY	5-1	Turnbull, Bauchop 3, Peel	7000			9	3		4				5				8				11	6	2				10	1		7
25	Feb	11	Coventry City	2-2	Kirkland, D McLean	17000	4			3						5				8				11	6	2	9			10	1		7
26		15	COVENTRY CITY	1-2	D McLean	7000	4			3						5				8				11	6	2	9			10	1		7
27		18	Derby County	3-1	Kirkland,D McLean,Bauchop	10000	4		11	3										8		5			6	2	9			10	1		7
28		25	Barnsley	0-2		10000	4		11	3										8		5			6	2	9			10	1		7
29		28	NOTTS COUNTY	2-1	Turnbull, Peel	7000	4		11	3												5		7	6	2	9			10	1		8
30	Mar	4	WOLVERHAMPTON W.	0-0		12000	6		11	2		4	3							8		5					9			10	1		7
31		11	Wolverhampton Wan.	0-5		15000	6		11	2		4	3							8		5		7			9			10	1		
32		18	Nottingham Forest	1-4	Scattergood	10000	6		9				3		5					8				11		2				10	1	4	7
33		22	BARNSLEY	2-3	Kirkland, D McLean	7000						4	3		5					8				11		2	9		6	10	1		7
34		25	NOTTM. FOREST	1-0	D McLean	12000			11			4	3		5					8				7		2	9		6	10	1		
35	Apr	8	BRISTOL CITY	2-1	D McLean, Peel	7000						4	3		5	6			11	8						2	9			10	1		7
36		11	Bristol City	0-1		5000	4	11					3		5	6				8						2	9			10	1		7
37		15	South Shields	0-1		10000			10			4	3		5	6				8				11		2		9			1		7
38		17	Crystal Palace	1-1	Fell	14000		10		2		4	3		5	6					1			11			8	9					7
39		18	CRYSTAL PALACE	0-0		12000				3		4			5	6			11							2	8	9		10	1		7
40		22	SOUTH SHIELDS	1-0	D McLean	10000		8				4	3		5	6			11					7		2	9				1		10
41		29	Port Vale	0-1		10000		8				4	3		5	6			11					7		2	9			10	1		
42	May	6	PORT VALE	2-0	Turnbull, D McLean	12000							3		5	6			11	8				7	4	2	9				1		10
						Apps	16	14	24	27	7	22	35	8	11	29	7	3	5	18	2	6	9	29	22	22	22	7	17	28	40	4	28
						Goals			14			1			1	2	1			3			2	2			9	1		4	3		3

F.A. Cup

#	Date		Opponent	Score	Scorers	Att.	Barnett LH	Batten J	Bauchop JR	Blackham S	Brown TE	Crozier J	Dickenson W	Donaghy J	Fell G	Howie D	Humphrey D	Keetley T	Kennie G	Kirkland A	Laycock A	Loughran T	Lowson F	McCandless J	McDonald DR	McGloughlin FJ	McLean DP	McLean G	Nicholson H	Peel HB	Scattergood EO	Taylor HW	Turnbull RJ
R1	Jan	7	SHEFFIELD WEDNESDAY	1-0	Batten	21880		8	9	2		4	3		5									11	6					10	1		7
R2		28	ARSENAL	2-3	D McLean, Bauchop	12000			9	2		4	3		5									11	6		8			10	1		7

		P	W	D	L	F	A	W	D	L	F	A	Pts
1	Nottingham Forest	42	13	7	1	29	9	9	5	7	22	21	56
2	Stoke	42	9	11	1	31	11	9	5	7	29	33	52
3	Barnsley	42	14	5	2	43	18	8	3	10	24	34	52
4	West Ham United	42	15	3	3	39	13	5	5	11	13	26	48
5	Hull City	42	13	5	3	36	13	6	5	10	15	28	48
6	South Shields	42	11	7	3	25	13	6	5	10	18	25	46
7	Fulham	42	14	5	2	41	8	4	4	13	16	30	45
8	Leeds United	42	10	8	3	31	12	6	5	10	17	26	45
9	Leicester City	42	11	6	4	30	16	3	11	7	9	18	45
10	Sheffield Wednesday	42	12	4	5	31	24	3	10	8	16	26	44
11	Bury	42	11	3	7	35	19	4	7	10	19	36	40
12	Derby County	42	11	3	7	34	22	4	6	11	26	42	39
13	Notts County	42	10	7	4	34	18	2	8	11	13	33	39
14	Crystal Palace	42	9	6	6	28	20	4	7	10	17	31	39
15	Clapton Orient	42	12	4	5	33	18	3	5	13	10	32	39
16	Rotherham County	42	8	9	4	17	7	6	2	13	15	36	39
17	Wolverhampton Wan.	42	8	7	6	28	19	5	4	12	16	30	37
18	Port Vale	42	10	5	6	28	19	4	3	14	15	38	36
19	Blackpool	42	11	1	9	33	27	4	4	13	11	30	35
20	Coventry City	42	8	5	8	31	21	4	5	12	20	39	34
21	BRADFORD	42	10	5	6	32	22	2	4	15	14	40	33
22	Bristol City	42	10	3	8	25	18	2	6	13	12	40	33

1922/23

2nd in Division Three (North)

						Batten J	Bradley A	Brandon WT	Fell G	Hodgson H	Howie D	Hubbert H	Keetley T	Kennie G	Kirkland A	Lowson F	McCandless J	McCluggage A	McDonald DR	McGloughlin FJ	McLean G	Nicholson H	Peel HB	Scattergood EC	Taylor HW	Thompson EG	Turnbull RJ	Wilcox JC
1	Aug 26	NELSON	6-2	Howie, Kirkland 2, Peel, Turnbull 2	10000			3	5		6				8		11		4	2	9		10	1			7	
2	Sep 2	Nelson	0-1		6000			3	5		6		9		8		11		4	2			10	1			7	
3	9	HALIFAX TOWN	2-2	Kirkland, Treasure (og)	14000			3	5		6		9		8		11		4	2			10	1			7	
4	16	Halifax Town	0-3		17000			2	5		6		7		8		11			3			10	1	4		9	
5	23	WALSALL	2-2	McLean 2	9000	8		2	6		5			11		10		3			9			1	4	7		
6	30	Walsall	0-1		7884			2	5		6			11	8	10		3			9			1	4	7		
7	Oct 7	Tranmere Rovers	0-0		8000			2			6			11				3			8	5		1	4	7	10	9
8	14	TRANMERE ROVERS	3-0	McLean 3	7000		9	2	4		6							3			8	5	11	1		7	10	
9	21	LINCOLN CITY	4-1	Turnbull 2, Peel 2	10000		9	2	4		5	6						3			8		11	1		7	10	
10	28	Lincoln City	0-0		5000		9	3	4		6									2	8	5	11	1		7	10	
11	Nov 4	DURHAM CITY	4-1	Peel, Bradley 2, Turnbull	8000		9	2	4			6						3			8	5	11	1		7	10	
12	11	Durham City	0-0		1500		9	2	4			6						3	5		8		11	1		7	10	
13	18	STALYBRIDGE CELTIC	1-0	McCluggage	9000		9	2	4			6						3	5		8		11	1		7	10	
14	25	Wigan Borough	2-3	McLean, Bradley	12000		9	2	4		5	6						3			8		11	1		7	10	
15	Dec 9	Chesterfield	2-2	Turnbull 2	7000		9	2	4		5	6						3			8		11	1		7	10	
16	16	Crewe Alexandra	1-0	Bradley	6000		9	2	4		5	6						3			8		11	1		7	10	
17	23	CREWE ALEXANDRA	3-0	McLean 2, Bradley	9000		9	2	4		5	6						3			8		11	1		7	10	
18	25	CHESTERFIELD	1-0	Turnbull	16000		9	2	4		5	6						3			8		11	1		7	10	
19	26	Stalybridge Celtic	0-1		5000			2	4			6	9			8		3				5	11	1		7	10	
20	30	Grimsby Town	1-0	Bradley	8000		9	2	4		5	6						3			8		11	1		7	10	
21	Jan 6	GRIMSBY TOWN	2-1	Turnbull, Miller (og)	12000		9	2	4		5	6						3			8		11	1		7	10	
22	20	Accrington Stanley	3-4	McLean, Howie, McCluggage	7500		9		5		10	6			7			3		2	8		11	1	4			
23	27	ACCRINGTON STANLEY	5-1	Bradley, Howie, McLean 3	14000		9	2	5		10	6			7			3			8		11	1	4			
24	Feb 10	Hartlepools United	1-0	McLean	4000			2	5	3	8	6			7						9		11	1	4		10	
25	17	DARLINGTON	2-1	McLean, Bradley	9000		9	2	5	3		6									8		11	1	4	7	10	
26	24	Darlington	0-2		4000			2	5	3	8	6									9		11	1	4	7	10	
27	Mar 3	WREXHAM	0-1		10000			2	5		8	6						3			9		11	1	4	7	10	
28	10	Wrexham	0-3		7000			2	4		5	6						3			8		11	1		7	10	9
29	14	HARTLEPOOLS UNITED	1-1	Turnbull	5000			2	5			6			8			3			9		11	1	4	7	10	
30	17	Rochdale	3-0	Turnbull 2, Bradley	5000		9	2		3	5	6									8		11	1	4	7	10	
31	24	ROCHDALE	3-0	McLean, Turnbull 2	12000		9	2		3	5	6									8		11	1	4	7	10	
32	31	Barrow	2-1	Hubbert, Turnbull	3000			2	6	3	5	10									8		11	1	4	7	9	
33	Apr 2	WIGAN BOROUGH	1-1	Turnbull	15000			2	6	3	5	10									8		11	1	4	7	9	
34	7	BARROW	3-0	McLean 2, Turnbull	12000			2	6	3	5	10									8		11	1	4	7	9	
35	14	Ashington	1-2	Fell	4000			2	6	3	5	10									8		11	1	4	7	9	
36	21	ASHINGTON	3-0	McLean 2, Howie	10000			2	5		10	6						3			8		11	1	4	7	9	
37	28	Southport	0-0		4000			2	5		10	6						3			8		11	1	4	7	9	
38	May 5	SOUTHPORT	5-1	McLean, Turnbull 3, Peel	5000				4	3	5	6								2	8		11	1		7	10	9
					Apps	1	18	36	35	10	32	29	4	3	9	3	4	23	5	7	34	5	35	38	19	31	34	3
					Goals		9		1		4	1			3			2			20		5				20	

Two own goals

F.A. Cup

						Batten J	Bradley A	Brandon WT	Fell G	Hodgson H	Howie D	Hubbert H	Keetley T	Kennie G	Kirkland A	Lowson F	McCandless J	McCluggage A	McDonald DR	McGloughlin FJ	McLean G	Nicholson H	Peel HB	Scattergood EC	Taylor HW	Thompson EG	Turnbull RJ	Wilcox JC
R1	Jan 13	Everton	1-1	Peel	18755		9	2	4		5	6						3			8		11	1		7	10	
rep	17	EVERTON	1-0	McLean	15000		9	2	5		10	6						3			8		11	1	4	7		
R2	Feb 3	Plymouth Argyle	1-4	Fell	24500			2	4		5	6	9		7			3			8		11	1			10	

		P	W	D	L	F	A	W	D	L	F	A	Pts
1	Nelson	38	15	2	2	37	10	9	1	9	24	31	51
2	BRADFORD	38	14	4	1	51	15	5	5	9	16	23	47
3	Walsall	38	13	4	2	32	14	6	4	9	19	30	46
4	Chesterfield	38	13	5	1	49	18	6	2	11	19	34	45
5	Wigan Borough	38	14	3	2	45	11	4	5	10	19	28	44
6	Crewe Alexandra	38	13	3	3	32	9	4	6	9	16	29	43
7	Halifax Town	38	11	4	4	29	14	6	3	10	24	32	41
8	Accrington Stanley	38	14	2	3	40	21	3	5	11	19	44	41
9	Darlington	38	13	3	3	43	14	2	7	10	16	32	40
10	Wrexham	38	13	5	1	29	12	1	5	13	9	36	38
11	Stalybridge Celtic	38	13	2	4	32	18	2	4	13	10	29	36
12	Rochdale	38	8	5	6	29	22	5	5	9	13	31	36
13	Lincoln City	38	9	7	3	21	11	4	3	12	18	44	36
14	Grimsby Town	38	10	3	6	35	18	4	2	13	20	34	33
15	Hartlepools United	38	10	6	3	34	14	0	6	13	14	40	32
16	Tranmere Rovers	38	11	4	4	41	21	1	4	14	8	38	32
17	Southport	38	11	3	5	21	12	1	4	14	11	34	31
18	Barrow	38	11	2	6	31	17	2	2	15	19	43	30
19	Ashington	38	10	3	6	34	33	1	5	13	17	44	30
20	Durham City	38	7	9	3	31	19	2	1	16	12	40	28

1923/24

5th in Division Three (North)

							Bradley A	Brandon WT	Fell G	Hodgson H	Howie D	Hubbert H	Kennie G	Laycock A	McCluggage A	McDonald K	McGloughlin FJ	McLean G	Myerscough J	Peel HB	Scattergood EC	Tasker H	Taylor HW	Thompson EG	Turnbull RJ	Walker R	Wilcox JC
1	Aug	25	NEW BRIGHTON	1-1	og	8000		2	4		5	6			3			8		11	1			7	10		9
2		27	Grimsby Town	0-2		6000		2	4		5	6			3			8		11	1			7	10		9
3	Sep	1	New Brighton	0-1		7000		2	4		5	6			3			8		11	1	9		7	10		
4		3	GRIMSBY TOWN	2-1	Thompson, Atter (og)	5000		3	4		5	6		1			2	8		11		9		7	10		
5		8	ROCHDALE	4-2	McLean 2, Turnbull, Peel	9000		3	4		5	6		1			2	8		11		9		7	10		
6		15	Rochdale	0-3		7000		3	5		8	6					2	9		11	1		4	7	10		
7		22	SOUTHPORT	2-0	Thompson, Turnbull	9000		3			5	6	11				2	8		9	1		4	7	10		
8		29	Southport	0-1		6000				3	5	6					2	8		11	1	9	4	7	10		
9	Oct	6	BARROW	3-0	McLean 2, Wilcox	6000		3			5	6					2	8		11	1		4	7	10		9
10		13	Barrow	1-1	Wilcox	4500		3			5	6					2	8		11	1		4	7	10		9
11		20	WOLVERHAMPTON W.	0-1		10000		3			5	6					2	8		11	1		4	7	10		9
12		27	Wolverhampton Wan.	0-2		17000		3			5	6				9	2		8	11	1		4	7	10		
13	Nov	3	LINCOLN CITY	3-1	Myerscough, Turnbull, McDonald	5000		3			5	6				9	2		8	11	1		4		7		10
14		10	Lincoln City	3-2	McDonald, Myerscough, Peel	7000		3			5	6				9	2		8	11	1		4		7		10
15		17	Darlington	1-3	McDonald	5000		3			5	6				9	2		8	11	1		4		7		10
16		24	TRANMERE ROVERS	2-0	McDonald, Wilcox	8000		2	5			6				9			8	11	1		4		7	3	10
17	Dec	8	DARLINGTON	1-0	McDonald	7000		2	5			6			3	9			8	11	1		4		7		10
18		22	Chesterfield	3-2	Wilcox, McDonald 2	4122		2	5			6			3	9			8	11	1		4		7		10
19		25	Doncaster Rovers	1-1	McDonald	6000		2	5			6			3	9			8	11	1		4	7			10
20		26	DONCASTER ROVERS	4-2	Myerscough, McDonald 2, Hubbert	10000		2			5	6			3	9			8	11	1		4		7		10
21	Jan	1	Tranmere Rovers	1-2	Myerscough	6000		2			5	6			3	9			8	11	1		4		7		10
22		5	ROTHERHAM COUNTY	2-0	McDonald, Turnbull	7000		2	5			6			3	9			8	11	1		4		7		10
23		19	HALIFAX TOWN	1-0	Peel	15000		3			5	6				9			8	11	1		4		7	2	10
24		26	Halifax Town	0-0		10000		3			5	6				9			8	11	1		4		7	2	10
25	Feb	2	HARTLEPOOLS UNITED	4-0	Peel, Wilcox, Turnbull 2	6000		3			5	6				9			8	11	1		4		7	2	10
26		6	CHESTERFIELD	2-1	McDonald, McLean	4000		3			5	6				9	2	10	8	11	1		4		7		
27		9	Hartlepools United	0-0		2485		3	6		5					9	2	10	8	11	1		4		7		
28		16	ACCRINGTON STANLEY	1-1	Fell	7000		3	6		5					9	2	10	8	11	1		4		7		
29		23	Accrington Stanley	2-2	Myerscough, McDonald	6000		3	6		5					9	2		8	11	1		4	7	10		
30	Mar	1	CREWE ALEXANDRA	1-1	Myerscough	5000		3	6		5					9	2		8	11	1		4	7	10		
31		8	Crewe Alexandra	1-1	McDonald	6000			6	3	5			1	2	9			8	11			4	7	10		
32		15	Durham City	0-2		3000			6		5			1	3	9	2		8	11			4	7	10		
33		22	DURHAM CITY	3-0	Myerscough, Peel, Bradley	6000	9		5			6			3		2		8	10	1		4	7	11		
34		24	Rotherham County	0-1		9000	7		5			6			3	9	2		8	10	1		4		11		
35		29	Wigan Borough	1-0	Fell	7000	9		5			6			3		2	7	8	10	1		4		11		
36	Apr	5	WIGAN BOROUGH	4-0	Peel, Bradley 3	5000	9		5			6	11		3		2		8	10	1		4	7			
37		12	Ashington	0-1		2000	9			5	6				3	10	2	7	8	11	1		4				
38		19	ASHINGTON	3-1	Myerscough, Bradley, McDonald	6000	9	6			5				3	10	2		8	11	1		4		7		
39		21	Wrexham	2-2	Peel, McDonald	6000	9	6			5				3	10	2	7	8	11	1		4				
40		22	WREXHAM	2-0	Bradley, McDonald	7000	9	6			5				3	10	2		8	11	1		4		7		
41		26	Walsall	3-2	Bradley 2, Peel	1887	9	6			5				3	10	2		8	11	1		4		7		
42	May	3	WALSALL	5-0	Myerscough 2, Bradley 2, Turnbull	2000	9		5		6				3	10	2		8	11	1		4		7		
						Apps	10	33	22	3	33	30	2	4	21	28	28	17	31	42	38	4	37	19	38	4	18
						Goals	10		2			1				17		5	10	8				2	7		5

Two own goals

F.A. Cup

							Bradley A	Brandon WT	Fell G	Hodgson H	Howie D	Hubbert H	Kennie G	Laycock A	McCluggage A	McDonald K	McGloughlin FJ	McLean G	Myerscough J	Peel HB	Scattergood EC	Tasker H	Taylor HW	Thompson EG	Turnbull RJ	Walker R	Wilcox JC
R1	Jan	12	Swindon Town	0-4		15227		2			5	6			3	9			8	11	1		4		7		10

		P	W	D	L	F	A	W	D	L	F	A	Pts
1	Wolverhampton Wan.	42	18	3	0	51	10	6	12	3	25	17	63
2	Rochdale	42	17	4	0	40	8	8	8	5	20	18	62
3	Chesterfield	42	16	4	1	54	15	6	6	9	16	24	54
4	Rotherham County	42	16	3	2	46	13	7	3	11	24	30	52
5	BRADFORD	42	17	3	1	50	12	4	7	10	19	31	52
6	Darlington	42	16	5	0	51	19	4	3	14	19	34	48
7	Southport	42	13	7	1	30	10	3	7	11	14	32	46
8	Ashington	42	14	4	3	41	21	4	4	13	18	40	44
9	Doncaster Rovers	42	13	4	4	41	17	2	8	11	18	36	42
10	Wigan Borough	42	12	5	4	39	15	2	9	10	16	38	42
11	Grimsby Town	42	11	9	1	30	7	3	4	14	19	40	41
12	Tranmere Rovers	42	11	5	5	32	21	2	10	9	19	39	41
13	Accrington Stanley	42	12	5	4	35	21	4	3	14	13	40	40
14	Halifax Town	42	11	4	6	26	17	4	6	11	16	42	40
15	Durham City	42	12	5	4	40	23	3	4	14	19	37	39
16	Wrexham	42	8	11	2	24	12	2	7	12	13	32	38
17	Walsall	42	10	5	6	31	20	4	3	14	13	39	36
18	New Brighton	42	9	9	3	28	10	2	4	15	12	43	35
19	Lincoln City	42	8	8	5	29	22	2	4	15	19	37	32
20	Crewe Alexandra	42	6	7	8	20	24	1	6	14	12	34	27
21	Hartlepools United	42	5	7	9	22	24	2	4	15	11	46	25
22	Barrow	42	7	7	7	25	24	1	2	18	10	56	25

1924/25

5th in Division Three (North)

	Date		Opponent	Score	Scorers	Att	Bradley A	Brandon WT	Cook C	Dailey WS	Fell G	Hodgson H	Howie D	Hubbert H	Laycock A	McCluggage A	McDonald K	McGloughlin FJ	McLean G	Myerscough J	O'Rourke M	Peacock LV	Peel HB	Quantrill AE	Scattergood EO	Taylor HW	Turnbull RJ	Wilson RS
1	Aug	30	New Brighton	0-0		9000	9				5		6			3	10	2		8			11		1	4	7	
2	Sep	1	ACCRINGTON STANLEY	3-0	Myerscough, McDonald 2	7000	9			6	5					3	10	2		8			11		1	4	7	
3		6	GRIMSBY TOWN	0-1		12000	9			6	5					3	10	2		8			11		1	4	7	
4		8	Accrington Stanley	2-2	Turnbull, Myerscough	6000					5			6		3	9	2	10	8			11		1	4	7	
5		13	Hartlepools United	2-2	McLean, Scattergood	5500					5			6		3	9	2	10	8			11		1	4	7	
6		20	ROCHDALE	0-0		12000	9				5			6		3	10	2		8			11		1	4	7	
7		27	Darlington	1-2	McGloughlin	6000	9			4	5			6		3		2	10	8			11		1		7	
8	Oct	4	DURHAM CITY	4-1	O'Rourke 2, Myerscough, Bradley	10000	9	2		4	5			6		3				8	10		11	7	1			
9		11	WREXHAM	3-0	Myerscough, Dailey, McDonald	10000		2		4	5			6		3	9			8	10		11	7	1			
10		18	Rotherham County	1-1	McDonald	5000		2		4	5			6		3	9		10	8			11	7	1			
11		25	Crewe Alexandra	1-2	Myerscough	6000	9	2		4	5			6		3				8	10		11	7	1			
12	Nov	1	WIGAN BOROUGH	2-2	Peel, Bradley	6000	9	2		4	5			6		3				8			10	11	1		7	
13		8	Walsall	2-0	Myerscough, Wilson	4187		2			5			6		3				8			10	11	1	4	7	9
14		15	HALIFAX TOWN	2-1	Wilson, Quantrill	14000		2			5			6		3				8			10	11	1	4	7	9
15		22	Lincoln City	4-0	Wilson 2, Turnbull, Quantrill	10000		2			5			6		3				8			10	11	1	4	7	9
16	Dec	6	Nelson	2-2	Peel, Wilson	6000		2			5			6		3				8			10	11	1	4	7	9
17		17	ASHINGTON	7-1	* see below	5000		2			5			6		3				8			10	11	1	4	7	9
18		20	Southport	0-3		4000		2			5			6		3				8			10	11	1	4	7	9
19		25	DONCASTER ROVERS	4-1	* see below	15000		2			5			6		3				8			10	11	1	4	7	9
20		26	Doncaster Rovers	0-1		8000		2			5			6		3				8			10	11	1	4	7	9
21		27	NEW BRIGHTON	5-2	Hubbert,Howie,Quantrill,Taylor,Wilson	7000		2			5		8	6		3							10	11	1	4	7	9
22	Jan	1	BARROW	1-1	Howie	2000		2			5		8	6		3							10	11	1	4	7	9
23		3	Grimsby Town	0-2		5000		2	11		5			6		3				8			10		1	4	7	9
24		17	HARTLEPOOLS UNITED	3-0	Wilson, Myerscough, Peel	10000					5		6			3		2		8			10	11	1	4	7	9
25		24	Rochdale	2-2	Quantrill, Peel	8000			11		5			6		3		2		8			10	7	1	4		9
26	Feb	7	Durham City	0-1		5000					5			6		3		2		8			10	11	1	4	7	9
27		14	Wrexham	3-1	Turnbull, Wilson 2	7000					5			6		3		2		8			10	11	1	4	7	9
28		21	ROTHERHAM COUNTY	3-0	Wilson 2, Quantrill	7000					5			6		3		2		8			10	11	1	4	7	9
29		24	DARLINGTON	0-0		3000					5			6		3		2		8			10	11	1	4	7	9
30		28	CREWE ALEXANDRA	6-1	Wilson 2,Turnbull 2,Peel,Myerscough	8000					5			6		3		2		8			10	11	1	4	7	9
31	Mar	4	TRANMERE ROVERS	5-1	McDonald 2,Myerscough,Peel,Quantrill	4000					5			6		3	9	2	10	8			11	7	1	4		
32		7	Wigan Borough	0-1		7000					5			6		3	9	2		8			10	11	1	4	7	
33		14	WALSALL	2-0	McDonald, Peel	7000					5					3	9	2	8				10	11	1	4	7	6
34		21	Tranmere Rovers	0-2		6000					5			6		3	9	2	8				10	11	1	4	7	
35		28	LINCOLN CITY	4-0	McLean 3, Peel	6000					5	2		6		3			8				10	11	1	4	7	9
36	Apr	4	Barrow	1-2	Turnbull	4000					5	2		6	1	3			8	10				11		4	7	9
37		10	Chesterfield	1-1	Myerscough	8000					5	2				3			8	10		6		11	1	4	7	9
38		11	NELSON	1-1	Wilson	10000					5	2				3				8		6	10	11	1	4	7	9
39		13	CHESTERFIELD	3-0	Turnbull 2, Wilson	7000					5	2				3			8			6	10	11	1	4	7	9
40		18	Ashington	0-1		2000					5	2				3				8		6	10	11	1	4	7	9
41		25	SOUTHPORT	1-0	McLean	6000					5	2				3			8			6	10	11	1	4	7	9
42	May	2	Halifax Town	3-1	McLean, Wilson 2	8000					5	3						2	8	10		6	11		1	4	7	9
						Apps	8	16	2	8	42	8	4	31	1	41	12	19	13	35	3	6	40	33	41	36	36	27
						Goals	2			1	1		2	1			7	1	6	12	2		8	7	2	1	8	22

Scorers in game 17: Wilson 4, Hamilton (og), Myerscough, Fell
In game 19: Wilson, Scattergood, Quantrill, Myerscough

One own goal

F.A. Cup

	Date		Opponent	Score	Scorers	Att	Bradley A	Brandon WT	Cook C	Dailey WS	Fell G	Hodgson H	Howie D	Hubbert H	Laycock A	McCluggage A	McDonald K	McGloughlin FJ	McLean G	Myerscough J	O'Rourke M	Peacock LV	Peel HB	Quantrill AE	Scattergood EO	Taylor HW	Turnbull RJ	Wilson RS
Q5	Nov	29	Wigan Borough	1-0	Wilson	8000		2	11		5			6		3				8			10		1	4	7	9
Q6	Dec	13	Crook Town	4-0	Myerscough 2, Wilson 2	4700		2	11		5			6		3				8			10		1	4	7	9
R1	Jan	10	MIDDLESBROUGH	1-0	Turnbull	28000			11		5			6		3		2		8			10		1	4	7	9
R2		31	BLACKPOOL	1-1	Hubbert	23172			11		5			6		3		2		8			10		1	4	7	9
rep	Feb	14	Blackpool	1-2	Scattergood (p)	13745					5			6		3		2	10	8			11		1	4	7	9

		P	W	D	L	F	A	W	D	L	F	A	Pts
1	Darlington	42	16	4	1	50	14	8	6	7	28	19	58
2	Nelson	42	18	2	1	58	14	5	5	11	21	36	53
3	New Brighton	42	17	3	1	56	16	6	4	11	19	34	53
4	Southport	42	17	2	2	41	7	5	5	11	18	30	51
5	BRADFORD	42	15	5	1	59	13	4	7	10	25	29	50
6	Rochdale	42	17	2	2	53	16	4	5	12	22	37	49
7	Chesterfield	42	14	3	4	42	15	3	8	10	18	29	45
8	Lincoln City	42	13	4	4	39	19	5	4	12	14	39	44
9	Halifax Town	42	11	5	5	36	22	5	6	10	20	30	43
10	Ashington	42	13	4	4	41	24	3	6	12	27	52	42
11	Wigan Borough	42	10	7	4	39	16	5	4	12	23	49	41
12	Grimsby Town	42	10	6	5	38	21	5	3	13	22	39	39
13	Durham City	42	11	6	4	38	17	2	7	12	12	51	39
14	Barrow	42	14	4	3	39	22	2	3	16	12	52	39
15	Crewe Alexandra	42	11	7	3	35	24	2	6	13	18	54	39
16	Wrexham	42	11	5	5	37	21	4	3	14	16	40	38
17	Accrington Stanley	42	12	5	4	43	23	3	3	15	17	49	38
18	Doncaster Rovers	42	12	5	4	36	17	2	5	14	18	48	38
19	Walsall	42	10	6	5	27	16	3	5	13	17	37	37
20	Hartlepools United	42	9	8	4	28	21	3	3	15	17	42	35
21	Tranmere Rovers	42	11	3	7	40	29	3	1	17	19	49	32
22	Rotherham County	42	6	5	10	27	31	1	2	18	15	57	21

1925/26

2nd in Division Three (North)

No	Month	Day	Opponent	Score	Scorers	Att	Bradley A	Crowther GE	Duffield A	Fell G	Hodgson H	Hubbert H	Johnson M	Matthews RW	McDonald K	McGloughlin F	McLean G	McVee W	Myerscough J	Peacock LV	Peel HB	Potts JF	Poyntz WI	Quantrill AE	Rogers CW	Schofield HW	Taylor HW	Walker W
1	Aug	29	ROTHERHAM UNITED	6-1	McDonald 3, Peel 2, Taylor	11290				5	3	6			9		8		10		11	2		7			4	1
2		31	CHESTERFIELD	1-0	McDonald	7653				5	3	6			9		8		10		11	2		7			4	1
3	Sep	5	Halifax Town	2-1	Myerscough 2	10890				5	3	6			9		8		10		11	2		7			4	1
4		7	Chesterfield	1-1	McDonald	4174				5	3	6			9				10		11	2	8	7			4	1
5		12	ACCRINGTON STANLEY	3-0	Myerscough 2, McLean	12388				5	3	6			9		8		10		11	2		7			4	1
6		14	WALSALL	8-0	* see below	7678				5	3	6			9		8		10		11	2		7			4	1
7		19	Durham City	1-2	McDonald	4953				5	3	6			9		8		10		11	2		7			4	1
8		24	Walsall	1-3	McDonald	2302				5	3	6			9		8		10		11	2		7			4	1
9		26	HARTLEPOOLS UNITED	4-0	McLean, Quantrill, Bradley, Myerscough	9849	9			5	3	6					8		10		11	2		7			4	1
10	Oct	3	Rochdale	0-2		16295	9			5	3	6					8		10		11	2		7			4	1
11		10	TRANMERE ROVERS	3-0	Quantrill, Myerscough, Poyntz	10060				5	3				9				10		11	2	8	7	6		4	1
12		17	LINCOLN CITY	4-1	Fell, McDonald 2, Peel	7772				5					9				10		11	2	8	7	6	3	4	1
13		24	Crewe Alexandra	2-1	Myerscough, McDonald	7546				5					9				10		11	2	8	7	6	3	4	1
14		31	WREXHAM	1-1	Quantrill	7100				5					9				10		11	2	8	7	6	3	4	1
15	Nov	7	Doncaster Rovers	3-0	Myerscough, McDonald 2	3880			2	5		6			9			3	10		11		8	7			4	1
16		14	ASHINGTON	1-0	McDonald	12135			2	5		6			9			3	10		11		8	7			4	1
17		21	Barrow	1-0	McDonald	3759			2	5		6			9				10		11	3	8	7			4	1
18	Dec	5	Coventry City	2-2	Taylor, Quantrill	12261	9		2	5		6						3	10		11		8	7			4	1
19		16	NEW BRIGHTON	1-0	Myerscough	4895		1	2	5					9				10	6	11	3	8	7			4	
20		19	Wigan Borough	3-1	McDonald 3	7197		1	2	5					9				10	6	11	3	8	7			4	
21		25	Grimsby Town	0-3		13230		1		5					9	2			10	6	11	3	8	7			4	
22		26	GRIMSBY TOWN	0-1		18599		1		5		6			9			3	10		11	2	8	7			4	
23	Jan	2	Rotherham United	3-2	Quantrill, McDonald 2	6624		1	2	5		6			9			3	10		11		8	7			4	
24		9	NELSON	3-0	Myerscough, McDonald, Quantrill	20946		1	2	5		6			9			3	10		11		8	7			4	
25		16	HALIFAX TOWN	2-2	McDonald, Myerscough	20836		1	2	5		6			9			3	10		11		8	7			4	
26		23	Accrington Stanley	4-1	Poyntz, Quantrill, McDonald 2	5575			2	5		6			9			3	10		11		8	7			4	1
27		30	DURHAM CITY	2-1	Myerscough, McDonald	15902			2	6				5	9			3	10		11		8	7			4	1
28	Feb	6	Hartlepools United	3-0	McDonald, Myerscough, Quantrill	7491			2	6				5	9			3	10		11		8	7			4	1
29		13	ROCHDALE	3-1	McDonald, Poyntz, Hubbert	24893			2	5		6			9			3	10		11		8	7			4	1
30		20	Tranmere Rovers	2-3	Myerscough, Quantrill	8774			2	5		6			9			3	10		11		8	7			4	1
31		27	Lincoln City	1-1	McDonald	6905			2	5		6	10		9				8		11	3		7			4	1
32	Mar	6	CREWE ALEXANDRA	3-0	Morris (og), McDonald, Quantrill	12702			2	5		6	10		9				8		11	3		7			4	1
33		13	Wrexham	2-4	McDonald, Johnson	7805			2	5		6	10		9				8		11	3		7			4	1
34		20	DONCASTER ROVERS	2-0	Myerscough, Quantrill	12766			2	5		6			9			3	10		11		8	7			4	1
35		27	Ashington	1-1	McDonald	5517			2	5		6			9		8	3	10		11			7			4	1
36	Apr	2	Southport	1-2	McDonald	6399			2	5		6			9			3	10		11		8	7			4	1
37		3	BARROW	3-0	McDonald 2, McLean	13841			2	6				5	9		10				11	3	8	7			4	1
38		6	SOUTHPORT	6-1	McDonald 3, McLean 2, Glover (og)	17523			2	6				5	9		10				11	3	8	7			4	1
39		10	Nelson	2-2	One og, Quantrill	14143			2	6			10	5	9						11	3	8	7			4	1
40		17	COVENTRY CITY	3-0	McDonald 3	11572			2	6			10	5	9						11	3	8	7			4	1
41		24	New Brighton	1-1	Peel	6368			2	6			10	5	9						11	3	8	7			4	1
42	May	1	WIGAN BOROUGH	6-1	Peel 2, Poyntz, McDonald 2, Taylor	9293		1	2	6			10	5	9						11	3	8	7			4	
						Apps	3	8	26	42	11	27	7	8	39	1	12	15	36	3	42	28	29	42	4	3	42	34
						Goals	1			1		1	1		43		7		17		8		4	12			3	

Scorers in game 6: Myerscough 2, Peel 2, McDonald 2, McLean 2

Three own goals

F.A. Cup

Rd	Month	Day	Opponent	Score	Scorers	Att	Bradley A	Crowther GE	Duffield A	Fell G	Hodgson H	Hubbert H	Johnson M	Matthews RW	McDonald K	McGloughlin F	McLean G	McVee W	Myerscough J	Peacock LV	Peel HB	Potts JF	Poyntz WI	Quantrill AE	Rogers CW	Schofield HW	Taylor HW	Walker W
R1	Nov	28	LINCOLN CITY	2-2	McDonald 2	12459			2	5					9				10	6	11	3	8	7			4	1
rep	Dec	2	Lincoln City	1-1	(aet) McDonald	5857			2	5		6			9				10		11	3	8	7			4	1
rep2		7	Lincoln City	2-1	Peel 2	5500		1	2	5					9				10	6	11	3	8	7			4	
R2		12	Boston	0-1		5041		1	2	5					9				10	6	11	3	8	7			4	

R1 replay 2 at Bramall Lane

		P	W	D	L	F	A	W	D	L	F	A	Pts
1	Grimsby Town	42	20	1	0	61	8	6	8	7	30	32	61
2	BRADFORD	42	18	2	1	65	10	8	6	7	36	33	60
3	Rochdale	42	16	1	4	55	25	11	4	6	49	33	59
4	Chesterfield	42	18	2	1	70	19	7	3	11	30	35	55
5	Halifax Town	42	12	5	4	34	19	5	6	10	19	31	45
6	Hartlepools United	42	15	5	1	59	23	3	3	15	23	50	44
7	Tranmere Rovers	42	15	2	4	45	27	4	4	13	28	56	44
8	Nelson	42	12	8	1	67	29	4	3	14	22	42	43
9	Ashington	42	11	6	4	44	23	5	5	11	26	39	43
10	Doncaster Rovers	42	11	7	3	52	25	5	4	12	28	47	43
11	Crewe Alexandra	42	14	3	4	43	23	3	6	12	20	38	43
12	New Brighton	42	13	4	4	51	29	4	4	13	18	38	42
13	Durham City	42	14	5	2	45	19	4	1	16	18	51	42
14	Rotherham United	42	13	3	5	44	28	4	4	13	25	64	41
15	Lincoln City	42	14	2	5	42	28	3	3	15	24	54	39
16	Coventry City	42	13	6	2	47	19	3	0	18	26	63	38
17	Wigan Borough	42	12	5	4	53	22	1	6	14	15	52	37
18	Accrington Stanley	42	14	0	7	49	34	3	3	15	32	71	37
19	Wrexham	42	9	6	6	39	31	2	4	15	24	61	32
20	Southport	42	9	6	6	37	34	2	4	15	25	58	32
21	Walsall	42	9	4	8	40	34	1	2	18	18	73	26
22	Barrow	42	4	2	15	28	49	3	2	16	22	49	18

1926/27

3rd in Division Three (North)

No	Date		Opponent	Result	Scorers	Att	Aitken FMcK	Batt E	Carrick JH	Clough JH	Croot J	Dickinson S	Duffield A	Fell G	Hubbert H	Johnson M	Matthews RW	McDonald K	McLean G	McNestry G	McVee W	Myerscough J	Peel HB	Potts JF	Poyntz WI	Quantrill AE	Rawlings A	Schofield HW	Smith JA	Taylor HW	Turnbull G
1	Aug	28	Stoke City	0-0		11525				1			2	6			5	9		7		10	11	3	8					4	
2		30	NEW BRIGHTON	1-1	McDonald	10560				1			2	6			5	9		7		10	11	3	8					4	
3	Sep	4	ROTHERHAM UNITED	2-2	Johnson, Peel	13060				1			2	6		10	5	9		7	3		8			11				4	
4		8	New Brighton	1-3	Johnson	4397			3	1			2	5	6	10		9		7		8	11							4	
5		11	Barrow	3-0	McDonald 2, Peel	5314			2	1				5	6	10		9		7		8	11	3						4	
6		18	Walsall	0-1		8494			3	1			2	5	6	10		9				8	11			7				4	
7		20	Wigan Borough	2-1	Myerscough, Poyntz	3835	7		3	1			2	5	6	10						8	11		9					4	
8		25	NELSON	2-2	McDonald 2	11992	7		3	1			2	5	6	10		9					11		8					4	
9	Oct	2	Chesterfield	2-3	McDonald 2	8571	7		3	1			2	5	6	10		9	8				11							4	
10		9	ASHINGTON	2-0	McLean, Peel	7080	7		3	1			2	5	6	10		9	8				11							4	
11		16	LINCOLN CITY	3-1	McDonald 2, McLean	11032	7		3	1			2	5	6	10		9	8				11							4	
12		23	Halifax Town	0-2		17850	7			1			2	5	6			9	8				10	3		11				4	
13		30	CREWE ALEXANDRA	2-0	McDonald, Peel	10738	7		2	1				5	6	10		9	8				11							4	3
14	Nov	6	Hartlepools United	4-2	Taylor 2, Myerscough, Matthews	1278	7			1			2	5	6	10	9					8	11							4	3
15		13	STOCKPORT COUNTY	3-1	Matthews, Myerscough, Quantrill	9002			2	1				5	6	10	9					8	11			7				4	3
16		20	Southport	1-2	Myerscough	3953			2	1				5	6	10	9					8	11			7				4	3
17	Dec	4	Tranmere Rovers	2-1	McLean, McDonald	5457		10	2	1	4			5				9	8				11			7			6		3
18		11	DURHAM CITY	3-0	Batt, McDonald 2	9443		10		1	4			5				9	8	7			11	2					6		3
19		18	Accrington Stanley	3-2	Batt, McDonald 2	4407		10		1	4			5				9	8	7				2		11			6		3
20		25	DONCASTER ROVERS	7-3	* see below	17533		10	2	1	4			5				9	8	7						11			6		3
21		27	Doncaster Rovers	1-4	McDonald	8107			2	1				5				9	8	7		10				11			6	4	3
22	Jan	1	WIGAN BOROUGH	2-1	McLean, McDonald	9710		10		1	4		2	5				9	8	7						11			6		3
23		8	ROCHDALE	5-1	McDonald 3, Taylor, McLean	7423				1			2	5	6	10		9	8	7						11				4	3
24		15	STOKE CITY	3-0	McDonald 2, Quantrill	20180	7			1			2	5	6	10		9	8							11				4	3
25		22	Rotherham United	1-1	Johnson	4023			2	1					6	10	5	9	8	7						11				4	3
26		29	BARROW	1-0	McDonald	7111				1			2	5	6	10		9	8	7						11				4	3
27	Feb	5	WALSALL	5-1	McLean 2, McDonald 3	8766				1			2	5	6	10		9	8	7						11				4	3
28		12	Nelson	0-1		12415				1		6	2	5		10		9	8							11	7			4	3
29		19	CHESTERFIELD	5-0	McDonald 2, Johnson 2, Rawlings	11693	11			1		6	2	5		10		9	8								7			4	3
30		26	Ashington	2-2	McDonald 2	3499				1		6	2	5		10		9	8							11	7			4	3
31	Mar	5	Lincoln City	1-5	Taylor	6358				1		6	2	5		10		9	8							11	7			4	3
32		12	HALIFAX TOWN	2-1	McLean, Quantrill	26543				1		6	2	5		10		9	8							11	7			4	3
33		19	Crewe Alexandra	1-1	Shaw (og)	5606			2	1		6				10	5	9	8							11	7			4	3
34		26	HARTLEPOOLS UNITED	4-1	Quantrill, Myerscough, McLean, Taylor	5796				1		6	2			10	5		8			9				11	7	3		4	
35	Apr	2	Stockport County	2-1	Rawlings 2	7883				1		6	2			10	5		8			9				11	7	3		4	
36		9	SOUTHPORT	6-2	McLean 3, Myerscough 2, Quantrill	5292				1		6				10	5		8			9		2		11	7	3		4	
37		15	Wrexham	0-1		8207			2	1		6				10	5		8			9				11	7	3		4	
38		16	Rochdale	0-3		8871	11		2	1						10	5		8			9					7	3	6	4	
39		18	WREXHAM	5-0	McDonald 3, McLean, Quantrill	7278				1		6				10	5	9	8					2		11	7			4	3
40		23	TRANMERE ROVERS	5-3	McLean 2, Quantrill 2, McDonald	5954				1		6					5	9	8			10		2		11	7			4	3
41		30	Durham City	1-2	Rawlings	1858				1		6					5	9	8			10		2		11	7			4	3
42	May	7	ACCRINGTON STANLEY	6-1	McDonald 3, McLean 2, Myerscough	4470				1		6					5	9	8			10				11	7	2		4	3
						Apps	11	5	18	42	5	14	24	31	18	30	17	33	31	14	1	18	18	10	4	28	15	6	7	37	25
						Goals		3								5	2	39	17	1		8	4		1	10	4		1	5	

Scorers in game 20: Quantrill 2, McDonald 2, McNestry, Batt, Smith

One own goal

F.A. Cup

Rd	Date		Opponent	Result	Scorers	Att	Aitken FMcK	Batt E	Carrick JH	Clough JH	Croot J	Dickinson S	Duffield A	Fell G	Hubbert H	Johnson M	Matthews RW	McDonald K	McLean G	McNestry G	McVee W	Myerscough J	Peel HB	Potts JF	Poyntz WI	Quantrill AE	Rawlings A	Schofield HW	Smith JA	Taylor HW	Turnbull G
R1	Nov	27	Walsall	0-1		10995			2	1				5	6	10			9			8	11			7				4	3

		P	W	D	L	F	A	W	D	L	F	A	Pts
1	Stoke City	42	17	3	1	57	11	10	6	5	35	29	63
2	Rochdale	42	18	2	1	72	22	8	4	9	33	43	58
3	BRADFORD	42	18	3	0	74	21	6	4	11	27	38	55
4	Halifax Town	42	13	6	2	46	23	8	5	8	24	30	53
5	Nelson	42	16	2	3	64	20	6	5	10	40	55	51
6	Stockport County	42	13	4	4	60	31	9	3	9	33	38	49
7	Chesterfield	42	15	4	2	65	24	6	1	14	27	44	47
8	Doncaster Rovers	42	13	4	4	58	27	5	7	9	23	38	47
9	Tranmere Rovers	42	13	5	3	54	22	6	3	12	31	45	46
10	New Brighton	42	14	2	5	49	21	4	8	9	30	46	46
11	Lincoln City	42	9	5	7	50	33	6	7	8	40	45	42
12	Southport	42	11	5	5	54	32	4	4	13	26	53	39
13	Wrexham	42	10	5	6	41	26	4	5	12	24	47	38
14	Walsall	42	10	4	7	35	22	4	6	11	33	59	38
15	Crewe Alexandra	42	11	5	5	46	28	3	4	14	25	53	37
16	Ashington	42	9	8	4	42	30	3	4	14	18	60	36
17	Hartlepools United	42	11	4	6	43	26	3	2	16	23	55	34
18	Wigan Borough	42	10	6	5	44	28	1	4	16	22	55	32
19	Rotherham United	42	8	6	7	41	35	2	6	13	29	57	32
20	Durham City	42	9	4	8	35	35	3	2	16	23	70	30
21	Accrington Stanley	42	9	3	9	45	38	1	4	16	17	60	27
22	Barrow	42	5	6	10	22	40	2	2	17	12	77	22

1927/28

Champions of Division Three (North): Promoted

	Date	Opponent	Score	Scorers	Att	Cartwright HP	Clough JH	Croot J	Davis H	Dickinson S	Duckett DT	Duffield A	Fell G	Hart J	Hawes AR	Little J(2)	Lloyd T	Manderson R	Matthews RW	McDonald K	McLean G	Millership W	Quantrill AE	Rawlings A	Schofield HW	Smith JA	Taylor HW	Turnbull G
1	Aug 27	DURHAM CITY	4-0	McDonald 3, Lloyd	14040		1			6					10		3	2	5	9	8		11	7			4	
2	30	Southport	1-2	Hawes	6457		1			6					10		3	2	5	9	8		11	7			4	
3	Sep 3	Wrexham	1-1	Hawes	7579		1	4							10		3	2	5	9	8		11	7		6		
4	5	SOUTHPORT	5-3	McDonald 3, McLean, Rawlings	10429		1	4							10		3	2	5	9	8		11	7		6		
5	10	CHESTERFIELD	1-0	McLean	12816	7	1			6					10		3	2	5	9	8		11				4	
6	17	Bradford City	3-2	McLean, McDonald, Quantrill	37059	7	1			6					10		3	2	5	9	8		11			4		
7	24	Tranmere Rovers	2-2	Hawes, McDonald	5370	7	1			6					10		3	2	5	9	8		11			4		
8	Oct 1	STOCKPORT COUNTY	2-0	McDonald, Hawes	9838	7	1			6					10		2		5	9	8		11			4		3
9	8	Barrow	0-0		8316	7	1			6					10		3	2	5	9	8		11			4		
10	15	NELSON	3-2	Quantrill, McLean, McDonald	14833	7	1						4		10		3	2	5	9	8		11			6		
11	22	ASHINGTON	5-0	McLean, McDonald 2, Lloyd, Hawes	7315	7	1								10		3	2	5	9	8		11			6	4	
12	29	Crewe Alexandra	3-1	Quantrill, McDonald 2	5207	7	1								10		3	2	5	9	8		11			6	4	
13	Nov 5	HALIFAX TOWN	3-2	Hawes, Smith, McDonald	15727	7	1								10		3	2	5	9	8		11			6	4	
14	12	Darlington	3-1	Hawes, Cartwright, McDonald	7976	7	1								10		3	2	5	9	8		11			6	4	
15	19	DONCASTER ROVERS	0-2		22202	7	1								10		3	2	5	9	8		11			6	4	
16	Dec 3	ACCRINGTON STANLEY	3-3	Little, Davis, Smith	10337	7	1		8						10	11	2		5	9						6	4	3
17	17	LINCOLN CITY	3-0	McLean 2, Cartwright	10977	7	1		9	6					10		3	2	5		8		11				4	
18	24	New Brighton	2-1	McDonald (og), Hart	2589	7	1			6				9	10		3	2	5		8		11				4	
19	27	ROCHDALE	4-1	Taylor, Quantrill, Hart 2	21762		1			6				9	10		3	2	5		8		11	7			4	
20	31	Durham City	1-0	McLean	2262		1			6				9	10	11	3	2	5		8			7			4	
21	Jan 3	Rochdale	4-0	Quantrill, Hart 3	5481		1		7	6				9	10		3	2	5		8		11				4	
22	7	WREXHAM	2-0	Hart, Hawes	13060		1		7	6				9	10		3	2	5		8		11				4	
23	14	Hartlepools United	1-1	Matthews	5023		1		7	6				9	10		3	2	5		8		11				4	
24	21	Chesterfield	0-0		6465		1		7	6					10		3	2	5	9	8		11				4	
25	28	BRADFORD CITY	5-0	McDonald 2, McLean, Hawes, Lloyd	21876		1		7		6				10		3	2	5	9	8		11				4	
26	Feb 1	Wigan Borough	3-1	McLean 2, Quantrill	2406		1		7	6					10		3	2	5	9	8		11				4	
27	4	TRANMERE ROVERS	6-2	McLean 2, McDonald 3, Hawes	13815		1		7		6				10		3	2	5	9	8		11				4	
28	11	Stockport County	2-2	McLean, Matthews	15775		1		7		6				10		3	2	5	9	8		11				4	
29	18	BARROW	1-1	Hawes	11176		1		7	6					10		3	2	5	9	8		11				4	
30	25	Nelson	2-1	McDonald 2	8096		1		7		6				10		3	2	5	9		8	11				4	
31	Mar 3	Ashington	3-0	McDonald 2, Davis	4052		1		7		6				10		3	2	5	9	8		11				4	
32	10	CREWE ALEXANDRA	2-0	McLean 2	9504		1		7		6				10		3	2	5	9	8		11				4	
33	17	Halifax Town	1-1	Hawes	15842		1		7		6				10		3	2	5	9	8		11				4	
34	24	DARLINGTON	6-3	Hawes, McLean, Quantrill 3, McDonald	16294		1		7		6				10		3	2	5	9	8		11				4	
35	31	Doncaster Rovers	0-2		14176		1		7		6				10		3	2	5	9	8		11				4	
36	Apr 7	HARTLEPOOLS UNITED	3-0	Millership, McDonald, McLean	12715		1		7		6						3	2	5	9	8	10	11				4	
37	9	Rotherham United	0-1		6288		1		7		6							2	5	9	8	10	11		3		4	
38	10	ROTHERHAM UNITED	3-1	Hart 2, McLean	14311		1		7	6	4			9	10		3	2	5		8		11					
39	14	Accrington Stanley	1-2	Hawes	4948		1		7		6			9	10		3	2	5		8		11				4	
40	21	WIGAN BOROUGH	5-1	McLean 3, McDonald 2	11236		1		7		6				10		3	2	5	9	8		11				4	
41	28	Lincoln City	0-2		9785		1		7		6				10		3	2	5	9	8		11				4	
42	May 5	NEW BRIGHTON	2-1	McLean, McDonald (og)	9538		1		7		6	2			10		3		5	9	8		11				4	
					Apps	14	42	2	24	18	16	1	1	8	40	2	41	39	42	33	40	3	40	6	1	13	34	2
					Goals	2			2					9	14	1	3		2	29	23	1	9	1		2	1	

Two own goals

F.A. Cup

	Date	Opponent	Score	Scorers	Att	Cartwright HP	Clough JH	Croot J	Davis H	Dickinson S	Duckett DT	Duffield A	Fell G	Hart J	Hawes AR	Little J(2)	Lloyd T	Manderson R	Matthews RW	McDonald K	McLean G	Millership W	Quantrill AE	Rawlings A	Schofield HW	Smith JA	Taylor HW	Turnbull G
R1	Nov 26	Nelson	3-0	Cartwright 2, Hawes	9000	7	1								10	11	2		5	9	8					6	4	3
R2	Dec 10	SOUTHPORT	0-2		9226	7	1								10		3	2	5	9	8		11			6	4	

		P	W	D	L	F	A	W	D	L	F	A	Pts
1	BRADFORD	42	18	2	1	68	22	9	7	5	33	23	63
2	Lincoln City	42	15	4	2	53	20	9	3	9	38	44	55
3	Stockport County	42	16	5	0	62	14	7	3	11	27	37	54
4	Doncaster Rovers	42	15	4	2	59	18	8	3	10	21	26	53
5	Tranmere Rovers	42	14	6	1	68	28	8	3	10	37	44	53
6	Bradford City	42	15	4	2	59	19	3	8	10	26	41	48
7	Darlington	42	15	1	5	63	28	6	4	11	26	46	47
8	Southport	42	15	2	4	55	24	5	3	13	24	46	45
9	Accrington Stanley	42	14	4	3	49	22	4	4	13	27	45	44
10	New Brighton	42	10	7	4	45	22	4	7	10	27	40	42
11	Wrexham	42	15	1	5	48	19	3	5	13	16	48	42
12	Halifax Town	42	11	7	3	47	24	2	8	11	26	47	41
13	Rochdale	42	13	4	4	45	24	4	3	14	29	53	41
14	Rotherham United	42	11	6	4	39	19	3	5	13	26	50	39
15	Hartlepools United	42	10	3	8	41	35	6	3	12	28	46	38
16	Chesterfield	42	10	4	7	46	29	3	6	12	25	49	36
17	Crewe Alexandra	42	10	6	5	51	28	2	4	15	26	58	34
18	Ashington	42	10	5	6	54	36	1	6	14	23	67	33
19	Barrow	42	10	8	3	41	24	0	3	18	13	78	31
20	Wigan Borough	42	8	5	8	30	32	2	5	14	26	65	30
21	Durham City	42	10	5	6	37	30	1	2	18	16	70	29
22	Nelson	42	8	4	9	50	49	2	2	17	26	87	26

1928/29

3rd in Division Two

#	Month	Day	Opponent	Score	Scorers	Att.	Atherton WJ	Buckley W	Cartwright HP	Clough JH	Cookson S	Davis H	Dickinson S	Dinsdale WA	Duckett DT	Elwood JH	Hart J	Hawes AR	Lloyd T	Matthews RW	McCandless TB	McLean G	Millership W	Parris JE	Quantrill AE	Reid A	Rhodes WT	Robinson WA	Schofield HW	Scott H	Taylor HW
1	Aug	25	Barnsley	2-1	Lloyd, Hart	11072				1		7			6		9	10	3	5	2	8			11						4
2		27	CHELSEA	1-2	Quantrill	20801				1		7			6		9	10		5	3	8			11	2					4
3	Sep	1	BRISTOL CITY	3-2	McLean, Cartwright, Robinson	19708			11	1		7			6			10		5	3	8				2		9			4
4		5	Chelsea	1-3	McLean	21556			11	1		7			6			10		5		8				2		9	3		4
5		8	Nottingham Forest	2-3	McLean 2	9679			11	1		7			6			10		5		8				2		9	3		4
6		15	WEST BROMWICH ALB.	4-1	Dickinson 2, McLean 2	20487			11	1		7	10		6		9		3	5		8				2					4
7		22	Clapton Orient	0-1		10798			11	1		7	10		6		9		3	5		8				2					4
8		29	STOKE CITY	2-1	McLean, Quantrill	17221			7	1	2		6					10	3	5		8			11			9			4
9	Oct	6	Grimsby Town	2-4	Atherton 2	11360	9			1	2	7			6	5		10	3			8			11						4
10		13	TOTTENHAM HOTSPUR	4-1	McLean, Quantrill, Hawes, Atherton	22688	9			1	2	7			6	5		10	3			8			11						4
11		20	Reading	0-4		11169	9			1	2	7			6	5		10	3			8			11						4
12		27	PRESTON NORTH END	7-2	* see below	20558	9			1	2	7			6	5			3			8			11					10	4
13	Nov	3	Middlesbrough	3-5	Quantrill 2, McLean	18783	9			1	2	7			6	5			3			8			11					10	4
14		10	HULL CITY	5-1	McLean,Atherton,Lloyd,Quantrill,Davis	17877	9			1	2	7			6	5			3			8			11					10	4
15		17	Southampton	2-2	McLean, Scott	14406	9			1	2	7			6	5			3			8			11					10	4
16		24	WOLVERHAMPTON W.	4-1	McLean, Quantrill, Atherton 2	6958	9			1	2	7	6			5			3			8			11					10	4
17	Dec	1	Notts County	3-3	McLean 2, Quantrill	14875	9			1	2	7			6	5			3			8			11					10	4
18		8	MILLWALL	4-0	Scott 2, McLean 2	17667	9			1	2	7			6	5			3			8			11					10	4
19		15	Port Vale	1-0	Atherton	7339	9			1	2	7			6	5			3			8			11					10	4
20		22	OLDHAM ATHLETIC	2-0	McLean, Atherton	14116	9			1	2	7			6	5			3			8			11					10	4
21		25	SWANSEA TOWN	3-1	McLean, Davis, Quantrill	26925	9			1	2	7			6	5			3			8			11					10	4
22		26	Swansea Town	1-3	Quantrill	15197	9			1	2	7			6					5		8			11				3	10	4
23		29	BARNSLEY	2-1	Atherton 2	17706	9			1	2	7	6			5						8			11	3				10	4
24	Jan	5	Bristol City	0-1		10956	9			1	2	7	6			5						8			11				3	10	4
25		19	NOTTM. FOREST	1-1	Quantrill	19211	9			1	2	7	6			5						8			11				3	10	4
26	Feb	2	CLAPTON ORIENT	2-1	Davis, Quantrill	12701	9			1	2	7	6							5		8			11				3	10	4
27		9	Stoke City	0-2		12093	9			1	2	7	6			5						8			11				3	10	4
28		23	Tottenham Hotspur	2-3	Millership, Hawes	19910				1	2	7						10		5	3		8	11				9			4
29	Mar	2	READING	1-0	Hawes	15376		4		1	2	7						10		5	3		8	11			9				
30		9	Preston North End	0-2		13912		4		1	2	7		9				10		5	3	8		11							
31		11	West Bromwich Albion	2-1	Dinsdale, Scott	4696		4		1	2	7	6	9					3	5		8			11					10	
32		16	MIDDLESBROUGH	3-2	McLean 2, Davis	26109		4		1	2	7	6	9					3	5		8			11					10	
33		23	Hull City	0-1		6980		4		1	2	7	6	9					3	5		8		11						10	
34		29	Blackpool	0-3		17977				1	2	7	6	9		5			3			8		11						10	4
35		30	SOUTHAMPTON	4-1	Scott, Parris 2, Davis	15420				1	2	7	6			5			3			8		11			9			10	4
36	Apr	1	BLACKPOOL	5-2	Rhodes 2, Scott, Parris 2	14125				1	2	7	6						3	5		8		11			9			10	4
37		6	Wolverhampton Wan.	1-3	McLean	12165				1	2	7	6			5			3			8		11			9			10	4
38		13	NOTTS COUNTY	2-2	McLean 2	15104				1	2	7		9					3	5		8			11					10	4
39		20	Millwall	3-1	Dinsdale 2, McLean	15082				1	2	7	6	9					3	5		8			11					10	4
40		27	PORT VALE	2-0	McLean, Quantrill	9132				1	2	7	6	9						5		8			11	3				10	4
41		29	GRIMSBY TOWN	1-0	McLean	12143				1	2	7	6	9						5		8			11	3				10	4
42	May	4	Oldham Athletic	1-2	McLean	6880				1	2	7	6	9						5		8			11	3				10	4
						Apps	19	5	6	42	35	41	20	10	20	20	4	12	26	22	6	40	2	8	29	10	4	5	7	28	37
						Goals	12		1			5	2	3			1	3	3			28	1	4	15		2	1		7	

JA Smith played in game 28 at 6

C Godfrey played at 6 in 3 games, 29, 30 and 38

Scorers in game 12: Atherton 2, Lloyd, Quantrill 2, Scott, McLean

F.A. Cup

Rd	Month	Day	Opponent	Score	Scorers	Att.	Atherton WJ	Buckley W	Cartwright HP	Clough JH	Cookson S	Davis H	Dickinson S	Dinsdale WA	Duckett DT	Elwood JH	Hart J	Hawes AR	Lloyd T	Matthews RW	McCandless TB	McLean G	Millership W	Parris JE	Quantrill AE	Reid A	Rhodes WT	Robinson WA	Schofield HW	Scott H	Taylor HW
R3	Jan	12	Hull City	1-1	Parris	23000	9			1	2	7	6			5						8		11					3	10	4
rep		16	HULL CITY	3-1	Davis, Atherton, McLean	21072	9			1	2	7	6			5						8		11					3	10	4
R4		26	Plymouth Argyle	1-0	Davis	33050	9			1	2	7	6			5						8			11				3	10	4
R5	Feb	16	West Bromwich Albion	0-6		30307				1	2	7			6	5						8			11			9	3	10	4

		P	W	D	L	F	A	W	D	L	F	A	Pts
1	Middlesbrough	42	14	4	3	54	22	8	7	6	38	35	55
2	Grimsby Town	42	16	2	3	49	24	8	3	10	33	37	53
3	BRADFORD	42	18	2	1	62	22	4	2	15	26	48	48
4	Southampton	42	12	6	3	48	22	5	8	8	26	38	48
5	Notts County	42	13	4	4	51	24	6	5	10	27	41	47
6	Stoke City	42	12	7	2	46	16	5	5	11	28	35	46
7	West Bromwich Albion	42	13	4	4	50	25	6	4	11	30	54	46
8	Blackpool	42	13	4	4	49	18	6	3	12	43	58	45
9	Chelsea	42	10	6	5	40	30	7	4	10	24	35	44
10	Tottenham Hotspur	42	16	3	2	50	26	1	6	14	25	55	43
11	Nottingham Forest	42	8	6	7	34	33	7	6	8	37	37	42
12	Hull City	42	8	8	5	38	24	5	6	10	20	39	40
13	Preston North End	42	12	6	3	58	27	3	3	15	20	52	39
14	Millwall	42	10	4	7	43	35	6	3	12	28	51	39
15	Reading	42	12	3	6	48	30	3	6	12	15	56	39
16	Barnsley	42	12	4	5	51	28	4	2	15	18	38	38
17	Wolverhampton Wan.	42	9	6	6	41	31	6	1	14	36	50	37
18	Oldham Athletic	42	15	2	4	37	24	1	3	17	17	51	37
19	Swansea Town	42	12	3	6	46	26	1	7	13	16	49	36
20	Bristol City	42	11	6	4	37	25	2	4	15	21	47	36
21	Port Vale	42	14	1	6	53	25	1	3	17	18	61	34
22	Clapton Orient	42	10	4	7	29	25	2	4	15	16	47	32

1929/30

4th in Division Two

No	Date	Opponent	Score	Scorers	Att	Atherton WJ	Bentley A	Clough JH	Cookson S	Davis H	Dickinson S	Dinsdale WA	Elwood JH	Geldard A	Godfrey C	Harwood I	Kilcar SP	Lloyd T	Matthews RW	McLean G	Millership W	Moody J	Parris JE	Pringle CR	Quantrill AE	Rhodes WT	Scott H	Taylor HW
1	Aug 31	TOTTENHAM HOTSPUR	2-1	Quantrill, Scott	18771			1	2	7	6	9						3	5	8					11		10	4
2	Sep 4	NOTTM. FOREST	5-1	Dinsdale, Quantrill, Davis, McLean 2	14593			1	2	7	6	9						3	5	8					11		10	4
3	7	West Bromwich Albion	0-5		17168			1	2	7		9						3	5	8					11		10	4
4	14	BRADFORD CITY	0-2		28880			1	2	7		9						3	5	8					11		10	4
5	16	Millwall	2-1	Millership, Quantrill	9143			1	2			9	5	7	6			3		10	8				11			4
6	21	BARNSLEY	4-4	Rhodes 2, Millership, McLean	14516			1	2				5	7	6			3		10	8				11	9		4
7	28	Blackpool	0-1		18870			1	2					7	6				5	10	8				11	9		4
8	Oct 3	Nottingham Forest	1-1	Quantrill	4430			1	2					7	6			3	5	10	8				11	9	4	
9	5	BURY	2-1	Davis, Parris	15185			1	2	7	6	9						3	5	8	10		11					4
10	12	Chelsea	2-1	Millership, Atherton	27171	9		1	2	7								3	5	8	10		11	6				4
11	19	Swansea Town	4-2	Parris, McLean 2, Millership	13215	9		1	2	7								3	5	8	10		11	6				4
12	26	CARDIFF CITY	2-0	Davis, McLean	18455	9		1	2	7								3	5	8	10		11	6				4
13	Nov 2	Preston North End	1-4	Atherton	10226	9		1	2	7								3	5	8	10		11	6				4
14	9	BRISTOL CITY	3-1	Atherton, Pringle, Davis	10305	9		1	2	7								3	5	8	10		11	6				4
15	16	Notts County	1-1	Atherton	8034	9		1	2	7								3	5	8	10		11	6				4
16	23	READING	5-2	McLean,Atherton 2,Matthews,Millership	9243	9	2	1		7								3	5	8	10			6	11			4
17	30	Charlton Athletic	0-2		11959	9		1	2	7								3	5	8	10			6	11			4
18	Dec 7	HULL CITY	4-2	og, McLean, Lloyd, Taylor	6930	9			2	7								3	5	8	10	1		6	11			4
19	14	Stoke City	1-2	Millership	8676	9			2	7								3	5	8	10	1	11	6				4
20	21	WOLVERHAMPTON W.	0-0		12567	9			2		11							3	5	8	10	1		6				4
21	25	Oldham Athletic	1-5	Dickinson	18235	7			2		11							3	5	8	10	1		6		9		4
22	26	OLDHAM ATHLETIC	2-2	Rhodes 2	27257		2			7	11		5				10	3		8		1		6		9		4
23	28	Tottenham Hotspur	1-1	McLean	20726		2			7	10		5					3		8		1	11	6		9		4
24	Jan 4	WEST BROMWICH ALB.	5-1	McLean 2, Harwood, Millership 2	17740		2	1		7			5			9		3		8	10		11	6				4
25	18	Bradford City	2-1	Harwood 2	34172		2	1		7	11		5			9		3		8	10			6				4
26	Feb 1	BLACKPOOL	5-0	Millership 2, Davis 2, McLean	17970		2	1		7	6					9		3		8	10			5	11			4
27	5	Barnsley	1-1	Harwood	5932		2	1		7	6		5			9		3		8	10				11			4
28	8	Bury	1-5	Harwood	11789		2	1		7	6					9		3		8	10			5	11			4
29	22	SWANSEA TOWN	3-0	McLean 2, Lloyd	13489			1	2	7	11		5			9		3		8	10			6				4
30	Mar 1	Cardiff City	0-2		11442	8	2	1		7	11	9	5					3			10			6				4
31	8	PRESTON NORTH END	5-2	Harwood, McLean 2, Davis, Millership	14396			1	2	7	11					9			5	8	10			6				4
32	12	CHELSEA	1-3	Kilcar	11087			1	2	7						9	10	3	5	8				6	11			4
33	15	Bristol City	0-0		5961		2	1		7						9	10	3	5	8			11	6				4
34	22	NOTTS COUNTY	3-3	Parris, Harwood, McLean	10497		2	1		7	6					9	10	3	5	8			11					4
35	29	Reading	0-1		9908			1	2	7			5			9		3		8				6	11		10	4
36	Apr 5	CHARLTON ATHLETIC	4-0	Harwood 2, Scott, Davis	8523			1	2	7			5			9		3		8				6	11		10	4
37	12	Hull City	2-0	Harwood 2	5594			1	2	7			5			9		3		8				6	11		10	4
38	19	STOKE CITY	3-2	Harwood 2, Scott	4840			1	2	7			5			9		3		8				6	11		10	4
39	21	Southampton	2-2	Davis, Harwood	15302			1	2	7			5			9		3		8			11	6			10	4
40	22	SOUTHAMPTON	1-1	McLean	10038			1	2	7			5			9		3		10			11	6				4
41	26	Wolverhampton Wan.	4-4	Taylor, Harwood, McLean, Scott	6474			1	2	7			5			9		3		8			11	6			10	4
42	May 3	MILLWALL	6-0	Scott, Parris 2, Davis, McLean, Harwood	7057			1	2	7			5			9		3		8			11	6			10	4
					Apps	13	11	36	31	36	15	7	17	4	4	18	4	40	23	41	25	6	16	31	19	6	12	41
					Goals	6				10	1	1				16	1	2	1	20	11		5	1	4	4	5	2

Played in one game: H Parrish (20, at 7), T Hogg (40, at 8)

A Reid played in games 7 and 31 at 3

C Sullivan played in games 3 and 4 at 6

One own goal

F.A. Cup

Rd	Date	Opponent	Score	Scorers	Att	Atherton WJ	Bentley A	Clough JH	Cookson S	Davis H	Dickinson S	Dinsdale WA	Elwood JH	Geldard A	Godfrey C	Harwood I	Kilcar SP	Lloyd T	Matthews RW	McLean G	Millership W	Moody J	Parris JE	Pringle CR	Quantrill AE	Rhodes WT	Scott H	Taylor HW
R3	Jan 11	Barnsley	1-0	Quantrill	19700		2	1		7			5			9		3		8	10				11			4
R4	25	Derby County	1-1	Harwood	26659		2	1		7	6		5			9		3		8	10				11			4
rep	29	DERBY COUNTY	2-1	Millership, Davis	29738		2	1		7	6		5			9		3		8	10				11			4
R5	Feb 15	Sheffield Wednesday	1-5	McLean	53268		2	1		7	6		5			9		3		8	10		11					4

Played at 6 in R3: Smith

		P	W	D	L	F	A	W	D	L	F	A	Pts
1	Blackpool	42	17	1	3	63	22	10	3	8	35	45	58
2	Chelsea	42	17	3	1	49	14	5	8	8	25	32	55
3	Oldham Athletic	42	14	5	2	60	21	7	6	8	30	30	53
4	BRADFORD	42	14	5	2	65	28	5	7	9	26	42	50
5	Bury	42	14	2	5	45	27	8	3	10	33	40	49
6	West Bromwich Albion	42	16	1	4	73	31	5	4	12	32	42	47
7	Southampton	42	14	6	1	46	22	3	5	13	31	54	45
8	Cardiff City	42	14	4	3	41	16	4	4	13	20	43	44
9	Wolverhampton Wan.	42	14	3	4	53	24	2	6	13	24	55	41
10	Nottingham Forest	42	9	6	6	36	28	4	9	8	19	41	41
11	Stoke City	42	12	4	5	41	20	4	4	13	33	52	40
12	Tottenham Hotspur	42	11	8	2	43	24	4	1	16	16	37	39
13	Charlton Athletic	42	10	6	5	39	23	4	5	12	20	40	39
14	Millwall	42	10	7	4	36	26	2	8	11	21	47	39
15	Swansea Town	42	11	5	5	42	23	3	4	14	15	38	37
16	Preston North End	42	7	7	7	42	36	6	4	11	23	44	37
17	Barnsley	42	12	7	2	39	22	2	1	18	17	49	36
18	Bradford City	42	7	7	7	33	30	5	5	11	27	47	36
19	Reading	42	10	7	4	31	20	2	4	15	23	47	35
20	Bristol City	42	11	4	6	36	30	2	5	14	25	53	35
21	Hull City	42	11	3	7	30	24	3	4	14	21	54	35
22	Notts County	42	8	7	6	33	26	1	8	12	21	44	33

1930/31

6th in Division Two

	Date	Opponent	Score	Scorers	Att	Allcock CW	Atherton WJ	Clough JH	Cookson S	Crayston WJ	Davis H	Dickinson S	Ellwood JH	Geldard A	Godfrey C	Harwood I	Hogg T	Kilcar SP	Lloyd T	McLean G	McMillan G	Parris JE	Pringle CR	Rhodes WT	Robertson A	Scott H	Smith JA	Spooner PG	Taylor HW	Ward RA
1	Aug 30	Oldham Athletic	0-2		13762			1	2		7		5			9			3	8			6			10		11	4	
2	Sep 1	Stoke City	1-1	Atherton	12756		9	1	2		7		5						3	8		11	6			10			4	
3	6	NOTTM. FOREST	4-1	McLean, Kilcar 2, Davis	14313			1	2	5	7					9		10	3	8		11	6						4	
4	8	PORT VALE	5-1	Taylor, Kilcar, Atherton, Parris 2	10296		9	1	2	5	7							10	3	8		11	6						4	
5	13	Tottenham Hotspur	2-3	Kilcar, Parris	18828		9	1	2	5	7							10	3	8		11	6						4	
6	20	PRESTON NORTH END	2-2	Taylor, Kilcar	16466			1	2	5				7		9		10	3	8		11	6						4	
7	22	Port Vale	2-8	McLean, Rhodes	8623			1	2	5	7							10	3	8		11	6	9					4	
8	27	Burnley	2-3	Rhodes 2	13132			1	2	5	7							10	3	8		11	6	9					4	
9	Oct 4	SOUTHAMPTON	1-1	Geldard	12825				2				5	7	6			10		8		11		9	1				4	3
10	11	Reading	0-3		8887			1	2	5	7	6				9			3	8		11				10			4	
11	18	CHARLTON ATHLETIC	3-2	Rhodes 2, Dickinson	9962			1	2		7	11	5					10		8			6	9					4	3
12	25	Bradford City	4-0	Davis, McLean, Rhodes 2	28378			1	2		7	11	5					10		8				9			6		4	3
13	Nov 1	PLYMOUTH ARGYLE	7-1	Smith, Kilcar 2, McLean 3, Rhodes	9697			1	2		7	11	5					10		8				9			6		4	3
14	8	Bury	1-3	Rhodes	9173			1	2		7		5					10		8		11		9			6		4	3
15	15	BRISTOL CITY	5-2	McLean 3, Rhodes, Davis	7538			1	2		7	11	5					10		8				9			6		4	3
16	22	Cardiff City	3-0	Kilcar, Rhodes, Davis	5475			1	2		7	11	5					10	3					9		8	6		4	
17	29	EVERTON	4-1	Rhodes 2, Scott, Davis	18686			1	2		7	11	5					10	3					9		8	6		4	
18	Dec 6	Barnsley	0-1		8177			1	2		7	11	5			9		10	3							8	6		4	
19	13	WEST BROMWICH ALB.	3-1	Lloyd, Harwood 2	14790			1	2		7	11	5			9		10	3		8						6		4	
20	20	Swansea Town	1-2	Dickinson	9612			1	2		7	11	5			9		10	3		8						6		4	
21	25	Millwall	1-1	Taylor	13053			1	2	4	7	11	5			9		10	3		8						6			
22	26	MILLWALL	6-0	* see below	11714			1	2	5	7					9			3		8	11				10	6		4	
23	27	OLDHAM ATHLETIC	4-0	Harwood, Davis, Scott 2	16728			1	2	5	7					9			3		8	11				10	6		4	
24	Jan 3	Nottingham Forest	0-1		3819			1		5	7					9			3		8	11				10	6		4	2
25	17	TOTTENHAM HOTSPUR	4-1	Rhodes 2, Davis, Scott	15229			1	2		7	11	5						3		8		6	9		10			4	
26	29	Preston North End	1-1	Davis	7001			1	2		7	11	5						3		8			9		10	6		4	
27	31	BURNLEY	4-1	Dickinson 3, Rhodes	7954			1	2		7	11	5						3		8			9		10	6		4	
28	Feb 7	Southampton	3-2	Davis 3	11093			1	2		7	11	5					10	3		8			9			6		4	
29	18	READING	1-3	Rhodes	5259			1	2		7	11	5					10	3		8			9			6		4	
30	21	Charlton Athletic	1-3	Davis	10609			1	2		7	11	5			8		10	3					9			6		4	
31	28	BRADFORD CITY	1-2	Dickinson	17012			1	2		7	11	5			9			3		8					10	6		4	
32	Mar 7	Plymouth Argyle	0-0		13123	4	7	1	2			11	5			9		10			8		6							3
33	14	BURY	5-1	Rhodes 2,McMillan,Davis,Dickinson	9077	4		1	2	10	7	11	5								8		6	9						3
34	21	Bristol City	0-2		8719	4		1	2	10	7	11	5								8		6	9						3
35	28	CARDIFF CITY	3-0	Spooner, Crayston 2	6557	4		1	2	9	7		5		6	10			3		8							11		
36	Apr 4	Everton	2-4	Crayston, McMillan	32213			1	2	9	7		5						3		8			10			6	11	4	
37	6	WOLVERHAMPTON W.	1-1	Crayston	7712	4				5	7						8		3		10			9	1		6	11		
38	7	Wolverhampton Wan.	1-1	Crayston	11899	4			2	5	7						8		3		10			9	1		6	11		
39	11	BARNSLEY	1-0	Harwood	9124	4			2	5	7	11				9			3		8				1	10	6			
40	18	West Bromwich Albion	1-1	McMillan	20979	4			2	9	7	11	5						3		8				1	10	6			
41	25	SWANSEA TOWN	5-1	Scott 2, Crayston 2, McMillan	4372	4			2	9	7	11	5						3		8				1	10	6			
42	May 2	STOKE CITY	2-2	Crayston, Scott	6767	4			2	9	7	11	5						3		8				1	10	6			
					Apps	10	4	35	40	21	39	25	29	2	2	16	2	22	33	15	23	13	13	21	7	17	26	5	31	10
					Goals		2			9	14	7		1		6		8	1	9	6	3		19		7	1	1	3	

Scorers in game 22: McMillan 2, Harwood 2, Davis, Crayston

Played in one game: A Bentley (37, at 2)

F.A. Cup

	Date	Opponent	Score	Scorers	Att	Allcock CW	Atherton WJ	Clough JH	Cookson S	Crayston WJ	Davis H	Dickinson S	Ellwood JH	Geldard A	Godfrey C	Harwood I	Hogg T	Kilcar SP	Lloyd T	McLean G	McMillan G	Parris JE	Pringle CR	Rhodes WT	Robertson A	Scott H	Smith JA	Spooner PG	Taylor HW	Ward RA
R3	Jan 10	Aldershot	1-0	Scott	7987			1	2		7		5					10	3			11		9		8	6		4	
R4	24	BURNLEY	2-0	McMillan, Rhodes	26444			1	2		7	11	5						3		8			9		10	6		4	
R5	Feb 14	Southport	0-1		17508			1	2		7	11	5					10	3		8			9			6		4	

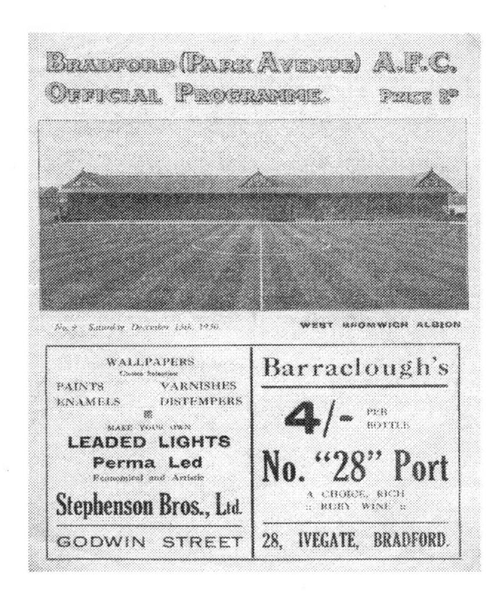

		P	W	D	L	F	A	W	D	L	F	A	Pts
1	Everton	42	18	1	2	76	31	10	4	7	45	35	61
2	West Bromwich Albion	42	14	3	4	40	16	8	7	6	43	33	54
3	Tottenham Hotspur	42	15	5	1	64	20	7	2	12	24	35	51
4	Wolverhampton Wan.	42	15	2	4	56	25	6	3	12	28	42	47
5	Port Vale	42	15	3	3	39	16	6	2	13	28	45	47
6	BRADFORD	42	15	4	2	71	24	3	6	12	26	42	46
7	Preston North End	42	12	5	4	55	31	5	6	10	28	33	45
8	Burnley	42	13	5	3	55	30	4	6	11	26	47	45
9	Southampton	42	13	4	4	46	22	6	2	13	28	40	44
10	Bradford City	42	12	5	4	39	26	5	5	11	22	37	44
11	Stoke City	42	11	6	4	34	17	6	4	11	30	54	44
12	Oldham Athletic	42	13	5	3	45	28	3	5	13	16	44	42
13	Bury	42	14	3	4	44	20	5	0	16	31	62	41
14	Millwall	42	12	4	5	47	25	4	3	14	24	55	39
15	Charlton Athletic	42	11	4	6	35	33	4	5	12	24	53	39
16	Bristol City	42	11	5	5	29	23	4	3	14	25	59	38
17	Nottingham Forest	42	12	6	3	54	35	2	3	16	26	50	37
18	Plymouth Argyle	42	10	3	8	47	33	4	5	12	29	51	36
19	Barnsley	42	13	3	5	42	23	0	6	15	17	56	35
20	Swansea Town	42	11	5	5	40	29	1	5	15	11	45	34
21	Reading	42	11	2	8	47	33	1	4	16	25	63	30
22	Cardiff City	42	7	6	8	32	31	1	3	17	15	56	25

1931/32

6th in Division Two

							Allcock CW	Bell JC	Clough JH	Cookson S	Crayston WJ	Davis H	Dick WR	Dickinson S	Elwood JH	Geldard A	Godfrey C	Harwood I	Kilcar SP	Leedham FA	Lloyd T	McMillan G	Morfitt JW	Morton R	Parris JE	Purdon JS	Rhodes WT	Robertson A	Scott H	Smith JA	Taylor HW	Ward RA
1	Aug	29	MANCHESTER UNITED	3-1	Leedham, Dickinson, Rhodes	16239	4		1	2		7		6	5					10		8		11		3	9					
2		31	STOKE CITY	2-1	Leedham, Dickinson	11692			1	2		7		6	5					10	3	8		11			9				4	
3	Sep	5	Tottenham Hotspur	3-3	Davis, Parris 2	27108	4		1	2		7		6	5			9		10	3	8			11							
4		7	Charlton Athletic	2-2	Harwood, Dickinson	9789	4		1			7		6	5			9		10	3	8			11	2						
5		12	NOTTM. FOREST	4-1	Harwood 3, Dickinson	13161			1			7	4	6	5			9		10	3	8			11	2						
6		16	CHARLTON ATHLETIC	3-0	Parris, Davis, Harwood	11304			1			7	4	6	5			9		10	3	8			11	2						
7		19	Chesterfield	2-3	McMillan 2	11398			1			7	4	6	5			9		10	3	8			11	2						
8		26	BURNLEY	2-0	Wood (og), Parris	15426					9		4	6	5	7				10	3	8			11	2		1				
9	Oct	3	Preston North End	0-1		10240							4	6	5	7		9		10	3	8			11	2		1				
10		10	SOUTHAMPTON	2-1	Crayston 2	13539				2	9	7		6	5					10	3	8		11				1			4	
11		17	Swansea Town	0-1		11279				2	9	7		6	5					10	3	8		11				1			4	
12		24	BARNSLEY	1-0	Parris	10857				2	9	7		6	5					10	3	8			11			1			4	
13		31	Notts County	2-0	Parris, Davis	12687				2	9	7		6	5					10	3	8			11			1			4	
14	Nov	7	BRADFORD CITY	1-0	Leedham	21035				2		7			5			9		10	3	8			11			1		6	4	
15		14	Bristol City	0-0		8213				2	9	7			5				10		3				11			1	8	6	4	
16		21	OLDHAM ATHLETIC	5-0	Davis, Rhodes 3, Parris	11794				2		7			5					10	3				11		9	1	8	6	4	
17		28	Bury	2-4	McMillan, Scott	8257				2		7			5						3	10			11		9	1	8	6	4	
18	Dec	5	PORT VALE	2-2	Rhodes 2	10281				2		7		6	5						3	10		11			9	1	8		4	
19		12	Millwall	0-3		13602				2		7		6	5					10	3				11		9	1	8	4		
20		19	PLYMOUTH ARGYLE	2-0	McMillan, Crayston	11900			1	2	4	7		6			5	10			3	8			11		9					
21		25	LEEDS UNITED	3-0	Rhodes, Parris, Dickinson	32421			1	2	4	7		6			5	10			3	8			11		9					
22		26	Leeds United	2-3	Davis, G Milburn (og)	34009			1	2	4	7		6			5	10			3	8			11		9					
23	Jan	2	Manchester United	2-0	Parris, Rhodes	6056			1	2	4	7		6	5			10			3				11		9		8			
24		16	TOTTENHAM HOTSPUR	2-1	Rhodes, Dickinson	12596				2	4	7		6	5			10			3	8			11		9	1				
25		27	Nottingham Forest	1-6	Geldard	4550					5	8		6		7		9		10	3			11		2		1			4	
26		30	CHESTERFIELD	1-0	Crayston	12007				2	9	8		6	5	7		10			3	4			11			1				
27	Feb	6	Burnley	2-3	Crayston, Davis	7942					9	8		6	5	7		10			2	4			11			1				3
28		17	PRESTON NORTH END	1-5	Geldard	7617					4	7	5	6		8					3				11		9	1	10			2
29		20	Southampton	3-0	Parris, Rhodes 2	8013					4			6	5	7				10	3	8			11		9	1				2
30		27	SWANSEA TOWN	2-1	Parris, Dickinson	10126					4			6	5	7				10	3	8			11		9	1				2
31	Mar	5	Barnsley	2-2	Parris, Geldard	5727				2				6		7	5			10	3	8			11		9	1			4	
32		12	NOTTS COUNTY	1-1	Dickinson	12015				2				6	5	7				10	3	8	9		11			1			4	
33		19	Bradford City	0-0		27784				2				6	5	7				10	3	8	9		11			1			4	
34		26	BRISTOL CITY	2-0	Davis, Leedham	10100		1				7		6	5					10	3	8			11		9				4	2
35		28	Wolverhampton Wan.	0-6		27902		1				7		6	5					10	3				11		9		8		4	2
36		29	WOLVERHAMPTON W.	2-1	Morfitt 2	12509					4	8	6			7	5			10	3		9		11			1				2
37	Apr	2	Oldham Athletic	1-2	Morfitt	6365					4	8	6			7	5			10	3		9		11			1				2
38		9	BURY	2-1	Elwood, Parris	9127				2	4	8	6		5	7				10	3		9		11			1				
39		16	Port Vale	3-1	Morfitt, Davis 2	6672				2	4	7	6		5					10	3		9		11			1	8			
40		23	MILLWALL	1-2	Lloyd	6785				2	4		6		5	7				10	3		9		11			1	8			
41		30	Plymouth Argyle	1-4	Morfitt	9356				2	4			6	5	7				10	3		9		11			1	8			
42	May	7	Stoke City	0-1		6473		1		2	4				5	7				10	3		9		11	6			8			
						Apps	3	3	11	27	24	32	11	32	34	17	6	15	1	31	41	28	9	6	36	9	17	28	12	5	16	8
						Goals					5	9		8	1	3		5		4	1	4	5		13		11		1			

Two own goals

F.A. Cup

							Allcock CW	Bell JC	Clough JH	Cookson S	Crayston WJ	Davis H	Dick WR	Dickinson S	Elwood JH	Geldard A	Godfrey C	Harwood I	Kilcar SP	Leedham FA	Lloyd T	McMillan G	Morfitt JW	Morton R	Parris JE	Purdon JS	Rhodes WT	Robertson A	Scott H	Smith JA	Taylor HW	Ward RA
R3	Jan	9	CARDIFF CITY	2-0	Harwood, Rhodes	18343				2	4	7		6	5			10			3	8			11		9	1				
R4		23	NORTHAMPTON T	4-2	* see below	20487				2	4	11		6		7	5	9		10	3							1	8			
R5	Feb	13	Watford	0-1		23457				2	9	7	4	6	5						3	8			11			1	10			

Scorers in R4: Leedham, Harwood, Dickinson, Davis

		P	W	D	L	F	A	W	D	L	F	A	Pts
1	Wolverhampton Wan.	42	17	3	1	71	11	7	5	9	44	38	56
2	Leeds United	42	12	5	4	36	22	10	5	6	42	32	54
3	Stoke City	42	14	6	1	47	19	5	8	8	22	29	52
4	Plymouth Argyle	42	14	4	3	69	29	6	5	10	31	37	49
5	Bury	42	13	4	4	44	21	8	3	10	26	37	49
6	BRADFORD	42	17	2	2	44	18	4	5	12	28	45	49
7	Bradford City	42	10	7	4	53	26	6	6	9	27	35	45
8	Tottenham Hotspur	42	11	6	4	58	37	5	5	11	29	41	43
9	Millwall	42	13	3	5	43	21	4	6	11	18	40	43
10	Charlton Athletic	42	11	5	5	38	28	6	4	11	23	38	43
11	Nottingham Forest	42	13	4	4	49	27	3	6	12	28	45	42
12	Manchester United	42	12	3	6	44	31	5	5	11	27	41	42
13	Preston North End	42	11	6	4	37	25	5	4	12	38	52	42
14	Southampton	42	10	5	6	39	30	7	2	12	27	47	41
15	Swansea Town	42	12	4	5	45	22	4	3	14	28	53	39
16	Notts County	42	10	4	7	43	30	3	8	10	32	45	38
17	Chesterfield	42	11	3	7	43	33	2	8	11	21	53	37
18	Oldham Athletic	42	10	4	7	41	34	3	6	12	21	50	36
19	Burnley	42	7	8	6	36	36	6	1	14	23	51	35
20	Port Vale	42	8	4	9	30	33	5	3	13	28	56	33
21	Barnsley	42	8	7	6	35	30	4	2	15	20	61	33
22	Bristol City	42	4	7	10	22	37	2	4	15	17	41	23

1932/33

8th in Division Two

	Month	Day	Opponent	Score	Scorers	Att.	Allcock CW	Barrett C	Bedford H	Bell JC	Collins D	Cookson S	Crayston WJ	Danskin R	Dickinson S	Elwood JH	Geldard A	Godfrey C	Hawthorn W	Leedham FA	Lloyd T	McMillan G	Parris JE	Purdon JS	Rhodes WT	Robertson A	Robertson JH	Robson J	Scaife S	Smith JA	Suggett EJ	Ward RA
1	Aug	27	Preston North End	3-2	Leedham, Rhodes, Parris	15343			8	1		2	4		6	5				10	3		11		9						7	
2		31	OLDHAM ATHLETIC	1-3	Parris	15877			8	1		2	4		6	5				10	3		11		9						7	
3	Sep	3	BURNLEY	0-4		11020			9	1		2	4		6	5				10	3	8	11								7	
4		5	Oldham Athletic	3-1	Bedford 2, Suggett	11262			8				4		6		7	5			3	10	11			1					9	2
5		10	Bradford City	0-1		28110			8				4		6		7	5			3	10	11			1					9	2
6		17	Plymouth Argyle	2-3	Dickinson, Suggett	21240			8				4		6		7	5		10	3		11			1					9	2
7		24	NOTTM. FOREST	3-1	Parris, Suggett 2	11357			8				4		6		7	5		10	3		11			1					9	2
8	Oct	1	Charlton Athletic	2-0	Suggett 2	13361			8				4		6		7	5		10	3		11			1					9	2
9		8	STOKE CITY	2-2	Suggett, Parris	9003			8				4		6		7	5		10	3		11			1					9	2
10		15	Manchester United	1-2	Bedford	18918			8				4		6		7	5		10	3		11			1					9	2
11		22	CHESTERFIELD	5-1	Geldard, Bedford, Suggett 3	9748			8				4		6		7	5			3		10			1					9	2
12		29	Fulham	2-5	Geldard, Bedford	20326			8				4		6		7	5			3		10			1					9	2
13	Nov	5	WEST HAM UNITED	3-0	Bedford, Robson, Parris	14861			10	1			4		6	5	7				3		11					9			8	2
14		12	Swansea Town	1-3	Crayston	9668			10	1			4		6	5	7				3		11					9			8	2
15		19	MILLWALL	3-0	Robson, Lloyd, Suggett	9775			8	1			5		6			4		10	3		11					9			7	2
16		26	Southampton	0-2		11693			8	1			5		6			4		10	3		11					9			7	2
17	Dec	3	BURY	4-0	Bedford 2, Suggett, Rhodes	8952			8	1			5		10			4			3		11		9					6	7	2
18		10	Port Vale	1-3	Rhodes	6114			8	1					10	5		4			3		11		9					6	7	2
19		17	NOTTS COUNTY	3-4	Suggett 2, Collins	8678			10	1	7		4	5	6						3		11				8				9	2
20		24	Lincoln City	2-2	Suggett, Bedford	9239			10	1	7		4	5	6						3		11				8				9	2
21		26	TOTTENHAM HOTSPUR	3-3	Parris 2, Robertson	25318			8	1			4	5	6					10	3		11				7				9	2
22		27	Tottenham Hotspur	0-2		48478		3		1	7		4	5	6					10			11	2			8				9	
23		31	PRESTON NORTH END	2-0	Suggett, Robertson	8699	4	3	8	1				5	6						2		11		10		7				9	
24	Jan	7	Burnley	0-2		7640	4	3	8	1				5	6						2		11		10		7				9	
25		21	BRADFORD CITY	2-0	Suggett, Robertson	22602	4	3		1			5		10						2		11				8	9		6	7	
26	Feb	1	PLYMOUTH ARGYLE	1-0	Suggett	3708	4			1			5	6	10						2		11	3			8	9			7	
27		4	Nottingham Forest	1-1	Robertson	9690	4			1				5	10			6			2		11	3			8	9			7	
28		11	CHARLTON ATHLETIC	3-0	Suggett, Robson, Collins	9032	4			1	11			5	10			6			2			3			8	9			7	
29		18	Stoke City	0-4		8118	4			1	11			5	10			6			2			3			8	9			7	
30	Mar	4	Chesterfield	1-2	Lloyd	8280	4	3	8	1	11			5							2						10	9		6	7	
31		11	FULHAM	1-4	Parris	10478	4	3			7		5	6	10						2		11			1		8			9	
32		20	West Ham United	1-2	Robertson	7258		3	8				4	5					1	10	2		11				7			6	9	
33		25	SWANSEA TOWN	1-0	Robson	8260	6		8				4	5					1	10	3		11	2				9			7	
34	Apr	1	Millwall	1-1	Lloyd	12415	6		8				4	5					1	10	3		11	2				9			7	
35		5	MANCHESTER UNITED	1-1	Leedham	6314	6		8				4	5					1	10	3		11	2				9			7	
36		8	SOUTHAMPTON	2-1	Danskin, Parris	7504	6		8				4	5					1	10	3		11	2	9						7	
37		14	Grimsby Town	1-5	Bedford	16836	6	3	8				4	5					1	10			11	2				9			7	
38		15	Bury	0-0		9167	6	3					4	5				10	1				11	2	9		8				7	
39		17	GRIMSBY TOWN	1-1	Godfrey	8961	6	3					4	5				10	1				11	2	9		8				7	
40		22	PORT VALE	4-2	Robertson 2, Bedford, Suggett	5757	6	3	9					5				10	1		2		11				8		4		7	
41		29	Notts County	4-1	Robertson 2, Parris, Bedford	3306	6		9					5				10	1		3		11	2			8		4		7	
42	May	6	LINCOLN CITY	6-0	Suggett 2,Bedford 3,Robertson	5709	6		9				4	5				10	1		3		11	2			8				7	
						Apps	19	11	33	21	7	3	33	23	30	6	11	21	11	18	38	3	39	14	9	10	18	15	2	5	42	18
						Goals			15		2		1	1	1		2	1		2	3		10		3		10	4			22	

MA Coleman played at 11 in games 11 and 12

F.A. Cup

	Month	Day	Opponent	Score	Scorers	Att.	Allcock CW	Barrett C	Bedford H	Bell JC	Collins D	Cookson S	Crayston WJ	Danskin R	Dickinson S	Elwood JH	Geldard A	Godfrey C	Hawthorn W	Leedham FA	Lloyd T	McMillan G	Parris JE	Purdon JS	Rhodes WT	Robertson A	Robertson JH	Robson J	Scaife S	Smith JA	Suggett EJ	Ward RA
R3	Jan	14	PLYMOUTH ARGYLE	5-1	* see below	10554	4	3		1			5		10						2		11				8	9		6	7	
R4		28	Brighton & Hove Albion	1-2	Robson	18248	4			1			5		10			6			2		11				8	9			7	3

Scorers in R3: Dickinson, Robertson 2, Robson 2

The team en route for Brighton, January 28 1933. From left: Crayston, Robson, Robertson, Lloyd, Allcock, unknown, manager Claude Ingram, Suggett, Bell, Parris and trainer Nuttall.

		P	W	D	L	F	A	W	D	L	F	A	Pts
1	Stoke City	42	13	3	5	40	15	12	3	6	38	24	56
2	Tottenham Hotspur	42	14	7	0	58	19	6	8	7	38	32	55
3	Fulham	42	12	5	4	46	31	8	5	8	32	34	50
4	Bury	42	13	7	1	55	23	7	2	12	29	36	49
5	Nottingham Forest	42	9	8	4	37	28	8	7	6	30	31	49
6	Manchester United	42	11	5	5	40	24	4	8	9	31	44	43
7	Millwall	42	11	7	3	40	20	5	4	12	19	37	43
8	BRADFORD	42	13	4	4	51	27	4	4	13	26	44	42
9	Preston North End	42	12	2	7	53	36	4	8	9	21	34	42
10	Swansea Town	42	17	0	4	36	12	2	4	15	14	42	42
11	Bradford City	42	10	6	5	43	24	4	7	10	22	37	41
12	Southampton	42	15	3	3	48	22	3	2	16	18	44	41
13	Grimsby Town	42	8	10	3	49	34	6	3	12	30	50	41
14	Plymouth Argyle	42	13	4	4	45	22	3	5	13	18	45	41
15	Notts County	42	10	4	7	41	31	5	6	10	26	47	40
16	Oldham Athletic	42	10	4	7	38	31	5	4	12	29	49	38
17	Port Vale	42	12	3	6	49	27	2	7	12	17	52	38
18	Lincoln City	42	11	6	4	46	28	1	7	13	26	59	37
19	Burnley	42	8	9	4	35	20	3	5	13	32	59	36
20	West Ham United	42	12	6	3	56	31	1	3	17	19	62	35
21	Chesterfield	42	10	5	6	36	25	2	5	14	25	59	34
22	Charlton Athletic	42	9	3	9	35	35	3	4	14	25	56	31

1933/34

5th in Division Two

No	Date	Opponents	Score	Scorers	Att	Allcock CW	Barker D	Barrett C	Bell JC	Blackmore HA	Bowater G	Carson J	Crayston WJ	Danskin R	Dickinson S	Field FS	Godfrey C	Hawthorn W	Hogan J	Kelso J	Lewis TH	Lloyd T	McClelland J	Parris JE	Purdon JS	Robertson JH	Suggett EJ	Torrance G	Ward RA	Wilson J
1	Aug 26	OLDHAM ATHLETIC	4-2	Parris,Blackmore,McClelland,Lloyd	13908	6			1	9			4	5							10	3	8	11	2		7			
2	31	Brentford	0-2		13667	6			1	9			4	5							10	3	8	11	2		7			
3	Sep 2	Preston North End	1-3	McClelland	16488	6			1	9			4	5							10	3	8	11	2		7			
4	6	BRENTFORD	5-2	Blackmore 3, Parris 2	11982	6				9			4	5				1			10	3	8	11	2		7			
5	9	BRADFORD CITY	2-1	Blackmore, Suggett	22120	6				9			4	5				1			10	3	8	11	2		7			
6	16	GRIMSBY TOWN	2-1	Blackmore 2	15672	6				9			4	5				1			10	3	8	11	2		7			
7	23	Nottingham Forest	0-3		8157	6				9			4	5				1			10	3	8	11	2		7			
8	30	WEST HAM UNITED	0-0		11865	4				9				5	6			1				3	10	11	2	8	7			
9	Oct 7	Plymouth Argyle	1-4	Suggett	18127	4				9				5	6			1			10	3	8	11			7		2	
10	14	MANCHESTER UNITED	6-1	Lewis 2, Robertson 3, Blackmore	11033	4		3		9				5				1		6	10			11		8	7		2	
11	21	Port Vale	1-3	Lewis	13122	4		3		9				5				1		6	10			11		8	7		2	
12	28	NOTTS COUNTY	3-2	Blackmore 3	8628	4		3		9	11			5				1		6	10					8	7		2	
13	Nov 4	Swansea Town	1-5	Lewis	7402	4		3		9	11			5				1		6	10					8	7		2	
14	11	MILLWALL	4-0	Blackmore 2, Sweetman(og), Lewis	9205	4				9		7		5				1		6	10	3	8	11	2					
15	18	Lincoln City	1-2	McClelland	5951	4				9		7		5				1		6		3	8	11	2	10				
16	25	BURY	0-1		7291					9		7	4	5				1		6	10	3	8	11	2					
17	Dec 2	Hull City	2-1	Suggett, Blackmore	9030	6				8		7	4	5				1			10	3		11	2		9			
18	9	FULHAM	3-1	Lloyd, Blackmore 2	8085	6				8	11	7	4	5				1			10	3			2		9			
19	16	Southampton	0-5		8482	6				8	11	7	4	5				1			10	3			2		9			
20	23	BLACKPOOL	1-2	Bowater	10465					8	11	7	4	5			6				10	3			2		9			1
21	25	BOLTON WANDERERS	1-4	Blackmore	17527					8	11	7	4	5			6	1	9			3		10	2					
22	30	Oldham Athletic	3-1	Lewis 2, Blackmore	6513					9		7	4				5	1		6	10	3	8	11	2					
23	Jan 1	Bolton Wanderers	1-0	Blackmore	19433					9		7					5	1		6	10	3	4	11	2	8				
24	6	PRESTON NORTH END	2-1	Blackmore, Robertson	10655					9		7					5	1		6	10	3	4	11	2	8				
25	20	Bradford City	0-3		22774					9		7					5	1		6	10	3	4	11	2		8			
26	30	Grimsby Town	2-3	Robertson 2	7486	6			1	9				5							10	3	4	11		8	7		2	
27	Feb 3	NOTTM. FOREST	6-2	* see below	7126	6	10		1	9				5							11	3	4			8	7		2	
28	10	West Ham United	1-0	Lewis	16630	6	10		1	9				5							11	3	4			8	7		2	
29	17	PLYMOUTH ARGYLE	4-1	Robertson 3, Blackmore	9428	6	10		1	9				5							11	3	4			8	7		2	
30	24	Manchester United	4-0	Blackmore 2, Lewis, Suggett	13389	6	10		1	9				5							11	3	4			8	7		2	
31	Mar 3	PORT VALE	2-2	Robertson, Lloyd	11548	6	10		1	9				5							11	3	4			8	7		2	
32	17	SWANSEA TOWN	5-1	* see below	7175	6	10		1	9				5							11	3	4			8	7		2	
33	24	Millwall	1-0	Barker	9882	6	10	3	1	9				5							11		4			8	7		2	
34	30	Burnley	0-1		18721	6	10	3	1	9				5							11		4			8	7		2	
35	31	LINCOLN CITY	2-1	Robertson, Suggett	10855	6		3	1	9				5							11		4			8	7	10	2	
36	Apr 3	BURNLEY	5-0	Lewis, Suggett 3, Blackmore	15360	6	10	3	1	9				5							11		4			8	7		2	
37	7	Bury	1-2	Lewis	7952	6	10	3	1	9							5				11		4			8	7		2	
38	14	HULL CITY	3-1	Lewis, Robertson 2	8406	6	10	3	1	9			5								11		4			8	7		2	
39	16	Notts County	0-1		9141	6	10	3	1	9			5								11		4			8	7		2	
40	21	Fulham	2-0	Lewis, Robertson	11193				1	9			4	5					10		11		6		3	8	7		2	
41	28	SOUTHAMPTON	3-1	Robertson, Blackmore, Hogan	5378			3	1	9			4				5		10		11		6			8	7		2	
42	May 5	Blackpool	1-1	Field	8252			3	1	8			4	5		9			10		11		6				7		2	
					Apps	32	12	13	20	42	6	12	19	34	2	1	8	21	4	11	39	28	33	21	21	24	35	1	22	1
					Goals		3			27	1					1			1		13	4	4	3		17	11			

Scorers in game 27: Barker, Robertson 2, Suggett, Blackmore, Lloyd

Scorers in game 32: Blackmore, Suggett 2, Barker, McClelland

One own goal

F.A. Cup

Rd	Date	Opponents	Score	Scorers	Att	Allcock CW	Barker D	Barrett C	Bell JC	Blackmore HA	Bowater G	Carson J	Crayston WJ	Danskin R	Dickinson S	Field FS	Godfrey C	Hawthorn W	Hogan J	Kelso J	Lewis TH	Lloyd T	McClelland J	Parris JE	Purdon JS	Robertson JH	Suggett EJ	Torrance G	Ward RA	Wilson J
R3	Jan 13	Stoke City	0-3		22306					9		7					5	1		6	10	3	4	11	2	8				

		P	W	D	L	F	A	W	D	L	F	A	Pts
1	Grimsby Town	42	15	3	3	62	28	12	2	7	41	31	59
2	Preston North End	42	15	3	3	47	20	8	3	10	24	32	52
3	Bolton Wanderers	42	14	2	5	45	22	7	7	7	34	33	51
4	Brentford	42	15	2	4	52	24	7	5	9	33	36	51
5	BRADFORD	42	16	2	3	63	27	7	1	13	23	40	49
6	Bradford City	42	14	4	3	46	25	6	2	13	27	42	46
7	West Ham United	42	13	3	5	51	28	4	8	9	27	42	45
8	Port Vale	42	14	4	3	39	14	5	3	13	21	41	45
9	Oldham Athletic	42	12	5	4	48	28	5	5	11	24	32	44
10	Plymouth Argyle	42	12	7	2	43	20	3	6	12	26	50	43
11	Blackpool	42	10	8	3	39	27	5	5	11	23	37	43
12	Bury	42	12	4	5	43	31	5	5	11	27	42	43
13	Burnley	42	14	2	5	40	29	4	4	13	20	43	42
14	Southampton	42	15	2	4	40	21	0	6	15	14	37	38
15	Hull City	42	11	4	6	33	20	2	8	11	19	48	38
16	Fulham	42	13	3	5	29	17	2	4	15	19	50	37
17	Nottingham Forest	42	11	4	6	50	27	2	5	14	23	47	35
18	Notts County	42	9	7	5	32	22	3	4	14	21	40	35
19	Swansea Town	42	10	9	2	36	19	0	6	15	15	41	35
20	Manchester United	42	9	3	9	29	33	5	3	13	30	52	34
21	Millwall	42	8	8	5	21	17	3	3	15	18	51	33
22	Lincoln City	42	7	7	7	31	23	2	1	18	13	52	26

1934/35

15th in Division Two

	Date		Opponent	Score	Scorers	Att.	Barker D	Barrett C	Bell JC	Blackmore HA	Danskin R	Doran S	Farr TF	Godfrey C	Harrison FP	Lewis TH	Lloyd T	McClelland J	McGrath J	Meek J	Murfin C	Postlethwaite T	Robertson JH	Sellars W	Suggett EJ	Thompson A	Wallbanks J	Ward RA	Wesley JC	Wightman JR
1	Aug	25	BARNSLEY	3-2	Lewis, Suggett, Robertson	14960	10		1	9	5					11	3	4				6	8		7			2		
2	Sep	1	Plymouth Argyle	2-2	Blackmore, Barker	17298	10		1	9	5					11	3	4				6	8		7			2		
3		3	NOTTM. FOREST	1-1	Robertson	8797	10		1	9	5					11	3	4				6	8	7				2		
4		8	NORWICH CITY	1-1	Sellars	9349	10		1	9	5					11	3	4				6	8	7				2		
5		15	Newcastle United	1-0	Robertson	26504	10		1	9	5					11	3	4				6	8		7			2		
6		22	WEST HAM UNITED	1-3	Blackmore	7089	10		1	9	5					11	3	4				6	8		7			2		
7		29	Blackpool	0-1		15354			1	8	5					11	3	4				10			7			2	9	6
8	Oct	4	Nottingham Forest	2-2	Wesley 2	7302			1	10	5					11	3					6	8		7			2	9	4
9		6	BURY	2-1	Blackmore 2	8823			1	10	5					11	3	7				6	8					2	9	4
10		13	Hull City	0-2		10256			1	10	5					11	3	7		8		6						2	9	4
11		20	SHEFFIELD UNITED	1-3	Robertson	11581	10		1					5		11	3	6		8			7					2	9	4
12		27	Bradford City	1-3	Robertson	14234	10		1						6	11	3	5		8			7					2	9	4
13	Nov	3	NOTTS COUNTY	0-0		6581	10	2			5		1			11	3					6	8		7				9	4
14		10	Southampton	1-4	Lewis	9785		2		10	5		1			11	3	8				6	7						9	4
15		17	BOLTON WANDERERS	4-0	* see below	12627				10	5		1		6	11	3	8					7					2	9	4
16		24	Oldham Athletic	1-1	Wesley	5805				10	5		1		6	11	3	8					7					2	9	4
17	Dec	1	BURNLEY	1-1	Wesley	8803				10	5		1		6		3	8	11				7					2	9	4
18		8	Swansea Town	0-0		5892				10	5		1		6		3	8	11				7					2	9	4
19		15	MANCHESTER UNITED	1-2	Robertson	8405				9	5		1			11	3	6	7				8					2	10	4
20		22	Port Vale	1-1	McClelland	6251					5		1	6			3	9	11				8		7			2	10	4
21		25	FULHAM	0-0		11798					5		1	6			3	9	11				8		7			2	10	4
22		26	Fulham	2-2	Wesley, Robertson	26906	10				5		1	6			3		11				8		7			2	9	4
23		29	Barnsley	1-1	Suggett	7783	10			8	5		1	6			3	4	11						7			2	9	
24	Jan	5	PLYMOUTH ARGYLE	2-2	Suggett 2	8836				8	5		1	6		11	3	4	7						9			2	10	
25		19	Norwich City	0-3		10390					5	9	1				3	4				11	8		7			2	10	6
26		30	NEWCASTLE UNITED	1-3	Postlethwaite	4487	10				5		1			11	3	4	7			6	8					2	9	
27	Feb	2	West Ham United	1-2	McGrath	20593	10	3	1		5			4		11		8	7			6						2	9	
28		9	BLACKPOOL	0-0		9019	10	3			5		1	4		11		8	7			6						2	9	
29		16	Bury	4-2	Meek 2, McGrath, Lewis	6731		3			5		1	4		11			7	8		6				9		2	10	
30		23	HULL CITY	1-2	Suggett	6779		3			5		1	4		11			7	8		6			9			2	10	
31	Mar	2	Sheffield United	1-3	Lewis	12056		3			5		1	4		11			7	8		6					9	2	10	
32		9	BRADFORD CITY	2-1	Lewis 2	13685		3			5		1			11		4	6	8					7		9	2	10	
33		16	Notts County	1-1	Wallbanks	9199		3			5		1			11		4	6	8					7		9	2	10	
34		23	SOUTHAMPTON	3-1	Danskin, Suggett, Meek	4038		3			5		1			11		4	6	8					7		9	2	10	
35		30	Bolton Wanderers	2-1	Meek, Lewis	19357		3			5		1			11		4	6	8					7		9	2	10	
36	Apr	6	OLDHAM ATHLETIC	2-0	Wesley, Suggett	6093		3			5		1			11		4	6	8					7		9	2	10	
37		13	Burnley	2-1	Murfin, Suggett	5833		3			5		1					4	6	8	11				7		9	2	10	
38		19	Brentford	0-1		20447		3			5		1			11		4	6	8					7		9	2	10	
39		20	SWANSEA TOWN	3-1	Lewis, Wallbanks, Danskin	5795		3			5		1			11		4	6				8		7		9	2	10	
40		22	BRENTFORD	2-3	Robertson, Lewis	12729		3			5		1			11		4	6				8		7		9	2	10	
41		27	Manchester United	0-2		8606		3			5		1			11		4	6				8		7	9		2	10	
42	May	4	PORT VALE	1-1	Gunn (og)	3634					5		1			11	3	4	6				8		7		9	2	10	

Scorers in game 15: Robertson, Wesley, Blackmore, McClelland

	Barker D	Barrett C	Bell JC	Blackmore HA	Danskin R	Doran S	Farr TF	Godfrey C	Harrison FP	Lewis TH	Lloyd T	McClelland J	McGrath J	Meek J	Murfin C	Postlethwaite T	Robertson JH	Sellars W	Suggett EJ	Thompson A	Wallbanks J	Ward RA	Wesley JC	Wightman JR
Apps	14	17	13	18	40	1	29	11	5	34	27	36	25	13	1	19	26	2	25	2	11	40	36	17
Goals	1			5	2					9		2	2	4	1	1	9	1	8		2		7	

One own goal

F.A. Cup

	Date		Opponent	Score	Scorers	Att.	Barker D	Barrett C	Bell JC	Blackmore HA	Danskin R	Doran S	Farr TF	Godfrey C	Harrison FP	Lewis TH	Lloyd T	McClelland J	McGrath J	Meek J	Murfin C	Postlethwaite T	Robertson JH	Sellars W	Suggett EJ	Thompson A	Wallbanks J	Ward RA	Wesley JC	Wightman JR
R3	Jan	12	Leeds United	1-4	Suggett	35400				8	5		1				3	4	7			11			9			2	10	6

		P	W	D	L	F	A	W	D	L	F	A	Pts
1	Brentford	42	19	2	0	59	14	7	7	7	34	34	61
2	Bolton Wanderers	42	17	1	3	63	15	9	3	9	33	33	56
3	West Ham United	42	18	1	2	46	17	8	3	10	34	46	56
4	Blackpool	42	16	4	1	46	18	5	7	9	33	39	53
5	Manchester United	42	16	2	3	50	21	7	2	12	26	34	50
6	Newcastle United	42	14	2	5	55	25	8	2	11	34	43	48
7	Fulham	42	15	3	3	62	26	2	9	10	14	30	46
8	Plymouth Argyle	42	13	3	5	48	26	6	5	10	27	38	46
9	Nottingham Forest	42	12	5	4	46	23	5	3	13	30	47	42
10	Bury	42	14	1	6	38	26	5	3	13	24	47	42
11	Sheffield United	42	11	4	6	51	30	5	5	11	28	40	41
12	Burnley	42	11	2	8	43	32	5	7	9	20	41	41
13	Hull City	42	9	6	6	32	22	7	2	12	31	52	40
14	Norwich City	42	11	6	4	51	23	3	5	13	20	38	39
15	BRADFORD	42	7	8	6	32	28	4	8	9	23	35	38
16	Barnsley	42	8	10	3	32	22	5	2	14	28	61	38
17	Swansea Town	42	13	5	3	41	22	1	3	17	15	45	36
18	Port Vale	42	10	7	4	42	28	1	5	15	13	46	34
19	Southampton	42	9	8	4	28	19	2	4	15	18	56	34
20	Bradford City	42	10	7	4	34	20	2	1	18	16	48	32
21	Oldham Athletic	42	10	3	8	44	40	0	3	18	12	55	26
22	Notts County	42	8	3	10	29	33	1	4	16	17	64	25

1935/36

16th in Division Two

No	Month	Day	Opponent	Score	Scorers	Att.	Barker D	Barrett C	Bell JC	Danskin R	Doran S	Farr TF	Harrison FP	Johnstone R	Lewis TH	Lloyd T	Marshall W	McClelland J	McGrath J	Meek J	Murfin C	Nolan TG	Robertson JH	Sanaghan J	Strange AH	Suggett EJ	Talbot AD	Tewkesbury KC	Thompson A	Ward RA	Wesley JC	Whyte C	Wright D
1	Aug	31	Newcastle United	3-3	Lewis 2, Nolan	27843									11				6			9	8		4	7	5	1		2		3	10
2	Sep	2	WEST HAM UNITED	2-0	Nolan, Robertson	16224				5					11				6			9	8		4	7		1		2		3	10
3		7	SHEFFIELD UNITED	3-3	Nolan, Lewis, Suggett	18850									11				6			9	8		4	7	5	1		2		3	10
4		9	West Ham United	0-1		17709												4	6			9	8			7	5	1		2	11	3	10
5		14	Southampton	0-3		15318								11				4	6			9	8			7	5	1		2		3	10
6		16	SWANSEA TOWN	1-1	Wright	7931				5				11				4	6			9	8			7		1		2		3	10
7		21	NORWICH CITY	1-0	Robertson	10719				5				7	11	3			6			9	8		4			1		2			10
8		28	Nottingham Forest	0-2		10885				5				7	11	3			6				8		4			1		2	9		10
9	Oct	5	BLACKPOOL	3-2	Robertson 2, Talbot	11410							6	7	11	3		4				9	8				5	1		2			10
10		12	Doncaster Rovers	2-3	Nolan 2	13989				5			6	7	11	3		4				9	8					1		2	10		
11		19	Tottenham Hotspur	0-4		37796						1		7	4	3		6			11	9	8				5			2			10
12		26	MANCHESTER UNITED	1-0	McClelland	12216				5		1		7	11	3		6				9	8		4					2			10
13	Nov	2	Port Vale	2-3	Nolan, Johnstone	8571				5		1		7	11	3		6				9	8		4					2			10
14		9	FULHAM	1-1	Robertson	8905				5		1		7	11	3		6				9	8		4					2			10
15		16	Burnley	1-1	McClelland	10047				5		1		7	11	3		4	6	8		9								2			10
16		23	BRADFORD CITY	1-1	Meek	22321				5		1		7	11	3		4	6	8		9								2			10
17		30	Hull City	1-1	Denby (og)	5557				5		1		7	11	3		4	6	8		9								2			10
18	Dec	7	BARNSLEY	3-0	Meek, Wesley 2	9774				5	7	1			11	3		4	6	8									9	2	10		
19		14	Plymouth Argyle	0-2		14673		3		5	7	1			11			4	6	8									9	2	10		
20		21	CHARLTON ATHLETIC	3-0	Meek, Thompson, Lewis	8707				5	7	1			11	3		4	6	8									9	2	10		
21		25	Leicester City	0-5		18097				5	7	1			11	3		4	6	8									9	2	10		
22		28	NEWCASTLE UNITED	3-2	Wesley 3	12609			1	5	7				11	3		4	6	8		9								2	10		
23	Jan	1	LEICESTER CITY	3-1	Meek 2, Lewis	9218			1	5	7				11	3		4	6	8		9								2	10		
24		4	Sheffield United	1-2	Nolan	23634			1	5	7				11	3		4	6	8		9								2	10		
25		18	SOUTHAMPTON	2-1	Meek, Nolan	8549				5	7				11	3		4	6	8		9						1		2	10		
26	Feb	1	NOTTM. FOREST	1-4	Meek	12369				5	7		6		11	3				8		9			4			1		2	10		
27		8	Blackpool	2-4	Barker 2	9936	10		1		7					3	5		6	8	11	9			4					2			
28		22	TOTTENHAM HOTSPUR	2-5	McClelland, Nolan	6987			1	5	7					3		4	6	8	11	9								2	10		
29		26	DONCASTER ROVERS	3-1	Barker, Doran, Nolan	4237	10			5	7				11			4	6	8		9						1		2		3	
30	Mar	4	Barnsley	1-5	Barker	5929	10			5	7				11			4	6	8		9						1		2		3	
31		7	BURNLEY	2-0	Barker 2	5120	10		1	5	7				11	3		4	6	8									9	2			
32		14	Fulham	1-4	Lewis	16792	10	2	1	5	7				11	3		4	6	8		9											
33		21	PORT VALE	3-0	Lewis 2, Nolan	4332	10	2	1	5	7				11	3			6			9		4									8
34		28	Bradford City	1-2	Nolan	16066		2	1	5	7				11	3		4	6			9									10		8
35	Apr	4	HULL CITY	2-1	Barker 2	4746	10	2		5	7	1			11	3		4	6			9											8
36		10	Bury	0-1		6493	10			5	7	1			11	2		4	6			9										3	8
37		11	Manchester United	0-4		33517	10			5	7	1				3	4		6		11	9	8	2									
38		13	BURY	1-1	Robertson	5716	10				7	1			11	3	5	4	6			9	8	2									
39		18	PLYMOUTH ARGYLE	2-2	McClelland, Wesley	5774	10				7	1		4	11	3	2	5	6				8								9		
40		25	Charlton Athletic	1-3	Nolan	20682	10	2		5	7	1		4	11	3			6			9									8		
41		30	Norwich City	1-4	Nolan	9263	10			5	7	1		4	11	3			6			9		2							8		
42	May	2	Swansea Town	2-1	Robertson, Lewis	5471	10			5	7	1		2	11	3		4	6			9	8										
						Apps	14	6	9	33	25	19	3	17	36	33	4	31	35	18	4	35	18	4	10	6	6	14	5	31	17	9	20
						Goals	8				1			1	9			4		7		14	7			1	1		1		6		1

One own goal

F.A. Cup

Rd	Month	Day	Opponent	Score	Scorers	Att.	Barker D	Barrett C	Bell JC	Danskin R	Doran S	Farr TF	Harrison FP	Johnstone R	Lewis TH	Lloyd T	Marshall W	McClelland J	McGrath J	Meek J	Murfin C	Nolan TG	Robertson JH	Sanaghan J	Strange AH	Suggett EJ	Talbot AD	Tewkesbury KC	Thompson A	Ward RA	Wesley JC	Whyte C	Wright D
R3	Jan	11	WORKINGTON	3-2	Lewis, Nolan, Doran	10706			1	5	7				11	3		4	6	8		9								2	10		
R4	Jan	29	WEST BROMWICH ALB.	1-1	Wesley	14938				5	7				11	3		4	6	8		9						1		2	10		
rep	Feb	3	West Bromwich Albion	1-1	Meek	27503			1	5	7					3		4	6	8	11	9								2	10		
rep2		10	West Bromwich Albion	2-0	Nolan, Doran	11685			1	5	7					3		4	6	8	11	9								2	10		
R5		15	TOTTENHAM HOTSPUR	0-0		24053			1	5	7					3		4	6	8	11	9								2	10		
rep	Feb	17	Tottenham Hotspur	1-2	Nolan	35442			1	5	7					3		4	6	8	11	9								2	10		

R4 replay a.e.t. R4 replay 2 at Old Trafford

A subdued cover for the programme of January 25 1936, after the death of King George V.

		P	W	D	L	F	A	W	D	L	F	A	Pts
1	Manchester United	42	16	3	2	55	16	6	9	6	30	27	56
2	Charlton Athletic	42	15	6	0	53	17	7	5	9	32	41	55
3	Sheffield United	42	15	4	2	51	15	5	8	8	28	35	52
4	West Ham United	42	13	5	3	51	23	9	3	9	39	45	52
5	Tottenham Hotspur	42	12	6	3	60	25	6	7	8	31	30	49
6	Leicester City	42	14	5	2	53	19	5	5	11	26	38	48
7	Plymouth Argyle	42	15	2	4	50	20	5	6	10	21	37	48
8	Newcastle United	42	13	5	3	56	27	7	1	13	32	52	46
9	Fulham	42	11	6	4	58	24	4	8	9	18	28	44
10	Blackpool	42	14	3	4	64	34	4	4	13	29	38	43
11	Norwich City	42	14	2	5	47	24	3	7	11	25	41	43
12	Bradford City	42	12	7	2	32	18	3	6	12	23	47	43
13	Swansea Town	42	11	3	7	42	26	4	6	11	25	50	39
14	Bury	42	10	6	5	41	27	3	6	12	25	57	38
15	Burnley	42	9	8	4	35	21	3	5	13	15	38	37
16	BRADFORD	42	13	6	2	43	26	1	3	17	19	58	37
17	Southampton	42	11	3	7	32	24	3	6	12	15	41	37
18	Doncaster Rovers	42	10	7	4	28	17	4	2	15	23	54	37
19	Nottingham Forest	42	8	8	5	43	22	4	3	14	26	54	35
20	Barnsley	42	9	4	8	40	32	3	5	13	14	48	33
21	Port Vale	42	10	5	6	34	30	2	3	16	22	76	32
22	Hull City	42	4	7	10	33	45	1	3	17	14	66	20

1936/37

20th in Division Two

			Opponent	Score	Scorers	Att.	Bailey LA	Barker D	Breakwell T	Cainey WP	Danskin R	Doran S	Farr TF	Flowers GA	Foulkes JB	Green GF	Harvey JH	Johnstone R	Jones H	Lewis AN	Lewis TH	Lloyd T	Marshall W	Martin WJ	McGrath J	McPhee MG	Nolan TG	Picken W	Robertson JH	Ross AC	Sharp W	Stabb GH	Thompson A	Wesley JC
1	Aug	29	BRADFORD CITY	2-1	Robertson, Thompson	19005		10			5	7	1					2			11	3			6				8		4		9	
2		31	Leicester City	0-5		8036		10			5	7	1					2			11	3			6				8		4		9	
3	Sep	5	Barnsley	1-2	Foulkes	10387		10			5		1	4	7			2			11	3			6				8				9	
4		9	LEICESTER CITY	1-2	Danskin	9223		10		11	5			4	7					1		2			6		9	3						8
5		12	SHEFFIELD UNITED	0-3		8678	4			11					7					1		2	5		6			3	8			9		10
6		14	NEWCASTLE UNITED	0-3		7921	6					9	1	4	7			2			11	3										8	5	10
7		19	Tottenham Hotspur	1-5	Robertson	33177				11		9	1	6	7			2				3	5						8		4	10		
8		26	BLACKPOOL	2-1	Barker, Robertson	11256		10		11	5		1	4	7			2				3			6				8			9		
9	Oct	3	Blackburn Rovers	1-1	Cainey	13610		10		11	5		1	4	7			2				3			6				8			9		
10		10	BURY	0-1		12249	4	10		11	5		1		7			2				3			6				8			9		
11		17	ASTON VILLA	3-3	Hardy (og), Wesley, Stabb	12001	4	8			5		1		7			2			11	3			6							9		10
12		24	Chesterfield	2-4	Barker, Wesley	13263	4	8			5		1		7			2			11	3			6							9		10
13		31	NOTTM. FOREST	3-2	Munro (og), McPhee 2	11902	4	8			5		1		7			2							6	9		3				10		11
14	Nov	7	Plymouth Argyle	0-2		11372	4	8			5		1		7			2			11				6	9		3						10
15		14	COVENTRY CITY	1-3	McPhee	9292	4	8			5		1		7			2			11				6	9		3						10
16		21	Doncaster Rovers	3-1	McPhee 2, Barker	9729	4	8	6		5	7	1					2			11	3				9								10
17		28	FULHAM	1-1	Doran	10192	4	8	6		5	7	1					2			11	3				9								10
18	Dec	5	Burnley	2-2	McPhee 2	7360	4		6		5	7	1					2			11	3				9			8					10
19		12	SOUTHAMPTON	3-1	Robertson 2, McPhee	7441	4		6		5	7	1					2			11	3				9			8					10
20		19	Swansea Town	0-3		7193	4		6		5	7	1					2			11	3				9			8					10
21		25	WEST HAM UNITED	2-1	McPhee, Bailey	17203	4		6		5				7			2	1			3				9			8			10		11
22		26	Bradford City	3-2	McPhee 2, Wesley	28236	4		6	11	5				7			3	1							9			8		2			10
23		28	West Ham United	0-1		12901	4		6	11	5				7			3	1							9			8		2			10
24	Jan	1	Newcastle United	1-1	Robertson	29327	4	10	6	11					7			3	1				5			9			8		2			
25		2	BARNSLEY	2-1	McPhee 2	6636	4		6	11					7			3	1				5			9			8		2			10
26		9	Sheffield United	0-3		17274	4		6	11	5				7			3	1							9			8		2			10
27		23	TOTTENHAM HOTSPUR	3-2	Lewis 2, McPhee	7481	4		6		5				7			3	1		11					9			8		2			10
28		30	Blackpool	0-6		8923	4		6		5				7			3	1		11					9			8		2			10
29	Feb	6	BLACKBURN ROVERS	1-2	Lewis	11419	4		6		5				7	8		2	1		11	3				9								10
30		13	Bury	1-3	McPhee	8681					2	7				8		3	1		11		5	10	6	9						4		
31		20	Aston Villa	1-4	Foulkes	28775			6		2		1		7			3			11		5	8		9						4		10
32		27	CHESTERFIELD	4-5	* See below	9198					5		1	6	7			2			11	3				9			8			4		10
33	Mar	6	Nottingham Forest	2-3	Martin, Robertson	10809					5	7	1	6				3			11			10		9			8		2	4		
34		13	PLYMOUTH ARGYLE	0-0		7337					9	7	1	6				3			11		5	10		8					2	4		
35		20	Coventry City	0-4		15726					8	7	1	6				3			11		5	10		9				2		4		
36		27	DONCASTER ROVERS	1-0	McPhee	9458			6		5		1		7			3			11					9			8	2		4		10
37		29	Norwich City	1-3	Sharp	25267			6		5		1		7						11	3		8		9				2	4			10
38		30	NORWICH CITY	1-0	Lewis	9681			4		5	7	1					3			11				6	9			8	2				10
39	Apr	3	Fulham	0-0		12813					5	7	1					3			11				6	9			8	2	4			10
40		10	BURNLEY	2-0	McPhee, Wesley	9697					5	7	1				8	3			11				6	9				2	4			10
41		17	Southampton	0-0		9584					5	7	1				8	3			11				6	9				2	4			10
42		24	SWANSEA TOWN	1-1	Doran	11590					5	7	1				8	3			11				6	9				2	4			10
						Apps	22	15	18	11	37	18	30	10	26	2	3	39	10	2	29	21	8	6	19	30	1	5	24	8	17	17	4	30
						Goals	1	3		1	1	2		1	2						4			1		18			9		1	1	1	4

Scorers in game 32: Flowers, Robertson 2, McPhee

Two own goals

F.A. Cup

			Opponent	Score	Scorers	Att.	Bailey LA	Barker D	Breakwell T	Cainey WP	Danskin R	Doran S	Farr TF	Flowers GA	Foulkes JB	Green GF	Harvey JH	Johnstone R	Jones H	Lewis AN	Lewis TH	Lloyd T	Marshall W	Martin WJ	McGrath J	McPhee MG	Nolan TG	Picken W	Robertson JH	Ross AC	Sharp W	Stabb GH	Thompson A	Wesley JC
R3	Jan	16	DERBY COUNTY	0-4		21155	4		6	11	5				7			3	1							9			8		2			10

		P	W	D	L	F	A	W	D	L	F	A	Pts
1	Leicester City	42	14	4	3	56	26	10	4	7	33	31	56
2	Blackpool	42	13	4	4	49	19	11	3	7	39	34	55
3	Bury	42	13	4	4	46	26	9	4	8	28	29	52
4	Newcastle United	42	11	3	7	45	23	11	2	8	35	33	49
5	Plymouth Argyle	42	11	6	4	42	22	7	7	7	29	31	49
6	West Ham United	42	14	5	2	47	18	5	6	10	26	37	49
7	Sheffield United	42	16	4	1	48	14	2	6	13	18	40	46
8	Coventry City	42	11	5	5	35	19	6	6	9	31	35	45
9	Aston Villa	42	10	6	5	47	30	6	6	9	35	40	44
10	Tottenham Hotspur	42	13	3	5	57	26	4	6	11	31	40	43
11	Fulham	42	11	5	5	43	24	4	8	9	28	37	43
12	Blackburn Rovers	42	11	3	7	49	32	5	7	9	21	30	42
13	Burnley	42	11	5	5	37	20	5	5	11	20	41	42
14	Barnsley	42	11	6	4	30	23	5	3	13	20	41	41
15	Chesterfield	42	12	3	6	54	34	4	5	12	30	55	40
16	Swansea Town	42	14	2	5	40	16	1	5	15	10	49	37
17	Norwich City	42	8	6	7	38	29	6	2	13	25	42	36
18	Nottingham Forest	42	10	6	5	42	30	2	4	15	26	60	34
19	Southampton	42	10	8	3	38	25	1	4	16	15	52	34
20	BRADFORD	42	10	4	7	33	33	2	5	14	19	55	33
21	Bradford City	42	8	8	5	36	31	1	4	16	18	63	30
22	Doncaster Rovers	42	6	6	9	18	29	1	4	16	12	55	24

1937/38

7th in Division Two

No.	Month	Day	Opponent	Score	Scorers	Att	Cringan JA	Danskin R	Doran S	Doyle W	Farr TF	Foulkes JB	Gallon JW	Graham A	Hallard W	Henson GH	Johnstone R	Keeling AJ	Law WGMcK	Lewis TH	Lindley U	Marshall W	Martin WJ	McCall J	McGrath J	Picken W	Robertson JH	Ross AC	Stabb GH	Wesley JC
1	Aug	28	BARNSLEY	4-3	Lewis 2, Henson 2	12802		5	7		1					9	3			11					6		8	2	4	10
2	Sep	1	Norwich City	1-1	Robertson	17491		5	7		1					9	3			11					6		8	2	4	10
3		4	West Ham United	1-3	Robertson	22467		5	7		1					9	3			11	2				6		8		4	10
4		6	NORWICH CITY	3-0	Robertson 2, Lewis	7678		5			1	7			6	9	3			11	2						8		4	10
5		11	SOUTHAMPTON	2-0	Martin, Henson	10845		5			1	7			6	9	3				2		10				8		4	11
6		13	Swansea Town	1-0	Henson	8268		5			1	7			6	9	3				2		10				8		4	11
7		18	Blackburn Rovers	0-0		15167		5			1	7			6	9	3				2		10				8		4	11
8		25	SHEFFIELD WEDNESDAY	1-1	Hallard	17674		5			1	7			6	9	3				2		10				8		4	11
9	Oct	2	Fulham	1-1	Robertson	15136		5			1	7			6	9	3			11	2						8		4	10
10		9	PLYMOUTH ARGYLE	2-0	Robertson, Lewis	12748		5			1	7			6	9	3			11	2						8		4	10
11		16	LUTON TOWN	1-1	Henson	15397		5	7		1				6	9	3			11	2						8		4	10
12		23	Newcastle United	0-3		21280		5	7		1				6	9	3			11	2		10				8		4	
13		30	NOTTM. FOREST	2-2	Foulkes, Lewis	9801					1	7		8	6	9	3			11	2	5	10						4	
14	Nov	6	Coventry City	0-0		29604		5			1	7		8	6	9	3			11	2		10						4	
15		13	BURY	1-1	Lewis	10683		5			1	7		8	6	9	3			11	2		10						4	
16		20	Sheffield United	1-3	Lewis	19162		5			1	7			6	9	3			11	2		10				8		4	
17		27	TOTTENHAM HOTSPUR	3-1	Lewis, Hallard, Wesley	10794		5			1				6	9	3			11	2		8				7		4	10
18	Dec	4	Burnley	1-1	Lewis	9453		5			1				6	9	3			11	2		8				7		4	10
19		11	MANCHESTER UNITED	4-0	Lewis, Wesley, Henson, og	12004		5			1				6	9	3			11	2		8				7		4	10
20		18	Stockport County	2-1	Wesley, Henson	10375		5			1				6	9	3			11	2		8				7		4	10
21		27	ASTON VILLA	1-2	Lewis	20129		5			1				6	9	3			11	2		8				7		4	10
22	Jan	1	Barnsley	1-0	Henson	16654		5			1				6	9				11	2		8			3	7		4	10
23		15	WEST HAM UNITED	2-1	C Walker (og), Henson	8611		5	3		1				6	9				11	2		8				7		4	10
24		29	BLACKBURN ROVERS	7-1	Henson 6, Martin	11730		5			1	7			6	9				11	2		8					3	4	10
25	Feb	2	Southampton	1-2	Lewis	7960		5			1	7			6	9				11	2		8					3	4	10
26		5	Sheffield Wednesday	0-1		24838		5			1	7		4		9				11	2		8		6			3		10
27		16	FULHAM	1-2	Lewis	6394		5			1	7			6	9	3			11			8					2	4	10
28		19	Plymouth Argyle	0-1		15349	4	5		9	1	7	10	8			3			11								2	6	
29		26	Luton Town	2-4	Lewis, Henson	14494	4				1	7			6	9	3			11			8					2	5	10
30	Mar	5	NEWCASTLE UNITED	2-0	Doran, Henson	12187	4	5	7		1			8		9	3			11								2	6	10
31		12	Nottingham Forest	0-1		13924	4	5	7		1					9	3			11			8					2	6	10
32		19	COVENTRY CITY	0-1		10675	4	5			1	7	9	6			3			11			8					2		10
33		26	Bury	1-5	Henson	8344	4	5			1					9	3	7		11			8					2	6	10
34	Apr	2	SHEFFIELD UNITED	5-1	Henson 3, Law, Lewis	11191		5			1		8		6	7	2		9	11						3			4	10
35		9	Tottenham Hotspur	1-2	Lewis	17967		5			1		8		6	7	2		9	11						3			4	10
36		15	Chesterfield	3-0	Lewis 3	13404		5	7		1		8		6	9	2			11				10		3			4	
37		16	BURNLEY	3-1	Lewis, McCall, Henson	10180		5	7		1		8		6	9	2			11				10		3			4	
38		18	CHESTERFIELD	3-2	Henson 2, Lewis	8676		5			1		8		6	9	2			11				10		3			4	7
39		23	Manchester United	1-3	Lewis	28919		5			1		8		6	9	2			11				10		3			4	7
40		27	Aston Villa	0-2		41966		5			1	7	8		6	9	2			11						3			4	10
41		30	STOCKPORT COUNTY	4-1	Henson 3, Lewis	6215		5			1	7			6	9	2			11			8			3			4	10
42	May	7	SWANSEA TOWN	0-1		7021		5			1	7			6	9	2			11			8			3			4	10
						Apps	6	40	10	1	42	21	9	7	33	40	37	1	2	38	24	1	26	4	4	10	20	12	40	34
						Goals			1			1			2	27			1	23			2	1			6			3

Two own goals

F.A. Cup

Round	Month	Day	Opponent	Score	Scorers	Att	Cringan JA	Danskin R	Doran S	Doyle W	Farr TF	Foulkes JB	Gallon JW	Graham A	Hallard W	Henson GH	Johnstone R	Keeling AJ	Law WGMcK	Lewis TH	Lindley U	Marshall W	Martin WJ	McCall J	McGrath J	Picken W	Robertson JH	Ross AC	Stabb GH	Wesley JC
R3	Jan	8	NEWPORT COUNTY	7-4	Martin, Henson 4, Lewis 2	12710		5			1				6	9				11	2		8			3	7		4	10
R4		22	STOKE CITY	1-1	Wesley	31347		5			1				6	9	3			11	2		8				7		4	10
rep		26	Stoke City	2-1	Stabb, Henson	30680		5			1	7			6	9				11	2		8					3	4	10
R5	Feb	12	Sunderland	0-1		59326		5			1	7			6	9	3			11			8					2	4	10

		P	*W*	*D*	*L*	*F*	*A*	*W*	*D*	*L*	*F*	*A*	*Pts*
1	Aston Villa	42	17	2	2	50	12	8	5	8	23	23	57
2	Manchester United	42	15	3	3	50	18	7	6	8	32	32	53
3	Sheffield United	42	15	4	2	46	19	7	5	9	27	37	53
4	Coventry City	42	12	5	4	31	15	8	7	6	35	30	52
5	Tottenham Hotspur	42	14	3	4	46	16	5	3	13	30	38	44
6	Burnley	42	15	4	2	35	11	2	6	13	19	43	44
7	BRADFORD	42	13	4	4	51	22	4	5	12	18	34	43
8	Fulham	42	10	7	4	44	23	6	4	11	17	34	43
9	West Ham United	42	13	5	3	34	16	1	9	11	19	36	42
10	Bury	42	12	3	6	43	26	6	2	13	20	34	41
11	Chesterfield	42	12	2	7	39	24	4	7	10	24	39	41
12	Luton Town	42	10	6	5	53	36	5	4	12	36	50	40
13	Plymouth Argyle	42	10	7	4	40	30	4	5	12	17	35	40
14	Norwich City	42	11	5	5	35	28	3	6	12	21	47	39
15	Southampton	42	12	6	3	42	26	3	3	15	13	51	39
16	Blackburn Rovers	42	13	6	2	51	30	1	4	16	20	50	38
17	Sheffield Wednesday	42	10	5	6	27	21	4	5	12	22	35	38
18	Swansea Town	42	12	6	3	31	21	1	6	14	14	52	38
19	Newcastle United	42	12	4	5	38	18	2	4	15	13	40	36
20	Nottingham Forest	42	12	3	6	29	21	2	5	14	18	39	36
21	Barnsley	42	7	11	3	30	20	4	3	14	20	44	36
22	Stockport County	42	8	6	7	24	24	3	3	15	19	46	31

1938/39

17th in Division Two

			Opponent	Score	Scorers	Att.	Brown J	Bruce R	Danskin R	Davies J	Farr TF	Gallon JW	Hallard W	Hays CJ	Henson GH	Johnstone R	Jones TC	Kaye G	Kelly JE	Lewis TH	Lindley U	Martin WJ	McCall J	McGarry T	Padgett JM	Paton HM	Phillips D	Picken W	Smith FA	Stabb GH	Wesley JC
1	Aug	27	Norwich City	3-1	Martin, Lewis, Wesley	16443			5		1		6		9	3				11	2	8				7				4	10
2		29	SWANSEA TOWN	1-1	Paton	9339			5		1		6		9	3				11	2	8				7				4	10
3	Sep	3	MANCHESTER CITY	4-2	Gallon, Martin, Wesley, Stabb	16738			5		1	11	6		9	3					2	8				7				4	10
4		10	Millwall	1-3	Henson	27812			5		1		6		9	3				11	2	8				7				4	10
5		17	BLACKBURN ROVERS	0-4		13608			5	7	1		6		9	2				11		8						3		4	10
6		19	TRANMERE ROVERS	3-0	Lewis, Smith, Martin	5120			5	7	1		6			3			2	11		8							9	4	10
7		24	Fulham	0-4		17607			5	7	1		6			3			2	11		8							9	4	10
8	Oct	1	SHEFFIELD WEDNESDAY	3-1	Lewis 2, Martin	13002			5		1		6		9	3				11	2	8	10			7				4	
9		8	Bury	1-0	Lewis	8936			5		1		6		9	3				11	2	8	10			7				4	
10		15	Luton Town	2-2	Henson, McCall	14955			5		1		6		9	3				11	2	8	10			7				4	
11		22	PLYMOUTH ARGYLE	2-2	Lewis, Hallard	10807			5		1		6		9	3				11	2	8	10			7				4	
12		29	Newcastle United	0-1		40758			5		1		6		9	3				11	2	8	10			7				4	
13	Nov	5	BURNLEY	2-2	Smith 2	12408			5		1		6		7	3				11	2	8	10						9	4	
14		12	Tottenham Hotspur	2-2	Martin, Smith	24132			5		1		6			3				11	2	8	10			7			9	4	
15		19	SOUTHAMPTON	2-1	McCall, Lewis	10748					1		6			3		5		11	2	8	10			7			9	4	
16		26	Coventry City	1-3	Lewis	17263				7	1		6			3		5		11	2	8	10						9	4	
17	Dec	3	NOTTM. FOREST	1-2	Henson	8945					1		6		9	3	7	5		11	2	8								4	10
18		10	Sheffield United	1-3	Smith	20304			5	7	1		6			3				11	2	8	10						9	4	
19		17	WEST BROMWICH ALB.	4-4	Smith 3, Gallon	8637			5		1	7	6	11							2	8	10					3	9	4	
20		24	NORWICH CITY	3-0	Smith 3	8766			5		1	7	6	11							2	8	10					3	9	4	
21		26	CHESTERFIELD	0-0		15236			5		1	7	6	11							2		10					3	9	4	8
22		27	Chesterfield	2-2	Wesley, McCall	17211		10			1	7	5	11							2		8					3	9	4	6
23		31	Manchester City	1-5	Padgett	33741					1	7	5	11							2		10		8			3	9	4	6
24	Jan	2	Tranmere Rovers	1-2	Hallard	9523					1	7	6	11							2		10				5	3	9	4	8
25		14	MILLWALL	1-0	Smith	7118					1	7	5	11	9	2							10					3	8	4	6
26		23	Blackburn Rovers	4-6	Smith 2, Henson, Stabb	7547			5		1	7	6	11	9	2												3	8	4	10
27		28	FULHAM	1-5	Wesley	8722					1	7	5	11	9	2							10					3	8	4	6
28	Feb	4	Sheffield Wednesday	0-2		25452			5		1	7	6	11	9						2		10					3	8	4	
29		11	BURY	3-2	Henson, Smith 2	9059	4		5		1	7		11	9						2		10					3	8	6	
30		18	LUTON TOWN	2-1	Henson, Smith	8215	4		5		1	7		11	9	3					2		10						8	6	
31		25	Plymouth Argyle	1-4	Gallon	14424	4		5		1	7		11	9	3					2		10						8	6	
32	Mar	4	NEWCASTLE UNITED	0-1		10148	4		5		1	7	6		9	3					2		10						8		11
33		11	Burnley	0-0		8473	4		5		1		6	11							2		8	7				3	9		10
34		18	TOTTENHAM HOTSPUR	0-0		8202	4		5		1	11	6								2		8	7				3	9		10
35		25	Southampton	2-3	McGarry 2	9679	4		5		1	7	6	11							2	8	10	9				3			
36	Apr	1	COVENTRY CITY	0-2		7166	4		5		1	7	6	11							2	8	10	9				3			
37		7	West Ham United	2-0	Gallon, Smith	23336	4		5		1	7									2	10		9				3	8	6	11
38		8	Nottingham Forest	0-2		13351	4		5		1	7									2	10		9				3	8	6	11
39		11	WEST HAM UNITED	1-2	Smith	9177	4		5		1	7									2	10		9				3	8	6	11
40		15	SHEFFIELD UNITED	0-3		8954			5		1	7	4	11		3					2	8							9	6	10
41		22	West Bromwich Albion	2-0	Smith, Wesley	6950	4		5		1		6			3					2	10		9		7			8		11
42		29	Swansea Town	2-2	Smith, Hallard	7393	4		5		1		6			3					2	10		9		7			8		11
						Apps	13	1	34	5	42	22	36	17	20	27	1	3	2	17	36	28	27	9	1	13	1	19	29	35	24
						Goals						4	3		6					8		5	3	2	1	1			21	2	5

F.A. Cup

			Opponent	Score	Scorers	Att.	Brown J	Bruce R	Danskin R	Davies J	Farr TF	Gallon JW	Hallard W	Hays CJ	Henson GH	Johnstone R	Jones TC	Kaye G	Kelly JE	Lewis TH	Lindley U	Martin WJ	McCall J	McGarry T	Padgett JM	Paton HM	Phillips D	Picken W	Smith FA	Stabb GH	Wesley JC
R3	Jan	7	Wolverhampton Wan.	1-3	Gallon	23845					1	7	5	11	9	3					2		10						8	4	6

		P	W	D	L	F	A	W	D	L	F	A	Pts
1	Blackburn Rovers	42	17	1	3	59	23	8	4	9	35	37	55
2	Sheffield United	42	9	9	3	35	15	11	5	5	34	26	54
3	Sheffield Wednesday	42	14	4	3	47	18	7	7	7	41	41	53
4	Coventry City	42	13	4	4	35	13	8	4	9	27	32	50
5	Manchester City	42	13	3	5	56	35	8	4	9	40	37	49
6	Chesterfield	42	16	1	4	54	20	4	8	9	15	32	49
7	Luton Town	42	13	4	4	47	27	9	1	11	35	39	49
8	Tottenham Hotspur	42	13	6	2	48	27	6	3	12	19	35	47
9	Newcastle United	42	13	3	5	44	21	5	7	9	17	27	46
10	West Bromwich Albion	42	15	3	3	54	22	3	6	12	35	50	45
11	West Ham United	42	10	5	6	36	21	7	5	9	34	31	44
12	Fulham	42	12	5	4	35	20	5	5	11	26	35	44
13	Millwall	42	12	6	3	44	18	2	8	11	20	35	42
14	Burnley	42	13	3	5	32	20	2	6	13	18	36	39
15	Plymouth Argyle	42	9	7	5	24	13	6	1	14	25	42	38
16	Bury	42	9	5	7	48	36	3	8	10	17	38	37
17	BRADFORD	42	8	6	7	33	35	4	5	12	28	47	35
18	Southampton	42	9	6	6	35	34	4	3	14	21	48	35
19	Swansea Town	42	8	6	7	33	30	3	6	12	17	53	34
20	Nottingham Forest	42	8	6	7	33	29	2	5	14	16	53	31
21	Norwich City	42	10	5	6	39	29	3	0	18	11	62	31
22	Tranmere Rovers	42	6	4	11	26	38	0	1	20	13	61	17

1939/40

Football League (games 1 to 3), Regional League North East Division (games 4 to 17, 20 to 24), League Cup (games 18, 19)

#	Month	Day	Opponent	Score	Att											
1	Aug	26	Chesterfield	0-2	11679	Farr	Johnstone	Hepworth	Brown	Danskin	Stabb	Hughes	Martin	Smith FA	Wesley	Cochrane
2		30	LUTON TOWN	0-3	7319	Farr	Stephen	Hepworth	Stabb	Danskin	Dann	Hughes	McKenzie	McGarry	Norton	Cochrane
3	Sep	2	MILLWALL	2-2	6319	Farr	Stephen	Hepworth	Stabb	Danskin	Hallard	Hughes	McGarry 1	Smith FA	Watson 1	Cochrane
4	Oct	21	Huddersfield Town	1-4	3862	Farr	Ward	Hepworth	Stabb	Danskin	Kaye	Johnstone	McGarry 1	Smith FA	Watson	Cochrane
5	Nov	4	Bradford City	3-4	3495	Farr	Stephen	Carr	Stabb	Danskin	Kaye	Johnstone	Smith FA 1	McGarry	Wesley 1	Cochrane 1
6		11	MIDDLESBROUGH	3-0	4634	Gilroy	Stephen	Carr	Gordon	Danskin	Smith G	Davis	McCall	McGarry 1	Wesley 2	Cochrane
7		18	Newcastle United	3-2	5700	Gilroy	Stephen	Carr	Stabb	Danskin	Smith G	Davis	Martin	McGarry 1	Wesley 1	Juliussen 1
8		25	HULL CITY	2-1	1259	Gilroy	Stephen	Johnstone	Stabb	Danskin	Smith G	Davis	Martin	Watson	Wesley 1	Juliussen 1
9	Dec	9	LEEDS UNITED	3-1	3546	Gilroy	Stephen	Carr	Stabb	Danskin	Smith G	Davis	Barton 1	McGarry 2	Wesley	Cochrane
10		25	Halifax Town	3-2	5000	Gilroy	Stephen	Carr	Stabb 1	Davidson	Kaye	Davis	Barton 1	McGarry 1	Wesley	Juliussen
11		26	HALIFAX TOWN	3-0	5490	Gilroy	Stephen	Carr	Stabb	Danskin	Smith G	Davis 2	Barton	McGarry 1	Watson	Wesley
12	Mar	9	Middlesbrough	3-3	600	Gilroy	Stephen	Johnstone	Stabb	Danskin	Kaye	Davis 1	Curry 1	Smith FA	Wesley 1	Juliussen
13		16	NEWCASTLE UNITED	2-1	3605	Gilroy	Stephen	Johnstone	Stabb	Danskin	Kaye	Davis 1	Curry	McGarry 1	Wesley	Juliussen
14		22	Hartlepools United	4-0	3500	Gilroy	Stephen	Johnstone	Stabb	Danskin	Kaye	Davis	Curry 1	McGarry 3	Wesley	Stephenson
15		23	Hull City	1-4	4000	Gilroy	Stephen	Johnstone	Stabb	Danskin	Kaye	Davis	Smith FH	McGarry 1	Wesley	Spivey
16	Apr	6	Leeds United	2-5	4000	Gilroy	Stephen	Johnstone	Stabb	Danskin	Kaye	Davis 1	Barton	McGarry	Curry 1	Stephenson
17		13	Huddersfield Town	1-2	4156	Farr	Stephen	Johnstone	Stabb	Danskin	Kaye	Davis	Barton	Sheen 1	Curry	Stephenson
18		20	NEWCASTLE UNITED	2-0	5208	Gilroy	Stephen	Johnstone	Stabb	Danskin	Kaye	Davis 1	Martin	Milne 1	Wesley	Cochrane
19		27	Newcastle United	0-3	9470	Gilroy	Stephen	Johnstone	Stabb	Danskin	Kaye	Davis	Sheen	Kuhnel	Wesley	Cochrane
20	May	4	York City	2-3	2500	Farr	Stephen	Blenkinsop	Stabb	Danskin	Kaye	Davis 1	Norton	Sheen	Wesley 1	Cochrane
21		11	BRADFORD CITY	2-1	3364	Farr	Stephen	Bailey	Stabb	Danskin	Kaye	Davis 1	Barton	Sheen 1	Hutchinson	Wesley
22		18	Darlington	2-2	1500	Farr	Stephen	Bailey	Stabb	Danskin	Kaye	Davis	Sheen 1	Barton	Hutchinson 1	Wesley
23		20	HARTLEPOOLS UNITED	2-0	469	Farr	Stephen	Bailey	Stabb 1	Danskin	Kaye	Davis	Shackleton 1	Coxon	Offord	Wesley
24		25	YORK CITY	2-3	500	Farr	Stephen	Wharton	Palmer	Danskin	Kaye	Davis	Shackleton	Sheen 2	Hutchinson	Page

The Football League season was cancelled after the games of September 2 1939. Appearances in the three games played are not counted in a player's record.
The home game with Darlington in the Regional League was not played.

Guest players include:

Bailey (Huddersfield Town)
Barton (Sheffield United)
W Carr (Sheffield United)
Coxon (Yorkshire CCC)
Curry (Gainsborough Trinity)
Davis (Crystal Palace)
Gordon (Huddersfield Town)
Hutchinson (Sheffield United)
Juliussen (Huddersfield Town)
Milne
Sheen
Spivey (Southport)
Stephenson (Luton Town)
Ward (Tottenham Hotspur)

Friendly games were played as follows:

Aug 19 v BRADFORD CITY 3-2 (Hallard, Wesley, Martin) 4,843 (FL Jubilee Fund)
Sep 16 v Doncaster Rovers 0-0 2,000
Sep 23 v Halifax Town 3-3 (Smith, Martin, Stabb) 3,000
Sep 30 v GRIMSBY TOWN 4-2 (McGarry 3, Smith) 3,731
Oct 7 v Hull City 2-2 (Watson 2) 2,500
Oct 14 v CHESTERFIELD 0-1 2,549
Oct 28 v ARMY XI 2-0 (Pepper, Watson) 1,168
Dec 2 v Scunthorpe United 1-2 (Cochrane) 1,200
Dec 16 v Barnsley 3-2 (Davis, Stabb, McGarry) 1,000
Dec 23 v Rotherham United 2-1
Dec 30 v Stockport County 4-7 (McCall, Wesley, Davis, Watson) 1,000
Jan 1 v Bury 3-3 (Wesley, McGarry, Davis) 5,000
Jan 13 v Chesterfield 0-5 200
Feb 24 v Accrington Stanley 3-3 (Stabb, Wesley, Curry) 700
Mar 25 v Halifax Town 1-2 (Curry) 2,000
Mar 30 v DONCASTER ROVERS 1-1 (Davis) 1,568

1940/41

League North (games 1 to 22, 25 to 33), League Cup (games 23, 24)

1	Aug	31	Newcastle United	2-0	5000	Farr	Stephen	Firth	Stabb	Danskin	Wesley	Davis	Shackleton 1	Dodd	Offord	Miller 1	
2	Sep	7	Huddersfield Town	1-1	1971	Farr	Stephen	Firth	Stabb 1	Danskin	Wesley	Davis	Shackleton	Dodd	Offord	Miller	
3		14	HALIFAX TOWN	0-0	1394	Farr	Stephen	Firth	Palmer	Danskin	Wesley	Bannister	Shackleton	Dodd	Offord	Miller	
4		21	Hull City	1-2	2000	Farr	Stephen	Firth	Palmer	Danskin	Wesley	Bannister	Shackleton 1	Dodd	Offord	Miller	
5		28	BRADFORD CITY	0-2	2987	Farr	Stephen	Firth	Palmer	Danskin	Wesley	Bannister	Shackleton	Brook	Offord	Miller	
6	Oct	5	Halifax Town	3-2	2000	Farr	Stephen	Firth	Palmer	Danskin	Carte	Wesley 1	Shackleton 1	Dodd 1	McCall	Miller	
7		12	MIDDLESBROUGH	0-2	1768	Farr	Stephen	Firth	Palmer	Danskin	Carte	Keeling	Shackleton	Greaves	Offord	Wesley	
8		19	Middlesbrough	2-6	2500	Farr	Stephen	Firth	Carte	Danskin	Harrison	Keeling	Shackleton	Greaves 1	Offord	Cochrane 1	
9		26	NEWCASTLE UNITED	0-1	1571	Farr	Stephen	Firth	Carte	Danskin	Harrison	Conroy	Shackleton	Futter	Wesley	Dodds	
10	Nov	2	Rochdale	1-1	500	Farr	Stephen	Firth	Carte	Danskin	Harrison	Shackleton	Carr 1	Stabb	Offord	Wesley	
11		9	Oldham Athletic	4-4	1000	Farr	Stephen	Firth	Carte	Danskin	Stabb 1	Harrison	Carr	Futter 1	Shackleton 2	Wesley	
12		16	SHEFFIELD UNITED	1-2	1276	Farr	Stephen	Firth	Carte	Danskin 1	Stabb	Harrison	Carr	Baines	Shackleton	Wesley	
13		23	Sheffield United	4-3	3000	Farr	Stephen	Firth	Palmer	Danskin	Stabb	Barton	Carr 1	Carte	Shackleton 1	Tomlinson 2	
14		30	Sheffield Wednesday	3-4	3000	Farr	Stephen	Firth	Palmer	Danskin	Stabb	Barton	Carr 1	Carte	Shackleton 2	Tomlinson	
15	Dec	7	ROCHDALE	2-4	838	Farr	Stephen	Firth	Palmer	Danskin 1	Stabb 1	Kelly	Carr	Carte	Shackleton	Tomlinson	
16		14	Bradford City	2-4	575	Farr	Stephen	Carte	Goslin	Danskin	Stabb	Kelly	Barton	Carr	Shackleton 1	Laycock	1 og
17		21	HUDDERSFIELD T	3-2	1349	Farr	Stephen	Firth	Stabb 1	Danskin	Carte	Barton	Shackleton 1	Murphy	Hastie 1	Smailes	
18		25	Leeds United	1-2	4500	Farr	Stephen	Farrell	Stabb	Danskin	Carte	Barton	Shackleton	Carr	Wesley	Tomlinson 1	
19		28	York City	0-0	2000	Farr	Stephen	Firth	Stabb	Danskin	Carte	Shackleton	Carr	McGarry	Wesley	Tomlinson	
20	Jan	11	YORK CITY	4-2	1165	Gilroy	Stephen	Firth	Stabb	Danskin	Carte	Shackleton 1	McCall	Carr 2	Wesley	Tomlinson 1	
21		18	Middlesbrough	3-5	700	Nicholls	Stephen	Firth	Palmer	Danskin	Carte	Paton	Shackleton 1	Stabb 2	Carr	Wesley	
22	Feb	1	Grimsby Town	3-0	2000	Nicholls	Stephen	Firth	Palmer	Danskin	Carte	Prior	Shackleton 1	Stabb 1	Wesley 1	Tomlinson	
23		15	York City	2-3	3000	Nicholls	Stephen	Firth	Stabb	Danskin	Carte	Barton	Shackleton 1	Carr 1	Wesley	Tomlinson	
24		22	York City	3-4	1500	Nicholls	Stephen	Firth	Palmer	Danskin	Carte	Harrison	Shackleton 1	Stabb 2	Wesley	Tomlinson	
25	Mar	1	LINCOLN CITY	4-0	831	Farr	Stephen	Farrell	Firth	Danskin	Carte	Palmer	Shackleton 1	Carr 1	Stabb 2	Wesley	
26		8	Bradford City	2-2	1009	Farr	Stephen	Farrell	Firth	Danskin	Carte	Palmer	Shackleton	Carr 1	Stabb 1	Tomlinson	
27		15	Halifax Town	2-2	1000	Farr	Stephen	Farrell	Firth	Danskin	Carte	Cross	Shackleton	Carr 1	Stabb	Tomlinson 1	
28		29	BRADFORD CITY	4-1	1184	Farr	Stephen	Farrell	Palmer	Danskin	Carte	Prior	Shackleton 2	Carr 1	Stabb	Tomlinson 1	
29	Apr	5	Tranmere Rovers	4-6	800	Farr	Stephen	Farrell	Palmer 1	Baker	Carte	Prior	Shackleton	Carr 2	Stabb 1	Tomlinson	
30		14	Mansfield Town	1-5	1000	Farr	Stephen	Farrell	Palmer	Carte	Wharton	Prior	Shackleton	Carr 1	Stabb	Tomlinson	
31		19	Lincoln City	2-6	2000	Farr	Stephen	Farrell	Firth	Danskin	Carte	Steele	Shackleton	Stabb	McCall 1	Tomlinson 1	
32		26	Rotherham United	0-2	500	Farr	Stephen	Farrell	Firth	Danskin	Kaye	Palmer	Shackleton	Carr	Wharton	Tomlinson	
33	May	3	ROTHERHAM UNITED	5-1	300	Farr	Stokes	Stephen	Palmer	Danskin	Elliott	Farrell 1	Shackleton 1	Carr 2	Stabb 1	Miller	

Games 22 and 24 played at Scunthorpe

Guest players include:

Baines (Halifax Town)
Barton (Sheffield United)
E Carr (Arsenal)
Davis (Crystal Palace)
Dodd (New Brighton)
Dodds (Hartlepools United)

Goslin (Bolton Wanderers)
Hastie (Bradford City)
Keeling (Manchester City)
Kelly (Southampton)
Murphy (Bradford City)
Smailes (Bradford City)

1941/42

League North First Competition (games 1 to 18), League North Second Competition (games 19 to 29, 36,37), League Cup (games 30 to 35)

1	Aug	30 GATESHEAD	2-2	1253	Farr	Stephen	Farrell	Palmer	Danskin	Elliott	Davis	Carr	Priestley	Shackleton 2	Tomlinson
2	Sep	6 Gateshead	2-2	3000	Farr	Moore	Stephen	Palmer	Danskin	Elliott	Farrell 1	Stabb	Carr 1	Offord	Wesley
3		13 Sunderland	2-1	10000	Farr	Moore	Stephen	Palmer	Danskin	Elliott	Deplidge 1	Shackleton 1	Carr	Stabb	Wesley
4		20 SUNDERLAND	2-2	4940	Farr	Moore	Stephen	Palmer	Danskin	Elliott	Deplidge	Shackleton 1	Carr 1	Stabb	Wesley
5		27 Mansfield Town	2-1	1500	Farr	Moore	Stephen	Palmer	Danskin	Elliott	Deplidge	Shackleton 1	Carr	Stabb 1	Wesley
6	Oct	4 MANSFIELD TOWN	3-0	3000	Farr	Moore	Stephen	Palmer	Danskin 1	Elliott	Deplidge	Shackleton 2	Carr	Stabb	Wesley
7		11 LEEDS UNITED	6-0	3850	Farr	Moore	Stephen	Palmer	Danskin	Elliott	Deplidge	Shackleton 4	Carr 1	Stabb 1	Wesley
8		18 Leeds United	0-4	2000	Farr	Moore	Stephen	Palmer	Danskin	Elliott	Deplidge	Shackleton	Carr	Stabb	Wesley
9		25 Middlesbrough	2-0	4500	Farr	Moore	Stephen	Palmer	Danskin	Elliott	Deplidge	Stabb	Carr 1	Offord	Wesley 1
10	Nov	1 MIDDLESBROUGH	1-0	4268	Farr	Moore	Wharton L	Palmer	Danskin	Elliott	Geldard	Shackleton	Carr	McCall	Wesley 1
11		8 NEWCASTLE UNITED	0-0	4703	Farr	Moore	Wharton L	Palmer	Danskin	Elliott	Deplidge	Shackleton	Carr	Stabb	Wesley
12		15 Newcastle United	1-3	5000	Farr	Moore	Stephen	Palmer	Danskin	Elliott	Deplidge	Shackleton	Carr 1	Stabb	Wesley
13		22 Bradford City	1-2	4407	Farr	Moore	Stephen	Palmer	Danskin	Elliott	Davis	Shackleton	Carr	Stabb 1	Wesley
14		29 BRADFORD CITY	3-1	3456	Farr	Moore	Stephen	Palmer 1	Danskin	Wharton F	Davis	Shackleton	Carr	Stabb 1	Miller 1
15	Dec	13 Huddersfield Town	0-3	2500	Farr	Moore	Stephen	Palmer	Danskin	Elliott	Deplidge	Shackleton	Carr	Stabb	Miller
16		20 York City	3-2	2000	Farr	Stephen	Wharton L	Palmer	Danskin	Stabb	Deplidge	Shackleton	McGarry 1	Carr 2	Miller
17		25 YORK CITY	2-2	2080	Farr	Coxon	Stephen	Wharton F	Stabb	Elliott	Davis	Bedford 1	McGarry 1	Gibson	Wesley
18		25 HUDDERSFIELD T	1-3	5300	Farr	Moore	Stephen	Palmer	Danskin	Gill	Deplidge	Shackleton	Priestley	Carr	Miller 1
19		27 Barnsley	2-5	5000	Farr	Stephen	Wharton L	Palmer	Danskin	Stabb	Deplidge	Shackleton 1	McGarry 1	Carr	Miller
20	Jan	3 BARNSLEY	1-1	3202	Nicholls	Moore	Stephen	Palmer	Danskin	Stabb	Deplidge	Shackleton 1	Carr	Wesley	Miller
21		10 MIDDLESBROUGH	1-1	3100	Farr	Stephen	Wharton L	Palmer	Stabb	Elliott	Davis	Shackleton 1	McGarry	Carr	Lewis
22		17 Middlesbrough	2-1	4000	Farr	Stephen	Wharton L	Harvey	Stabb	Elliott	Deplidge	Shackleton	Carr 1	Green 1	Lewis
23		31 ROTHERHAM UNITED	5-5	1359	Farr	Moore	Stephen	Palmer	Stabb	Elliott	Deplidge	Shackleton 1	Carr 3	Green	Lewis 1
24	Feb	14 OLDHAM ATHLETIC	3-1	3010	Farr	Stephen	Farrell	Palmer	Danskin	Stabb	Deplidge	Shackleton	Carr 2	Baird 1	Lewis
25		21 SUNDERLAND	3-0	2101	Farr	Stephen	Farrell	Palmer	Danskin	Elliott	Deplidge	Shackleton 3	Carr	Green	Steele
26		28 Sunderland	2-4	8000	Farr	Stephen	Farrell	Palmer	Danskin	Elliott	Deplidge	Shackleton 1	Carr	Stabb	Green 1
27	Mar	14 Oldham Athletic	2-5	3000	Farr	Stephen	Farrell	Palmer	Danskin	Stabb 1	Deplidge 1	Shackleton	Carr	Green	Offord
28		21 Rotherham United	1-3	2400	Farr	Stephen	Farrell	Palmer	Danskin	Elliott	Deplidge	Shackleton	Mills	Stabb	Green 1
29		28 Bradford City	2-2	2500	Farr	Stephen	Farrell	Palmer	Danskin	Stabb	Deplidge 1	Shackleton 1	McGarry	Green	Walker J
30	Apr	4 Middlesbrough	2-3	5000	Farr	Stephen	Farrell	Palmer	Danskin	Stabb	Deplidge	Shackleton	Brenen	Green	Lee 2
31		6 MIDDLESBROUGH	2-0	6016	Farr	Stephen	Farrell	Palmer	Danskin	Stabb	Deplidge	Shackleton 1	Carr	Green 1	Lee
32		11 SHEFFIELD UNITED	2-0	6000	Farr	Stephen	Farrell	Palmer	Danskin	Stabb	Deplidge	Shackleton	Carr 1	Green 1	Walker RG
33		18 Sheffield United	1-2	10000	Farr	Stephen	Farrell	Palmer	Danskin	Stabb	Deplidge	Shackleton 1	Carr	Green	Lee
34		25 SUNDERLAND	0-1	7640	Farr	Stephen	Farrell	Stabb	Danskin	Elliott	Deplidge	Shackleton	Carr	Green	Lee
35	May	2 Sunderland	2-2	15000	Farr	Stephen	Farrell	Stabb	Danskin	Elliott	Deplidge	Shackleton 1	Carr 1	Green	Lee
36		9 CHESTERFIELD	0-2	1970	Farr	Stephen	Farrell	Stabb	Danskin	Elliott	Deplidge	Shackleton	Carr	Green	Walker RG
37		16 Huddersfield Town	2-2	917	Farr	Stephen	Farrell	Stabb	Danskin	Elliott	Deplidge 1	Shackleton 1	Crowther	Carr	Walker RG

Guest players include:

Brenen (York City)
E Carr (Arsenal)
Davis (Crystal Palace)
Geldard (Bolton Wanderers)

Harvey (Bradford City)
Lee (York City)
Lewis (Blackpool)
Mills (Chelsea)

1942/43

League North First Competition (games 1 to 18), League North Second Competition (games 19 to 27, 32 to 37), League Cup (games 28 to 31)

1	Aug	29	Newcastle United	4-1	8000	Farr	Moore	Farrell	Stabb	Danskin	Green	Deplidge	Walker T 1	Carr 1	Shackleton 1	Walker RG 1
2	Sep	5	NEWCASTLE UNITED	0-0	4500	Farr	Moore	Farrell	Stabb	Danskin	Elliott	Deplidge	Shackleton	Carr	Green	Walker RG
3		12	MIDDLESBROUGH	0-0	3700	Farr	Moore	Farrell	Elliott	Danskin	Green	Deplidge	Shackleton	McGarry	Carr	Miller
4		19	Middlesbrough	2-2	4000	Farr	Hirst	Stephen	Stabb	Danskin	Elliott	Deplidge	Shackleton 2	McGarry	Green	Walker RG
5		26	Sheffield Wednesday	0-1	7000	Farr	Hirst	Stephen	Stabb	Danskin	Elliott	Deplidge	Shackleton	McGarry	Green	Walker RG
6	Oct	3	SHEFFIELD WEDNESDAY	3-3	3500	Farr	Stephen	Farrell	Palmer	Danskin	Elliott	Downie	Shackleton 2	Steele DM 1	Green	Walker RG
7		10	SUNDERLAND	4-2	3500	Farr	Hirst	Stephen	Stabb 1	Danskin	Green	Deplidge	Shackleton 3	McGarry	Barclay	Walker RG
8		17	Sunderland	1-2	5000	Farr	Hirst	Stephen	Stabb	Danskin	Green	Deplidge	Warburton	McGarry 1	Short	Walker RG
9		24	GATESHEAD	6-0	1850	Farr	Hirst	Stephen	Stabb	Danskin	Green	Deplidge 1	Shackleton 3	McGarry 1	Barclay 1	Walker RG
10		31	Gateshead	1-1	3000	Farr	Hirst	Stephen	Stabb	Danskin	Green	Deplidge	Shackleton 1	McGarry	Flatley	Walker RG
11	Nov	7	Leeds United	1-1	3000	Farr	Stephen	Farrell	Stabb	Danskin	Cabrelli	Downie	Shackleton 1	McGarry	Green	Walker RG
12		14	LEEDS UNITED	1-0	4465	Farr	Hirst	Farrell	Stabb	Danskin	Green	Doran	Shackleton	McGarry 1	Johnson	Walker RG
13		21	BARNSLEY	1-1	3500	Farr	Hirst	Farrell	Stabb	Danskin	Cabrelli	Davis	Shackleton	McGarry	Green 1	Walker RG
14		28	Barnsley	1-3	2820	Dawson	Hirst	Farrell	Stabb	Danskin	Cabrelli	McKellor	Shackleton 1	McGarry	Williamson	Walker RG
15	Dec	5	York City	6-3	2800	Dawson	Hirst	Farrell	Stabb	Danskin	Johnson	Bannister	Shackleton 5	McGarry 1	Green	Walker RG
16		12	YORK CITY	3-1	3539	Farr	Hirst	Farrell	Stabb	Danskin	Green	Flatley 1	Shackleton 1	McGarry	Johnson	Walker RG 1
17		19	Bradford City	10-0	3634	Farr	Hirst	Farrell	Stabb	Danskin	Green 1	Flatley 1	Shackleton 2	McGarry 2	Johnson 3	Walker RG 1
18		25	BRADFORD CITY	2-0	10000	Farr	Hirst	Farrell	Stabb	Danskin	Green	Flatley	Shackleton	McGarry 1	Johnson 1	Walker RG
19	Jan	2	HUDDERSFIELD T	2-3	4062	Farr	Hirst	Farrell	Stabb	Danskin	Green	Deplidge	Shackleton 2	McGarry	Johnson	Walker RG
20		9	HALIFAX TOWN	5-1	2773	Farr	Hirst	Farrell	Stabb 1	Danskin	Brophy	Flatley	Shackleton 2	McGarry	Johnson 1	Walker RG 1
21		16	Halifax Town	2-0	3500	Farr	Hirst	Farrell	Stabb	Danskin	Brophy	Flatley	Shackleton 1	Green 1	Johnson	Walker RG
22		23	Bradford City	1-2	4670	Farr	Hirst	Farrell	Stabb	Danskin	Green	Flatley	Shackleton	Brophy 1	Johnson	Walker RG
23		30	BRADFORD CITY	2-0	5046	Farr	Firth	Farrell	Stabb	Danskin	Elliott	Deplidge	Shackleton 1	Johnson	Green 1	Walker RG
24	Feb	6	LEEDS UNITED	2-1	4500	Farr	Stabb	Farrell	Green	Danskin	Elliott	Deplidge	Shackleton 2	Hatfield	Johnson	Walker RG
25		13	Leeds United	2-2	3000	Farr	Firth	Farrell	Stabb	Danskin	Elliott	Flatley	Shackleton 1	Anderson	Johnson 1	Walker RG
26		20	Sunderland	1-1	12000	Farr	Hirst	Farrell	Stabb	Danskin	Elliott	Deplidge	Shackleton 1	Hatfield	Johnson	Walker RG
27		27	SUNDERLAND	1-1	6915	Farr	Stephen	Farrell	Stabb	Danskin	Elliott	Deplidge	Shackleton 1	Hatfield	Johnson	Walker RG
28	Mar	6	HUDDERSFIELD T	0-0	8440	Farr	Stephen	Farrell	Stabb	Danskin	Elliott	Flatley	Shackleton	Hatfield	Dickie	Walker RG
29		13	Huddersfield Town	3-2	8813	Farr	Stephen	Farrell	Stabb	Danskin	Elliott	Simpson 1	Shackleton	Steele FC 2	Dickie	Walker RG
30		20	York City	1-2	11000	Farr	Stephen	Farrell	Stabb	Danskin	Elliott	Simpson 1	Shackleton	Steele FC	Dickie	Walker RG
31		27	YORK CITY	0-3	14000	Farr	Stephen	Farrell	Stabb	Danskin	Elliott	Simpson	Shackleton	Steele FC	Dickie	Walker RG
32	Apr	3	Leeds United	0-2	3000	Farr	Stephen	Farrell	Dobson	Danskin	Elliott	Simpson	Shackleton	Hatfield	Smith	Walker RG
33		10	LEEDS UNITED	5-2	3908	Farr	Stephen	Farrell	Stabb	Danskin	Elliott	Simpson 1	Shackleton 1	Steele FC 3	Asquith	Walker RG
34		17	SUNDERLAND	0-1	4030	Farr	Farrell	Stephen	Stabb	Danskin	Elliott	Downie	Shackleton	Steele FC	Smith	Walker RG
35		24	Sunderland	2-2	7000	Farr	Stabb	Stephen	Devlin	Danskin	Elliott	Simpson	Shackleton	Hatfield 2	Smith	Walker RG
36		26	Chesterfield	3-2	3000	Farr	Stephen	Farrell	Stabb	Danskin	Elliott	Downie	Shackleton 1	Green 2	Smith	Hawksworth
37	May	1	Oldham Athletic	3-4	1000	Farr	Stephen	Farrell	Knight	Danskin	Green	Walker J	Shackleton 1	Hatfield 2	Smith	Walker RG

Guest players include:

Anderson (Hibernian)
Asquith (Manchester United)
Barclay (Huddersfield Town)
Brophy (Southampton)
Cabrelli (Raith Rovers)
E Carr (Arsenal)
Davis (Crystal Palace)
J Dawson (York City)
Devlin (Gateshead)
Dickie (Blackburn Rovers)
Doran (Halifax Town)
Flatley (Port Vale)
Johnson (Everton)
McKellor (Huddersfield Town)
Short (Leeds United)
Simpson (Darlington)
Steele FC (Stoke City)
Walker T (Hearts)
Warburton (QPR)
Williamson (Falkirk)

1943/44

League North First Competition (games 1 to 18), League North Second Competition (games 19 to 28, 35 to 38), League Cup (games 29 to 34)

1	Aug	28	Huddersfield Town	4-7	2576	Farr	Stephen	Farrell	Hodgson	Danskin	Stabb	Downie	Shackleton 2	Carr 2	Smith J	Walker RG	
2	Sep	4	HUDDERSFIELD T	1-2	4957	Farr	Stephen	Farrell	Stabb	Danskin	Knight	Downie	Shackleton	Carr 1	Smith J	Walker RG	
3		11	NEWCASTLE UNITED	1-0	2763	Farr	Stephen	Farrell	Hodgson	Danskin	Stabb	Downie	Ainsley	Shackleton 1	Smith J	Walker RG	
4		18	Newcastle United	1-2	12000	Farr	Stephen	Farrell	Hodgson	Danskin	Stabb	Taylor	Shackleton 1	Carr	Smith J	Walker RG	
5		25	SHEFFIELD WEDNESDAY	3-1	4305	Farr	Stephen	Farrell	Hodgson	Danskin	Stabb	Taylor	Ainsley	Shackleton 3	Smith J	Walker RG	
6	Oct	2	Sheffield Wednesday	3-2	9750	Farr	Firth	Farrell	Knight	Hodgson	Stabb 2	Smith J	Ainsley 1	Shackleton	Green	Walker RG	
7		9	Middlesbrough	8-1	2440	Farr	Farrell	Compton	Stabb	Danskin	Knight	Smith J	Ainsley 1	Carr 1	Shackleton 3	Walker RG 3	
8		16	MIDDLESBROUGH	1-1	4596	Farr	Farrell	Compton	Stabb	Danskin	Knight	Smith J	Ainsley	Carr	Shackleton	Walker RG 1	
9		23	Sunderland	1-1	9000	Farr	Farrell	Compton	Ainsley	Danskin	Stabb	Smith J	Shackleton 1	Smith F	Carr	Walker RG	
10		30	SUNDERLAND	0-0	7216	Farr	Stephen	Farrell	Firth	Danskin	Stabb	Smith J	Shackleton	Carr	Haines	Walker RG	
11	Nov	6	LEEDS UNITED	6-1	5301	Farr	Stephen	Farrell	Jones T	Danskin	Knight	Smith J 1	Shackleton 2	Stabb 1	Carr 1	Walker RG 1	
12		13	Leeds United	2-2	4500	Farr	Stephen	Farrell 1	Stirland	Danskin	Davidson	Smith J	Ainsley	Stabb 1	Carr	Walker RG	
13		20	Barnsley	5-1	3746	Farr	Stephen	Farrell	Stabb	Danskin	Knight	Smith J	Shackleton 1	Ainsley 2	Carr 2	Walker RG	
14		27	BARNSLEY	5-3	3370	Farr	Stephen	Farrell	Stabb	Danskin	Knight	Smith J 1	Shackleton	Ainsley 2	Carr 2	Walker RG	
15	Dec	4	YORK CITY	6-1	4655	Farr	Stephen	Farrell 1	Stabb	Danskin	Knight	Smith J	Shackleton 1	Ainsley 2	Carr 2	Hawksworth	
16		11	York City	4-2	40000	Farr	Stephen	Farrell	Stabb	Danskin	Knight	Smith J	Shackleton 2	Ainsley 1	Carr	Walker RG 1	
17		18	BRADFORD CITY	8-0	6191	Farr	Stephen	Compton	Elliott	Danskin	Farrell	Smith J	Shackleton 5	Ainsley 3	Carr	Walker RG	
18		25	Bradford City	6-1	11053	Farr	Stephen 1	Compton 1	Stabb	Danskin	Farrell	Smith J 1	Shackleton 2	Ainsley 1	Carr	Walker RG	
19		27	LEEDS UNITED	2-1	13186	Farr	Stephen	Compton 1	Stabb	Danskin	Dobson	Smith J	Farrell	Ainsley 1	Carr	Walker RG	
20	Jan	1	Leeds United	1-3	7108	Farr	Stephen	Compton	Stabb	Danskin	Knight	Smith J	Farrell	Ainsley	Carr	Walker RG	1 og
21		8	Huddersfield Town	2-1	5359	Farr	Stephen	Farrell	Stabb	Danskin	Green	Smith J 1	Ainsley	Compton	Carr 1	Walker RG	
22		15	HUDDERSFIELD T	1-1	6569	Farr	Stephen	Farrell	Stabb	Danskin	Green	Smith J	Ainsley	Compton 1	Carr	Walker RG	
23		22	BRADFORD CITY	1-0	3500	Farr	Stephen	Farrell	Stabb	Danskin	Dobson	Smith J	Ainsley	Horsman 1	Carr	Walker RG	
24		29	Bradford City	5-1	7802	Farr	Stephen	Compton	Stabb	Danskin	Farrell	Smith J	Ainsley	Haddington	Carr 5	Walker RG	
25	Feb	5	York City	1-0	6560	Farr	Stephen	Firth	Stabb	Danskin	Farrell 1	Smith J	Ainsley	Jones G	Carr	Walker RG	
26		12	YORK CITY	4-1	6766	Farr	Stephen	Firth	Palmer	Danskin	Farrell	Smith J	Stabb	Ainsley 3	Offord 1	Walker RG	
27		19	BARNSLEY	3-3	5621	Farr	Hepworth	Farrell	Stabb	Danskin	Stirland	Smith J	Ainsley 1	Horsman 2	Carr	Walker RG	
28		26	Barnsley	3-3	8311	Farr	Stephen	Farrell	Stabb	Danskin	Knight	Downie 1	Shackleton 1	Carr 1	Smith J	Walker RG	
29	Mar	4	SHEFFIELD WEDNESDAY	5-0	11209	Farr	Stephen	Compton	Stabb	Danskin	Farrell	Smith J 1	Shackleton 1	Ainsley 1	Carr 1	Walker RG 1	
30		11	Sheffield Wednesday	2-1	12500	Farr	Stephen	Firth	Stabb	Danskin	Farrell	Smith J	Shackleton 1	Carr	Smith F 1	Walker RG	
31		18	York City	5-1	11977	Farr	Stephen	Farrell	Stabb	Danskin	Baird	Downie	Shackleton 2	Ainsley 2	Carr 1	Walker RG	
32		25	YORK CITY	2-1	12393	Farr	Stephen	Compton	Stabb	Danskin	Farrell	Smith J	Shackleton 2	Carr	Baird	Walker RG	
33	Apr	1	Blackpool	2-2	17000	Farr	Stephen	Farrell 1	Stabb	Danskin	Green	Smith J	Shackleton 1	Ainsley	Carr	Walker RG	
34		8	BLACKPOOL	1-2	32810	Farr	Stephen	Compton	Stabb	Danskin	Farrell	Smith J	Shackleton	Ainsley 1	Carr	Walker RG	
35		15	DONCASTER ROVERS	3-4	6973	Farr	Stephen	Farrell 1	Stabb	Danskin	Ainsley	Taylor	Smith J	Carr 1	Shackleton 1	Walker RG	
36		22	Doncaster Rovers	1-3	4600	Farr	Shotton	Farrell	Stabb	Danskin	Logan	Smith J	Shackleton	Ainsley 1	Carr	Walker RG	
37		29	MANCHESTER CITY	5-0	3724	Farr	Stephen	Farrell	Stabb	Danskin	Logan	Smith J	Shackleton 1	Ainsley 4	Asquith	Walker RG	
38	May	6	Manchester City	1-2	3000	Farr	Stephen	Farrell	Stabb	Danskin	Stirland	Smith J	Henry 1	Horsman	Shackleton	Thorogood	

April 8: New ground attendance record

Game 22 abandoned after 45 mins: result stood

Guest players include:

Ainsley (Leeds United)
Asquith (Manchester United)
Baird (Huddersfield Town)
E Carr (Arsenal)
Compton (Arsenal)
Haines (Swansea Town)
Henry (Leeds United)
Hodgson (Grimsby Town)
Jones G (Doncaster Rovers)
Jones TC (Bradford City)
Logan (Barnsley)
Shotton (Barnsley)
Stirland (Doncaster Rovers)
Thorogood (Millwall)

1944/45

League North First Competition (games 1 to 18), League North Second Competition (games 19 to 30, 33 to 40), League Cup (games 31, 32)

No	Month	Date/Opponent	Score	Att	1	2	3	4	5	6	7	8	9	10	11
1	Aug	26 LEEDS UNITED	4-3	8416	Farr	Stephen	Farrell	Stabb	Knight	Hallard	Smith	Shackleton 1	Flatley	Broadis 1	Walker RG 2
2	Sep	2 Leeds United	3-3	5480	Farr	Stephen	Farrell	Stabb 1	Danskin	Hallard	Flatley	Shackleton 2	Haddington	Smith	Walker RG
3		9 Newcastle United	2-0	16112	Farr	Stephen	Farrell	Stabb	Danskin	Hallard	Smith	Shackleton 2	Flatley	Dix	Walker RG
4		16 NEWCASTLE UNITED	1-0	8309	Farr	Stephen	Farrell	Stabb	Danskin	Hallard	Smith	Shackleton	Horsman 1	Hawksworth	Walker RG
5		23 BRADFORD CITY	4-1	11762	Farr	Stephen	Farrell 2	Stabb	Danskin	Hallard 1	Smith	Shackleton 1	Flatley	Hawksworth	Walker RG
6		30 Bradford City	3-1	12053	Farr	Stephen	Farrell	Stabb 1	Danskin	Hallard	Smith	Shackleton 2	Flatley	Hawksworth	Walker RG
7	Oct	7 Harlepools United	0-0	8000	Farr	Stephen	Farrell	Stabb	Danskin	Hallard	Smith	Shackleton	Flatley	Hawksworth	Walker RG
8		14 HARTLEPOOLS UTD.	4-1	7184	Farr	James	Farrell	Stabb 1	Danskin	Hallard	Smith	Shackleton 2	Flatley 1	Hawksworth	Walker RG
9		21 HUDDERSFIELD T	2-2	15628	Farr	Stephen	Farrell 1	Stabb 1	Danskin	Hallard	Smith	Shackleton	Murphy	Flatley	Walker RG
10		28 Huddersfield Town	1-1	13130	Farr	Stephen	Farrell	Stabb	Danskin	Hallard	Smith 1	Shackleton	Murphy	Flatley	Walker RG
11	Nov	4 York City	1-4	6000	Farr	Stephen	Farrell	Stabb	Danskin	Hallard	Smith	Shackleton 1	Flatley	Conway	Walker RG
12		11 YORK CITY	5-3	7596	Farr	Stephen	Farrell	Stabb	Danskin	Flatley	Smith	Shackleton 2	Downie 2	Hawksworth 1	Walker RG
13		18 DARLINGTON	0-3	8652	Farr	Stephen	Farrell	Stabb	Danskin	Flatley	Smith	Shackleton	Downie	Hawksworth	Walker RG
14		25 Darlington	2-3	8725	Farr	Farrell	James	Stabb	Danskin	Britton	Smith	Shackleton	Downie 1	Dix	Walker RG 1
15	Dec	2 Gateshead	2-1	4000	Farr	Stephen	James	Hallard	Britton	Farrell	Smith	Shackleton	Downie	Miller	Walker RG 2
16		9 GATESHEAD	1-4	2250	Farr	Stephen	James	Dickens	Farrell	Hallard	Downie 1	Flatley	Haddington	Smith	Dix
17		16 Hull City	4-0	4000	Farr	Stephen	Farrell	Stabb	Danskin	James	Dickinson	Shackleton 3	Noble	Downie 1	Walker RG
18		23 HULL CITY	6-1	6562	Farr	Stephen	Farrell	Stabb	Danskin	Hallard	Smith	Shackleton 5	Rodgers 1	Downie	Walker RG
19		25 BARNSLEY	3-1	11962	Farr	Stephen	Farrell	Stabb	Danskin	Hallard	Smith	Shackleton	Murphy 2	Downie	Walker RG 1
20		26 Burnley	2-4	11000	Clarke	Stephen	Farrell 1	Hallard	Stabb	Elliott	Smith	Shackleton 1	Murphy	Hawksworth	Walker RG
21		30 Barnsley	1-2	9300	Farr	Stephen	Farrell	Stabb	Danskin	Hallard	Smith	Shackleton 1	Britton	Downie	Walker RG
22	Jan	6 YORK CITY	4-2	7648	Farr	Stephen	James	Stabb 1	Danskin	Hallard	Deplidge	Shackleton 2	Murphy	Downie 1	Walker RG
23		27 HULL CITY	2-1	4791	Farr	Stephen	Farrell 1	Stabb	Danskin	Hallard	Smith	Shackleton 1	Murphy	Downie	Walker RG
24	Feb	3 BRADFORD CITY	2-2	10536	Farr	Shotton	Farrell	Stabb	Danskin	Hallard	Smith	Shackleton 1	Flatley	Downie	Dix 1
25		10 Bradford City	1-3	12135	Farr	Stephen	Farrell	Stabb	Danskin	Hallard	Smith	Shackleton	Rodgers	Downie 1	Dix
26		17 LEEDS UNITED	5-2	10198	Farr	Stephen	Farrell	Stabb	Danskin	Dobson	Smith 2	Shackleton 1	Flatley	Downie 2	McGarry
27		24 Leeds United	2-0	15807	Farr	Stephen	Farrell	Stabb	Danskin	Dobson	Smith 1	Shackleton	Murphy 1	Downie	Deplidge
28	Mar	3 York City	1-6	4250	Farr	Stephen	Farrell	Stabb	Danskin	Dobson	Smith 1	Shackleton	Flatley	Downie	Dix
29		10 Hull City	2-0	5000	Farr	Stephen	Farrell	McTaff	Danskin	Stabb	Smith	Shackleton 1	Gibbons 1	Downie	Walker RG
30		17 HUDDERSFIELD T	5-0	13032	Farr	Stephen	Farrell	McTaff	Danskin	Stabb	Dix	Shackleton 3	Gibbons 2	Downie	Walker RG
31		24 DONCASTER ROVERS	1-1	16007	Farr	Stephen	Farrell	Willingham	Danskin	Stabb	Downie 1	Shackleton	Gibbons	Dawson	Walker RG
32		31 Doncaster Rovers	0-2	19549	Farr	Stephen	Farrell	McTaff	Danskin	Stabb	Willingham	Shackleton	Gibbons	Downie	Walker RG
33	Apr	2 PRESTON NORTH END	6-1	7812	Clarke	Stephen	Farrell	McTaff	Danskin	Stabb	Shackleton 4	Downie 1	Gibbons 1	Hawksworth	Walker RG
34		7 MIDDLESBROUGH	3-1	6000	Farr	Stephen	Farrell	McTaff	Danskin	Stabb	Deplidge	Shackleton 1	Gibbons 1	Downie	Walker RG 1
35		14 Middlesbrough	0-1	4100	Farr	Shotton	Farrell	McTaff	Danskin	Stabb	Deplidge	Shackleton	Downie	Hawksworth	Walker RG
36		21 Sheffield Wednesday	1-3	9734	Farr	Shotton	Farrell	Flynn	Danskin	Stabb	Downie	Shackleton	Cummings 1	Naylor	Walker RG
37		28 SHEFFIELD WEDNESDAY	5-3	3578	Farr	Stephen	Farrell	McTaff	Danskin	Stabb	Downie	Shackleton 2	Cummings	Naylor 2	Dix 1
38	May	5 Burnley	1-1	2000	Farr	Stephen	Farrell 1	Stabb	Danskin	Elliott	Flatley	Shackleton	Hatfield	Naylor	Walker RG
39		19 CHESTERFIELD	2-2	3079	Clarke	Stephen	Farrell	McTaff 1	Danskin	Stabb	Flatley	Shackleton 1	Kendall	Downie	Walker RG
40		26 Chesterfield	0-1	2000	Farr	Stephen	Farrell	McTaff	Danskin	Leonard	Kendall	Shackleton	Flatley	Stabb	Walker RG

Game 16 played at York City as Park Avenue hosting FA XI v Army XI

Guest players include:

Broadis (Tottenham Hotspur)
T Dawson (Charlton Athletic)
Dickinson (Hull City)
Gibbons (Tottenham Hotspur)
McGarry (Barnsley)
Murphy (Bradford City)
Noble (Huddersfield Town)
Rodgers (Huddersfield Town)
Shotton (Barnsley)
Willingham (Huddersfield Town)

1945/46

League North

No	Month	Date	Opponent	Score	Att	1	2	3	4	5	6	7	8	9	10	11	
1	Aug	25	STOKE CITY	1-0	13275	Farr	Stephen	Farrell	Stabb	Danskin	Greenwood	Smith J	Shackleton	Hepworth	Downie	Walker RG 1	
2		27	CHESTERFIELD	1-0	6924	Farr	Stephen	Farrell	Stabb	Ruecroft	Dobson	Smith J	Shackleton	Downie	Hawksworth 1	Walker RG	
3	Sep	1	Stoke City	0-3	14000	Farr	Stephen	Farrell	Stabb	Greenwood	Dobson	Smith J	Shackleton	Hepworth	Hawksworth	Walker RG	
4		8	Grimsby Town	1-2	8950	Farr	Stephen	Farrell	Stabb	Danskin	Dobson	Smith J	Shackleton	Hepworth 1	Downie	Walker RG	
5		12	HUDDERSFIELD T	2-2	10868	Farr	Stephen	Farrell	Stabb	Danskin	Dobson	Smith J	Shackleton	Rodi 2	Downie	Walker RG	
6		15	GRIMSBY TOWN	2-3	10869	Farr	Stephen	Hepworth	Stabb	Greenwood	Farrell	Smith J 1	Shackleton	Haddington	Hawksworth 1	Walker RG	
7		22	BLACKPOOL	3-0	15897	Farr	Stephen	Farrell 1	McTaff	Danskin	Greenwood	Smith J	Stabb 1	Whittingham	Downie 1	Walker RG	
8		29	Blackpool	1-0	15600	Farr	Stephen	Farrell	McTaff	Danskin	Greenwood	Smith J	Stabb	Hepworth	Downie 1	Walker RG	
9	Oct	6	Liverpool	1-4	30000	Farr	Stephen	Farrell	McTaff	Danskin	Greenwood	Smith J	Stabb	Horsman 1	Downie	Walker RG	
10		13	LIVERPOOL	0-2	18308	Farr	Hepworth	Farrell	McTaff	Danskin	Greenwood	Smith J	Downie	Knott	Poole	Walker RG	
11		20	BURY	6-0	10168	Farr	Hepworth	Farrell	McTaff	Danskin	Greenwood	Smith J 2	Hallard	Flatley	Downie 1	Walker RG 3	
12		27	Bury	3-2	7000	Farr	Hepworth	Farrell	McTaff	Danskin	Greenwood	Smith J	Shackleton 1	Flatley	Downie 1	Walker RG 1	
13	Nov	3	BLACKBURN ROVERS	2-1	11289	Farr	Hepworth	Farrell	Stabb 1	Danskin	Hallard	Smith J	Shackleton 1	Flatley	Downie	Walker RG	
14		10	Blackburn Rovers	2-1	8000	Farr	Hepworth	Farrell	Stabb	Danskin	Hallard	Smith J	Shackleton 1	Knott	Downie 1	Walker RG	
15		17	BURNLEY	7-0	11331	Farr	Hepworth	Farrell	Stabb	Danskin	Hallard	Smith J	Shackleton 1	Knott 2	Downie 3	Walker RG 1	
16		24	Burnley	1-2	11000	Farr	Hepworth	Farrell	Stabb	Danskin	Hallard	Smith J	Shackleton	Knott 1	Downie	Flatley	
17	Dec	1	MANCHESTER CITY	2-3	14012	Farr	Hepworth	Firth	McTaff	Danskin	Greenwood	Smith J	Shackleton 1	Knott	Downie 1	Walker RG	
18		8	Manchester City	0-6	18525	Farr	Hepworth	Farrell	McTaff	Danskin	Greenwood	Smith J	Shackleton	Stabb	Downie	Hawksworth	
19		15	Newcastle United	0-4	38881	Farr	Hepworth	Farrell	Greenwood	Danskin	Hallard	Smith J	Shackleton	Knott	Downie	Dix	
20		25	SHEFFIELD WEDNESDAY	3-2	19000	Farr	Hepworth	Farrell 1	Greenwood	Danskin	Britton	Smith J 1	Shackleton 1	Horsman	Downie	Dix	
21		26	Sheffield Wednesday	0-3	32078	Farr	Hepworth	Farrell	McTaff	Greenwood	Britton	Smith J	Shackleton	Horsman	McCall	Hawksworth	
22		29	Huddersfield Town	1-1	14283	Farr	Hepworth	Leonard	McTaff	Ruecroft	Greenwood	Smith J	Shackleton	Gibbons	Downie	Walker RG	1 og
23	Jan	12	Barnsley	0-3	14700	Farr	Leonard	Farrell	McTaff	Danskin	Greenwood	Colley	Shackleton	Gibbons	Shirley	Smith J	
24		19	BARNSLEY	2-1	8643	Farr	Leonard	James	Greenwood	Danskin	Britton	Smith J	Shackleton	Knott	Gibbons 2	Offord	
25	Feb	2	Everton	0-0	28832	Farr	Hepworth	Farrell	Greenwood	Danskin	Hallard	Knott	Shackleton	Gibbons	Downie	Dix	
26		16	BOLTON WANDERERS	0-5	20358	Farr	Hepworth	Farrell	Greenwood	Danskin	Hallard	Shackleton	Stabb	Gibbons	Downie	Dix	
27		23	PRESTON NORTH END	3-1	11587	Farr	Hepworth	Farrell 1	McTaff	Kaye	Britton	Dix	Shackleton	Gibbons 1	Downie 1	Walker RG	
28	Mar	13	Bolton Wanderers	0-0	5162	Farr	Greenwood	Hepworth	Stabb	Kaye	White	Colley	Shackleton	Gibbons	McCall	Walker RG	
29		16	LEEDS UNITED	9-4	11302	Farr	Greenwood	Hepworth	McTaff	Kaye	Britton	Downie	Shackleton 3	Gibbons 4	McCall 1	Walker RG 1	
30		23	MANCHESTER UNITED	2-1	13498	Farr	Greenwood	Hepworth	McTaff	Danskin	Hallard	Colley 1	Shackleton	Gibbons 1	McCall	Walker RG	
31		27	NEWCASTLE UNITED	5-3	9397	Farr	Stephen	Hepworth	White	Danskin	Greenwood	Smith G 1	Shackleton 2	Gibbons 2	McCall	Walker RG	
32		30	Manchester United	0-4	36791	Farr	Greenwood	Hepworth	White	Danskin	Kaye	Downie	Shackleton	Gibbons	Sperrin	Walker RG	
33	Apr	3	EVERTON	1-2	10072	Farr	Greenwood	Hepworth	McTaff	Danskin	White	Smith J	Shackleton 1	Gibbons	McCall	Walker RG	
34		6	Sunderland	0-1	13000	Farr	Stephen	Hepworth	White	Danskin	Greenwood	Smith J	Downie	Gibbons	McCall	Walker RG	
35		11	Preston North End	6-4	6000	Farr	Stephen	Hepworth	McTaff	Danskin	White	Smith J 2	Downie 2	Gibbons 2	Chisholm	Walker RG	
36		13	SUNDERLAND	1-0	12660	Farr	Stephen	Hepworth	McTaff	Danskin	White	Smith J	Downie	Gibbons	McCall	Walker RG 1	
37		19	SHEFFIELD UNITED	0-4	18841	Farr	Stephen	Hepworth	White	Danskin	Greenwood	Smith J	Shackleton	Gibbons	Downie	Walker RG	
38		20	Middlesbrough	0-3	20000	Farr	Stephen	Hepworth	McTaff	Greenwood	Downie	Glasby	Shackleton	Gibbons	McCall	Walker RG	
39		22	Sheffield United	1-1	25455	Farr	Stephen	Hepworth	McTaff	Greenwood	Hallard	Glasby	Downie	Gibbons	McCall 1	Walker RG	
40		27	MIDDLESBROUGH	1-1	7143	Farr	Stephen	Hepworth	Downie	Greenwood	Hallard	Glasby	McCall	Horsman 1	Gibbons	Walker RG	
41	May	1	Leeds United	1-3	10000	Farr	Stephen	Hepworth	Greenwood	Danskin	Hallard	Glasby	Downie	Gibbons	McCall 1	Dix	
42		4	Chesterfield	0-2	10000	Farr	Stephen	Greenwood	Downie	Kaye	Hallard	Smith J	Gibbons	Horsman	McCall	Dix	

FA Cup

Rd	Month	Date	Opponent	Score	Att	1	2	3	4	5	6	7	8	9	10	11
R3/1	Jan	5	PORT VALE	2-1	14822	Farr	Hepworth	Farrell	McTaff	Greenwood	Hallard	Smith J	Shackleton	Gibbons 1	Downie 1	Dix
R3/2		7	Port Vale	1-1	11066	Farr	Hepworth	Farrell	McTaff	Greenwood	Hallard	Smith J	Shackleton	Gibbons 1	Downie	Dix
R4/1		26	MANCHESTER CITY	1-3	25014	Farr	Hepworth	James	Greenwood	Danskin	Britton	Downie	Shackleton	Knott	Gibbons 1	Walker RG
R4/2		30	Manchester City	8-2	15026	Farr	Hepworth	Farrell 1	Greenwood	Danskin	Hallard	Knott 1	Shackleton	Gibbons 4	Downie	Dix 2
R5/1	Feb	9	Barnsley	1-0	37770	Farr	Hepworth	Farrell	Greenwood	Danskin	Hallard	Knott	Shackleton 1	Gibbons	Downie	Dix
R5/2		13	BARNSLEY	1-1	29341	Farr	Hepworth	Farrell	Greenwood	Danskin	Hallard	Flatley	Shackleton	Gibbons 1	Downie	Dix
R6/1	Mar	2	BIRMINGHAM CITY	2-2	19732	Farr	Hepworth	Farrell	Greenwood	Danskin	Hallard 1	Dix 1	Shackleton	Gibbons	Downie	Walker RG
R6/2		9	Birmingham City	0-6	50000	Farr	Hepworth	Leonard	Greenwood	Danskin	Hallard	Dix	Shackleton	Knott	Gibbons	Walker RG

Guest players (League North only - no guest players permitted in the F.A. Cup)

Chilsholm (QPR)
Colley (Arsenal)
Greenwood (Chelsea)
Poole (Huddersfield Town)
Rodi (Grimsby Town)
Ruecroft (Halifax Town)
Shirley (Halifax Town)
Smith G (Barnsley)
White (Tottenham Hotspur)

LEAGUE TABLES 1939/40 TO 1945/46

1939/40 Regional League North East Division

		p	w	d	l	f	a	pts
1	Huddersfield Town	20	15	4	1	54	22	34
2	Newcastle United	20	12	0	8	58	39	24
3	BRADFORD	19	10	2	7	44	38	22
4	Middlesbrough	20	9	4	7	49	42	22
5	Leeds United	18	9	3	6	36	27	21
6	Bradford City	19	9	3	7	41	36	21
7	Hull City	20	8	1	11	35	41	17
8	York City	20	8	1	11	36	51	17
9	Darlington	19	6	3	10	44	57	15
10	Hartlepools United	20	6	1	13	27	47	13
11	Halifax Town	19	3	2	14	29	53	8

Some fixtures not played

1940/41 League North

Bradford finished 22nd out of 36 with this record;

p	w	d	l	f	a	Goal av.
31	9	7	15	64	74	0.864

Positions decided on goal average

1941/42

League North

Bradford finished 12th out of 38 with this record;

p	w	d	l	f	a	pts
18	8	5	5	33	28	21

League Championship

Bradford finsished 18th out of 51 with this record;

p	w	d	l	f	a	pts	Av.
19	5	6	8	35	40	16	19.360

Average points calculated assuming 23 games played

League Cup Qualifiers:

p	w	d	l	f	a	pts	Av.
10	3	3	4	22	26	9	9

Average points calculated assuming 10 games played

Bradford finished 32nd out of 51 clubs and qualified for the knock-out stage

1942/43

League North First Championship

Bradford finsished 10th out of 48 with this record;

p	w	d	l	f	a	pts
18	8	7	3	46	21	23

League North Second Championship

Bradford finsished 24th out of 56 with this record;

p	w	d	l	f	a	pts
19	7	5	7	35	31	19

League North Cup

Bradford finsished 24th out of 54 and qualified for the knock-out stages

p	w	d	l	f	a	pts
9	4	3	2	18	11	19

1943/44 Football League North

First Championship (top 12 clubs only)

		p	w	d	l	f	a	pts
1	Blackpool	18	12	4	2	46	20	28
2	Manchester United	18	13	2	3	56	30	28
3	Liverpool	18	13	1	4	72	26	27
4	Doncaster	18	11	5	2	45	25	27
5	BRADFORD	18	11	4	3	65	28	26
6	Huddersfield T	18	12	2	4	48	35	26
7	Northampton T	18	10	5	3	43	25	25
8	Aston Villa	18	11	3	4	43	27	25
9	Sunderland	18	10	3	5	46	30	23
10	Hartlepools United	18	10	3	5	44	31	23
11	Everton	18	9	4	5	60	34	22
12	Blackburn Rovers	18	10	2	6	47	32	22

Second Championship (top 12 clubs only)

		p	w	d	l	f	a	pts
1	Bath	21	16	2	3	78	26	34
2	Wrexham	21	15	4	2	62	29	34
3	Liverpool	21	14	2	5	71	38	30
4	Birmingham	20	12	5	3	47	19	29
5	Rotherham United	21	12	5	4	54	30	29
6	Aston Villa	21	13	3	5	50	34	29
7	Blackpool	20	12	3	5	53	27	27
8	Cardiff City	21	13	1	7	53	28	27
9	Manchester United	21	10	7	4	55	38	27
10	BRADFORD	20	11	4	5	50	30	26
11	Newcastle United	20	13	0	7	47	36	26
12	Everton	21	12	1	8	73	39	25

League North Cup

Bradford finished 6th out of 56 and qualified for the knock-out stages

p	w	d	l	f	a	pts
10	6	3	1	23	14	15

1944/45 Football League North

First Championship (top 10 clubs only)

		p	w	d	l	f	a	pts
1	Huddersfield Town	18	14	3	1	50	22	31
2	Derby County	18	14	1	3	54	19	29
3	Sunderland	18	12	4	2	52	25	28
4	Aston Villa	18	12	3	3	54	19	27
5	Everton	18	12	2	4	58	25	26
6	Wrexham	18	11	3	4	40	18	25
7	Doncaster Rovers	18	12	0	6	48	27	24
8	BRADFORD	18	10	4	4	45	31	24
9	Bolton Wanderers	18	9	6	3	34	22	24
10	Manchester City	18	9	4	5	53	31	22

Second Championship

Finished mid-table with the following record:

p	w	d	l	f	a	pts
22	10	4	8	49	39	24

and qualifed for the knock-out stages of the League North Cup:

p	w	d	l	f	a	pts
10	6	3	1	27	15	13

1945/46 League North

		p	w	d	l	f	a	w	d	l	f	a	pts
1	Sheffield United	42	14	3	4	61	29	13	3	5	51	33	60
2	Everton	42	14	5	2	58	23	9	4	8	30	31	55
3	Bolton Wanderers	42	11	6	4	32	18	9	5	7	35	27	51
4	Manchester United	42	13	4	4	61	29	6	7	8	37	33	49
5	Sheffield Wednesday	42	13	5	3	39	20	7	3	11	28	40	48
6	Newcastle United	42	13	4	4	68	27	8	1	12	38	43	47
7	Chesterfield	42	9	8	4	29	16	8	4	9	39	33	46
8	Barnsley	42	11	5	5	44	33	6	6	9	32	35	45
9	Blackpool	42	13	4	4	56	34	5	5	11	38	58	45
10	Manchester City	42	12	0	9	43	37	8	4	9	35	38	44
11	Liverpool	42	10	5	6	47	36	7	4	10	33	34	43
12	Middlesbrough	42	12	2	7	44	43	5	7	9	31	44	43
13	Stoke City	42	14	2	5	60	24	4	4	13	28	55	42
14	BRADFORD	42	13	2	6	53	35	4	4	13	18	49	40
15	Huddersfield Town	42	13	2	6	50	33	4	2	15	40	56	38
16	Burnley	42	9	5	7	42	36	4	5	12	21	48	36
17	Grimsby Town	42	8	6	7	32	34	5	3	13	29	55	35
18	Sunderland	42	12	2	7	33	27	3	3	15	22	56	35
19	Preston North End	42	10	2	9	50	34	4	4	13	20	43	34
20	Bury	42	8	6	7	35	35	4	4	13	25	50	34
21	Blackburn Rovers	42	7	5	9	31	44	4	2	15	29	67	29
22	Leeds United	42	7	4	10	36	42	2	3	16	30	76	25

The programme for the game with Blackpool April 8 1944, the record attendance at Park Avenue

1946/47

16th in Division Two

No	Month	Day	Opponent	Score	Scorers	Att	Britton J	Danskin R	Davidson DBL	Deplidge W	Dix R	Donaldson W	Downie JD	Elliott WH	Farr TF	Farrell A	Gibbons AH	Glasby H	Greenwood R	Hepworth R	Horsman L	Layton WH	McCall J	McIlvenny HJ	McTaff S	Nicholls JH	Shackleton LF	Smith JW	Stabb GH	Stephen JF	White RBW	Wilkins GE	Woods W
1	Aug	31	Chesterfield	1-1	Shackleton	14473		5	6			11			1		10	7		3	9						8			2	4		
2	Sep	4	LUTON TOWN	2-1	Gibbons, Glasby	16931		5	6			11			1		10	7		3	9						8			2	4		
3		7	MILLWALL	0-0		20509		5	6			11			1		10	7		3	9						8			2	4		
4		14	Swansea Town	6-1	* see below	16217		5				11			1		9	7	6	3			10				8			2	4		
5		21	Manchester City	2-7	Gibbons 2	40087		5				11			1		9	7	6	3			10				8			2	4		
6		25	BURY	2-2	McCall, Gibbons	9673			6			11			1	3	9	7			5		10				8			2	4		
7		28	WEST HAM UNITED	0-1		21360			6			11			1		9		5	3			10				8	7		2	4		
8	Oct	5	Sheffield Wednesday	2-1	Gibbons, Smith	20591			6			11			1		9		5	3			10		4			7	8	2			
9		12	FULHAM	1-2	Stabb	15479			6	10		11			1		9		5	3					4			7	8	2			
10		19	NEWCASTLE UNITED	2-1	Horsman, Downie	26433		5	6			11	8		1	3	10		2		9				4			7					
11		26	West Bromwich Albion	1-1	Horsman	22979		5	6			11	8		1	3	10				9				4			7		2			
12	Nov	2	BIRMINGHAM CITY	2-0	Horsman 2	21638		5	6			11	8		1	3	10				9				4			7		2			
13		9	Coventry City	0-0		19164		5	6			11	8		1	3	10				9				4			7		2			
14		16	NOTTM. FOREST	0-1		16034		5				11	8		1	3	10				9				4			7		2	6		
15		23	Southampton	2-3	Farrell, Danskin	16249		5			11		8		1	3	10				9				4			7		2	6		
16		30	NEWPORT COUNTY	2-1	Downie, Horsman	12555		5			11		10		1	3	9				8				4			7		2	6		
17	Dec	7	Barnsley	1-3	Charlesworth (og)	13448		5	6			11	10		1	3	9				8				4			7		2			
18		14	BURNLEY	0-1		10731		5	6	11			10		1	3	9			2	8				4			7					
19		21	Tottenham Hotspur	3-3	Downie, Dix, Smith	24779		5			11		8	6	1	3	10				9				4			7		2			
20		25	LEICESTER CITY	1-2	Danskin	14939		5			11		8	6	1	3	10			2	9				4			7					
21		26	Leicester City	1-2	Horsman	36075	6				11		8	4	1	2	10		5	3	9							7					
22		28	CHESTERFIELD	0-0		19221						11		6	1	3	9		5		8		10					7		2	4		
23	Jan	1	Bury	3-6	Gibbons 2, Horsman	19203					11		8	6	1	2	9		5	3	7		10								4		
24		4	Millwall	1-0	Gibbons	26773						11			1	3	9		5	6	8		10					7		2	4		
25		18	SWANSEA TOWN	0-0		14336						11	8		1	3	9		5			6						7		2	4		10
26	Feb	1	West Ham United	1-1	Gibbons	16593					11			8	1	3	9		5			6						7		2	4		10
27	Mar	12	SHEFFIELD WEDNESDAY	1-1	Gibbons	5180					11				1	3	9		5			6			4			7		2		8	10
28		15	COVENTRY CITY	5-1	Wilkins, Gibbons 4	13516					11				1	3	9		5			6			4			7		2		8	10
29		29	SOUTHAMPTON	2-3	Smith, Dix	10133					11				1	3	9		5			6			4			7		2		8	10
30	Apr	7	Plymouth Argyle	4-2	Wilkins, Smith, Dix, White	23201					11				1	3	9		5			10			4			7		2	6	8	
31		12	BARNSLEY	1-3	Gibbons	18412					11				1	3	9		5			10			4			7		2	6	8	
32		19	Burnley	2-1	Downie, Dix	32905					11		10		1		9		5	3				8	4			7		2	6		
33		26	TOTTENHAM HOTSPUR	2-1	Stephen, McIlvenny	11371					11		10		1		9		5	3				8	4			7		2	6		
34	May	3	Birmingham City	0-4		23083					11			8	1		9		5	3			10		4			7		2	6		
35		10	Newcastle United	0-5		33131						11		8	1		9		5	3					4			7		2	6	10	
36		14	MANCHESTER CITY	1-1	Gibbons	15162								7	1	3	9		5	11				8	4					2	6	10	
37		17	Newport County	3-1	Layton, McIlvenny, Wilkins	10159								7		3	9		5	11		6		8		1				2	4	10	
38		24	Luton Town	0-3		10805					11			7		3	9		5			6		8		1				2	4	10	
39		26	PLYMOUTH ARGYLE	3-2	Wilkins, Gibbons 2	7996								7		3	9		5	11				8	4	1				2	6	10	
40		27	WEST BROMWICH ALB.	2-4	Gibbons, Elliott	10777								7		3	9		5			6		8	4	1		11		2		10	
41		31	Fulham	3-0	Gibbons, Elliott, McIlvenny	9662		5				11	10	7		3	9		6					8	4	1				2			
42	Jun	14	Nottingham Forest	0-4		8429		5				11		7		3	9		6					8	4	1				2		10	
						Apps	1	18	13	2	16	21	17	15	36	30	42	6	28	20	19	10	9	9	27	6	7	29	2	37	25	12	5
						Goals		2			4	2	4	2		1	21	1			7	1	1	3			4	4	1	1	1	4	

Scorers in game 4: Shackleton 3, Donaldson 2, Gibbons

One own goal

F.A. Cup

Round	Month	Day	Opponent	Score	Att	Britton J	Danskin R	Davidson DBL	Deplidge W	Dix R	Donaldson W	Downie JD	Elliott WH	Farr TF	Farrell A	Gibbons AH	Glasby H	Greenwood R	Hepworth R	Horsman L	Layton WH	McCall J	McIlvenny HJ	McTaff S	Nicholls JH	Shackleton LF	Smith JW	Stabb GH	Stephen JF	White RBW	Wilkins GE	Woods W
R1	Jan	11	MANCHESTER UNITED	0-3	24370		5				11			1	3	10		6		8			9				7		2	4		

		P	W	D	L	F	A	W	D	L	F	A	Pts
1	Manchester City	42	17	3	1	49	14	9	7	5	29	21	62
2	Burnley	42	11	8	2	30	14	11	6	4	35	15	58
3	Birmingham City	42	17	2	2	51	11	8	3	10	23	22	55
4	Chesterfield	42	12	6	3	37	17	6	8	7	21	27	50
5	Newcastle United	42	11	4	6	60	32	8	6	7	35	30	48
6	Tottenham Hotspur	42	11	8	2	35	21	6	6	9	30	32	48
7	West Bromwich Albion	42	12	4	5	53	37	8	4	9	35	38	48
8	Coventry City	42	12	8	1	40	17	4	5	12	26	42	45
9	Leicester City	42	11	4	6	42	25	7	3	11	27	39	43
10	Barnsley	42	13	2	6	48	29	4	6	11	36	57	42
11	Nottingham Forest	42	13	5	3	47	20	2	5	14	22	54	40
12	West Ham United	42	12	4	5	46	31	4	4	13	24	45	40
13	Luton Town	42	13	4	4	50	29	3	3	15	21	44	39
14	Southampton	42	11	5	5	45	24	4	4	13	24	52	39
15	Fulham	42	12	4	5	40	25	3	5	13	23	49	39
16	BRADFORD	42	7	6	8	29	28	7	5	9	36	49	39
17	Bury	42	11	6	4	62	34	1	6	14	18	44	36
18	Millwall	42	7	7	7	30	30	7	1	13	26	49	36
19	Plymouth Argyle	42	11	3	7	45	34	3	2	16	34	62	33
20	Sheffield Wednesday	42	10	5	6	39	28	2	3	16	28	60	32
21	Swansea Town	42	9	1	11	36	40	2	6	13	19	43	29
22	Newport County	42	9	1	11	41	52	1	2	18	20	81	23

1947/48

14th in Division Two

	Date		Opponent	Score	Scorers	Att	Ainsley GE	Danskin R	Deplidge W	Dix R	Donaldson W	Downie JD	Elliott WH	Farr TF	Farrell A	Glasby H	Glover A	Greenwood R	Henry GR	Hepworth R	Horsman L	Layton WH	Leonard H	McCall J	McIlvenny HJ	McTaff S	Neil WM	Nicholls JH	Smith JW	Stephen JF	White RBW	Wilkins GE
1	Aug	23	WEST HAM UNITED	4-1	McIlvenny 2, Downie 2	14523						10	11		3			5				6			9			1	7	2	4	8
2		27	Nottingham Forest	2-1	Smith 2	22365						10	11		3			5				6			9			1	7	2	4	8
3		30	Chesterfield	1-0	Smith	12601						10	11		3			5				6			9			1	7	2	4	8
4	Sep	3	NOTTM. FOREST	3-1	Downie, McIlvenny, Elliott	16246						10	11		3			5				6			9			1	7	2	4	8
5		6	MILLWALL	4-0	Downie 2, Farrell, Layton	18164		5				10	11		3							6			9			1	7	2	4	8
6		10	DONCASTER ROVERS	4-0	McIlvenny, Downie, Wilkins, Smith	18942						10	11		3						5	6			9			1	7	2	4	8
7		13	Tottenham Hotspur	1-3	Farrell	44004						10	11		3						5	6			9			1	7	2	4	8
8		18	Doncaster Rovers	0-3		22207						10	11		3			5		2	9	6						1	7	4		8
9		20	SHEFFIELD WEDNESDAY	2-0	McIlvenny, Wilkins	21818						10	11	1	3			5				6			9	4			7	2		8
10		27	Cardiff City	0-1		39796						10	11	1	3			5				6			9				7	2	4	8
11	Oct	4	LUTON TOWN	2-2	McIlvenny, Downie	21568						10	11	1	3			5				6			9				7	2	4	8
12		11	Brentford	1-2	Downie	24682						10	11	1	3			5				6			9				7	2	4	8
13		18	LEICESTER CITY	0-2		16406						10	11	1	3			5			9	6		8					7	2	4	
14		25	Leeds United	0-2		31532			6		11	10		1	3			5			9				8				7	2	4	
15	Nov	1	FULHAM	3-0	Dix, Horsman, Bacuzzi (og)	16390			6	11				1	3			5		2	9	10							7		4	8
16		8	Coventry City	0-5		21577			6	11				1	3			5			9	10							7	2	4	8
17		15	NEWCASTLE UNITED	0-3		24654			6			10	11	1	3	7		5		2	9										4	8
18		22	Birmingham City	3-4	Smith, Downie 2	29020			6			10	11	1		7		5		3	9								8	2	4	
19		29	WEST BROMWICH ALB.	3-1	Ainsley 2, Downie	19297	9		6			10	11	1	3			5	8	2									7		4	
20	Dec	6	Barnsley	2-2	Downie, Ainsley	17327	9		6			10	11	1	3			5	8	2									7		4	
21		13	PLYMOUTH ARGYLE	3-0	Ainsley, Henry 2	14851	9		6			10	11		3			5	8	2								1	7		4	
22		20	West Ham United	0-0		24412	9		6		7	10	11		3			5	8				2					1			4	
23		26	SOUTHAMPTON	1-3	Downie	22823	9		6			10	11		3	7		5	8	2								1			4	
24		27	Southampton	2-1	Henry, Donaldson	24893			6		7	10	11	1	3			5	8	2	9										4	
25	Jan	3	CHESTERFIELD	1-3	Henry	19887	9		6		7	10	11	1	3			5	8	2											4	
26		17	Millwall	1-0	Smith	19039	9		6			10	11	1	3			5	8	2									7		4	
27		31	TOTTENHAM HOTSPUR	0-2		20807	9		6			10	11	1	3			5	8	2						4			7			
28	Feb	7	Sheffield Wednesday	1-3	Downie	36376	9					10	11	1	3	7		5	6	2							8				4	
29		14	CARDIFF CITY	0-1		14756			7			10	11	1	3			5	6	2	9						8				4	
30		21	Luton Town	3-3	Horsman 2, Downie	11418			7			10	11	1				5	6	3	9						8			2	4	
31		28	BRENTFORD	1-1	Henry	11666			6			10	11	1				5	8	3	9								7	2	4	
32	Mar	6	Leicester City	0-2		22291			6			10	11	1			7	5	8	3	9									2	4	
33		13	LEEDS UNITED	3-1	Ainsley 3	21060	9					10	11	1	3		7	5	8			6								2	4	
34		20	Fulham	0-0		16896	9					10	11	1	3		7		8		5	6								2	4	
35		26	Bury	4-0	G Griffiths (og), Henry 2, Ainsley	20260	9				11	10	6	1	3		7		8		5									2	4	
36		27	COVENTRY CITY	2-2	Ainsley, Downie	16700	9		6			10	11	1	3		7		8		5									2	4	
37		29	BURY	5-3	Downie 2, Ainsley 2, Henry	13638	9		6			10	11		3		7	5	8									1		2	4	
38	Apr	3	Newcastle United	0-2		50367	9		6			10	11		3		7		8		5							1		2	4	
39		10	BIRMINGHAM CITY	1-2	Henry	16782			6			10	11		3		7		8		5				9			1		2	4	
40		17	West Bromwich Albion	0-6		13349	9		6			10	11	1	3		7		8		5									2	4	
41		24	BARNSLEY	3-2	Layton, Ainsley, Downie	10440	9					10	11	1	3		7		8		5	6								2	4	
42	May	1	Plymouth Argyle	2-2	Layton, Ainsley	18398	9					10	11	1	3		7		8		5	6								2	4	
						Apps	18	1	23	2	5	40	39	28	38	4	11	31	24	17	22	19	1	1	13	2	3	14	23	29	39	15
						Goals	13			1	1	19	1		2				9		3	3			6				6			2

Two own goals

F.A. Cup

	Date		Opponent	Score	Scorers	Att	Ainsley GE	Danskin R	Deplidge W	Dix R	Donaldson W	Downie JD	Elliott WH	Farr TF	Farrell A	Glasby H	Glover A	Greenwood R	Henry GR	Hepworth R	Horsman L	Layton WH	Leonard H	McCall J	McIlvenny HJ	McTaff S	Neil WM	Nicholls JH	Smith JW	Stephen JF	White RBW	Wilkins GE
R3	Jan	10	Arsenal	1-0	Elliott	47738	9		6			10	11	1	3			5	8	2									7		4	
R4		24	Colchester United	2-3	Elliott, Ainsley	17000	9		6			10	11	1	3			5	8	2									7		4	

		P	W	D	L	F	A	W	D	L	F	A	Pts
1	Birmingham City	42	12	7	2	34	13	10	8	3	21	11	59
2	Newcastle United	42	18	1	2	46	13	6	7	8	26	28	56
3	Southampton	42	15	3	3	53	23	6	7	8	18	30	52
4	Sheffield Wednesday	42	13	6	2	39	21	7	5	9	27	32	51
5	Cardiff City	42	12	6	3	36	18	6	5	10	25	40	47
6	West Ham United	42	10	7	4	29	19	6	7	8	26	34	46
7	West Bromwich Albion	42	11	4	6	37	29	7	5	9	26	29	45
8	Tottenham Hotspur	42	10	6	5	36	24	5	8	8	20	19	44
9	Leicester City	42	10	5	6	36	29	6	6	9	24	28	43
10	Coventry City	42	10	5	6	33	16	4	8	9	26	36	41
11	Fulham	42	6	9	6	24	19	9	1	11	23	27	40
12	Barnsley	42	10	5	6	31	22	5	5	11	31	42	40
13	Luton Town	42	8	8	5	31	25	6	4	11	25	34	40
14	BRADFORD	42	11	3	7	45	30	5	5	11	23	42	40
15	Brentford	42	10	6	5	31	26	3	8	10	13	35	40
16	Chesterfield	42	8	4	9	32	26	8	3	10	22	29	39
17	Plymouth Argyle	42	8	9	4	27	22	1	11	9	13	36	38
18	Leeds United	42	12	5	4	44	20	2	3	16	18	52	36
19	Nottingham Forest	42	10	5	6	32	23	2	6	13	22	37	35
20	Bury	42	6	8	7	27	28	3	8	10	31	40	34
21	Doncaster Rovers	42	7	8	6	23	20	2	3	16	17	46	29
22	Millwall	42	7	7	7	27	28	2	4	15	17	46	29

1948/49

17th in Division Two

	Date		Opponent	Score	Scorers	Att.	Ainsley GE	Crowther K	Deplidge W	Donaldson W	Downie JD	Elliott WH	Farr TF	Farrell A	Glasby H	Glover A	Henry GR	Hepworth R	Hodgson D	Horsman L	Layton WH	McIlvenny HJ	Mordue J	Smith JW	Stephen JF	Stevens LWG	White RBW
1	Aug	21	CARDIFF CITY	3-0	Ainsley, Downie 2	15048	9				10	11	1	3		7	8			5	6				2		4
2		23	Blackburn Rovers	3-2	Ainsley, Henry, Downie	27786	9				10	11	1	3		7	8			5	6				2		4
3		28	Queen's Park Rangers	0-1		27666	9				10	11	1	3		7	8			5	6				2		4
4	Sep	1	BLACKBURN ROVERS	2-0	Henry, Ainsley	17749	9				10	11	1			7	8	3		5	6				2		4
5		4	LUTON TOWN	4-1	Henry, Ainsley 3	18697	9				10	11	1			7	8	3		5	6				2		4
6		8	Plymouth Argyle	0-3		18580	9				10	11	1			7	8	3		5	6				2		4
7		11	Coventry City	0-2		16372	9				10	11	1			7	8	3		5	6				2		4
8		15	PLYMOUTH ARGYLE	2-2	Ainsley, Downie	10624	9				10	11	1	3		7	8			5	6				2		4
9		18	Southampton	2-2	Ainsley 2	26559	9				10	11	1	3		7				5	6			8	2		4
10		25	BARNSLEY	0-2		23145	9				10	11	1			7		3		5	6			8	2		4
11	Oct	2	Grimsby Town	3-0	Downie 2, Deplidge	15931	9	4	8		10	11	1	3		7				5	6				2		
12		9	LEEDS UNITED	1-1	Downie	25587	9	4			10	11	1	3		7	8			5	6				2		
13		16	Leicester City	2-2	Glover, Crowther	27154	9	4		11	10		1	3		7	8			5	6				2		
14		23	BRENTFORD	3-1	Henry, Downie, Ainsley	14906	9	4		11	10		1	3		7	8			5	6				2		
15		30	Tottenham Hotspur	1-5	Ainsley	47955	9	4		11	10		1	3		7	8			5	6				2		
16	Nov	6	WEST HAM UNITED	2-3	Downie, Donaldson	15913	9	4		11	10		1	3		7	8			5	6				2		
17		13	Bury	1-2	McIlvenny	9923			6		10	11	1	3		7	8			5		9			2		4
18		20	WEST BROMWICH ALB.	4-1	McIlvenny, Farrell, Deplidge, Glover	18064			10	11	8	6	1	3		7				5		9			2		4
19		27	Chesterfield	3-2	McIlvenny, Deplidge, Glover	12585			10	11	8	6	1	3		7				5		9			2		4
20	Dec	4	Lincoln City	6-3	McIlvenny 2, Deplidge 2, White, Glover	14171			10	11	8	6	1	3		7				5		9			2		4
21		11	Sheffield Wednesday	1-2	McIlvenny	36683			10	11	8	6	1	3		7				5		9			2		4
22		18	Cardiff City	1-6	Downie	28002			10	11	8	6	1	3		7			9	5					2		4
23		25	FULHAM	1-1	Deplidge	20742			10	11	8	6	1	3		7				5		9			2		4
24		27	Fulham	0-2		22242			10	11	8	6	1	3		7				5		9			2		4
25	Jan	1	QUEEN'S PARK RANGERS	0-0		15178				11	10	6	1	3		7	8			5		9			2		4
26		15	Luton Town	1-0	Henry	16071			11		10	6	1	3		7	8			5		9			2		4
27		22	COVENTRY CITY	2-1	Ainsley, Henry	17624	9		11		10		1	3		7	8			5			6		2		4
28	Feb	19	Barnsley	0-0		21535				11	10	6	1	3		7	9	2	8	5							4
29		26	GRIMSBY TOWN	0-1		15139					10	6	1	3		7	9	2	8	5						11	4
30	Mar	5	Leeds United	2-4	Stevens, Deplidge	22477			10			6	1	3		7	8	2	9	5						11	4
31		12	LEICESTER CITY	3-3	Henry, Layton, Ainsley	14770	9					6	1	3			8	2		5	10			7		11	4
32		19	Brentford	0-1		18413	9					6	1	3			8	2		5	10			7		11	4
33		26	TOTTENHAM HOTSPUR	1-1	Deplidge	13304	9		10			6	1	3			8	2		5				7		11	4
34	Apr	2	West Ham United	1-4	Deplidge	18645	9		10			6	1	3			8	2		5				7		11	4
35		4	SOUTHAMPTON	2-0	White, Ainsley	9293	9		10			6	1	3			8	2		5				7		11	4
36		9	BURY	4-1	Henry 3, Ainsley	13064	9		10			6	1	3			8	2		5				7		11	4
37		15	Nottingham Forest	0-2		21229	9		10			6	1	3			8	2		5				7		11	4
38		16	West Bromwich Albion	1-7	Ainsley	39241	9		10			6	1	3			8	2		5				7		11	4
39		18	NOTTM. FOREST	1-2	Donaldson	12032				11		6	1	3	9		8	2		5				7		10	4
40		23	CHESTERFIELD	1-1	Deplidge	10581			10	11		6	1	3			8	2	9	5				7			4
41	May	4	LINCOLN CITY	0-3		6054	9		10				1	3			8			5			6	7	2	11	4
42		7	SHEFFIELD WEDNESDAY	1-1	Henry	7132				11		6	1	3		10	8	2	9	5				7			4
						Apps	26	6	20	16	29	36	42	37	1	31	32	19	6	42	18	9	2	14	28	12	36
						Goals	16	1	10	2	10			1		4	11				1	6				1	2

F.A. Cup

	Date		Opponent	Score	Scorers	Att.	Ainsley GE	Crowther K	Deplidge W	Donaldson W	Downie JD	Elliott WH	Farr TF	Farrell A	Glasby H	Glover A	Henry GR	Hepworth R	Hodgson D	Horsman L	Layton WH	McIlvenny HJ	Mordue J	Smith JW	Stephen JF	Stevens LWG	White RBW
R3	Jan	8	Newcastle United	2-0	Downie, McIlvenny	47196			11		10	6	1	3		7	8			5		9			2		4
R4		29	Manchester United	1-1	(aet) Henry	82771			11		10	6	1	3		7	8			5		9			2		4
rep	Feb	5	MANCHESTER UNITED	1-1	(aet) Farrell (p)	29092			11		10	6	1	3		7	8			5		9			2		4
rep2		7	Manchester United	0-5		70434	9		11		10	6	1	3		7	8			5					2		4

R4 and R4 second replay played at Maine Road

		P	W	D	L	F	A	W	D	L	F	A	Pts
1	Fulham	42	16	4	1	52	14	8	5	8	25	23	57
2	West Bromwich Albion	42	16	3	2	47	16	8	5	8	22	23	56
3	Southampton	42	16	4	1	48	10	7	5	9	21	26	55
4	Cardiff City	42	14	4	3	45	21	5	9	7	17	26	51
5	Tottenham Hotspur	42	14	4	3	50	18	3	12	6	22	26	50
6	Chesterfield	42	9	7	5	24	18	6	10	5	27	27	47
7	West Ham United	42	13	5	3	38	23	5	5	11	18	35	46
8	Sheffield Wednesday	42	12	6	3	36	17	3	7	11	27	39	43
9	Barnsley	42	10	7	4	40	18	4	5	12	22	43	40
10	Luton Town	42	11	6	4	32	16	3	6	12	23	41	40
11	Grimsby Town	42	10	5	6	44	28	5	5	11	28	48	40
12	Bury	42	12	5	4	41	23	5	1	15	26	53	40
13	Queen's Park Rangers	42	11	4	6	31	26	3	7	11	13	36	39
14	Blackburn Rovers	42	12	5	4	41	23	3	3	15	12	40	38
15	Leeds United	42	11	6	4	36	21	1	7	13	19	42	37
16	Coventry City	42	12	3	6	35	20	3	4	14	20	44	37
17	BRADFORD	42	8	8	5	37	26	5	3	13	28	52	37
18	Brentford	42	7	10	4	28	21	4	4	13	14	32	36
19	Leicester City	42	6	10	5	41	38	4	6	11	21	41	36
20	Plymouth Argyle	42	11	4	6	33	25	1	8	12	16	39	36
21	Nottingham Forest	42	9	6	6	22	14	5	1	15	28	40	35
22	Lincoln City	42	6	7	8	31	35	2	5	14	22	56	28

1949/50

Bottom of Division Two: Relegated

#	Month	Day	Opponent	Score	Scorers	Att	Crosbie RC	Currie CJ	Deplidge W	Donaldson W	Elliott WH	Farr TF	Farrell A	Glover A	Haines JTW	Henry GR	Hepworth R	Hodgson D	Horsman L	James JS	Leuty LH	McIlvenny HJ	Nicholls JH	Sirrel J	Smith A(2)	Smith JW	Stevens LWG	Suddards J	White RBW
1	Aug	20	Plymouth Argyle	1-1	Smith	25698	9				6	1	3	8			2		5					10		7	11		4
2		24	LEICESTER CITY	2-2	Glover, Crosbie	14624	9				6	1	3	11		8	2		5					10		7			4
3		27	SHEFFIELD WEDNESDAY	1-3	Deplidge	18745	9	5	10		6	1	3	11		8	2									7			4
4		29	Leicester City	1-4	Deplidge	26938	9	5	10	11	6	1	3											8	2	7			4
5	Sep	3	Hull City	3-3	Henry, Smith, Deplidge	41624	9		10		6	1	3	11		8	2		5							7			4
6		7	LUTON TOWN	1-0	Deplidge	11201	9		10		6	1	3	11		8	2		5							7			4
7		10	BRENTFORD	0-2		12754	9		10		6	1	3	11		8	2		5							7			4
8		17	Blackburn Rovers	1-0	Deplidge	23106	9		10		6	1	3			8	2		5							7	11		4
9		24	CARDIFF CITY	3-3	McIlvenny, Henry, Deplidge	13187			10		6	1	3			8	2		5			9				7	11		4
10	Oct	1	Tottenham Hotspur	0-5		54905			10		6	1				8	2		5			9			3	7	11		4
11		8	Barnsley	2-3	Henry, Elliott	21642		2	10		6	1				8	3		5			9				7	11		4
12		15	WEST HAM UNITED	2-1	Deplidge, Henry	13863		2	10		6	1				8	3		5			9				7	11		4
13		22	Sheffield United	1-2	Chisholm (og)	25313		2	10		6	1				8	3		5			9				7	11		4
14		29	GRIMSBY TOWN	4-1	Smith, Deplidge, Henry 2	15369			10		6	1	2			8	3		5			9				7	11		4
15	Nov	5	Queen's Park Rangers	1-0	Deplidge	8873			10		6	1	2			8	3		5			9				7	11		4
16		12	PRESTON NORTH END	1-2	Stevens	14017			10		6	1	2			8	3		5			9				7	11		4
17		19	Swansea Town	0-2		18729		2	10		6	1	3			8			5			9				7	11		4
18		26	LEEDS UNITED	1-2	Elliott	18401		2	10		6	1	3			8			5			9				7	11		4
19	Dec	3	Southampton	1-3	Henry	20876	9	2	10		6	1	3			8			5							7	11		4
20		10	COVENTRY CITY	2-2	Currie 2	9928		9	10		6		2			8	3		5				1			7	11		4
21		17	PLYMOUTH ARGYLE	3-2	Smith, Henry 2	7708		9			6		2			10	3	8	5				1			7	11		4
22		24	Sheffield Wednesday	1-1	Henry	38369		9			6		2		10	8	3		5				1			7	11		4
23		26	BURY	1-2	McIlvenny	23341					6		2		10	8	3		5			9	1			7	11		4
24		27	Bury	0-1		22700		2	8		6				10		3		5			9	1			7	11		4
25		31	HULL CITY	5-1	Stevens 2, Henry, Crosbie, Haines	27020	9	2			6				10	8	3		5				1			7	11		4
26	Jan	14	Brentford	0-2		19781	9	2			6				10	8	3		5				1			7	11		4
27		21	BLACKBURN ROVERS	2-2	Crosbie,Deplidge	13707	9	2	8		6				10		3		5				1			7	11		4
28	Feb	4	Cardiff City	2-1	Crosbie, Haines	25164	9	2	8		6		3		10				5				1			7	11		4
29		18	TOTTENHAM HOTSPUR	1-3	Crosbie	20287	9	2	8		6		3		10				5				1			7	11		4
30		25	BARNSLEY	1-3	Elliott	11134	9		11		6		3		10		2	8	5				1			7			4
31	Mar	4	West Ham United	0-1		17587	9				6		3		10		2		5				1	8		7	11		4
32		11	SHEFFIELD UNITED	1-1	Haines	18115	9		8		6		3		10		2		5				1			7	11		4
33		18	Grimsby Town	0-4		15336	9		8		6		3		10		2				5		1			7	11		4
34		25	QUEEN'S PARK RANGERS	1-0	Smith	18063	8	2			6		3		10				9		5		1			7	11		4
35	Apr	1	Leeds United	0-0		31062	8	2			6		3		10				9		5		1			7	11	4	
36		7	Chesterfield	1-1	Horsman	14680	8	2			6	1	3		10				9		5					7	11	4	
37		8	SOUTHAMPTON	0-0		16359	8	2		11	6	1	3		10				9		5					7		4	
38		11	CHESTERFIELD	2-0	Elliott, Crosbie	19596	9	2			6	1	3		10						5					7	11	4	8
39		15	Preston North End	0-3		19251	9	2			6	1	3		10						5					7	11	4	8
40		22	SWANSEA TOWN	0-2		16169		2	8		6	1	3		10			9			5					7	11	4	
41		29	Coventry City	1-3	Horsman	12611		2	6		11	1	3		10			8	9		5					7		4	
42	May	6	Luton Town	1-3	Sirrel	11232		2	6		11	1			10				9	3	5			8		7		4	
						Apps	24	26	28	2	42	26	33	6	21	23	27	4	36	1	10	12	16	5	2	42	32	8	36
						Goals	6	2	10		4			1	3	11			2			2		1		5	3		

One own goal

F.A. Cup

Rd	Month	Day	Opponent	Score	Scorers	Att	Crosbie RC	Currie CJ	Deplidge W	Donaldson W	Elliott WH	Farr TF	Farrell A	Glover A	Haines JTW	Henry GR	Hepworth R	Hodgson D	Horsman L	James JS	Leuty LH	McIlvenny HJ	Nicholls JH	Sirrel J	Smith A(2)	Smith JW	Stevens LWG	Suddards J	White RBW
R3	Jan	7	BOURNEMOUTH	0-1		19709	9				6		2		10	8	3		5				1			7	11		4

		P	W	D	L	F	A	W	D	L	F	A	Pts
1	Tottenham Hotspur	42	15	3	3	51	15	12	4	5	30	20	61
2	Sheffield Wednesday	42	12	7	2	46	23	6	9	6	21	25	52
3	Sheffield United	42	9	10	2	36	19	10	4	7	32	30	52
4	Southampton	42	13	4	4	44	25	6	10	5	20	23	52
5	Leeds United	42	11	8	2	33	16	6	5	10	21	29	47
6	Preston North End	42	12	5	4	37	21	6	4	11	23	28	45
7	Hull City	42	11	8	2	39	25	6	3	12	25	47	45
8	Swansea Town	42	11	3	7	34	18	6	6	9	19	31	43
9	Brentford	42	11	5	5	21	12	4	8	9	23	37	43
10	Cardiff City	42	13	3	5	28	14	3	7	11	13	30	42
11	Grimsby Town	42	13	5	3	53	25	3	3	15	21	48	40
12	Coventry City	42	8	6	7	32	24	5	7	9	23	31	39
13	Barnsley	42	11	6	4	45	28	2	7	12	19	39	39
14	Chesterfield	42	12	3	6	28	16	3	6	12	15	31	39
15	Leicester City	42	8	9	4	30	25	4	6	11	25	40	39
16	Blackburn Rovers	42	10	5	6	30	15	4	5	12	25	45	38
17	Luton Town	42	8	9	4	28	22	2	9	10	13	29	38
18	Bury	42	10	8	3	37	19	4	1	16	23	46	37
19	West Ham United	42	8	7	6	30	25	4	5	12	23	36	36
20	Queen's Park Rangers	42	6	5	10	21	30	5	7	9	19	27	34
21	Plymouth Argyle	42	6	6	9	19	24	2	10	9	25	41	32
22	BRADFORD	42	7	6	8	34	34	3	5	13	17	43	31

1950/51

6th in Division Three (North)

No	Date	Opponent	Score	Scorers	Att	Brickley D	Crosbie RC	Currie CJ	Deplidge W	Donaldson W	Downie M	Elliott WH	Farrell A	Haines JTW	Hepworth R	Hindle FJ	Hodgson D	Horsfield A	Horsman L	Hudson GA	James JS	Leuty LH	Lynn S	Reid DA	Sirrel J	Smith A(2)	Smith JW	Suddards J	Wheat AB	White RBW
1	Aug 19	BARROW	5-0	Elliott 4, Haines	16623			2	6		1	11	3	10			8		9			5					7			4
2	21	ROCHDALE	0-1		19058			2	6		1	11	3	10			8		9			5					7			4
3	26	York City	3-1	Horsman, Wheat, Haines	12572			2	6		1	11	3	8					9			5					7		10	4
4	29	Rochdale	2-1	Wheat, Elliott	10743			2	6		1	11	3	8					9			5					7		10	4
5	Sep 2	CARLISLE UNITED	0-2		16655			2	6		1	11	3	8					9			5					7		10	4
6	4	Mansfield Town	2-3	Horsman, Wheat	13447	7		2	6		1	11	3	8					9			5							10	4
7	9	Accrington Stanley	3-3	Deplidge, Donaldson, Haines	6503	7		2	10	11	1	6		8	3				9			5			4					
8	13	MANSFIELD TOWN	1-0	Sirrel	11174		9	2	6		1	11		10	3							5			8		7	4		
9	16	SOUTHPORT	2-0	Crosbie, Elliott	14916		9	2	6		1	11		10	3							5			8		7	4		
10	23	Tranmere Rovers	2-2	Deplidge, Elliott	12140	7	9	2	10		1	11			3				5					6	8					4
11	30	BRADFORD CITY	3-1	Smith, Crosbie 2	25655		9	2	10		1	11		8	3				5					6			7			4
12	Oct 7	Stockport County	1-2	Crosbie	10640		9		10		1	11		8	3									6	7	2		5		4
13	14	HALIFAX TOWN	2-1	Elliott, Deplidge	14621	7	9		10		1	11	2	8	3				5					6						4
14	21	Lincoln City	3-1	Deplidge 2, Haines	10929	7	9		10		1	11	2	8	3				5					6						4
15	28	DARLINGTON	2-1	Deplidge, Elliott	12046		9		10		1	11	2	8	3				5					6			7			4
16	Nov 4	Chester	0-2		7362		9		10		1	11	2	8	3				5					6			7			4
17	11	SHREWSBURY TOWN	2-4	Elliott, Smith	10807		9		10		1	11	2	8	3				5					6			7			4
18	18	Hartlepools United	1-3	Crosbie	7536		9	2	10		1	11							5		3			6	8		7			4
19	Dec 2	Crewe Alexandra	4-2	Crosbie 3, Brickley	7649	7	9	2	10		1	11		8			4		5		3								6	
20	16	Barrow	3-2	Horsfield, Haines, Crosbie	4579	7	9	2			1	11		8			4	10	5		3								6	
21	23	YORK CITY	4-0	Haines 2, Crosbie, Horsfield	9348	7	9	2			1	11		10			4	8	5		3								6	
22	25	ROTHERHAM UNITED	0-4		23195	7	9	2			1	11		10			4	8	5		3								6	
23	26	Rotherham United	1-2	Crosbie	17888	7	9		10		1	11		8			4		5		3							2	6	
24	30	Carlisle United	0-1		10656	7	9		10		1	11		8			4		5		3							2	6	
25	Jan 6	Scunthorpe United	1-1	Deplidge	6760	7	9		10		1	11		8			4		5		3							2	6	
26	13	ACCRINGTON STANLEY	3-0	Elliott 2, Crosbie	8883	7	9				1	11		10			4	8	5		3							2	6	
27	20	Southport	4-2	Crosbie 2, Deplidge, Haines	4043	7	9		10		1	11		8			4		5		3							2	6	
28	27	SCUNTHORPE UNITED	2-2	Hodgson, Deplidge	10246	7	9		10		1	11		8			4		5		3							2	6	
29	Feb 3	TRANMERE ROVERS	4-1	Haines 2, Crosbie, Hodgson	12986	7	9		10		1	11	3	8			4		5									2	6	
30	10	Wrexham	1-3	Crosbie	8572	7	9		10		1	11	3	8			4		5									2	6	
31	17	Bradford City	1-4	Brickley	18454	7	9		10		1	11	3	8			4		5									2	6	
32	24	STOCKPORT COUNTY	3-0	Hodgson, Deplidge, Crosbie	10477	7	9		6		1	11			3		8		5				4					2	10	
33	Mar 3	Halifax Town	2-2	Hodgson, Deplidge	10533				6		1	11		9	3		8		5				4				7	2	10	
34	10	LINCOLN CITY	2-1	Crosbie 2	10203	7	9		6		1	11		10	3		8		5				4					2		
35	17	Darlington	4-1	Elliott, Crosbie 2, James	5126	7	9				1	11		10			8		5		3		4					2	6	
36	23	Oldham Athletic	3-2	Crosbie 2, Brickley	21112	7	9		6		1	11		10	3		8		5				4					2		
37	24	CHESTER	2-0	Hodgson, Deplidge	11679	7	9		6		1	11	2	10	3		8		5				4							
38	26	OLDHAM ATHLETIC	3-1	Crosbie 2, Haines	9728		9		6		1	11	3	10			8		5				4				7	2		
39	31	Shrewsbury Town	0-1		7598		9		6		1	11	3	10			8		5				4				7	2		
40	Apr 7	HARTLEPOOLS UNITED	1-1	Haines	6910		9		6		1	11		10	3		8		5				4			2	7			
41	11	NEW BRIGHTON	2-1	J Smith, Elliott	5227		9		6		1	11	3	10			8		5				4			2	7			
42	14	Gateshead	0-5		4717		9		6		1	11		10	3				5				4		8		7	2		
43	18	GATESHEAD	2-0	Hodgson, Crosbie	7003		9		11		1	6		10			8		5	3			4				7	2		
44	21	CREWE ALEXANDRA	1-1	Deplidge	9427		9		11		1	6		10		3	8		5				4				7	2		
45	28	New Brighton	3-3	Hodgson, Haines, Crosbie	2450		9		11		1			10			8		5	3			4	6			7	2		
46	30	WREXHAM	0-1		4945		9		11		1			10		3	8		5				4	6			7	2		
					Apps	23	38	16	41	1	46	44	18	43	18	2	29	4	43	2	12	9	15	11	7	3	22	24	20	15
					Goals	3	27		13	1		14		13			7	2	2		1				1		3		3	

F.A. Cup

Rd	Date	Opponent	Score	Scorers	Att	Brickley D	Crosbie RC	Currie CJ	Deplidge W	Donaldson W	Downie M	Elliott WH	Farrell A	Haines JTW	Hepworth R	Hindle FJ	Hodgson D	Horsfield A	Horsman L	Hudson GA	James JS	Leuty LH	Lynn S	Reid DA	Sirrel J	Smith A(2)	Smith JW	Suddards J	Wheat AB	White RBW
R1	Nov 25	Chester	2-1	Elliott, Deplidge	4604		9	2	10		1	11		8			4		5		3						7		6	
R2	Dec 9	Millwall	1-1	Crosbie	22774	7	9	2	10		1	11		8			4		5		3								6	
rep	13	MILLWALL	0-1		11527	7	9	2	10		1	11		8			4		5		3								6	

BRADFORD v. BARROW SATURDAY, AUGUST 19th, 1950

		P	W	D	L	F	A	W	D	L	F	A	Pts
1	Rotherham United	46	16	3	4	55	16	15	6	2	48	25	71
2	Mansfield Town	46	17	6	0	54	19	9	6	8	24	29	64
3	Carlisle United	46	18	4	1	44	17	7	8	8	35	33	62
4	Tranmere Rovers	46	15	5	3	51	26	9	6	8	32	36	59
5	Lincoln City	46	18	1	4	62	23	7	7	9	27	35	58
6	BRADFORD	46	15	3	5	46	23	8	5	10	44	49	54
7	Bradford City	46	13	4	6	55	30	8	6	9	35	33	52
8	Gateshead	46	17	1	5	60	21	4	7	12	24	41	50
9	Crewe Alexandra	46	11	5	7	38	26	8	5	10	23	34	48
10	Stockport County	46	15	3	5	45	26	5	5	13	18	37	48
11	Rochdale	46	11	6	6	38	18	6	5	12	31	44	45
12	Scunthorpe United	46	10	12	1	32	9	3	6	14	26	48	44
13	Chester	46	11	6	6	42	30	6	3	14	20	34	43
14	Wrexham	46	12	6	5	37	28	3	6	14	18	43	42
15	Oldham Athletic	46	10	5	8	47	36	6	3	14	26	37	40
16	Hartlepools United	46	14	5	4	55	26	2	2	19	9	40	39
17	York City	46	7	12	4	37	24	5	3	15	29	53	39
18	Darlington	46	10	8	5	35	29	3	5	15	24	48	39
19	Barrow	46	12	3	8	38	27	4	3	16	13	49	38
20	Shrewsbury Town	46	11	3	9	28	30	4	4	15	15	44	37
21	Southport	46	9	4	10	29	25	4	6	13	27	47	36
22	Halifax Town	46	11	6	6	36	24	0	6	17	14	45	34
23	Accrington Stanley	46	10	4	9	28	29	1	6	16	14	72	32
24	New Brighton	46	7	6	10	22	32	4	2	17	18	58	30

1951/52

8th in Division Three (North)

No	Month	Day	Opponent	Score	Scorers	Att	Brickley D	Crosbie RC	Currie CJ	Deplidge W	Downie M	Haines JTW	Heffron CA	Hindle FJ	Hodgson D	Horsman L	Hudson GA	Lynn S	Lyons T	Parkinson A	Reid DA	Smith JW	Suddards J	Turner PS	Wheat AB	Wright AM
1	Aug	18	BARROW	3-1	Turner 2, Crosbie	12793	7	9		6	1	10		3		5		4				11	2	8		
2		20	Stockport County	0-1		11277	7	9		6	1	10		3		5		4				11	2	8		
3		25	Grimsby Town	0-3		17476	7	9		6	1	10		3		5		4				11	2	8		
4		27	STOCKPORT COUNTY	4-2	Turner 2, Haines, Wright	12150	7			6	1	10		3	4	5							2	8	11	9
5	Sep	1	WREXHAM	5-0	Turner, Brickley, Deplidge, Wright 2	14146	7			6	1	10		3		5		4				11	2	8		9
6		6	Carlisle United	0-1		14793				6	1	10		3		5		4	11			7	2	8		9
7		8	Chesterfield	0-0		10151	7			6	1	10		3		5		4	11				2	8		9
8		15	Bradford City	2-2	Turner, Lyons	23135	7			6	1	10		3		5		4	11				2	8		9
9		17	CARLISLE UNITED	0-1		13701	7			6	1	10		3	8	5		4	11				2			9
10		22	HALIFAX TOWN	6-1	Turner 3, Deplidge, Wright, Lyons	16068	7			6	1	10		3		5		4	11				2	8		9
11		29	Mansfield Town	0-1		11567	7			6	1	10		3		5		4	11				2	8		9
12	Oct	6	CHESTER	3-0	Lyons, Wright, Haines	11795	7			10	1	8		3		5		4	11		6		2			9
13		13	Lincoln City	0-2		12013	7			10	1			3		5		4	11		6		2	8		9
14		20	SCUNTHORPE UNITED	2-2	Turner, Haines	11207	7	9		6	1	10		3		5		4	11				2	8		
15		27	Tranmere Rovers	2-1	Wright, Crosbie	8529	7	9	4	6	1	10		3		5			11				2			8
16	Nov	3	SOUTHPORT	2-2	Crosbie 2	10035	7	9	4	6	1	10		3		5			11				2			8
17		10	Crewe Alexandra	4-3	Crosbie 3, Haines	5966		9	4	6	1	10		3		5			11			7	2			8
18		17	GATESHEAD	2-0	Crosbie, Wright	13611	7	9	4	6	1	10		3		5			11				2			8
19	Dec	1	OLDHAM ATHLETIC	1-0	Haines	17194		9	4			10	1	3		5		6	11				2	7		8
20		8	Hartlepools United	1-2	Turner	5973		9	4		1	10		3		5		6					2	7	11	8
21		22	GRIMSBY TOWN	3-2	Crosbie, Haines, Lyons	12169		9	4		1	10		3		5		6	11				2	7		8
22		25	York City	0-1		8786		9	4		1	10		3		5		6	11				2	7		8
23		26	YORK CITY	2-1	Crosbie, Deplidge	15125	7	9	4	11	1	10		3		5		6					2	8		
24		29	Wrexham	2-3	Deplidge, Smith	8148		9	4	11	1			3		5		6				7	2	8		10
25	Jan	5	CHESTERFIELD	3-3	Smith, Turner, Deplidge	12359			4	11	1	10		3		5		6				7	2	8		9
26		19	BRADFORD CITY	2-1	Turner, Crosbie	21730		9	4	11	1	10		3		5		6				7	2	8		
27		24	Workington	3-2	Deplidge 2, Turner	3932		9	4	11	1	10		3		5		6				7	2	8		
28	Feb	9	MANSFIELD TOWN	0-1		10516		9	4	11	1	10		3		5		6				7	2	8		
29		13	WORKINGTON	2-1	McAlone (og), Haines	4179			4		1	10		3		5		6	11			7	2	8		9
30		16	Chester	2-4	Turner, Wright	5691			4		1	10		3		5		6	11			7	2	8		9
31		23	ACCRINGTON STANLEY	1-1	Turner	10897			4				1	3		5		6	11	10		7	2	8		9
32	Mar	1	LINCOLN CITY	1-1	Haines	17468		9	4	11		10	1	3		5		6				7	2	8		
33		8	Scunthorpe United	0-0		8445		9	4	11			1	3		5		6				7	2	8		10
34		10	Halifax Town	0-0		6429		9	4	11			1	3		5		6				7	2	8		10
35		15	TRANMERE ROVERS	2-3	Crosbie 2	9508		9	4				1	3		5		6	11			7	2	8		10
36		22	Southport	0-0		4559		9		6		11	1	5			3	4				7	2	8		10
37		27	Barrow	2-0	Turner 2	3647		9		6		11	1	5		3		4				7	2	8		10
38		29	CREWE ALEXANDRA	3-2	Turner 2, Wright	4495		9		6		11	1	5		3		4				7	2	8		10
39	Apr	5	Gateshead	1-0	Lyons	2803				6		9	1	5		3		4	11			7	2	8		10
40		12	DARLINGTON	2-0	Turner, Smith	9538		9		6			1	5		3		4	11			7	2	8		10
41		14	Rochdale	1-1	Wright	5540		9	4	6			1	5		3			11			7	2	8		10
42		15	ROCHDALE	1-1	Smith	10235		9	4			10	1	5		3		6	11			7	2	8		
43		19	Oldham Athletic	2-1	Crosbie, Wright	11418		9		6			1	5		3		4	11			7	2	8		10
44		26	HARTLEPOOLS UNITED	1-2	Turner	7415	7	9	4	6			1	5		3						11	2	8		10
45		30	Accrington Stanley	1-5	Wright	5598	7	9	4	6	1			5		3						11	2	8		10
46	May	3	Darlington	0-3		2235	7	9		6			1	5		2	3					11	4	8		10
						Apps	20	31	25	37	30	34	16	46	2	45	2	37	25	1	2	29	46	40	2	36
						Goals	1	14		7		8							5			4		22		12

One own goal

F.A. Cup

Rd	Month	Day	Opponent	Score	Scorers	Att	Brickley D	Crosbie RC	Currie CJ	Deplidge W	Downie M	Haines JTW	Heffron CA	Hindle FJ	Hodgson D	Horsman L	Hudson GA	Lynn S	Lyons T	Parkinson A	Reid DA	Smith JW	Suddards J	Turner PS	Wheat AB	Wright AM
R1	Nov	24	York City	1-1	Crosbie	12015	7	9	4	6	1	10		3		5			11				2			8
rep		28	YORK CITY	1-1	(aet) Lyons	8659	7	9	4	6	1	10		3		5			11				2			8
rep2	Dec	3	York City	4-0	Haines 2, Turner, Crosbie	10000		9	4			10	1	3		5		6	11				2	7		8
R2		15	BRADFORD CITY	3-2	Turner 2, Lyons	24430		9	4		1	10		3		5		6	11				2	7		8
R3	Jan	12	SHEFFIELD WEDNESDAY	2-1	Turner 2	28449		9	4	11	1	10		3		5		6				7	2	8		
R4	Feb	2	Leeds United	0-2		50645		9	4	11	1	10		3		5		6				7	2	8		

R1 replay 2 at Elland Road, Leeds

		P	W	D	L	F	A	W	D	L	F	A	Pts
1	Lincoln City	46	19	2	2	80	23	11	7	5	41	29	69
2	Grimsby Town	46	19	2	2	59	14	10	6	7	37	31	66
3	Stockport County	46	12	9	2	47	17	11	4	8	27	23	59
4	Oldham Athletic	46	19	2	2	65	22	5	7	11	25	39	57
5	Gateshead	46	14	7	2	41	17	7	4	12	25	32	53
6	Mansfield Town	46	17	3	3	50	23	5	5	13	23	37	52
7	Carlisle United	46	10	7	6	31	24	9	6	8	31	33	51
8	BRADFORD	46	13	6	4	51	28	6	6	11	23	36	50
9	Hartlepools United	46	17	3	3	47	19	4	5	14	24	46	50
10	York City	46	16	4	3	53	19	2	9	12	20	33	49
11	Tranmere Rovers	46	17	2	4	59	29	4	4	15	17	42	48
12	Barrow	46	13	5	5	33	19	4	7	12	24	42	46
13	Chesterfield	46	15	7	1	47	16	2	4	17	18	50	45
14	Scunthorpe United	46	10	11	2	39	23	4	5	14	26	51	44
15	Bradford City	46	12	5	6	40	32	4	5	14	21	36	42
16	Crewe Alexandra	46	12	6	5	42	28	5	2	16	21	54	42
17	Southport	46	12	6	5	36	22	3	5	15	17	49	41
18	Wrexham	46	14	5	4	41	22	1	4	18	22	51	39
19	Chester	46	13	4	6	46	30	2	5	16	26	55	39
20	Halifax Town	46	11	4	8	31	23	3	3	17	30	74	35
21	Rochdale	46	10	5	8	32	34	1	8	14	15	45	35
22	Accrington Stanley	46	6	8	9	30	34	4	4	15	31	58	32
23	Darlington	46	10	5	8	39	34	1	4	18	25	69	31
24	Workington	46	8	4	11	33	34	3	3	17	17	57	29

1952/53

7th in Division Three (North)

No.	Month	Day	Opponent	Score	Scorers	Att.	Brickley D	Calow CJH	Crosbie RC	Crowe MJ	Currie CJ	Deplidge W	Downie M	Haddington H	Haines JTW	Heffron CA	Hindle FJ	Horsman L	Hudson GA	Johnson T	Kevan DT	Lynn S	Lyons T	Milburn J	Rafferty J	Redfearn B	Smith IW	Suddards J	Turner PS	Vandermotten W	Wright AM
1	Aug	23	York City	1-3	Milburn	10246			9		6					1	5	2					11	3			7	4	8		10
2		25	ROCHDALE	2-1	Horsman, Turner	12060									10	1	5	2					11	3	6		7	4	8		9
3		30	GRIMSBY TOWN	0-3		16998	7				4				10	1	3	5						9	6		11	2	8		
4	Sep	2	Rochdale	0-1		6647	7				4				10	1	3	5						9			11	2	8		6
5		6	Barrow	0-2		5516			9		4				11	1		5		8				3			7	2	10		6
6		10	TRANMERE ROVERS	1-0	Wright	7127			9		4					1		5				6		3		11	7	2	8		10
7		13	WREXHAM	1-2	Haines	9787			9		4				8	1		5				6		3		11	7	2			10
8		16	Tranmere Rovers	0-4		8507		1	9		4				8			5				6		3		11	7	2			10
9		20	BRADFORD CITY	2-2	Horsman, Wright	15702					4				8	1	5	9	6				11	3			7	2			10
10		22	Port Vale	0-1		12553			9		4	6			8	1	5		3				11	2			7				10
11		27	Oldham Athletic	1-2	Deplidge	16180	7					6	1		8		5	9	3			4		2		11					10
12	Oct	4	MANSFIELD TOWN	1-1	Smith	9623						6	1		8		5		3		9	4		2		11	7				10
13		11	Darlington	3-1	Kevan 2, Redfearn	7417						6	1		8		5		3		9	4		2		11	7				10
14		18	GATESHEAD	3-0	Kevan, Haines, Wright	13022						6	1		8		5		3		9	4	11	2			7				10
15		25	Hartlepools United	1-0	Wright	9554						6	1		8		5		3		9	4	11	2			7				10
16	Nov	1	CARLISLE UNITED	2-2	Kevan, Haines	13834						6	1		8		5		3		9	4	11	2			7				10
17		8	Southport	2-2	Crosbie, Smith	4466			10		2	6	1		8		5		3		9	4	11				7				
18		15	CREWE ALEXANDRA	1-0	Kevan	8877					2	6	1		8		5		3		9	4	11				7				10
19		29	CHESTER	1-0	Haines	8145					2	6	1		8		5		3		9	4				11	7				10
20	Dec	13	STOCKPORT COUNTY	1-1	Kevan	7838			10		2	6	1		8		5		3		9	4				11	7				
21		20	YORK CITY	2-3	Andrews (og), Lyons	6506			9			6	1		8		5		3			4	11	2			7				10
22		26	HALIFAX TOWN	1-2	Horsman	22252			10			6	1		8		5	2	3		9	4				11	7				
23		27	Halifax Town	4-2	Kevan 2, Redfearn, Milburn	18597			10		4	6	1				5	2			9			3		11	7				8
24	Jan	1	Accrington Stanley	2-3	Wright 2	5638			10		4	6	1				5	2			9			3		11	7				8
25		3	Grimsby Town	3-2	Haines 2, Crosbie	12201			9		4		1		10		5	2	3			6	11				7				8
26		10	Chesterfield	1-1	Haines	8997			9		4		1	2	8		5	3				6	11				7				10
27		17	BARROW	1-0	Crosbie	9362	11		10		4	6	1		8		5	2	3		9						7				
28		24	Wrexham	3-0	Smith, Brickley, Crosbie	10120	11		9		4	6	1		8		5	2	3								7				10
29		31	CHESTERFIELD	0-1		7559	11		9	10	4	6	1		8		5	2	3								7				
30	Feb	7	Bradford City	1-2	Haines	18661	11		10		4	6	1		8		5	2	3		9						7				
31		21	Mansfield Town	1-1	Horsman	6219			10		4	6	1				5	9	3			4	11				7				8
32		28	DARLINGTON	3-0	Deplidge 3	6551			9		4	10	1				5	2	3			6				11	7			8	
33	Mar	7	Gateshead	2-3	Wright 2	7303			9		4	6	1		10		5	2	3							11	7				8
34		11	OLDHAM ATHLETIC	0-0		6898	11				4	6	1		10		5	2			9			3			7				8
35		14	HARTLEPOOLS UNITED	1-1	Wright	6006			9		4	6	1		10		5	2						3		11	7				8
36		21	Carlisle United	3-1	Redfearn, Crosbie 2	8923			8		4	10	1				5		3					9		11	7	2			6
37		26	Scunthorpe United	2-1	Milburn, Delplidge	6119			8		4	10	1				5		3					9		11	7	2			6
38		28	SOUTHPORT	1-0	Redfearn	5755			8		4	10	1				5		3					9		11	7	2			6
39	Apr	3	Workington	2-2	Smith, Milburn	6698			8		4	10	1				5	2	3					9		11	7				6
40		4	Crewe Alexandra	3-2	Crosbie 2, Deplidge	7739			8		4	10	1				5	2	3					9		11	7				6
41		6	WORKINGTON	6-1	Crosbie 3, Milburn, Brickley 2	8407	11		8		4	10	1				5	2	3			6		9			7				
42		11	PORT VALE	2-2	Crosbie 2	11790	11		9		4	10	1		8		5	2	3			6					7				
43		18	Chester	3-0	Haines, Crosbie 2	4441	11		8		4		1		10		5	2	3					9			7				6
44		22	ACCRINGTON STANLEY	4-0	Milburn 2, Brickley, Haines	6067	11		8		4		1	2	10		5	3						9			7				6
45		25	SCUNTHORPE UNITED	1-1	Crosbie	8571	11		8		4		1		10		5	2	3					9			7				6
46		29	Stockport County	0-2		3619	11		8			6	1		10		5	3						9			7	2			4
						Apps	14	1	33	1	36	32	36	2	34	9	42	32	31	1	15	21	13	31	2	19	45	13	6	1	36
						Goals	4		16			6			10			4			8		1	7		4	4		1		9

One own goal

F.A. Cup

Round	Month	Day	Opponent	Score	Scorers	Att.	Brickley D	Calow CJH	Crosbie RC	Crowe MJ	Currie CJ	Deplidge W	Downie M	Haddington H	Haines JTW	Heffron CA	Hindle FJ	Horsman L	Hudson GA	Johnson T	Kevan DT	Lynn S	Lyons T	Milburn J	Rafferty J	Redfearn B	Smith IW	Suddards J	Turner PS	Vandermotten W	Wright AM
R1	Nov	22	ROCHDALE	2-1	Haines, Lyons	13524					2	6	1		8		5		3		9	4	11				7				10
R2	Dec	6	GATESHEAD	1-2	Smith	13149					2	6	1		8		5		3		9	4				11	7				10

		P	W	D	L	F	A	W	D	L	F	A	Pts
1	Oldham Athletic	46	15	4	4	48	21	7	11	5	29	24	59
2	Port Vale	46	13	9	1	41	10	7	9	7	26	25	58
3	Wrexham	46	18	3	2	59	24	6	5	12	27	42	56
4	York City	46	14	5	4	35	16	6	8	9	25	29	53
5	Grimsby Town	46	15	5	3	47	19	6	5	12	28	40	52
6	Southport	46	16	4	3	42	18	4	7	12	21	42	51
7	BRADFORD	46	10	8	5	37	23	9	4	10	38	38	50
8	Gateshead	46	13	6	4	51	24	4	9	10	25	36	49
9	Carlisle United	46	13	7	3	57	24	5	6	12	25	44	49
10	Crewe Alexandra	46	13	5	5	46	28	7	3	13	24	40	48
11	Stockport County	46	13	8	2	61	26	4	5	14	21	43	47
12	Tranmere Rovers	46	16	4	3	45	16	5	1	17	20	47	47
12	Chesterfield	46	13	6	4	40	23	5	5	13	25	40	47
14	Halifax Town	46	13	5	5	47	31	3	10	10	21	37	47
15	Scunthorpe United	46	10	6	7	38	21	6	8	9	24	35	46
16	Bradford City	46	14	7	2	54	29	0	11	12	21	51	46
17	Hartlepools United	46	14	6	3	39	16	2	8	13	18	45	46
18	Mansfield Town	46	11	9	3	34	25	5	5	13	21	37	46
19	Barrow	46	15	6	2	48	20	1	6	16	18	51	44
20	Chester	46	10	7	6	39	27	1	8	14	25	58	37
21	Darlington	46	13	4	6	33	27	1	2	20	25	69	34
22	Rochdale	46	12	5	6	41	27	2	0	21	21	56	33
23	Workington	46	9	5	9	40	33	2	5	16	15	58	32
24	Accrington Stanley	46	7	9	7	25	29	1	2	20	14	60	27

1953/54

9th in Division Three (North)

No	Date	Opponent	Score	Scorers	Att	Beattie G	Begg JA	Brickley D	Carlin P	Conroy R	Crosbie RC	Currie CJ	Deplidge W	Downie M	Dunlop WL	Fagan JF	Haines JTW	Hindle FJ	Hirst KRH	Hudson GA	Jordan C	Keating PJ	Milburn J	Miles D	Parkinson A	Pickard LJ	Redfearn B	Roberts C	Suddards J	Turner PS	Whitaker C	Wright AM
1	Aug 22	BRADFORD CITY	4-0	Beattie, Crosbie 2, Whitaker	19376	8		7			9		6	1	10			5					3						2		11	4
2	26	Crewe Alexandra	1-1	Dunlop	6873	8		7			9		6	1	10			5					3						2		11	4
3	29	Barnsley	1-2	Thomas (og)	7480	8					9		6	1	10		7	5					3						2		11	4
4	31	CREWE ALEXANDRA	1-1	Dunlop	6134	8		7					6	1	10			5		3			9						2		11	4
5	Sep 5	DARLINGTON	2-2	Crosbie, Milburn	12295	8					9		6	1	10			5					3						2	7	11	4
6	7	Port Vale	0-2		19270	9					8		6	1		5	10						3		7				2		11	4
7	12	Hartlepools United	2-0	Brickley, Crosbie	8409	8		7			9		6	1	10			5					3						2		11	4
8	16	PORT VALE	1-2	Beattie	10960	8		7			9		6	1	10			5				11	3						2			4
9	19	GATESHEAD	3-1	Dunlop, Beattie, Crosbie	12581	8		7			9	2	6	1	10			5					3								11	4
10	23	Chester	3-2	Dunlop 2, Crosbie	4906			7			9	2	6	1	8		10	5				11	3									4
11	26	Workington	1-1	Crosbie	6140			7			9	4	6	1	8		10	5					3						2		11	
12	30	CHESTER	5-0	Deplidge 2, Dunlop, Crosbie 2	5333	8		7			9	4	11	1	10			5		3									2			6
13	Oct 3	SCUNTHORPE UNITED	2-2	Dunlop, Whitaker	13686	8		7			9	4	6	1	10			5		3									2		11	
14	10	Tranmere Rovers	1-1	Beattie	6720	8		7			9	4		1	10			5		3									2		11	6
15	17	HALIFAX TOWN	4-2	Whitaker, Beattie 2, Brickley	14261	8		7					6	1	10			5					3			9			2		11	4
16	24	Carlisle United	1-0	Pickard	7873	8		7		5			6	1				3					2			9				10	11	4
17	31	ACCRINGTON STANLEY	6-4	Beattie, Pickard 4, Whitaker	11108	8		7		5			6	1	10								3			9			2		11	4
18	Nov 7	Grimsby Town	0-0		8551	8		7		5			6	1	10								3			9	11		2			4
19	14	STOCKPORT COUNTY	3-2	Dunlop, Beattie, Pickard	12253	8		7		5			6	1	10								3			9			2		11	4
20	28	WREXHAM	2-0	Wright, Dunlop	12272	8				5		4	7	1	10								3			9			2		11	6
21	Dec 5	Mansfield Town	1-1	Pickard	5493	8				5		4	7	1	10								3			9			2		11	6
22	19	Bradford City	0-3		17526	8		7		5			6	1	10								3			9			2		11	4
23	25	Southport	0-1		5166			7		5			6	1	10								3			9			2	8	11	4
24	28	SOUTHPORT	1-1	Pickard	18156			7		5			6	1	10								3			9			2	8	11	4
25	Jan 1	Barrow	1-4	Beattie	8845	8		7		5		4	11	1	10								3			9			2			6
26	2	BARNSLEY	0-2		11141	8				5		4		1				3	7						9	10			2		11	6
27	16	Darlington	1-2	Dunlop	3792	8		7		5		2	6	1	10			3								9					11	4
28	23	HARTLEPOOLS UNITED	5-0	* see below	5998	10		7		5			6	1				3			2					9	11			8		4
29	Feb 20	Scunthorpe United	1-4	Pickard	8097	10		7		5			6	1						3						9	11		2	8		4
30	24	WORKINGTON	3-1	Milburn, Redfearn, Beattie	3221	10							6	1	7	5		3					9				11		2	8		4
31	27	TRANMERE ROVERS	1-2	Deplidge	7490	10						4	6	1	7	5		3					9				11		2	8		
32	Mar 6	Halifax Town	2-2	Beattie, Redfearn	5308	10		7		5				1	8			3								9	11	6	2			4
33	10	CHESTERFIELD	1-1	Dunlop	2371	10		7		5			11	1	8			3								9		6	2			4
34	13	CARLISLE UNITED	2-4	Beattie, Redfearn	6346	10		7	2	5				1	8			3							9		11	6				4
35	17	BARROW	2-1	Pickard 2	1881	10	1	7	2			4	11					5					3			9		6				8
36	20	Accrington Stanley	0-0		6814	10	1	7	2			4			8			5					3			9	11	6				
37	24	Chesterfield	1-5	Dunlop	2118	10		7	2			4	11	1	8			5					3			9		6				
38	27	GRIMSBY TOWN	4-1	Deplidge, Redfearn, Pickard 2	5302			7	2	5			10	1	8			3								9	11	6				4
39	Apr 3	Stockport County	1-4	Brickley	4676			7	2	5			10	1	8			3								9	11	6				4
40	7	Gateshead	1-0	Pickard	2228	8		7					10	1				5		6			3			9	11	4	2			
41	10	ROCHDALE	2-2	Pickard 2	7099	8		7					10	1				5		6			3			9	11	4	2			
42	16	York City	0-0		6362	8		7					11	1	10			5		6			3			9		4	2			
43	17	Wrexham	0-2		8216	8		7					10	1				5		6			3			9	11	4	2			
44	19	YORK CITY	2-0	Deplidge, Pickard	5378			7					10	1				5		6			3			9	11	4	2	8		
45	24	MANSFIELD TOWN	1-0	Brickley	5437			7					10	1	8			5		6			3			9	11	4	2			
46	27	Rochdale	1-0	Pickard	3818			7					10	1	8			5		6			3	11		9		4	2			
					Apps	37	2	38	6	19	13	15	41	44	36	3	4	35	1	12	1	2	34	1	3	29	15	15	35	9	22	34
					Goals	12		4			9		6		12								2			20	5			1	4	1

Scorers in game 28: Redfearn, Pickard 2, Deplidge, Turner

One own goal

F.A. Cup

Rd	Date	Opponent	Score	Scorers	Att	Beattie G	Begg JA	Brickley D	Carlin P	Conroy R	Crosbie RC	Currie CJ	Deplidge W	Downie M	Dunlop WL	Fagan JF	Haines JTW	Hindle FJ	Hirst KRH	Hudson GA	Jordan C	Keating PJ	Milburn J	Miles D	Parkinson A	Pickard LJ	Redfearn B	Roberts C	Suddards J	Turner PS	Whitaker C	Wright AM
R1	Nov 21	Selby Town	2-0	Dunlop, Pickard	5000	8				5			6	1	10								3	7		9			2		11	4
R2	Dec 12	Cambridge United	2-1	Pickard, Whitaker	10000	8		7		5			6	1	10								3			9			2		11	4
R3	Jan 9	MANCHESTER CITY	2-5	Pickard, Beattie	22194	8		7		5		2	6	1	10			3								9					11	4

Back; P. Carlin, J. Milburn, C. Whitaker, J. Begg, R. Lee, J. Stainton.
Front; G. Beattie, D. Brickley, W. Dunlop, C. Roberts, P. Hall

		P	W	D	L	F	A	W	D	L	F	A	Pts
1	Port Vale	46	16	7	0	48	5	10	10	3	26	16	69
2	Barnsley	46	16	3	4	54	24	8	7	8	23	33	58
3	Scunthorpe United	46	14	7	2	49	24	7	8	8	28	32	57
4	Gateshead	46	15	4	4	49	22	6	9	8	25	33	55
5	Bradford City	46	15	6	2	40	14	7	3	13	20	41	53
6	Chesterfield	46	13	6	4	41	19	6	8	9	35	45	52
7	Mansfield Town	46	15	5	3	59	22	5	6	12	29	45	51
8	Wrexham	46	16	4	3	59	19	5	5	13	22	49	51
9	BRADFORD	46	13	6	4	57	31	5	8	10	20	37	50
10	Stockport County	46	14	6	3	57	20	4	5	14	20	47	47
11	Southport	46	12	5	6	41	26	5	7	11	22	34	46
12	Barrow	46	12	7	4	46	26	4	5	14	26	45	44
13	Carlisle United	46	10	8	5	53	27	4	7	12	30	44	43
14	Tranmere Rovers	46	11	4	8	40	34	7	3	13	19	36	43
15	Accrington Stanley	46	12	7	4	41	22	4	3	16	25	52	42
16	Crewe Alexandra	46	9	8	6	30	26	5	5	13	19	41	41
17	Grimsby Town	46	14	5	4	31	15	2	4	17	20	62	41
18	Hartlepools United	46	10	8	5	40	21	3	6	14	19	44	40
19	Rochdale	46	12	5	6	40	20	3	5	15	19	57	40
20	Workington	46	10	9	4	36	22	3	5	15	23	58	40
21	Darlington	46	11	3	9	31	27	1	11	11	19	44	38
22	York City	46	8	7	8	39	32	4	6	13	25	54	37
23	Halifax Town	46	9	6	8	26	21	3	4	16	18	52	34
24	Chester	46	10	7	6	39	22	1	3	19	9	45	32

1954/55

16th in Division Three (North)

No	Date	Opponent	Score	Scorers	Att	Adey AL	Beattie G	Begg JA	Brickley D	Brocklehurst JF	Conroy R	Deplidge W	Hindle FJ	Horton H	Hudson GA	Jordan C	Marron C	McLaren A	Milburn J	Miles D	Parkinson A	Pickard LJ	Redfearn B	Roberts C	Suddards J	Taylor JB	Whitaker C	Worsman RH	Wright AM
1	Aug 21	Bradford City	1-1	Deplidge	17838		8		7			10	5	6					3			9	11	4	2	1			
2	23	BARNSLEY	1-0	Marron	12774				7			10	5	6			8		3			9	11	4	2	1			
3	28	ROCHDALE	1-1	Brickley	10819				7			10	5	6			8		3			9	11	4	2	1			
4	Sep 1	Barnsley	1-2	Parkinson	12679		10		7				5	6					3	11	9			4	2	1		8	
5	4	Tranmere Rovers	3-3	Beattie, Brickley, Worsman	7272		9		7				5	8					3	11				4	2	1		10	6
6	6	CARLISLE UNITED	0-2		6874		9		7		5			8	3					11				4	2	1		10	6
7	11	STOCKPORT COUNTY	2-1	Pickard 2	9275							8	5						3	7		9	11	4	2	1		10	6
8	14	Carlisle United	2-3	Deplidge, Worsman	7120							8	5						3	7		9	11	4	2	1		10	6
9	18	Hartlepools United	1-0	Parkinson	8279							8	5						3	7	9		11	4	2	1		10	6
10	20	CHESTERFIELD	1-3	Deplidge	5093					4		11	5						3	7	9			6	2	1		10	8
11	25	GATESHEAD	2-2	Deplidge, Worsman	8779			1		4		11	5						3	7	9			6	2			10	8
12	27	Chesterfield	3-1	Deplidge, Parkinson 2	9735			1	7			11	5	6					3		9			4	2			10	8
13	Oct 2	Darlington	0-3		12875			1	7	4		11	5	6					3		9				2			10	8
14	9	SCUNTHORPE UNITED	0-0		14402		10		7			11	5	6					3			8		4	2	1			9
15	16	Wrexham	0-1		8112		8					11	5	6					3	7	9			4	2	1		10	
16	23	ACCRINGTON STANLEY	3-2	Adey, McLaren, Wright	13731	9				4			5					8	3	7			11	6	2	1			10
17	30	Mansfield Town	1-2	Adey	9221	9				4			5					8	3	7			11	6	2	1			10
18	Nov 6	WORKINGTON	3-1	McLaren 2, Wright	9202	9				4			5					8	3	7			11	6	2	1			10
19	13	Barrow	1-3	Miles	3467	9				4			5					8	3	7			11	6	2	1			10
20	27	York City	2-1	Adey, McLaren	8727	9				4			5					8	3	7			11	6	2	1			10
21	Dec 4	HALIFAX TOWN	0-1		10330	9				4			5					8	3	7			11	6	2	1			10
22	18	BRADFORD CITY	2-0	McLaren 2	13975	9	10	1		4		11	5	6				8	3	7					2				
23	25	Chester	0-2		3203	9	10	1		4			5	6	3			8		7					2		11		
24	27	CHESTER	3-0	Readfearn 2, Whitaker	8454			1		4		10	5	6				8	3	7			9		2		11		
25	Jan 1	Rochdale	2-3	Brickley, Deplidge	6976			1	7	4		10	5	6				8	3	11	9				2				
26	8	Crewe Alexandra	1-2	Milburn	4288			1	7	4		11	5	6				8	3				9		2				10
27	22	Stockport County	0-6		6370	9				4	5			6				8	3	7			11		2	1			10
28	29	CREWE ALEXANDRA	2-1	Worsman, Deplidge	6964	9			7	4	5	8	3										11	6	2	1		10	
29	Feb 5	HARTLEPOOLS UNITED	1-0	Pickard	7373				7	4	5	8	3									9	11	6	2	1		10	
30	19	DARLINGTON	1-1	Redfearn	6884				7	4	5	8	3									9	11	6	2	1		10	
31	Mar 5	WREXHAM	0-0		5106				7	4	5	8	3									9	11	6	2	1		10	
32	9	Gateshead	2-3	og, Adey	1813	9	8		7	4	5		3										11	6	2	1			10
33	12	Accrington Stanley	3-4	Beattie 3	8430	9	8		7	4	5		3										11	6	2	1			10
34	19	MANSFIELD TOWN	0-0		5527	9	8		7	4	5		3	6						11					2	1			10
35	26	Workington	3-1	Pickard 3	4820		8		7	4	5		3	6								9	11		2	1			10
36	30	TRANMERE ROVERS	0-0		2726		8		7	4	5	11	3	6								9			2	1			10
37	Apr 2	BARROW	3-0	Brickley, Pickard, Wright	5329		8		7	4	5		3	6								9	11		2	1			10
38	8	Grimsby Town	0-1		11610		8			4	5		3							7		9	11	6	2	1			10
39	9	Southport	0-1		3415						5	6	3					8		7		9	11	4	2	1		10	
40	11	GRIMSBY TOWN	2-1	McLaren, Bridkley	5850				7	4	5	8	3	6				10				9	11		2	1			
41	16	YORK CITY	1-3	Redfearn	9993				7	4	5	8	3	6				10				9	11		2	1			
42	18	Oldham Athletic	0-5		16634				7	4	5	8	3	6				10				9	11		2	1			
43	23	Halifax Town	0-0		6875				7		5	8	3	6		2		10				9	11	4		1			
44	25	SOUTHPORT	1-0	Pickard	3036				7		5	8	3	6				10				9	11	4	2	1			
45	30	OLDHAM ATHLETIC	0-2		5297		10		7		5	8	3	6							9		11	4	2	1			
46	May 5	Scunthorpe United	1-1	Worsman	5136				7		5	8	3		6							9	11	4	2	1		10	
					Apps	13	16	8	28	29	21	29	44	26	3	1	2	18	25	23	9	20	32	32	45	38	2	17	25
					Goals	4	4		5			7					1	7	1	1	4	8	4				1	5	3

One own goal

F.A. Cup

Rd	Date	Opponent	Score	Scorers	Att	Adey AL	Beattie G	Begg JA	Brickley D	Brocklehurst JF	Conroy R	Deplidge W	Hindle FJ	Horton H	Hudson GA	Jordan C	Marron C	McLaren A	Milburn J	Miles D	Parkinson A	Pickard LJ	Redfearn B	Roberts C	Suddards J	Taylor JB	Whitaker C	Worsman RH	Wright AM
R1	Nov 20	SOUTHPORT	2-0	Adey, Wright	11217	9				4			5					8	3	7			11	6	2	1			10
R2	Dec 11	SOUTHEND UNITED	2-3	McLaren, Miles	12094	9				4			5					8	3	7			11	6	2	1			10

		P	W	D	L	F	A	W	D	L	F	A	Pts
1	Barnsley	46	18	3	2	51	17	12	2	9	35	29	65
2	Accrington Stanley	46	18	2	3	65	32	7	9	7	31	35	61
3	Scunthorpe United	46	14	6	3	45	18	9	6	8	36	35	58
4	York City	46	13	5	5	43	27	11	5	7	49	36	58
5	Hartlepools United	46	16	3	4	39	20	9	2	12	25	29	55
6	Chesterfield	46	17	1	5	54	33	7	5	11	27	37	54
7	Gateshead	46	11	7	5	38	26	9	5	9	27	43	52
8	Workington	46	11	7	5	39	23	7	7	9	29	32	50
9	Stockport County	46	13	4	6	50	27	5	8	10	34	43	48
10	Oldham Athletic	46	14	5	4	47	22	5	5	13	27	46	48
11	Southport	46	10	9	4	28	18	6	7	10	19	26	48
12	Rochdale	46	13	7	3	39	20	4	7	12	30	46	48
13	Mansfield Town	46	14	4	5	40	28	4	5	14	25	43	45
14	Halifax Town	46	9	9	5	41	27	6	4	13	22	40	43
15	Darlington	46	10	7	6	41	28	4	7	12	21	45	42
16	BRADFORD	46	11	7	5	29	21	4	4	15	27	49	41
17	Barrow	46	12	4	7	39	34	5	2	16	31	55	40
18	Wrexham	46	9	6	8	40	35	4	6	13	25	42	38
19	Tranmere Rovers	46	9	6	8	37	30	4	5	14	18	40	37
20	Carlisle United	46	12	1	10	53	39	3	5	15	25	50	36
21	Bradford City	46	9	5	9	30	26	4	5	14	17	29	36
22	Crewe Alexandra	46	8	10	5	45	35	2	4	17	23	56	34
23	Grimsby Town	46	10	4	9	28	32	3	4	16	19	46	34
24	Chester	46	10	3	10	23	25	2	6	15	21	52	33

1955/56

23rd in Division Three (North)

No	Date	Opponent	Score	Scorers	Att	Batty FR	Bradley G	Brickley D	Brocklehurst JF	Brydon IF	Conroy R	Deplidge W	Fazackerley MA	Hindle FJ	Houghton HB	Hudson GA	Jordan C	Loftus R	Pickard LJ	Pilling VJ	Redfearn B	Reilly TJ	Roberts C	Smith JB	Suddards J	Taylor JB	Ward D	Ward LW	Whitaker C	Worsman RH
1	Aug 20	SCUNTHORPE UNITED	2-0	Ward, Pickard	12624			7		8	5	6							9		11	3	4		2	1		10		
2	25	Barrow	2-2	Brydon, Redfearn	5837			7		8	5	6							9		11	3	4		2	1		10		
3	27	Rochdale	2-4	Deplidge, Brickley	4648			7		8	5	6							9		11	3	4		2		1	10		
4	29	BARROW	3-2	Whitaker, Brickley, Brydon	8485			7	6	8	5											3	4	9	2	1		10	11	
5	Sep 3	CHESTERFIELD	0-5		10328			7	4	8	5											3		9	2	1		10	11	6
6	7	Chester	0-0		8801					9	4	6		5		3				7	11				2	1		10		8
7	10	Tranmere Rovers	1-4	Deplidge	5850					9	4	6		5		3				7				11	2	1		10		8
8	12	CHESTER	1-1	Brydon	4081			7		9		6		5		3			8				4		2	1		10	11	
9	17	SOUTHPORT	0-3		6661			7	4	9		8		5		3				11			6		2	1		10		
10	24	Gateshead	0-3		2905			7	4			6	3	5					9		11				2	1		8		
11	26	Accrington Stanley	0-7		9553			7		9	4	6	3	5					8		11				2		1			
12	Oct 1	DARLINGTON	3-0	Deplidge, Brickley, Ward	6790			7			4	6		5							11	3		9	2		1	8	10	
13	8	Workington	0-4		6339			7			4	6		5							11	3		9	2	1		8	10	
14	15	BRADFORD CITY	1-1	Brickley	19396			7			4	6		5		3					11			9	2	1		8	10	
15	22	Derby County	0-4		17139			7			4	6		5		3			10		11			9	2	1		8		
16	29	CREWE ALEXANDRA	2-0	Ward 2	6441			7	10		4	6		5	9	3					11				2	1		8		
17	Nov 5	Hartlepools United	1-3	Ward	6383			7	10		4			5	9	3					11		6		2	1		8		
18	12	STOCKPORT COUNTY	2-0	Houghton 2	6711			7	10					5	9	3			4		11		6		2	1		8		
19	26	WREXHAM	4-2	Redfearn, og, Brocklhurst, Whitaker	6624			7	10					5		3			4		9		6		2	1		8	11	
20	Dec 3	Halifax Town	0-6		8421			7	10					5		3			4		9		6		2	1		8	11	
21	17	Scunthorpe United	2-4	Ward 2	5942				8	7	5					3		4	9		11	2	6					10		
22	24	ROCHDALE	3-3	Readfearn, Ward, Whitaker	7743				8					5	9	3			6		10	2			4	1		7	11	
23	26	Grimsby Town	0-2		17908						9					3		8	6		10	2	4		5	1		7	11	
24	27	GRIMSBY TOWN	2-1	Ward 2	12102			7							9	3			6		10	2	4		5	1		8	11	
25	31	Chesterfield	1-5	Readfearn	7287			7							9	3			6		10	2	4		5	1		8	11	
26	Jan 2	Carlisle United	1-4	Whitaker	6188					7						3			6		10	2	4		5		1	8	11	9
27	21	Southport	0-3		4050			7	4					3	9	2		8	6		11				5	1		10		
28	Feb 4	GATESHEAD	3-1	Brickley, Houghton 2	4357	5	4	7							8	3							6	9	2	1		10	11	
29	11	Darlington	1-4	Redfearn	2962	5	4	7							8	3					11		6	9	2		1	10		
30	18	WORKINGTON	4-0	Ward, Smith 3	5133			7						5	8	3			4				6	9	2	1		10	11	
31	Mar 3	DERBY COUNTY	2-4	Smith, Houghton	11530	5	4	7							8	3					11		6	9	2	1		10		
32	10	Crewe Alexandra	2-4	Smith 2	6384			7				10		5		3			4		11		6	9	2	1		8		
33	14	YORK CITY	2-1	Smith, Brickley	3055	5		7	4							3	2		10		11		6	9		1		8		
34	17	MANSFIELD TOWN	0-3		5912	5		7	4						8	3	2		10		9		6			1			11	
35	24	Stockport County	0-0		5381				4					5	9	3	2		6		11		10				1	8		7
36	31	HARTLEPOOLS UNITED	1-3	Redfearn	6579			7	4					5		3	2		6		11		10	9			1	8		
37	Apr 2	Oldham Athletic	1-5	Ward	7381		4	7						5	8	3	2						6	9			1	10	11	
38	3	OLDHAM ATHLETIC	4-1	Pickard 2, Whitaker, Brickley	5590	5	4	7				10		3			2		9				6				1	8	11	
39	7	Wrexham	0-1		4744	5	4					10		3			2		9		7		6				1	8	11	
40	9	Mansfield Town	0-5		6382	5	4							3		6	2		9	7	10						1	8	11	
41	14	HALIFAX TOWN	1-1	Ward	5775	5	4					6			8	3	2		9	7				11			1	10		
42	16	Bradford City	0-5		11658			7			4	6		5	8	3	2							9			1	10	11	
43	18	TRANMERE ROVERS	4-5	Smith 3, Pilling	2651	5	4					10				2				7		3	6	9			1	8	11	
44	21	York City	0-5		8006	5	4					8		3		6	2			7	10			9			1		11	
45	23	ACCRINGTON STANLEY	1-0	Redfearn	4606	5	4		8					3		6	2			7	10			9			1		11	
46	28	CARLISLE UNITED	2-1	Redfearn, Bradley	5320	5	4		8					3		6	2			7	10			9			1		11	
					Apps	13	12	32	18	12	17	21	2	29	16	35	13	3	27	9	34	14	28	21	31	28	17	41	25	5
					Goals		1	7	1	3		3			5				3	1	8			10				13	5	

K Featherstone played at 1 in game 21

JA Pickup played at 10 in games 10 and 11

All Ward's goals are LW Ward

One own goal

F.A. Cup

Rd	Date	Opponent	Score	Scorers	Att	Batty FR	Bradley G	Brickley D	Brocklehurst JF	Brydon IF	Conroy R	Deplidge W	Fazackerley MA	Hindle FJ	Houghton HB	Hudson GA	Jordan C	Loftus R	Pickard LJ	Pilling VJ	Redfearn B	Reilly TJ	Roberts C	Smith JB	Suddards J	Taylor JB	Ward D	Ward LW	Whitaker C	Worsman RH
R1	Nov 19	Rhyl	3-0	Brickley, Ward, Houghton	7000			7	10					5	9	3			4				6		2	1		8	11	
R2	Dec 10	WORKINGTON	4-3	Houghton 2, Whitaker, Ward	7096			7						5	9	3			4		11		6		2	1		8	10	
R3	Jan 7	MIDDLESBROUGH	0-4		18524			7						3	9	2			6		10		4		5	1		8	11	

Back: Hudson, Suddards, Conroy, Roberts, Reilly, Taylo

Front: Brickley, Brydon, Smith, Deplidge, Redfearn

		P	W	D	L	F	A	W	D	L	F	A	Pts
1	Grimsby Town	46	20	1	2	54	10	11	5	7	22	19	68
2	Derby County	46	18	4	1	67	23	10	3	10	43	32	63
3	Accrington Stanley	46	17	4	2	61	19	8	5	10	31	38	59
4	Hartlepools United	46	18	2	3	47	15	8	3	12	34	45	57
5	Southport	46	12	9	2	39	18	11	2	10	27	35	57
6	Chesterfield	46	18	1	4	61	21	7	3	13	33	45	54
7	Stockport County	46	16	4	3	65	22	5	5	13	25	39	51
8	Bradford City	46	16	5	2	57	25	2	8	13	21	39	49
9	Scunthorpe United	46	12	4	7	40	26	8	4	11	35	37	48
10	Workington	46	13	4	6	47	20	6	5	12	28	43	47
11	York City	46	12	4	7	44	24	7	5	11	41	48	47
12	Rochdale	46	13	5	5	46	39	4	8	11	20	45	47
13	Gateshead	46	15	4	4	56	32	2	7	14	21	52	45
14	Wrexham	46	11	5	7	37	28	5	5	13	29	45	42
15	Darlington	46	11	6	6	41	28	5	3	15	19	45	41
16	Tranmere Rovers	46	11	4	8	33	25	5	5	13	26	59	41
17	Chester	46	10	8	5	35	33	3	6	14	17	49	40
18	Mansfield Town	46	13	6	4	59	21	1	5	17	25	60	39
19	Halifax Town	46	10	6	7	40	27	4	5	14	26	49	39
20	Oldham Athletic	46	7	12	4	48	36	3	6	14	28	50	38
21	Carlisle United	46	11	3	9	45	36	4	5	14	26	59	38
22	Barrow	46	11	6	6	44	25	1	3	19	17	58	33
23	BRADFORD	46	13	4	6	47	38	0	3	20	14	84	33
24	Crewe Alexandra	46	9	4	10	32	35	0	6	17	18	70	28

1956/57

20th in Division Three (North)

							Anders J	Atkinson C	Batty FR	Bradley G	Brickley D	Brolls N	Brown GD	Cameron JA	Gleadall D	Hindle FJ	Houghton HB	Hudson GA	Hughes WCJ	Jordan C	Keen A	Kendall HA	Malan NF	Perry A	Redfearn B	Robinson C	Smith JB	Suddards J	Ward D	Ward LW
1	Aug	18	Crewe Alexandra	0-2		5029		8		4		7	10		5								1	3	11	6	9	2		
2		20	STOCKPORT COUNTY	3-2	Redfearn 2, Smith	11152		8		4		7	10		5								1	3	11	6	9	2		
3		25	DERBY COUNTY	3-2	Redfearn, Smith, Ward	13762		4	5			7	10										1	3	11	6	9	2		8
4		27	Stockport County	0-4		8355		7				11	10	6	5								1	3		4	9	2		8
5	Sep	1	Wrexham	0-2		8467		4					10		5		9					7	1	3		6	11	2		8
6		3	SCUNTHORPE UNITED	1-2	Atkinson	8564		8					10			5	9	4		3		7	1		11	6		2		
7		8	GATESHEAD	0-1		9431	11	8					10			5		4		3		7	1			6	9	2		
8		13	Scunthorpe United	2-2	Anders, Smith	7855	11	8							5			4		3		7	1			6	9	2		10
9		15	Bradford City	0-2		20523	11	4				8			5			3				7	1			6	9	2		10
10		17	HULL CITY	4-1	Kendall, Smith 2, Ward	7102	11	8							5			4				7	1	3		6	9	2		10
11		22	Darlington	5-0	Smith 3, Ward, Anders	6326	11	8							5			4				7	1	3		6	9	2		10
12		24	Hull City	0-2		8349	11	8							5			4				7	1	3		6	9	2		10
13		29	BARROW	4-1	Atkinson 2, Kendall, Anders	8694	11	8							5			4				7	1	3		6	9	2		10
14	Oct	6	Carlisle United	1-2	Smith	4713	11	8							5			4				7	1	3		6	9	2		10
15		13	ACCRINGTON STANLEY	2-0	Brown, Smith	12415	7	4					10		5								1	3	11	6	9	2		8
16		20	Chester	0-2		5385	7	4					10		5								1	3	11	6	9	2		8
17		27	YORK CITY	0-2		9206	11	4					10		5							7	1	3		6	9	2		8
18	Nov	3	Oldham Athletic	1-3	Ward	9813		4					10		5		9					7	1	3	11	6		2		8
19		10	MANSFIELD TOWN	1-4	Kendall	6456	11	8		4			10			5	9					7	1	3		6		2		
20		24	CHESTERFIELD	2-0	Smith 2	6895	11	4	5		7		8							2		10	1	3		6	9			
21	Dec	1	Tranmere Rovers	3-0	Smith 3	5611	11	4	5		7		8							2		10	1	3		6	9			
22		15	CREWE ALEXANDRA	4-3	Anders, Smith 3	4791	11	4	5		7									2		10	1	3		6	9			8
23		22	Derby County	1-6	Robinson	7655	11	4	5		7									2		8	1	3		6	9			10
24		25	Workington	1-0	Smith	4631	11	4	5		7						8			2				3		6	9		1	10
25		26	WORKINGTON	1-3	Houghton	5310	11	4	5		7						8			2			1	3		6	9			10
26		29	WREXHAM	0-4		8712		8	5	4	7			6						2		11		3	10		9		1	
27	Jan	1	Southport	1-5	Redfearn	4743	11			4	7			6				3		2		8			10		9	5	1	
28		5	HALIFAX TOWN	2-1	Redfearn, Robinson	6796		4				7			5							11		3	10	6	9	2	1	8
29		12	Gateshead	3-1	Smith 3	2593		4				7			5							11		3	10	6	9	2	1	8
30		19	BRADFORD CITY	2-0	og, Smith	22010	11	4							5							7		3	10	6	9	2	1	8
31		26	Halifax Town	1-3	Smith	6405		4				7			5							11		3	10	6	9	2	1	8
32	Feb	2	DARLINGTON	3-1	Brown, Redfearn, Smith	8802		4			7		10		5									3	11	6	9	2	1	8
33		9	Barrow	0-1		5935		4			7		10		5									3	11	6	9	2	1	8
34		16	CARLISLE UNITED	1-3	Ward	7376		8		4	7				5					11				3		6	9	2	1	10
35	Mar	2	CHESTER	3-1	Ward, Keen, Robinson	7547		4			7				5						8			3	11	6	9	2	1	10
36		9	York City	2-1	Smith 2	8857		4							5						8	7		3	11	6	9	2	1	10
37		16	OLDHAM ATHLETIC	2-2	Ward, Redfearn	7854		4							5						8	7		3	11	6	9	2	1	10
38		23	Mansfield Town	1-2	Atkinson	7621		4							5						8	7		3	11	6	9	2	1	10
39		25	Accrington Stanley	0-5		8553		4							5						8	7		3	11	6	9	2	1	10
40		30	SOUTHPORT	2-3	Kendall, Smith	5273		4				7			5						8	11		3		6	9	2	1	10
41	Apr	6	Chesterfield	1-4	og	7641		4				7				5					8			3	11	6	9	2	1	10
42		13	TRANMERE ROVERS	1-2	Redfearn	4520		4	5			7										11		3	10	6	9	2	1	8
43		20	Hartlepools United	1-2	Redfearn	8102		4	5		7						11				8			3	10	6	9	2	1	
44		22	Rochdale	1-2	Houghton	5007		4	5								11		7		8			3	10	6	9	2	1	
45		23	ROCHDALE	0-0		6280		4	3		11					5	10		7		8					6	9	2	1	
46		27	HARTLEPOOLS UNITED	0-2		6193		4	3				10			5			7		8	11				6	9	2	1	
						Apps	20	45	13	6	14	11	17	3	28	6	9	10	3	12	11	30	24	39	24	44	43	39	22	33
						Goals	4	4					2				2				1	4			9	3	28			7

All Ward's goals are LW Ward

Two own goals

F.A. Cup

							Anders J	Atkinson C	Batty FR	Bradley G	Brickley D	Brolls N	Brown GD	Cameron JA	Gleadall D	Hindle FJ	Houghton HB	Hudson GA	Hughes WCJ	Jordan C	Keen A	Kendall HA	Malan NF	Perry A	Redfearn B	Robinson C	Smith JB	Suddards J	Ward D	Ward LW
R1	Nov	17	Boston United	2-0	Kendall, Smith	8674	7	4				10				5				2		8	1	3	11	6	9			
R2	Dec	8	Peterborough United	0-3		18618	11	4	5		7	8								2		10	1	3		6	9			

		P	W	D	L	F	A	W	D	L	F	A	Pts
1	Derby County	46	18	3	2	69	18	8	8	7	42	35	63
2	Hartlepools United	46	18	4	1	56	21	7	5	11	34	42	59
3	Accrington Stanley	46	15	4	4	54	22	10	4	9	41	42	58
4	Workington	46	16	4	3	60	25	8	6	9	33	38	58
5	Stockport County	46	16	3	4	51	26	7	5	11	40	49	54
6	Chesterfield	46	17	5	1	60	22	5	4	14	36	57	53
7	York City	46	14	4	5	43	21	7	6	10	32	40	52
8	Hull City	46	14	6	3	45	24	7	4	12	39	45	52
9	Bradford City	46	14	3	6	47	31	8	5	10	31	37	52
10	Barrow	46	16	2	5	51	22	5	7	11	25	40	51
11	Halifax Town	46	16	2	5	40	24	5	5	13	25	46	49
12	Wrexham	46	12	7	4	63	33	7	3	13	34	41	48
13	Rochdale	46	14	6	3	38	19	4	6	13	27	46	48
14	Scunthorpe United	46	9	5	9	44	36	6	10	7	27	33	45
15	Carlisle United	46	9	9	5	44	36	7	4	12	32	49	45
16	Mansfield Town	46	13	3	7	58	38	4	7	12	33	52	44
17	Gateshead	46	9	6	8	42	40	8	4	11	30	50	44
18	Darlington	46	11	5	7	47	36	6	3	14	35	59	42
19	Oldham Athletic	46	9	7	7	35	31	3	8	12	31	43	39
20	BRADFORD	46	11	2	10	41	40	5	1	17	25	53	35
21	Chester	46	8	7	8	40	35	2	6	15	15	49	33
22	Southport	46	7	8	8	31	34	3	4	16	21	60	32
23	Tranmere Rovers	46	5	9	9	33	38	2	4	17	18	53	27
24	Crewe Alexandra	46	5	7	11	31	46	1	2	20	12	64	21

1957/58

22nd in Division Three (North)

No	Month	Day	Opponent	Score	Scorers	Att	Atkinson C	Bailey M	Bates E	Batty FR	Booth KK	Buchanan J	Clegg MB	Dean J	Devlin J	France P	Gleadall D	Houghton HB	Hughes WCJ	Kendall HA	Lawton HM	Maxwell K	Minshull R	Perry A	Redfearn B	Robinson C	Rushby A	Suddards J	Taylor JE	Ward D	Ward LW	Whittle E	Williams A	Williams HT
1	Aug	24	Bury	0-1		11724	4			2	10					1		9		7				3		6			8				5	11
2		26	GATESHEAD	2-2	Whittle, og	10568	4				8							9		7				3		6		2		1		10	5	11
3		31	ACCRINGTON STANLEY	1-3	Taylor	12820	4				8					1				7				3		6		2	9			10	5	11
4	Sep	2	Gateshead	4-2	Whittle, Booth 2, Taylor	7631			4		8					1	6			7				3				2	9			10	5	11
5		7	Chester	2-1	Taylor 2	8353			4		8					1	6			7	3							2	9			10	5	11
6		9	BARROW	1-1	Whittle	8513			4		8					1	6			7				3				2	9			10	5	11
7		14	CHESTERFIELD	2-0	Whittle, Taylor	11158	6		4		8					1			7		3							2	9			10	5	11
8		16	Barrow	0-0		3774	6		4		8					1			7					3				2	9			10	5	11
9		21	Tranmere Rovers	0-5		8259	6		4		8					1			7		3				11			2	9			10	5	
10		25	YORK CITY	0-2		5045			4		8					1	6	9	7					3				2				10	5	11
11		28	HARTLEPOOLS UNITED	2-3	Taylor, LW Ward	9220			4		8					1			7					3		6		2	9		10		5	11
12		30	York City	0-3		4407	4		6	5	8					1			7									2	9		10		3	11
13	Oct	5	Mansfield Town	1-2	A Williams	7753	6		4	5	8					1			7					3				2			10		9	11
14		12	BRADFORD CITY	0-0		22899	4				8					1			7					3	9	6		2				10	5	11
15		19	Scunthorpe United	2-6	Redfearn, Booth	7591	4				8					1			7					3	9	6		2				10	5	11
16		26	WREXHAM	2-0	Redfearn, A Williams	7337	4				8						6		7						11	10		3	9	1			5	
17	Nov	2	Crewe Alexandra	0-3		5464	4				8				11		6		7						9	10		3		1			5	
18		9	ROCHDALE	2-2	A Williams, Whittle	8965	4				8				11				7					3		6		2		1	10	9	5	
19		23	STOCKPORT COUNTY	1-0	Devlin	8422			4		8				11				7					3		6	5	2		1		10	9	
20		30	Hull City	3-3	A Williams 2, Whittle	11042						9		4	11				7					3		6	5	2		1		10	8	
21	Dec	7	HALIFAX TOWN	0-2		8516						9		4	11				7					3		6	5	2		1		10	8	
22		14	Workington	2-1	Buchanan, A Williams	6633					8	7		4	11									3		6	5	2		1		10	9	
23		21	BURY	1-4	Dean	9858					7	9		4	11									3		6	5	2		1		10	8	
24		25	SOUTHPORT	3-5	LW Ward 2, A Williams	6363	7				8	9		4										3			6	2		1	10		5	11
25		26	Southport	1-2	Buchanan	3907			6			9		4	7	1			10			2		3	11		5						8	
26		28	Accrington Stanley	2-5	A Williams 2	7212	8		6					4					7	11		3	1				5	2				10	9	
27	Jan	1	Carlisle United	3-2	LW Ward, Kendall, A Williams	7202	8		3	5				4	11					7			1			6		2			10		9	
28		4	CARLISLE UNITED	4-1	LW Ward, A Williams 2, og	5849	8		3	5				4	11					7			1			6		2			10		9	
29		11	CHESTER	3-0	Kendall, A Williams 2	7341	8		3	5				4	11					7			1			6		2			10		9	
30		18	Chesterfield	1-1	Devlin	7295	8		3	5				4	11					7			1			6		2			10		9	
31	Feb	1	TRANMERE ROVERS	1-0	LW Ward	9708	8		3	5				4	11					7			1			6		2			10		9	
32		8	Hartlepools United	0-0		4805	8		3	5				4	11					7			1			6		2			10		9	
33		15	MANSFIELD TOWN	0-2		8629	8		3	5				4	11					7			1			6		2			10		9	
34		22	Stockport County	0-3		8035	8		3	5		9		4	11					7			1			6		2			10			
35	Mar	1	SCUNTHORPE UNITED	1-2	Kendall	13467	8		3	5			9	4	11					7			1			6		2			10			
36		8	Wrexham	1-1	Atkinson	8721	8		3	5	11		9	4						7						6		2		1	10			
37		15	CREWE ALEXANDRA	3-1	A Williams 2, LW Ward	6552	8		3	5			7	4						11			1			6		2			10		9	
38		22	Bradford City	1-2	A Williams	16698	8		3	5			7	4						11			1			6		2			10		9	
39		29	Halifax Town	0-2		6358	8		3	5			7	4						11			1			6		2			10		9	
40	Apr	4	Oldham Athletic	2-4	Buchanan, Booth	5981	8			5	10	7		4						11			1	3		6		2	9					
41		5	Darlington	0-4		3281	8			5	10			4	11					7			1	3		6		2					9	
42		7	OLDHAM ATHLETIC	1-3	Atkinson	5420	8	11	3	5			9	4		1				7						6		2			10			
43		12	HULL CITY	4-4	Atkinson 2, Buchanan 2	5910	8	11	3	5	10	9		4						7			1			6		2						
44		14	DARLINGTON	4-1	Booth, Buchanan 2, Bailey	3273	8	11	3	5	10	9		4						7			1			6		2						
45		19	Rochdale	2-1	Booth, Buchanan	4912	8	11	3	5	10	9		4						7			1			6		2						
46		26	WORKINGTON	3-3	Buchanan 2, Kendall	5283	8	11	3	5	10	9		4						7			1			6		2						
						Apps	35	5	31	23	29	12	6	27	18	16	6	3	17	27	3	2	19	21	6	34	8	44	12	11	19	18	37	15
						Goals	4	1			6	10		1	2					4					2				6		7	6	17	

G Baker played at 2 in games 16 and 17

Two own goals

F.A. Cup

Rd	Month	Day	Opponent	Score	Scorers	Att	Atkinson C	Bailey M	Bates E	Batty FR	Booth KK	Buchanan J	Clegg MB	Dean J	Devlin J	France P	Gleadall D	Houghton HB	Hughes WCJ	Kendall HA	Lawton HM	Maxwell K	Minshull R	Perry A	Redfearn B	Robinson C	Rushby A	Suddards J	Taylor JE	Ward D	Ward LW	Whittle E	Williams A	Williams HT
R1	Nov	16	Oldham Athletic	0-2		9272	7		4		8				11	1								3		6		2			10	9	5	

OFFICIAL PROGRAMME

BRADFORD PARK AVENUE A.F.C.

PRICE 3ᴰ

At Park Avenue. Football League Div. 3 (North)
GATESHEAD
MONDAY, 26th AUGUST Kick-off 6-30 p.m.

AUSTIN RETAIL DEALERS ALL MAKES OF CARS SUPPLIED
BAYLEY MOTOR CO.
DUDLEY HILL, BRADFORD 4
SALES REPAIRS AND ALL SERVICES

FOR COMPLETE RESULTS YOU MUST GET
YORKSHIRE SPORTS
EVERY SATURDAY NIGHT
THE COMPLETE SPORTS PAPER

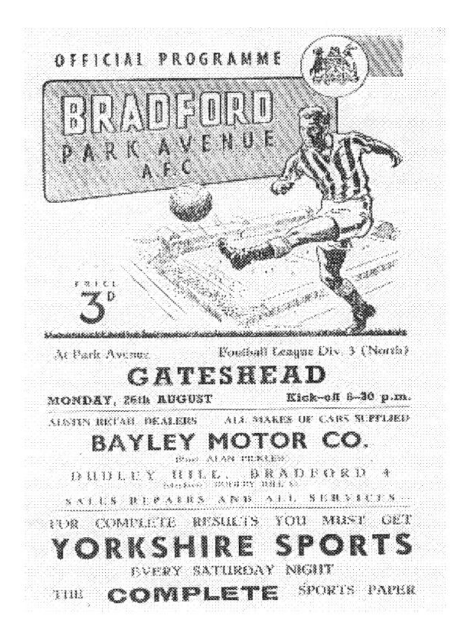

		P	W	D	L	F	A	W	D	L	F	A	Pts
1	Scunthorpe United	46	16	5	2	46	19	13	3	7	42	31	66
2	Accrington Stanley	46	16	4	3	53	28	9	5	9	30	33	59
3	Bradford City	46	13	7	3	42	19	8	8	7	31	30	57
4	Bury	46	17	4	2	61	18	6	6	11	33	44	56
5	Hull City	46	15	6	2	49	20	4	9	10	29	47	53
6	Mansfield Town	46	16	3	4	68	42	6	5	12	32	50	52
7	Halifax Town	46	15	5	3	52	20	5	6	12	31	49	51
8	Chesterfield	46	12	8	3	39	28	6	7	10	32	41	51
9	Stockport County	46	15	4	4	54	28	3	7	13	20	39	47
10	Rochdale	46	14	4	5	50	25	5	4	14	29	42	46
11	Tranmere Rovers	46	12	6	5	51	32	6	4	13	31	44	46
12	Wrexham	46	13	8	2	39	18	4	4	15	22	45	46
13	York City	46	11	8	4	40	26	6	4	13	28	50	46
14	Gateshead	46	12	5	6	41	27	3	10	10	27	49	45
15	Oldham Athletic	46	11	7	5	44	32	3	10	10	28	52	45
16	Carlisle United	46	13	3	7	56	35	6	3	14	24	43	44
17	Hartlepools United	46	11	6	6	45	26	5	6	12	28	50	44
18	Barrow	46	9	7	7	36	32	4	8	11	30	42	41
19	Workington	46	11	6	6	46	33	3	7	13	26	48	41
20	Darlington	46	15	3	5	53	25	2	4	17	25	64	41
21	Chester	46	7	10	6	38	26	6	3	14	35	55	39
22	BRADFORD	46	8	6	9	41	41	5	5	13	27	54	37
23	Southport	46	8	3	12	29	40	3	3	17	23	48	28
24	Crewe Alexandra	46	6	5	12	29	41	2	2	19	18	52	23

1958/59

14th in Division Four

No	Month	Day	Opponent	Score	Scorers	Att	Allan J	Atkinson C	Bailey M	Baker G	Bates E	Batty FR	Booth KK	Brims D	Buchanan J	Byrom R	Dean J	Devlin J	Dick PW	Harvey WJ	Heenan T	Kendall HA	Lawton HM	Lightowler GB	McGregor C	Minshull R	Robinson C	Routledge RW	Rushby A	Suddards J	Ward LW	Williams A
1	Aug	23	WORKINGTON	3-2	Atkinson, Booth, 2	9333		8	11		3	5	10		9		4					7				1	6			2		
2		25	Hartlepools United	0-3		6994		8	11		3	5	10		9		4					7					6	1		2		
3		30	York City	0-4		8497		8			3	5	10		9		4	11				7					6	1		2		
4	Sep	1	HARTLEPOOLS UNITED	4-1	Ward, Buchanan, Booth, Williams	7688		6	11				10	4	9							7	3					1		2	8	5
5		6	Gateshead	4-1	Booth 4	6399		6	11				10	4	9							7	3					1		2	8	5
6		9	Southport	0-1		3880		6	11				10	4	9							7	3					1		2	8	5
7		13	PORT VALE	0-2		9683		6			3		10	4	9							7					11	1		2	8	5
8		15	SOUTHPORT	3-0	Buchanan 2, Heenan	5744		6		3			10		9		4				7	11						1		2	8	5
9		20	Crystal Palace	0-2		14134		6			3		10	4	9						7	11						1		2	8	5
10		22	Torquay United	1-2	Williams	4515		10			3		7	4	9		6					11						1		2	8	5
11		27	CHESTER	3-0	Williams, Buchanan 2	7274		10						4	9		6				7	11						1	3	2	8	5
12		29	TORQUAY UNITED	3-1	Kendall 2, Buchanan	4969		10						4	9		6				7	11						1	3	2	8	5
13	Oct	4	Watford	1-2	Ward	6661		6					10	4	9		3				7	11						1	5	2	8	
14		8	Crewe Alexandra	1-4	Devlin	8099		6						4	9		3	11				10			7			1	5	2	8	
15		11	BARROW	0-2		7115		6					10	4	9		5	11				7	3					1		2	8	
16		18	Carlisle United	1-1	Atkinson	8844		10				5		4	8		3	11				7					6	1		2		
17		25	GILLINGHAM	2-0	Brims, Atkinson	7459		10			3	5		8	9		4	11				7					6	1		2		
18	Nov	1	Exeter City	0-4		10808		10			3	5		8	9		4	11				7					6	1		2		
19		8	COVENTRY CITY	2-0	Buchanan, 2	8619		10			3		8	4	9		5	11				7					6	1		2		
20		22	DARLINGTON	1-2	Atkinson	7376		10			3	5	8	4	9			11				7					6	1		2		
21		29	Walsall	2-3	Booth, Atkinson	6702		8					10	4	9		5	11				7	3				6	1		2		
22	Dec	13	Aldershot	3-3	Atkinson, Ward, Buchanan	3154		8			3			4	9		5	11				7						1		2	10	
23		20	Workington	1-2	Atkinson	3366		8			3		10	4	9		5	11				7					6	1		2		
24		26	OLDHAM ATHLETIC	2-1	Buchanan, Ward	9692		6			3			4	9	11	5	7	10									1		2	8	
25		27	Oldham Athletic	0-1		5942		8						4		11	6	7	9				3					1		2	10	5
26	Jan	1	CREWE ALEXANDRA	0-2		3177		8						4	9	11	6	7	10				3			1				2		5
27		3	YORK CITY	2-1	Byrom, Atkinson	7715		8						4	9	11	6	7	10				3			1				2		5
28		10	Shrewsbury Town	1-0	Buchanan	5175		8						4	9	11		7	6	10			3			1				2		5
29		17	GATESHEAD	4-1	Byrom, Buchanan, Harvey, Atkinson	5918		8						4	9	11			6	10		7	3			1				2		5
30		24	MILLWALL	4-1	Atkinson, Byrom, Kendall, Brims	8925		8						4	9	11			6	10		7	3			1				2		5
31		31	Port Vale	2-4	Byrom, Atkinson	12377		8						4	9	11			6	10		7	3			1				2		5
32	Feb	7	CRYSTAL PALACE	5-0	Buchanan 4, Kendall	6267		8						4	9	11			6	10		7	3			1				2		5
33		14	Chester	0-2		6089		8						4	9	11			6	10		7	3			1				2		5
34		21	WATFORD	1-1	Allan	6304	9	8						4	10	11			6			7	3					1		2		5
35		28	Barrow	3-2	Buchanan, Atkinson, Byrom	3124	8	7						4	9	11			6	10			3					1		2		5
36	Mar	7	CARLISLE UNITED	0-3		6329	8	7						4	9	11			6	10			3					1		2		5
37		14	Gillingham	1-1	Atkinson	6371		8						4	9	11	5		6	10		7	3					1		2		
38		21	EXETER CITY	0-3		7203		8						4	9	11	5		6	10		7	3					1		2		
39		27	NORTHAMPTON T	1-2	Williams	5898		8						4	9	11	2		6	10		7	3					1				5
40		28	Coventry City	0-0		16399	9	7						4	8	11	2		6	10			3					1				5
41		31	Northampton Town	1-4	Buchanan	7544	9	7						4	8	11	2		6	10			3					1				5
42	Apr	4	SHREWSBURY TOWN	3-1	Allan 2, Buchanan	7262	9	7						4	8	11			6	10			3					1		2		5
43		11	Darlington	1-1	Atkinson	4106	9	7						4	8	11			6	10			3					1		2		5
44		18	WALSALL	3-2	Buchanan, Allan 2	6054	9	7						4	8	11			6	10			3					1		2		5
45		25	Millwall	1-1	Byrom	6446	9	4		2					8	11			6	10		7	3					1				5
46		27	ALDERSHOT	5-1	Allan 3, Atkinson, Buchanan	5360	9	4							8				6	10			3	11	7			1		2		5

Played in one game: P Flynn (22, at 6), K Whaley (16, 9)

	Allan J	Atkinson C	Bailey M	Baker G	Bates E	Batty FR	Booth KK	Brims D	Buchanan J	Byrom R	Dean J	Devlin J	Dick PW	Harvey WJ	Heenan T	Kendall HA	Lawton HM	Lightowler GB	McGregor C	Minshull R	Robinson C	Routledge RW	Rushby A	Suddards J	Ward LW	Williams A
Apps	10	46	5	2	13	7	16	40	45	22	26	16	23	18	5	33	27	1	2	9	11	37	4	42	15	29
Goals	8	15					8	2	21	6		1		1	1	4									4	4

F.A. Cup

Rd	Month	Day	Opponent	Score	Scorers	Att	Allan J	Atkinson C	Bailey M	Baker G	Bates E	Batty FR	Booth KK	Brims D	Buchanan J	Byrom R	Dean J	Devlin J	Dick PW	Harvey WJ	Heenan T	Kendall HA	Lawton HM	Lightowler GB	McGregor C	Minshull R	Robinson C	Routledge RW	Rushby A	Suddards J	Ward LW	Williams A
R1	Nov	15	Gateshead	4-1	Buchanan 2, Atkinson, Booth	6006		10			3		8	4	9		5	11				7					6	1		2		
R2	Dec	6	BRADFORD CITY	0-2		19962		8			3		10	4	9		5	11				7					6	1		2		

		P	W	D	L	F	A	W	D	L	F	A	Pts
1	Port Vale	46	14	6	3	62	30	12	6	5	48	28	64
2	Coventry City	46	18	4	1	50	11	6	8	9	34	36	60
3	York City	46	12	10	1	37	17	9	8	6	36	35	60
4	Shrewsbury Town	46	15	5	3	59	24	9	5	9	42	39	58
5	Exeter City	46	16	4	3	55	24	7	7	9	32	37	57
6	Walsall	46	13	5	5	56	25	8	5	10	39	39	52
7	Crystal Palace	46	12	8	3	54	27	8	4	11	36	44	52
8	Northampton Town	46	14	5	4	48	25	7	4	12	37	53	51
9	Millwall	46	13	6	4	46	23	7	4	12	30	46	50
10	Carlisle United	46	11	6	6	37	30	8	6	9	25	35	50
11	Gillingham	46	14	6	3	53	27	6	3	14	29	50	49
12	Torquay United	46	11	5	7	45	32	5	7	11	33	45	44
13	Chester	46	10	5	8	39	33	6	7	10	33	51	44
14	BRADFORD	46	15	1	7	51	29	3	6	14	24	48	43
15	Watford	46	10	6	7	46	36	6	4	13	35	43	42
16	Darlington	46	7	8	8	37	36	6	8	9	29	32	42
17	Workington	46	9	10	4	40	32	3	7	13	23	46	41
18	Crewe Alexandra	46	11	5	7	52	32	4	5	14	18	50	40
19	Hartlepools United	46	11	4	8	50	41	4	6	13	24	47	40
20	Gateshead	46	11	3	9	33	30	5	5	13	23	55	40
21	Oldham Athletic	46	15	0	8	39	29	1	4	18	20	55	36
22	Aldershot	46	8	4	11	37	45	6	3	14	26	52	35
23	Barrow	46	6	6	11	34	45	3	4	16	17	59	28
24	Southport	46	7	8	8	26	25	0	4	19	15	61	26

1959/60

11th in Division Four

No	Month	Day	Opponent	Score	Scorers	Att	Allan J	Atkinson C	Baker G	Brims D	Buchanan J	Byrom R	Cade D	Dick PW	Gibson IS	Harvey WJ	Hooley JW	Hough H	Lawton HM	McGregor C	McAllister J	McCalman DS	McHard A	Reilly F	Storey S	Walker J	Williams A
1	Aug	22	Oldham Athletic	0-2		9100	9			4	8	11		6		10		1	3				7			2	5
2		24	WATFORD	1-1	Atkinson	8052	9	7		4	8	11		6				1	3		10					2	5
3		29	CARLISLE UNITED	1-1	Buchanan	8357		8		4	9	11		6	7			1	3		10					2	5
4	Sep	1	Watford	0-1		8801		4	2		9	11		6		10		1			8	3	7				5
5		5	Notts County	1-0	McAllister	12139			2	4	9	11		6		10		1			8	3	7				5
6		7	MILLWALL	1-1	Byrom	7204			2	4	9	11		6		10		1			8	3	7				5
7		12	WALSALL	1-3	Allan	8048	9		2	4		11		6		10		1			8	3	7				5
8		14	Millwall	0-2		15162		2		4	9	11		6		8		1	3		10	5	7				
9		19	Hartlepools United	0-3		4109		8	2	4	9	11		6				1			10	3	7				5
10		21	EXETER CITY	1-0	McAllister	4615		8		4	9	11		6				1		7	10	3				2	5
11		26	CREWE ALEXANDRA	2-2	Atkinson, McAllister	6209		8		4	9	11		6				1			10	3	7			2	5
12		30	Exeter City	1-3	Buchanan,	6414	9	6		4	8	11						1	3		10		7			2	5
13	Oct	3	Chester	1-1	Byrom	6806		6		4	9	11						1	3		8		7		10	2	5
14		7	CRYSTAL PALACE	3-1	McAllister, Buchanan, Byrom	3220		6		4	9	11						1	3		8	5	7		10	2	
15		10	GILLINGHAM	3-0	og, Allan, Buchanan	6104	9	6		4	8	11						1	3		10	5	7			2	
16		17	Barrow	3-3	Allan 2, McAllister	4318	9	6		4	8	11						1	3		10		7			2	5
17		24	ALDERSHOT	3-2	Brims, Buchanan, Allan	5741	9	6		4	8	11						1	3		10	5	7			2	
18		31	Darlington	3-4	McAllister 2, og	4782	9	6		4	8	11						1	3		10	5	7			2	
19	Nov	7	GATESHEAD	4-2	Byrom 2, Allan, McHard	5702	9	6		4	8	11		5				1	3		10		7			2	
20		21	WORKINGTON	3-2	Allan, McAllister, Buchanan	6967	9	6		4	8	11		5				1	3		10		7			2	
21		28	Doncaster Rovers	0-2		4229	9	6		4	8	11		5				1	3		10		7			2	
22	Dec	12	Torquay United	1-1	Atkinson	5424	9	8		4		11		6		10		1	3				7			2	5
23		19	OLDHAM ATHLETIC	2-0	Allan 2	5266	9	10		4	8	11		6				1	3				7			2	5
24		26	SOUTHPORT	3-0	McHard, Allan 2	8109	9	10		4	8	11		6				1	3				7			2	5
25		28	Southport	1-1	McAllister	2949	9	10		4		11		6				1	3		8		7			2	5
26	Jan	2	Carlisle United	3-1	Allan 2, McAllister	4076	9	4			8	11		6				1	3		10		7			2	5
27		16	NOTTS COUNTY	1-1	Allan	8114	9	4			8	11		6				1	3		10		7			2	5
28		23	Walsall	1-2	McAllister	8630	9	4				11		6		10	7	1	3		8					2	5
29	Feb	6	HARTLEPOOLS UNITED	6-2	Allan 3, Byrom, Gibson, Atkinson	6921	9	4			8	11		6	7			1	3		10					2	5
30		13	Crewe Alexandra	1-4	Allan	5656	9	4			8	11		6	7			1	3		10					2	5
31		20	CHESTER	1-1	McAllister	5167	9	4			8	7	11	6				1	3		10					2	5
32		27	Gillingham	0-2		7281		8		4	9	11		6	7			1			10	3				2	5
33	Mar	5	BARROW	2-0	Buchanan, Byrom	6223		8		4	9	11		6	7			1			10	3				2	5
34		12	Aldershot	1-6	Gibson	5185	9	8		4		11		6	7			1			10	3				2	5
35		15	Rochdale	1-0	Reilly	3814	9	4				11		6	7		8	1	3			5		10		2	
36		19	DARLINGTON	1-0	Reilly	5411	9	4				11		6	7		8	1	3			5		10		2	
37		26	Gateshead	2-1	Allan 2	1488	9	4				11		6	7		8	1	3			5		10		2	
38	Apr	2	ROCHDALE	0-0		5955	9	6	2	4		11		3	7		8	1				5		10			
39		7	NORTHAMPTON T	3-0	Allan 3	4916	9	6		4	8	11		3	7			1				5		10		2	
40		9	Workington	1-0	Allan	2748	9	6		4	8	11		3	7			1				5		10		2	
41		15	Stockport County	0-0		4458	9	6		4	8	11		3	7			1				5		10		2	
42		16	DONCASTER ROVERS	3-3	Allan 2, Gibson	8032	9	6		4	8	11		3	7			1				5		10		2	
43		19	STOCKPORT COUNTY	1-1	Gibson	7579	9			4	8	11		6	7			1	3			5		10		2	
44		23	Northampton Town	1-3	Reilly	8667	9			4	8	11		6				1	3			5	7	10		2	
45		27	Crystal Palace	0-1		9920		6		4	9	7		10				1	3		8	5		11		2	
46		30	TORQUAY UNITED	2-2	Reilly, Byrom	5274	9	6		4		7		10				1	3		8	5		11		2	
						Apps	33	40	6	36	36	46	1	39	15	8	5	46	31	1	32	27	25	12	2	39	26
						Goals	26	4		1	7	8			4						12		2	4			

Two own goals

F.A. Cup

Rd	Month	Day	Opponent	Score	Scorers	Att	Allan J	Atkinson C	Baker G	Brims D	Buchanan J	Byrom R	Cade D	Dick PW	Gibson IS	Harvey WJ	Hooley JW	Hough H	Lawton HM	McGregor C	McAllister J	McCalman DS	McHard A	Reilly F	Storey S	Walker J	Williams A
R1	Nov	14	SCARBOROUGH	6-1	Buchanan 4, Allan 2	8786	9	6		4	8	11		5				1	3		10		7			2	
R2	Dec	5	South Shields	5-1	Allan 2, Harvey 2, Buchanan	10200	9	4			8	11		6		10		1	3				7			2	5
R3	Jan	9	Chelsea	1-5	Allan	32212	9	4			8	11		6				1	3		10		7			2	5

		P	W	D	L	F	A	W	D	L	F	A	Pts
1	Walsall	46	14	5	4	57	33	14	4	5	45	27	65
2	Notts County	46	19	1	3	66	27	7	7	9	41	42	60
3	Torquay United	46	17	3	3	56	27	9	5	9	28	31	60
4	Watford	46	17	2	4	62	28	7	7	9	30	39	57
5	Millwall	46	12	8	3	54	28	6	9	8	30	33	53
6	Northampton Town	46	13	6	4	50	22	9	3	11	35	41	53
7	Gillingham	46	17	4	2	47	21	4	6	13	27	48	52
8	Crystal Palace	46	12	6	5	61	27	7	6	10	23	37	50
9	Exeter City	46	13	7	3	50	30	6	4	13	30	40	49
10	Stockport County	46	15	6	2	35	10	4	5	14	23	44	49
11	BRADFORD	46	12	10	1	48	25	5	5	13	22	43	49
12	Rochdale	46	15	4	4	46	19	3	6	14	19	41	46
13	Aldershot	46	14	5	4	50	22	4	4	15	27	52	45
14	Crewe Alexandra	46	14	3	6	51	31	4	6	13	28	57	45
15	Darlington	46	11	6	6	40	30	6	3	14	23	43	43
16	Workington	46	10	8	5	41	20	4	6	13	27	40	42
17	Doncaster Rovers	46	13	3	7	40	23	3	7	13	29	53	42
18	Barrow	46	11	8	4	52	29	4	3	16	25	58	41
19	Carlisle United	46	9	6	8	28	28	6	5	12	23	38	41
20	Chester	46	10	8	5	37	26	4	4	15	22	51	40
21	Southport	46	9	7	7	30	32	1	7	15	18	60	34
22	Gateshead	46	12	3	8	37	27	0	6	17	21	59	33
23	Oldham Athletic	46	5	7	11	20	30	3	5	15	21	53	28
24	Hartlepools United	46	9	2	12	40	41	1	5	17	19	68	27

1960/61

4th in Division Four: Promoted

	Date		Opponent	Score	Scorers	Att.	Allan J	Anders J	Atkinson C	Baillie J	Baker G	Buchanan J	Byrom R	Dick PW	Dick TW	Flynn P	Gebbie RBR	Gibson IS	Hooley JW	Hough H	Lawton HM	Lightbown TJ	Lightowler GB	McAllister J	McCalman DS	McHard A	Reilly F	Routledge RW	Scoular J	Spratt T	Walker J
1	Aug	20	Workington	3-1	Buchanan 2, Allan	4646	9		4	3		8	11	6				7		1					5		10				2
2		22	CHESTER	1-0	Buchanan	8244	9		4	3		8	11	6				7		1					5		10				2
3		27	OLDHAM ATHLETIC	5-1	Reilly 2, Baillie, Allan, Buchanan	9303	9		4	3		8		6				7		1		11			5		10				2
4		31	Chester	1-3	Gibson	5246	9		4	3		8		6				7		1		11			5		10				2
5	Sep	3	Aldershot	0-3		6502		11	4	3				6	9			8		1				10	5	7					2
6		5	YORK CITY	3-3	Anders, Atkinson, Buchanan	7782		11	4	3		8		6	9			7		1					5		10				2
7		10	NORTHAMPTON T	1-3	Gibson	7616		11	4	3		8		6	9			7		1					5		10				2
8		12	York City	0-2		9704		11	4		2			6	9		1	7	8		3			10	5						
9		17	EXETER CITY	5-2	Reilly, Anders 2, Buchanan 2	6124	9	11	4		2	8		6			1	7			3				5		10				
10		19	CREWE ALEXANDRA	2-0	Allan 2	4395	9	11			2	8		4		6	1	7			3				5		10				
11		24	Gillingham	4-3	Reilly 3, Buchanan	6998	9	11	4		2	8		6				7		1	3				5		10				
12		28	Crewe Alexandra	1-1	Allan	7157	9	11	4			8		6				7		1	3		2		5		10				
13	Oct	1	BARROW	4-0	Hooley 2, Allan 2	7417	9	11	4			8		6					7	1	3		2		5		10				
14		3	Millwall	1-5	Anders	9815	9	11	4			8		6					7	1	3		2		5		10				
15		8	Southport	3-2	Hooley, Buchanan, Anders	5586	9	11	4			8		6					7		3		2		5		10	1			
16		15	DARLINGTON	1-0	Anders	8925	9	11	4			8		6			1		7		3		2		5		10				
17		22	Crystal Palace	1-4	Hooley	14946	9	11	4			8		6			1	10	7		3		2		5						
18		29	DONCASTER ROVERS	1-1	Buchanan	8422	9	11	4			8		6			1	10	7		3		2		5						
19	Nov	12	WREXHAM	3-1	Allan 2, Gibson	6990	9	11	4			8		6			1	7			3			10	5						2
20		19	Carlisle United	2-2	Allan, Buchanan	4160	9	11	4			8		6			1	7			3			10	5						2
21		26	Barrow	0-5		3397	9	11	4			8		6			1	7			3			10	5						2
22	Dec	10	STOCKPORT COUNTY	4-2	McAllister, Buchanan 2, Allan	6099	9	11	4			8		6			1	7			3		2	10	5						
23		17	WORKINGTON	4-0	McHard, Allan 2, McAllister	6367	9	11	4					6			1	8			3		2	10	5	7					
24		24	Accrington Stanley	2-1	Allan, Buchanan	5040	9	11	4			8		6			1	7			3		2	10	5						
25		31	Oldham Athletic	0-4		16060	9	11	4			8		6			1	7			3		2	10	5						
26	Jan	7	ROCHDALE	2-1	Gibson, Buchanan	7375	9	11	4			8		6			1	7			3		2	10	5						
27		14	ALDERSHOT	1-0	Buchanan	12718	9	11	10			8		6			1	7			3		2		5				4		
28		21	Northampton Town	1-0	Allan	9749	9	11	10			8		6			1	7			3		2		5				4		
29		28	Hartlepools United	4-2	Anders, Atkinson, Allan, Buchanan	3207	9	11	10			8		6			1	7			3		2		5				4		
30	Feb	4	Exeter City	2-4	Allan, Atkinson	4916	9	11	10			8		6			1	7			3		2		5				4		
31		11	GILLINGHAM	0-0		7483	9	11	7			8		6			1	10			3		2		5				4		
32		25	SOUTHPORT	1-0	Spratt	8447		11	7			9		6			1	8			3		2		5				4	10	
33	Mar	4	Darlington	0-0		7135		11	7			9		6			1	8			3		2		5				4	10	
34		11	CRYSTAL PALACE	3-1	Buchanan, Atkinson, Anders	17017		11	7			9				6	1	8			3		2		5				4	10	
35		18	Doncaster Rovers	0-2		6494		11	7			9				6	1	8			3		2		5				4	10	
36		25	HARTLEPOOLS UNITED	1-3	Spratt	8975		11	7			9		6			1	8			3		2		5				4	10	
37	Apr	1	Wrexham	1-0	Buchanan	5183		11	7			9		6			1	10			3				5				4	8	2
38		3	Peterborough United	1-3	Scoular	16459			7			9		6			1	10			3		11		5				4	8	2
39		8	CARLISLE UNITED	0-0		10467			7			9		6			1	10			3		11		5				4	8	2
40		12	Mansfield Town	2-1	Gibson, Reilly	4703			7			9		6			1	8			3				5		10		4	11	2
41		15	Rochdale	3-2	Spratt, Gibson, Walker	5342			7					6			1	8	9		3				5		10		4	11	2
42		20	PETERBOROUGH UTD.	1-0	Reilly	20461			4		3	9		6			1	8						7	5		10			11	2
43		22	MANSFIELD TOWN	2-1	Gibson, McCalman	10249		11	4		3	9		6			1	8							5		10			7	2
44		24	MILLWALL	2-1	Spratt, Buchanan	12339		11	7			9		6			1	8			3				5				4	10	2
45		29	Stockport County	3-2	Scoular, Spratt 2	4147		11	7			9		6			1	8			3				5				4	10	2
46	May	1	ACCRINGTON STANLEY	2-2	Buchanan, Spratt	8589		11	7			9		6			1	8			3				5				4	10	2
						Apps	27	37	45	7	6	42	2	44	4	3	34	42	8	11	37	2	24	11	46	2	18	1	18	15	20
						Goals	17	8	4	1		21						7	4					2	1	1	8		2	7	1

F.A. Cup

	Date		Opponent	Score	Scorers	Att.	Allan J	Anders J	Atkinson C	Baillie J	Baker G	Buchanan J	Byrom R	Dick PW	Dick TW	Flynn P	Gebbie RBR	Gibson IS	Hooley JW	Hough H	Lawton HM	Lightbown TJ	Lightowler GB	McAllister J	McCalman DS	McHard A	Reilly F	Routledge RW	Scoular J	Spratt T	Walker J
R1	Nov	5	York City	0-0		7808	9	11	4					6	10		1	7	8		3				5						2
rep		9	YORK CITY	0-2		5813	9	11	4					6	10		1	7	8		3				5						2

F.L. Cup

	Date		Opponent	Score	Scorers	Att.	Allan J	Anders J	Atkinson C	Baillie J	Baker G	Buchanan J	Byrom R	Dick PW	Dick TW	Flynn P	Gebbie RBR	Gibson IS	Hooley JW	Hough H	Lawton HM	Lightbown TJ	Lightowler GB	McAllister J	McCalman DS	McHard A	Reilly F	Routledge RW	Scoular J	Spratt T	Walker J
R1	Oct	12	Lincoln City	2-2	Hooley, Allan	1737	9	11	4			8		6					7		3		2		5		10				
rep		19	LINCOLN CITY	1-0	Anders	3145	9	11	4					6	8		1		7		3		2	10	5						
R2		31	Birmingham City	0-1		4736	9	11	4					6	10		1	7	8		3		2		5						

Played in goal in R1: Alexander

Back: Scoular, Walker, Lawton, Gebbie, Dick, McCalman
Front: Atkinson, Buchanan, Spratt, Gibson, Anders

		P	W	D	L	F	A	W	D	L	F	A	Pts
1	Peterborough United	46	18	3	2	85	30	10	7	6	49	35	66
2	Crystal Palace	46	16	4	3	64	28	13	2	8	46	41	64
3	Northampton Town	46	16	4	3	53	25	9	6	8	37	37	60
4	BRADFORD	46	16	5	2	49	22	10	3	10	35	52	60
5	York City	46	17	3	3	50	14	4	6	13	30	46	51
6	Millwall	46	13	3	7	56	33	8	5	10	41	53	50
7	Darlington	46	11	7	5	41	24	7	6	10	37	46	49
8	Workington	46	14	3	6	38	28	7	4	12	36	48	49
9	Crewe Alexandra	46	11	4	8	40	29	9	5	9	21	38	49
10	Aldershot	46	16	4	3	55	19	2	5	16	24	50	45
11	Doncaster Rovers	46	15	0	8	52	33	4	7	12	24	45	45
12	Oldham Athletic	46	13	4	6	57	38	6	3	14	22	50	45
13	Stockport County	46	14	4	5	31	21	4	5	14	26	45	45
14	Southport	46	12	6	5	47	27	7	0	16	22	40	44
15	Gillingham	46	9	7	7	45	34	6	6	11	19	32	43
16	Wrexham	46	12	4	7	38	22	5	4	14	24	34	42
17	Rochdale	46	13	7	3	43	19	4	1	18	17	47	42
18	Accrington Stanley	46	12	4	7	44	32	4	4	15	30	56	40
19	Carlisle United	46	10	7	6	43	37	3	6	14	18	42	39
20	Mansfield Town	46	10	3	10	39	34	6	3	14	32	44	38
21	Exeter City	46	12	3	8	39	32	2	7	14	27	62	38
22	Barrow	46	10	6	7	33	28	3	5	15	19	51	37
23	Hartlepools United	46	10	4	9	46	40	2	4	17	25	63	32
24	Chester	46	9	7	7	38	35	2	2	19	23	69	31

1961/62

11th in Division Three

#	Date	Opponent	Score	Scorers	Att	Alexander A	Anders J	Ashworth JM	Atkinson C	Bird RP	Bleanch NWS	Buchanan J	Dick PW	Flynn P	Gebbie RBR	Gibson IS	Ham RS	Hannigan JL	Lawton HM	March JE	Maxwell H	McCalman DS	Reilly F	Routledge RW	Scoular J	Spratt T	Walker J
1	Aug 19	Southend United	1-2	Spratt	13049				7	11			6		1	8		9		3		5			4	10	2
2	23	LINCOLN CITY	2-0	Atkinson, Spratt	10854				7	11			6		1	8		9		3		5			4	10	2
3	26	NOTTS COUNTY	3-2	Hannigan 2, Spratt	11476				7	11			6		1	8		9		3		5			4	10	2
4	30	Lincoln City	2-3	Bird, Heward (og)	5948				7	11			6		1	8		9		3		5			4	10	2
5	Sep 2	Shrewsbury Town	1-4	Gibson	6664				4	11			6		1	8		7		3		5	9			10	2
6	6	READING	1-3	Spratt	7358		11		7				6		1	8		9		3		5			4	10	2
7	9	PETERBOROUGH UTD.	6-2	Spratt 2, Atkinson, Dick, Buchanan, Hannigan	11866		7		4			9	6		1	10		11		3		5				8	2
8	16	Port Vale	2-3	Hannigan, Spratt	9279				7			9	6		1	10		11		3		5			4	8	2
9	18	Newport County	2-1	Gibson, Hannigan	10458				7	11			6		1	10		9		3		5			4	8	2
10	23	BRISTOL CITY	2-0	Atkinson, Spratt	10432				7	11			6		1	10		9		3		5			4	8	2
11	30	Torquay United	3-1	Atkinson, Gibson, Spratt	4826				7	11			6		1	8		9		3		5			4	10	2
12	Oct 7	NORTHAMPTON T	1-2	Atkinson,	10738				7	11		9	6		1	10				3		5			4	8	2
13	9	Coventry City	0-3		7195				7	11			6		1	10		9		3		5			4	8	2
14	14	Hull City	1-0	Gibson	12096				7			9	6		1	10		11		3		5			4	8	2
15	16	COVENTRY CITY	0-0		8681				7			9	6		1	10		11		3		5			4	8	2
16	21	HALIFAX TOWN	2-0	Atkinson, Buchanan	11996				7			9	6		1	10		11		3		5			4	8	2
17	25	NEWPORT COUNTY	4-1	Hannigan, Gibson, Dick, Spratt	9370				7			9	6		1	10		11		3		5			4	8	2
18	28	Swindon Town	2-3	Buchanan, Gibson	9400				7			9	6		1	10		11		3		5			4	8	2
19	Nov 11	Portsmouth	2-4	Bleanch 2	11546				7		9		6		1	10		11		3		5			4	8	2
20	18	BARNSLEY	3-2	Atkinson, Spratt 2	12104				7		9		6		1	10		11		3		5			4	8	2
21	Dec 2	WATFORD	1-1	Spratt	8948				7		9		6		1	10		11		3		5			4	8	2
22	9	Bournemouth	2-2	March, Bleanch	9401				7		9		6		1	10		11		3		5			4	8	2
23	23	Notts County	2-4	Hannigan, Gibson	6868			4	7		9		6			10		11		3		5		1		8	2
24	26	Brentford	0-2		5043	1			4	11	9		6			10		7		3		5				8	2
25	Jan 13	SHREWSBURY TOWN	1-1	Spratt	7242	1			7		9		6			10		11		3		5			4	8	2
26	Feb 3	PORT VALE	2-1	Spratt, Buchanan	9294	1			7			9	6			10		11		3		5			4	8	2
27	10	Bristol City	1-6	Spratt	16217	1			7			9	6			10		11		3		5			4	8	2
28	17	TORQUAY UNITED	3-1	Bird 2, Atkinson	7804	1		8	7	11	9		6			10				3		5			4		2
29	24	Northampton Town	0-2		7563				7	11	9		6		1	10				3		5			4	8	2
30	Mar 3	HULL CITY	1-0	Spratt	7736				9				6		1	10	7	11		3		5			4	8	2
31	7	CRYSTAL PALACE	2-0	Ham, Atkinson	3583				9				6		1	10	7	11		3		5			4	8	2
32	14	SOUTHEND UNITED	4-0	Hannigan 2, Atkinson, Spratt	2802				9			8	6		1		7	11		3		5			4	10	2
33	17	SWINDON TOWN	2-2	Hannigan, og	8184				9			8	6		1		7	11		3		5			4	10	2
34	19	Peterborough United	0-1		8732				9			8	6		1		7	11		3		5			4	10	2
35	24	Crystal Palace	0-0		8527			10	9			8	6		1		7	11		3		5			4		2
36	31	PORTSMOUTH	2-1	Hannigan 2	10154				9			8	6		1		7	11	3			5			4	10	2
37	Apr 4	BRENTFORD	1-2	Atkinson	4812				9			8	6		1		7	11		3		5			4	10	2
38	7	Barnsley	2-1	Ham, Hannigan	5367				9			8	6	4	1		7	11		3		5				10	2
39	11	Queen's Park Rangers	2-1	Atkinson, Hannigan	11462				9			8	6	4	1		7	11		3		5				10	2
40	14	QUEEN'S PARK RANGERS	3-3	Atkinson, Spratt, Buchanan	8744				9			8	6	4	1		7	11		3		5				10	2
41	18	Halifax Town	3-2	Spratt 3	4196				9			8	6	4	1		7	11		3		5				10	2
42	21	Watford	2-0	Atkinson 2	6360				9				6	4	1		7	11		3	10	5				8	2
43	23	Grimsby Town	2-3	Buchanan 2	14408				9			8	6	4	1		7	11		3		5				10	2
44	24	GRIMSBY TOWN	0-1		11753				9			8	6	4	1		7	11		3		5				10	2
45	28	BOURNEMOUTH	1-2	Flynn,	8107				9			8	6	4	1		7	11		3		5				10	2
46	May 2	Reading	1-3	Maxwell	4847				9				6	4	1		7	11		3	10	5				8	2
					Apps	5	2	3	46	13	9	23	46	9	40	31	17	43	1	45	2	46	1	1	33	44	46
					Goals				15	3	3	7	2	1		7	2	14		1	1					22	

Two own goals

F.A. Cup

#	Date	Opponent	Score	Scorers	Att	Alexander A	Anders J	Ashworth JM	Atkinson C	Bird RP	Bleanch NWS	Buchanan J	Dick PW	Flynn P	Gebbie RBR	Gibson IS	Ham RS	Hannigan JL	Lawton HM	March JE	Maxwell H	McCalman DS	Reilly F	Routledge RW	Scoular J	Spratt T	Walker J
R1	Nov 4	PORT VALE	0-1		12127				7			9	6		1	10		11		3		5			4	8	2

F.L. Cup

#	Date	Opponent	Score	Scorers	Att	Alexander A	Anders J	Ashworth JM	Atkinson C	Bird RP	Bleanch NWS	Buchanan J	Dick PW	Flynn P	Gebbie RBR	Gibson IS	Ham RS	Hannigan JL	Lawton HM	March JE	Maxwell H	McCalman DS	Reilly F	Routledge RW	Scoular J	Spratt T	Walker J
R1	Sep 11	Hull City	2-4	Anders, Hannigan	10401		7		4			9	6		1	10		11		3		5				8	2

		P	W	D	L	F	A	W	D	L	F	A	Pts
1	Portsmouth	46	15	6	2	48	23	12	5	6	39	24	65
2	Grimsby Town	46	18	3	2	49	18	10	3	10	31	38	62
3	Bournemouth	46	14	8	1	42	18	7	9	7	27	27	59
4	Queen's Park Rangers	46	15	3	5	65	31	9	8	6	46	42	59
5	Peterborough United	46	16	0	7	60	38	10	6	7	47	44	58
6	Bristol City	46	15	3	5	56	27	8	5	10	38	45	54
7	Reading	46	14	5	4	46	24	8	4	11	31	42	53
8	Northampton Town	46	12	6	5	52	24	8	5	10	33	33	51
9	Swindon Town	46	11	8	4	48	26	6	7	10	30	45	49
10	Hull City	46	15	2	6	43	20	5	6	12	24	34	48
11	BRADFORD	46	13	5	5	47	27	7	2	14	33	51	47
12	Port Vale	46	12	4	7	41	23	5	7	11	24	35	45
13	Notts County	46	14	5	4	44	23	3	4	16	23	51	43
14	Coventry City	46	11	6	6	38	26	5	5	13	26	45	43
15	Crystal Palace	46	8	8	7	50	41	6	6	11	33	39	42
16	Southend United	46	10	7	6	31	26	3	9	11	26	43	42
17	Watford	46	10	9	4	37	26	4	4	15	26	48	41
18	Halifax Town	46	9	5	9	34	35	6	5	12	28	49	40
19	Shrewsbury Town	46	8	7	8	46	37	5	5	13	27	47	38
20	Barnsley	46	9	6	8	45	41	4	6	13	26	54	38
21	Torquay United	46	9	4	10	48	44	6	2	15	28	56	36
22	Lincoln City	46	4	10	9	31	43	5	7	11	26	44	35
23	Brentford	46	11	3	9	34	29	2	5	16	19	64	34
24	Newport County	46	6	5	12	29	38	1	3	19	17	64	22

1962/63

21st in Division Three: Relegated

No	Month	Day	Opponent	Result	Scorers	Att	Atkinson C	Bird RP	Buchanan J	Dick PW	Dine JMcQ	Flynn P	Gebbie RBR	Gould G	Green HR	Ham RS	Hannigan JL	Hector KJ	Jones K	Lawrie S	Lawton HM	Lightowler GB	March JE	Maxwell H	McCalman DS	Scoular J	Spratt T	Walker J	Williams D	Williamson IJ
1	Aug	18	COLCHESTER UNITED	1-1	Maxwell	9482	6					4	1		9		11						3	10	5		8	2	7	
2		22	Bournemouth	2-2	Spratt 2	12132	6						1		9		11	7					3	10	5	4	8	2		
3		25	Southend United	1-3	Green	7931	6						1		9		11	7					3	10	5	4	8	2		
4		29	BOURNEMOUTH	1-1	Bird	9808	7	11					1		9								3	10	5	4	8	2		6
5	Sep	1	MILLWALL	2-2	Green, Spratt	8567	10	11					1		9		7						3		5	4	8	2		6
6		7	Shrewsbury Town	2-1	Hector, Green	6507	10	11					1		9			7					3		5	4	8	2		6
7		12	CARLISLE UNITED	3-1	McBain (og), Spratt, Green	7429	10	11					1		9			7					3		5	4	8	2		6
8		15	PORT VALE	2-1	Green, Hector	8935	10	11					1		9			7					3		5	4	8	2		6
9		18	Coventry City	1-3	Curtis (og)	13038	10	11					1		9			7					3		5	4	8	2		6
10		21	Reading	1-4	Green	7051	10	11					1		9			7				3			5	4	8	2		6
11		24	COVENTRY CITY	0-0		7664		11	8				1		9		7						3	10	5	4		2		6
12		29	BRISTOL CITY	2-5	Buchanan, Maxwell	8917		11	8	6			1		9		7						3	10	5	4		2		
13	Oct	2	Watford	2-3	Spratt, Williams	12136		11		6		4	1		9		7						3		5		8	2	10	
14		6	Peterborough United	0-2		10142		11		6		4	1		9		7						3		5		8	2	10	
15		10	WATFORD	1-0	Maxwell	6492		11			1				9			7					3	8	5	4	10	2		6
16		13	BARNSLEY	1-1	Scoular	9325		11			1				9			7					3	8	5	4	10	2		6
17		20	Northampton Town	1-3	Spratt	12634	10				1			11	9			7				2	3		5	4	8			6
18		27	QUEEN'S PARK RANGERS	0-3		8552	10				1			11						7		2	3		5	4	8		9	6
19	Nov	10	CRYSTAL PALACE	2-1	Atkinson, Ham	5811	9				1					8	11			7	3	2		10	5	4				6
20		17	Wrexham	1-3	Maxwell	6887	9				1					8	11			7	3	2		10	5	4				6
21	Dec	1	Bristol Rovers	3-3	Spratt 2, Ham	6593	4	11			1				9	8				7		3			5		10	2		6
22		8	BRIGHTON & HOVE ALB	1-5	Ham	4765	4	11			1				9	8				7		3			5		10	2		6
23		15	Colchester United	4-1	Walker, Hector, Hannigan, Bird	2896	6	11			1	4				10	7	8			3				5			2	9	
24		26	SWINDON TOWN	2-0	Williams 2	6691	6	11			1	4				10	7	8			3				5			2	9	
25	Jan	4	HALIFAX TOWN	1-1	Williams	3806	6	11				4	1			10	7	8			3				5			2	9	
26	Feb	16	Bristol City	2-4	Hector, McCalman	7805	6	11			1	4					7	8			3				5			2	9	10
27	Mar	6	PETERBOROUGH UTD.	2-2	Hector, Flynn	6457	6	11			1	10						8		7	3				5	4		2	9	
28		9	NORTHAMPTON T	2-3	Scoular, Flynn	6551	6	11				10	1					8		7	3				5	4		2	9	
29		13	Hull City	0-1		7635	6	11			1	10						8	2	7	3				5	4	9			
30		16	Queen's Park Rangers	2-1	Scoular, Hector	7355	6	11			1	10					9	8	2	7	3				5	4				
31		19	SOUTHEND UNITED	2-2	Bird, Flynn	7054	6	11			1	10					7	8	2		3				5	4			9	
32		23	HULL CITY	3-1	Flynn, Ham, Hannigan	7529	6	11			1	10				7	9	8	2		3				5	4				
33		26	SHREWSBURY TOWN	2-1	Hector, Bird	6890	6	11			1	10					9	8	2	7	3				5	4				
34		30	Crystal Palace	0-6		9146	6	11			1	10					9	8	2	7	3				5	4				
35	Apr	2	Swindon Town	1-2	Gould	14709	6					10	1	11			7	8	2			3			5	4			9	
36		6	WREXHAM	3-1	Williams 2, Hector	6432	6					10	1	11			7	8	2			3			5	4			9	
37		12	Notts County	2-3	Bird, Hector	6382	6	11				10	1				7	8	2			3			5	4			9	
38		13	Halifax Town	4-4	Hector, Flynn, Williams 2	4470	6	11				10	1				7	8	2			3			5	4			9	
39		16	NOTTS COUNTY	5-0	Hector 3, Hannigan, Bird	8258	6	11				10	1				7	8	2			3			5	4			9	
40		20	BRISTOL ROVERS	2-2	Hector 2	6794	6	11				10	1				7	8	2			3			5	4			9	
41		23	Carlisle United	0-3		4845	6	11				10	1				7	8	2			3			5	4			9	
42		27	Brighton & Hove Albion	1-3	Hannigan	2333	6	11				10	1				7	8	2			3			5	4			9	
43		30	Barnsley	4-1	Hannigan, Hector 2, Spratt	6556	6	11	9				1				7	8	2			3			5	4	10			
44	May	4	READING	3-2	Hector, Hannigan 2	8209	6	11	9				1				7	8	2			3			5	4	10			
45		6	Port Vale	1-2	Hector	6680	6	11	9				1				7	8	2			3			5	4	10			
46		11	Millwall	1-3	Spratt	8906	6		9				1	11			7	8	2			3			5	4	10			
						Apps	40	36	6	3	18	23	28	5	19	8	31	34	18	11	14	19	17	10	46	37	23	24	19	17
						Goals	1	6	1			5		1	6	4	7	19						4	1	3	10	1	8	

Two own goals

F.A. Cup

Rd	Month	Day	Opponent	Result	Scorers	Att	Atkinson C	Bird RP	Buchanan J	Dick PW	Dine JMcQ	Flynn P	Gebbie RBR	Gould G	Green HR	Ham RS	Hannigan JL	Hector KJ	Jones K	Lawrie S	Lawton HM	Lightowler GB	March JE	Maxwell H	McCalman DS	Scoular J	Spratt T	Walker J	Williams D	Williamson IJ
R1	Nov	3	Halifax Town	0-1		11386	10	11			1							7			3	2			5	4	8		9	6

F.L. Cup

Rd	Month	Day	Opponent	Result	Scorers	Att	Atkinson C	Bird RP	Buchanan J	Dick PW	Dine JMcQ	Flynn P	Gebbie RBR	Gould G	Green HR	Ham RS	Hannigan JL	Hector KJ	Jones K	Lawrie S	Lawton HM	Lightowler GB	March JE	Maxwell H	McCalman DS	Scoular J	Spratt T	Walker J	Williams D	Williamson IJ
R2	Sep	26	HUDDERSFIELD T	3-1	Bird, Maxwell, Buchanan	6931		11	8	6			1		9		7						3	10	5	4		2		
R3	Oct	16	CHARLTON ATHLETIC	2-2	Spratt, Atkinson	8700	10	11			1			7	9								3		5	4	8	2		6
rep		23	Charlton Athletic	0-1		8747	10				1			11	9			7				2	3		5	4	8			6

		P	W	D	L	F	A	W	D	L	F	A	Pts
1	Northampton Town	46	16	6	1	64	19	10	4	9	45	41	62
2	Swindon Town	46	18	2	3	60	22	4	12	7	27	34	58
3	Port Vale	46	16	4	3	47	25	7	4	12	25	33	54
4	Coventry City	46	14	6	3	54	28	4	11	8	29	41	53
5	Bournemouth	46	11	12	0	39	16	7	4	12	24	30	52
6	Peterborough United	46	11	5	7	48	33	9	6	8	45	42	51
7	Notts County	46	15	3	5	46	29	4	10	9	27	45	51
8	Southend United	46	11	7	5	38	24	8	5	10	37	53	50
9	Wrexham	46	14	6	3	54	27	6	3	14	30	56	49
10	Hull City	46	12	6	5	40	22	7	4	12	34	47	48
11	Crystal Palace	46	10	7	6	38	22	7	6	10	30	36	47
12	Colchester United	46	11	6	6	41	35	7	5	11	32	58	47
13	Queen's Park Rangers	46	9	6	8	44	36	8	5	10	41	40	45
14	Bristol City	46	10	9	4	54	38	6	4	13	46	54	45
15	Shrewsbury Town	46	13	4	6	57	41	3	8	12	26	40	44
16	Millwall	46	11	6	6	50	32	4	7	12	32	55	43
17	Watford	46	12	3	8	55	40	5	5	13	27	45	42
18	Barnsley	46	12	6	5	39	28	3	5	15	24	46	41
19	Bristol Rovers	46	11	8	4	45	29	4	3	16	25	59	41
20	Reading	46	13	4	6	51	30	3	4	16	23	48	40
21	BRADFORD	46	10	9	4	43	36	4	3	16	36	61	40
22	Brighton & Hove Albion	46	7	6	10	28	38	5	6	12	30	46	36
23	Carlisle United	46	12	4	7	41	37	1	5	17	20	52	35
24	Halifax Town	46	8	3	12	41	51	1	9	13	23	55	30

1963/64

13th in Division Four

	Date	Opponent	Score	Scorers	Att	Atkinson C	Bird RP	Blackhall S	Burns EO	Church G	Cook MI	Dine JMcQ	Evans R	Flynn P	Fryatt JE	Gebbie RBR	Gould G	Hannigan JL	Hardie JC	Hector KJ	I'Anson P	Jones K	Lawrie S	Lightowler GB	McCalman DS	Scoular J	Spratt T	Thomas GP	Walker J
1	Aug 24	Gillingham	0-2		8562		11				6		10		9	1		7		8		2		3	5	4			
2	26	NEWPORT COUNTY	2-5	Spratt, Hannigan	6312	6	11								9	1		7		8		2		3	5	4	10		
3	31	CHESTERFIELD	0-1		5765	6	11				5				9	1		7		8		3				4	10		2
4	Sep 7	Doncaster Rovers	2-3	Hector, Cook	6484	6					5				9	1	11	7		8		2		3		4	10		
5	9	Newport County	0-4		4453	6		9		4	5					1	11	7		8		3		2			10		
6	14	BRIGHTON & HOVE ALB	2-1	Hannigan, McCalman	4974	6	11		7	4						1		8		9		3			5		10		2
7	17	STOCKPORT COUNTY	2-2	Spratt, Beighton (og)	6382	6	11		7	4						1		9		8		3			5		10		2
8	21	Chester	0-1		5569	6	11		7	4		1						9		8		3			5		10		2
9	28	YORK CITY	1-3	Bird	5843	6	11					1			9			7		8		3			5	4	10		2
10	30	Stockport County	1-2	Bird	6370	6	11					1	9					7		10		3			5	4	8		2
11	Oct 5	Barrow	2-2	Fryatt, Hannigan	2983		11					1		6	9			7		10		3			5	4	8		2
12	8	OXFORD UNITED	5-2	Hannigan 2, Bird 2, Fryatt	5213	6	11					1			9			7		10		3			5	4	8		2
13	12	BRADFORD CITY	1-3	Hector	10954	6	11					1			9			7		10		3			5	4	8		2
14	16	Oxford United	1-2	Jones (og)	6518	6	11								9	1		7		10		3			5	4	8		2
15	19	Aldershot	3-0	Hector, Bird, Fryatt	6396	6	11		7						9	1				10		3			5	4	8		2
16	23	ROCHDALE	2-2	Burns, Fryatt	5484	6	11		7						9	1				10		3			5	4	8		2
17	26	CARLISLE UNITED	1-1	Burns	6448	6	11		7			1			9					10		3			5	4	8		2
18	30	Rochdale	0-0		2490	6	11		7			1	9							10		3			5	4	8		2
19	Nov 2	Torquay United	2-6	Evans 2	4850	6	11				2	1	8		9			7		10		3			5	4			2
20	9	HALIFAX TOWN	4-4	Evans, Bird, Hector, Atkinson	8060	10	11		7			1	9	6						8		3			5	4			
21	23	DARLINGTON	4-1	Flynn, Hector 2, Evans	4541	10	11					1	9	6				7		8		3			5	4		2	
22	30	Hartlepools United	2-4	Hector, Bird	5632	10	11					1	9	6				7		8		3			5	4		2	
23	Dec 14	GILLINGHAM	1-0	Bird	4930	9	11					1	10	6				7		8		3			5	4		2	
24	21	Chesterfield	2-1	Evans, Bird	3724	4	11						10	6	9			7	1	8		3			5			2	
25	26	Lincoln City	0-3		6606	4	11						10	6	9			7	1	8		3			5			2	
26	28	LINCOLN CITY	0-1		6939	9	11		7		4		10	6					1	8		3			5			2	
27	Jan 3	Tranmere Rovers	1-3	Atkinson	4815	9	11		7				10	6					1	8		3			5	4		2	
28	11	DONCASTER ROVERS	3-1	Atkinson, Cook, Hector	6963	9	11		7		4			6					1	10		3			5		8	2	
29	18	Brighton & Hove Albion	1-0	Hector	9706	9	11		7		4			6					1	10		3			5		8	2	
30	25	EXETER CITY	3-2	Spratt, Bird, Hector	6273	9	11		7		4			6					1	10		3			5		8	2	
31	Feb 1	CHESTER	4-0	Hector 2, Flynn, Bird	6071	9	11		7		4			6					1	10		3			5		8	2	
32	8	York City	0-2		4344	9	11				4			6				7	1	10		3			5		8	2	
33	15	BARROW	1-0	Bird	5009	9	11		7		4			6					1	10		3			5		8	2	
34	22	Bradford City	0-1		12164	4	11		7					6				9	1	10		3			5		8	2	
35	29	ALDERSHOT	2-1	Burns, Bird	5785		11		7				9	4					1	10	6	3			5		8	2	
36	Mar 7	Carlisle United	0-4		7175		11		7					4	9				1	10	6	3			5		8	2	
37	21	Halifax Town	1-2	Fryatt	5135	9	11				4			6	8				1	7				3	5		10	2	
38	27	Workington	1-1	Hector	4843	4	11							6	9				1	8			7	3	5		10	2	
39	28	SOUTHPORT	3-0	Lawrie, Fryatt, Spratt	4402	4	11							6	9				1	8			7	3	5		10	2	
40	30	WORKINGTON	1-0	Fryatt	6246	4	11							6	9				1	8			7	3	5		10	2	
41	Apr 4	Darlington	2-2	Fryatt, Spratt	2458	4	11							6	9				1	8			7	3	5		10	2	
42	11	HARTLEPOOLS UNITED	3-1	Lawrie, Hector, Fryatt	5104	4	11							6	9				1	8			7	3	5		10	2	
43	18	Exeter City	3-2	Hector, Spratt, Lawrie	9714	4	11							6	9				1	8			7	3	5		10	2	
44	21	Southport	1-0	Lawrie	2553	4	11							6	9				1	8		3	7		5		10	2	
45	25	TRANMERE ROVERS	4-2	Fryatt, Hector 2, Bird	5111	4	11							6	9				1	8		3	7		5		10	2	
46	27	TORQUAY UNITED	1-1	Fryatt	5262	4	11							6	9				1	8		3	7		5		10	2	
					Apps	42	44	1	18	4	13	13	13	28	26	10	2	22	23	46	2	39	9	11	43	20	36	26	15
					Goals	3	14		3		2		5	2	11			5		17			4		1		6		

Two own goals

F.A. Cup

	Date	Opponent	Score	Scorers	Att	Atkinson C	Bird RP	Blackhall S	Burns EO	Church G	Cook MI	Dine JMcQ	Evans R	Flynn P	Fryatt JE	Gebbie RBR	Gould G	Hannigan JL	Hardie JC	Hector KJ	I'Anson P	Jones K	Lawrie S	Lightowler GB	McCalman DS	Scoular J	Spratt T	Thomas GP	Walker J
R1	Nov 16	HEANOR TOWN	3-1	Evans, Atkinson, Flynn	5799	10	11				2	1	9	6				7		8		3			5	4			
R2	Dec 7	Oldham Athletic	0-2		17600	10	11					1	9	6				7		8		3			5	4		2	

F.L. Cup

	Date	Opponent	Score	Scorers	Att	Atkinson C	Bird RP	Blackhall S	Burns EO	Church G	Cook MI	Dine JMcQ	Evans R	Flynn P	Fryatt JE	Gebbie RBR	Gould G	Hannigan JL	Hardie JC	Hector KJ	I'Anson P	Jones K	Lawrie S	Lightowler GB	McCalman DS	Scoular J	Spratt T	Thomas GP	Walker J
R1	Sep 4	BRADFORD CITY	7-3	* se below	6593	6					5				9	1	11	7		8		3		2		4	10		
R2	25	MIDDLESBROUGH	2-2	Hector, Spratt	9273	6	11					1			9			7		10		3			5	4	8		2
rep	Oct 2	Middlesbrough	3-2	Fryatt 2, Bird	11991	6	11					1			9			7		10		3			5	4	8		2
R3	Nov 5	Notts County	2-3	Hector, Bird	4002	10	11		7		2	1	9	6						8		3			5	4			

Scorers in R1: Cook, Fryatt 2, Hector 2, Hannigan, Spratt

		P	W	D	L	F	A	W	D	L	F	A	Pts
1	Gillingham	46	16	7	0	37	10	7	7	9	22	20	60
2	Carlisle United	46	17	3	3	70	20	8	7	8	43	38	60
3	Workington	46	15	6	2	46	19	9	5	9	30	33	59
4	Exeter City	46	12	9	2	39	14	8	9	6	23	23	58
5	Bradford City	46	15	3	5	45	24	10	3	10	31	38	56
6	Torquay United	46	16	6	1	60	20	4	5	14	20	34	51
7	Tranmere Rovers	46	12	4	7	46	30	8	7	8	39	43	51
8	Brighton & Hove Albion	46	13	3	7	45	22	6	9	8	26	30	50
9	Aldershot	46	15	3	5	58	28	4	7	12	25	50	48
10	Halifax Town	46	14	4	5	47	28	3	10	10	30	49	48
11	Lincoln City	46	15	2	6	49	31	4	7	12	18	44	47
12	Chester	46	17	3	3	47	18	2	5	16	18	42	46
13	BRADFORD	46	13	5	5	50	34	5	4	14	25	47	45
14	Doncaster Rovers	46	11	8	4	46	23	4	4	15	24	52	42
15	Newport County	46	12	3	8	35	24	5	5	13	29	49	42
16	Chesterfield	46	8	9	6	29	27	7	3	13	28	44	42
17	Stockport County	46	12	7	4	32	19	3	5	15	18	49	42
18	Oxford United	46	10	7	6	37	27	4	6	13	22	36	41
19	Darlington	46	8	9	6	40	37	6	3	14	26	56	40
20	Rochdale	46	9	8	6	36	24	3	7	13	20	35	39
21	Southport	46	12	6	5	42	29	3	3	17	21	59	39
22	York City	46	9	3	11	29	26	5	4	14	23	40	35
23	Hartlepools United	46	8	7	8	30	36	4	2	17	24	57	33
24	Barrow	46	4	10	9	30	36	2	8	13	21	57	30

1964/65

7th in Division Four

	Date		Opponent	Score	Scorers	Att.	Bird RP	Burns EO	Cook MI	Dine JMcQ	Flynn P	Fryatt JE	Gould G	Ham RS	Hardie JC	Hector KJ	Hunter WN	I'Anson P	Jones K	Lawrie S	Lightowler GB	McCalman DS	Symonds A	Taylor K	Thomas GP
1	Aug	22	DONCASTER ROVERS	5-2	Lawrie, Hector 3, Fryatt	7293	11		4		6	9			1	8	10		3	7		5			2
2		26	Aldershot	1-1	Bird	6916	11				6	9			1	8	10		3	7	4	5			2
3		29	Chesterfield	4-2	Hector 3, Fryatt	7450	11				6	9			1	8	10		3	7	4	5			2
4		31	ALDERSHOT	3-1	Fryatt, McCalman, Bird	9036	11			1	6	9				8	10		3	7	4	5			2
5	Sep	5	NOTTS COUNTY	2-2	Lawrie, Bird	7064	11		4		6	9			1	8	10		3	7		5			2
6		9	Bradford City	2-0	Hector, Gould	9436			4		6	9	11		1	8	10		3	7	2	5			
7		12	Halifax Town	3-2	Hector, Fryatt, Lawrie	7319			4		6	9	11		1	8	10		3	7	2	5			
8		15	BRADFORD CITY	3-3	Flynn, Jones, Hector	12976			4		6	9	11		1	8	10		3	7	2	5			
9		19	NEWPORT COUNTY	2-2	Hector, Lawrie	8003			4		6	9	11		1	8	10		3	7	2	5			
10		26	Crewe Alexandra	1-1	Hector	3741			4		6	9	11		1	8	10		3	7	2	5			
11		29	WREXHAM	0-0		8588			4		6	9	11		1	8	10		2	7	3	5			
12	Oct	3	DARLINGTON	3-1	Gould, Fryatt 2	8055			4		6	9	11		1	8	10		2	7	3	5			
13		7	Wrexham	1-4	Hector	5454			4		6	9	11		1	8	10		2	7	3	5			
14		10	Torquay United	1-1	Bird	4179	11	10	4		6	9	7		1	8			2		3	5			
15		13	SOUTHPORT	0-0		7337	11	10	4		6	9	7		1	8			2		3	5			
16		17	STOCKPORT COUNTY	1-0	Hector	6542	11	10	4		6	9	7		1	8			2		3	5			
17		19	Southport	1-1	Jones	3089	11	10	4		6	9	7		1	8			2		3	5			
18		24	York City	1-0	Bird	7604	11		4		6	9	7		1	8			2	10	3	5			
19		27	MILLWALL	4-0	Hector, Lawrie, Bird, Fryatt	10459	11		4		6	9	7		1	8			2	10	3	5			
20		31	LINCOLN CITY	3-1	Bird, Hector 2	7984	11		4		6	9	7		1	8			2	10	3		5		
21	Nov	7	Brighton & Hove Albion	2-2	Lawrie, McCalman	20722	11		4		6	9	7		1	8			2	10	3	5			
22		21	Barrow	1-2	Hector	4181	11		4		6	9	7		1	8			2	10	3	5			
23		28	HARTLEPOOLS UNITED	4-0	Lawrie, Gould, Bird, Fryatt	5721	11		4		6	9	7		1	8			2	10	3	5			
24	Dec	5	HALIFAX TOWN	5-1	Hector 2, Lawrie 2, Jones	6042	11		4		6	9	7		1	8			2	10	3	5			
25		12	Doncaster Rovers	1-1	Bird	8446	11		4		6	9	7		1	8			2	10	3	5			
26		22	CHESTERFIELD	1-0	Bird	6726	11		4		6	9	7		1	8			2	10	3	5			
27		26	Chester	0-3		10057	11		4		6	9	7		1	8			2	10	3	5			
28		28	CHESTER	3-1	Fryatt, Lawrie, Hector	9968			4		6	9	11	7	1	8			2	10	3	5			
29	Jan	2	Notts County	3-3	Lawrie, Hector, Fryatt	6205			4		6	9	11	7	1	8			2	10	3	5			
30		9	Rochdale	3-4	Ham, Lawrie, Hector	4377					6	9	11	7	1	8	4		2	10	3	5			
31		23	Newport County	3-4	Fryatt, Hector, Ham	3417			4		6	9	11	7	1	8			2	10	3	5			
32		30	OXFORD UNITED	1-0	Hector	6727			4		6	9	11	7	1	8			2	10	3	5			
33	Feb	6	CREWE ALEXANDRA	2-3	Fryatt 2	6526	11		4		6	9		7	1	8			2	10	3	5			
34		13	Darlington	2-1	Greener (og), Hector	3087	11		4		10	9			1	8		6	2	7	3	5			
35		20	TORQUAY UNITED	4-2	Bird 2, Fryatt, Hector	6896	11					9		7	1	8		6	2	10	3	5		4	
36		27	Stockport County	2-0	Bird, Ham	5255	11					9		7	1	8		6	2	10	3	5		4	
37	Mar	6	YORK CITY	0-0		13745	11					9		7	1	8		6		10	3	5		4	2
38		12	Lincoln City	2-2	Hector 2	3772	11					9		7	1	8		6	2	10	3	5		4	
39		20	BRIGHTON & HOVE ALB	2-0	Bird, I'Anson	6288	11					9		7	1	8		6	2	10	3	5		4	
40		27	Oxford United	0-3		7692	11		2			9		10	1	8		6		7	3	5		4	
41	Apr	3	BARROW	3-2	Bird, Fryatt 2	7003	11		2			9		7	1	8		6		10	3	5		4	
42		10	Hartlepools United	0-2		4697	11					9		7	1	8		6	2	10	3		5	4	
43		16	Tranmere Rovers	0-0		17430	11	7			6	9		10	1	8			2		3	5		4	
44		17	ROCHDALE	0-0		10636	11	7			6	9		10	1	8			2		3	5		4	
45		21	TRANMERE ROVERS	1-1	Hector	12806	11	7			6	9		10	1	8			2		3	5		4	
46		24	Millwall	0-1		14205	11	7			6	9		10	1	8		4	2		3	5			
						Apps	33	8	32	1	38	46	27	18	45	46	14	10	43	38	44	44	2	11	6
						Goals	15				1	16	3	3		29		1	3	12		2			

One own goal

F.A. Cup

	Date		Opponent	Score	Scorers	Att.	Bird RP	Burns EO	Cook MI	Dine JMcQ	Flynn P	Fryatt JE	Gould G	Ham RS	Hardie JC	Hector KJ	Hunter WN	I'Anson P	Jones K	Lawrie S	Lightowler GB	McCalman DS	Symonds A	Taylor K	Thomas GP
R1	Nov	14	Doncaster Rovers	2-3	Fryatt, Hector	12372	11		4		6	9	7		1	8			2	10	3	5			

F.L. Cup

	Date		Opponent	Score	Scorers	Att.	Bird RP	Burns EO	Cook MI	Dine JMcQ	Flynn P	Fryatt JE	Gould G	Ham RS	Hardie JC	Hector KJ	Hunter WN	I'Anson P	Jones K	Lawrie S	Lightowler GB	McCalman DS	Symonds A	Taylor K	Thomas GP
R1	Sep	2	Doncaster Rovers	0-1		7684	11		4	1	6	9		10		8			3	7		5			2

		P	W	D	L	F	A	W	D	L	F	A	Pts
1	Brighton & Hove Albion	46	18	5	0	68	20	8	6	9	34	37	63
2	Millwall	46	13	10	0	45	15	10	6	7	33	30	62
3	York City	46	20	1	2	63	21	8	5	10	28	35	62
4	Oxford United	46	18	4	1	54	13	5	11	7	33	31	61
5	Tranmere Rovers	46	20	2	1	72	20	7	4	12	27	36	60
6	Rochdale	46	15	4	4	46	22	7	10	6	28	31	58
7	BRADFORD	46	14	8	1	52	22	6	9	8	34	40	57
8	Chester	46	19	1	3	75	26	6	5	12	44	55	56
9	Doncaster Rovers	46	13	6	4	46	25	7	5	11	38	47	51
10	Crewe Alexandra	46	11	8	4	55	34	7	5	11	35	47	49
11	Torquay United	46	11	5	7	41	33	10	2	11	29	37	49
12	Chesterfield	46	13	5	5	36	22	7	3	13	22	48	48
13	Notts County	46	12	7	4	43	23	3	7	13	18	50	44
14	Wrexham	46	12	5	6	59	37	5	4	14	25	55	43
15	Hartlepools United	46	11	10	2	44	28	4	3	16	17	57	43
16	Newport County	46	14	5	4	54	26	3	3	17	31	55	42
17	Darlington	46	14	2	7	52	30	4	4	15	32	57	42
18	Aldershot	46	14	3	6	46	25	1	4	18	18	59	37
19	Bradford City	46	9	2	12	37	36	3	6	14	33	52	32
20	Southport	46	5	9	9	35	45	3	7	13	23	44	32
21	Barrow	46	9	4	10	30	38	3	2	18	29	67	30
22	Lincoln City	46	8	4	11	35	33	3	2	18	23	66	28
23	Halifax Town	46	9	4	10	37	37	2	2	19	17	66	28
24	Stockport County	46	8	4	11	30	34	2	3	18	14	53	27

1965/66

11th in Division Four

						Bird RP	Broadbent AH	Burns EO	Flynn P	Fryatt JE	Geddes JG	Gilpin J	Gordon HA	Gould G	Ham RS	Hardie JC	Hector KJ	I'Anson P	Lawrie S	Lightowler GB	McCalman DS	McGrath M	Oliver J	Rodger W	Symonds A	Taylor K	Thomas GP
1	Aug 21	Luton Town	1-3	Ham	6182	11		12	6	9			2		10	1	8	4	7	3	5						
2	24	ROCHDALE	1-2	Hector	5486	11			6	9			2		7	1	8	4	10	3	5						
3	28	BARROW	2-3	Hector, Bird	4365	11			6	9	4		2		7	1	8		10	3					5		
4	Sep 4	Hartlepools United	3-2	Fryatt, Hector 2	4205				6	9			2	11	7	1	8		10	3	5				4		
5	11	DONCASTER ROVERS	0-1		7257				6	9			2	11	7	1	8		10	3	5					4	
6	14	Rochdale	3-2	Hector, Ham 2	4806				6	9		12	2	11	7	1	8		10	3	5					4	
7	17	Southport	1-2	Hector	4622				3	9		6	2	11	7	1	8		10		5					4	
8	25	WREXHAM	4-2	Hector 2, Fryatt 2	3399				4	9			2	11	7	1	8	6	10		5			12			3
9	Oct 1	Halifax Town	0-1		3960		10		4	9				11		1	8		7	3	5				6		2
10	4	TORQUAY UNITED	1-1	Fryatt	5119		10		4	9				11	7	1	8			3	5				6		2
11	9	NOTTS COUNTY	4-0	Hector, Fryatt 2, Ham	4501		10		4	9			2	11	7	1	8			3	5				6		
12	15	Lincoln City	1-1	Hector	6426		10		4	9			2	11	7	1	8			3	5				6		
13	23	DARLINGTON	0-2		5104		10		4	9			2	11	7	1	8			3	5				6		
14	29	Stockport County	3-2	Ham 2, Gould	9989		10			9			2	11	7	1	8	6		3	5					4	
15	Nov 1	ALDERSHOT	5-1	Hector 3, Fryatt, Broadbent	2849		10			9			4	11	7	1	8	6	12	3	5						2
16	6	TRANMERE ROVERS	1-1	Hector	6507		9						4	11	7	1	8	6	10	3	5						2
17	20	BARNSLEY	7-2	Hector 5, Ironside (og), Fryatt	5833		10			9			4	11	7	1	8	6		3	5						2
18	23	Torquay United	1-2	Hector	3892		10			9			4	11	7	1	8	6		3	5						2
19	Dec 11	Port Vale	3-3	Fryatt, I'Anson, Ham	4419		10	12		9			4	11	7	1	8	6		3	5						2
20	18	LINCOLN CITY	4-2	Broadbent, Gould, Ham 2	4576		10			9			4	11	7	1	8	6		3	5						2
21	27	Chesterfield	3-0	Hector 2, Broadbent	6460		10			9			4	11	7	1	8	6		3	5						2
22	Jan 1	Notts County	0-2		6277		10			9			4	11	7	1	8	6		3	5						2
23	4	CHESTERFIELD	3-1	Fryatt 2, Broadbent	6280		10			9			4	11	7	1	8	6		3	5						2
24	8	COLCHESTER UNITED	1-0	Hector	5867		10			9			4	11	7	1	8	6		3	5						2
25	29	LUTON TOWN	1-3	Gould	6451		10			9			4	11	7	1	8	6		3	5						2
26	Feb 5	Barrow	2-5	Taylor, Hector	4221		10						4	11	7	1	8	6		3	5					9	2
27	12	NEWPORT COUNTY	6-1	Ham 4, Gould, Hector	4358		10			9			4	11	7	1	8			3	5					6	2
28	16	Bradford City	0-3	,	9004		10			9			4	11	7	1	8			3	5					6	2
29	25	Doncaster Rovers	2-6	Hector 2	10252		9							11	10	1	8	6	7	3	5					4	2
30	28	Colchester United	3-6	Hector 2, Broadbent	4921		11		3	9					7	1	8	6	10		5				2	4	
31	Mar 7	Newport County	1-3	Hector	2817		10		4	9				11	7	1	8	6		3	5				2		
32	12	SOUTHPORT	2-1	Symonds, Ham	4905		10		4	9				11	7	1	8			3	6	5			2		
33	14	Darlington	1-4	Broadbent	7579		10							11	9	1	8		7	3	5	6				4	2
34	19	Wrexham	2-3	Hector 2	7103		10		7					11	9	1	8	4		3	2	6				5	
35	26	HALIFAX TOWN	2-1	Hector, Broadbent	4594		10		12			11	4	7	9	1	8			3	2	6				5	
36	Apr 1	Tranmere Rovers	2-1	Ham, Hector	6127		10		4			11		7	9	1	8			3	2	6				5	
37	8	Chester	4-2	Broadbent, Hector 3	9526		10		4			11		7	9	1	8			3	2	6				5	
38	9	CREWE ALEXANDRA	2-1	Hector, Ham	4616		10		4			11		7	9	1	8			3	2	6				5	
39	12	CHESTER	0-1		7030		10		4			11		7	9	1	8			3	2	6				5	
40	15	Barnsley	1-1	Broadbent	2057		10		4			11		7	9	1	8			3	2	6				5	
41	19	HARTLEPOOLS UNITED	4-1	Hector 2, Ham 2	3755		10		4			11		7	9	1	8			3	2	6				5	
42	23	BRADFORD CITY	5-1	Hector 2, McGrath, Gilpin, Ham	10202		10		4			11		7	9	1	8			3	2	6				5	
43	27	Aldershot	1-5	Ham	3308		10		4			11		7	9	1	8			3	2	6			5		
44	30	Crewe Alexandra	5-2	Ham 2, Gould, Hector 2	3484		10		4					7	9	1	8	11		3	5	6					2
45	May 7	PORT VALE	1-2	Ham	4978		10		4					11	9	1	8			2	5	6	3	7			
46	24	STOCKPORT COUNTY	3-1	Ham, Gould, Broadbent	3563		10		4					11	9	1	8		7	3	5				6		2
					Apps	3	38	2	29	29	1	11	27	42	45	46	46	21	15	43	45	14	1	2	12	19	21
					Goals	1	10			11		1		6	24		44	1				1			1	1	

One own goal

F.A. Cup

						Bird RP	Broadbent AH	Burns EO	Flynn P	Fryatt JE	Geddes JG	Gilpin J	Gordon HA	Gould G	Ham RS	Hardie JC	Hector KJ	I'Anson P	Lawrie S	Lightowler GB	McCalman DS	McGrath M	Oliver J	Rodger W	Symonds A	Taylor K	Thomas GP
R1	Nov 13	HULL CITY	2-3	Lightowler, Hector	11487		10						4	11	8	1	9	6	7	3	5						2

F.L. Cup

						Bird RP	Broadbent AH	Burns EO	Flynn P	Fryatt JE	Geddes JG	Gilpin J	Gordon HA	Gould G	Ham RS	Hardie JC	Hector KJ	I'Anson P	Lawrie S	Lightowler GB	McCalman DS	McGrath M	Oliver J	Rodger W	Symonds A	Taylor K	Thomas GP
R1	Sep 1	HALIFAX TOWN	1-0	Lawrie	3433				6	9			2	11	7	1	8		10	3	5				4		
R2	22	Chesterfield	0-3		5820				3	9		10	2	11	7	1	8	6			5					4	

No. 16 FOOTBALL LEAGUE—FOURTH DIVISION

BRADFORD (PARK AVENUE)

v.

COLCHESTER UNITED

SATURDAY, JANUARY 8th, 1966 Kick-off 3-0 p.m.

OFFICIAL PROGRAMME 6d.

PRINT PROBLEMS?

—WRITE—CALL—OR PHONE

LEWIS HODGSON and SONS

DOWKER STREET . MILNSBRIDGE . HUDDERSFIELD

Telephone: Huddersfield 53117

		P	W	D	L	F	A	W	D	L	F	A	Pts
1	Doncaster Rovers	46	15	6	2	49	21	9	5	9	36	33	59
2	Darlington	46	16	3	4	41	17	9	6	8	31	36	59
3	Torquay United	46	17	2	4	43	20	7	8	8	29	29	58
4	Colchester United	46	13	7	3	45	21	10	3	10	25	26	56
5	Tranmere Rovers	46	15	1	7	56	32	9	7	7	37	34	56
6	Luton Town	46	19	2	2	65	27	5	6	12	25	43	56
7	Chester	46	15	5	3	52	27	5	7	11	27	43	52
8	Notts County	46	9	8	6	32	25	10	4	9	29	28	50
9	Newport County	46	14	6	3	46	24	4	6	13	29	51	48
10	Southport	46	15	6	2	47	20	3	6	14	21	49	48
11	BRADFORD	46	14	2	7	59	31	7	3	13	43	61	47
12	Barrow	46	12	8	3	48	31	4	7	12	24	45	47
13	Stockport County	46	12	4	7	42	29	6	2	15	29	41	42
14	Crewe Alexandra	46	12	4	7	42	23	4	5	14	19	40	41
15	Halifax Town	46	11	6	6	46	31	4	5	14	21	44	41
16	Barnsley	46	11	6	6	43	24	4	4	15	31	54	40
17	Aldershot	46	12	6	5	47	27	3	4	16	28	57	40
18	Hartlepools United	46	13	4	6	44	22	3	4	16	19	53	40
19	Port Vale	46	12	7	4	38	18	3	2	18	10	41	39
20	Chesterfield	46	8	9	6	37	35	5	4	14	25	43	39
21	Rochdale	46	12	1	10	46	27	4	4	15	25	60	37
22	Lincoln City	46	9	7	7	37	29	4	4	15	20	53	37
23	Bradford City	46	10	5	8	37	34	2	8	13	26	60	37
24	Wrexham	46	10	4	9	43	43	3	5	15	29	61	35

1966/67

23rd in Division Four

#	Month	Day	Opponent	Score	Scorers	Att	Barnes W	Broadbent AH	Deakin P	Gordon HA	Gould G	Ham RS	Hardie JC	Hector KJ	I'Anson P	Lightowler GB	Liney P	Madden P	McGillivray F	McGrath M	Milner J	Peel T	Robinson PB	Rodger W	Sumpner RA	Symonds A	Taylor K	Waddell R
1	Aug	20	NOTTS COUNTY	4-1	Hector, Gould, Robinson, Lightowler	6283		10		4	11	9		8		3	1	5	2	6			7					
2		27	Chester	3-0	Hector, Gould 2	6402		10		4	11	9		8		3	1	5	2	6			7					
3	Sep	3	Bradford City	3-2	Broadbent, Ham 2	9856		10		4	11	9		8		3	1	5	2	6			7					
4		6	TRANMERE ROVERS	2-3	Hector 2	7384		10		4	11	9		8		3	1	5	2	6			7	12				
5		10	PORT VALE	1-1	Ham	5246		10		4	11	9			7	3	1	5	2	6				8				
6		16	Crewe Alexandra	3-1	Madden, Ham 2	5457		10		4	11	8				3	1	9	2	6			7			12	5	
7		24	BARROW	0-1		5584		10	8	4	11	9				3	1		2	6			7				5	
8		26	Tranmere Rovers	2-2	Gould, Ham	5834		10	8	4	11	9				3	1	12	2	6			7				5	
9		30	York City	1-3	Gordon	5453		10	8	4	11	9				3	1		2	6			7				5	
10	Oct	8	SOUTHEND UNITED	1-2	Deakin	5391		10	8	4	11	9				3	1	12	2	6			7				5	
11		15	Wrexham	0-6		7079		10	8		11	9				3	1	4	2	6			7				5	
12		18	STOCKPORT COUNTY	0-1		4878	5	10			11	8	1			3		9	2				7			6	4	
13		22	ALDERSHOT	1-1	Ham	3889	3		10		11	8	1					9	2	4			7			6	5	
14		29	Luton Town	2-2	Ham, Deakin	4566	3		10		11	8	1					9	2	4			7			6	5	
15	Nov	5	BRADFORD CITY	2-0	Ham, Deakin	9870			10	4	11	8	1			3			2				7			6	5	9
16		12	Newport County	0-0		3144			10	4	11	8	1			3			2				7			6	5	9
17		14	Stockport County	0-4		7526			10	4	11	8	1			3			2				7			6	5	9
18		19	BRENTFORD	2-2	Waddell, Ham	4182			10	4	11	8	1			3		12	2				7			6	5	9
19	Dec	3	HARTLEPOOLS UNITED	1-2	Waddell	4309			10	4	11	8	1			3			2				7			6	5	9
20		10	Exeter City	1-4	Waddell	3372			10	4	11	8	1			3		5	2				7			6		9
21		17	Notts County	1-2	Coates (og)	3051	3	10	8	4	11	7	1						2	6			12				5	9
22		27	Chesterfield	1-4	Gould,	6081	3	10	8	4	11	7	1						2	6							5	9
23		31	CHESTER	2-3	Deakin 2	3966		10	8		11	7	1			3		5	2	6			12				4	9
24	Jan	14	Port Vale	0-0		4798		10	8	4		7	1			3			2	6			11			9	5	
25		21	CREWE ALEXANDRA	1-4	Deakin	4781		10	8			7	1			3		9	2	6			11			4	5	
26	Feb	4	Barrow	0-1		6425		10	8	4		7	1			3		5	2	6			11					9
27		8	CHESTERFIELD	2-0	Deakin, Ham	3940			8	4	10	7	1			3		5	2	6			11					9
28		11	YORK CITY	1-0	Deakin	4572			8	4	11	10	1			3		5	2	6			7					9
29		15	BARNSLEY	1-3	McGrath	4962			8	3	11	9	1					5	2	6	4		7	10				
30		18	ROCHDALE	0-3		4823	3			4		8	1					5	2	6	10		11	7				9
31		25	Southend United	0-4		7749	3		8	4	12		1					5	2	6	10		11	7			9	
32	Mar	4	WREXHAM	1-3	Turner (og)	3388			8	4			1			3		5	2		6		11	7			9	10
33		11	Rochdale	0-1		2143					11	8	1		6	3		5	2	4	10		7					9
34		18	Aldershot	2-1	Robinson, Symonds	3610					11	9	1		6	3		5	2	4			7			10		8
35		25	HALIFAX TOWN	1-0	Ham	5623					11	9	1		6	3		5	2	4	12		7			10		8
36		27	Southport	0-1		5960			8		11	9	1		6	3		5	2	4			7			10		
37		28	SOUTHPORT	0-0		3923			8	4	11	9	1		6	3		5	2		10		7					
38	Apr	1	Barnsley	0-2		5936	5		8	4	11	9	1		6	3			2				7					10
39		8	NEWPORT COUNTY	3-1	Gordon, Deakin, Ham	2724	5		10	8	11	9	1		6	3				4		2	7					
40		11	LINCOLN CITY	2-1	Robinson, Ham	3713	5		10	8	11	9	1		6	3				4	12	2	7					
41		15	Brentford	1-1	Gould	10021	5		10	8	11	9	1		6	3			12	4		2	7					
42		22	LUTON TOWN	0-0		3760	5		10	8	11	9	1		6	3				4		2	7					
43		26	Lincoln City	2-2	Ham, Robinson	2155	5		10		11	9	1		6	3				4		2	7					8
44		29	Hartlepools United	0-2		3567	5		10		11	9	1		6	3				4		2	7					8
45	May	6	EXETER CITY	2-2	Sumpner, Ham	3262	5		10	4	11	8	1		12	3				6		2	7		9			
46		13	Halifax Town	0-0		2829	5		10	4	11	8	1			3				6		2	7		9			
						Apps	16	18	35	34	41	44	35	4	14	39	11	28	39	36	8	8	44	6	2	15	21	20
						Goals		1	9	2	6	16		4		1		1		1			4		1	1		3

Two own goals

F.A. Cup

Rd	Month	Day	Opponent	Score	Scorers	Att	Barnes W	Broadbent AH	Deakin P	Gordon HA	Gould G	Ham RS	Hardie JC	Hector KJ	I'Anson P	Lightowler GB	Liney P	Madden P	McGillivray F	McGrath M	Milner J	Peel T	Robinson PB	Rodger W	Sumpner RA	Symonds A	Taylor K	Waddell R
R1	Nov	26	WITTON ALBION	3-2	Symonds, Robinson, Waddell	5318			10	4	11	8	1			3			2				7			6	5	9
R2	Jan	11	WORKINGTON	3-1	Symonds 2, Madden	9510		10	8		11	7	1			3		9	2	6			12			4	5	
R3		28	FULHAM	1-3	Robinson	14710		10	8	4	11	9	1			3		5	2	6			7					

F.L. Cup

Rd	Month	Day	Opponent	Score	Scorers	Att	Barnes W	Broadbent AH	Deakin P	Gordon HA	Gould G	Ham RS	Hardie JC	Hector KJ	I'Anson P	Lightowler GB	Liney P	Madden P	McGillivray F	McGrath M	Milner J	Peel T	Robinson PB	Rodger W	Sumpner RA	Symonds A	Taylor K	Waddell R
R1	Aug	23	HARTLEPOOLS U	2-2	Hector, Ham	4128		10		4	11	9		8		3	1	5	2	6			7					
rep		31	Hartlepools United	2-1	Hector, Gordon	4835		10		4		9		8	11	3	1	5	2	6			7					
R2	Sep	14	GRIMSBY TOWN	0-0		3304		10		4	11	8				3	1	9	2	6			7				5	
rep		21	Grimsby Town	1-3	Symonds	6877		10			11	8				3	1	9	2	6			7			4	5	

	Team	P	W	D	L	F	A	W	D	L	F	A	Pts
1	Stockport County	46	16	5	2	41	18	10	7	6	28	24	64
2	Southport	46	19	2	2	47	15	4	11	8	22	27	59
3	Barrow	46	12	8	3	35	18	12	3	8	41	36	59
4	Tranmere Rovers	46	14	6	3	42	20	8	8	7	24	23	58
5	Crewe Alexandra	46	14	5	4	42	26	7	7	9	28	29	54
6	Southend United	46	15	5	3	44	12	7	4	12	26	37	53
7	Wrexham	46	11	12	0	46	20	5	8	10	30	42	52
8	Hartlepools United	46	15	3	5	44	29	7	4	12	22	35	51
9	Brentford	46	13	7	3	36	19	5	6	12	22	37	49
10	Aldershot	46	14	4	5	48	19	4	8	11	24	38	48
11	Bradford City	46	13	4	6	48	31	6	6	11	26	31	48
12	Halifax Town	46	10	11	2	37	27	5	3	15	22	41	44
13	Port Vale	46	9	7	7	33	27	5	8	10	22	31	43
14	Exeter City	46	11	6	6	30	24	3	9	11	20	36	43
15	Chesterfield	46	13	6	4	33	16	4	2	17	27	47	42
16	Barnsley	46	8	7	8	30	28	5	8	10	30	36	41
17	Luton Town	46	15	5	3	47	23	1	4	18	12	50	41
18	Newport County	46	9	9	5	35	23	3	7	13	21	40	40
19	Chester	46	8	5	10	24	32	7	5	11	30	46	40
20	Notts County	46	10	7	6	31	25	3	4	16	22	47	37
21	Rochdale	46	10	4	9	30	27	3	7	13	23	48	37
22	York City	46	11	5	7	45	31	1	6	16	20	48	35
23	BRADFORD	46	7	6	10	30	34	4	7	12	22	45	35
24	Lincoln City	46	7	8	8	39	39	2	5	16	19	43	31

1967/68

Bottom of Division Four

	Date	Opponent	Score	Scorers	Att.	Andrews G	Barnes W	Burgin T	Clancy JP	Deakin P	Dinsdale P	Down DF	Draper D	Drury CE	Gibson JS	Giles JE	Gould G	Haddock AER	Ham RS	Hardie JC	Hibbitt K	Hudson GP	Hughes RI	I'Anson P	Lawson D	Lightowler GB	Lloyd RG	Lyons B	McBride PP	Peel T	Robinson PB	Rowley J	Tanner GG	Turner A
1	Aug 19	Swansea Town	1-1	Turner	7418				8	10	5						12			1			7	6		3			4	2	11			9
2	26	HARTLEPOOLS UNITED	0-1		3780		5	12	8										9	1			7			3	10		4	2	11			6
3	Sep 2	Newport County	0-4		3700		5		8										11	1			7			4	9		6		2	3		10
4	4	BARNSLEY	1-1	Lloyd	4428		5	12											9	1			7	4		2	10		6		11	3		8
5	9	YORK CITY	1-1	Turner	3664		5	12											9	1			7	4		2	10		6		11	3		8
6	16	Rochdale	1-1	Ham	2579		5	6											9	1			7			4	10			2	11	3		8
7	23	BRENTFORD	1-0	Lloyd	3403	2	5	6											9	1			7			4	10				11	3		8
8	26	Barnsley	0-2		7884	2	5	6											9	1			7			4	10		12		11	3		8
9	30	BRADFORD CITY	1-2	Robinson	9552	2	5		7		6		10						9	1						4					11	3		8
10	Oct 2	Southend United	1-2	Ham	11732	2	5	6				9	10						7	1						4					11	3		8
11	7	Notts County	0-0		7355	2	5	6				9	10						7	1						4			12		11	3		8
12	14	PORT VALE	2-2	Turner, Ham	3648	2	5						10						7	1						4	9				11	3	6	8
13	21	Chester	0-0		3717	2	5					9	10						7	1						4					11	3	6	8
14	23	SOUTHEND UNITED	0-1		3923	2					5	9	10						7	1						4					11	3	6	8
15	28	CHESTERFIELD	2-1	Lloyd, Robinson	4369	2					5	9	10						7	1						4	8				11	3	6	
16	Nov 11	DARLINGTON	1-2	Robinson	3278	2					5	9	10						7	1						4	8				11	3	6	
17	13	NEWPORT COUNTY	0-2		2991	2					5	9	10						7	1						4	8				11	3	6	
18	18	Aldershot	1-1	Lloyd	5143	2	5	4	8				10				11		7	1							9					3	6	
19	25	WORKINGTON	1-1	Lloyd	2745	2	5	4	8				10				11		7	1							9					3	6	
20	Dec 2	Lincoln City	1-5	Lloyd	5015		5	4	8				10		6				7	1						2	9				11	3		
21	16	SWANSEA TOWN	1-2	Down	3875	2	5					10	8						7	1						4	9				11	3	6	
22	22	Hartlepools United	0-2		4268	2	5				4	9	10					7	11	1							8				12	3	6	
23	26	Luton Town	0-2		16699	2			7		5	9	10						8	1						4					11	3	6	
24	30	LUTON TOWN	2-1	Lloyd, Down	3674		2		7		5	9	10						11	1						3	8				4		6	
25	Jan 20	ROCHDALE	0-0		3334	5	2		11			9	10						7	1						3	8				4		6	
26	27	CREWE ALEXANDRA	1-2	Lloyd	3234		5		11			9	10						7	1						2	8				12	3	6	4
27	Feb 3	Brentford	1-2	Down	4313	2	5		11			9	10					7	8	1												3	6	4
28	10	Bradford City	2-1	Ham, Down	11513	2	5					9	10					7	11	1							8					3	6	4
29	17	DONCASTER ROVERS	1-1	Down	4813	2	5		11			9	10					7		1						4					12	3	6	8
30	24	ALDERSHOT	1-1	Down	3181	2	5		11			9	10					7		1						12	8					3	6	4
31	Mar 2	Port Vale	0-4		3938	2	5		7			9	10			8				1						12					11	3	6	4
32	9	Crewe Alexandra	0-4		5150	2	5		11			9	10	4		8				1			7			3							6	
33	16	CHESTER	0-2		3050	2	5		11			9	10	4		8				1						3	7				12		6	
34	23	Chesterfield	0-2		7337							9	7	4		8				1	10							5			11	3	6	
35	25	York City	2-6	Tanner, Draper	4009							9	7	4		8				1	10							5			11	3	6	12
36	30	EXETER CITY	0-1		1956							9	7			8				1	10							5			11	3	6	4
37	Apr 6	Darlington	0-0		3153		2					9	12	5		10				1	8						7				11	3	6	4
38	12	Wrexham	0-3		5533		2					9	12	5		8				1	10						7				11	3	6	4
39	13	NOTTS COUNTY	1-4	Lloyd	2165		2	5				9				8				1			7				10				11	3	6	4
40	16	WREXHAM	0-1		2451		2		7			9	12		6					1	10						8				11	3	5	4
41	20	Workington	2-2	Draper, Turner	1650		2		12				8		6					1	10		7				9				11	3	5	4
42	22	HALIFAX TOWN	0-1		3224		2	12	11				8		6					1			7				9				3		5	4
43	27	LINCOLN CITY	1-5	Lloyd	2259		2	12					10		6					1	11		7				9				3		5	4
44	May 1	Exeter City	0-0		3535		2	5				9	10	4	6							3			1		8				11			7
45	4	Halifax Town	0-1		2827		2	4				8	10	6	5							3			1		9				11			7
46	10	Doncaster Rovers	0-2		5526		2	5	8			9	10	4	6							3			1		7				11			12
					Apps	24	37	17	21	1	9	30	37	9	8	9	3	5	27	43	8	3	13	3	3	28	32	3	7	3	40	35	31	32
					Goals							6	2						4								10				3		1	4

D Blunt played in game 42 at 10 and game 43 at 8
PA Hart played at 2 in three games 34 to 36

F.A. Cup

	Date	Opponent	Score	Scorers	Att.	Andrews G	Barnes W	Burgin T	Clancy JP	Deakin P	Dinsdale P	Down DF	Draper D	Drury CE	Gibson JS	Giles JE	Gould G	Haddock AER	Ham RS	Hardie JC	Hibbitt K	Hudson GP	Hughes RI	I'Anson P	Lawson D	Lightowler GB	Lloyd RG	Lyons B	McBride PP	Peel T	Robinson PB	Rowley J	Tanner GG	Turner A
R1	Dec 9	Grimsby Town	1-1	Down	2388	2	5					9	10						7	1						6	8				11	3	4	
R1	Dec 11	GRIMSBY TOWN	4-1	Lloyd 2, Ham, Down	5243	2	5				12	9	10						7	1						4	8				11	3	6	
R2	Jan 6	TRANMERE ROVERS	2-3	Ham, og	4967		2		11		5	9	10						7	1						3	8				4		6	

F.L. Cup

	Date	Opponent	Score	Scorers	Att.	Andrews G	Barnes W	Burgin T	Clancy JP	Deakin P	Dinsdale P	Down DF	Draper D	Drury CE	Gibson JS	Giles JE	Gould G	Haddock AER	Ham RS	Hardie JC	Hibbitt K	Hudson GP	Hughes RI	I'Anson P	Lawson D	Lightowler GB	Lloyd RG	Lyons B	McBride PP	Peel T	Robinson PB	Rowley J	Tanner GG	Turner A
R1	Aug 23	Halifax T	0-5		4810		5		8	10									9	1			7	4		3			6	2	11			12

		P	W	D	L	F	A	W	D	L	F	A	Pts
1	Luton Town	46	19	3	1	55	16	8	9	6	32	28	66
2	Barnsley	46	17	6	0	43	14	7	7	9	25	32	61
3	Hartlepools United	46	15	7	1	34	12	10	3	10	26	34	60
4	Crewe Alexandra	46	13	10	0	44	18	7	8	8	30	31	58
5	Bradford City	46	14	5	4	41	22	9	6	8	31	29	57
6	Southend United	46	12	8	3	45	21	8	6	9	32	37	54
7	Chesterfield	46	15	4	4	47	20	6	7	10	24	30	53
8	Wrexham	46	17	3	3	47	12	3	10	10	25	41	53
9	Aldershot	46	10	11	2	36	19	8	6	9	34	36	53
10	Doncaster Rovers	46	12	8	3	36	16	6	7	10	30	40	51
11	Halifax Town	46	10	6	7	34	24	5	10	8	18	25	46
12	Newport County	46	11	7	5	32	22	5	6	12	26	41	45
13	Lincoln City	46	11	3	9	41	31	6	6	11	30	37	43
14	Brentford	46	13	4	6	41	24	5	3	15	20	40	43
15	Swansea Town	46	11	8	4	38	25	5	2	16	25	52	42
16	Darlington	46	6	11	6	31	27	6	6	11	16	26	41
17	Notts County	46	10	7	6	27	27	5	4	14	26	52	41
18	Port Vale	46	10	5	8	41	31	2	10	11	20	41	39
19	Rochdale	46	9	8	6	35	32	3	6	14	16	40	38
20	Exeter City	46	9	7	7	30	30	2	9	12	15	35	38
21	York City	46	9	6	8	44	30	2	8	13	21	38	36
22	Chester	46	6	6	11	35	38	3	8	12	22	40	32
23	Workington	46	8	8	7	35	29	2	3	18	19	58	31
24	BRADFORD	46	3	7	13	18	35	1	8	14	12	47	23

1968/69

Bottom of Division Four

No	Date	Opponent	Score	Scorers	Att	Andrews G	Atkinson TJ	Booker M	Brannan P	Brown L	Charnley RO	Clancy JP	Cockburn K	Conley BJ	Darfield S	Dolan TP	Down DF	Draper D	Drury CE	Gibson JS	Gould G	Hardie JC	Harris AT	Hemstock B	Henderson T	Hibbitt K	Hopkins M	Hudson GP	Lawson D	Penrose C	Robinson PB	Saville PW	Singleton TW	Tanner GG
1	Aug 10	SWANSEA TOWN	1-1	Draper	2819	2						7						9	4			1	5	8		10		3			11		6	
2	17	Wrexham	0-3		6676			8				7					10	9	4			1	5					3			11		2	6
3	24	NOTTS COUNTY	1-1	Singleton	2395			12									8	9	4			1	6	10		7		3			11		2	5
4	26	ALDERSHOT	0-1		2427			10					11				7	9	4			1	5	8				3					2	6
5	31	Halifax Town	0-3		4876	2		12					11		10		7	9	4			1	5	8				3					6	
6	Sep 7	GRIMSBY TOWN	1-1	Draper	2263			3				8	11		12		7	9	4			1	5					2					6	
7	9	EXETER CITY	2-1	Draper, Penrose	2591			3				8	11		6		7	9	4			1	5							10			2	
8	14	Workington	1-3	Draper	2870			3				10	11		6		7	9	4	2		1	5							8				
9	16	LINCOLN CITY	1-1	Down	3433	12		3				10			6		7	9	4	2		1				11				8			5	
10	21	NEWPORT COUNTY	1-5	Drury	3007			3				10			6		7	9	4	2		1				11				8			5	
11	28	Darlington	0-2		5788			3	10			7	6					9	4	2	11	1											5	8
12	Oct 5	York City	2-4	Clancy, Draper	5250			3	10			7	11		12			9	4	2		1									8		6	5
13	9	Aldershot	1-4	Clancy	5577				10			8	11		6			9	4	2		1									7		3	5
14	12	CHESTER	1-1	Tanner	2969				10			8	11		6			9	4	2		1				12					7		3	5
15	18	Doncaster Rovers	1-4	Cockburn	11007			3	10			8	11					9	4	2		1				12					7		6	5
16	26	CHESTERFIELD	0-1		3088				10			12	11		6			9		5		1				8		2			7		3	4
17	Nov 2	Rochdale	0-6		2795				11						7			8	4	3		1	5					2			12		10	6
18	6	Bradford City	0-1		8178			3	9			7	10					8	4		11	1									6		2	5
19	9	COLCHESTER UNITED	2-1	Brannan, Gould	2011				10			8	11					9	4	3	7	1									6		2	5
20	23	BRENTFORD	0-2		2391	5			10			8						9	6	3	11	1								7	4		2	
21	30	Peterborough United	1-6	Gould	5419	4			12			7			10			9	5	3	11	1								8	6		2	
22	Dec 6	Scunthorpe United	0-1		3158					5		7			10			9	4	3	11	1									6		2	8
23	14	Chester	1-4	Andrews	3182	9				5		7	11		6			10	4	3		1									8		2	
24	21	DONCASTER ROVERS	2-1	Draper, Andrews	3911	9				5			11	4	10			8		3	7	1									6		2	
25	28	Chesterfield	1-1	Draper	5036	9				5		10	11	6				8		3	7	1									4		2	
26	Jan 11	ROCHDALE	1-4	Andrews	5453	10				5	9			6	8			4			11	1					3				7		2	
27	18	Colchester United	0-3		5914	8	4			5	9			6							11	1			10		3	12			7		2	
28	25	BRADFORD CITY	0-0		10784		4		11	9	8	7		6								1			10		5	2			12		3	
29	Feb 1	SCUNTHORPE UNITED	2-2	Andrews, Henderson	3050	7	5		11	9	8	12		6								1			10			2			4		3	
30	24	Exeter City	2-4	Andrews, Charnley	3767	10	4		11	9	8	7		6						12							5	2	1				3	
31	Mar 1	Swansea Town	0-3		4365	8	4			5	9			6							11		10				3	2	1		7			
32	8	WREXHAM	1-2	Charnley	2980	7	4			10	9	8		6		5				12					11		3	2	1					
33	15	Notts County	0-5		3629	11	4			5	9	10				6									8		3	2	1			7		
34	26	YORK CITY	1-0	Charnley	2449	9	4			5	8	12		6						11					10		3	2	1			7		
35	29	Grimsby Town	0-2		4549	10	2			6	9	11								4					8		3	5	1			7		
36	Apr 2	PETERBOROUGH UTD.	0-2		2471	9	4			5	8	11								6					10		3	2	1			7		
37	5	DARLINGTON	1-3	Henderson	2825	9	4			5	8	7								12					10		3	2	1		6	11		
38	7	Lincoln City	2-3	Henderson, Robinson	8092		4			5	9	11				6									10		3	2	1		8	7		
39	8	SOUTHEND UNITED	0-3		2543		5				9	7			6	4				12					10		3	2	1		8	11		
40	12	Newport County	0-1		1192		4		11	5	9					6						1			10		3	2			7	8		
41	14	Southend United	0-5		7684				11	5	9	8				6						1			10		3	2			4	7		
42	19	WORKINGTON	1-0	Atkinson	1780	10	4			5	9					6						1			11		3	2			8	7		
43	21	Brentford	0-3		4137	9	4			5	8					6						1			11		3	2			10	7		
44	25	Port Vale	1-1	Andrews	3873	9	4				8	11				6						1					5	2			10	7	3	
45	May 5	PORT VALE	0-1		1572	9	4			8		7				6						1					5	2			10	11	3	
46	12	HALIFAX TOWN	0-0		6057	9	4					7				6						1			10		5	2			8	11	3	
					Apps	24	19	13	16	22	19	35	16	10	17	11	9	26	22	24	11	36	10	4	16	7	20	28	10	6	32	14	32	13
					Goals	6	1		1		3	2	1				1	7	1		2				3					1	1		1	1

Played in one game: G Halliday (31, at 12) , J Hellawell (17, 9), J Sykes (6, at 10, subbed), M Walker (35, 12)

F.A. Cup

Rd	Date	Opponent	Score	Scorers	Att	Andrews G	Atkinson TJ	Booker M	Brannan P	Brown L	Charnley RO	Clancy JP	Cockburn K	Conley BJ	Darfield S	Dolan TP	Down DF	Draper D	Drury CE	Gibson JS	Gould G	Hardie JC	Harris AT	Hemstock B	Henderson T	Hibbitt K	Hopkins M	Hudson GP	Lawson D	Penrose C	Robinson PB	Saville PW	Singleton TW	Tanner GG
R1	Nov 16	Stockport County	0-3		8413				10			8	11					9	4	3	7	1									6		2	5

F.L. Cup

Rd	Date	Opponent	Score	Scorers	Att	Andrews G	Atkinson TJ	Booker M	Brannan P	Brown L	Charnley RO	Clancy JP	Cockburn K	Conley BJ	Darfield S	Dolan TP	Down DF	Draper D	Drury CE	Gibson JS	Gould G	Hardie JC	Harris AT	Hemstock B	Henderson T	Hibbitt K	Hopkins M	Hudson GP	Lawson D	Penrose C	Robinson PB	Saville PW	Singleton TW	Tanner GG
R1	Aug 13	DARLINGTON	0-3		2560	2						7					8	9	4			1	5			10		3			11		6	

		P	W	D	L	F	A	W	D	L	F	A	Pts
1	Doncaster Rovers	46	13	8	2	42	16	8	9	6	23	22	59
2	Halifax Town	46	15	5	3	36	18	5	12	6	17	19	57
3	Rochdale	46	14	7	2	47	11	4	13	6	21	24	56
4	Bradford City	46	11	10	2	36	18	7	10	6	29	28	56
5	Darlington	46	11	6	6	40	26	6	12	5	22	19	52
6	Colchester United	46	12	8	3	31	17	8	4	11	26	36	52
7	Southend United	46	15	3	5	51	21	4	10	9	27	40	51
8	Lincoln City	46	13	6	4	38	19	4	11	8	16	33	51
9	Wrexham	46	13	7	3	41	22	5	7	11	20	30	50
10	Swansea Town	46	11	8	4	35	20	8	3	12	23	34	49
11	Brentford	46	12	7	4	40	24	6	5	12	24	41	48
12	Workington	46	8	11	4	24	17	7	6	10	16	26	47
13	Port Vale	46	12	8	3	33	15	4	6	13	13	31	46
14	Chester	46	12	4	7	43	24	4	9	10	33	42	45
15	Aldershot	46	13	3	7	42	23	6	4	13	24	43	45
16	Scunthorpe United	46	10	5	8	28	22	8	3	12	33	38	44
17	Exeter City	46	11	8	4	45	24	5	3	15	21	41	43
18	Peterborough United	46	8	9	6	32	23	5	7	11	28	34	42
19	Notts County	46	10	8	5	33	22	2	10	11	15	35	42
20	Chesterfield	46	7	7	9	24	22	6	8	9	19	28	41
21	York City	46	12	8	3	36	25	2	3	18	17	50	39
22	Newport County	46	9	9	5	31	26	2	5	16	18	48	36
23	Grimsby Town	46	5	7	11	25	31	4	8	11	22	38	33
24	BRADFORD	46	5	8	10	19	34	0	2	21	13	72	20

1969/70

Bottom of Division Four

	Date		Opponent	Res	Scorers	Att	Atkinson TJ	Beanland A	Brannan P	Brodie J	Brown L	Campbell D	Carr WG	Charnley RO	Conley BJ	Dolan TP	Eyre SF	Fitzsimmons EJ	Hardie JC	Henderson T	Hickman GB	Hopkins M	Hudson GP	Massie L	Rafferty B	Roberts A	Saville PW	Tewley AB	Thom LM	Walker M	Woolmer AJ	Wright RL
1	Aug	9	ALDERSHOT	2-0	Atkinson, Beanland	2901	4	7	8	3	5		6	9		10			1				2						11			
2		16	Peterborough United	1-2	Saville	6303	4	7	10	3	5		6	9					1				2				8		11			
3		23	GRIMSBY TOWN	1-1	Brown	3384	4	10	7	3	5		6	9					1				2	8					11			
4		26	Scunthorpe United	0-2		3300	4	10	7	3			5	9		6			1				2	8					11			
5		30	Exeter City	0-3		4457	4	10	7	2	5		6	9	12				1			3		8					11			
6	Sep	6	CHESTERFIELD	1-1	Atkinson	2867	4	10		2	5		6	9	12				1			3		8			7		11			
7		13	York City	1-4	Brannan	4743	4	7	10	2	5		6	9					1			3		8					11			
8		15	WORKINGTON	2-0	Atkinson, og	2685	4	7	10	2	5		6	9					1			3		8					11			
9		20	BRENTFORD	0-1		2887	4	7	10	2	5		6	9					1			3		8					11			
10		27	Southend United	1-1	Charnley	6174	4	7	10	2	5		6	9					1			3		8					11			
11	Oct	1	Chester	0-1		3203	4	7	10	2	5		6	9		12			1			3		8					11			
12		4	NORTHAMPTON T	1-2	Atkinson	2555	4	10		2	6		5	9		12			1	7		3		8					11			
13		6	PETERBOROUGH UTD.	2-3	Charnley 2	2568	2	12	11	3			6	9	4	10			1			5		8			7					
14		11	Colchester United	1-2	Massie	4497	2	10		3	5		6	9		4			1			12		8			7		11			
15		18	Hartlepool	2-5	Massie, Woolmer	2816	2	10		3	5		4	9					1					8					11		7	6
16		25	NOTTS COUNTY	1-3	Charnley	3219	12			3	5		2	9		4			1	10					8		7				11	6
17	Nov	1	Darlington	1-1	Carr	3331	2	8		3			4	9		5				10	1				12		11				7	6
18		8	PORT VALE	1-2	Charnley	3498	2	4		3			6	9		5				11	1			8	12		10				7	
19		22	SWANSEA TOWN	0-2		3500		12		2			4	9		6					1				8	3	11	7		5	10	
20		24	WREXHAM	2-3	Charnley, Woolmer	2671	6	4	12	2				9		5					1				7	3		10	11		8	
21		29	Newport County	1-5	Tewley	2724	6	4		2			7	9		5					1				12	3		10	11		8	
22	Dec	13	YORK CITY	2-0	Woolmer, Charnley	3084	6	10		2			4	9		5			1							3		7	11		8	
23		26	Grimsby Town	2-2	Tewley, Woolmer	6805	6	10		2			4	9		5			1							3		7	11		8	
24		27	EXETER CITY	2-1	Thom, Woolmer	5758	6	10		2			4			5			1							3	8	7	11		9	
25	Jan	10	Brentford	1-1	Tewley	5847	6	10		2			4	9		5			1							3		7	11		8	
26		17	SOUTHEND UNITED	1-0	Woolmer	4524	6	10		2			4	9		5			1							3		7	11		8	
27		19	CHESTER	1-2	Charnley	5997	6	10		2			4	9		5			1							3		7	11		8	
28		24	Oldham Athletic	0-0		4444	6	10		2			4	9		5			1							3		7	11		8	
29		31	Northampton Town	0-3		12972	6	10	12	2			4	9		5			1							3		7	11		8	
30	Feb	7	COLCHESTER UNITED	0-1		2972	6	10		2			4	9		5			1							3	11	7			8	12
31		21	Port Vale	1-4	Wright	4416	6		11	2			4			5			1						10	3		7			8	9
32		28	DARLINGTON	0-1		2635	2			3			4	9		5			1						10	6		7	11		8	
33	Mar	2	CREWE ALEXANDRA	0-0		2141	4		12	2			10	9		5			1							3	11	7			8	6
34		7	Swansea Town	0-5		7355	4			2			10	9		5	3		1								11	7			8	6
35		13	NEWPORT COUNTY	1-1	Carr	1864	4		3	2			5			9			1						8		11	7		12	10	6
36		16	OLDHAM ATHLETIC	0-0		3163	4		3			5	10	9		2			1								11	7			8	6
37		21	Crewe Alexandra	0-0		2568	4		3			5	10	9		2			1						12			7	11		8	6
38		23	Lincoln City	2-5	Charnley, Tewley	4350			3			5	10	9		4			1									7	11	2	8	6
39		28	LINCOLN CITY	0-3		2427	6		3	2		5	9			4			1								7	8	11		10	
40		30	Notts County	2-5	Charnley, Rafferty	8897	4		10	3		5	6	9		2					1				12		7	8	11			
41		31	HARTLEPOOL	3-0	Charnley 2, Atkinson	2294	4		10	3		5		9		2					1							8	11		7	6
42	Apr	4	SCUNTHORPE UNITED	0-5		2563	4		10	3		5	6	9		2					1							8	11		7	
43		6	Wrexham	0-4		8972	4		11	3			10	9		5					1		2		7			8				6
44		15	Workington	0-1		2246				3		5	4	9		6			1				2		7		11	8			10	
45		17	Chesterfield	0-4		11178		6	10	3		5				4		8	1	11			2					7			9	
46		20	Aldershot	2-4	Woolmer, Campbell	4861		8	10	3		5				4			1	11			2					7			9	6
						Apps	41	31	26	43	14	10	42	40	3	37	1	1	37	6	9	10	8	14	13	15	17	28	31	3	30	14
						Goals	5	1	1		1	1	2	12										2	1		1	4	1		7	1

One own goal

F.A. Cup

	Date		Opponent	Res	Scorers	Att	Atkinson TJ	Beanland A	Brannan P	Brodie J	Brown L	Campbell D	Carr WG	Charnley RO	Conley BJ	Dolan TP	Eyre SF	Fitzsimmons EJ	Hardie JC	Henderson T	Hickman GB	Hopkins M	Hudson GP	Massie L	Rafferty B	Roberts A	Saville PW	Tewley AB	Thom LM	Walker M	Woolmer AJ	Wright RL
R1	Nov	15	South Shields	1-2	Brannan	2000		4	12	3			6	9		5				10	1				8		11			2	7	

F.L. Cup

	Date		Opponent	Res	Scorers	Att	Atkinson TJ	Beanland A	Brannan P	Brodie J	Brown L	Campbell D	Carr WG	Charnley RO	Conley BJ	Dolan TP	Eyre SF	Fitzsimmons EJ	Hardie JC	Henderson T	Hickman GB	Hopkins M	Hudson GP	Massie L	Rafferty B	Roberts A	Saville PW	Tewley AB	Thom LM	Walker M	Woolmer AJ	Wright RL
R1	Aug	12	ROTHERHAM UNITED	0-2		3980	4	7	8	3	5		6	9					1	10		12	2						11			

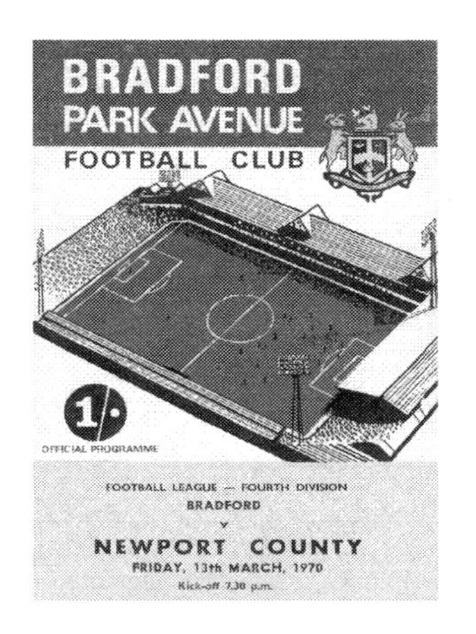

		P	W	D	L	F	A	W	D	L	F	A	Pts
1	Chesterfield	46	19	1	3	55	12	8	9	6	22	20	64
2	Wrexham	46	17	6	0	56	16	9	3	11	28	33	61
3	Swansea Town	46	14	8	1	43	14	7	10	6	23	31	60
4	Port Vale	46	13	9	1	39	10	7	10	6	22	23	59
5	Brentford	46	14	8	1	36	11	6	8	9	22	28	56
6	Aldershot	46	16	5	2	52	22	4	8	11	26	43	53
7	Notts County	46	14	4	5	44	21	8	4	11	29	41	52
8	Lincoln City	46	11	8	4	38	20	6	8	9	28	32	50
9	Peterborough United	46	13	8	2	51	21	4	6	13	26	48	48
10	Colchester United	46	14	5	4	38	22	3	9	11	26	41	48
11	Chester	46	14	3	6	39	23	7	3	13	19	43	48
12	Scunthorpe United	46	11	6	6	34	23	7	4	12	33	42	46
13	York City	46	14	7	2	38	16	2	7	14	17	46	46
14	Northampton Town	46	11	7	5	41	19	5	5	13	23	36	44
15	Crewe Alexandra	46	12	6	5	37	18	4	6	13	14	33	44
16	Grimsby Town	46	9	9	5	33	24	5	6	12	21	34	43
17	Southend United	46	12	8	3	40	28	3	2	18	19	57	40
18	Exeter City	46	13	5	5	48	20	1	6	16	9	39	39
19	Oldham Athletic	46	11	4	8	45	28	2	9	12	15	37	39
20	Workington	46	9	9	5	31	21	3	5	15	15	43	38
21	Newport County	46	12	3	8	39	24	1	8	14	14	50	37
22	Darlington	46	8	7	8	31	27	5	3	15	22	46	36
23	Hartlepool	46	7	7	9	31	30	3	3	17	11	52	30
24	BRADFORD	46	6	5	12	23	32	0	6	17	18	64	23

Name		D.O.B	Place of Birth	Died	First Season	Last Season	lin	Previous Club	Next Club	Appearances Lge	FAC	FLC	Oth.	Goals Lge	FAC	FLC	Oth.
Adey AL	Arthur	01/03/1930	Glasgow		1954			Gillingham		13	2	0	0	4	1	0	0
Ainsley GE	George	15/04/1915	South Shields	1985	1947	1948		Leeds United	Coach	44	3	0	0	29	1	0	0
Aitken FMcK	Fergie	05/06/1896	Glasgow	1989	1926			Southport	retired	11	0	0	0	0	0	0	0
Alexander A	Alan	01/11/1941	Cumbernauld		1960	1961		Amateur	Corby Town	5	0	1	0	0	0	0	0
Allan J	John	23/03/1931	Stirling		1958	1960		Third Lanark	Halifax Town	70	5	3	0	51	5	1	0
Allcock CW	Bill	18/07/1907	Codnor	1971	1930	1933		Grantham	Barrow	64	2	0	0	0	0	0	0
Anders J	Jimmy	08/03/1928	St Helens		1956	1961		Rochdale	Accrington Stanley	59	4	4	0	12	0	2	0
								Buxton	Tranmere Rovers								
Andrews G	Glen	11/02/1945	Dudley		1967	1968		Wolves	Chelmsford City	48	2	1	0	6	0	0	0
Ashworth JM	Joe	06/01/1943	Huddersfield	2002	1961			Juniors	York City	3	0	0	0	0	0	0	0
Atherton WJ	Billy	04/05/1905	Bradford	1976	1928	1930		Amateur	Doncaster Rovers	36	3	0	0	20	1	0	0
Atkinson C	Charlie	17/12/1932	Hull		1956	1963		Hull City	Bradford City	339	14	10	0	50	2	1	0
Atkinson TJ	Trevor	23/11/1942	Bishop Auckland		1968	1970		Darlington	retired	60	2	1	29	6	0	0	4
Baddeley T	Tom	02/11/1874	Bycars	1946	1907	1908	e	Wolves	Stoke	9	1	0	33	0	0	0	0
Bailey LA	Les	02/10/1916	Worksop	1980	1936			Gainsborough Trin.	Derby County	22	1	0	0	1	0	0	0
Bailey M	Malcolm	07/05/1937	Halifax		1957	1958		Luddendenfoot	Leeds United	10	0	0	0	1	0	0	0
Baillie J	Joe	26/02/1929	Dumfries	1966	1960			Leicester City	retired	7	0	0	0	1	0	0	0
Baker G	Gerry	22/04/1939	South Hiendley		1957	1960		Juniors	King's Lynn	16	0	0	0	0	0	0	0
Barker D	Don	17/06/1911	Long Eaton	1979	1933	1936		Notts Alliance	Millwall	55	0	0	0	15	0	0	0
Barnes W	Billy	16/03/1939	Dumbarton		1966	1967		Scarborough	Arnold Town	53	3	1	0	0	0	0	0
Barnett LH	Laurie	08/05/1903	Bramley	1982	1920	1921			Barnsley	33	0	0	0	0	0	0	0
Barrett C	Claude	05/12/1907	Rawdon	1976	1932	1935		Amateur	Port Vale	47	1	0	0	0	0	0	0
Bates E	Ernie	10/06/1935	Huddersfield	1995	1957	1958		Huddersfield T		44	3	0	0	0	0	0	0
Batt E	Edgar	20/02/1909	Bradford	1969	1926			Amateur	Doncaster Rovers	5	0	0	0	3	0	0	0
Batten J	John	28/05/1899	Galston		1920	1922		Amateur	Exeter City	33	2	0	0	5	1	0	0
Batty FR	Fred	20/12/1934	Stanley		1955	1958		Stanley United		56	1	0	0	0	0	0	0
Bauchop JR	Jimmy	22/05/1886	Sauchie	1948	1913	1921		Tottenham H	Lincoln City	157	13	0	0	68	7	0	0
Beanland A	Tony	11/01/1944	Bradford		1969	1970		Wrexham	Kirkby Town	31	3	1	21	1	0	0	0
Beattie G	George	16/06/1925	Aberdeen		1953	1954		Newport County		53	3	0	0	16	1	0	0
Bedford H	Harry	15/10/1899	Calow	1976	1932		e	Sunderland	Chesterfield	33	0	0	0	15	0	0	0
Begg JA	Jim	14/02/1930	Dumfries		1953	1954		Liverpool		10	0	0	0	0	0	0	0
Bell DS	Donald	03/12/1890	Harrogate	1916	1912	1913		Newcastle United		5	0	0	0	0	0	0	0
Bell JC	Jack	24/10/1905	Seaham Harbour		1931	1935		Accrington Stanley		66	7	0	0	0	0	0	0
Bentley A	Alec	02/06/1908	Shipley		1929	1930		Amateur		12	4	0	0	0	0	0	0
Bingham S	Sam		Northern Ireland		1920			Amateur		7	0	0	0	0	0	0	0
Bird RP	Ronnie	27/12/1941	Erdington		1961	1965		Birmingham City	Bury	129	4	6	0	39	0	3	0
Blackburn G	George	1888	Worksop		1909			Denaby United	Huddersfield T	11	0	0	0	6	0	0	0
Blackhall S	Sid	25/09/1945	Ashington		1963			App.	Ashington	1	0	0	0	0	0	0	0
Blackham S	Sam	19/08/1890	Edmonton	1956	1911	1921		Barrow	Halifax Town	221	21	0	0	0	0	0	0
Blackmore HA	Harold	13/05/1904	Silverton	1989	1933	1934		Middlesbrough	Bury	60	2	0	0	32	0	0	0
Bleanch NWS	Norman	19/08/1940	Houghton-le-Spring		1961			Southend Utd.	King's Lynn	9	0	0	0	3	0	0	0
Blunt D	David	29/04/1949	Goldthorpe		1967			Amateur	Chester	2	0	0	0	0	0	0	0
Bolton H	Hugh		Port Glasgow		1908	1909		Everton	Morton	30	0	0	0	7	0	0	0
Booker M	Mike	22/10/1947	Barnsley		1968			Barnsley	Bangor City	13	0	0	0	0	0	0	0
Booth KK	Ken	22/11/1934	Blackpool		1957	1958		Blackpool	Workington	45	3	0	0	14	1	0	0
Bowater GA	George	26/10/1911	Shirebrook	1966	1933			Mansfield Town	York City	6	0	0	0	1	0	0	0
Boyle O	Owen		South Bank	1959	1919			Amateur		1	0	0	0	0	0	0	0
Bracey FC	Fred	20/07/1887	Derby	1960	1908			Leicester Fosse		7	1	0	0	0	1	0	0
Bradley A	Albert	10/05/1896	Bradford	1969	1922	1925		Amateur	Southport	39	2	0	0	22	0	0	0
Bradley G	Gordon	23/11/1933	Easington		1955	1956		Stanley United	Carlisle Utd.	18	0	0	0	1	0	0	0
Brandon WT	Tom	28/05/1893	Blackburn	1956	1922	1924		Hull City	Wigan Borough	85	4	0	0	0	0	0	0
Brannan P	Peter	07/04/1947	Bradford		1968	1973		Juniors	Gainsborough Trin.	42	12	1	145	2	2	0	18
Breakwell T	Tom	03/07/1915	Stourport		1936			Bolton Wanderers	Wrexham	18	1	0	0	0	0	0	0
Brickley D	Dennis	09/09/1929	Bradford	1983	1950	1956		Huddersfield T		169	10	0	0	24	1	0	0
Brims D	Don	08/01/1934	Auchendinny		1958	1959		Motherwell	Third Lanark	76	3	0	0	3	0	0	0
Britton J	Jimmy	27/05/1920	Salford		1945	1946		Lowestoft	Rochdale	1	1	0	0	0	0	0	0
Broadbent AH	Albert	20/08/1934	Dudley		1965	1966		Doncaster Rovers	Hartlepool Utd.	56	3	4	0	11	0	0	0
Brocklehurst JF	John	15/12/1927	Horwich		1954	1955		Stalybridge Celtic		47	3	0	0	1	0	0	0
Brodie J	John	08/06/1947	Bedlington		1969	1970		Carlisle Utd.	Port Vale	43	3	1	20	0	0	0	0
Brolls N	Norman	26/09/1933	Wigtown		1956			Third Lanark	Scarborough	11	2	0	0	0	0	0	0
Brown GD	George	08/05/1928	Airdrie		1956			Clyde	Poole	17	0	0	0	2	0	0	0
Brown J	Jimmy	1907	Motherwell		1938			Manchester Utd.		13	0	0	0	0	0	0	0
Brown L	Laurie	22/08/1937	Shildon	1998	1968	1969		Norwich City	Altrincham	36	0	1	0	1	0	0	0
Brown TE	Tommy	27/03/1897	Sheffield		1919	1921		Amateur	Rotherham Town	19	0	0	0	0	0	0	0
Bruce R	Ron	04/03/1915	Walker		1938			North Shields	Consett	1	0	0	0	0	0	0	0
Brydon IF	Ian	22/03/1927	Edinburgh	1973	1955			Accrington Stanley		12	0	0	0	3	0	0	0
Buchanan G	George		Paisley	1944	1910	1912		Hearts	Morton	52	2	0	0	9	0	0	0
Buchanan J	Jock	09/06/1928	Underwood, Stirling	2000	1957	1962		Derby County	retired	164	6	3	0	67	7	1	0
Buckley W	Walter	30/04/1906	Eccleshall		1928			Mansfield Town	Lincoln City	5	0	0	0	0	0	0	0
Burgin T	Trevor	28/08/1943	Darfield		1967			Amateur		17	0	0	0	0	0	0	0
Burkinshaw JDL	Jack	12/05/1890	Kilnhurst	1947	1920			Sheffield Wed.	Accrington Stanley	23	2	0	0	2	1	0	0
Burnison S	Sam	1891	Belfast		1910		i	Distillery	Distillery	15	0	0	0	0	0	0	0
Burns EO	Eric	08/03/1945	Newton Stewart		1963	1965		App.	Barnsley	28	0	1	0	3	0	0	0
Byrom R	Ray	02/01/1935	Blackburn		1958	1960		Accrington Stanley	retired	70	3	0	0	14	0	0	0
Cade D	David	29/09/1938	Hemsworth		1959			Barnsley	Scarborough	1	0	0	0	0	0	0	0
Cainey WP	Percy	12/12/1908	Bristol	1960	1936			Bristol City	Bath City	11	1	0	0	1	0	0	0
Calow CJH	Charlie	30/09/1931	Belfast		1952			Cliftonville		1	0	0	0	0	0	0	0
Cameron JA	John	29/11/1929	Greenock		1956			Motherwell		3	0	0	0	0	0	0	0
Campbell D	Danny	03/02/1944	Oldham		1969	1970		Stockport Co.	Port Elizabeth (SA)	10	2	0	25	1	0	0	1

Name		D.O.B	Place of Birth	Died	First Season	Last Season	lin	Previous Club	Next Club	Appearances Lge	FAC	FLC	Oth.	Goals Lge	FAC	FLC	Oth.
Carlin P	Pat	17/12/1929	Dunscroft		1953			Dunscroft		6	0	0	0	0	0	0	0
Carr WG	Graham	25/10/1944	Newcastle		1969			York City	Altrincham	42	1	1	0	2	0	0	0
Carrick JH	Jim	17/02/1901	Boothstown		1926			Barrow	Accrington Stanley	18	1	0	0	0	0	0	0
Carson J	Jim	1912	Clydebank		1933			Yoker Athletic	Crystal Palace	12	1	0	0	0	0	0	0
Cartwright HP	Phil	08/02/1908	Scarborough	1974	1927	1928		Middlesbrough	Hull City	20	2	0	0	3	2	0	0
Cawdry W	Walter				1908			Amateur		1	1	0	0	0	1	0	0
Charnley RO	Ray	29/05/1935	Lancaster		1968	1969	e	Wrexham	Morecambe	59	1	1	0	15	0	0	0
Church G	Garry	20/09/1944	Pontefract		1963			Gt Preston Jnrs	Bournemouth	4	0	0	0	0	0	0	0
Clancy JP	John	05/07/1949	Perivale		1967	1968		Bristol City	Yeovil	56	2	2	0	2	0	0	0
Clark DC	David				1909			West Ham U		7	0	0	0	0	0	0	0
Clegg MB	Malcolm	09/04/1936	Leeds		1957			Bradford Rovers		6	0	0	0	0	0	0	0
Clough JH	Jack	13/05/1902	Murton		1926	1931		Middlesbrough	Mansfield Town	208	14	0	0	0	0	0	0
Cockburn K	Keith	02/09/1948	Barnsley		1968			Barnsley	Grimsby Town	16	1	0	0	1	0	0	0
Coleman MA	Arthur	1910			1932			Gainsborough Trin.	Gainsborough Trin.	2	0	0	0	0	0	0	0
Collins D	David	1912			1932			Dumbarton	Dumbarton	7	0	0	0	2	0	0	0
Conley BJ	Brian	21/11/1948	Thurnscoe		1968	1969		Sheffield Utd.		13	0	0	0	0	0	0	0
Conroy R	Dick	29/07/1927	Bradford	1991	1953	1955		Bradford City	Grantham	57	3	0	0	0	0	0	0
Cook C	Charlie	03/06/1898	Glasgow		1924			Coventry City	(USA)	2	4	0	0	0	0	0	0
Cook MI	Malcolm	24/05/1943	Glasgow		1963	1964		Motherwell	Newport County	45	2	3	0	2	0	1	0
Cookson S	Sam	22/11/1896	Manchester	1955	1928	1932		Manchester City	Barnsley	136	10	0	0	0	0	0	0
Craig CT	Charlie	11/07/1876	Dundee	1933	1907	1908		Nottm. Forest	Norwich City	6	0	0	30	0	0	0	0
Crayston WJ	Jack	09/10/1910	Grange-over-Sands	1992	1930	1933	e	Barrow	Arsenal	97	5	0	0	15	0	0	0
Cringan JA	Jimmy	1918	Douglas Water		1937			Armadale Thistle	Wolves	6	0	0	0	0	0	0	0
Croot J	Jimmy	24/06/1904	Smalley Green		1926	1927		Denaby United		7	0	0	0	0	0	0	0
Crosbie RC	Bob	02/09/1925	Glasgow	1994	1949	1953		Bury	Hull City	139	10	0	0	72	3	0	0
Crosson D	Danny	1887		1918	1908	1909		Abercorn		23	2	0	0	0	0	0	0
Crowe MJ	Matt	04/07/1932	Bathgate		1952			Bathgate Thistle	Norwich City	1	0	0	0	0	0	0	0
Crowther GE	George		Pudsey		1925			Leeds United	York City	8	2	0	0	0	0	0	0
Crowther GL	George	1892	Bishop Middleham		1919			Amateur	West Ham Utd.	9	0	0	0	0	0	0	0
Crowther K	Ken	17/12/1924	Halifax	1994	1948			Burnley	Rochdale	6	0	0	0	1	0	0	0
Crozier J	Joe	04/12/1889	Middlesbrough	1960	1914	1921		Middlesbrough	Grimsby Town	115	9	0	0	4	0	0	0
Currie CJ	Charlie	17/04/1920	Belfast		1949	1953		Belfast Celtic	Derry City	118	12	0	0	2	0	0	0
Curtis T	Tom	1901	South Bank		1920			South Bank		9	0	0	0	0	0	0	0
Dailey WS	Bill		Coatbridge		1924			Shieldmuir Celtic	Coventry City	8	0	0	0	1	0	0	0
Dainty HC	Herbert	02/06/1879	Rushton	1961	1911	1913		Dundee	Ayr United	63	8	0	0	1	0	0	0
Danskin R	Bob	28/05/1908	Scotswood	1985	1932	1947		Leeds United	retired	260	19	0	0	6	0	0	0
Darfield SC	Stuart	12/12/1950	Leeds		1968			Wolves		17	0	0	0	0	0	0	0
Davidson DBL	Dave	25/03/1920	Lanark	1954	1946			Juniors	Leyton Orient	13	0	0	0	0	0	0	0
Davies J	Joe	10/11/1917	Burslem		1938			Wolves		5	0	0	0	0	0	0	0
Davis H	Bert	11/08/1906	Bradford	1981	1927	1931		Guiseley	Sunderland	172	14	0	0	40	4	0	0
Deakin P	Peter	25/03/1938	Normanton		1966	1967		Peterborough Utd.	Peterborough Utd.	36	3	1	0	9	0	0	0
Dean J	Joby	25/11/1934	Chesterfield		1957	1958		Sutton Town		53	2	0	0	1	0	0	0
Dempsey M	Mark	14/10/1887			1914					1	0	0	0	0	0	0	0
Deplidge W	Bill	12/11/1924	Bradford		1946	1955		App.	Yeovil Town	274	18	0	0	62	1	0	0
Devlin J	Joe	12/03/1931	Cleland		1957	1958		Rochdale	Carlisle Utd.	34	3	0	0	3	0	0	0
Dick PW	Wattie	28/02/1927	Newmains		1958	1962		Accrington Stanley	retired	155	6	5	0	2	0	0	0
Dick TW	Tom	19/07/1936	Glasgow		1960			Third Lanark	Ramsgate	4	2	2	0	0	0	0	0
Dick WR	William		Harthill		1931			Hibernian		11	1	0	0	0	0	0	0
Dickenson W	Wally	22/12/1895	Sheffield	1968	1919	1921		Amateur	Sheffield Wed.	113	7	0	0	0	0	0	0
Dickinson S	Syd	17/08/1906	Nottingham	1984	1926	1933		Mansfield Town	Port Vale	156	13	0	0	19	2	0	0
Dilly T	Tommy	1882	Arbroath	1960	1908			Derby County	Walsall	1	1	0	0	0	0	0	0
Dine JMcQ	John	03/05/1940	Newton Stewart		1962	1964		Bulford United	Stranraer	32	3	6	0	0	0	0	0
Dinsdale P	Peter	19/10/1938	Bradford		1967			Huddersfield T		9	2	0	0	0	0	0	0
Dinsdale WA	Billy	12/07/1903	Guisborough	1984	1928	1929		Lincoln City	Lincoln City	17	0	0	0	4	0	0	0
Dix R	Richard	17/01/1924	South Shields	1990	1945	1947		North Shields	Bradford City	18	7	0	0	5	3	0	0
Dixon A	Arthur	05/10/1879	Barrowford	1946	1908	1912		Burnley	Nelson	115	5	0	0	2	0	0	0
Dolan TP	Terry	11/06/1950	Bradford		1968	1970		Bradford City	Huddersfield T	48	1	0	15	0	0	0	1
Donaghy J	John		Grangetown		1921			Middlesbrough		8	0	0	0	0	0	0	0
Donald DM	Davie	21/07/1885	Coatbridge	1932	1908	1909		Albion Rovers	Derby County	27	1	0	0	2	0	0	0
Donaldson JMcF	John				1908			Preston NE		6	1	0	0	0	0	0	0
Donaldson W	Willie	20/01/1920	Wallacetown	1977	1946	1950		Leith Athletic	Mansfield Town	45	1	0	0	6	0	0	0
Doran S	Sam	22/12/1912	Bradford		1934	1937		Sunfield Rovers	Reading	54	6	0	0	4	2	0	0
Down DF	David	07/07/1948	Bristol		1967	1968		Bristol City	Oldham Athletic	39	3	1	0	7	2	0	0
Downie JD	Johnny	19/07/1925	Lanark		1945	1948		Lanark ATC	Manchester Utd.	86	13	0	0	33	3	0	0
Downie M	Mitch	09/02/1923	Troon	2001	1950	1953		Airdrie	Lincoln City	156	13	0	0	0	0	0	0
Doyle W	Bill	19/11/1913	Wishaw		1937			Forth Wanderers		1	0	0	0	0	0	0	0
Drabble F	Frank	08/07/1888	Southport	1964	1913	1914		Burnley	Bolton Wanderers	32	2	0	0	0	0	0	0
Draper D	Derek	11/05/1943	Swansea		1967	1968		Derby County	Chester City	63	4	1	0	9	0	0	0
Drury CE	Chuck	04/07/1937	Darlaston		1967	1968		Bristol City	Tamworth	31	1	1	0	1	0	0	0
Duckett DT	Don	20/04/1894	Bradford	1970	1927	1928		Halifax Town		36	1	0	0	0	0	0	0
Duffield A	Bert	03/03/1894	Owston Ferry	1981	1925	1927		Leeds United		51	4	0	0	0	0	0	0
Dunlop WL	Billy	20/02/1926	Airdrie		1953			Bristol Rovers	Darlington	36	3	0	0	12	1	0	0
Eccles AP	Arthur				1908			Amateur		1	1	0	0	0	1	0	0
Elliott WH	Billy	20/03/1925	Bradford		1946	1950	e	Juniors	Burnley	176	10	0	0	21	3	0	0
Elwood JH	Jimmy	12/06/1901	Belfast	1937	1928	1932	i	Chesterfield	Derry City	106	13	0	0	1	0	0	0
Evans R	Reuben	19/03/1941	Dublin		1963			Rangers	Scarborough	13	2	1	0	5	1	0	0
Eyre SF	Fred	03/02/1944	Manchester		1969			Chorley	Oswestry Town	1	0	0	0	0	0	0	0
Fagan JF	Joe	12/03/1921	Liverpool	2001	1953			Manchester City		3	0	0	0	0	0	0	0
Farr TF	Chick	19/02/1914	Bathgate	1980	1934	1949		Blackburn Ath.	retired	294	21	0	0	0	0	0	0

Name		D.O.B	Place of Birth	Died	First Season	Last Season	lin	Previous Club	Next Club	Appearances Lge	FAC	FLC	Oth.	Goals Lge	FAC	FLC	Oth.
Farrell A	Arthur	01/10/1920	Huddersfield		1945	1950		Amateur	Barnsley	156	14	0	0	4	2	0	0
Fazackerley MA	Mick	08/04/1932	Manchester		1955			Bradford City		2	0	0	0	0	0	0	0
Featherstone K	Keith	30/08/1935	Bradford		1955			Wyke Celtic		1	0	0	0	0	0	0	0
Fell G	Gerry	03/12/1898	Barnsley	1977	1921	1927		Barnsley	Chesterfield	184	15	0	0	6	1	0	0
Field FS	Fred	12/06/1914	Mansfield		1933			Welbeck Colliery	Mansfield Town	1	0	0	0	1	0	0	0
Fitzsimmons EJ	Eric	23/10/1948	Oldham		1969	1970		Amateur	retired	1	0	0	17	0	0	0	3
Flowers GA	George	07/05/1907	Darlaston		1936			Doncaster Rovers	Tranmere Rovers	10	0	0	0	1	0	0	0
Flynn P	Peter	11/10/1936	Glasgow		1958	1965		Leeds United	retired	131	3	4	0	9	1	0	0
Foulkes JB	Jabez	28/08/1913	Fryston		1936	1937		Stockport Co.	Halifax Town	47	3	0	0	3	0	0	0
France P	Peter	27/03/1936	Huddersfield		1957			Huddersfield T		16	1	0	0	0	0	0	0
Fraser A	Alec	1883	Inverness		1907	1908		Fulham	Middlesbrough	17	3	0	6	5	5	0	0
Freeborough J	Jimmy	13/02/1879	Stockport	1961	1908			Leeds City	Rochdale	10	3	0	0	0	0	0	0
Fryatt JE	Jim	02/09/1940	Swaythling		1963	1965		Southend Utd.	Southport	101	1	6	0	38	1	4	0
Gallon JW	Jack	12/02/1914	Burradon	1993	1937	1938		Bradford City	Swansea Town	31	1	0	0	4	1	0	0
Garry E	Ted	1885	Dumbarton	1955	1913	1914		Derby County	Dumbarton	44	2	0	0	0	0	0	0
Gebbie RBR	Bert	18/11/1934	Cambuslang		1960	1963		Queen of the South	Morecambe	112	3	5	0	0	0	0	0
Geddes JG	Jim	25/05/1942	Burntisland		1965			Third Lanark	Cape Town (SA)	1	0	0	0	0	0	0	0
Geldard A	Albert	11/04/1914	Bradford	1989	1929	1932	e	Juniors	Everton	34	1	0	0	6	0	0	0
Gibbons AH	Jackie	10/04/1914	Fulham		1945	1946		Tottenham H	Brentford	42	9	0	0	21	8	0	0
Gibson IS	Ian	30/03/1943	Newton Stewart		1959	1961		Accrington Stanley	Middlesbrough	88	3	2	0	18	0	0	0
Gibson JS	Steve	02/05/1949	Huddersfield		1967	1968		Huddersfield T	Bridlington Trin.	32	1	0	0	0	0	0	0
Giles JE	John	07/11/1947	Bristol		1967			Bristol City (loan)		9	0	0	0	0	0	0	0
Gilpin J	Jim	12/06/1945	Edinburgh		1965			Raith Rovers	Brora Rangers	11	0	1	0	1	0	0	0
Glasby H	Herbert	21/09/1919	Bradford		1946	1948		Amateur		11	0	0	0	1	0	0	0
Gleadall D	Dennis	15/02/1934	Sheffield		1956	1957		Bury		34	0	0	0	0	0	0	0
Glover A	Alec	28/02/1922	Glasgow		1947	1949		Partick Thistle	Luton Town	48	4	0	0	5	0	0	0
Godfrey C	Cliff	17/02/1909	Baildon		1928	1934		Guiseley	Cardiff City	55	3	0	0	1	0	0	0
Gordon D	Dan	1883	West Calder		1908	1909		Middlesbrough	Hull City	50	3	0	0	0	0	0	0
Gordon HA	Alec	25/07/1940	Livingston	1996	1965	1966		Dundee United	St Johnstone	61	3	5	0	2	0	1	0
Gough HC	Harold	31/12/1890	Chesterfield	1970	1910		e	Spital Olympic	Sheffield Utd.	3	0	0	0	0	0	0	0
Gould G	Geoff	07/01/1945	Blackburn		1962	1968		App.	Notts County	131	6	8	0	18	0	0	0
Graham A	Alex		Coatbridge		1937			Rochdale	Halifax Town	7	0	0	0	0	0	0	0
Green GF	George	22/12/1914	Northowram	1995	1936			Juniors	Huddersfield T	2	0	0	0	0	0	0	0
Green HR	Rodney	24/06/1939	Halifax		1962			Halifax Town	Bradford City	19	0	3	0	6	0	0	0
Green WJ	Billy	1882	Gravesend		1908	1909		Burnley		31	0	0	0	0	0	0	0
Greenwood R	Ron	11/11/1921	Burnley		1945	1947		Chelsea	Brentford	59	11	0	0	0	0	0	0
Grierson RT	Bob				1908			Newcastle United	Rochdale	4	1	0	0	1	3	0	0
Haddington H	Harry	07/08/1931	Scarborough		1952			Scarborough	West Bromwich A.	2	0	0	0	0	0	0	0
Haddock AER	Andy	05/05/1946	Edinburgh		1967			Rotherham Utd.	Chester	5	0	0	0	0	0	0	0
Haines JTW	Jack	24/04/1920	Wickhamford	1987	1949	1953	e	West Bromwich A.	Rochdale	136	12	0	0	34	3	0	0
Hallard W	Billy	28/08/1913	St Helens	1980	1937	1945		Bury	Rochdale	69	12	0	0	5	1	0	0
Halley G	George	29/10/1887	Cronberry		1911	1912		Kilmarnock	Burnley	62	8	0	0	8	0	0	0
Halliday G	Gary	09/05/1951	Bradford		1968			Juniors		1	0	0	0	0	0	0	0
Ham RS	Bobby	29/03/1942	Bradford		1961	1967		Juniors	Huddersfield T	159	7	8	0	53	2	1	0
								Grimsby Town	Bradford City								
Handley TH	Tom	1882	Birmingham		1909	1910		Birmingham		26	1	0	0	0	0	0	0
Hannigan JL	Johnny	17/02/1933	Barrhead		1961	1963		Derby County	Weymouth	96	3	5	0	26	0	2	0
Hanson W	Bill	1887	Rushall		1910			Coventry City		1	0	0	0	0	0	0	0
Hardie JC	John	07/02/1938	Edinburgh		1963	1970		Chester	Crystal Palace	265	9	5	1	0	0	0	0
Harris AT	Tony	20/12/1945	Berrington		1968			Shrewsbury Town	Gloucester City	10	0	1	0	0	0	0	0
Harrison FP	Fred	21/06/1911	Bradford	1986	1934	1935		Amateur	Halifax Town	8	0	0	0	0	0	0	0
Hart J	Jimmy	02/01/1903	Glasgow		1927	1928		Flint	Crewe Alexandra	12	0	0	0	10	0	0	0
Hart PA	Peter	06/09/1949	Wickersley		1967			Rotherham Utd.		3	0	0	0	0	0	0	0
Hartles W	Wilf	1890	Warrington		1920			Runcorn	Accrington Stanley	2	0	0	0	1	0	0	0
Hartwell AW	Ambrose	28/06/1883	Exeter		1908			Birmingham	QPR	21	2	0	0	2	0	0	0
Harvey JH	Jack	06/04/1915	Maidenlaw		1936			Manchester City	Bristol City	3	0	0	0	0	0	0	0
Harvey WJ	William	23/11/1929	Clydebank		1958	1959		Dunfermline Ath.	Arbroath	26	1	0	0	1	2	0	0
Harwood I	Irvine	05/12/1905	Bradford	1973	1929	1931		Amateur	Bradford City	49	6	0	0	27	3	0	0
Hawes AR	Arthur	02/10/1895	Swanton Morley	1963	1927	1928		Sunderland	Accrington Stanley	52	2	0	0	17	1	0	0
Hawthorn W	Willie	1910	Glasgow		1932	1933		Scottish jnr	New Brighton	32	1	0	0	0	0	0	0
Hayes JV	Vince	1879	Miles Platting		1910	1911		Manchester Utd.	Coach (Norway)	29	2	0	0	0	0	0	0
Hays CJ	Jack	12/12/1918	Ashington	1983	1938			Ipswich Town	Burnley	17	1	0	0	0	0	0	0
Hector KJ	Kevin	02/11/1944	Leeds		1962	1966	e	Juniors	Derby County	176	5	10	0	113	2	6	0
Heenan T	Tommy	16/06/1932	Glasgow		1958			Stirling Albion		5	0	0	0	1	0	0	0
Heffron CA	Charlie	13/08/1927	Belfast		1951	1952		Belfast Celtic		25	1	0	0	0	0	0	0
Hellawell JR	John	20/12/1943	Keighley		1968			Darlington	Bromsgrove Rovers	1	0	0	0	0	0	0	0
Hemstock B	Brian	09/02/1949	Goldthorpe		1968			Barnsley	Worksop Town	4	0	0	0	0	0	0	0
Henderson T	Tommy	06/04/1949	Consett		1968	1970		Tow Law Town	York City	22	4	1	51	3	1	0	23
					1972			York City									
Henry GR	Gerry	05/10/1920	Hemsworth	1979	1947	1949		Leeds United	Sheffield Wed.	79	7	0	0	31	1	0	0
Henson GH	George	25/12/1911	Stony Stratford		1937	1938		Swansea Town	Sheffield Utd.	60	5	0	0	33	5	0	0
Hepworth R	Ronnie	25/01/1919	Barnsley		1945	1950		Chesterfield		101	11	0	0	0	0	0	0
Hibbitt K	Ken	03/01/1951	Bradford		1967	1968		Juniors	Wolves	15	0	1	0	0	0	0	0
Hickman GB	Geoff	07/01/1950	West Bromwich		1969			West Bromwich A.		9	1	0	0	0	0	0	0
Hindle FJ	Frank	22/06/1925	Blackburn		1950	1956		Chester	Barrow	204	15	0	0	0	0	0	0
Hirst KRH	Keith	15/10/1932	Bradford		1953			Amateur		1	0	0	0	0	0	0	0
Hodgson D	Don	22/12/1922	Liversedge	1995	1948	1951		Bradford United	York City	41	3	0	0	7	0	0	0
Hodgson H	Harold	24/10/1903	Bradford		1922	1925		Amateur	retired	32	0	0	0	0	0	0	0
Hogan J	Jimmy	02/07/1911	Dublin		1933			Bray Unknowns		4	0	0	0	1	0	0	0

Name		D.O.B	Place of Birth	Died	First Season	Last Season	lin	Previous Club	Next Club	Appearances Lge	FAC	FLC	Oth.	Goals Lge	FAC	FLC	Oth.
Hogg T	Tommy	21/03/1908	Brampton	1965	1929	1930		Amateur	Rochdale	3	0	0	0	0	0	0	0
Hooley JW	Joe	26/12/1938	Hoyland		1959	1960		Workington	Accrington Stanley	13	2	3	0	4	0	1	0
Hopkins M	Mel	07/11/1934	Ystrad Rhondda		1968	1969	w	Ballymena		30	0	1	0	0	0	0	0
Horsfield A	Alec	04/08/1921	Selby	1981	1950			Arsenal		4	0	0	0	2	0	0	0
Horsman L	Les	26/05/1920	Burley-in-Wharfedale	1996	1946	1952		Guiseley	Halifax Town	239	15	0	0	18	0	0	0
Horton H	Henry	18/04/1923	Malvern	1998	1954			Southampton	Hereford	26	0	0	0	0	0	0	0
Hough H	Harry	26/09/1924	Chapeltown		1959	1960		Barnsley	Denaby U (p/mgr)	57	3	0	0	0	0	0	0
Houghton HB	Brian 'Bud'	01/09/1936	Madras, India	1994	1955	1957		Amateur	Birmingham City	28	3	0	0	7	3	0	0
Howie D	David	15/07/1886	Galston	1930	1911	1924		Kilmarnock	retired	306	21	0	0	21	1	0	0
Howling E	Teddy	1885	Stockton	1955	1919	1920		Bristol City		2	0	0	0	0	0	0	0
Hubbert H	Hugh	12/10/1899	Bradford	1966	1922	1926		Amateur	Halifax Town	135	11	0	0	4	1	0	0
Hudson GA	Geoff	14/10/1931	Leeds		1950	1956		Juniors	Bradford City	95	5	0	0	0	0	0	0
Hudson GP	Gary	25/02/1951	Bradford		1967	1970		Juniors		39	0	2	3	0	0	0	0
Hughes RI	Ian	17/03/1946	Cefn Mawr		1967			Wrexham	Rhyl	13	0	1	0	0	0	0	0
Hughes WCJ	Wally	15/03/1934	Dingle		1956	1957		Wisbech Town	Southport	20	0	0	0	0	0	0	0
Humphrey D	Duggie	27/09/1900	Skipton		1921			Amateur	Stockport Co.	7	0	0	0	1	0	0	0
Hunter WN	Willie	07/04/1942	Cambuslang		1964			Rangers	Queen of the South	14	0	0	0	0	0	0	0
I'Anson P	Paul	03/05/1946	Shipley		1963	1967		App.		50	1	3	0	2	0	0	0
James JS	Stan	12/09/1923	South Shields		1945	1950		South Shields		13	4	0	0	1	0	0	0
Jobey G	George	1885	Heddon	1962	1914			Arsenal	Leicester City	14	1	0	0	3	0	0	0
Johnson M	Martin	09/10/1904	Windy Nook		1925	1926		Durham City	Sheffield Utd.	37	1	0	0	6	0	0	0
Johnson T	Tom	05/03/1926	Stockton		1952			Darlington		1	0	0	0	0	0	0	0
Johnstone R	Bob	18/09/1908	Coldstream		1935	1938		Hearts		120	4	0	0	1	0	0	0
Jones H	Herbert	1915	St Helens		1936			Warrington	Sheffield Utd.	10	1	0	0	0	0	0	0
Jones K	Ken	26/06/1944	Havercroft		1962	1964		Monkton Colliery	Southampton	100	3	5	0	3	0	0	0
Jones TC	Tommy		Trehafod		1938			Guildford City		1	0	0	0	0	0	0	0
Jordan C	Colin	02/06/1934	Hemsworth		1953	1956		Fitzwilliam YC	Oldham Athletic	27	2	0	0	0	0	0	0
Kaye G	George		Huddersfield		1938			Juniors	Liverpool	3	0	0	0	0	0	0	0
Keating PJ	Pat	17/09/1930	Cork		1953			Swindon Town	Chesterfield	2	0	0	0	0	0	0	0
Keeling AJ	Alf	14/12/1920	Bradford		1937			Juniors	Portsmouth	1	0	0	0	0	0	0	0
Keen A	Alan	29/05/1930	Barrow		1956			Chesterfield	Carlisle Utd.	11	0	0	0	1	0	0	0
Keetley T	Tom	16/11/1898	Derby	1958	1919	1922		Derby County	Doncaster Rovers	21	2	0	0	5	0	0	0
Kelly JE	Jimmy 'Ned'	29/12/1907	Seaham Harbour	1984	1938			Grimsby Town	York City	2	0	0	0	0	0	0	0
Kelso J	Jimmy	08/12/1910	Cardross	1987	1933			Dumbarton	Port Vale	11	1	0	0	0	0	0	0
Kendall HA	Arnold	06/04/1925	Halifax	2003	1956	1958		Rochdale	Bradford City	90	4	0	0	12	1	0	0
Kennie G	George	17/05/1904	Bradford		1921	1923		Amateur	Mansfield Town	10	0	0	0	0	0	0	0
Kenyon J	Jimmy	1889			1910			Stockport Co.	Stockport Co.	1	0	0	0	0	0	0	0
Kevan DT	Derek	06/03/1935	Ripon		1952		e	Ripon YMCA	West Bromwich A.	15	2	0	0	8	0	0	0
Kilcar SP	Steve	22/12/1907	Bo'ness		1929	1931		East Stirling	Coventry City	27	2	0	0	9	0	0	0
Kirby F	Fred		County Durham		1914			Middlesbrough		10	0	0	0	3	0	0	0
Kirkland A	Alex	26/08/1897	Dublin		1921	1922	r	Pontypridd		27	1	0	0	6	0	0	0
Kivlichan WF	Willie	11/03/1890	Galashiels	1937	1911	1914		Celtic	retired	88	8	0	0	5	0	0	0
Law WGMcK	Billy	26/04/1914	Leith		1937			Penicuik Ath.	Stockport Co.	2	0	0	0	1	0	0	0
Lawrie S	Sam	15/12/1934	Denistoun	1979	1962	1965		Charlton Ath.	retired	73	2	2	0	16	0	1	0
Lawson D	David	22/12/1947	Wallsend		1967	1968		Shrewsbury Town	Huddersfield T	13	0	0	0	0	0	0	0
Lawton HM	Malcolm	07/11/1935	Leeds		1957	1962		Leeds United	retired	113	6	3	0	0	0	0	0
Laycock A	Alf	29/09/1895	Low Moor	1964	1921	1924		Amateur	Southport	7	0	0	0	0	0	0	0
Layton WH	Bill	13/01/1915	Shirley	1984	1946	1948		Reading	Colchester Utd.	47	0	0	0	5	0	0	0
Leavey HJ	Bert	1886	Guildford		1913			Barnsley	Portsmouth	19	1	0	0	1	0	0	0
Leedham FA	Fred	21/02/1909	Lye	1996	1931	1932		Kidderminster Harr.	Accrington Stanley	49	1	0	0	6	1	0	0
Leonard H	Harry	19/05/1924	Jarrow		1945	1947		Darlington	Hartlepool Utd.	1	1	0	0	0	0	0	0
Leuty LH	Leon	23/10/1920	Meole Brace	1955	1949	1950		Derby County	Notts County	19	0	0	0	0	0	0	0
Lewis AN	Norman	13/06/1908	Wolverhampton		1936			Stoke City	Tranmere Rovers	2	0	0	0	0	0	0	0
Lewis TH	Tommy	11/10/1909	Ellesmere Port		1933	1938		Wrexham	Blackpool	193	7	0	0	66	3	0	0
Lightbown TJ	Trevor	21/11/1939	Blackburn		1960			Accrington Stanley		2	0	0	0	0	0	0	0
Lightowler GB	Gerry	05/09/1940	Bradford		1958	1967		Amateur	Bradford City	209	9	11	0	1	1	0	0
Lindley U	Urban	07/12/1912	Sheffield		1937	1938		Preston NE		60	4	0	0	0	0	0	0
Liney P	Pat	14/07/1936	Paisley		1966	1973		St Mirren	Bradford City	11	1	4	6	0	0	0	0
Little J	Joe		Dumfries		1912					6	0	0	0	0	0	0	0
Little J	Joe	25/01/1902	Leeds	1965	1927			Darlington	Rotherham Utd.	2	1	0	0	1	0	0	0
Little TSC	Tommy	27/02/1890	Ilford		1908	1920		Southend Utd.	Stoke City	231	16	0	0	106	5	0	0
Lloyd RG	Geoff	18/08/1942	Wrexham		1967			Wrexham	Rhyl	32	3	0	0	10	2	0	0
Lloyd T	Tommy	17/11/1903	Wednesbury	1984	1927	1936		Sunderland	Burton Town	328	22	0	0	17	0	0	0
Loftus R	Bob	15/12/1931	Liverpool		1955			Llanelly		3	0	0	0	0	0	0	0
Logan JH	Jimmy	17/10/1885	Dunbar		1909	1911		Bradford City	Raith Rovers	59	2	0	0	3	1	0	0
Loughran T	Tommy	02/11/1893	South Bank	1972	1919	1921		Amateur		22	0	0	0	3	0	0	0
Lowson F	Frank	13/12/1895	Forfar	1969	1921	1922		Dundee	Exeter City	12	0	0	0	2	0	0	0
Lynn S	Sammy	25/12/1920	St Helens	1995	1950	1952		Manchester Utd.		73	6	0	0	0	0	0	0
Lyons B	Brian	03/12/1948	Darfield		1967			Houghton Main		3	0	0	0	0	0	0	0
Lyons T	Terry	14/04/1929	Bradford		1951	1952		Burnley		38	5	0	0	6	3	0	0
McAllister J	Jimmy	30/10/1931	Barrhead		1959	1960		Morton	Bangor City	43	2	1	0	14	0	0	0
McBride PP	Peter	22/12/1946	Motherwell		1967			Southport	Morecambe	7	0	1	0	0	0	0	0
McCall J	Johnny	29/09/1918	Glasgow	1992	1937	1947		Workington		41	1	0	0	5	0	0	0
McCalman DS	Don	18/10/1935	Greenock		1959	1965		Hibernian	Barrow	297	8	13	0	5	0	0	0
McCandless J	Jack	29/02/1888	Coleraine	1940	1911	1922	i	Linfield	Accrington Stanley	190	11	0	0	21	2	0	0
McCandless TB	Tom		Belfast		1928			Barn FC	Charlton Ath.	6	0	0	0	0	0	0	0
McClarence JP	Joe	1885	Newcastle		1908	1910		Bolton Wanderers	Distillery	63	5	0	0	31	2	0	0
McClelland J	Jim	11/05/1902	Dysart		1933	1935		Blackpool	Manchester Utd.	100	8	0	0	10	0	0	0
McCluggage A	Andy	01/09/1900	Larne	1954	1922	1924	i	Cliftonville	Burnley	85	9	0	0	2	0	0	0

Name		D.O.B	Place of Birth	Died	First Season	Last Season	lin	Previous Club	Next Club	Appearances Lge	FAC	FLC	Oth.	Goals Lge	FAC	FLC	Oth.
McConnell WG	Bill		Ireland		1912	1914		Amateur		10	0	0	0	0	0	0	0
McCulloch A	Alex	1886	Edinburgh		1908			Brentford	Lincoln City	7	1	0	0	1	0	0	0
McDonald DR	Roy	12/04/1894	East Wemyss	1970	1921	1922		Tottenham H		27	2	0	0	0	0	0	0
McDonald HL	Hugh	20/12/1881	Kilwinning	1920	1911	1912		Oldham Athletic	Arsenal	26	3	0	0	0	0	0	0
McDonald K	Ken	24/04/1898	Llanrwst		1923	1927		Manchester Utd.	Hull City	145	7	0	0	135	3	0	0
McGarry T	Tommy	28/09/1918	Heworth	1983	1938			Hartlepool Utd.		9	0	0	0	2	0	0	0
McGillivray F	Findlay	19/03/1940	Newtongrange		1966			Rangers	St Johnstone	39	3	4	0	0	0	0	0
McGloughlin FJ	Frank	04/07/1898	Dublin		1921	1925		Pontypridd	Bristol Rovers	77	3	0	0	1	0	0	0
McGrath J	Jimmy	04/03/1907	Washington		1934	1937		Notts County	retired	83	7	0	0	2	0	0	0
McGrath M	Mick	07/04/1936	Dublin		1965	1966	r	Blackburn Rovers	Bangor C (p/mgr)	50	2	4	0	2	0	0	0
MacGregor C	Colin	13/11/1940	Bradford		1958	1959		Bradford City		3	0	0	0	0	0	0	0
McHard A	Archie	10/06/1934	Dumbarton		1959	1960		Clyde		27	3	0	0	3	0	0	0
McIlvenny HJ	Harry	05/10/1922	Bradford		1946	1949		Yorkshire Ams.	Bishop Auckland	43	4	0	0	17	1	0	0
McLaren A	Andy	24/01/1922	Larkhall	1996	1954		s	Barrow	Southport	18	2	0	0	7	1	0	0
McLaughlin J	Jimmy				1913			Amateur		1	0	0	0	0	0	0	0
McLean DP	David	13/12/1887	Forfar	1967	1919	1921	s	Sheffield Wed.	Dundee	85	7	0	0	49	6	0	0
McLean G	George	24/08/1897	Forfar	1970	1921	1930		Forfar	Huddersfield T	250	15	0	0	136	3	0	0
McMillan G	George	28/03/1904	Armadale		1930	1932		Rangers	Bath City	54	4	0	0	10	1	0	0
McNestry G	George	07/01/1908	Chopwell	1998	1926			Amateur	Doncaster Rovers	14	0	0	0	1	0	0	0
MacPhee MG	Tony	30/04/1914	Edinburgh	1960	1936			Workington	Coventry City	30	1	0	0	18	0	0	0
McTaff S	Steve	11/03/1922	Tanfield	1983	1945	1947		Eden Colliery	New Brighton	29	2	0	0	0	0	0	0
McVee W	Bill	26/11/1901	Blackwood, Lanarks.	1977	1925	1926		Scottish am.	Weymouth	16	0	0	0	0	0	0	0
Madden P	Peter	31/10/1934	Bradford		1966			Rotherham Utd.	Aldershot	28	2	4	0	1	1	0	0
Malan NF	Norman	23/11/1923	Johannesburg, SA		1956			Scunthorpe Utd.		24	2	0	0	0	0	0	0
Manderson R	Bertie	09/05/1893	Belfast	1946	1927		i	Rangers	retired	39	1	0	0	0	0	0	0
Manning JT	Jack	1886	Boston	1946	1907	1909		Hull City	Rochdale	47	3	0	31	9	3	0	5
March JE	John	12/05/1940	Norwich		1961	1962		Norwich City	retired	62	1	4	0	1	0	0	0
Marron C	Chris	07/02/1925	Jarrow	1986	1954			Mansfield Town		2	0	0	0	1	0	0	0
Marshall W	Bill	13/04/1914	Falkirk		1935	1937		Blackburn Ath.	retired	13	0	0	0	0	0	0	0
Martin WJ	Billy	12/06/1913	Glasgow		1936	1938		Shawfield Jnrs.		60	4	0	0	8	1	0	0
Mason R	Bob		Burnbank		1909	1913		Clyde	Stalybridge Celtic	118	9	0	0	0	0	0	0
Massie L	Les	20/07/1935	Aberdeen		1969	1971		Halifax Town	Workington	14	0	0	34	2	0	0	9
Matthews RW	Billy	04/04/1897	Plas Bennion	1987	1925	1929	w	Barrow	Stockport Co.	112	2	0	0	5	0	0	0
Maven 'Mavin' FJ	Fred	1884	Newcastle	1957	1913	1914		Fulham	Reading	13	2	0	0	1	0	0	0
Maxwell H	Hugh	14/05/1938	Rigghead		1961	1962		Stirling Albion	Falkirk	12	0	1	0	5	0	1	0
Maxwell K	Ken	11/02/1928	Glasgow		1957			Northampton Town		2	0	0	0	0	0	0	0
Meek J	Joe	31/05/1910	Hazlerigg	1976	1934	1935		Gateshead	Tottenham H	31	6	0	0	11	1	0	0
Milburn J	Jim	21/06/1919	Ashington	1985	1952	1954		Leeds United		90	4	0	0	10	0	0	0
Miles D	Denis	06/08/1936	Normanton		1953	1954		Juniors	Southport	24	3	0	0	1	1	0	0
Millership W	Walter	08/06/1910	Warsop Vale	1978	1927	1929		Amateur	Sheffield Wed.	30	4	0	0	13	1	0	0
Milner J	John	14/05/1942	Huddersfield		1966			Lincoln City	Boston Beacons (USA)	8	0	0	0	0	0	0	0
Milnes C	Charlie	1885	Manchester	1956	1907	1910		Grimsby Town	Huddersfield T	83	6	0	29	4	1	0	2
Milsom P	Percy				1908			Millwall		2	0	0	0	0	0	0	0
Minshull R	Ray	15/07/1920	Bolton		1957	1958		Southport	Wigan Rovers (p/mgr)	28	0	0	0	0	0	0	0
Moody J	Jack	10/11/1903	Heeley		1929			Arsenal	Doncaster Rovers	6	0	0	0	0	0	0	0
Mordue J	Jimmy	18/02/1924	Seaton Delaval		1948			North Shields		2	0	0	0	0	0	0	0
Morfitt JW	Jack	28/09/1908	Sheffield	1973	1931			Blackpool	Southend Utd.	9	0	0	0	5	0	0	0
Morgan C	Charlie	1882	Bootle		1909			Tottenham H		1	0	0	0	0	0	0	0
Morton R	Bobby	03/03/1906	Widdrington	1990	1931			Newark Town	Port Vale	6	0	0	0	0	0	0	0
Munro D	Dan		Forres		1910	1913		Celtic	Port Vale	85	10	0	0	3	0	0	0
Murfin C	Clarrie	02/04/1909	Barnsley	1954	1934	1935		Gainsborough Trin.	Brighton & Hove A.	5	4	0	0	1	0	0	0
Myerscough J	Joe	08/08/1893	Galgate	1975	1923	1926		Manchester Utd.		120	11	0	0	47	2	0	0
Neil WM	Billy	20/04/1924	Lanark		1947			Morton Workington	Workington	3	0	0	0	0	0	0	0
Newton LF	Frank	28/10/1883	Denaby	1959	1909	1910	w	Oldham Athletic	Burnley	33	2	0	0	13	3	0	0
Nicholls JH	Jim	27/11/1919	Coseley		1946	1949		Amateur	Rochdale	36	1	0	0	0	0	0	0
Nicholson H	Horace	19/07/1895	Mexborough		1920	1922		Mexborough T	Wath Ath.	25	0	0	0	0	0	0	0
Noble WD	Bill	1883	Wellingborough	1947	1909			Barnsley	Rotherham Town	2	0	0	0	0	0	0	0
Nolan TG	Tommy 'Wilf'	13/06/1909	Preston		1935	1936		Port Vale	Port Vale	36	6	0	0	14	3	0	0
O'Donnell D	Dennis	1880	Willington Quay		1908			Notts County		10	3	0	0	1	3	0	0
Oliver J	Jack	21/09/1946	Bradford		1965			Bradford City	Heanor Town	1	0	0	0	0	0	0	0
O'Rourke H	Harry				1907	1908		Bathgate		11	2	0	38	0	0	0	3
O'Rourke P	Peter	14/03/1903	Newmains		1924			Juniors	Northampton Town	3	0	0	0	2	0	0	0
Padgett JM	Jack	30/11/1916	Ilkeston		1938			Bradford City		1	0	0	0	1	0	0	0
Parker J	Jonathan 'Jim'		Barrow		1908	1912		Burnley	Barrow	80	1	0	0	4	0	0	0
Parkinson A	Alan	05/05/1932	Normanton		1951	1954		Juniors		13	0	0	0	4	0	0	0
Parris JE	Eddie	31/01/1911	Pwllmeyric	1971	1928	1933	w	Trialist	Bournemouth	133	9	0	0	38	1	0	0
Parrish H	Bert		Shelf		1929			Amateur		1	0	0	0	0	0	0	0
Paton HM	Hugh	08/09/1918	Glasgow		1938			Shettleston		13	0	0	0	1	0	0	0
Peacock LV	Leo	1903	Apperley Bridge		1924	1925		Apperley B		9	3	0	0	0	0	0	0
Peel HB	Harold	26/03/1900	Bradford	1976	1920	1926		Calverley	Arsenal	207	16	0	0	37	3	0	0
Peel T	Trevor	25/10/1945	Huddersfield		1966	1967		Huddersfield T	Chorley	11	0	1	0	0	0	0	0
Penrose CR	Colin	01/11/1949	Bradford		1968			Sedburgh YC	Oldham Athletic	6	0	0	0	1	0	0	0
Perry A	Arthur	15/10/1932	Doncaster		1956	1957		Hull City	Rotherham Utd.	60	3	0	0	0	0	0	0
Phillips D	David	25/12/1917	Glasgow		1938			Haddon United		1	0	0	0	0	0	0	0
Pickard LJ	Len	29/11/1924	Barnstaple		1953	1955		Bristol City		76	6	0	0	31	3	0	0
Picken W	Billy	29/03/1916	Glasgow		1936	1938		Bridgeton Waverley		34	1	0	0	0	0	0	0
Pickup JA	Tony	03/12/1931	Wakefield		1955			Frickley Colliery		2	0	0	0	0	0	0	0
Pilling VJ	Vince	08/01/1932	Bolton		1955			Bolton Wanderers		9	0	0	0	1	0	0	0

Name		D.O.B	Place of Birth	Died	First Season	Last Season	lin	Previous Club	Next Club	Appearances Lge	Appearances FAC	Appearances FLC	Appearances Oth.	Goals Lge	Goals FAC	Goals FLC	Goals Oth.
Postlethwaite TW	Tom	04/09/1909	Haverthwaite		1934			Barrow	Northampton Town	19	1	0	0	1	0	0	0
Potts JF	Joe	25/02/1891	Newcastle		1925	1926		Chesterfield		38	4	0	0	0	0	0	0
Poyntz WI	Billy	18/03/1894	Tylorstown	1966	1925	1926		Northampton Town	Crewe Alexandra	33	4	0	0	5	0	0	0
Pringle CR	Charlie	18/10/1894	Nilshill		1929	1930	s	Manchester Central	Lincoln City	44	0	0	0	1	0	0	0
Purdon JS	Jimmy	14/03/1906	Springburn	1985	1931	1933		Rangers	Crystal Palace	44	1	0	0	0	0	0	0
Quantrill AE	Alf	22/01/1897	Punjab, India	1968	1924	1929	e	Preston NE	Nottm. Forest	191	11	0	0	57	1	0	0
Rafferty B	Bernard	09/07/1948	Manchester		1969	1970		Amateur		13	2	0	4	1	0	0	3
Rafferty J	Jim	07/11/1930	Manchester		1952			Manchester City		2	0	0	0	0	0	0	0
Rawlings A	Archie	02/10/1891	Leicester	1952	1926	1927	e	Walsall	Southport	21	0	0	0	5	0	0	0
Redfearn B	Brian	20/02/1935	Bradford		1952	1957		Juniors	Blackburn Rovers	130	6	0	0	32	0	0	0
Reeves G	George	1884	Hucknall	1954	1909	1912		Aston Villa	Blackpool	58	5	0	0	17	5	0	0
Reid A	Andy		Aberdeen		1928	1929		Burnley	Reading	12	0	0	0	0	0	0	0
Reid DA	David	03/01/1923	Glasgow		1950	1951		Rochdale	Workington	13	0	0	0	0	0	0	0
Reid GT	Geordie		Blackland Mill		1907	1908		Middlesbrough	Brentford	5	1	0	32	0	3	0	15
Reilly FMcC	Felix	12/09/1933	Wallyford		1959	1961		Portsmouth	Crewe Alexandra	31	0	1	0	12	0	0	0
Reilly TJ	Terry	01/07/1924	High Valleyfield		1955			Southport	Dunfermline	14	0	0	0	0	0	0	0
Rhodes WT	Trevor	10/11/1909	Leeds		1928	1932		Amateur	Port Vale	57	4	0	0	39	2	0	0
Roberts A	Alan	23/04/1946	Bury		1969	1970		Mossley	Mossley	15	2	0	35	0	0	0	0
Roberts C	Colin	16/09/1933	Castleford		1953	1955		Altofts Wed.	Frickley Colliery	75	5	0	0	0	0	0	0
Robertson AJ	Alf	02/07/1908	Sunderland	1984	1930	1932		Grantham	Leyton Orient	45	3	0	0	0	0	0	0
Robertson JH	Jimmy	22/03/1913	Berwick-on-Tweed	1973	1932	1937		Welbeck Colliery	Bradford City	130	6	0	0	58	2	0	0
Robinson C	Cyril	04/03/1929	Nottingham		1956	1958		Northwich Vic.	Southport	89	5	0	0	3	0	0	0
Robinson PB	Phil	21/11/1942	Doncaster		1966	1968		Doncaster Rovers	Darlington	116	7	6	0	8	2	0	0
Robinson WA	Billy	30/12/1898	Pegswood Colliery	1975	1928			Hartlepools Utd.	Lincoln City	5	1	0	0	1	0	0	0
Robson J	Joe	21/03/1903	Gateshead	1969	1932			Huddersfield T	Gainsborough Trin.	15	2	0	0	4	3	0	0
Rodger W	Willie	24/06/1947	Dalkeith		1965	1966		Newton Grange Star		8	0	0	0	0	0	0	0
Rogers CW	Bill	09/10/1901	Bradford	1977	1925			Liverpool		4	0	0	0	0	0	0	0
Ross AC	Albert	07/10/1916	York		1936	1937		Middlesbrough	Chester	20	2	0	0	0	0	0	0
Routledge RW	Ron	14/10/1937	Ashington		1958	1961		Sunderland	Ashington	39	2	0	0	0	0	0	0
Rowley J	John	23/06/1944	Wolverhampton		1967			Shrewsbury Town	Buxton	35	2	0	0	0	0	0	0
Rushby A	Alan	27/12/1933	Doncaster		1957	1958		Mansfield Town		12	0	0	0	0	0	0	0
Sanaghan J	Joe	12/12/1914	Motherwell	1951	1935			Blantyre Celtic	Bournemouth	4	0	0	0	0	0	0	0
Saville PW	Peter	29/08/1948	Dalbeattie		1968	1969		Hawick RA		31	1	0	0	1	0	0	0
Scaife S	Sam	10/02/1909	Otley	1981	1932			Yeadon Celtic	Rochdale	2	0	0	0	0	0	0	0
Scattergood EO	Ernie	29/05/1887	Riddings	1932	1914	1924	e	Derby County	Alfreton Town	268	20	0	0	5	1	0	0
Schofield HW	Harold	22/05/1903	Manchester	1975	1925	1928		Amateur	Chesterfield	17	4	0	0	0	0	0	0
Scott H	Harry	04/08/1897	Newburn		1928	1931		Hull City	Swansea Town	69	8	0	0	20	1	0	0
Scott JMA	Jack		Motherwell		1909	1920		Hamilton Ac.	Manchester Utd.	245	21	0	0	3	0	0	0
Scoular J	Jimmy	11/01/1925	Livingston	1998	1960	1963	s	Newcastle United	Cardiff C (mgr)	108	4	7	0	5	0	0	0
Sellars W	Billy	07/10/1907	Sheffield	1987	1934			Burnley	Lincoln City	2	0	0	0	1	0	0	0
Shackleton LF	Len	03/05/1922	Bradford	2000	1945	1946	e	Arsenal	Newcastle United	7	8	0	0	4	1	0	0
Sharp W	Wilf	08/04/1907	Bathgate		1936			Sheffield Wed.		17	1	0	0	1	0	0	0
Shearer S	Sammy				1912			Nithsdale Wan.	(to USA)	1	0	0	0	0	0	0	0
Simpson RA	Bobby	1888	Chorlton-cum-Hardy		1910	1912		Aberdeen	Brighton & Hove A.	53	3	0	0	8	1	0	0
Singleton TW	Tommy	08/09/1940	Blackpool		1968			Chester	Fleetwood	32	1	1	0	1	0	0	0
Sirrel J	Jimmy	02/02/1922	Glasgow		1949	1950		Celtic	Brighton & Hove A.	12	0	0	0	2	0	0	0
Smith A	Albert	28/04/1887	Burnley		1908	1909		Burnley	Grimsby Town	55	1	0	0	10	2	0	0
Smith A	Alec	04/09/1927	Dundee	1991	1949	1950		Blackpool		5	0	0	0	0	0	0	0
Smith CF	Cliff		Bradford		1919			Amateur		3	0	0	0	1	0	0	0
Smith FA	Fred	16/04/1914	Liverpool	1982	1938			Bury		29	1	0	0	21	0	0	0
Smith J	Jimmy	1889	Stafford	1918	1912	1914		Brighton		90	10	0	0	52	8	0	0
Smith JA	John	27/08/1905	West Melton		1926	1932		Amateur		57	7	0	0	4	0	0	0
Smith JB	Barry	15/03/1934	South Kirkby		1955	1956		Leeds United	Wrexham	64	2	0	0	38	1	0	0
Smith JW	Jackie	27/05/1920	St Pancras	1991	1945	1952		Avro Works	Grantham	204	11	0	0	26	1	0	0
Speedie FB	Finlay	18/08/1880	Dumbarton	1953	1908		s	Oldham Athletic	Dumbarton	5	0	0	0	1	0	0	0
Spooner PG	Peter	30/08/1910	Hepscott	1987	1930			Ashington	York City	5	0	0	0	1	0	0	0
Spratt T	Tommy	20/12/1941	Cambois		1960	1963		Manchester Utd.	Torquay United	118	2	6	0	45	0	3	0
Stabb GH	George	26/09/1912	Paignton	1994	1936	1946		Port Vale	training staff	94	5	0	0	4	1	0	0
Stephen JF	Jimmy	23/08/1922	Fettercairn		1946	1948	s	Johnshaven	Portsmouth	94	5	0	0	1	0	0	0
Stevens LWG	Les	15/08/1920	Croydon	1991	1948	1949		Tottenham H	Crystal Palace	44	1	0	0	4	0	0	0
Stirling J	Jock		Clydebank	1924	1914			Middlesbrough	Stoke City	31	3	0	0	2	0	0	0
Storey S	Sid	25/12/1919	Darfield		1959			Accrington Stanley	York C (training staff)	2	0	0	0	0	0	0	0
Strange AH	Alf	02/04/1900	Marehay	1978	1935		e	Sheffield Wed.	Ripley Town	10	0	0	0	0	0	0	0
Suddards J	Jeff	17/01/1929	Bradford		1949	1958		Hull City	Cambridge City	327	16	0	0	0	0	0	0
Suggett EJ	Ernie	03/12/1907	Pelaw	1971	1932	1935		Barrow	ret	108	3	0	0	42	1	0	0
Sullivan C	Con	06/06/1903	Tynemouth		1929			Hull City	Carlisle Utd.	2	0	0	0	0	0	0	0
Sumpner RA	Richard	12/04/1947	Leeds		1966			Leeds United	Frickley Colliery	2	0	0	0	1	0	0	0
Sykes J	John	02/11/1950	Huddersfield		1968			App.	Wrexham	1	0	0	0	0	0	0	0
Symonds A	Tony	10/11/1944	Wakefield		1964	1966		Gt Preston Jnrs	Fulham	29	2	2	0	2	3	1	0
Talbot AD	Alec	13/07/1902	Cannock	1975	1935			Aston Villa	Stourbridge	6	0	0	0	1	0	0	0
Tanner GG	Graham	04/09/1947	Bridgwater		1967	1968		Bristol City	Scarborough	44	4	0	0	2	0	0	0
Tasker H	Hiram	06/11/1898	Bradford	1968	1923			Amateur		4	0	0	0	0	0	0	0
Taylor HW	Harold	18/11/1902	Frizinghall	1963	1921	1931		Amateur	Southport	334	25	0	0	15	0	0	0
Taylor JB	Brian	07/10/1931	Rossington		1954	1955		King's Lynn		66	5	0	0	0	0	0	0
Taylor JE	Jack	11/09/1924	Chilton		1957			Notts County	ret	12	0	0	0	6	0	0	0
Taylor K	Ken	21/08/1935	Huddersfield		1964	1966		Huddersfield T	ret	51	2	3	0	1	0	0	0
Tewkesbury KC	Ken	10/04/1909	Hove	1970	1935			Aston Villa	Walsall	14	1	0	0	0	0	0	0
Tewley AB	Alan	22/01/1945	Leicester		1969	1970		Leicester City	Crewe Alexandra	28	0	0	5	4	0	0	2
Thackeray J	Jim		Hebburn		1910			Middlesbrough	West Stanley (p/mgr)	33	2	0	0	3	1	0	0

Name		D.O.B	Place of Birth	Died	First Season	Last Season	lin	Previous Club	Next Club	Appearances				Goals			
										Lge	FAC	FLC	Oth.	Lge	FAC	FLC	Oth.
Thom LMcD	Lewis	10/04/1944	Stornoway		1969			Lincoln City	Altrincham	31	0	1	0	1	0	0	0
Thomas GP	Geoff	12/03/1946	Bradford		1963	1965		App.		53	2	1	0	0	0	0	0
Thompson A	Albert	1912	Llanbradach		1934	1936		Barry	York City	11	0	0	0	2	0	0	0
Thompson EG	Ernie	1892	Rotherham		1922	1923		Sheffield Wed.	Grimsby Town	50	2	0	0	2	0	0	0
Thomson J	John				1912	1913		Amateur		8	0	0	0	0	0	0	0
Tomlinson T	Tommy	1890	Sheffield		1909			Chesterfield	Mexborough	4	1	0	0	4	0	0	0
Torrance G	George	01/03/1914	Glasgow		1933			Benburb		1	0	0	0	0	0	0	0
Turnbull G	George	21/08/1899	South Shields	1928	1926	1927		Durham City		27	2	0	0	0	0	0	0
Turnbull JMcL	Jimmy	23/05/1884	Bannockburn		1910	1911		Manchester Utd.	Chelsea	49	3	0	0	19	2	0	0
Turnbull RJ	Bobby	17/12/1895	South Bank	1952	1919	1924	e	South Bank	Leeds United	207	16	0	0	47	2	0	0
Turner A	Alan	05/07/1943	Hull		1967			Shrewsbury Town	Wigan Athletic	32	0	1	0	4	0	0	0
Turner PS	Phil	20/02/1927	Frodsham		1951	1953		Carlisle Utd.	Scunthorpe Utd.	55	4	0	0	24	5	0	0
Vandermotten W	Willie	26/08/1930	Glasgow	1979	1952			Third Lanark		1	0	0	0	0	0	0	0
Waddell R	Bobby	05/09/1939	Kirkcaldy		1966			Blackpool	East Fife	20	1	0	0	3	1	0	0
Waite GH	George	01/03/1894	Bradford	1972	1919			Amateur	Raith Rovers	6	0	0	0	0	0	0	0
Walker J	Jimmy	25/08/1933	Aberdeen		1959	1963		Aberdeen	Corby Town	144	6	5	0	2	0	0	0
Walker M	Mick	08/03/1952	Mexborough		1968	1969		App.		4	1	0	0	0	0	0	0
Walker R	Bob	06/04/1903	Bradford	1952	1923			Bradford City	New Brighton	4	0	0	0	0	0	0	0
Walker W	Willis	24/11/1892	Gosforth	1991	1925			South Shields	Stockport Co.	34	2	0	0	0	0	0	0
Wallace H	Hugh				1911			Dumbarton		4	0	0	0	0	0	0	0
Wallbanks J	John	13/07/1905	Hindley	1979	1934			Chester	Glenavon	11	0	0	0	2	0	0	0
Walton RW	Bob				1907	1908		Newcastle United		8	2	0	22	0	0	0	0
Ward D	Denis	25/10/1924	Burton Joyce		1955	1957		Stockport Co.		50	0	0	0	0	0	0	0
Ward LW	Whelan 'Polly'	15/06/1929	Ovenden		1955	1958		King's Lynn	Nelson	108	4	0	0	31	2	0	0
Ward R	Bob	1881	Glasgow		1908			Sunderland		7	3	0	0	0	0	0	0
Ward RA	Ralph	05/02/1911	Oadby		1930	1935		Hinckley United	Tottenham H	129	8	0	0	0	0	0	0
Ward W	Wilkie	1884	Rochdale		1907	1908		Oldham Athletic	Rossendale U	18	3	0	6	2	2	0	1
Waterall TW	Tommy	24/10/1884	Radford	1951	1908			Notts County	Leicester City	4	2	0	0	0	2	0	0
Watson A	Alex	02/08/1889	Stirling		1911	1919		Clyde	Halifax Town	151	14	0	0	0	0	0	0
Wesley JC	Jack	19/01/1908	Cheltenham		1934	1938		Gateshead		141	13	0	0	25	2	0	0
Whaley K	Ken	22/06/1935	Leeds		1958			Amateur		1	0	0	0	0	0	0	0
Wheat AB	Arthur	26/10/1921	Selston		1950	1951		Montrose	York City	22	3	0	0	3	0	0	0
Whitaker C	Colin	14/06/1932	Leeds		1953	1955		Sheffield Wed.	Shrewsbury Town	49	6	0	0	10	2	0	0
White RBW	Ray	13/08/1918	Bootle	1988	1946	1950		Tottenham H		151	8	0	0	3	0	0	0
Whittle E	Ernie	25/11/1925	Lanchester	1998	1957			Chesterfield	Scarborough	18	1	0	0	6	0	0	0
Whyte C	Crawford	04/12/1907	Wallsend	1984	1935			Blackburn Rovers	Tranmere Rovers	9	0	0	0	0	0	0	0
Wightman JR	Jock	02/11/1912	Duns	1964	1934			York City	Huddersfield T	17	1	0	0	0	0	0	0
Wilcox JC	Joe	19/01/1894	Coleford	1956	1922	1923		Bristol City	New Brighton	21	1	0	0	5	0	0	0
Wilkins EG	George	27/10/1917	Hackney		1946	1947		Brentford	Nottm. Forest	27	0	0	0	6	0	0	0
Williams A	Alvan	21/11/1932	Penmon		1957	1959		Wrexham	Exeter City	92	3	0	0	21	0	0	0
Williams D	Derek	28/01/1937	Wardley		1962			Grimsby Town	Skegness	19	1	0	0	8	0	0	0
Williams HT	Harold	17/06/1924	Britton Ferry		1957		w	Newport County	retired	15	0	0	0	0	0	0	0
Williamson JI	Ian	14/03/1939	Larbert		1962			Norwich City	King's Lynn	17	1	2	0	0	0	0	0
Wilson JE	Jimmy	01/01/1909	Garforth		1933			Sutton Town	Bristol City	1	0	0	0	0	0	0	0
Wilson RS	Bob		Cambuslang		1924			Third Lanark	(USA)	27	5	0	0	22	3	0	0
Wolstenholme T	Tom				1908	1909		Burnley	Nelson	39	4	0	0	1	0	0	0
Woods W	Billy	12/03/1926	Farnworth		1946			Rochdale	Rochdale	5	0	0	0	0	0	0	0
Woolmer AJ	Tony	25/03/1946	Swardeston		1969	1970		Norwich City	Scunthorpe Utd.	30	1	0	13	7	0	0	4
Worsman RH	Reg	19/03/1933	Bradford		1954	1955		Juniors	Bradford City	22	0	0	0	5	0	0	0
Wright AM	Alex	18/10/1925	Kirkcaldy		1951	1954		Tottenham H	Falkirk	131	11	0	0	25	1	0	0
Wright D	Dave	05/10/1905	Kirkcaldy	1955	1935			Hull City		20	0	0	0	1	0	0	0
Wright RL	Ralph	03/08/1947	Newcastle		1969			Norwich City	Hartlepool Utd.	14	0	0	0	1	0	0	0

1939/40 Season Only

Name		D.O.B	Place of Birth	Died	First Season	Last Season	lin	Previous Club	Next Club
Dann RW	Reg	06/06/1916	Maidstone	1948				Tottenham H	
McKenzie CL	Crawford		Newtongrange					Dalkeith Thistle	
Norton JG	George	18/11/1916	Stockton					Leicester City	
Watson E	Edwin	28/05/1914	Pittenweem					Huddersfield T	
Cochrane T	Tom	07/10/1908	Newcastle	1976				Middlesbrough	
Hughes JH	Jack	25/09/1912	Oswestry	1991				Chesterfield	

1945/46 FA Cup Only

Name		D.O.B	Place of Birth	Died	First Season	Last Season	lin	Previous Club	Next Club	Lge	FAC	FLC	Oth.	Lge	FAC	FLC	Oth.
Flatley A	Albert	05/09/1919	Bradford	1987	1945			York City	Bury	0	1	0	0	0	0	0	0
Knott A	Bert		Goole		1945			Sheffield United	Hull City	0	4	0	0	0	0	0	0
Walker G	Geoff	29/09/1926	Bradford		1945			Juniors	Middlesbrough	0	3	0	0	0	0	0	0

BRADFORD AGAINST OTHER CLUBS (LEAGUE MEETINGS ONLY)

		Home:					*Away:*					*Totals:*		
	p	*w*	*d*	*l*	*f*	*a*	*w*	*d*	*l*	*f*	*a*	*f*	*a*	*% won*
Accrington Stanley	30	10	4	1	44	18	3	4	8	28	46	72	64	43.33
Aldershot	20	7	2	1	23	9	2	3	5	15	28	38	37	45.00
Arsenal	6	0	1	2	2	4	0	0	3	1	7	3	11	0.00
Ashington	12	6	0	0	21	2	1	2	3	7	7	28	9	58.33
Aston Villa	10	2	2	1	16	8	1	0	4	4	12	20	20	30.00
Barnsley	52	14	5	7	50	41	5	6	15	26	54	76	95	36.54
Barrow	42	15	3	3	46	16	6	6	9	28	38	74	54	50.00
Birmingham City	16	4	2	2	19	7	3	1	4	11	16	30	23	43.75
Blackburn Rovers	16	3	2	3	19	14	2	4	2	14	15	33	29	31.25
Blackpool	26	9	3	1	31	14	2	3	8	13	25	44	39	42.31
Bolton Wanderers	14	3	1	3	12	10	4	0	3	8	8	20	18	50.00
Bournemouth	4	0	1	1	2	3	0	2	0	4	4	6	7	0.00
Bradford City	52	14	7	5	48	24	7	4	15	30	48	78	72	40.38
Brentford	20	3	2	5	15	16	0	2	8	4	17	19	33	15.00
Brighton & Hove Albion	6	2	0	1	5	6	1	1	1	4	5	9	11	50.00
Bristol City	20	8	0	2	27	16	0	3	7	3	17	30	33	40.00
Bristol Rovers	2	0	1	0	2	2	0	1	0	3	3	5	5	0.00
Burnley	36	8	4	6	34	25	3	6	9	24	33	58	58	30.56
Bury	36	10	4	4	40	25	3	3	12	22	39	62	64	36.11
Cardiff City	10	3	1	1	11	4	2	0	3	6	10	17	14	50.00
Carlisle United	26	3	4	6	16	22	4	2	7	17	25	33	47	26.92
Charlton Ath	10	5	0	0	16	2	1	1	3	6	10	22	12	60.00
Chelsea	14	3	1	3	9	9	2	0	5	5	16	14	25	35.71
Chester	36	11	3	4	37	13	5	3	10	20	30	57	43	44.44
Chesterfield	60	17	6	7	49	31	8	11	11	45	57	94	88	41.67
Colchester United	8	2	1	1	4	3	1	0	3	8	12	12	15	37.50
Coventry City	24	4	4	4	18	14	0	5	7	7	27	25	41	16.67
Crewe Alexandra	44	13	5	4	44	25	8	6	8	36	42	80	67	47.73
Crystal Palace	12	5	1	0	15	3	0	2	4	2	14	17	17	41.67
Darlington	42	13	3	5	41	22	5	5	11	29	41	70	63	42.86
Derby County	18	5	1	3	18	13	2	1	6	9	21	27	34	38.89
Doncaster Rovers	30	10	3	2	40	19	2	2	11	16	35	56	54	40.00
Durham City	12	6	0	0	20	3	1	1	4	3	7	23	10	58.33
Everton	8	1	1	2	8	8	0	1	3	4	11	12	19	12.50
Exeter City	16	5	1	2	15	12	1	1	6	9	24	24	36	37.50
Fulham	34	5	5	7	22	25	3	4	10	21	36	43	61	23.53
Gainsborough Trin.	8	4	0	0	16	1	1	1	2	4	6	20	7	62.50
Gateshead	22	8	2	1	26	10	6	0	5	19	20	45	30	63.64
Gillingham	8	3	1	0	6	0	1	1	2	5	8	11	8	50.00
Glossop	12	4	2	0	18	5	1	2	3	7	10	25	15	41.67
Grimsby Town	44	13	3	6	41	23	4	5	13	18	42	59	65	38.64
Halifax Town	44	12	6	4	43	27	5	8	9	26	40	69	67	38.64
Hartlepool United	46	13	3	7	57	25	8	4	11	30	40	87	65	45.65
Huddersfield Town	10	3	1	1	8	5	1	2	2	2	5	10	10	40.00
Hull City	34	13	2	2	43	17	5	4	8	22	34	65	51	52.94
Leeds City	12	3	1	2	10	7	3	0	3	9	12	19	19	50.00
Leeds United	10	2	1	2	8	5	0	1	4	4	12	12	17	20.00
Leicester City	24	3	4	5	20	22	1	1	10	8	35	28	57	16.67
Leyton Orient	16	7	0	1	17	5	0	0	8	0	10	17	15	43.75
Lincoln City	46	17	2	4	61	24	5	9	9	38	46	99	70	47.83
Liverpool	6	1	0	2	3	5	1	1	1	5	5	8	10	33.33
Luton Town	18	5	3	1	15	10	1	3	5	12	22	27	32	33.33
Manchester City	12	4	1	1	13	7	1	0	5	8	22	21	29	41.67
Manchester United	18	5	1	3	24	13	4	0	5	12	17	36	30	50.00
Mansfield Town	18	3	2	4	6	12	1	2	6	9	18	15	30	22.22
Middlesbrough	8	3	1	0	9	3	2	0	2	9	9	18	12	62.50
Millwall	28	10	3	1	42	7	5	3	6	14	22	56	29	53.57
Nelson	10	3	2	0	15	7	1	2	2	6	7	21	14	40.00
New Brighton	12	4	2	0	12	6	1	3	2	7	9	19	15	41.67

	Home:						Away:				Totals:		
	p	w	d	l	f	a	w	d	l	f	a	f	a	% won
Newcastle United	20	4	0	6	9	16	1	3	6	7	22	16	38	25.00
Newport County	18	4	2	3	21	19	2	1	6	10	23	31	42	33.33
Northampton Town	12	1	0	5	9	12	1	0	5	4	15	13	27	16.67
Norwich City	10	4	1	0	9	1	1	1	3	6	12	15	13	50.00
Nottm Forest	36	11	3	4	45	24	2	3	13	15	40	60	64	36.11
Notts County	38	7	7	5	39	32	6	5	8	29	37	68	69	34.21
Oldham Ath.	46	13	5	5	49	30	4	4	15	25	55	74	85	36.96
Oxford United	4	2	0	0	6	2	0	0	2	1	5	7	7	50.00
Peterborough United	10	2	1	2	11	9	0	0	5	3	14	14	23	20.00
Plymouth Argyle	26	8	5	0	33	14	1	4	8	14	30	47	44	34.62
Port Vale	36	7	6	5	33	24	2	4	12	21	44	54	68	25.00
Portsmouth	2	1	0	0	2	1	0	0	1	2	4	4	5	50.00
Preston North End	20	4	3	3	24	20	2	2	6	14	23	38	43	30.00
Queen's Park Rangers	8	1	2	1	4	6	3	0	1	5	3	9	9	50.00
Reading	10	3	0	2	11	10	0	0	5	2	15	13	25	30.00
Rochdale	44	7	11	4	36	28	8	4	10	31	39	67	67	34.09
Rotherham United	14	5	1	1	20	10	1	2	4	6	10	26	20	42.86
Scunthorpe United	20	1	6	3	13	18	1	4	5	11	22	24	40	10.00
Sheffield United	18	4	2	3	15	14	0	1	8	9	23	24	37	22.22
Sheffield Wednesday	18	4	4	1	15	9	2	1	6	7	18	22	27	33.33
Shrewsbury Town	8	2	1	1	8	7	2	0	2	4	6	12	13	50.00
Southampton	30	10	3	2	30	16	3	4	8	21	34	51	50	43.33
Southend United	12	2	1	3	8	8	0	1	5	4	17	12	25	16.67
Southport	42	14	4	3	49	22	3	5	13	18	34	67	56	40.48
Stalybridge Celtic	2	1	0	0	1	0	0	0	1	0	1	1	1	50.00
Stockport County	46	16	3	4	49	28	6	3	14	20	44	69	72	47.83
Stoke City	14	4	2	1	16	12	1	2	4	3	10	19	22	35.71
Sunderland	6	1	2	0	5	4	0	1	2	4	10	9	14	16.67
Swansea City	32	7	5	4	27	16	4	3	9	20	34	47	50	34.38
Swindon Town	4	1	1	0	4	2	0	0	2	3	5	7	7	25.00
Torquay United	12	3	3	0	14	8	1	2	3	9	13	23	21	33.33
Tottenham Hotspur	32	8	4	4	33	26	0	4	12	17	49	50	75	25.00
Tranmere Rovers	38	11	3	5	49	26	4	7	8	25	38	74	64	39.47
Walsall	14	5	1	1	26	8	2	0	5	9	12	35	20	50.00
Watford	8	1	3	0	4	3	1	0	3	5	6	9	9	25.00
West Bromwich Albion	26	6	3	4	30	27	3	2	8	9	30	39	57	34.62
West Ham United	24	7	1	4	21	13	2	2	8	8	16	29	29	37.50
Wigan Borough	12	4	2	0	20	6	4	0	2	11	7	31	13	66.67
Wolverhampton Wan.	24	6	3	3	20	11	1	6	5	10	24	30	35	29.17
Workington	28	11	2	1	37	15	6	4	4	21	21	58	36	60.71
Wrexham	44	11	3	8	41	24	3	3	16	20	51	61	75	31.82
York City	32	8	3	5	24	20	4	1	11	15	40	39	60	37.50

TOTALS

	Home:						Away:				Totals:		
	p	w	d	l	f	a	w	d	l	f	a	f	a	Points
	2190	604	239	252	2272	1335	233	237	625	1244	2247	3516	3582	2150
Comprising:														
Division One	122	25	15	21	100	81	15	12	34	72	123	172	204	107
Division Two	900	257	92	101	967	555	88	95	267	481	916	1448	1471	877
Division Three (North)	616	194	61	53	716	338	78	72	158	374	577	1090	915	677
Division Three	92	23	14	9	90	63	11	5	30	69	112	159	175	87
Division Four	460	105	57	68	399	298	41	53	136	248	519	647	817	402

1970/71

14th in the Northern Premier League

#	Month	Date / Opponent	Score	Comp	Att	1	2	3	4	5	6	7	8	9	10	11	12	
1	Aug	15 NETHERFIELD	0-2	L	2216	Hardie	Hudson	Brodie	Atkinson	Dolan	Roberts	Brown	Tewley	Leighton	Henderson	Brannan		
2		19 Wigan Athletic	0-3	L	4533	Aubrey	Brodie	Roberts	Tewley	Dolan	Beanland	Brown	Henderson	Campbell	Leighton	Ham		
3		22 South Liverpool	1-1	L	637	Aubrey	Brodie	Roberts	Tewley	Campbell	Beanland	Ham	Henderson	Dolan	Leighton 1	Brannan		
4		26 Gainsborough Trinity	4-2	LC	2000	Aubrey	Hudson	Brodie	Dolan	Campbell	Beanland	Lester	Tewley 1	Leighton	Woolmer 2	Brannan 1	Henderson	
5		29 Fleetwood	0-5	L	1135	Aubrey	Hudson	Brodie	Atkinson	Campbell	Beanland	Lester	Dolan	Leighton	Woolmer	Brannan		
6		31 MATLOCK TOWN	4-1	L	1609	Aubrey	Atkinson	Brodie	Roberts	Dolan	Leighton	Henderson	Beanland	Woolmer	Rafferty 3	Brannan 1		
7	Sep	5 Morecambe	2-0	L	1326	Aubrey	Atkinson 1	Brodie	Roberts	Dolan	Leighton	Henderson	Beanland	Woolmer	Rafferty	Brannan 1		
8		7 WIGAN ATHLETIC	1-1	L	3387	Aubrey	Atkinson	Brodie	Roberts	Dolan	Leighton	Henderson 1	Beanland	Woolmer	Rafferty	Brannan		
9		12 KIRKBY TOWN	1-0	LC	2590	Aubrey	Atkinson	Brodie	Roberts	Dolan	Leighton	Ham	Henderson 1	Woolmer	Beanland	Brannan		
10		17 Matlock Town	1-1	L	1400	Aubrey	Atkinson	Brodie	Roberts	Dolan	Leighton	Ham	Henderson 1	Woolmer	Beanland	Brannan		
11		19 SOUTH SHIELDS	2-1	L	1773	Aubrey	Atkinson 1	Brodie	Roberts	Dolan	Leighton	Ham	Henderson 1	Woolmer	Beanland	Brannan	Rafferty	
12		26 Great Harwood	3-2	L	1733	Aubrey	Atkinson	Brodie	Roberts	Dolan	Leighton 1	Ham	Henderson 1	Woolmer 1	Beanland	Brannan		
13		28 MACCLESFIELD T	0-1	L	3713	Aubrey	Atkinson	Brodie	Roberts	Dolan	Leighton	Ham	Henderson	Woolmer	Beanland	Brannan		
14	Oct	3 RUNCORN	3-1	L	1958	Aubrey	Atkinson	Brodie	Roberts	Dolan	Leighton	Ham	Henderson 3	Woolmer	Beanland	Brannan	Tewley	
15		10 ALTRINCHAM	4-1	L	3139	Aubrey	Atkinson	Brodie	Roberts	Dolan 1	Leighton 1	Ham	Henderson 1	Woolmer	Beanland	Brannan	Tewley 1	
16		17 Netherfield	3-1	L	865	Aubrey	Hudson	Brodie	Roberts	Dolan	Leighton	Tewley 1	Henderson 1	Woolmer 1	Beanland	Brannan	Wood	
17		24 Lancaster City	1-0	L	650	Aubrey	Campbell	Brodie	Beanland	Dolan	Roberts	Tewley	Henderson	Woolmer	Wood 1	Brannan		
18		31 MORECAMBE	4-0	L	2416	Aubrey	Balmforth	Brodie	Beanland	Campbell	Roberts	Ham	Woolmer 2	Leighton 1	Wood	Brannan		1og
19	Nov	7 Washington	3-0	FAC	2000	Aubrey	Atkinson	Brodie	Beanland	Campbell	Roberts	Ham 3	Wood	Leighton	Brown	Brannan		
20		21 Barnsley	0-1	FAC	7198	Aubrey	Atkinson	Brodie	Beanland	Campbell	Leighton	Ham	Rafferty	Roberts	Wood	Brown	Walker	
21		28 Northwich Victoria	0-3	L	930	Aubrey	Atkinson	McCaffery	Beanland	Campbell	Walker	Ham	Rackstraw	Leighton	Roberts	Brannan	Brodie	
22	Dec	1 Fleetwood	1-3	LC		Aubrey	Atkinson	Brodie	Beanland	Campbell	Leighton	Ham	Brown	Walker 1	Williams	Brannan	Thornton	
23		5 KIRKBY TOWN	2-1	L	1362	Smith	Atkinson 1	Brodie	Beanland	Campbell	Leighton	Ham 1	Williams	Walker	Rackstraw	Brannan		
24		19 Bangor City	1-2	L	1106	Aubrey	Atkinson	Brodie	Beanland	Campbell	Roberts	Williams 1	Thornton	Walker	Fitzsimmons	Brannan	Leighton	
25		26 BANGOR CITY	2-2	L	1346	Aubrey	Roberts	Brodie	Beanland	Campbell	Leighton	Ham	Thornton	Rackstraw	Fitzsimmons	Brannan 2		
26	Jan	2 GOOLE TOWN	2-1	L	1971	Aubrey	Brodie	Brannan	Beanland	Campbell	Roberts	Ham	Thornton 1	Rackstraw	Wood	Fitzsimmons		1og
27		9 SELBY TOWN	4-0	CC	1800	Aubrey	Kay	Brodie	Beanland 1	Campbell 1	Atkinson I	Ham	Thornton	Rackstraw	Wood	Fitzsimmons	Brannan 1	
28		16 Telford United	1-6	FAT	1475	Aubrey	Brodie	Atkinson	Beanland	Campbell	Walker	Ham	Thornton	Rackstraw	Wood 1	Brannan	Fitzsimmons	
29		23 Goole Town	1-0	L	850	Smith	Kay	Atkinson	Roberts	Campbell	Leighton	Wood	Rackstraw	Thornton 1	Beanland	Ham		
30	Feb	1 Boston United	0-0	L		Smith	Kay	Campbell	Leighton	Brannan	Rackstraw	Atkinson	Roberts	Fitzsimmons	Wood	Ham		
31		6 Stafford Rangers	0-4	L	1699	Smith	Kay	Brannan	Roberts	Campbell	Beckwith	Fitzsimmons	Rackstraw	Thornton	Wood	Ham		
32		13 BOSTON UNITED	1-2	L	1222	Smith	Kay	Mackay	Roberts	Campbell 1	Leighton	Fitzsimmons	Atkinson	Thornton	Beckwith	Ham		
33		16 Gainsborough Trinity	2-2	L		Smith	Kay	Mackay	Roberts	Campbell	Beckwith	Fitzsimmons 2	Atkinson	Thornton	Leighton	Ham		
34		20 Kirkby Town	3-1	L	173	Smith	Kay	Mackay	Roberts	Campbell	Beckwith	Wood	Atkinson 1	Leighton	Thornton 1	Fitzsimmons 1	Ham	
35	Mar	6 LANCASTER CITY	1-4	L	1243	Smith	Kay	Mackay	Roberts	Campbell	Beckwith	Wood	Atkinson	Leighton 1	Thornton	Fitzsimmons		
36		8 Macclesfield Town	0-4	L		Smith	Roberts	Mackay	Wood	Campbell	Beckwith	Thornton	Wilkinson	Leighton	Fitzsimmons	Ham	Brannan	
37		13 Farsley Celtic	0-0	CC	600	Smith	Kay	Mackay	Wilkinson	Campbell	Roberts	Fitzsimmons	Wood	Leighton	Thornton	Brannan		
38		20 Scarborough	0-4	L	2300	Smith	Roberts	Campbell	Wood	Atkinson	Leighton	Ham	Wilkinson	Thornton	Mackay	Brannan	Rafferty	
39		22 FARSLEY CELTIC	1-1	CC	800	Smith	Kay	Roberts	Rackstraw 1	Atkinson	Leighton	Ham	Wilkinson	Fitzsimmons	Mackay	Brannan	Wood	
40		27 STAFFORD RANGERS	1-2	L	1299	Aubrey	Kay	Roberts	Wilkinson	Atkinson	Campbell	Ham	Fitzsimmons	Thornton 1	Mackay	Brannan	Leighton	
41		29 SCARBOROUGH	0-1	L	1443	Aubrey	Ham	Mackay	Kay	Roberts	Beckwith	Wilkinson	Leighton	Thornton	Fitzsimmons	Brannan		
42	Apr	3 GREAT HARWOOD	2-1	L	857	Aubrey	Ham	Mackay	Kay	Roberts	Beckwith	Rackstraw	Doman 2	Thornton	Moriarty	Brannan	Leighton	
43		5 FLEETWOOD	2-2	L	1184	Aubrey	Ham	Mackay	Kay	Roberts	Beckwith 2	Fitzsimmons	Doman	Thornton	Moriarty	Foster	Leighton	
44		6 Farsley Celtic	1-2	CC	956	Aubrey	Ham	Mackay	Kay	Roberts	Beckwith	Fitzsimmons	Moriarty	Thornton	Wilkinson	Foster	Leighton 1	
45		9 South Shields	1-5	L	1300	Aubrey	Ham	Mackay	Kay	Campbell	Leighton	Wilkinson	Fitzsimmons	Brannan	Atkinson	Foster 1		
46		10 Runcorn	1-2	L	647	Aubrey	Balmforth	Atkinson	Kay	Peel	Beckwith	Rafferty	Moriarty 1	Thornton	Ham	Wilkinson	Mackay	
47		12 GAINSBOROUGH TR.	1-0	L	727	Aubrey	Balmforth	Atkinson	Kay	Peel	Leighton	Foster	Moriarty	Beckwith	Ham	Mackay 1		
48		17 Altrincham	0-1	L	1119	Aubrey	Balmforth	Atkinson	Kay	Peel	Campbell	Foster	Moriarty	Beckwith	Ham	Mackay	Fitzsimmons	
49		19 CHORLEY	0-1	L	1031	Aubrey	Balmforth	Atkinson	Kay	Peel	Campbell	Stebbings	Fitzsimmons	Thornton	Ham	Mackay		
50		24 SOUTH LIVERPOOL	2-2	L	777	Aubrey	Kay	Mackay	Atkinson	Peel	Campbell	Fitzsimmons	Roberts	Thornton	Ham 1	Stebbings		1og
51		26 NORTHWICH VIC.	0-2	L	809	Smith	Kay	Mackay	Atkinson	Peel	Campbell	Fitzsimmons	Roberts	Thornton	Ham	Stebbings		
52		30 Chorley	0-3	L		Aubrey	Ham	Hardman	Kay	Roberts	Leighton	Brannan	Thornton	Beckwith	Stuart	Stebbings	Ambler	

NW Floodlit League Matches

Game 44 played at Valley Parade

Oct 5 CHORLEY 1-0 (Woolmer) 1,559
Oct 14 Macclesfield Town 0-3
Oct 19 Hude United 2-3 (Woolmer, Dolan)
Oct 26 HYDE UNITED 3-1 (Tewley, Brannan, Woolmer) 1,894

Nov 10 Chorley 3-0 (Brannan 2, Rafferty)
Nov 16 MACCLESFIELD TOWN 1-0 (Rafferty) 1,530
Nov 25 Witton Albion 2-3 (Walker, Rafferty)
Jan 11 WITTON ALBION 0-3 1,084

1971/72

18th in the Northern Premier League

No	Month	Opponent	Score	Comp	Att	1	2	3	4	5	6	7	8	9	10	11	12	
1	Aug	14 MACCLESFIELD T	1-0	L	1488	Aubrey	Ham 1	Mackay	Massie	Beckwith	Harrity	Thornton	Jones	Pamment	Cawthra	Brannan		
2		16 SOUTH SHIELDS	0-1	L	2085	Aubrey	Ham	Mackay	Beckwith	Massie	Harrity	Thornton	Jones	Pamment	Cawthra	Brannan	Leighton	
3		21 Matlock Town	1-0	L		Aubrey	Ham	Mackay	Massie	Harrity	Beckwith	Jones	Thornton	Pamment	Mills 1	Brannan		
4		23 Altrincham	1-2	L		Aubrey	Ham	Mackay	Massie	Harrity	Beckwith	Thornton	Jones 1	Pamment	Mills	Brannan		
5		28 GREAT HARWOOD	0-1	L	1151	Aubrey	Ham	Mackay	Beckwith	Massie	Harrity	Wilkinson	Jones	Thornton	Mills	Brannan	Leighton	
6	Sep	4 South Liverpool	1-1	L		Aubrey	Ham	Mackay	Beckwith	Massie	Harrity	Wilkinson	Jones	Leighton	Pamment 1	Brannan		
7		8 Boston United	1-5	L		Aubrey	Ham	Mackay	Wilkinson	Harrity	Beckwith	Jones	Massie	Pamment	Leighton	Brannan 1		
8		11 SOUTH SHIELDS	2-1	LC	1175	Aubrey	Ham	Mackay	Massie	Leighton	Beckwith	Jones	Thornton	Pamment 1	Wilkinson 1	Brannan		
9		13 NETHERFIELD	0-0	L	1380	Aubrey	Ham	Mackay	Massie	Leighton	Beckwith	Jones	Mills	Pamment	Fitzsimmons	Brannan	Wilkinson	
10		20 ALTRINCHAM	2-1	L	1632	Aubrey	Harrity	Stuart	Thornton	Leighton	Beckwith	Massie	Brannan	Pamment 2	Mackay	Ham		
11		25 Skelmersdale United	1-2	L	751	Aubrey	Harrity	Stuart	Thornton	Leighton	Beckwith	Massie	Brannan	Pamment	Mackay	Ham	Mills	1og
12		27 South Shields	0-0	L		Aubrey	Ham	Stuart	Mackay	Leighton	Harrity	Pamment	Jones	Massie	Mills	Brannan		
13	Oct	2 BANGOR CITY	0-2	L	1517	Aubrey	Ham	Stuart	Myers	Leighton	Harrity	Jones	Mills	Pamment	Mackay	Brannan	Massie	
14		4 BOSTON UNITED	1-0	L	1336	Aubrey	Harrity	Stuart	Myers 1	Leighton	Beckwith	Ham	Moriarty	Pamment	Massie	Brannan		
15		9 Northwich Victoria	2-1	L		Aubrey	Wright B	Stuart	Myers	Leighton	Harrity	Ham	Moriarty	Pamment 1	Massie	Brannan 1		
16		12 Netherfield	0-1	L	550	Aubrey	Wright B	Stuart	Myers	Leighton	Peel	Ham	Moriarty	Pamment	Massie	Brannan		
17		16 RUNCORN	1-1	L	1323	Aubrey	Ham	Stuart	Wright B	Peel	Beckwith 1	Smith A	Leighton	Pamment	Brannan	Gomersall	Thornton	
18		18 LANCASTER CITY	3-3	L	1043	Rose	Wright B	Stuart	Ham	Leighton	Beckwith	Moriarty	Thornton	Pamment	Brannan 2	Jones 1		
19		30 Kirkby Town	1-2	L	177	Rose	Wright B	Stuart	Ham	Harrity	Beckwith	Moriarty	Thornton 1	Pamment	Brannan	Jones	Massie	
20	Nov	6 SOUTH SHIELDS	0-1	FAC	1940	Aubrey	Myers	Massie	Wright	Leighton	Harrity	Thornton	Moriarty	Brannan	Ham	Pamment		
21		9 Gainsborough Trinity	0-3	LC		Aubrey	Myers	Stuart	Thornton	Leighton	Harrity	Moriarty	Ham	Brannan	Wright B	Mackay	Pamment	
22		13 Macclesfield Town	1-3	L	1378	Aubrey	Wright B	Stuart	Ham	Leighton	Harrity	Moriarty	Gilfillan	Thornton	Brannan	Mackay		1og
23		20 KIRKBY TOWN	1-0	L	880	Aubrey	Myers	Wright K	Leighton	Taylor	Harrity	Ham 1	Pamment	Gilfillan	Brannan	Wright B		
24		27 Wigan Athletic	0-1	L	3061	Aubrey	Myers	Wright K	Wright B	Taylor	Harrity	Ham	Pamment	Gilfillan	Jones	Brannan	Stuart	
25	Dec	4 ELLESMERE PORT T	1-0	L	1140	Aubrey	Wright B	Wright K	Pamment	Taylor	Harrity	Jones	Ham	Gilfillan	Myers	Massie 1		
26		11 Goole Town	3-1	L	750	Aubrey	Wright B	Wright K	Pamment	Taylor	Harrity	Jones	Ham 2	Massie	Myers 1	Mackay		
27		13 Scarborough	1-4	L	1733	Aubrey	Wright B	Wright K	Pamment	Taylor	Harrity 1	Jones	Ham	Massie	Myers	Mackay	Thornton	
28		23 Chorley	1-4	L		Aubrey	Wright B	Wright K	Wilkinson	Taylor	Crook	Smith A 1	Ham	Massie	Myers	Brannan		
29		27 GOOLE TOWN	5-2	L	1285	Aubrey	Wright B	Wright K	Harrity	Taylor	Crook	Smith A 1	Wilkinson	Massie 3	Myers 1	Brannan		
30	Jan	1 MATLOCK TOWN	2-4	L	1151	Aubrey	Wright B	Wright K	Harrity	Taylor	Crook 1	Smith A	Wilkinson	Massie	Myers	Brannan 1		
31		4 Fleetwood	1-2	L		Rose	Wright B	Wright K	Crook	Taylor	Harrity	Ham	Wilkinson	Massie	Moriarty	Brannan 1	Leighton	
32		8 Ossett Town	5-0	CC	450	Rose	Ham	Mackay	Harrity	Taylor	Wright K	Smith A 2	Crook	Wilkinson	Myers 2	Brannan	Kay	
33		16 SOUTH LIVERPOOL	2-1	L	889	Rose	Wright B	Mackay	Harrity	Kay	Wright K	Ham	Crook	Massie 2	Myers	Smith A	Brannan	
34		22 STAFFORD RANGERS	1-1	FAT	1875	Rose	Kay	Mackay	Harrity	Leighton	Wright K	Ham	Crook	Massie 1	Myers	Brannan	Smith	
35		25 Stafford Rangers	0-1	FAT	2209	Rose	Kay	Mackay	Harrity	Leighton	Wright K	Crook	Ham	Massie	Myers	Brannan		
36		31 GAINSBOROUGH TRIN.	4-2	L	718	Rose	Kay	Mackay	Harrity	Leighton 1	Wright K	Ham 1	Crook	Massie 1	Myers 1	Wright B		
37	Feb	5 Bangor City	1-3	L	1216	Aubrey	Kay	Mackay	Harrity	Leighton	Wright B	Smith A	Crook	Massie 1	Myers	Wright K		
38		7 Skelmersdale United	0-1	L	1182	Rose	Kay	Mackay	Harrity	Leighton	Wright B	Smith A	Crook	Massie	Wright K	Myers		
39		12 NORTHWICH VIC.	1-1	L	936	Rose	Kay	Mackay	Harrity	Peel	Wright B	Smith A	Crook	Massie	Wright K	Myers 1	Brannan	
40		19 Runcorn	2-2	L	443	Rose	Wright B 1	Wright K	Ham	Kay	Leighton	Crook	Myers 1	Harrity	Brannan	Massie		
41		26 SCARBOROUGH	0-0	L	1049	Rose	Kay	Wright K	Harrity	Brannan	Wright B	Ham	Crook	Massie	Fleming	Smith A	Leighton	
42	Mar	4 FLEETWOOD	1-0	L	1030	Rose	Kay	Wright K	Harrity	Brannan	Wright B	Smith A	Crook	Leighton	Fleming	Myers 1		
43		5 Great Harwood	1-1	L	714	Rose	Kay	Wright K	Harrity	Brannan 1	Wright B	Ham	Crook	Leighton	Fleming	Smith A		
44		11 Gainsborough Trin.	2-1	L	1008	Rose	Kay	Wright K	Harrity 1	Brannan	Wright B	Ham 1	Crook	Myers	Fleming	Smith A		
45		18 MORECAMBE	0-2	L	1209	Rose	Kay	Wright K	Harrity	Brannan	Wright B	Ham	Crook	Myers	Fleming	Smith A	Massie	
46		25 Morecambe	1-1	L	710	Rose	Kay	Wright K	Harrity	Brannan	Wright B	Ham 1	Crook	Corner	Fleming	Massie	Myers	
47		26 Goole Town	2-3	CC	1000	Rose	Kay	Wright B	Harrity	Brannan	Fleming	Ham	Crook	Massie 2	Myers	Smith A		
48		31 Lancaster City	0-3	L	650	Leighton	Smith P	Mackay	Saunders	Balmforth	Fleming	Gomersall	Simpson	Bottomley	Myers	Smith A	Renshaw	
49	Apr	1 WIGAN ATHLETIC	0-0	L	1489	Rose	Kay	Wright B	Harrity	Brannan	Fleming	Ham	Crook	Corner	Massie	Myers	Wright K	
50		8 Ellemere Port T	3-3	L	150	Rose	Kay	Wright B	Harrity	Brannan	Fleming 2	Ham	Crook	Corner	Massie	Leighton	Myers	1og
51		17 Stafford Rangers	2-3	L	5589	Rose	Kay	Wright B	Harrity	Taylor	Fleming	Ham	Crook	Corner	Myers 1	Massie 1		
52		22 CHORLEY	1-1	L	1012	Rose	Kay	Wright B	Harrity	Taylor	Fleming	Ham	Massie	Corner 1	Myers	Legg	Crook	
53	May	1 STAFFORD RANGERS	1-2	L	1571	Rose	Kay	Wright B	Harrity	Taylor	Fleming	Ham	Crook	Corner 1	Myers	Massie		

NW Floodlit League Matches

Oct 25 BUXTON 2-1 (og, Pamment) 1,075
Nov 1 Hude United 2-2 (Ham 2)
Nov 22 Buxton 2-2 (Ham, Brannan) 832
Dec 6 Northwich Victoria 1-0 (Mackay) 835
Dec 18 Macclesfield Town 0-3
Dec 20 NORTHWICH VICTORIA 2-1 Massie, og) 726
Jan 17 MACCLESFIELD TOWN 1-0 (Crook) 915
Feb 20 HYDE UNITED 3-3 (Massie, Crook, Ham) 1,142

1972/73

5th in the Northern Premier League

#	Month	Match	Score	Comp	Att	1	2	3	4	5	6	7	8	9	10	11	12	
1	Aug	12 Wigan Athletic	0-2	L	1956	Rose	Kay	Wright	Cartwright	Brannan	Fleming	Myers	Walker	Corner	Riordan	Henderson		
2		14 Gainsborough Tr.	2-0	L		Rose	Kay	Wright	Harrity	Brannan	Fleming	Myers	Corner 1	Walker	Beaumont	Henderson 1	Leighton	
3		19 ELLESMERE PORT T	1-2	L	1256	Rose	Kay	Wright	Harrity 1	Brannan	Fleming	Myers	Leighton	Corner	Beaumont	Henderson	Riordan	
4		21 BOSTON UNITED	1-1	L	1285	Rose	Riordan	Wright	Harrity	Brannan	Fleming 1	Myers	Leighton	Corner	Beaumont	Henderson		
5		25 Macclesfield Town	2-2	L	2170	Rose	Kay	Wright	Harrity	Brannan	Fleming	Myers	Riordan	Gomersall D	Beaumont	Henderson 2		
6		28 Goole Town	0-1	LC		Rose	Kay	Wright	Harrity	Brannan	Riordan	Leighton	Henderson	Gomersall D	Beaumont	Legg		
7	Sep	2 FLEETWOOD	1-0	L	949	Rose	Kay	Wright	Harrity	Brannan	Fleming	Lee	Myers	Gomersall D 1	Beaumont	Henderson		
8		4 GAINSBOROUGH TR.	1-0	L	1072	Rose	Kay	Wright	Harrity	Brannan	Fleming	Gomersall D 1	Myers	Corner	Beaumont	Henderson	Cartwright	
9		9 Altrincham	1-1	L	878	Rose	Kay	Wright	Cartwright	Brannan	Fleming	Myers	Gomersall D	Harrity	Beaumont	Henderson		1og
10		13 Boston United	0-3	L	1500	Rose	Kay	Wright	Cartwright	Brannan	Fleming	Smith A	Myers	Harrity	Beaumont	Henderson	Corner	
11		16 Stocksbridge Works	3-1	FAC	500	Rose	Kay	Wright	Harrity	Cartwright	Brannan	Gomersall B 1	Walker 2	Fleming	Beaumont	Henderson		
12		23 Fleetwood	0-0	L	663	Rose	Kay	Wright	Beaumont	Brannan	Fleming	Myers	Gomersall D	Leighton	Corner	Walker	Henderson	
13		25 GOOLE TOWN	2-1	L	1117	Rose	Leighton	Wright	Myers	Brannan	Corner	Smith A	Peel	Walker	Beaumont 1	Henderson 1		
14		30 BANGOR CITY	0-1	L	1128	Rose	Leighton	Wright	Myers	Brannan	Corner	Smith A	Peel	Walker	Beaumont	Henderson		
15	Oct	2 SOUTH SHIELDS	2-1	L	1052	Rose	Myers	Wright	Leighton	Brannan	Corner	Beaumont	Peel	Walker 1	Henderson 1	Smith A		
16		7 STALYBRIDGE CELTIC	2-1	FAC	1507	Rose	Myers	Wright	Peel	Brannan 1	Leighton	Gomersall B	Henderson 1	Walker	Corner	Smith	Beaumont	
17		11 South Shields	1-2	L		Rose	Myers	Leighton	Brannan	Wright	Smith P	Corner	Peel	Henderson	Walker 1	Smith A		
18		14 South Liverpool	1-1	L	597	Rose	Myers	Wright	Leighton	Brannan	Kay	Peel	Corner	Henderson	Walker 1	Smith A		
19		18 Scarborough	0-0	L	1600	Rose	Peel	Brannan	Beaumont	Leighton	Myers	Corner	Henderson	Walker	Fleming	Smith A		
20		21 Macclesfield Town	0-1	FAC	1805	Rose	Myers	Kay	Peel	Brannan	Leighton	Beaumont	Henderson	Walker	Corner	Fleming	Smith	
21	Nov	4 Stafford Rangers	2-1	L	2430	Rose	Kay	Wright	Beaumont	Leighton	Myers	Peel	Henderson 2	Walker	Corner	Brannan		
22		6 SCARBOROUGH	1-0	L	1373	Liney	Kay	Wright	Beaumont	Brannan	Myers	Fleming 1	Corner	Walker	Henderson	Leighton		
23		11 ALFRETON TOWN	7-0	FAT	1208	Rose	Kay	Wright	Peel 1	Brannan	Myers	Fleming 3	Henderson	Walker 2	Corner	Beaumont	Leighton 1	
24		18 MACCLEFIELD T	1-1	L	1091	Rose	Kay	Wright	Myers	Cartwright	Fleming	Peel	Henderson	Walker 1	Corner	Beaumont		
25		20 BARROW	4-2	L	831	Rose	Kay	Wright	Myers	Cartwright	Fleming 2	Peel	Henderson	Walker 2	Corner	Beaumont		
26		27 NETHERFIELD	2-0	L	1060	Rose	Kay	Wright	Peel	Cartwright	Myers	Leighton	Beaumont 1	Walker 1	Corner	Fleming	Jones	
27	Dec	2 ILKESTON TOWN	2-0	FAT	1253	Rose	Kay	Wright	Peel	Cartwright	Myers	Walsh	Beaumont	Walker 1	Corner	Fleming	Leighton	1og
28		9 Runcorn	4-1	L	530	Rose	Kay	Wright	Peel	Cartwright	Myers	Fleming 1	Beaumont 2	Walker	Corner 1	Jones		
29		23 Ellesmere Port T	0-0	L	580	Rose	Kay	Wright	Peel	Cartwright	Myers	Beaumont	Henderson	Walker	Corner	Fleming		
30		26 MATLOCK TOWN	4-0	L	1535	Rose	Kay	Wright	Peel	Cartwright	Myers	Beaumont 1	Henderson 3	Walker	Corner	Fleming	Brannan	
31		30 Great Harwood	3-2	L	765	Rose	Kay	Brannan	Peel	Cartwright	Myers	Beaumont 1	Henderson	Walker 2	Corner	Fleming	Leighton	
32	Jan	6 ALTRINCHAM	2-3	L	1177	Rose	Kay	Wright 1	Peel	Cartwright	Myers	Beaumont	Brannan	Walker	Corner	Fleming	Gomersall D 1	
33		13 Bangor City	0-0	L	1102	Rose	Kay	Wright	Peel	Brannan	Cartwright	Beaumont	Henderson	Gomersall D	Corner	Myers	Gomersall B	
34		13 Goole Town	0-1	CC	750	Liney	Smith P	Burke	Wood	Stuart	Jones	Smith A	Hall	Morgan	Ambler	Walsh		
35		20 Morecambe	1-3	FAT	1100	Rose	Kay	Wright	Peel	Brannan	Cartwright	Beaumont	Henderson	Walker 1	Corner	Myers	Fleming	
36		27 SKELMERSDALE U	2-1	L	1224	Rose	Kay	Wright	Peel	Brannan	Myers	Cartwright	Henderson	Gomersall D	Corner 2	Beaumont		
37	Feb	3 MORECAMBE	1-1	L	1349	Rose	Kay	Wright	Peel	Brannan	Myers	Gomersall B	Henderson 1	Gomersall D	Corner	Beaumont		
38		10 NORTHWICH VIC.	1-0	L	962	Rose	Kay	Wright	Peel	Brannan	Myers	Beaumont	Gomersall D	Walker	Corner	Jones 1	Fleming	
39		12 LANCASTER CITY	2-2	L	644	Rose	Kay	Wright	Peel	Brannan	Myers	Beaumont	Fleming 1	Walker 1	Corner	Jones		
40		17 WIGAN ATHLETIC	2-1	L	1515	Rose	Kay	Wright	Peel	Brannan	Cartwright	Myers 1	Fleming	Walker	Corner	Jones 1		
41		24 Mossley	2-4	L	758	Rose	Kay	Fleming	Peel	Brannan	Cartwright	Smith A	Beaumont	Walker 1	Corner 1	Jones		
42	Mar	3 MOSSLEY	2-2	L	1177	Rose	Kay	Wright	Peel	Brannan	Jones 1	Beaumont	Fleming	Walker 1	Corner	Henderson	Myers	
43		10 RUNCORN	1-0	L	1137	Rose	Kay	Wright	Myers	Brannan	Jones	Beaumont	Henderson 1	Walker	Corner	Fleming		
44		14 Lancaster City	2-0	L	411	Rose	Kay	Wright	Peel	Brannan	Myers	Beaumont	Henderson 1	Walker	Corner 1	Jones		
45		17 Barrow	4-0	L	479	Rose	Kay	Wright	Peel	Brannan	Myers	Beaumont 1	Henderson 1	Walker 1	Corner	Jones 1		
46		24 STAFFORD RANGERS	1-1	L	1326	Rose	Kay	Wright	Peel	Brannan	Myers	Beaumont	Henderson	Walker	Corner 1	Jones		
47		31 Northwich Victoria	1-1	L	615	Rose	Kay	Wright	Peel	Brannan	Myers	Beaumont 1	Henderson	Walker	Corner	Jones		
48	Apr	3 Netherfield	0-5	L		Rose	Kay	Wright	Peel	Brannan	Myers	Beaumont	Henderson	Walker	Corner	Jones		
49		7 Morecambe	1-1	L	685	Rose	Kay	Wright	Peel	Brannan 1	Myers	Beaumont	Henderson	Walker	Corner	Jones		
50		12 Goole Town	0-1	L		Rose	Kay	Wright	Myers	Brannan	Cartwright	Beaumont	Henderson	Walker	Foster	Jones		
51		14 SOUTH LIVERPOOL	0-1	L	895	Rose	Kay	Wright	Peel	Brannan	Myers	Beaumont	Foster	Walker	Cartwright	Jones	Henderson	
52		17 Skelmersdale United	0-0	L		Rose	Kay	Wright	Peel	Brannan	Cartwright	Beaumont	Henderson	Walker	Myers	Jones		
53		21 GREAT HARWOOD	2-1	L	1413	Rose	Kay	Wright 1	Peel	Brannan	Cartwright	Beaumont	Henderson	Walker	Myers	Leighton 1	Foster	
54		23 Matlock Town	1-1	L		Rose	Kay	Wright	Peel	Brannan	Cartwright	Beaumont	Myers	Walker 1	Corner	Henderson	Foster	

NW Floodlit League Matches

Oct 30 MACCLESFIELD TOWN 3-1 (Corner, Walker, Henderson) 1,044
Nov 7 Buxton 1-2 (Henderson)
Nov 13 BUXTON 2-3 (Walker, Henderson)
Nov 29 Witton Albion 1-0 (Myers)

Dec 4 WITTON ALBION 3-0 (Fleming, Jones, Corner) 711
Jan 1 Mossley 0-2
Jan 8 MOSSLEY 2-0 (Corner, Walker) 629
Feb 7 Macclesfield Town 0-3

1973/74

21st in the Northern Premier League

	Month	Date / Opponent	Score	Comp	Att	1	2	3	4	5	6	7	8	9	10	11	12	
1	Aug	11 NORTHWICH VIC.	2-2	L	1022	Rose	Kay	Woodhall	Peel	Brannan	Myers	Ham	Fenton 1	Walker 1	Wright	Downing		
2		15 Scarborough	0-1	L	2500	Rose	Kay	Woodhall	Brannan	Cartwright	Myers	Ham	Fenton	Walker	Wright	Downing		
3		18 Morecambe	1-1	L	1110	Rose	Kay	Woodhall	Cartwright	Brannan	Myers	Brierley	Fenton	Walker 1	Wright	Downing	Ham	
4		21 GAINSBOROUGH TR.	1-1	L	761	Rose	Kay	Woodhall	Peel	Brannan	Leighton	Ham	Fenton	Walker	Wright	Downing 1	Smith	
5		25 SKELMERSDALE U	1-4	L	982	Rose	Wright	Peel	Brookes	Kay	Leighton	Ham	Fenton	Walker 1	Smith	Downing		
6		27 Great Harwood	0-1	L		Rose	Kay	Wright	Fenton	Cartwright	Leighton	Brierley	Walker	Downing	Brannan	Brookes		
7	Sep	1 Fleetwood	1-3	L	832	Rose	Burke	Kay	Wright	Fenton	Cartwright	Peel	Smith	Leighton 1	Walker	Downing		
8		4 GOOLE TOWN	1-3	L	634	Rose	Kay	Wright	Peel	Cartwright	Myers	Leighton	Fenton	Walker 1	Brannan	Downing		
9		8 STAFFORD RANGERS	1-7	L	634	Rose	Kay	Wright	Peel	Cartwright	Myers	Fenton	Smith	Walker	Manners	Downing	Leighton 1	
10		12 Boston United	1-1	L		Rose	Wright	Woodhall	Kay	Brannan	Myers	Leighton	Foster	Walker 1	Manners	Downing	Peel	
11		15 Barton Town	2-0	FAC	500	Liney	Wright	Woodhall	Kay 1	Cartwright	Brannan	Ham	Foster	Walker	Manners	Downing 1	Peel	
12		18 SOUTH SHIELDS	0-6	L	593	Liney	Wright	Woodhall	Kay	Brannan	Myers	Baker	Foster	Walker	Manners	Downing	Leighton	
13		22 SOUTH LIVERPOOL	0-2	L	575	Liney	Wright	Woodhall	Kay	Cartwright	Leighton	Baker	Peel	Walker	Brannan	Manners	Downing	
14		24 Gainsborough Trinity	0-4	L		Rose	Wright	Silverwood	Kay	Brannan	Leighton	Baker	Peel	Walker	Manners	Downing		
15		29 Matlock Town	1-1	L	430	Rose	Wright	Silverwood	Kay	Brannan	Cartwright	Dover	Walker	Leighton 1	Manners	Peel		
16	Oct	2 SCARBOROUGH	0-3	L	573	Rose	Wright	Myers	Kay	Brannan	Cartwright	Dover	Walker	Leighton	Downing	Peel		
17		6 Mexborough Town	1-1	FAC	350	Rose	Burke	Brannan	Kay	Cartwright	Myers	Dover	Walker 1	Leighton	Foster	Downing		
18		10 MEXBOROUGH T	4-2	FAC	673	Rose	Wright	Brannan	Kay	Peel	Myers	Dover 1	Leighton	Walker 3	Burke	Ham		
19		16 BOSTON UNITED	0-1	L	639	Rose	Wright	Brannan	Kay	Burke	Leighton	Dover	Griffin	Walker	Fleming	Myers		
20		20 GOOLE TOWN	3-3	FAC	876	Rose	Wright	Brannan	Kay	Burke	Leighton	Ham	Dover	Walker 2	Griffin	Myers 1		
21		24 Goole Town	1-4	FAC	1000	Rose	Wright	Brannan	Kay	Burke	Cartwright	Ham	Brierley	Walker 1	Griffin	Myers		
22		27 Runcorn	0-2	L	621	Rose	Wright	Burke	Kay	Cartwright	Brannan	Fenton	Ham	Leighton	Fleming	Brierley	Peel	
23	Nov	2 FLEETWOOD	1-0	L	511	Rose	Wright	Burke	Kay	Cartwright	Brannan	Woodhall	Fenton	Walker	Fleming	Leighton 1		
24		10 Altrincham	1-4	L	1140	Rose	Wright	Woodhall	Kay	Cartwright	Leighton	Burke	Fenton	Peel	Fleming	Brannan 1		
25		17 BANGOR CITY	0-3	L	604	Rose	Wright	Woodhall	Kay	Cartwright	Leighton	Brierley	Fenton	Walker	Fleming	Brannan		
26		24 Netherfield	1-2	L	350	Rose	Wright	Woodhall	Fenton	Cartwright	Leighton	Hollinshead	Kay	Walker 1	Fleming	Brannan		
27	Dec	1 KIMBERLEY TOWN	7-0	FAT	517	Rose	Wright	Burke	Kay	Cartwright	Myers 1	Hollinshead	Fenton 1	Walker 2	Fleming 3	Brannan		
28		8 Lancaster City	1-1	L	478	Rose	Kay	Wright	Schofield	Cartwright	Brannan	Myers 1	Fenton	Walker	Fleming	Bishop	Burke	
29		15 BARROW	3-1	L	508	Rose	Kay	Wright	Schofield 1	Myers	Brannan	South	Burke 2	Walker	Fleming	Bishop		
30		22 MORECAMBE	0-1	L	648	Rose	Kay	Wright	Schofield	Myers	Brannan	South	Burke	Walker	Fleming	Bishop		
31		26 Mossley	2-2	L		Rose	Kay	Wright	Schofield	Brannan 1	Myers	South	Fenton	Peel	Fleming	Bishop		1og
32		29 Skelmersdale United	2-2	L	400	Rose	Kay	Wright	Schofield	Brannan	Myers	South	Fenton 1	Peel	Fleming 1	Bishop		
33	Jan	2 BUXTON	0-1	FAT	825	Rose	Kay	Wright	Peel	Brannan	Myers	South	Fenton	Walker	Fleming	Bishop		
34		5 Buxton	1-3	L	602	Rose	Kay	Wright	Schofield	Brannan	Myers	South	Fenton	Walker	Fleming 1	Bishop		
35		14 OSSETT ALBION	5-1	CC	641	Rose	Kay	Wright	Schofield	Brannan 1	Myers	South 1	Fenton	Walker	Fleming 1	Bishop 2		
36		20 Bangor City	2-0	L	716	Rose	Kay	Wright	Fenton	Brannan	Myers	South	Peel	Walker 2	Fleming	Bishop		
37		26 MACCLESFIELD T	2-0	L	552	Rose	Kay	Wright	Fenton	Brannan 1	Myers	Schofield	Peel	Cartwright	Fleming 1	Bishop		
38	Feb	3 WIGAN ATHLETIC	0-0	L	1322	Rose	Kay	Wright	Fenton	Brannan	Myers	South	Peel	Walker	Fleming	Bishop		
39		9 Stafford Rangers	0-6	L	1912	Rose	Kay	Wright	Fenton	Brannan	Myers	South	Peel	Walker	Burke	Bishop		
40		16 LANCASTER CITY	1-0	L	631	Rose	Kay	Wright	Fenton	Brannan	Myers	South	Peel	Walker 1	Fleming	Bishop		
41		23 Barrow	0-1	L	359	Rose	Kay	Wright	Myers	Brannan	Fenton	Fleming	South	Walker	Peel	Bishop	Cartwright	
42	Mar	2 SKELMERSDALE U	0-2	LC	625	Rose	Kay	Wright	Burke	Cartwright	Myers	South	Peel	Brannan	Fleming	Bishop		
43		9 NETHERFIELD	2-0	L	393	Rose	Kay	Wright	Fenton	Cartwright	Myers	South	Peel	Brannan 1	Fleming	Bishop 1	Burke	
44		16 South Liverpool	1-1	L	400	Rose	Kay	Wright	Peel	Cartwright	Myers	South 1	Brannan	Walker	Fleming	Bishop		
45		23 ALTRINCHAM	0-0	L	707	Liney	Kay	Wright	Peel	Cartwright	Myers	South	Brannan	Walker	Fleming	Bishop		
46		24 South Shields	0-1	L		Liney	Kay	Wright	Peel	Cartwright	Myers	South	Brannan	Walker	Fleming	Bishop		
47		30 Thackley	2-4	CC	877	Liney	Kay	Wright	Peel	Cartwright	Myers	South	Brannan	Walker 1	Fleming 1	Bishop	Fenton	aet
48	Apr	1 Wigan Athletic	1-4	L	1085	Liney	Wright	Burke	Jones	Cartwright	Brannan	South	Peel	Walker 1	Fleming	Bishop		
49		6 RUNCORN	1-1	L	652	Rose	Wright	Burke	Jones	Cartwright	Brannan	South 1	Peel	Walker	Fenton	Bishop	Ambler	
50		13 Macclesfield Town	0-1	L	886	Rose	Kay	Wright	Cartwright	Myers	Peel	Brannan	South	Walker	Jones	Bishop		
51		15 MOSSLEY	1-1	L	408	Rose	Kay	Wright	Peel	Cartwright	Myers	Jones	Brannan 1	Walker	Burke	Bishop		
52		17 MATLOCK TOWN	2-1	L	338	Rose	Kay	Wright	Jones	Cartwright	Myers	South	Brannan 1	Walker	Burke	Bishop 1		
53		20 Northwich Victoria	2-2	L	604	Rose	Kay	Wright	Peel	Cartwright	Myers	Brannan	Burke	Walker 2	Jones	Bishop		
54		21 BUXTON	2-1	L	450	Rose	Kay	Wright	Peel	Cartwright	Myers	South	Brannan	Walker 1	Burke	Bishop 1		
55		30 Goole Town	2-2	L		Rose	Kay	Burke	Peel	Brannan	Cartwright	South	Jones	Walker	Fleming	Bishop 1	Ambler 1	
56	May	2 GREAT HARWOOD	1-0	L	698	Rose	Kay	Wright	Peel	Cartwright	Brannan	Myers	Jones	Walker	Fleming 1	Bishop		

NW Floodlit League Matches Oct 29 Hyde United 0-0 Nov 6 ASHTON UNITED 2-0 (Walker 2) 375 *Competition suspended due to power workers' industrial action.*

The final match (at Valley Parade) v Great Harwood, May 2 1974. Back, left to right: Andy Cartwright, Terry Burke, Mick Fleming, Wilson Rose, Alan Myers, Trevor Peel, Barry Wright. Front: Geoff Kay, Mick Walker, mascot, David Jones, Peter Brannan, Peter Bishop.

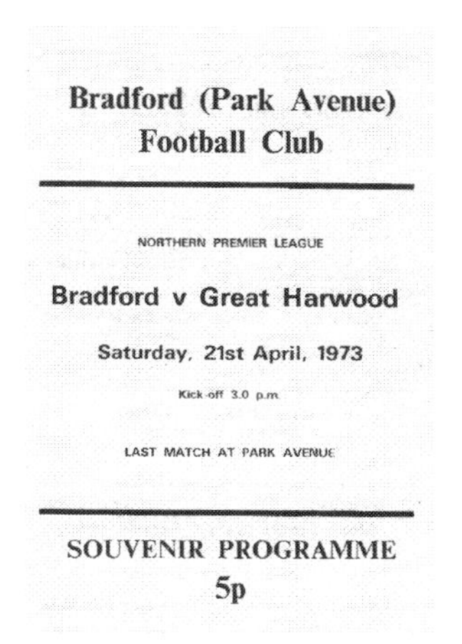

Bradford (Park Avenue)
Football Club

NORTHERN PREMIER LEAGUE

Bradford v Great Harwood

Saturday, 21st April, 1973

Kick-off 3.0 p.m.

LAST MATCH AT PARK AVENUE

SOUVENIR PROGRAMME
5p

The last match at Park Avenue, April 1973

May 1974; the Bradford players take to the field for the final match at Valley Parade.

The Old Club:

1970/71 Northern Premier League

		p	w	d	l	f	a	pts
1	Wigan Athletic	42	27	13	2	91	32	67
2	Stafford Rangers	42	27	7	8	87	51	61
3	Scarborough	42	23	12	7	83	40	58
4	Boston United	42	22	12	8	69	31	56
5	Macclesfield T	42	23	10	9	84	45	56
6	Northwich Vic.	42	22	5	15	71	55	49
7	Bangor City	42	19	10	13	72	61	48
8	Altrincham	42	19	10	13	80	76	48
9	South Liverpool	42	15	15	12	67	57	45
10	Chorley	42	14	14	14	58	61	42
11	Gainsborough Trin.	42	15	11	16	65	63	41
12	Morecambe	42	14	11	17	67	79	39
13	South Shields	42	12	14	16	67	66	38
14	BRADFORD	42	15	8	19	54	73	38
15	Lancaster C	42	12	12	18	53	76	36
16	Netherfield	42	13	9	20	59	57	35
17	Matlock Town	42	10	13	19	58	80	33
18	Fleetwood	42	10	11	21	56	90	31
19	Great Harwood	42	8	13	21	66	98	29
20	Runcorn	42	10	5	27	58	84	25
21	Kirkby Town	42	6	13	23	57	93	25
22	Goole Town	42	10	4	28	44	98	24

1971/72 Northern Premier League

		p	w	d	l	f	a	pts
1	Stafford Rangers	46	30	11	5	91	32	71
2	Boston United	46	28	13	5	87	37	69
3	Wigan Athletic	46	27	10	9	70	43	64
4	Scarborough	46	21	15	10	75	46	57
5	Northwich Vic.	46	20	14	12	65	59	54
6	Macclesfield T	46	18	15	13	61	50	51
7	Gainsborough Trin.	46	21	9	16	93	79	51
8	South Shields	46	18	14	14	75	57	50
9	Bangor City	46	20	8	18	93	74	48
10	Altrincham	46	18	11	17	72	58	47
11	Skelmersdale U	46	19	9	18	61	58	47
12	Matlock Town	46	20	7	19	67	75	47
13	Chorley	46	17	12	17	66	59	46
14	Lancaster C	46	15	14	17	85	84	44
15	Great Harwood	46	15	14	17	60	74	44
16	Ellesmere Port T	46	17	9	20	67	71	43
17	Morecambe	46	15	10	21	51	64	40
18	BRADFORD	46	13	13	20	54	71	39
19	Netherfield	46	16	5	25	51	73	37
20	Fleetwood	46	11	15	20	43	67	37
21	South Liverpool	46	12	12	22	61	73	36
22	Runcorn	46	8	14	24	48	80	30
23	Goole Town	46	9	10	27	51	97	28
24	Kirkby Town	46	6	12	28	38	104	24

1972/73 Northern Premier League

		p	w	d	l	f	a	pts
1	Boston United	46	27	16	3	88	34	70
2	Scarborough	46	26	9	11	72	39	61
3	Wigan Athletic	46	23	14	9	69	38	60
4	Altrincham	46	22	16	8	75	55	60
5	BRADFORD	46	19	17	10	63	50	55
6	Stafford Rangers	46	20	11	15	63	46	51
7	Gainsborough Trin.	46	18	13	15	70	50	49
8	Northwich Victoria	46	17	15	14	74	62	49
9	Netherfield	46	20	9	17	68	65	49
10	Macclesfield Town	46	16	16	14	58	47	48
11	Ellesmerre Port	46	18	11	17	52	56	47
12	Skelmersdale Utd.	46	15	16	15	58	59	46
13	Bangor City	46	16	13	17	70	60	45
14	Mossley	46	17	11	18	70	73	45
15	Morecambe	46	17	11	18	62	70	45
16	Great Harwood	46	14	15	17	63	74	43
17	South Liverpool	46	12	19	15	47	57	43
18	Runcorn	46	15	12	19	75	78	42
19	Goole Town	46	13	13	20	64	73	39
20	South Shields	46	17	4	25	64	81	38
21	Matlock Town	46	11	11	24	42	80	33
22	Lancaster City	46	10	11	25	53	78	31
23	Barrow	46	12	6	28	52	101	30
24	Fleetwood	46	5	15	26	31	77	25

1973/74 Northern Premier League

		p	w	d	l	f	a	pts
1	Boston United	46	27	11	8	69	32	65
2	Wigan Athletic	46	28	8	10	96	39	64
3	Altrincham	46	26	11	9	77	34	63
4	Stafford Rangers	46	27	9	10	101	45	63
5	Scarborough	46	22	14	10	62	43	58
6	South Shileds	46	25	6	15	87	48	56
7	Runcorn	46	21	14	11	72	47	56
8	Macclesfield Town	46	18	15	13	48	47	51
9	Bangor City	46	19	11	16	65	56	49
10	Gainsborough Trin.	46	18	11	17	77	64	47
11	South Liverpool	46	16	15	15	55	47	47
12	Skelmersdale Utd.	46	16	13	17	50	59	45
13	Goole Town	46	14	15	17	60	69	43
14	Fleetwood	46	14	15	17	48	68	43
15	Mossley	46	15	11	20	53	65	41
16	Northwich Victoria	46	14	13	19	68	75	41
17	Morecambe	46	13	13	20	62	84	39
18	Buxton	46	14	10	22	45	71	38
19	Matlock Town	46	11	14	21	50	79	36
20	Great Harwood	46	10	14	22	52	74	34
21	BRADFORD	46	9	15	22	42	84	33
22	Barrow	46	13	7	26	46	94	33
23	Lancaster City	46	10	12	24	52	67	32
24	Netherfield	46	11	5	30	42	88	27

The New:

1988/89 West Riding County Amateur League Division Three

		p	w	d	l	f	a	pts
1	Gatehouse	24	17	5	2	78	34	39
2	BRADFORD	24	18	1	5	93	50	37
3	Crag Road U Res	24	14	6	4	71	40	34
4	Salts Res	24	13	4	7	50	33	30
5	Pudsey Liberals	24	12	3	9	55	40	27
6	Ovenden WR Res	24	11	4	9	55	50	26
7	Littletown Res	24	10	6	8	51	51	26
8	Hall Green U Res	24	8	4	12	41	42	20
9	St Blaise	24	7	5	12	51	68	19
10	Trinity Ath Res	24	6	4	14	37	51	16
11	Field Res	24	6	4	14	34	55	16
12	Eccleshill U 3rds	24	4	3	17	49	77	11
13	Savile Arms	24	5	1	18	39	73	11

1989/90 Central Midlands League Supreme Divisior

		p	w	d	l	f	a	pts
1	Hucknall Town	38	30	3	5	102	39	93
2	Heanor Town	38	25	6	7	108	49	81
3	Arnold Town	38	23	7	8	76	32	76
4	Harworth CI	38	21	6	11	77	55	69
5	Long Eaton U	38	19	10	9	69	46	67
6	Ilkeston Town	38	17	15	6	56	31	66
7	Boston FC	38	19	7	12	67	42	64
8	Crookes FC	38	16	12	10	62	45	60
9	Lincoln United	38	18	6	14	57	62	60
10	Gainsborough Town	38	17	5	16	51	51	56
11	Borrowash Vic.	38	14	10	14	63	62	52
12	Louth United	38	14	9	15	52	50	51
13	Oakham United	38	14	5	19	54	66	47
14	Priory FC	38	12	7	19	54	69	43
15	Melton Town	38	11	10	17	58	74	43
16	BRADFORD	38	11	8	19	59	83	41
17	Stanton FC	38	7	9	22	33	69	30
18	Kimberley Town	38	8	4	26	48	110	28
19	Riossington Main	38	5	7	26	46	105	22
20	Girmsby Borough	38	4	4	30	32	84	16

1990/91 North West Counties League Division Twc

		p	w	d	l	f	a	pts
1	Gt Harwood Town	34	27	5	2	81	22	86
2	Blackpool Rovers	34	25	4	5	84	33	79
3	BRADFORD	34	20	9	5	72	41	69
4	Bamber Bridge	34	20	6	8	78	46	66
5	Blackpool Mech.	34	18	7	9	51	30	61
6	Newcastle Town	34	16	12	6	48	30	60
7	Cheadle Town	34	17	3	14	55	54	54
8	Glossop	34	12	10	12	47	42	46
9	Burscough	34	12	8	14	39	51	44
10	Westhoughton Town	34	11	10	13	50	64	43
11	Castleton Gabs	34	11	9	14	42	47	42
12	Chadderton	34	10	6	18	51	61	36
13	Maghull	34	9	8	17	37	54	35
14	Kidsgrove Ath.	34	7	10	17	37	65	31
15	Ashton Town	34	9	2	23	43	86	29
16	Oldham Town*	34	8	4	22	35	66	27
17	Formby	34	5	9	20	46	63	24
18	Atherton Col.	34	6	4	24	37	78	22

1991/92 North West Counties League Division One

		p	w	d	l	f	a	pts
1	Ashton United	34	24	5	5	61	31	77
2	Gt Harwood Town	34	22	8	4	68	38	74
3	Eastwood Hanley	34	18	9	7	54	35	63
4	Blackpool Rovers	34	16	7	11	73	57	55
5	Prescot	34	15	6	13	48	43	51
6	Penrith	34	15	5	14	57	58	50
7	Skelmersdale U	34	11	11	12	48	52	44
8	Flixton	34	11	9	14	46	50	42
9	Clitheroe	34	11	9	14	44	55	42
10	Darwen	34	10	11	13	56	55	41
11	Atherton LR	34	11	8	15	38	45	41
12	Nantwich Town*	34	11	10	13	44	49	40
13	Vauxhall GM	34	10	10	14	42	51	40
14	Bacup Borough	34	9	11	14	41	45	38
15	St Helens Town	34	9	9	16	49	55	36
16	Maine Road	34	9	9	16	40	60	36
17	BRADFORD	34	10	5	19	57	68	35
18	Bootle	34	9	8	17	41	61	35

1992/93 North West Counties League Division One

		p	w	d	l	f	a	pts
1	Atherton LR	42	33	7	2	75	25	106
2	Bamber Bridge	42	24	11	7	81	37	83
3	Chadderton	42	24	11	7	99	64	83
4	Prescot	42	20	12	10	68	44	72
5	Newcastle Town	42	20	8	14	70	57	68
6	BRADFORD	42	19	8	15	54	43	65
7	Clitheroe	42	17	8	17	61	40	59
8	St Helens Town	42	16	11	15	79	62	59
9	Salford City	42	15	13	14	58	61	58
10	Burscough	42	16	10	16	58	68	58
11	Flixton	42	14	15	13	50	42	57
12	Blackpool Rovers	42	16	9	17	66	64	57
13	Nantwich Town	42	14	15	13	60	60	57
14	Penrith	42	15	11	16	62	67	56
15	Bacup Borough	42	14	13	15	66	59	55
16	Glossop NE *	42	16	9	17	70	67	54
17	Darwen	42	14	10	18	54	61	52
18	Eastwood Hanley	42	14	10	18	45	57	52
19	Maine Road	42	12	9	21	55	63	45
20	Kidsgrove Ath.	42	9	8	25	53	94	35
21	Skelmersdale U	42	7	10	25	45	84	31
22	Blackpool Mech.	42	2	4	36	27	137	10

1993/94 North West Counties League Division One

		p	w	d	l	f	a	pts
1	Atherton LR	42	25	13	4	83	34	88
2	Rossendale U	42	25	9	8	76	46	84
3	Burscough	42	22	13	7	107	50	79
4	Nantwich Town	42	22	11	9	80	54	77
5	Eastwood Hanley	42	22	11	9	75	52	77
6	Bootle	42	21	10	11	77	61	73
7	Penrith	42	20	11	11	62	44	71
8	Blackpool Rovers	42	19	10	13	64	57	67
9	Clitheroe	42	19	9	14	75	58	66
10	Kidsgrove Ath.	42	16	10	16	70	61	58
10	St Helens Town	42	14	13	15	60	55	55
11	Prescot	42	14	13	15	46	47	55
12	Maine Road	42	14	13	15	58	64	55
13	Newcastle Town	42	14	10	18	66	67	52
14	BRADFORD	42	12	12	18	54	79	48
15	Darwen	42	12	8	22	38	61	44
16	Glossop NE	42	12	8	22	58	86	44
17	Salford City	42	11	10	21	50	67	43
18	Chadderton	42	10	8	24	49	85	38
19	Bacup Borough	42	9	9	24	57	85	36
21	Skelmersdale U	42	8	8	26	55	92	32
22	Flixton	42	9	5	28	35	90	32

1994/95 North West Counties League Division One

		p	w	d	l	f	a	pts
1	BRADFORD	42	30	4	8	96	43	94
2	Clitheroe	42	27	9	6	104	49	90
3	St Helens Town	42	27	8	7	86	42	89
4	Trafford	42	27	5	10	98	50	86
5	Newcastle Town	42	24	7	11	75	57	79
6	Glossop NE	42	23	8	11	88	59	77
7	Blackpool Rovers	42	22	7	13	81	64	73
8	Burscough	42	19	15	8	102	65	72
9	Prescot	42	16	8	18	47	47	56
10	Penrith	42	16	7	19	72	72	55
11	Chadderton	42	15	7	20	56	70	52
12	Maine Road	42	14	9	19	68	81	51
13	Holker OB	42	14	8	20	75	81	50
14	Kidsgrove Ath.	42	13	11	18	63	72	50
15	Eastwood Hanley	42	14	8	20	66	78	50
16	Nantwich Town	42	14	7	21	85	83	49
17	Darwen	42	14	5	23	65	82	47
18	Rossendale U	42	12	11	19	60	82	47
19	Bootle	42	11	10	21	46	68	43
20	Skelmersdale U	42	10	7	25	67	118	37
21	Salford City	42	9	9	24	45	85	36
22	Bacup Borough	42	3	6	33	35	132	15

1995/96 Northern Premier League Division One

		p	w	d	l	f	a	pts
1	Lancaster City	40	24	11	5	79	38	83
2	Alfreton Town	40	23	9	8	79	47	78
3	Lincoln United	40	22	7	11	80	56	73
4	Curzon Ashton	40	20	7	13	73	53	67
5	Farsley Celtic	40	19	9	12	66	61	66
6	Radcliffe Boro.	40	17	13	10	70	48	64
7	Eastwood Town	40	18	9	13	60	47	63
8	Whitley Bay	40	18	8	14	72	62	62
9	Ashton United *	40	19	7	14	73	65	60
10	Atherton LR	40	15	12	13	60	61	57
11	Worksop Town	40	16	8	16	84	90	56
12	Gretna	40	13	13	14	75	65	52
13	Warrington Town	40	13	10	17	75	72	49
14	Leigh	40	14	7	19	53	59	49
15	Netherfield	40	13	10	17	64	73	49
16	Workington	40	11	12	17	50	62	45
17	BRADFORD	40	9	14	17	57	72	41
18	Congleton Town*	40	11	11	18	36	59	41
19	Gt Harwood Town*	40	9	7	24	44	78	33
20	Fleetwood	40	7	10	23	41	81	31
21	Harrogate Town	40	7	10	23	54	96	31

** points deducted*

1996/97 Northern Premier League Division One

		p	w	d	l	f	a	w	d	l	f	a	pts
1	Radcliffe Borough	42	15	2	4	47	17	11	5	5	30	16	85
2	Leigh RMI	42	12	5	4	33	19	12	6	3	32	14	83
3	Lincoln United	42	13	3	5	43	26	12	5	4	35	21	83
4	Farsley Celtic	42	10	6	5	32	18	13	2	6	43	30	77
5	Worksop Town*	42	12	5	4	38	15	8	7	6	30	23	69
6	Stocksbidge PS	42	11	5	5	39	26	8	6	7	27	28	68
7	BRADFORD	42	11	2	8	28	25	9	6	6	30	25	68
8	Ashton United	42	10	7	4	38	24	7	7	7	35	28	65
9	Great Harwood T	42	10	5	6	30	17	6	7	8	26	29	60
10	Droylesden	42	7	7	7	38	35	8	7	6	31	32	59
10	Curzon Ashton	42	9	4	8	35	35	7	6	8	26	34	58
11	Matlock Town	42	8	7	6	26	21	6	5	10	21	33	54
12	Whitley Bay	42	7	5	9	26	27	8	2	11	31	45	52
13	Flixton	42	7	6	8	24	24	5	8	8	30	32	50
14	Netherfield	42	8	8	5	25	19	4	6	11	17	31	50
15	Eastwood Town	42	5	10	6	31	33	5	8	8	24	35	48
16	Gretna	42	6	5	10	30	39	7	3	11	25	37	47
17	Harrogate Town	42	8	4	9	31	31	4	5	12	16	33	45
18	Congleton Town	42	7	8	6	33	29	3	4	14	12	34	42
19	Workington	42	4	4	13	25	37	4	6	11	23	42	34
21	Warrington T	42	2	11	8	20	32	3	7	11	22	47	33
22	Atherton LR	42	3	4	14	22	40	4	5	12	23	45	30

1997/98 Northern Premier League Division One

		p	w	d	l	f	a	w	d	l	f	a	pts
1	Whitby Town	42	15	3	3	50	27	15	5	1	49	21	98
2	Worksop Town	42	14	4	3	49	21	14	3	4	44	23	91
3	Ashton United	42	16	2	3	50	24	10	7	4	43	19	87
4	Droylesden	42	13	3	5	39	25	11	5	5	31	24	80
5	Lincoln United	42	11	5	5	37	25	9	6	6	39	37	71
6	Farsley Celtic	42	11	6	4	41	28	9	4	8	31	38	70
7	Witton Albion	42	11	5	5	44	20	8	4	9	33	35	66
8	Eastwood Town	42	8	10	3	36	25	10	2	9	32	26	66
9	BRADFORD	42	9	5	7	37	24	9	6	6	25	22	65
10	Belper Town	42	10	2	9	37	38	8	5	8	31	28	61
11	Stocksbidge PS	42	10	5	6	38	29	7	4	10	30	34	60
12	Trafford	42	9	3	9	29	25	7	3	11	30	36	54
13	Whitley Bay	42	7	6	8	32	30	7	6	8	28	33	54
14	Matlock Town	42	10	4	7	44	28	4	7	10	24	36	53
15	Gretna	42	8	6	7	32	26	5	3	13	26	38	48
16	Netherfield	42	8	2	11	32	42	4	9	8	23	33	47
17	Flixton	42	6	6	9	22	27	4	6	11	23	46	42
18	Congleton Town	42	7	5	9	32	42	4	3	14	33	59	41
19	Harrogate Town	42	4	8	9	26	34	4	6	11	31	46	38
20	Great Harwood T	42	2	8	11	21	43	6	4	11	20	45	36
21	Workington	42	4	3	14	18	40	4	4	13	20	44	31
22	Buxton	42	4	2	15	24	40	3	1	17	17	47	24

1998/99 Northern Premier League Division One

		p	w	d	l	f	a	w	d	l	f	a	pts
1	Droylesden	42	16	3	2	54	24	10	5	6	43	31	86
2	Hucknall Town*	42	14	5	2	45	19	12	6	3	35	19	86
3	Ashton United	42	13	6	2	40	20	9	6	6	39	26	78
4	Lincoln United	42	13	3	5	57	32	7	9	5	37	33	72
5	Eastwood Town	42	11	7	3	39	24	9	1	11	26	45	68
6	Radcliffe Boro	42	11	4	6	45	33	8	4	9	33	29	65
7	Burscough	42	12	2	7	33	24	7	6	8	34	37	65
8	Witton Albion	42	11	4	6	45	25	7	5	9	25	38	63
9	BRADFORD	42	9	6	6	35	26	8	5	8	29	29	62
10	Stocksbidge PS	42	7	7	7	31	34	9	6	6	33	26	61
11	Harrogate Town	42	9	3	9	42	40	8	4	9	33	37	58
12	Gretna	42	8	7	6	40	38	8	3	10	33	42	58
13	Belper Town	42	10	6	5	34	25	5	5	11	24	32	56
14	Trafford	42	8	6	7	22	20	6	5	10	28	38	53
15	Netherfield Kendal	42	7	3	11	30	36	6	7	8	21	28	49
16	Flixton	42	8	6	7	31	28	4	6	11	19	36	48
17	Matlock Town	42	8	2	11	31	33	6	4	11	22	39	48
18	Farsley Celtic	42	8	6	7	31	27	3	7	11	25	46	46
19	Whitley Bay	42	6	5	10	26	31	4	4	13	27	46	39
20	Congleton Town	42	6	8	7	32	38	2	7	12	33	53	39
21	Great Harwood T	42	5	5	11	28	32	5	3	13	23	41	38
22	Alfreton Town	42	4	6	11	24	42	5	2	14	29	44	35

1999/2000 Northern Premier League Division One

		p	w	d	l	f	a	w	d	l	f	a	pts
1	Accrington Stanley	42	14	5	2	55	19	11	4	6	41	24	84
2	Burscough	42	13	6	2	46	18	9	12	0	35	17	84
3	Witton Albion	42	13	6	2	49	24	10	9	2	39	22	84
4	BRADFORD	42	15	5	1	48	19	8	4	9	29	29	78
5	Radcliffe Borough	42	11	7	3	36	21	11	5	5	35	27	78
6	Farsley Celtic	42	12	5	4	34	20	7	6	8	32	32	68
7	Matlock Town	42	10	7	4	44	30	7	9	5	28	25	67
8	Ossett Town	42	10	5	6	39	24	7	3	11	38	31	59
9	Stocksbridge PS	42	11	2	8	30	30	5	6	10	25	40	56
10	Eastwood Town	42	8	5	8	35	29	7	6	8	29	36	56
11	Harrogate Town	42	7	8	6	31	26	7	4	10	34	41	54
12	Congleton Town	42	8	5	8	31	30	6	7	8	32	43	54
13	Chorley	42	4	10	7	26	31	9	5	7	27	33	54
14	Ashton United	42	6	9	6	33	31	6	7	8	32	36	52
15	Workington	42	8	4	9	26	27	5	9	7	23	28	52
16	Lincoln United	42	8	5	8	31	37	5	7	9	21	43	51
17	Belper Town	42	8	5	8	31	31	5	6	10	28	41	50
18	Trafford	42	3	8	10	27	29	8	4	9	28	34	45
19	Gretna	42	7	5	9	32	34	4	2	15	16	44	40
20	Netherfield Kendal	42	5	6	10	26	36	3	3	15	20	46	33
21	Flixton	42	6	3	12	28	37	1	6	14	19	48	30
22	Whitley Bay	42	3	6	12	24	45	4	3	14	17	42	30

**points deducted*

2000/01 Northern Premier League Division One

		p	w	d	l	f	a	w	d	l	f	a	pts
1	BRADFORD	42	14	2	5	43	19	14	3	4	40	21	89
2	Vauxhall Motors	42	13	5	3	53	20	10	5	6	42	30	79
3	Ashton United	42	12	6	3	53	22	11	3	7	38	27	78
4	Stocksbridge PS	42	10	6	5	47	35	9	7	5	33	25	70
5	Trafford*	42	12	5	4	36	25	8	4	9	34	37	68
6	Belper Town	42	8	7	6	37	32	10	4	7	34	30	65
7	Witton Albion	42	10	7	4	29	20	5	9	7	22	30	61
8	Ossett Town	42	10	6	5	34	27	6	6	9	32	31	60
9	Radcliffe Borough	42	10	4	7	38	27	7	4	10	34	44	59
10	Chorley	42	7	9	5	40	34	8	5	8	31	36	59
11	Harrogate Town	42	9	6	6	39	30	6	4	11	21	40	55
12	Matlock Town	42	8	5	8	40	42	6	5	10	30	32	52
13	North Ferriby United	42	10	2	9	33	37	4	8	9	31	36	52
14	Workington	42	8	5	8	26	27	5	7	9	27	33	51
15	Lincoln United	42	11	5	5	35	25	2	7	12	25	50	51
16	Gretna	42	8	5	8	42	33	4	7	10	30	49	48
17	Guiseley	42	6	8	7	19	22	5	7	9	18	28	48
18	Kendal Town*	42	9	7	5	35	24	3	5	13	25	45	47
19	Farsley Celtic	42	7	3	11	26	31	5	8	8	27	40	47
20	Eastwood Town	42	7	5	9	21	29	6	3	12	19	34	47
21	Winsford United*	42	6	8	7	35	33	7	3	11	26	37	44
22	Congleton Town	42	6	2	13	24	44	2	4	15	19	50	30

2001/02 Northern Premier League

		p	w	d	l	f	a	w	d	l	f	a	pts
1	Burton Albion	44	17	5	0	59	12	14	6	2	47	18	104
2	Vauxhall Motors	44	16	3	3	50	26	11	5	6	36	29	89
3	Lancaster City	44	14	4	4	44	26	9	5	8	36	31	78
4	Worksop Town	44	13	4	5	40	22	10	5	7	34	29	78
5	Emley	44	15	4	3	43	24	7	5	10	26	30	75
6	Accrington Stanley	44	10	7	5	47	27	11	2	9	42	37	72
7	Runcorn FC Halton	44	11	2	9	36	26	10	6	6	40	27	71
8	Barrow	44	10	7	5	40	25	9	3	10	35	34	67
9	Altrincham	44	11	3	8	33	28	8	6	8	33	30	66
10	BRADFORD	44	11	2	9	45	37	7	3	12	32	39	59
11	Droylsden	44	11	3	8	32	34	6	5	11	33	44	59
12	Blyth Spartans	44	9	8	5	30	24	5	8	9	29	38	58
13	Frickley Ath*	44	10	4	8	37	37	6	7	9	26	32	58
14	Gateshead	44	7	8	7	24	30	7	6	9	34	41	56
15	Whitby Town	44	7	5	10	33	39	8	3	11	28	37	53
16	Hucknall Town	44	6	5	11	25	35	8	4	10	24	33	51
17	Marine	44	7	7	8	36	38	4	10	8	26	33	50
18	Burscough	44	9	4	9	40	38	6	1	15	29	48	50
19	Gainsborough Trin.	44	9	5	8	36	30	4	5	13	25	46	49
20	Colwyn Bay	44	7	6	9	27	39	5	5	12	22	43	47
21	Bishop Auckland	44	5	5	12	22	34	7	3	12	24	34	44
22	Hyde United	44	5	7	10	29	37	5	3	14	32	50	40
23	Bamber Bridge*	44	5	4	13	23	40	2	6	14	15	48	30

2002/03 Northern Premier League

		p	w	d	l	f	a	w	d	l	f	a	pts
1	Accrington Stanley	44	18	4	0	53	20	12	6	4	44	24	100
2	Barrow	44	14	5	3	41	21	10	7	5	43	31	84
3	Vauxhall Motors	44	14	3	5	46	19	8	7	7	35	27	76
4	Stalybridge C	44	14	5	3	52	26	7	8	7	25	25	76
5	Worksop Town	44	9	6	7	42	35	12	3	7	40	32	72
6	Harrogate Town	44	10	4	8	38	31	11	4	7	37	32	71
7	BRADFORD	44	12	6	4	42	27	8	4	10	31	43	70
8	Hucknall Town	44	8	8	6	32	28	9	7	6	40	34	66
9	Droylsden	44	11	4	7	31	21	7	6	9	31	31	64
10	Whitby Town	44	8	4	10	38	38	9	8	5	42	31	63
11	Marine	44	10	5	7	39	31	7	5	10	24	29	61
12	Wakefield & Emley	44	8	12	2	22	16	6	6	10	24	32	60
13	Runcorn FC Halton	44	9	6	7	33	37	6	9	7	36	37	60
14	Altrincham	44	9	7	6	34	27	8	2	12	24	36	60
15	Gainsborough Trin.	44	9	5	8	35	35	7	6	9	32	31	59
16	Ashton United	44	8	9	5	42	39	7	4	11	29	40	58
17	Lancaster City	44	8	1	13	33	39	8	8	6	37	36	57
18	Burscough	44	9	6	7	26	24	5	3	14	18	27	51
19	Blyth Spartans	44	9	3	10	34	40	5	6	11	33	47	51
20	Frickley Athletic	44	7	5	10	18	33	6	3	13	27	45	47
21	Gateshead	44	5	7	10	34	39	5	4	13	26	42	41
22	Colwyn Bay	44	3	5	14	28	47	2	4	16	24	52	24
23	Hyde United	44	3	4	15	22	47	2	4	16	18	51	23

2003/04 Northern Premier League

		p	w	d	l	f	a	w	d	l	f	a	pts
1	Hucknall Town	44	15	5	2	38	14	14	3	5	45	24	95
2	Droylsden	44	15	4	3	51	29	11	4	7	45	35	86
3	Barrow	44	14	4	4	41	20	8	10	4	41	32	80
4	Alfreton Town	44	14	5	3	45	18	9	4	9	28	25	78
5	Harrogate Town	44	15	2	5	44	26	9	3	10	35	37	77
6	Southport	44	10	7	5	36	25	10	3	9	35	27	70
7	Worksop Town	44	10	6	6	34	22	9	7	6	35	28	70
8	Lancaster City	44	12	4	6	40	25	8	5	9	22	24	69
9	Vauxhall Motors	44	12	5	5	44	32	7	5	10	34	43	67
10	Gainsborough Trin.	44	12	5	5	46	25	5	8	9	24	27	64
11	Stalybridge Celtic	44	8	6	8	35	33	10	4	8	37	33	64
12	Altrincham	44	9	8	5	36	24	7	7	8	30	27	63
13	Runcorn FC Halton	44	5	9	8	32	32	11	4	7	35	31	61
14	Ashton United	44	7	5	10	34	44	10	3	9	25	35	59
15	Whitby Town	44	9	3	10	24	34	5	8	9	31	36	53
16	Marine	44	8	5	9	32	31	5	7	10	30	43	51
17	BRADFORD	44	2	9	11	23	32	10	5	7	25	30	50
18	Spennymoor U	44	8	2	12	30	51	6	4	12	25	42	48
19	Burscough	44	6	8	8	27	30	4	7	11	20	37	45
20	Radcliffe Borough	44	9	1	12	39	46	3	5	14	35	53	42
21	Blyth Spartans	44	5	7	10	30	40	5	3	14	24	34	40
22	Frickley Athletic	44	8	4	10	29	32	3	3	16	22	51	40
23	Wakefield & Emley	44	4	2	16	18	45	4	4	14	27	54	30

1988/89

Second in the West Riding County Amateur League Division Three

#	Month	Date	Opponent	Score	Res	Att	1	2	3	4	5	6	7	8	9	10	11	12	13	
1	Aug	31	SALTS RESERVES	3-2	L	350	Pool	Burns	Carey	Taylor	Ellison	Sagar	McGregor	Barraclough	Jansen 1	Waters	Armitage 1	McDonald 1		
2	Sep	3	Crag Road Utd Res.	4-8	L	60	Pool	Weldon	Michallat	Taylor	Ellison	Sagar	McGregor	Barraclough	McDonald 3	Armitage 1	Burns			
3		7	Hall Green Utd Res.	8-3	L	40	Johnson	Carey	Waters 1	Taylor	Ellison	Burns	McGregor	Barraclough	Jansen 3	McDonald 1	Armitage 3			
4		10	Savile Arms	4-2	L	40	Johnson	Carey	Waters	Burns	Robinson	Wilkinson 2	McGregor 1	Taylor	McDonald 1	Jansen	Armitage	Howarth	Gadd	
5		17	Littletown Reserves	3-5	L	50	Pool	Waters	Wilkinson	Ellison	Carey	McGregor 1	Barraclough	Burns	Jansen 1	McDonald	Armitage 1			
6		24	ECCLESHILL U 3RDS	2-0	L	100	Clarke	Waters	Carey	Taylor	Dawson	Wilkinson	McGregor	Burns	Jansen	McDonald 2	Armitage			
7	Oct	1	Gatehouse	2-2	L	60	Pool	Carey	Waters	Taylor	Burns	Wilkinson	McGregor	Barraclough	Jansen 2	McDonald	Armitage			
8		8	GATEHOUSE	1-2	L	90	Martin	Waters	Carey	Taylor	Burns	Wilkinson	McGregor 1	Barraclough	Jansen	McDonald	Armitage			
9		15	Springfield YC	0-5	DC	40	Burns	Waters	Carey	Taylor	Robinson	Wilkinson	McGregor	Barraclough	Jansen	McDonald	Armitage			
10		22	PUDSEY LIBERAL	3-0	L	100	Hill	Burns 1	Hall M	Taylor	Tavernier	Carey	Byrne 1	Barraclough	Jansen	McDonald	Land 1			
11	Nov	5	TRINITY ATH. RES.	3-0	L	90	Hill	Waters	Carey	Wright 1	Hall M	Tavernier 1	Byrne	Land	Jansen 1	Robinson	Armitage			
12		12	St Blaise	6-1	L	30	Hill	Waters 1	March	Land 1	Hall M	Tavernier	Byrne 1	Jansen 2	Worthy	McGregor 1	Armitage	Robinson		
13		19	OVENDON W.R. RES.	4-1	L	80	Hill	Hall M	March	Tavernier	Land 1	Waters	Armitage	Wright	Jansen 1	Worthy	Byrne 2	Robinson		
14		26	Salts Reserves	1-2	LC	60	Hill	Waters	March	Tavernier	Hall M	Armitage	Wright	McGregor	Byrne 1	Worthy	Jansen	Robinson		
15	Dec	3	Ovenden W.R. Reserves	3-1	L	20	Hill	Waters	Wright	McGregor	Hall M 1	Tavernier	Land	Armitage	Brown	Margison 2	Byrne	March		
16		10	Field Reserves	3-5	L	30	Hill	Waters	Wigglesworth	Wright	Hall M	Tavernier 1	McGregor	Land 2	Jansen	Margison	Armitage	Benn		
17		17	Salts Reserves	2-1	L	50	Hill	Waters	Wigglesworth	Wright	Hall M	Tavernier 1	McGregor	Land	Benn 1	Worthy	March			
18	Jan	7	Eccleshill Utd. 3rds	8-3	L	50	Hill	Waters	Wigglesworth	Wright	Hall M 2	Dawson	McGregor 2	Land 1	Benn 3	Tavernier	March	Armitage		
19		14	HALL GREEN U RES.	5-0	L	70	Hill	Waters	Wigglesworth	March	Hall M 1	Tavernier	McGregor 2	Land	Benn 1	Margison	Armitage 1	Dawson		
20		21	Trinity Ath. Reserves	8-1	L	40	Hill	Waters	Wigglesworth	Wright	Hall M	Tavernier	McGregor	Land 2	Benn 4	Margison 1	Armitage 1	Rodgers		
21	Feb	4	SAVILLE ARMS	5-4	L	80	Hill	Waters	Wigglesworth	Rodgers	Tavernier	March	McGregor	Benn 2	Land	Hall M 1	Armitage 2	Hall A		
22		11	LIITTLETOWN RES.	3-2	L	50	Hill	Waters	Wigglesworth	Wright	Tavernier	Hall M 1	McGregor	Benn	Land	Margison 1	Armitage 1			
23		18	Pudsey Liberal	3-2	L	50	Hill	Waters	Wigglesworth	Margison	Tavernier	Hall M 1	McGregor	Benn	Land	Wright 2	Armitage			
24	Mar	4	ST BLAISE	4-1	L	80	Hill	Waters	Wigglesworth	Wright	Tavernier	Hall M 1	McGregor	Armitage	Land 1	Margison 1	Benn			1og
25		11	CRAG ROAD UTD. RES.	3-5	L	90	Hill	Waters	Wigglesworth	Wright 1	Tavernier 1	Hall M	Benn 1	Margison	Land	Rodgers	Armitage	Hall A	Sutcliffe	
26	Apr	11	FIELD RESERVES	3-1	L	50	Hill	Waters 1	Wigglesworth	Hall M	Tavernier	Wright 1	McGregor	Margison	Land 1	Benn	Armitage			

1989/90

16th in the Central Midlands League Supreme Division

						1	2	3	4	5	6	7	8	9	10	11	12	13	
1	Aug	12 Borrowash Victoria	1-1	L	170	Kennedy	Brook	Royston	Payton	Tavernier 1	Hall	Edmondson	Kershaw	Byrne	Wardman	Flanagan			
2		19 HEANOR TOWN	3-1	L	202	Kennedy	Hudson	Royston	Payton	Tavernier	Hall	Edmondson	Kershaw	Byrne 2	Wardman 1	Flanagan	Horne	Duxbury	
3		26 HUCKNALL TOWN	2-1	L	213	Kennedy	Brook	Royston	Payton	Tavernier	Hall	Byrne	Kershaw	Horne	Wardman 1	Flanagan 1			
4	Sep	2 Priory	1-3	L	100	Kennedy	Hudson	Royston	Payton	Horne	Hall	Land	Kershaw	Attenborough	Wardman	Tavernier 1	Duxbury		
5		9 ILKESTON TOWN	0-3	L	205	Kennedy	Hudson	Royston	Horne	Tavernier	Flanagan	Brook	Kershaw	Payton	Wardman	Kane	Duxbury	Hall	
6		16 Long Eaton United	0-3	L	110	Kennedy	Hudson	Brook	Payton	Royston	Hall	Byrne	Kershaw	Edmondson	Wardman	Flanagan	Duxbury		
7		23 MELTON TOWN	1-5	L	201	Kennedy	Hudson	Royston	Brook	Attenborough	Hall	Payton	Kershaw	Byrne 1	Wardman	Edmondson	Duxbury	Flanagan	
8		30 KIMBERLEY TOWN	5-0	L	151	Garrod	Royston	Hudson	Flanagan	Attenborough	Hall	Payton	Kershaw	Byrne 1	Wardman 2	Edmondson 2	Duxbury		
9	Oct	7 Oakham United	1-0	L	80	Garrod	Royston	Hudson	Payton	Attenborough	Hall	Duxbury	Kershaw	Byrne	McMann	Edmondson			1og
10		14 Lincoln United	1-1	L	85	Garrod	Royston	Hudson	Payton	Attenborough	Hall	Duxbury	Kershaw	Brook	Edmonson	Byrne 1			
11		21 GRIMSBY BOROUGH	0-1	L	168	Garrod	Royston	Hudson	Payton	McDonald	Hall	Edmondson	Kershaw	Byrne	Brook	Serop	Holmes		
12		28 LOUTH UNITED	1-1	L	124	Garrod	Royston	Hudson	Payton	McDonald	Hall	Byrne	Kershaw	Sykes 1	Brook	Edmondson	Duxbury		
13	Nov	4 CROOKES	2-3	L	138	Garrod	Royston	Hudson	Brook	McDonald	Hall	Holmes 1	Kershaw	Payton	Wardman	Kane 1	Edmondson		
14		11 BOSTON	2-3	L	131	Garrod	Hudson	Brook	Kane	McDonald	Hall	Pearson	Holmes	Edmondson 1	Wardman 1	Payton	Duxbury	Byrne	
15		17 Gainsborough Town	0-6	L	70	Garrod	Brook	Hudson	Payton	McDonald	Hall	Pearson	Kershaw	Byrne	Wardman	Kane	Holmes	Edmondson	
16		25 STANTON	1-1	L	149	Garrod	Royston	Hudson	Payton 1	Tavernier	Attenborough	Brook	Kershaw	Byrne	Wardman	Kane	Edmondson		
17	Dec	2 Heanor Town	1-4	L	163	Garrod	Royston	Hudson	Payton	Tavernier	McDonald	Pearson	Kershaw	Byrne 1	Wardman	Edmondson	Duxbury		
18		9 ARNOLD TOWN	1-4	L	103	Garrod	MacKay	Royston	Payton	McDonald	Tavernier 1	Padgett	Kershaw	Eli	Hirst	Wardman	Hudson	Duxbury	
19		13 Harworth C.I.	0-3	L	90	Garrod	Royston	Padgett	Tavernier	McDonald	Payton	MacKay	Kershaw	Eli	Hirst	Wardman	Byrne	Edmondson	
20		23 LONG EATON UTD.	4-1	L	145	Garrod	Hudson	Edmondson	Kershaw	Payton 1	Tavernier	MacKay	Eli 1	Watmuff 1	Wardman 1	Reape	Duxbury	Thorpe	
21		30 Crookes	0-3	L	100	Garrod	MacKay	Hudson	Kershaw	Tavernier	Payton	Reape	Eli	Watmuff	Edmondson	Wardman	Royston	Pearson	
22	Jan	3 ROSSINGTON MAIN	3-1	L	204	Allen	Royston	Edmondson	McDonald	Tavernier	Payton	MacKay 1	Kershaw	Watmuff	Eli	Wardman 2	Lilley	Byrne	
23		6 Grimsby Borough	2-0	L	85	Allen	Edmondson	Royston	McDonald	Tavernier	Payton	MacKay	Kershaw	Watmuff	Wardman	Byrne 1	Hudson	Pearson	1og
24		13 Ilkeston Town	1-2	L	325	Allen	Edmondson 1	Royston	McDonald	Tavernier	Hirst	MacKay	Kershaw	Eli	Wardman	Byrne	Pearson	Reape	
25		20 Kimberley Town	1-6	L	70	Pearson	Royston	Edmondson	Payton 1	Tavernier	McDonald	MacKay	Kershaw	Watmuff	Wardman	Byrne	Thorpe	Reape	
26		27 Melton Town	2-1	LC	80	Allen	McDonald	Henry	MacKay	Edmondson	Payton	Wardman 2	Kershaw	Watmuff	Hirst	Eli	Pearson		
27	Feb	3 LINCOLN UNITED	2-2	L	136	Allen	McDonald	Henry	MacKay	Edmondson	Payton	Wardman 1	Kershaw	Watmuff	Hirst	Eli 1	Byrne	Pearson	
28		10 GAINSBOROUGH TOWN	1-1	L	120	Allen	McDonald	Henry	Watmuff	Saunders	Payton	Wardman 1	Kershaw	Byrne	Hirst	Eli			
29		20 Louth United	1-2	FC	100	Allen	McDonald	Henry	Watmuff	Saunders	Payton	Wardman 1	Kershaw	Byrne	Hirst	Eli	Pearson		
30		24 Boston	2-1	L	80	Allen	McDonald	Henry	Watmuff 1	Saunders	Payton	Wardman	Kershaw	Byrne 1	Abrams	Edmondson			
31	Mar	10 Louth United	1-3	L	75	Allen	McDonald	Hudson	Kershaw	Saunders	Abrams	Eli	Hirst	Watmuff	Wardman 1	Byrne	Edmondson		
32		15 Grimsby Borough	0-1	LC	95	Allen	McDonald	Henry	Edmondson	Saunders	Kershaw	Wardman	MacKay	Watmuff	Hirst	Eli			
33		17 HARWORTH C.I.	2-2	L	125	Allen	McDonald	Henry	Edmondson	Saunders	Kershaw	Wardman 1	MacKay	Watmuff	Hirst	Eli 1	Byrne		
34		24 Stanton	2-4	L	75	Allen	Edmondson	Henry	Byrne	Saunders 1	Kershaw	Wardman 1	MacKay	Watmuff	Hirst	Eli	Hudson		
35		31 Arnold Town	1-2	L	200	Allen	Hudson	Henry	Edmondson	Saunders	Kershaw	Wardman	MacKay	Watmuff	Hirst	Eli	McDonald	Sandhu	1og
36	Apr	4 OAKHAM UNITED	3-3	L	155	Allen	Hudson	Henry	Edmondson	Saunders	Kershaw	Wardman	MacKay	Watmuff 2	Hirst	Eli 1	Payton	McDonald	
37		7 BORROWASH VIC.	2-3	L	101	Allen	McDonald	Edmondson	Payton	Saunders	Kershaw	Wardman	MacKay	Watmuff	Byrne	Eli 1	Hudson	Henry	1og
38		14 Melton Town	2-0	L	73	Allen	Hudson	Henry	McDonald	Saunders	Edmondson	Wardman 2	Payton	MacKay	Hirst	Eli	Sandhu		
39		16 Rossington Main	3-2	L	55	Allen	Thorpe	Reape	Sandhu	Edmondson 2	McDonald	Wardman 1	MacKay	Payton	Hirst	Eli			
40		21 Hucknall Town	0-1	L	465	Allen	Hudson	Henry	McDonald	Edmondson	Sandhu	Wardman	Watmuff	Payton	MacKay	Eli	Kalay	Waters	
41		28 PRIORY	4-2	L	95	Allen	Hudson	Henry	McDonald	Edmondson	Sandhu	Wardman 3	Watmuff	Byrne	MacKay 1	Eli	Kalay		

1990/91

Third in the NW Counties League Division Two: Promoted

						1	2	3	4	5	6	7	8	9	10	11	12	13	
1	Aug	18 Ashton Town	4-2	L	65	Allen	Eli Rupert	McDonald	Kershaw	Saunders	Clarke	Wardman 3	Mackay	Watmuff	Edmondson	Eli Rohan 1			
2		25 BURSCOUGH	2-2	L	108	Allen	Eli Rupert	McDonald	Kershaw	Saunders 2	Clarke	Wardman	Roberts	Watmuff	Abrams	Eli Rohan	Hudson		
3		27 Atherton Collieries	1-2	L	150	Allen	Eli Rupert	Hudson	Kershaw	Saunders 1	Edmondson	Wardman	Mackay	Watmuff	Abrams	Eli Rohan	McDonald	Pickles	
4	Sep	8 CHADDERTON	1-1	L	138	Allen	Payton	Eli Rupert	Kershaw	Saunders	Pickles	Wardman 1	Clarke	Watmuff	Roberts	Edmondson	Hudson	McDonald	
5		14 Great Harwood Town	3-0	LPT	225	Allen	Eli Rupert	Edmondson 1	Kershaw	Saunders	Pickles	Wardman	Clarke 2	Watmuff	Roberts	Eli Rohan	Payton		
6		22 Castleton Gabriels	2-2	LCC	78	Allen	Eli Rupert	Edmondson	Kershaw	Hudson	Pickles	Wardman 1	Clarke	Watmuff	Robers	Eli Rohan 1	Price		
7		25 GREAT HARWOOD T	3-0	LPT	181	Allen	Eli Rupert	Edmondson	Kershaw	McDonald	Pickles	Wardman	Clarke	Watmuff	Roberts	Eli Rohan 1			2og
8		29 CASTLETON GABRIELS	0-2	LCC	148	Allen	Eli Rupert	Edmondson	Kershaw	McDonald	Pickles	Wardman	Clarke	Watmuff	Roberts	Eli Rohan	Hudson		
9	Oct	13 Cheadle Town	2-1	L	100	Allen	Payton	McDonald	Kershaw	Hudson	Pickles	Wardman 1	Eli Rupert	Watmuff	Roberts	Edmondson	Jackson		1og
10		20 NEWCASTLE TOWN	0-0	L	152	Allen	Payton	Edmondson	Eli Rupert	Clarke	Pickles	Wardman	Kershaw	Watmuff	Roberts	Eli Rohan	Jackson		
11		27 GREAT HARWOOD T	2-0	L	127	Allen	Payton	Eli Rupert	Kershaw	Saunders	Pickles	Wardman 1	Clarke	Watmuff	Roberts	Eli Rohan			1og
12	Nov	24 BAMBER BRIDGE	1-0	L	130	Allen	Payton	Eli Rupert	Kershaw	Saunders	Pickles	Wardman 1	Jackson	Watmuff	Slater	Eli Rohan	Sidda	Mackay	
13		10 HATFIELD MAIN	5-2	CC	115	Allen	Payton	Eli Rupert 1	Kershaw	Saunders 1	Pickles	Wardman 1	Jackson	Watmuff 1	Roberts 1	Eli Rohan	Hudson	Mackay	
14	Dec	1 Oldham Town	1-0	L	60	Allen	Payton	Eli Rupert	Kershaw	Saunders	Pickles	Wardman	Sidda	Watmuff	Slater	Eli Rohan 1	Jackson		
15		15 GOOLE TOWN	3-0	CC	142	Allen	Payton 1	Eli Rupert	Kershaw	Saunders	Pickles	Wardman 2	Sidda	Watmuff	Slater	Eli Rohan			
16		22 WESTHOUGHTON	5-1	L	148	Allen	Payton	Eli Rupert	Hudson	Saunders	Jackson	Wardman 2	Sidda	Watmuff	Slater 2	Eli Rohan	Edmondson 1	Sandhu	
17		26 Blackpool Rovers	1-5	L	211	Allen	Payton	Eli Rupert	Kershaw	Saunders	Jackson	Wardman 1	Sidda	Watmuff	Slater	Eli Rohan			
18		29 OLDHAM TOWN	4-2	L	162	Allen	Payton	Eli Rupert	Kershaw	Saunders	Jackson	Wardman 2	Sidda	Edmondson	Slater 1	Eli Rohan 1	Hudson		
19	Jan	5 Newcastle Town	0-0	L	100	Allen	Payton	Eli Rupert	Kershaw	Rawnsly	Jackson	Wardman	Sidda	Edmondson	Slater	Eli Rohan	Goodman		
20		9 Farsley Celtic	2-1	CC	241	Allen	Jackson	Eli Rupert 1	Kershaw	Saunders	Sidda	Wardman	Slater 1	Watmuff	Edmondson	Eli Rohan	Hudson	Rawnsley	aet
21		12 ASHTON TOWN	3-2	L	144	Allen	Payton	Eli Rupert	Kershaw	Hudson	Sidda	Wardman	Edmondson	Watmuff 1	Slater 2	Eli Rohan	Rawnsley		
22		19 Maghull	3-0	L	101	Allen	Payton	Eli Rupert	Kershaw	Guest	Edmondson 1	Wardman 1	Rawnsley	Watmuff	Slater	Eli Rohan 1	Hudson	Jackson	
23		26 ATHERTON COLLIERY	4-0	L	214	Allen	Payton	Eli Rupert 1	Kershaw	Guest	Edmondson	Wardman 2	Rawnsley	Watmuff	Slater	Eli Rohan	Hudson	Jackson	1og
24	Feb	2 Chadderton	3-0	L	182	Allen	Payton	Eli Rupert	Wroot 1	Guest	Edmondson	Wardman 1	Jackson	Watmuff	Slater 1	Eli Rohan	Hudson		
25		23 Cheadle Town	2-1	LPT	90	Allen	Payton	Eli Rupert	Kershaw	Guest	Edmondson	Wardman 1	Jackson	Watmuff 1	Slater	Eli Rohan	Sidda		
26		27 Glossop North End	2-2	L	250	Allen	Payton	Eli Rupert	Kershaw	Sidda	Edmondson 1	Wardman 1	Wroot	Watmuff	Slater	Eli Rohan	Jackson		
27	Mar	2 CHEADLE TOWN	0-2	LPT	132	Allen	Payton	Eli Rupert	Kershaw	Sidda	Edmondson	Wardman	Wroot	Watmuff	Slater	Jackson	Mackay		
28		9 Bamber Bridge	2-2	L	350	Allen	Payton 1	Eli Rupert	Kershaw	Guest	Wroot	Wardman	Mackay	Edmondson	Slater 1	Eli Rohan			
29		16 MAGHULL	1-1	L	147	Allen	Payton	Eli Rupert	Kershaw	Guest	Wroot	Wardman	Mackay	Watmuff	Slater 1	Edmondson			
30		23 Kidsgrove Athletic	1-1	L	164	Allen	Payton	Eli Rupert	Kershaw	Guest	Wroot	Wardman	Mackay	Edmondson	Jackson 1	Eli Rohan			
31		30 Garforth Town	3-1	CC	317	Allen	Payton	Eli Rupert	Kershaw	Sidda	Wroot	Wardman 2	Mackay	Watmuff	Slater	Eli Rohan 1	Jackson		
32	Apr	1 Castleton Gabriels	3-0	L	215	Allen	Payton	Eli Rupert 1	Kershaw 1	Wroot	Hudson	Wardman	Edmondson	Watmuff	Jackson	Eli Rohan 1	Sandhu		
33		6 FORMBY	2-0	L	143	Allen	Payton	Eli Rupert	Kershaw	Wroot	Hudson	Wardman 1	Mackay	Jackson	Slater 1	Eli Rohan	Edmondson		
34		9 CASTLETON GABRIELS	5-4	L	169	Allen	Payton	Eli Rupert	Kershaw	Mackay	Sidda	Wardman 3	Jackson	Watmuff	Slater 2	Eli Rohan	Pickles	Edmondson	
35		13 Formby	1-1	L	110	Allen	Payton	Eli Rupert	Mackay	Wroot	Sidda	Wardman 1	Jackson	Watmuff	Slater	Pickles	Edmondson		
36		16 Burscough	1-0	L	85	Allen	Payton	Eli Rupert	Edmondson	Sidda	Pickles	Wardman	Mackay	Watmuff	Slater	Eli Rohan 1			
37		20 BLACKPOOL ROVERS	0-3	L	238	Allen	Sidda	Eli Rupert	Edmondson	Wroot	Pickles	Wardman	Mackay	Watmuff	Slater	Eli Rohan	Payton		
38		23 GLOSSOP NORTH END	1-2	L	123	Allen	Payton	Eli Rupert 1	Kershaw	Sidda	Pickles	Wardman	Mackay	Watmuff	Slater	Eli Rohan	Edmondson		
39		27 KIDSGROVE ATH.	4-0	L	129	Allen	Payton	Eli Rupert 1	Wroot 1	Sidda	Pickles 1	Wardman	Mackay	Edmondson	Guest	Eli Rohan 1	Kershaw	Hudson	
40		29 Westhoughton Town	3-0	L	70	Allen	Payton	Hudson	Kershaw	Wroot	Pickles	Wardman	Edmondson	Watmuff 1	Guest	Edwards	Eli Rupert	Eli Rohan 2	
41	May	1 Pontefract Collieries	5-1	CC	935	Allen	Payton	Eli Rupert	Sidda	Wroot	Pickles	Wardman 2	Mackay	Watmuff	Slater	Eli Rohan 1	Kershaw 1	Edmondson 1	
42		4 BLACKPOOL MECHANICS	3-2	L	184	Allen	Payton	Eli Rupert	Sidda	Wroot	Pickles	Wardman 1	Edmondson 1	Watmuff	Slater 1	Eli Rohan	Kershaw		
43		7 Great Harwood Town	3-2	L	250	Allen	Payton	Eli Rupert	Kershaw	Wroot	Pickles	Wardman 1	Saunders 2	Watmuff	Slater	Eli Rohan			
44		9 Blackpool Mechanics	0-1	L	150	Allen	Payton	Eli Rupert	Kershaw	Wroot	Pickles	Wardman	Saunders	Mackay	Slater	Eli Rohan	Edmondson		
45		11 CHEADLE TOWN	3-2	L	202	Allen	Sidda	Eli Rupert	Edmondson	Guest	Pickles	Wardman 2	Mackay	Watmuff	Slater	Eli Rohan 1			

Game 41: West Riding County Cup final played at Valley Parade

1991/92

17th in the NW Counties League Division One

No	Month	Date / Opponent	Score	Comp	Att	1	2	3	4	5	6	7	8	9	10	11	12	13	
1	Aug	24 Nantwich Town	0-3	L	116	Walsh	Edmondson	Eli Rupert	Stanley G	Pearson	Pattison	Wardman	Abrams	Watmuff	Slater	Eli Rohan	Cotton		
2		26 FLIXTON	1-1	L	283	Walsh	Edmondson	Eli Rupert	Stanley G	Pearson	Pattison	Wardman 1	Abrams	Adamson	Slater	Eli Rohan	Whyte		
3		31 Bootle	3-1	L	75	Allen	Payton	Eli Rupert 1	Stanley G	Pearson 1	Pickles	Wardman	Edmondson	Pattison	Slater	Eli Rohan 1	Whyte		
4	Sep	7 Winterton Rangers	1-4	FAV	113	Allen	Payton	Eli Rupert	Stanley G	Pearson	Pickles	Wardman	Edmondson	Pattison	Slater 1	Eli Rohan	Adamson		
5		11 BOOTLE	0-1	L	175	Allen	Payton	Edmondson	Stanley G	Pearson	Pickles	Wardman	Eli Rupert	Colville	Slater	Eli Rohan	Pattison		
6		14 ASHTON UNITED	1-1	L	151	Walsh	Payton	Eli Rupert	Stanley G	Pearson 1	Pickles	Wardman	Edmondson	Whyte	Slater	Eli Rohan			
7		21 SKELMERSDALE UNITED	2-2	L	169	Walsh	Payton	Eli Rupert	Stanley G	Pearson	Pickles	Wardman 1	Edmondson 1	Watmuff	Slater	Eli Rohan			
8		28 Vauxhall G.M.	2-4	L	55	Walsh	Payton	Eli Rupert	Stanley G	Pattison	Pickles	Wardman 1	Taylor	Watmuff	Slater	Eli Rohan	Edmondson 1		
9	Oct	1 Clitheroe	5-0	L	150	Walsh	Payton	Kershaw	Stanley G	Pearson 1	Wroot	Wardman	Taylor	Watmuff	Slater	Eli Rohan 3	Whyte		1og
10		5 Bacup Borough	2-1	L	155	Walsh	Payton 1	Eli Rupert	Edmondson	Stanley G	Pickles	Wardman	Taylor	Watmuff	Slater	Eli Rohan 1	Cotton	Sandhu	
11		12 Atherton LR	1-0	L	170	Walsh	Payton	Eli Rupert	Edmondson	Wroot	Pickles	Wardman	Taylor	Watmuff	Slater	Eli Rohan	Cotton		1og
12		19 Nantwich Town	1-1	LCC	105	Walsh	Payton	Eli Rupert	Edmondson	Wroot	Pickles	Wardman	Taylor	Watmuff	Slater	Eli Rohan	Cotton 1		
13		23 NANTWICH TOWN	1-3	LCC	116	Walsh	Payton	Eli Rupert 1	Edmondson	Wroot	Pickles	Wardman	Taylor	Watmuff	Slater	Cotton			
14		26 ST HELENS TOWN	1-2	L	132	Preston	Payton	Pickles	Edmondson	Wroot	Pattison	Wardman 1	Taylor	Watmuff	Slater	Eli Rohan	Cotton		
15	Nov	9 Great Harwood Town	1-3	L	190	Walsh	Payton	Eli Rupert	Edmondson 1	Pattison	Pickles	Wardman	Gilderdale	Stanley G	Slater	Eli Rohan	Cotton		
16		16 BACUP BOROUGH	2-2	L	152	Walsh	Payton	Eli Rupert 1	Jackson 1	Pattison	Stanley G	Wardman	Gilderdale	Cotton	Taylor	Eli Rohan	Stanley C		
17		23 BLACKPOOL ROVERS	1-2	L	125	Walsh	Payton	Eli Rupert	Jackson	Pattison	Stanley G	Wardman 1	Gilderdale	Taylor	Slater	Eli Rohan	Edmondson		
18		30 Darwen	2-2	L	73	Darville	Payton	Eli Rupert	Jackson	Pattison 1	Stanley G	Wardman 1	Gilderdale	Taylor	Pickles	Eli Rohan	Cotton	Edmondson	
19	Dec	7 Prescot	0-3	L	150	Booth	Gilderdale	Edmondson	Jackson	Pattison	Pickles	Wilkinson	Stanley G	Cotton	Slater	Stanley C	Wardman	Payton	
20		14 CLITHEROE	2-1	L	128	Booth	Gilderdale	Wroot	Stanley G	Pattison	Pickles	Wardman 2	Taylor	Watmuff	Craven	Eli Rohan			
21		17 Pontefract Colls	2-1	CC	100	Booth	Gilderdale	Wroot	Stanley G	Pattison	Pickles	Wardman	Taylor	Watmuff	Slater 1	Eli Rohan 1	Payton		
22		21 St Helens Town	1-2	L	75	Preston	Gilderdale	Pickles	Wroot	Stanley G	Craven	Wardman	Edmondson 1	Watmuff	Slater	Eli Rohan			
23		26 VAUXHALL G.M.	5-0	L	172	Preston	Gilderdale	Craven 1	Wright	Stanley G	Pickles	Wardman 2	Edmondson	Watmuff 1	Slater 1	Eli Rohan			
24		28 Flixton	2-5	L	144	Allen	Eli Rupert	Edmondson 1	Wright	Stanley G	Pickles	Wardman 1	Gilderdale	Watmuff	Wroot	Eli Rohan	Stanley C		
25	Jan	4 Blackpool Rovers	3-5	L	120	Booth	Eli Rupert	Edmondson	Wroot	Stanley G	Pickles	Wardman 2	Gilderdale	Watmuff	Craven	Eli Rohan	Taylor 1	Payton	
26		10 GARFORTH TOWN	2-0	CC	312	Booth	Gilderdale	Eli Rupert	Wroot	Stanley G 1	Pickles	Wardman 1	Craven	Watmuff	Taylor	Eli Rohan			
27		18 NANTWICH TOWN	5-1	L	102	Booth	Gilderdale	Eli Rupert	Kershaw	Stanley G	Pickles	Wardman 1	Taylor	Watmuff 1	Edmondson 2	Eli Rohan 1			
28	Feb	1 DARWEN	3-2	L	173	Booth	Gilderdale	Eli Rupert 1	Edmondson 1	Stanley G	Pickles	Wardman 1	Taylor	Watmuff	Craven	Eli Rohan	Adamson		
29		8 Maine Road	3-0	L	80	Booth	Gilderdale	Eli Rupert	Wroot	Stanley G	Pickles	Wardman 1	Taylor	Watmuff	Craven 2	Edmondson	Adamson	Eli Rohan	
30		22 Eastwood Hanley	2-3	L	67	Booth	Gilderdale	Eli Rupert	Edmondson	Stanley G	Adamson	Wardman 1	Taylor	Watmuff	Craven	Eli Rohan 1			
31		29 PRESCOT	1-3	L	169	Booth	Gilderdale	Edmondson	Wroot	Stanley G 1	Pickles	Wardman	Taylor	Watmuff	Craven	Eli Rohan	Adamson	Storey	
32	Mar	4 PENRITH	0-2	L	95	Booth	Gilderdale	Edmondson	Kershaw	Stanley G	Pickles	Wardman	Taylor	Watmuff	Singh	Eli Rohan	Adamson	Storey	
33		7 GREAT HARWOOD T	2-3	L	207	Walsh	Gilderdale	Edmondson	Kershaw	Stanley G	Pickles	Wardman	Adamson 1	Watmuff	Craven	Eli Rohan	Storey		1og
34		11 EASTWOOD HANLEY	0-5	L	113	Walsh	Gilderdale	Edmondson	Kershaw	Stanley G	Pickles	Wardman	Adamson	Payton	Storey	Eli Rohan	Singh	Stanley C	
35		14 Penrith	1-3	L	100	Allen	Payton	Edmondson	Adamson	Stanley G	Pickles	Wardman	Gilderdale	Storey	Craven	Eli Rohan 1			
36		21 MAINE ROAD	0-1	L	140	Booth	Gilderdale	Eli Rupert	Edmondson	Stanley G	Pickles	Wardman	Taylor	Watmuff	Craven	Eli Rohan	Adamson	Storey	
37		24 Goole Town	2-5	CC	197	Booth	Payton	Eli Rupert	Kershaw	Stanley G	Pickles	Gilderdale	Taylor	Watmuff	Edmondson	Eli Rohan 1	Wardman 1	Adamson	
38		28 Ashton United	1-2	L	260	Preston	Gilderdale	Edmondson	Kershaw	Wroot	Pickles	Wardman 1	Taylor	Watmuff	Stanley G	Eli Rohan	Adamson	Payton	
39	Apr	4 Skelmersdale United	2-1	L	110	Booth	Gilderdale	Eli Rupert	Wroot 1	Stanley G	Pickles	Wardman	Taylor	Adamson	Edmondson 1	Eli Rohan	Payton		
40		11 ATHERTON LR	0-1	L	191	Booth	Payton	Eli Rupert	Wroot	Stanley G	Pickles	Wardman	Taylor	Adamson	Edmondson	Eli Rohan	Watmuff		

1992/93

6th in the NW Counties League Division One

							1	2	3	4	5	6	7	8	9	10	11	12	13	
1	Aug	15	Atherton LR	0-2	L	125	Cox	Illingworth	Eli Rupert	Gilderdale	Stanley	Pickles	Wardman	Taylor	Watmuff	Edmondson	Dimbleby	Peel	Sandhu	
2		18	Flixton	0-2	L	131	Cox	Payton	Eli Rupert	Gilderdale	Stanley	Pickles	Wardman	Taylor	Watmuff	Edmondson	Dimbleby	Peel	Illingworth	
3		26	Glossop North End	2-1	L	340	Cox	Payton	Eli Rupert	Stanley	Pearson	Pickles	Wardman 1	Taylor	Dimbleby	Megson A	Eli Rohan 1	Peel	Sandhu	
4		29	Burscough	1-1	FAC	142	Cox	Payton	Eli Rupert	Stanley	Pearson	Pickles	Wardman 1	Taylor	Watmuff	Dimbleby	Eli Rohan	Megson A		At Burscough
5	Sep	1	Burscough	2-1	FAC	146	Cox	Kershaw	Eli Rupert	Stanley	Pearson	Megson A	Edmondson 1	Taylor	Watmuff 1	Dimbleby	Eli Rohan	Peel		aet
6		5	NANTWICH TOWN	2-0	L	124	Cox	Payton	Eli Rupert	Stanley	Pearson	Jones	Edmondson	Taylor	Watmuff 1	Dimbleby	Eli Rohan 1	Peel	Megson A	
7		8	Maine Road	2-0	L	100	Cox	Payton	Eli Rupert	Stanley	Pearson	Jones	Edmondson 1	Taylor	Watmuff 1	Dimbleby	Eli Rohan	Peel		
8		12	BELPER TOWN	2-0	FAC	161	Cox	Payton	Eli Rupert	Stanley	Pearson	Jones	Megson A	Taylor	Watmuff 1	Edmondson 1	Eli Rohan	Peel	Gilderdale	
9		16	FLIXTON	1-0	L	105	Cox	Payton	Eli Rupert	Stanley	Pearson	Jones	Megson A	Taylor	Watmuff 1	Edmondson	Eli Rohan	Dimbleby		
10		19	Penrith	6-0	L	125	Cox	Megson A	Eli Rupert	Stanley	Pearson 1	Jones	Dimbleby	Taylor 2	Watmuff	Edmondson	Eli Rohan 3	Gilderdale	Sandhu	
11		23	MAINE ROAD	2-0	L	127	Cox	Payton	Eli Rupert	Stanley	Pearson	Jones	Dimbleby 1	Taylor	Gilderdale	Edmondson	Eli Rohan 1	Wardman	Sandhu	
12		26	Accrington Stanley	0-2	FAC	707	Cox	Payton	Eli Rupert	Stanley	Pearson	Jones	Edmondson	Gilderdale	Watmuff	Dimbleby	Eli Rohan	Wardman	Megson A	
13	Oct	3	Blidworth MW	3-1	FAV	110	Cox	Payton	Eli Rupert	Stanley	Pearson	Jones	Wardman 1	Gilderdale	Watmuff	Edmondson	Eli Rohan 2			
14		10	Darwen	1-2	L	123	Cox	Payton 1	Eli Rupert	Stanley	Pearson	Jones	Wardman	Taylor	Watmuff	Edmondson	Eli Rohan	Gilderdale	Megson A	
15		14	BAMBER BRIDGE	0-2	L	180	Cox	Payton	Eli Rupert	Stanley	Pearson	Jones	Wardman	Taylor	Watmuff	Edmondson	Eli Rohan	Gilderdale	Megson A	
16		17	DARWEN	1-0	L	151	Cox	Payton 1	Eli Rupert	Stanley	Pearson	Jones	Wardman	Taylor	Megson A	Edmondson	Eli Rohan	Watmuff	Gilderdale	
17		20	Maine Road	2-1	FC	77	Cox	Payton	Eli Rupert	Gilderdale	Pearson	Jones	Wardman 1	Taylor	Megson A	Edmondson	Eli Rohan 1	Dimbleby	Sandhu	
18		24	St Helens Town	0-0	L	93	Cox	Payton	Eli Rupert	Stanley	Pearson	Jones	Wardman	Taylor	Megson A	Dimbleby	Eli Rohan	Pickles		
19		28	GLOSSOP N END	4-2	FC	85	Cox	Payton	Eli Rupert	Stanley	Gilderdale	Watmuff	Wardman 1	Taylor	Megson A 2	Dimbleby 1	Eli Rohan	Sandhu		
20		31	Brigg Town	1-2	FAV	156	Cox	Payton	Gilderdale	Stanley	Pearson	Jones	Wardman	Taylor	Watmuff	Dimbleby 1	Megson A			
21	Nov	7	NEWCASTLE TOWN	0-1	L	130	Cox	Payton	Eli Rupert	Stanley	Pearson	Jones	Gilderdale	Taylor	Watmuff	Dimbleby	Eli Rohan	Megson A		
22		11	MAINE ROAD	2-1	FC	93	Cox	Payton 1	Eli Rupert	Stanley 1	Pearson	Jones	Sandhu	Taylor	Gilderdale	Dimbleby	Eli Rohan	Pickles	Watmuff	
23		14	Blackpool Mechanics	2-0	L	65	Cox	Payton	Eli Rupert	Gilderdale	Pearson	Jones 2	Megson A	Taylor	Stanley	Dimbleby	Eli Rohan	Illingworth		
24		18	Glossop North End	2-2	FC	110	Cox	Payton	Eli Rupert	Gilderdale	Pearson	Jones	Megson A	Taylor	Stanley 1	Dimbleby 1	Sandhu	Shepherd	Eli Rohan	
25		28	MAINE ROAD	2-2	LCC	101	Cox	Payton	Eli Rupert	Gilderdale	Stanley	Jones	Sandhu	Taylor	Edmondson 1	Dimbleby	Eli Rohan 1	Pickles	Illingworth	
26	Dec	5	CLITHEROE	1-0	L	130	Cox	Payton	Eli Rupert	Gilderdale	Pearson	Jones	Stanley	Taylor	Edmondson	Dimbleby	Eli Rohan	Megson A		1og
27		8	Glasshoughton Welfare	0-4	CC	125	Cox	Payton	Eli Rupert	Gilderdale	Pearson	Jones	Stanley	Taylor	Edmondson	Dimbleby	Eli Rohan	Megson A	Sandhu	
28		12	Salford City	2-2	L	115	Cox	Payton 2	Pickles	Gilderdale	Pearson	Jones	Megson A	Eli Rupert	Stanley	Dimbleby	Eli Rohan	Edmondson		
29		15	Maine Road	1-0	LCC	90	Cox	Payton	Eli Rupert	Stanley	Pearson	Jones	Megson A	Taylor	Edmondson	Dimbleby	Eli Rohan 1			
30		19	EASTWOOD HANLEY	1-2	L	110	Cox	Payton	Eli Rupert	Stanley	Pearson	Jones	Megson A	Taylor	Pickles	Dimbleby 1	Eli Rohan	Wardman		
31	Jan	2	Burscough	2-2	L	107	Cox	Payton	Eli Rupert	Pickles	Pearson	Jones	Megson A	Taylor	Stanley 1	Dimbleby	Eli Rohan 1	Wardman	Edmondson	
32		6	ATHERTON LR	1-2	L	120	Preston	Payton	Eli Rupert	Stanley	Pearson	Jones	Wardman	Megson A	Pickles	Dimbleby	Eli Rohan 1	Edmondson	Sandhu	
33		9	Glossop North End	1-4	LCC	175	Preston	Payton	Eli Rupert	Sandhu	Pearson	Jones 1	Wardman	Megson A	Pickles	Illingworth	Edmondson	Sweeney		
34		23	Clitheroe	0-1	L	119	Cox	Payton	Pickles	Stanley	Pearson	Jones	Wardman	Megson A	Edmondson	Dimbleby	Sandhu	Illingworth	Megson S	
35	Feb	6	BLACKPOOL ROVERS	2-1	L	110	Cox	Megson A	Eli Rupert	Sandhu	Pearson	Jones	Pickles	Taylor	Edmondson 1	Dimbleby	Eli Rohan 1	Megson S	Illingworth	
36		10	CHADDERTON	0-4	FC	65	Cox	Megson A	Eli Rupert	Sandhu	Kershaw	Pickles	Megson S	Taylor	Edmondson	Dimbleby	Eli Rohan	Hudson	Sweeney	
37		13	Prescot	0-2	L	69	Cox	Payton	Pickles	Sandhu	Megson A	Jones	Illingworth	Taylor	Edmondson	Dimbleby	Eli Rohan	Sweeney		
38		20	SKELMERSDALE UNITED	2-0	L	113	Cox	Payton	Eli Rupert	Pickles	Pearson	Jones	Megson A 1	Taylor	Edmondson 1	Dimbleby	Eli Rohan			
39		24	Chadderton	2-3	L	120	Cox	Payton	Eli Rupert	Pickles	Pearson	Jones	Megson A	Taylor 1	Edmondson 1	Dimbleby	Eli Rohan	Gilderdale		
40		27	Kidsgrove Athletic	0-0	L	68	Cox	Payton	Eli Rupert	Pickles	Pearson	Jones	Megson A	Sandhu	Edmondson	Dimbleby	Eli Rohan	Illingworth	Gilderdale	
41	Mar	6	Skelmersdale United	1-0	L	67	Cox	Payton	Gilderdale	Pickles	Pearson	Jones	Eli Rupert 1	Taylor	Edmondson	Dimbleby	Eli Rohan	Megson A	Sandhu	
42		10	Chadderton	3-1	FC	116	Cox	Payton 1	Eli Rupert	Jones	Kershaw	Pickles	Megson A	Taylor	Edmondson 1	Dimbleby 1	Gilderdale	Mackay B		
43		13	BLACKPOOL MECHS	2-1	L	125	Cox	Megson A	Eli Rupert	Gilderdale	Pearson	Jones	Sandhu	Taylor	Edmondson	Dimbleby	Payton	Eli Rohan 1	Watmuff 1	
44		17	CHADDERTON	1-2	L	95	Cox	Payton	Eli Rupert 1	Gilderdale	Pearson	Jones	Megson A	Taylor	Edmondson	Stanley	Eli Rohan	Dimbleby		
45		20	Newcastle Town	1-2	L	90	Cox	Payton	Eli Rupert	Gilderdale	Pearson	Jones	Megson A 1	Taylor	Edmondson	Stanley	Dimbleby	Eli Rohan		
46		24	SALFORD CITY	3-0	L	85	Cox	Gilderdale	Eli Rupert	Stanley	Pearson 1	Jones 1	Megson A	Taylor	Edmondson 1	Dimbleby	Eli Rohan	Pickles	Sandhu	
47		27	PENRITH	1-0	L	110	Cox	Eli Rupert	Pickles	Gilderdale	Pearson	Jones	Megson A	Taylor	Edmondson	Stanley	Eli Rohan	Dimbleby 1		
48		31	Chadderton	0-3	FC	130	Cox	Taylor	Pickles	Gilderdale	Pearson	Jones	Megson A	Eli Rupert	Edmondson	Stanley	Eli Rohan	Dimbleby	Sandhu	
49	Apr	3	KIDSGROVE ATHLETIC	1-0	L	123	Cox	Megson A	Pickles	Gilderdale	Pearson	Jones	Sandhu	Taylor 1	Dimbleby	Stanley	Eli Rohan	Edmondson	Illingworth	
50		10	BURSCOUGH	1-2	L	113	Cox	Eli Rupert	Pickles	Gilderdale	Stanley	Jones	Megson A	Taylor	Edmondson	Dimbleby	Eli Rohan 1	Sandhu	Watmuff	
51		12	Bacup Borough	0-0	L	173	Cox	Gilderdale	Pickles	Stanley	Pearson	Jones	Sandhu	Eli Rupert	Edmondson	Dimbleby	Eli Rohan	Illingworth		
52		17	Eastwood Hanley	2-0	L	65	Cox	Taylor	Pickles	Stanley	Pearson	Jones	Sandhu	Eli Rupert	Edmondson 1	Dimbleby	Eli Rohan 1			
53		20	Nantwich Town	1-1	L	60	Cox	Illingworth	Eli Rupert	Stanley	Pearson	Jones	Sandhu	Taylor 1	Edmondson	Gilderdale	Eli Rohan			
54		24	ST HELENS TOWN	2-1	L	145	Cox	Illingworth	Eli Rupert	Stanley 1	Pearson	Pickles	Sandhu	Taylor	Edmondson	Gilderdale	Eli Rohan 1	Dimbleby	Watmuff	
55		26	PRESCOT	2-1	L	108	Cox	Payton	Pickles	Gilderdale	Pearson	Jones	Stanley	Taylor	Edmondson	Dimbleby	Eli Rohan 2	Sandhu	Watmuff	
56		28	GLOSSOP NORTH END	2-2	L	116	Cox	Payton	Edmondson	Stanley	Pearson 1	Pickles	Sandhu	Taylor 1	Watmuff	Dimbleby	Eli Rohan	Mackay B		
57	May	1	BACUP BOROUGH	1-3	L	122	Cox	Gilderdale	Sweeney	Stanley	Edmondson	Pickles	Sandhu	Taylor	Watmuff	Dimbleby	Eli Rohan	Mackay J		1og
58		3	Bamber Bridge	1-1	L	175	Cox	Payton	Dunn	Stanley	Edmondson	Pickles	Illingworth 1	Mackay B	Watmuff	Dimbleby	Eli Rohan	Preston	Mackay J	
59		8	Blackpool Rovers	0-2	L	75	Preston	Eli Rohan	Stanley	Pickles	Pearson	Dimbleby	Sandhu	Taylor	Jones	Gilderdale	Edmondson	Mackay J		

1993/94

15th in the NW Counties League Division One

							1	2	3	4	5	6	7	8	9	10	11	12	13
1	Aug	14	Prescot	0-2	L	110	Eloi	Hutchinson	Pickles	Gilderdale	Stanley	Jones	Edmondson	Taylor C	Watmuff A	Payton	Eli Rupert	Hazel	Taylor A
2		17	BOOTLE	1-1	L	152	Preston	Payton	Eli Rupert	Gilderdale	Pearson	Jones	Wardman	Stanley	Edmondson 1	Watmuff A	Eli Rohan		
3		21	SALFORD CITY	1-4	L	124	Preston	Gilderdale	Pickles	Hazel	Pearson	Jones	Wardman	Taylor C	Stanley	Eli Rupert 1	Eli Rohan	Taylor A	
4		24	Flixton	0-1	L	75	Preston	Payton	Pickles	Stanley	Pearson	Jones	Gilderdale	Taylor C	Eli Rupert	Watmuff A	Eli Rohan	Hutchinson	
5		28	Warrington Town	0-5	FAC	248	Preston	Payton	Eli Rupert	Stanley	Pearson	Jones	Hutchinson	Gilderdale	Watmuff A	Goddard	Eli Rohan	Taylor A	Price
6		30	PENRITH	0-0	L	132	Cox	Payton	Eli Rupert	Gilderdale	Pearson	Jones	Taylor C	Goddard	Edmondson	Dimbleby	Nazir	Taylor A	
7	Sep	4	ATHERTON LR	2-4	L	122	Cox	Payton	Eli Rupert	Gilderdale	Pearson	Jones	Taylor C	Stanley 1	Edmondson 1	Dimbleby	Nazir		
8		6	Clitheroe	1-1	L	250	Cox	Payton	Eli Rupert	Gilderdale	Pearson	Jones	Nazir	Taylor C	Edmondson 1	Dimbleby	Goddard	Taylor A	
9		11	PRESCOT	0-0	L	110	Preston	Gilderdale	Eli Rupert	Sandhu	Pearson	Jones	Nazir	Taylor C	Edmondson	Dimbleby	Stanley	Taylor A	
10		14	CHADDERTON	2-1	L	105	Preston	Gilderdale	Eli Rupert	Sandhu	Pearson	Jones	Stanley	Taylor C	Edmondson 1	Dimbleby 1	Nazir	Taylor A	Price
11		18	DARWEN	4-1	L	135	Preston	Gilderdale	Eli Rupert	Stanley	Pearson	Sandhu	Wardman 2	Taylor C	Edmondson 2	Payton	Nazir	Goddard	Taylor A
12		24	BACUP BOROUGH	2-4	L	181	Preston	Payton	Eli Rupert	Stanley	Pearson	Taylor C	Wardman	Goddard	Edmondson 2	Dimbleby	Nazir	Sandhu	Sacchetto
13		28	Skelmersdale United	0-6	L	80	Preston	Nazir	Eli Rupert	Gilderdale	Pearson	Sacchetto	Wardman	Taylor C	Edmondson	Dimbleby	Sandhu	Jones	
14	Oct	2	Belper Town	0-1	FAV	185	Preston	Gilderdale	Eli Rupert	Nazir	Pearson	Jones	Wardman	Taylor C	Edmondson	Dimbleby	Sacchetto		
15		5	Chadderton	2-1	L	92	Preston	Gilderdale	Eli Rupert	Sandhu	Pearson	Jones	Wardman 1	Taylor C	Edmondson	Dimbleby	Sacchetto 1	Taylor A	
16		9	Rossendale United	0-1	L	250	Preston	Gilderdale	Nazir	Stanley	Fry	Jones	Sandhu	Goddard	Watmuff A	Edmondson	Dimbleby	Singh	Taylor A
17		13	Chadderton	0-1	FC	51	Preston	Gilderdale	Nazir	Taylor C	Pearson	Jones	Eli Rupert	Singh	Edmondson	Dimbleby	Sacchetto	Sandhu	
18		16	EASTWOOD HANLEY	0-0	L	103	Preston	Gilderdale	Nazir	Taylor C	Pearson	Jones	Wardman	Singh	Edmondson	Dimbleby	Fry	Goddard	
19		23	St Helens Town	0-5	L	65	Preston	Gilderdale	Nazir	Stanley	Pearson	Taylor C	Singh	Sandhu	Edmondson	Dimbleby	Sacchetto	Goddard	Taylor A
20		26	CHADDERTON	1-2	FC	101	Preston	Gilderdale	Nazir	Fry	Pearson 1	Sandhu	Stanley	Edmondson	Eli Rupert	Dimbleby	Sacchetto	Singh	
21		30	Blackpool Rovers	1-1	L	75	Preston	Nazir	Dimbleby	Fry	Stanley	Pearson	Gilderdale	Sacchetto 1	Daykin	Mumby	Goddard	Edmondson	Singh
22	Nov	6	NANTWICH TOWN	3-1	L	153	Ward	Payton	Dimbleby 1	Goddard	Pearson	Stanley	Hudson J	Edmondson	Daykin 2	Mumby	Sacchetto	Nazir	Gilderdale
23		13	CASTLETON GABRIELS	6-4	LCC	110	Ward	Payton	Dimbleby	Goddard	Pearson	Stanley	Hudson J	Edmondson	Daykin 4	Mumby 1	Sacchetto 1	Nazir	Gilderdale
24		27	MAINE ROAD	1-2	L	112	Dennis	Dimbleby	Goddard	Hudson B	Pearson	Stanley	Roberts	Laycock 1	Daykin	Mumby	Sacchetto	Edmondson	Payton
25	Dec	4	CLITHEROE	2-3	L	108	Ward	Payton	Dimbleby	Hudson B	Pearson	Stanley	Goddard	Laycock	Daykin 1	Mumby	Sacchetto 1	Owen	Jones
26		21	Thackley	1-0	CC	126	Ward	Payton 1	Dimbleby	Goddard	Pearson	Stanley	Hudson J	Eli Rupert	Daykin	Mumby	Sacchetto	Hudson B	Jones
27	Jan	1	Glossop North End	1-3	L	175	Williams	Payton 1	Dimbleby	Goddard	Watmuff M	Tosney	Hudson J	Laycock	Daykin	Owen	Mumby	Fry	
28		8	North Trafford	1-1	LCC	80	Williams	Payton	Dimbleby	Stanley	Watmuff M	Tosney	Hudson J	Laycock 1	Aram	Mumby	Goddard	Owen	Pearson
29		11	Ossett Albion	2-3	CC	85	Williams	Payton	Goddard	Pearson	Watmuff M	Mumby 1	Dimbleby	Sacchetto	Daykin 1	Tosney	Taylor C	Eli Rupert	Stanley
30		22	NORTH TRAFFORD	0-6	LCC	87	Williams	Payton	Eli Rupert	Pearson	Watmuff M	Laycock	Dimbleby	Sacchetto	Tosney	Owen	Mumby	Hudson J	
31		29	KIDSGROVE ATHLETIC	3-2	L	84	Williams	Payton	Forrest	Walker	Tosney	Daibell	Dimbleby	Laycock 1	Mumby 1	Owen	Wilson 1	Sacchetto	
32	Feb	5	BURSCOUGH	2-2	L	103	Williams	Payton	Forrest	Walker	Tosney	Daibell	Dimbleby	Laycock	Mumby 1	Owen	Wilson 1		
33		8	Atherton LR	0-4	L	140	Williams	Payton	Forrest	Goddard	Tosney	Sacchetto	Dimbleby	Laycock	Mumby	Owen	Wilson	Quinn	
34		12	Kidsgrove Athletic	0-4	L	65	Williams	Payton	Forrest	Goddard	Tosney	Daibell	Dimbleby	Watmuff A	Mumby	Owen	Wilson	Rayner	
35		19	BLACKPOOL ROVERS	2-6	L	92	Preston	Eli Rupert	Forrest	Goddard	Pearson	Daibell	Dimbleby	Laycock 1	Mumby	Owen 1	Wilson		
36		26	Maine Road	1-1	L	60	Williams	Dimbleby	Forrest	Walker	Pearson	Daibell	Goddard	Mumby	Owen	Harvey	Wilson 1	Daykin	
37	Mar	1	Bootle	1-5	L	66	Williams	Dimbleby	Forrest	Walker	Pearson	Viner	Goddard 1	Mumby	Radford	Owen	Wilson		
38		5	Eastwood Hanley	0-2	L	55	Williams	Payton	Forrest	Walker	Pearson	Mumby	Goddard	Wilson	Viner	Harvey	Dimbleby	Owen	
39		9	Darwen	0-2	L	50	Williams	Payton	Forrest	Taylor K	Pearson	Daibell	Dimbleby	Laycock	Viner	Radford	Goddard	Mumby	Wilson
40		15	Salford City	3-2	L	45	Preston	Hudson J	Forrest	Walker	White	Pearson	Wilson 1	Laycock 1	Radford	Harvey	Daibell 1	Goddard	
41		19	NEWCASTLE TOWN	1-1	L	105	Williams	Hudson J	Forrest	Walker	Harvey	Pearson	Goddard	Laycock	Wilson	Owen 1	Daibell	Payton	
42		26	Nantwich Town	2-0	L	131	Williams	Hudson J	Forrest 1	Walker	Harvey	Pearson	Goddard	Mumby	Wilson 1	Owen	Daibell	Payton	Roberts
43		29	ST HELENS TOWN	2-0	L	85	Williams	Hudson J	Payton	Taylor K	Harvey	Pearson	Goddard	Mumby 2	Wilson	Walker	Daibell		
44	Apr	2	Newcastle Town	1-1	L	70	Williams	Hudson J	Forrest	Walker	Harvey	Pearson	Goddard	Mumby	Wilson	Viner 1	Laycock		
45		4	Burscough	1-1	L	161	Williams	Hudson J	Brame	Walker	Daibell	Pearson	Goddard	Payton 1	Wilson	Viner	Forrest		
46		16	SKELMERSDALE UNITED	0-0	L	120	Williams	Hudson J	Forrest	Watmuff A	Daibell	Pearson	Payton	Mumby	Wilson	Viner	Goddard	Owen	
47		23	Penrith	0-1	L	125	Williams	Watmuff A	Payton	Tosney	Daibell	Pearson	Laycock	Hudson J	Wilson	Owen	Mumby		
48		30	ROSSENDALE UNITED	3-0	L	124	Williams	Hudson J	Forrest	Watmuff A	Harvey	Pearson	Goddard	Laycock	Wilson 1	Owen	Mumby 1	Viner 1	Rayner
49	May	2	FLIXTON	2-1	L	116	Preston	Hudson J	Forrest	Payton	Daibell	Pearson	Laycock	Viner 2	Wilson	Owen	Mumby	Daykin	
50		6	Bacup Borough	3-1	L	85	Preston	Hudson J	Payton	Taylor K	Daibell	Pearson	Laycock 1	Viner	Wilson 2	Owen	Mumby		
51		11	GLOSSOP NORTH END	4-1	L	120	Dennis	Hudson J	Payton	Taylor K	Harvey	Pearson	Mumby 1	Viner 2	Wilson 1	Owen	Daibell	Forrest	

1994/95

Champions of the NW Counties League Division One: Promoted to UniBond League

						1	2	3	4	5	6	7	8	9	10	11	12	13	14	
1	Aug	13 NEWCASTLE TOWN	3-1	L	120	Williams	Hudson	Forrest	Taylor	Pearson	Bairstow 1	Goddard	Laycock 1	Viner 1	Roberts	Craven	Owen			
2		16 Burscough	2-1	L	221	Williams	Hudson	Forrest	Taylor	Margerison	Bairstow	Goddard	Laycock	Viner 2	Wilson	Craven	Owen	Mumby		
3		20 St Helens Town	0-3	L	118	Williams	Hudson	Forrest	Taylor	Pearson	Owen	Goddard	Laycock	Viner	Margerison	Craven	Daykin			
4		23 TRAFFORD	2-2	L	106	Williams	Sutcliffe	Forrest	Taylor	Pearson	Bairstow	Goddard	Laycock	Viner	Wilson 1	Craven 1	Owen	Daykin		
5		27 BURSCOUGH	0-3	FAC	130	Williams	Hudson	Forrest	Taylor	Pearson	Bairstow	Goddard	Owen	Daykin	Wilson	Craven	Ramsden			
6		29 Bacup Borough	2-0	L	120	Williams	Price	Forrest	Taylor	Pearson	Bairstow	Goddard	Owen 1	Margerison	Wilson 1	Craven	Sutcliffe			
7	Sep	3 NANTWICH TOWN	2-0	L	103	Williams	Price	Forrest	Taylor	Pearson	Bairstow	Goddard 1	Owen	Margerison 1	Wilson	Craven	Sutcliffe			
8		7 Darwen	3-1	L	125	Williams	Price	Forrest	Taylor	Pearson	Bairstow	Goddard 1	Owen	Margerison	Wilson 2	Craven	Edmonds			
9		10 PENRITH	2-1	L	127	Williams	Price	Forrest	Taylor	Pearson	Bairstow	Goddard 1	Owen	Margerison	Wilson	Craven 1	Edmonds	Morgan		
10		13 BURSCOUGH	2-2	L	104	Williams	Price	Forrest	Taylor	Pearson	Bairstow	Goddard	Morgan	Eli Rohan 1	Wilson	Craven 1	Margerison	Edmonds		
11		17 Nantwich Town	4-1	L	85	Williams	Edmonds	Forrest	Taylor	Pearson	Bairstow 1	Goddard	Morgan	Margerison 1	Wilson	Craven 2	Price	Laycock		
12		21 Rossendale United	4-0	L	210	Williams	Price	Forrest	Taylor	Pearson	Bairstow 1	Allen C	Morgan	Margerison 2	Wilson	Craven 1	Edmonds	Laycock		
13		24 GLOSSOP NORTH END	3-0	L	137	Williams	Noteman	Forrest 1	Taylor	Pearson	Bairstow	Allen C 1	Morgan	Margerison	Wilson	Craven 1	Edmonds	Price		
14		27 Maine Road	3-0	L	90	Williams	Noteman	Forrest	Taylor	Pearson	Price 1	Allen C 1	Morgan	Margerison	Wilson	Craven 1	Viner	Edmonds		
15	Oct	1 S NORMANTON ATH.	6-4	FAV	165	Williams	Noteman 1	Forrest	Taylor	Pearson 1	Bairstow	Allen C	Morgan 3	Viner	Wilson 1	Craven	Price	Edmonds		
16		8 BLACKPOOL ROVERS	3-0	L	155	Williams	Noteman 1	Edmonds	Taylor	Pearson	Price	Allen C	Morgan	Margerison 1	Wilson 1	Craven	Viner	Mumby		
17		11 FLIXTON	4-2	FC	106	Williams	Laycock	Edmonds	Taylor	Pearson	Price 1	Blair	Morgan 1	Viner 1	Mumby 1	Craven	Brown	Wilson		
18		15 Bootle	2-0	L	75	Williams	Noteman	Edmonds	Taylor	Pearson	Price 1	Bairstow	Morgan	Margerison	Wilson 1	Craven	Mumby	Viner		
19		22 ROSSENDALE UNITED	1-0	L	151	Williams	Mumby	Watson	Taylor	Pearson	Price	Bairstow	Morgan	Margerison 1	Wilson	Craven				
20		25 Flixton	1-2	FC	124	Williams	Hudson	Watson	Taylor	Pearson	Price	Laycock	Morgan	Viner	Mumby 1	Craven	Forrest	Blair		
21		29 ST HELENS TOWN	3-0	FAV	251	Williams	Forrest	Harrison	Taylor	Pearson	Price	Bairstow 1	Morgan	Margerison 1	Wilson	Craven	Mumby 1			
22	Nov	8 Pontefract Colls	5-1	CC	120	Williams	Forrest	Harrison	Taylor	Pearson 1	Price	Mumby 1	Morgan	Viner 2	Wilson	Craven 1	Daykin	Laycock		
23		19 Eastwood Hanley	1-3	FAV	148	Williams	Armitage	Harrison	Taylor	Pearson	Mumby	Bairstow	Morgan	Margerison	Wilson	Craven 1	Price			
24		23 Nantwich Town	2-4	FC	45	Williams	Armitage	Harrison	Taylor	Pearson 1	Price	Bairstow	Morgan 1	Viner	Wilson	Craven	Laycock	Mumby		
25		26 Prescot	1-0	L	130	Williams	Armitage	Harrison	Taylor	Pearson	Price 1	Bairstow	Morgan	Margerison	Wilson	Craven	Viner	Mumby		
26	Dec	3 CLITHEROE	1-3	L	226	Williams	Armitage	Harrison	Taylor	Pearson	Price	Bairstow	Morgan	Margerison	Wilson	Craven 1	Viner	Mumby		
27		7 Selby Town	1-0	CC	80	Williams	Armitage	Harrison	Taylor	Pearson	Laycock	Bairstow	Morgan	Viner 1	Mumby	Craven	Price	Wilson		
28		17 EASTWOOD HANLEY	3-2	L	145	Williams	Johnson	Harrison	Taylor	Noteman	Price	Bairstow	Morgan 1	Tunnacliffe 1	Margerison 1	Craven				
29		26 BACUP BOROUGH	4-1	LCC	134	Williams	Johnson	Harrison	Taylor 2	Noteman	Armitage	Bairstow	Morgan	Tunnacliffe 1	Margerison	Craven 1	Price	Forrest		
30	Jan	7 Chadderton	1-1	L	160	Williams	Price	Harrison	Taylor	Noteman	Armitage	Bairstow	Morgan	Tunnacliffe 1	Margerison	Craven	Forrest			
31		14 Kidsgrove Athletic	2-1	LCC	70	Williams	Price	Forrest	Taylor	Noteman	Morris	Bairstow	Morgan	Tunnacliffe	Margerison	Craven 1	Armitage 1			
32		24 Blackpool Rovers	0-4	L	105	Williams	Johnson	Forrest	Taylor	Noteman	Price	Armitage	Morgan	Tunnacliffe	Morris	Craven	Clarke			
33	Feb	4 BOOTLE	3-0	L	151	Williams	Clarke 1	Harrison	Johnson	Noteman	Sullivan	Bairstow	Morgan	Tunnacliffe	Morris 2	Craven				
34		7 Thackley	0-1	CC	150	Williams	Clarke	Harrison	Johnson	Noteman	Pearson	Bairstow	Morgan	Tunnacliffe	Morris	Craven	Price	Wilson		
35		11 Penrith	3-1	L	114	Williams	Clarke	Harrison	Johnson	Pearson	Sullivan	Bairstow	Morgan	Tunnacliffe	Morris 2	Craven 1	Price	Forrest		
36		14 Glossop North End	1-2	L	162	Williams	Price	Harrison	Johnson	Noteman	Sullivan	Goddard	Morgan	Clarke 1	Morris	Craven	Pearson	Forrest		
37		17 ST HELENS TOWN	1-3	L	174	Booth	Price	Harrison	Johnson	Noteman	Sullivan	Bairstow	Morgan	Allen C 1	Morris	Craven	Nesovic			*At Farsley*
38		21 Newcastle Town	1-1	L	115	Evans	Price	Harrison	Johnson	Noteman	Sullivan	Goddard	Morgan	Clarke	Morris 1	Forrest	Kettlewell			
39		25 DARWEN	1-2	L	124	Allen P	Clarke	Harrison	Johnson	Noteman	Sullivan 1	Bairstow	Morgan	Margerison	Goddard	Craven	Price			
40		28 Eastwood Hanley	1-2	L	51	Allen P	Price	Harrison	Johnson	Pearson	Sullivan	Goddard	Kettlewell	Cochrane	Morris	Forrest 1	Nesovic			*At Kidsgrove*
41	Mar	4 Nantwich Town	1-1	LCC	114	Allen P	Johnson	Harrison	Bairstow	Pearson	Sullivan	Noteman	Morgan	Daykin	Allen C	Morris 1				
42		11 Clitheroe	1-2	L	210	Allen P	Johnson	Harrison	Bairstow	Margerison	Sullivan	Noteman	Morgan	Clarke	Morris	Forrest	Price	Marshall 1		
43		21 NANTWICH TOWN	0-1	LCC	102	Allen P	Johnson	Forrest	Bairstow	Pearson	Sullivan	Noteman	Morgan	Margerison	Morris	Clarke	Price	Harrison		
44		25 HOLKER OLD BOYS	2-1	L	123	Allen P	Price 1	Forrest	Johnson	Pearson	Sullivan	Noteman	Morgan	Margerison	Marshall 1	Bairstow	Morris	Clarke		
45	Apr	1 Salford City	2-0	L	85	Allen P	Price	Forrest	Johnson	Pearson	Sullivan	Noteman	Morgan 1	Margerison 1	Marshall	Bairstow	Morris	Clarke		
46		15 PRESCOT	3-1	L	120	Allen P	Price	Forrest 2	Johnson	Roberts	Sullivan	Bairstow 1	Morgan	Margerison	Marshall	Clarke	Pearson	Morris		
47		17 Kidsgrove Athletic	2-0	L	95	Evans	Price	Forrest	Johnson	Roberts 1	Sullivan	Bairstow	Mumby	Margerison	Marshall 1	Clarke	Morris			
48		22 SKELMERSDALE UNITED	5-1	L	133	Williams	Price	Forrest	Johnson	Roberts	Sullivan	Bairstow	Mumby 3	Margerison	Marshall 1	Clarke	Morris 1			
49		25 SALFORD CITY	2-0	L	140	Williams	Price	Forrest	Johnson	Roberts	Sullivan 1	Harrison	Mumby	Brown	Marshall	Clarke	Cochrane 1	Morris		
50		29 Holker Old Boys	4-0	L	76	Williams	Price 1	Forrest	Johnson	Roberts	Sullivan	Bairstow	Morris	Margerison	Marshall 1	Harrison 2	Noteman	Ramsden	Allen P	
51	May	2 CHADDERTON	3-1	L	162	Williams	Price	Harrison	Johnson	Roberts	Sullivan	Bairstow 1	Morris 1	Margerison	Marshall	Harvey 1	Noteman			
52		4 Skelmersdale United	5-1	L	80	Williams	Price	Harrison	Johnson	Roberts	Sullivan	Bairstow	Morris 2	Margerison	Marshall 3	Harvey	Noteman	Daykin	Allen P	
53		6 MAINE ROAD	3-0	L	186	Williams	Price	Harrison	Johnson	Roberts	Sullivan 1	Bairstow	Morris	Margerison	Marshall	Harvey	Noteman	Daykin 2	Allen P	
54		8 KIDSGROVE ATHLETIC	3-1	L	212	Williams	Price 1	Harrison	Johnson	Roberts 1	Sullivan	Bairstow 1	Morris	Margerison	Marshall	Morgan	Allen P			
55		10 BACUP BOROUGH	2-0	L	275	Allen	Price	Harrison	Johnson	Roberts	Sullivan	Bairstow	Morris 2	Margerison	Marshall	Morgan	Daykin			
56		13 Trafford	4-2	L	388	Williams	Price 1	Harrison	Johnson	Roberts	Sullivan	Bairstow 1	Morris	Margerison	Marshall 1	Noteman	Daykin 1			
57		16 NANTWICH TOWN	4-1	LCT	183	Williams	Price	Harrison	Johnson	Roberts	Sullivan 1	Bairstow 1	Morris	Margerison	Marshall 2	Morgan	Noteman			

1995/96

17th in the UniBond League Division One

						1	2	3	4	5	6	7	8	9	10	11	12	13	14	
1	Aug	19 LANCASTER CITY	0-3	L	241	Wilkinson	Craven	Forrest	Brown T	Margerison	Sullivan	Bairstow	Noteman	Daykin	Mumby	Annan	Price	Brandon		
2		22 Worksop Town	1-4	L	460	Wilkinson	Craven	Price	Brown T	Bairstow	Sullivan	Woodhead	Roberts	Daykin	Mumby 1	Annan	Brandon			
3		26 Armthorpe Welfare	1-1	FAC	85	Williams	Craven 1	Price	Brown T	Pearson	Sullivan	Bairstow	Roberts	Annan	Mumby	Woodhead	Daykin			
4		30 ARMTHORPE WELFARE	1-0	FAC	148	Williams	Craven	Price	Brown T	Pearson	Sullivan	Annan	Roberts	Daykin 1	Mumby	Woodhead	Brandon			
5	Sep	2 WORKINGTON	3-0	L	155	Williams	Craven	Forrest	Johnson	Brown T	Morgan	Brandon 1	Roberts	Brown M 1	Mumby	Price	Annan 1	Woodhead		
6		5 Lincoln United	2-5	L	246	Williams	Craven	Forrest	Johnson	Brown T	Sullivan	Brandon	Roberts	Anann 1	Mumby 1	Price	Moris	Pearson		
7		9 Kowsley United	0-0	FAC	74	Williams	Craven	Forrest	Johnson	Morgan	Brown T	Woodhead	Roberts	Brown M	Mumby	Brandon	Dysart	Price		
8		13 KNOWSLEY UNITED	3-2	FAC	158	Williams	Craven	Forrest	Johnson	Morgan	Brown T 1	Margerison	Roberts 1	Brown M 1	Mumby	Brandon	Price	Dysart	Sullivan	aet
9		16 GRETNA	2-2	L	151	Williams	Craven 1	Forrest	Johnson	Moran	Brown T	Dysart	Roberts 1	Margerison	Morris	Brandon	Price	Sullivan	Annan	
10		18 Ashton United	1-0	L	283	Allen P	Craven 1	Forrest	Bairstow	Pearson	Margerison	Price	Roberts	Brown M	Marshall	Annan	Sullivan			
11		23 Accrington Stanley	2-1	FAC	553	Williams	Craven	Forrest	Bairstow	Pearson	Margerison	Price	Roberts	Brown M	Marshall	Annan	Brandon			
12		27 FARSLEY CELTIC	2-0	LC	177	Allen P	Craven	Brandon	Bairstow	Pearson	Brown T	Price	Roberts	Brown M 2	Marshall	Annan	Johnson			
13		30 Curzon Ashton	1-0	L	205	Allen P	Craven	Forrest	Johnson	Pearson	Bairstow	Price	Edmonds	Brown M	Marshall 1	Annan	Brandon	Dysart		
14	Oct	3 Whitley Bay	1-2	L	134	Allen P	Craven 1	Forrest	Johnson	Pearson	Brown T	Price	Daykin	Brandon	Marshall	Annan	Harrison			
15		7 CURZON ASHTON	2-1	FAC	202	Williams	Craven 1	Forrest	Johnson	Pearson	Brown T	Bairstow	Roberts	Brown M 1	Morris	Annan	Price	Brandon	Sullivan	
16		11 ALFRETON TOWN	1-1	L	183	Williams	Craven	Forrest	Johnson	Pearson	Brown T	Price	Brandon	Brown M	Edmonds 1	Annan				
17		14 Accrington Stanley	2-2	FAT	415	Allen P	Craven	Forrest	Johnson	Sullivan	Brown T	Price	Brandon	Brown M	Harrison	Annan 2	Morris	Edmonds		
18		18 ACCRINGTON STANLEY	2-3	FAT	258	Allen P	Craven	Harrison	Johnson	Pearson	Brown T	Price	Dysart	Brown M	Mumby	Annan 1	Morris 1	Edmonds		
19		21 Marine	0-2	FAC	626	Williams	Craven	Forrest	Bairstow	Pearson	Brown T	Price	Eli Roger	Brown M	Marshall	Annan	Harrison	Edmonds	Sullivan	
20		25 FRICKLEY ATHLETIC	1-1	LC	164	Williams	Craven	Harrison	Johnson	Sullivan	Price	Bairstow	Dysart	Brown M	Marshall 1	Annan	Forrest			
21		27 Radcliffe Borough	0-3	L	211	Williams	Craven	Forrest	Johnson	Sullivan	Pearson	Price	Harrison	Eli Roger	Marshall	Annan	Brandon	Edmonds	Dysart	
22		31 Frickley Athletic	1-3	LC	112	Allen P	Johnson	Edmonds	Forrest	Pearson	Price	Dysart	Roberts	Marshall	Harrison	Craven	Sullivan	Daykin 1	Williams	
23	Nov	4 Congleton Town	2-1	L	136	Allen P	Craven	Harrison	Johnson	Pearson	Sullivan	Price 1	Roberts	Higgins	Marshall 1	Dysart	Williams			
24		7 Lincoln United	0-2	FDC	108	Allen P	Craven	Harrison	Johnson	Pearson	Williams	Price	Roberts	Higgins	Marshall	Dysart	Sullivan			
25		11 LEIGH RMI	3-1	L	163	Allen P	Craven 1	Harrison	Johnson	Pearson	Price	Higgins 1	Roberts	Eli Roger	Marshall 1	Annan	Forrest			
26		18 Fleetwood	2-3	L	186	Stoney	Craven	Harrison	Brown T	Pearson	Price 1	Johnson	Roberts 1	Brandon	Marshall	Annan	Rae	Higgins		
27		22 EASTWOOD TOWN	2-2	L	133	Allen P	Craven	Harrison	Johnson	Pearson	Brown T	Rae 1	Roberts	Brown M 1	Marshall	Annan	Price	Brandon		
28		25 WARRINGTON TOWN	1-0	L	156	Allen P	Craven	Harrison	Johnson	Pearson	Sullivan	Rae	Roberts 1	Brown M	Marshall	Brandon	Price	Annan		
29		28 Harrogate Town	2-1	L	225	Allen P	Craven	Harrison	Johnson	Sullivan	Price 1	Brierley 1	Roberts	Laycock	Marshall	Annan	Brandon			
30	Dec	2 Netherfield	0-0	L	186	Williams	Craven	Harrison	Johnson	Pearson	Sullivan	Brierley	Roberts	Annan	Marshall	Price	Rae			
31		6 OSSETT ALBION	3-1	CC	101	Williams	Craven 1	Harrison	Johnson	Sullivan 1	Price	Brierley	Roberts	Annan	Marshall	Brandon 1	Rae	Brown T		
32		9 Lancaster City	0-1	L	278	Williams	Craven	Walker	Johnson	Rae	Price	Brierley	Roberts	Wolstenholme	Marshall	Brandon	Thompson	Cook		
33		15 RADCLIFFE BOROUGH	2-2	L	169	Williams	Craven	Walker	Johnson	Sullivan	Price 1	Brierley	Roberts	Wolstenholme	Marshall	Benn	Pearson 1			
34		26 Eastwood Town	1-0	L	182	Williams	Craven	Walker	Johnson	Sullivan	Margerison	Brierley	Benn	Brown M 1	Wolstenholme	Brandon				
35	Jan	6 Leigh RMI	0-1	L	161	Williams	Craven	Harrison	Johnson	Sullivan	Brierley	Benn	Roberts	Brown M	Annan	Brandon	Walker	Forrest	Marshall	
36		13 HARROGATE TOWN	1-1	L	228	Williams	Craven	Walker	Johnson	Pearson 1	Price	Benn	Roberts	Jackson	Hoy	Brandon	Brown M			
37		20 Workington	2-3	L	251	Williams	Craven 1	Walker	Johnson	Sullivan	Price	Benn	Roberts	Jackson	Hoy 1	Brandon	Forrest	Pearson		
38		24 FARSLEY CELTIC	1-1	L	152	Williams	Craven	Forrest	Johnson	Pearson	Price	Benn	Roberts 1	Jackson	Hoy	Brandon	Sullivan	Brierley	Walker	
39	Feb	3 GT HARWOOD TOWN	1-3	L	161	Williams	Craven	Forrest	Johnson	Sullivan	Price	Brierley 1	Bairstow	Brown M	Hoy	Brandon	Jackson	Walker	Moran	
40		13 Glasshoughton Welfare	2-0	CC	100	Williams	Price	Forrest	Johnson	Sullivan	Moran	Brierley 1	Brandon	Brown M	Harrison	Annan	Walker	Hoy	Jackson 1	
41		17 Atherton LR	1-3	L	176	Williams	Price	Harrison	Johnson	Goddard	Moran	Brierley	Brandon	Brown M	Sharpe 1	Annan	Forrest			
42		24 FLEETWOOD	2-2	L	172	Buxton	Price	Forrest	Johnson	Pearson	Moran	Benn 1	Roberts	Gabbiadini	Sharpe 1	Annan	Hoy	Brandon		
43	Mar	2 Gretna	1-1	L	93	Buxton	Price	Harrison	Johnson	Sullivan	Moran	Benn	Roberts	Sharpe 1	Brierley	Brandon	Jackson			
44		9 CURZON ASHTON	2-3	L	175	Buxton	Price	Harrison	Johnson	Sullivan	Moran	Benn	Gabbiadini	Sharpe 1	Brierley 1	Brandon	Forrest			
45		16 Great Harwood Town	3-1	L	120	Buxton	Price	Moran	Johnson	Sullivan	Brown T	Benn	Gabbiadini 2	Sharpe 1	Annan	Brandon	Jackson			
46		20 Farsley Celtic	0-1	CC	173	Williams	Price	Moran	Johnson	Sullivan	Brown T	Brandon	Jackson	Morgan	Brierley	Annan	Forrest	Pearson		
47		23 WORKSOP TOWN	4-4	L	187	Buxton	Price	Forrest	Johnson	Sullivan	Margerison	Benn	Gabbiadini 2	Sharpe 1	Brandon	Annan 1				
48		27 LINCOLN UNITED	2-3	L	176	Buxton	Price	Brierley 1	Johnson	Pearson	Margerison	Benn	Hoyle 1	Sharpe	Brandon	Annan	Daykin			
49		30 Warrington Town	1-1	L	103	Buxton	Price	Benn	Johnson	Morgan	Margerison 1	Brierley	Roberts	Sharpe	Brandon	Annan	Moran	Harrison		
50	Apr	3 ATHERTON LR	2-2	L	155	Williams	Price	Harrison	Moran	Margerison	Benn	Gabbiadini 1	Roberts	Sharpe	Brandon 1	Annan	Brierley			
51		8 Farsley Celtic	3-3	L	188	Buxton	Price 1	Harrison	Benn	Margerison	Sullivan	Gabbiadini	Roberts	Sharpe	Brandon	Annan	Brierley 1	Hoyle 1		
52		10 CONGLETON TOWN	0-0	L	171	Buxton	Price	Harrison	Morgan	Sullivan	Margerison	Gabbiadini	Roberts	Sharpe	Benn	Brierley				
53		13 NETHERFIELD	0-2	L	147	Buxton	Price	Harrison	Johnson	Sullivan	Margerison	Gabbiadini	Roberts	Sharpe	Benn	Brierley	Brandon	Annan		
54		20 ASHTON UNITED	0-1	L	175	Buxton	Brierley	Harrison	Brown T	Morgan	Margerison	Price	Roberts	Sharpe	Benn	Brandon	Annan			
55		27 Alfreton Town	2-3	L	364	Buxton	Brierley	Harrison	Morgan	Brown T	Sullivan	Price	Roberts	Sharpe	Benn 1	Brandon 1	Johnson	Annan	Gabbiadini	
56	May	4 WHITLEY BAY	2-3	L	198	Buxton	Price	Johnson	Brown T 1	Morgan	Benn	Annan	Roberts	Sharpe	Marshall	Gabbiadini 1	Brierley	Sullivan		

1996/97

7th in the UniBond League Division One

						1	2	3	4	5	6	7	8	9	10	11	12	13	14	
1	Aug	24 CURZON ASHTON	1-2	L	466	Redfern	Benn	Grayston	Brown T	Pallant	Price	Lanaghan 1	Cygan	Sharpe	Brandon	Mazurke	Richardson	Annan	Parke	
2		26 Flixton	1-2	L	228	Redfern	Richardson	Grayston	Brown T	Annan	Price	Lanaghan	Cygan	Sharpe	Brandon	Gabbiadini 1	Mazurke			
3		31 Lincoln United	1-2	L	247	Redfern	Richardson	Grayston	Brown T	Margerison	Sharpe	Mazurke	Price	Worboys 1	Benn	Gabbiadini	Cygan	Spencer		
4	Sep	4 HARROGATE TOWN	1-0	L	261	Redfern	Price	Grayston	Brown T	Margerison	Sharpe	Mazurke	Cygan	Worboys	Benn	Gabbiadini 1	Brandon			
5		7 RADCLIFFE BOROUGH	0-1	L	313	Redfern	Blair	Grayston	Price	Margerison	Sharpe	Mazurke	Cygan	Worboys	Benn	Gabbiadini	Roberts	Spencer		
6		10 Eastwood Town	1-1	L	137	Redfern	Spencer	Grayston	Hopley	Margerison	Blair	Richardson	Benn	Sharpe	Harrison	Gabbiadini 1	Kane			
7		14 ASHFIELD UNITED	1-0	FAC	349	Redfern	Spencer	Grayston	Brown T	Margerison	Blair	Richardson	Benn	Sharpe	Harrison	Gabbiadini 1	Warboys			
8		18 WORKSOP TOWN	1-1	L	302	Lenaghan	Blair	Harrison	Brown T	Margerison	Benn 1	Spivey	Mazurke	Sharpe	Worboys	Kane	Grayston	Spencer		
9		21 GT HARWOOD TOWN	2-1	L	283	Lenaghan	Blair	Grayston	Brown T	Margerison	Benn	Gabbiadini 1	Mazurke 1	Sharpe	Worboys	Richardson	Price	Kane		
10		24 Stocksbridge PS	2-3	L	258	Redfern	Price	Grayston	Brown T	Margerison 1	Blair	Gabbiadini	Mazurke	Sharpe 1	Benn	Kane	Worboys	Richardson		
11		28 Frickley Athletic	0-1	FAC	269	Redfern	Richardson	Grayston	Brown T	Margerison	Sharpe	Price	Mazurke	Warboys	Benn	Harrison	Spencer	Roberts		
12	Oct	2 ASHTON UNITED	0-0	LC	202	Lenaghan	Blair	Grayston	Brown T	Hopley	Benn	Price	Mazurke	Regan	Spencer	Gabbiadini	Warboys	Richardson		
13		5 Droylsden	2-2	L	180	Lenaghan	Blair	Grayston	Brown T	Sharpe	Megson 1	Richardson	Benn	Gabbiadini 1	Regan	Freeman	Price	Sykes		
14		9 WHITLEY BAY	1-2	L	215	Lenaghan	Blair	Grayston	Brown T	Sykes	Megson 1	Richardson	Benn	Gabbiadini	Price	Freeman	Hey			
15		12 Matlock Town	2-0	L	322	Lenaghan	Blair	Grayston	Brown T	Sharpe	Megson	Richardson 1	Benn	Gabbiadini 1	Price	Freeman				
16		14 Ashton United	2-4	LC	206	Lenaghan	Blair	Harrison 1	Hopley	Sharpe	Mazurke	Richardson	Benn	Gabbiadini 1	Price	Freeman				
17		23 LINCOLN UNITED	0-1	L	292	Lenaghan	Blair	Grayston	Price	Sharpe	Megson	Freeman	Benn	Brown M	Beddard	Harrison	Hey			
18		26 Atherton LR	3-1	L	138	Lenaghan	Blair	Grayston	Beddard	Sharpe	Megson	Harrison	Benn	Brown M 2	Chapman	Freeman	Richardson	Hey 1		
19	Nov	2 Leigh RMI	0-3	L	304	Lenaghan	Blair	Grayston	Price	Sharpe	Megson	Harrison	Benn	Brown M	Chapman	Freeman	Hey	Beddard		
20		9 Whitley Bay	1-0	FAT	214	Lenaghan	Blair	Grayston	Brown T	Sharpe	Megson	Hey	Benn 1	Brown M	Harrison	Freeman	Gabbiadini	Richardson		
21		16 ASHTON UNITED	0-1	L	293	Lenaghan	Blair	Grayston	Brown T	Sharpe	Megson	Hey	Benn	Brown M	Harrison	Freeman	Gabbiadini	Chapman		
22		30 BARROW	1-1	FAT	425	Lenaghan	Blair	Grayston	Brown T	Sharpe	Megson	Hendrick	Benn	Gabbiadini	Regan	Freeman				1og
23	Dec	3 Barrow	1-0	FAT	620	Lenaghan	Blair	Grayston	Brown T	Sharpe	Megson	Hey	Benn	Gabbiadini 1	Harrison	Freeman				
24		7 WARRINGTON TOWN	2-0	L	215	Lenaghan	Blair	Grayston	Brown T	Sharpe	Megson	Hey	Benn	Gabbiadini 2	Harrison	Freeman				
25		11 ECCLESHILL UNITED	3-1	CC	242	Lenaghan	Blair	Grayston	Brown T	Sharpe	Price	Hey 1	Harrison 1	Spencer	Regan 1	Freeman	Gabbiadini	Benn		
26		14 Netherfield	3-0	L	164	Lenaghan	Grayston	Ball	Brown T	Sharpe	Price	Blair 2	Benn	Gabbiadini 1	Harrison	Freeman	Barr			
27		21 Whitley Bay	4-3	L	190	Lenaghan	Grayston	Ball	Brown T 1	Sharpe	Price 1	Blair 1	Benn	Gabbiadini 1	Harrison	Freeman	Hendrick	Barr		
28		28 MATLOCK TOWN	1-0	L	289	Lenaghan	Grayston	Ball	Brown T	Sharpe	Price	Blair	Benn	Gabbiadini 1	Harrison	Freeman	Hendrick			
29	Jan	15 HARROGATE TOWN	0-2	UC	120	Lenaghan	Grayston	Ball	Price	Sharpe	Hendrick	Blair	Benn	Gabbiadini	Harrison	Freeman	Hey	Regan 1	Megson	
30		18 Gainsborough Trinity	3-1	FAT	631	Lenaghan	Grayston	Ball	Price	Sharpe	Barr	Blair 1	Benn	Gabbiadini 1	Harrison	Freeman	Hendrick	Regan 1		
31		22 FARSLEY CELTIC	2-1	L	228	Lenaghan	Megson 1	Ball	Price	Sharpe 1	Hendrick	Harrison	Benn	Gabbiadini	Regan	Freeman	Grayston	Hey	Barr	
32		25 Curzon Ashton	1-0	L	172	Lenaghan	Grayston	Ball	Brown T 1	Sharpe	Price	Blair	Benn	Gabbiadini	Harrison	Freeman	Megson			
33	Feb	1 Radcliffe Borough	0-2	L	288	Lenaghan	Grayston	Ball	Brown T	Sharpe	Price	Blair	Benn	Gabbiadini	Harrison	Freeman	Megson	Hendrick		
34		5 GUISELEY	4-3	CC	281	Lenaghan	Grayston 1	Ball	Brown T	Sharpe 1	Drury	Price	Benn	Regan	Megson 2	Hendrick	Gabbiadini	Barr	Richardson	
35		8 MORECAMBE	0-1	FAT	915	Lenaghan	Grayston	Ball	Brown T	Sharpe	Hendrick	Harrison	Benn	Regan	Megson	Freeman	Gabbiadini	Blair	Barr	
36		15 Great Harwood Town	2-1	L	224	Lenaghan	Grayston	Ball	Brown T	Sharpe	Drury	Blair	Benn	Hendrick	Megson 1	Harrison	Gabbiadini	Price 1		
37		22 CONGLETON TOWN	3-0	L	203	Lenaghan	Grayston	Ball	Brown T	Sharpe	Hendrick 2	Blair	Benn	Gabbiadini	Megson	Harrison 1	Freeman	Price	Hey	
38	Mar	1 Warrington Town	0-0	L	152	Lenaghan	Grayston	Ball	Brown T	Sharpe	Hendrick	Blair	Benn	Harrison	Megson	Freeman	Hey	Barr		
39		5 GRETNA	3-1	L	122	Lenaghan	Megson	Ball	Brown T	Sharpe	Hendrick	Blair 1	Benn	Harrison 1	Regan 1	Freeman	Price	Hey	Grayston	
40		8 Leigh RMI	2-1	L	162	Lenaghan	Megson	Ball	Brown T	Barr	Hendrick	Blair	Benn	Harrison	Regan 1	Freeman 1	Price	Sharpe		
41		15 DROYLSDEN	0-5	L	274	Lenaghan	Megson	Ball	Brown T	Barr	Hendrick	Blair	Benn	Harrison	Regan	Freeman	Price			
42		16 Workington	0-0	L	232	Lenaghan	Grayston	Ball	Brown T	Price	Barr	Blair	Benn	Harrison	Regan	Freeman	Hendrick			
43		22 Congleton Town	1-0	L	164	Lenaghan	Grayston	Ball	Brown T	Price	Barr	Hendrick	Benn	Harrison	Regan 1	Freeman	Gabbiadini			
44		26 ARMTHORPE WELFARE	0-1	CC	206	Lenaghan	Grayston	Ball	Brown T	Price	Richardson	Harrison	Benn	Regan	Gabbiadini	Freeman	Hendrick	Barr		
45		29 EASTWOOD TOWN	1-1	L	227	Lenaghan	Richardson	Grayston	Brown T	Sharpe	Hendrick	Harrison	Benn	Daws	Regan 1	Freeman	Gabbiadini	Blair	Price	
46		31 Farsley Celtic	0-1	L	347	Lenaghan	Richardson	Drury	Brown T	Hendrick	Barr	Ball	Benn	Daws	Regan	Freeman	Gabbiadini	Price	Grayston	
47	Apr	5 WORKINGTON	1-0	L	197	Lenaghan	Richardson	Ball	Hendrick	Price	Barr	Harrison	Benn	Daws 1	Regan	Freeman	Gabbiadini	Grayston	Blair	
48		8 Worksop Town	2-1	L	402	Lenaghan	Blair	Grayston	Price 1	Sharpe	Barr	Gabbiadini	Benn 1	Daws	Harrison	Freeman	Regan			
49		12 NETHERFIELD	3-2	L	206	Lenaghan	Blair	Grayston	Price 2	Sharpe	Barr	Gabbiadini	Benn	Daws	Harrison	Freeman	Regan 1	Ball		
50		16 STOCKSBRIDGE PS	2-0	L	162	Lenaghan	Grayston	Ball	Brown T 1	Sharpe	Price	Blair	Benn	Daws 1	Harrison	Freeman	Regan			
51		19 FLIXTON	0-1	L	155	Lenaghan	Grayston	Ball	Brown T	Sharpe	Price	Blair	Benn	Daws	Harrison	Freeman	Gabbiadini	Regan	Hendrick	
52		21 Ashton United	0-0	L	190	Lenaghan	Grayston	Ball	Brown T	Price	Barr	Blair	Benn	Daws	Harrison	Freeman	Gabbiadini			
53		26 ATHERTON LR	4-2	L	179	Lenaghan	Richardson	Harrison	Brown T	Sharpe	Price	Gabbiadini 1	Benn	Regan 1	Blair	Freeman	Hendrick	Annan 1	Barr	1og
54		29 Gretna	2-2	L	75	Lenaghan	Grayston 1	Ball	Brown T	Hendrick	Barr 1	Richardson	Benn	Daws	Harrison	Freeman	Annan			
55	May	3 Harrogate Town	1-3	L	260	Lenaghan	Grayston	Ball	Brown T	Sharpe	Price	Annan	Benn	Daws	Harrison	Freeman	Hendrick	Regan	Gabbiadini 1	

1997/98

9th in the UniBond League Division One

						1	2	3	4	5	6	7	8	9	10	11	12	13	14	
1	Aug	23 Buxton	1-0	L	225	Kenny	Ingram	Ball	Brown	Sharpe	Grayston	Lee	Benn	Daws	Annan	Freeman	Barr			1og
2		25 Lincoln United	0-0	L	154	Kenny	Ingram	Ball	Brown	Sharpe	Grayston	Lee	Benn	Daws	Harrison	Freeman	Annan	Regan		
3		30 Bootle	1-3	FAC	121	Kenny	Ingram	Ball 1	Brown	Sharpe	Price	Lee	Benn	Daws	Harrison	Freeman	Grayston	Annan	Regan	
4	Sep	3 TRAFFORD	0-1	L	232	Kenny	Barr	Ball	Brown	Price	Grayston	Lee	Benn	Gabbiadini	Daws	Freeman	Harrison	Annan		
5		5 Harrogate Town	4-1	L	224	Kenny	Price	Grayston	Brown	Harrison	Barr 1	Lee	Benn 1	Sharpe 1	Daws	Freeman	Annan 1	Gabbiadini		
6		9 Eastwood Town	1-1	L	167	Kenny	Barr	Harrison	Brown	Grayston 1	Annan	Lee	Benn	Sharpe	Daws	Freeman	Ball	Gabbiadini		
7		13 BUXTON	4-1	L	152	Kenny	Lee	Ball	Brown	Grayston	Barr	Annan	Benn	Sharpe 1	Daws 2	Freeman	Gabbiadini	Regan 1	Connor	
8		17 LINCOLN UNITED	1-1	L	192	Kenny	Lee	Ball	Brown	Connor	Barr	Grayston	Benn	Regan 1	Daws	Freeman	Gabbiadini	Annan		
9		20 Gretna	0-1	L	100	Kenny	Ingram	Ball	Brown	Connor	Grayston	Lee	Benn	Sharpe	Daws	Freeman	Regan	Annan		
10		24 WHITBY TOWN	1-1	L	318	Kenny	Ingram	Ball	Brown	Sharpe	Thornber	Price	Grayston 1	Regan	Pritchard	Freeman	Richardson			
11		27 NETHERFIELD	3-1	L	230	Kenny	Ingram	Ball 1	Connor	Sharpe	Grayston	Price	Benn 1	Regan 1	Pritchard	Freeman	Harrison	Richardson	Lee	
12	Oct	1 LINCOLN UNITED	1-0	LC	112	Kenny	Grayston	Ball	Connor	Sharpe	Thornber	Harrison	Benn 1	Lee	Pritchard	Freeman	Ingram			
13		4 Witton Albion	2-1	L	429	Kenny	Green	Grayston	Brown	Connor	Barr	Lee	Benn	Harrison	Pritchard 1	Freeman 1	Price			
14		8 Whitby Town	2-5	L	515	Kenny	Green	Grayston 1	Brown 1	Sharpe	Barr	Blair	Benn	Lee	Harrison	Freeman	Price	Richardson		
15		11 Stocksbridge PS	1-0	L	202	Kenny	Barr	Ball	Brown	Green	Grayston	Blair	Benn	Sharpe	Pritchard	Harrison 1				
16		15 EASTWOOD TOWN	0-1	L	186	Kenny	Freeman	Ball	Brown	Green	Price	Blair	Benn	Sharpe	Pritchard	Grayston	Richardson	Ingram		
17		18 ASHTON UNITED	0-0	L	278	Kenny	Grayston	Ball	Brown	Green	Lee	Blair	Benn	Sharpe	Pritchard	Freeman	Annan			
18		21 Worksop Town	0-1	L	321	Kenny	Green	Ball	Brown	Connor	Grayston	Lee	Benn	Sharpe	Pritchard	Freeman	Blair	Annan		
19		25 Trafford	1-1	L	234	Kenny	Green	Ball	Connor	Sharpe	Grayston	Annan	Benn	Blair	Pritchard	Freeman 1	Lee	Price		
20	Nov	1 Workington	1-0	L	169	Kenny	Grayston	Ball	Connor 1	Price	Green	Blair	Brandon	Sharpe	Harrison	Freeman	Richardson	Storton		
21		12 WORKSOP TOWN	2-3	L	228	Kenny	Grayston	Ball	Brown	Freeman	Green	Price	Thornber	Sharpe 1	Harrison	Brandon 1	Regan	Blair	Connor	
22		15 HARROGATE TOWN	3-1	L	251	Kenny	Freeman 1	Ball	Connor	Green	Barr	Brandon	Grayston 1	Sharpe	Regan 1	Harrison	Annan	Richardson		
23		19 FRICKLEY ATHLETIC	0-2	LC	135	Kenny	Blair	Grayston	Green	Freeman	Thornber	Richardson	Benn	Ward	Regan 1	Annan	Briggs	Connor	Ball	
24		22 STOCKSBRIDGE PS	2-3	L	177	Kenny	Blair	Grayston	Green	Freeman 1	Harrison	Ward	Benn	Sharpe	Pritchard	Brandon	Regan	Richardson	Ball 1	
25		26 Boston United	0-1	PC	306	Kenny	Richardson	Ball	Green	Sharpe	Briggs	Ward	Benn	Regan	Harrison	Freeman	Pritchard	Annan	Connor	
26	Dec	6 DROYLSDEN	1-0	L	158	Kenny	Richardson	Grayston	Connor	Sharpe	Green	Blair	Benn	Ward	Briggs	Harrison	Brandon	Ball 1		
27		8 LEIGH RMI	1-1	FAT	127	Kenny	Richardson	Grayston	Connor	Sharpe	Green	Blair	Thornber	Ward	Briggs 1	Harrison	Ball			
28		10 Leigh RMI	0-1	FAT	120	Kenny	Richardson	Ball	Connor	Sharpe	Green	Blair	Thornber	Ward	Grayston	Harrison	Freeman	Annan	Benn	
29		13 Whitley Bay	0-1	L	165	Kenny	Richardson	Ball	Connor	Freeman	Green	Brandon	Benn	Blair	Grayston	Harrison	Ward	Annan	Regan	
30		20 WORKINGTON	3-3	L	163	Kenny	Benn 1	Ball	Freeman	Sharpe 1	Green	Ward	Grayston	Regan 1	Briggs	Harrison	Blair			
31	Jan	1 Farsley Celtic	1-1	L	343	Kenny	Freeman	Ball	Connor 1	Sharpe	Green	Benn	Thornber	Regan	Grayston	Harrison	Blair			
32		10 Droylsden	2-2	L	162	Kenny	Freeman	Ball	Connor 1	Sharpe	Green	Benn	Briggs	Regan 1	Grayston	Harrison	Blair			
33		17 Netherfield	1-1	L	141	Kenny	Benn	Ball	Green	Sharpe	Barr	Briggs	Thornber	Regan	Blair 1	Harrison				
34		21 GUISELEY	2-2	CC	217	Kenny	Benn	Ball	Connor	Sharpe	Richardson	Briggs	Thornber	Brandon 1	Ward	Grayston	Blair	Regan 1	Harrison	aet
35		24 WITTON ALBION	1-2	L	214	Kenny	Benn	Ball	Clyde	Sharpe	Green	Briggs	Grayston	Regan	Blair 1	Harrison	Brandon			
36		27 Guiseley	0-1	CC	195	Kenny	Benn	Grayston	Green	Sharpe	Barr	Briggs	Thornber	Regan	Blair	Harrison	Ball	Connor	Brandon	
37		31 GT HARWOOD TOWN	1-2	L	162	Kenny	Grayston	Ball	Green	Sharpe	Barr	Blair	Benn 1	Regan	Briggs	Harrison	Freeman	Connor		
38	Feb	4 WHITBY TOWN	2-0	UC	134	Kenny	Richardson	Ball 1	Briggs	Clyde	Green	Blair	Benn	Regan	Harrison	Freeman	Lee			1og
39		7 Great Harwood Town	2-0	L	118	Kenny	Green	Ball	Clyde	Sharpe	Briggs	Blair 1	Benn	Regan	Harrison 1	Freeman	Brandon			
40		10 Droylsden	1-1	UC	134	Kenny	Green	Ball	Clyde	Sharpe	Briggs	Blair	Benn	Regan	Harrison	Freeman 1	Brandon			
41		14 Matlock Town	0-2	L	350	Kenny	Green	Harrison	Clyde	Sharpe	Briggs	Blair	Benn	Regan	Brandon	Freeman	Richardson	Grayston		
42		18 DROYLSDEN	3-1	UC	124	Kenny	Grayston	Ball	Briggs 1	Clyde	Harrison	Blair	Benn	Regan	Brandon 2	Freeman	Connor	Richardson	Green	
43		21 FLIXTON	1-0	L	123	Kenny	Richardson	Grayston	Clyde	Sharpe 1	Green	Briggs	Benn	Regan	Brandon	Harrison	Ball			
44		28 MATLOCK TOWN	1-2	L	130	Kenny	Grayston	Ball	Connor	Sharpe	Green	Brandon	Benn	Blair	Briggs	Harrison	Regan	Richardson	Lee 1	
45	Mar	14 Flixton	3-1	L	188	Kenny	Richardson 1	Grayston	Green	Sharpe	Briggs	Lee	Benn	Regan	Annan	Ball	Connor	Brandon 1	Blair 1	
46		17 Trafford	2-1	UC	153	Kenny	Richardson	Grayston	Green	Sharpe	Thornber	Brandon 1	Benn	Annan	Briggs	Ball 1	Regan	Connor	Harrison	
47		21 GRETNA	4-0	L	153	Kenny	Grayston	Freeman	Green	Sharpe 1	Thornber	Brandon	Benn	Annan 2	Briggs	Ball	Regan 1	Richardson		
48		25 TRAFFORD	0-2	UC	134	Kenny	Grayston	Freeman	Green	Sharpe	Richardson	Brandon	Benn	Annan	Briggs	Ball	Regan	Blair	Connor	
49		28 Ashton United	1-0	L	260	Kenny	Blair	Grayston	Green	Sharpe	Harrison	Brandon	Benn	Regan	Briggs	Ball 1	Richardson			
50	Apr	1 WHITLEY BAY	3-0	L	110	Kenny	Richardson	Grayston	Green	Connor	Harrison 1	Brandon 1	Benn	Regan 1	Briggs	Ball	Freeman	Thornber		
51		11 Congleton Town	1-2	L	173	Kenny	Blair	Grayston	Green	Sharpe	Harrison	Brandon	Benn	Annan 1	Briggs	Ball	Richardson	Freeman	Barr	
52		13 FARSLEY CELTIC	5-2	L	178	Kenny	Freeman 1	Grayston 1	Green	Connor 1	Thornber	Brandon	Benn	Annan 1	Harrison	Ball 1	Briggs			
53		25 BELPER TOWN	0-0	L	177	Kenny	Richardson	Grayston	Green	Connor	Harrison	Brandon	Freeman	Annan	Briggs	Ball	Blair			
54		29 CONGLETON TOWN	1-0	L	106	Kenny	Ingram	Ball 1	Brown	Connor	Briggs	Richardson	Brandon	Annan	Blair	Freeman	Grayston	Barr		
55	May	2 Belper Town	1-0	L	374	Kenny	Freeman	Grayston	Brown	Connor	Richardson	Brandon 1	Benn	Blair	Briggs	Ball	Regan	Harrison		

1998/99

9th in the UniBond League Division One

#	Month	Date / Opponent	Score	Comp	Att	1	2	3	4	5	6	7	8	9	10	11	12	13	14	
1	Aug	22 Congleton Town	0-0	L	160	Kenny	Connor	Grayston	Brown	Hutchinson	Green	Ward	Benn	Annan	Briggs	Ball	Richardson	Lee G	McClennon	
2		26 WHITLEY BAY	0-0	L	153	Lenaghan	Connor	Grayston	Brown	Hutchinson	Green	Richardson	Benn	McClennon	Lee G	Ball	Barr			
3		29 DROYLSDEN	0-5	L	177	Lenaghan	Connor	Grayston	Brown	Hutchinson	Benn	Richardson	Briggs	McClennon	Lee G	Ball	Annan	Ward	Green	
4		31 Radcliffe Borough	0-2	L	179	Lenaghan	Connor	Grayston	Brown	Hutchinson	Green	Briggs	Benn	Annan	Lee G	Ball	Richardson	Ward	McClennon	
5	Sep	5 EASINGTON COLLIERY	4-1	FAC	148	Lenaghan	Green	Grayston	Brown	Connor	Briggs	Ward 1	Benn	Annan 2	Pritchard	Ball 1	McClennon	Lee G	Richardson	
6		9 WHITLEY BAY	3-1	LC	74	Lenaghan	Green	Grayston	Brown	Connor	Briggs	Richardson	Benn	Annan	McClennon 3	Ball	Ward			
7		12 Netherfield Kendal	0-1	L	162	Lenaghan	Hutchinson	Grayston	Brown	Connor	Green	Richardson	Benn	Annan	McClennon	Ball	Ward			
8		15 Harrogate Town	1-0	L	166	Lenaghan	Green	Grayston	Brown	Connor	Richardson 1	Ward	Benn	Annan	McClennon	Ball	Lee G			
9		19 Bootle	3-2	FAC	109	Lenaghan	Green	Grayston	Brown	Connor	Richardson	Ward 1	Benn	McClennon 1	Annan 1	Ball	Lamb			
10		23 TRAFFORD	0-0	L	147	Lenaghan	Green	Grayston	Brown	Connor	Richardson	Ward	Benn	Annan	McClennon	Ball	Blair	Lee G		
11		26 BURSCOUGH	1-1	L	149	O'Connor	Green	Grayston	Hutchinson	Connor 1	Richardson	Ward	Benn	McClennon	Annan	Ball	Blair			
12		28 Ashton United	0-1	L	192	O'Connor	Blair	Grayston	Hutchinson	Hey	Richardson	Brandon	Benn	Ward	McClennon	Briggs	Harrison			
13	Oct	3 STOCKSBRIDGE PS	1-0	FAC	240	O'Connor	Grayston	Hutchinson	Brown	Connor	Briggs	Brandon	Benn	Blair	Richardson 1	Ball				
14		7 ALFRETON TOWN	2-1	L	166	Lenaghan	Grayston	Hutchinson	Brown	Connor 1	Harrison	Brandon	Benn	Blair	Richardson	Ball 1	Annan	Hey		
15		10 Witton Albion	1-2	L	383	Lenaghan	Richardson	Grayston	Brown	Connor	Green	Brandon 1	Benn	Blair	Briggs	Ball	Annan			
16		17 ASHTON UNITED	0-1	FAC	317	Lenaghan	Blair	Grayston	Brown	Richardson	Green	Briggs	Benn	Annan	Brandon	Ball	Pritchard	Connor		
17		21 HARROGATE TOWN	0-1	L	147	Lenaghan	Blair	Grayston	Brown	Green	Richardson	Brandon	Benn	Maxwell	Hey	Ball	Annan	Briggs		
18		31 Great Harwood Town	4-3	L	120	O'Connor	Blair	Grayston	Brown	Sharpe	Briggs 2	Brandon	Benn	Maxwell 1	Hey 1	Ball	Freeman	Connor		
19	Nov	2 STOURBRIDGE	3-0	FAT	140	O'Connor	Blair	Grayston	Brown	Hutchinson	Briggs	Brandon	Benn	Maxwell 2	Hey 1	Ball				
20		7 GRETNA	4-2	L	226	O'Connor	Blair	Grayston 2	Hutchinson	Sharpe	Briggs	Brandon 1	Benn	Maxwell	Hey 1	Ball	Richardson			
21		10 Harrogate Town	1-0	CC	144	O'Connor	Blair	Hutchinson	Harrison	Connor	Hey	Brandon	Benn	Ward 1	Richardson	Ball	Grayston	McClennon	Briggs	
22		14 Flixton	2-0	L	116	Lenaghan	Blair	Grayston	Brown	Sharpe	Connor 1	Hey 1	Benn	Maxwell	Briggs	Ball				
23		18 STOCKSBRIDGE PS	1-1	L	151	Lenaghan	Blair	Grayston	Brandon 1	Sharpe	Connor	Hey	Benn	Maxwell	Briggs	Ball	Freeman			
24		21 Witton Albion	2-0	FAT	279	Lenaghan	Blair	Grayston	Freeman 1	Hutchinson	Connor	Hey 1	Benn	Brandon	Briggs	Ball				
25	Dec	1 Blyth Spartans	1-3	LC	282	O'Connor	Blair	Grayston	Brandon	Hutchinson	Connor	Hey 1	Benn	Maxwell	Briggs	Ball	Ward			
26		5 RADCLIFFE BOROUGH	1-2	L	216	O'Connor	Blair	Grayston	Richardson	Hutchinson	Connor	Hey	Benn	Maxwell	Brandon	Ball 1	Brown	Freeman	Ward	
27		12 HUCKNALL TOWN	2-2	L	190	O'Connor	Blair	Grayston 1	Briggs	Hutchinson	Connor	Hey	Benn	Maxwell	Brandon	Ball	Freeman 1	Ward		
28		16 OSSETT TOWN	2-1	CC	103	Lenaghan	Blair	Freeman	Richardson	Briggs 1	Connor	Hey	Benn	McClennon	Ward	Ball 1	Brandon	Hutchinson	Harrison	
29		19 Gretna	2-3	L	85	O'Connor	Blair	Grayston	Freeman 1	Hutchinson	Connor	Hey	Benn	Maxwell	Briggs	Ball 1	Brandon	Lee D		
30		26 LINCOLN UNITED	3-1	L	196	Lenaghan	Blair	Grayston	Briggs 1	Hutchinson	Connor	Brandon 1	Benn	Maxwell	Hey 1	Ball	Lee D			
31		28 Stocksbridge PS	2-2	L	315	Lenaghan	Blair 1	Grayston	Briggs	Hutchinson	Connor	Brandon	Benn	Maxwell	Hey	Ball	Lee D	Freeman		1og
32	Jan	1 FARSLEY CELTIC	1-2	L	453	Lenaghan	Blair	Grayston	Briggs	Hutchinson	Connor	Brandon	Benn	Maxwell	Hey 1	Ball	Lee D	Freeman		
33		5 Eastwood Town	1-0	FDC	80	O'Connor	Blair	Grayston	Briggs	Bagshaw	Connor	Lee D	Benn	Maxwell	Hey	Ball	Richardson	McClennon		1og
34		9 Trafford	1-0	L	226	O'Connor	Blair	Grayston	Briggs 1	Bagshaw	Connor	Lee D	Benn	Maxwell	Hey	Ball				
35		16 Lincoln United	5-2	FAT	280	Lenaghan	Blair	Grayston	Briggs	Bagshaw	Connor 1	Lee D 2	Benn	Sharpe 1	Ward	Ball 1	Freeman			
36		23 NETHERFIELD KENDAL	1-1	L	154	Lenaghan	Blair	Grayston	Briggs	Bagshaw	Connor	Lee D 1	Benn	Maxwell	Hey	Ball	Sharpe			
37		30 BELPER TOWN	2-0	L	206	Lenaghan	Blair	Grayston	Briggs	Bagshaw	Connor	Lee D 1	Benn	Maxwell 1	Hey	Ball	Sharpe	Freeman		
38	Feb	2 Droylsden	0-1	FDC	129	Atkinson	Hand	Grayston	Briggs	Bagshaw	Connor	Richardson	Benn	Lamb	Jones	Ball	Spivey	Lee D	Maxwell	
39		6 Colwyn Bay	1-3	FAT	405	Lenaghan	Blair	Grayston	Briggs	Bagshaw	Connor	Lee D	Benn	Sharpe	Hey	Maxwell	Freeman 1	Brandon		
40		13 Eastwood Town	5-4	L	156	Atkinson	Blair	Grayston	Briggs	Sharpe	Connor	Lee D	Benn	Maxwell 1	Brandon 2	Freeman				2ogs
41		16 Selby Town	1-0	CC	107	Atkinson	Hand	Grayston	Briggs	Sharpe	Connor	Brandon 1	Benn	Maxwell	Freeman	Ball				
42		20 MATLOCK TOWN	3-1	L	192	Atkinson	Blair	Grayston	Briggs	Sharpe	Freeman	Brandon	Benn	Maxwell	Lee D 2	Ball	Jones 1			
43		27 Burscough	1-1	L	160	Atkinson	Blair	Grayston	Jones	Connor	Freeman	Brandon	Benn	Maxwell 1	Lee D	Ball				
44	Mar	13 FLIXTON	2-1	L	124	Atkinson	Blair	Grayston	Jones	Freeman	Connor	Brandon 1	Benn	Maxwell 1	Lee D	Ball				
45		17 LIVERSEDGE	2-0	CC	193	Atkinson	Blair	Grayston	Briggs	Connor	Freeman	Brandon 1	Benn	Maxwell	Lee D 1	Ball	Hey			
46		20 Lincoln United	3-1	L	220	Atkinson	Hand	Grayston	Briggs	Sharpe	Connor	Brandon	Benn	Maxwell 1	Lee D	Freeman 1	Jones 1	Ball		
47	Jan	24 GREAT HARWOOD T	0-1	L	134	Atkinson	Hand	Grayston	Briggs	Connor	Jones	Hey	Benn	Maxwell	Lee D	Ball	Freeman	Sharpe	Edge	
48		27 CONGLETON TOWN	4-0	L	156	O'Connor	Hand	Grayston	Jones 1	Connor	Freeman	Brandon 1	Benn	Sharpe	Lee D	Ball 1	Hey 1			
49		30 Whitley Bay	0-1	L	149	O'Connor	Hand	Grayston	Briggs	Connor	Jones	Brandon	Benn	Sharpe	Lee D	Hey	Edge			
50	Apr	3 WITTON ALBION	5-0	L	179	O'Connor	Hand	Grayston	Briggs 2	Sharpe	Jones	Brandon	Benn 1	Maxwell	Hey 2	Ball	Blair	Freeman	Edge	
51		5 Farsley Celtic	2-0	L	161	O'Connor	Blair	Grayston	Briggs	Sharpe	Connor	Jones	Benn	Maxwell 1	Hey 1	Ball				
52		10 Alfreton Town	2-2	L	164	O'Connor	Blair	Grayston	Briggs 1	Bagshaw	Connor	Jones	Benn	Maxwell	Hey	Ball 1				
53		14 ASHTON UNITED	0-3	L	140	O'Connor	Blair	Grayston	Briggs	Bagshaw	Jones	Hey	Benn	Maxwell	Brandon	Ball	Freeman			
54		17 EASTWOOD TOWN	3-1	L	139	O'Connor	Blair	Grayston	Jones	Bagshaw	Freeman 1	Brandon 1	Benn	Maxwell	Hey	Ball 1	Hand	Connor		
55		21 Ossett Albion	0-2	CC	393	O'Connor	Blair	Grayston	Briggs	Sharpe	Bagshaw	Brandon	Benn	Maxwell	Hey	Ball	Connor	Lee		At WR County Ground
56		24 Belper Town	1-3	L	213	O'Connor	Blair	Grayston	Briggs	Connor	Bagshaw	Jones	Benn	Sharpe	Maxwell	Freeman	Ball	Brandon 1		
57		27 Droylsden	0-2	L	138	Lenaghan	Blair	Grayston	Briggs	Sharpe	Jones	Brandon	Benn	Maxwell	Lee D	Hey	Freeman			
58		29 Matlock Town	1-0	L	193	O'Connor	Blair	Grayston	Briggs	Sharpe	Jones	Brandon 1	Benn	Richardson	Lee D	Ball	Maxwell			
59	May	1 Hucknall Town	1-1	L	494	O'Connor	Hand	Grayston	Freeman	Sharpe	Blair	Brandon	Benn	Maxwell	Briggs	Ball 1	Connor			

1999/2000

4th in UniBond League Division One

						1	2	3	4	5	6	7	8	9	10	11	12	13	14	
1	Aug	14 Congleton Town	1-2	L	152	Kelly	Freeman	Marquis	Hancock	Bagshaw	James	Jones	Benn	Maxwell	Lee	Ball 1	Francis	Richardson		
2		18 WHITLEY BAY	1-0	L	179	Kelly	Freeman	Marquis	Hancock	Bagshaw	James	Hey	Benn	Maxwell 1	Francis	Ball	Richardson			
3		21 PRESCOT CABLES	1-0	FAC	178	Kelly	Freeman	Marquis	Hancock	Bagshaw	Richardson	Hey	Benn	Maxwell 1	Francis	Ball	Hand	James		
4		24 Harrogate Town	3-0	L	369	Kelly	James	Marquis	Bagshaw	Sharpe	Hancock	Hey	Benn	Maxwell	Francis 3	Ball	Richardson	Hand		
5		28 Witton Albion	2-0	L	308	Kelly	James	Marquis	Bagshaw	Hand	Hancock	Hey 1	Benn	Maxwell	Donaldson	Ball	Richardson 1	Jones		
6		30 OSSETT TOWN	1-0	L	248	Kelly	James	Marquis	Bagshaw	Richardson	Hancock	Hey	Benn	Jones	Francis	Ball 1	Donaldson			
7	Sep	4 SKELMERSDALE U	2-1	FAC	261	Kelly	James	Marquis	Bagshaw	Richardson	Hancock 1	Hey	Benn	Maxwell 1	Francis	Ball	Donaldson	Lee	Jones	
8		7 Belper Town	0-0	L	183	Kelly	James	Marquis	Bagshaw	Richardson	Hancock	Hey	Benn	Maxwell	Francis	Donaldson	Lee			
9		11 Trafford	0-2	L	223	Kelly	James	Marquis	Bagshaw	Richardson	Hancock	Hey	Benn	Maxwell	Lee	Briggs	Francis	Jones		
10		13 Emley	0-0	LC	240	Kelly	James	Marquis	Freeman	Richardson	Jones	Hey	Briggs	Francis	Lee	Ball				
11		18 DROYLSDEN	2-2	FAC	251	Kelly	James	Marquis	Bagshaw	Briggs	Jones	Hey	Benn	Maxwell	Lee 1	Ball 1	Freeman			
12		21 Droylsden	1-2	FAC	261	Kelly	James	Marquis	Donaldson	Freeman	Jones	Hancock	Benn	Maxwell	Lee	Ball	Briggs	Francis 1		aet
13		25 Radcliffe Borough	1-2	L	240	Kelly	James	Marquis	Bagshaw	Donaldson	Jones	Hancock 1	Benn	Maxwell	Francis	Ball	Hey			
14		29 OSSETT TOWN	2-1	LC	103	Kelly	Verity	Freeman 1	Bagshaw	Marquis	Donaldson	Jones	Benn	Maxwell	Hey 1	James	Francis			
15	Oct	2 ACCRINGTON STANLEY	1-0	L	204	Kelly	Verity	Marquis	Bagshaw	James	Hancock	Francis	Benn	Denney 1	Pemberton	Ball	Donaldson	Hey		
16		6 HARROGATE TOWN	2-2	L	208	Kelly	Verity	Marquis	Blair 1	James	Hancock	Francis 1	Benn	Maxwell	Pemberton	Ball	Hey			
17		9 Gateshead	1-4	FAT	254	Kelly	Verity	Marquis	Blair	James	Doaldson	Hancock	Benn	Pemberton	Maxwell 1	Ball	Francis	Freeman		
18		12 Matlock Town	2-2	L	302	Kelly	Verity	James	Bagshaw	Marquis	Jones	Pemberton	Benn	Denney	Maxwell 1	Ball 1	Blair			
19		16 GRETNA	6-0	L	200	Kelly	Blair	James	Bagshaw	Marquis	Jones	Pemberton 2	Benn	Denney 1	Maxwell 1	Ball	Hancock 1	Francis	Freeman	1og
20		23 Burscough	2-1	L	185	Kelly	Blair	James	Bagshaw	Marquis	Jones	Pemberton	Benn	Denney 1	Maxwell 1	Ball	Hancock			
21		27 BELPER TOWN	2-1	L	172	Kelly	Blair	James	Bagshaw	Freeman	Jones 1	Pemberton	Benn	Denney	Maxwell 1	Ball	Hancock			
22		30 WORKINGTON	1-0	L	280	Kelly	Blair	James	Bagshaw	Hancock	Jones	Pemberton	Benn	Denney 1	Maxwell	Ball	Donaldson	Francis		
23	Nov	6 Stocksbridge PS	1-2	L	195	Kelly	Blair	James	Hancock	Marquis	Donaldson	Pemberton	Benn	Denney 1	Francis	Ball	Jones			
24		9 Blyth Spartans	0-4	LC	265	Kelly	Verity	James	Hancock	Marquis	Donaldson	Pemberton	Benn	Jones	Freeman	Ball	Blair			
25		12 FLIXTON	3-1	L	204	Kelly	Blair	James 1	Hancock	Marquis	Jones	Pemberton	Benn	Denney	Maxwell 2	Ball	Donaldson	Derefaka		
26		16 Lincoln United	1-2	L	145	Kelly	Freeman	James	Blair	Marquis	Hancock	Pemberton	Benn	Denney	Maxwell	Ball 1	Jones			
27		20 Netherfield Kendal	1-1	L	165	Kelly	Blair	James	Bagshaw	Marquis 1	Donaldson	Pemberton	Benn	Denney	Maxwell	Ball				
28		27 TRAFFORD	3-0	L	181	Kelly	Blair	James	Bagshaw	Edmunds	Hancock	Pemberton	Benn	Denney 1	Maxwell 2	Ball	Donaldson			
29	Dec	1 GUISELEY	6-2	LC	133	Kelly	Blair	Verity	Bagshaw	Donaldson	Hancock 1	Jones 1	Benn	McClennon 2	Maxwell 2	Ball				
30		8 HATFIELD MAIN	4-1	CC	61	Kelly	Verity	James	Bagshaw	Blair	Donaldson	Hancock	Benn	McClennon	Denney 2	Ball 1	Edmunds	Sharpe	Jones 1	
31		11 BURSCOUGH	1-1	L	192	Kelly	Verity	James	Bagshaw	Edmunds	Donaldson	Hancock	Benn	Denney 1	Maxwell	Ball	Wilson	Jones		
32		18 Ossett Town	1-3	L	225	Kelly	Freeman	James	Wilson 1	Edmunds	Marquis	Hancock	Benn	Denney	Maxwell	Ball	Pemberton	Jones		
33		27 LINCOLN UNITED	4-1	L	259	Kelly	James	Freeman	Bagshaw	Edmunds	Poopleton	Hancock	Benn	Denney 1	Maxwell	Ball 3				
34	Jan	3 Farsley Celtic	1-4	L	323	Kelly	Edmunds	Freeman	Bagshaw	Sharpe	James	Hancock	Benn	Poppleton	Maxwell	Ball 1				
35		8 Eastwood Town	1-0	L	196	Kelly	Verity	James	Bagshaw	Marquis	Donaldson	Poppleton	Benn	Wilson	Maxwell	Ball	Hancock	Pemberton 1		
36		15 RADCLIFFE BOROUGH	1-1	L	226	Kelly	James	Pemberton	Wilson	Marquis	Poppleton	Hancock	Benn	Denney	Maxwell 1	Ball	Donaldson	Francis	Edmunds	
37		22 Lancaster City	0-1	LC	198	Kelly	James	Pemberton	Bagshaw	Marquis	Hancock	Donaldson	Benn	McClennon	Francis	Ball				
38	Feb	5 Flixton	1-0	L	106	Baker	Wilson	James	Bagshaw	Marquis	Donaldson	Hancock	Benn	Denney	Maxwell	Pemberton 1	Ball	Edmunds		
39		11 STOCKSBRIDGE PS	2-0	L	208	Kelly	Wilson	James	Bagshaw	Pemberton	Verity	Hancock	Benn	McClennon	Maxwell	Ball 1	Denney	Edmunds 1		
40		15 Eccleshill United	0-3	CC	110	Baker	James	Freeman	Edmunds	Sharpe	Verity	McClennon	Benn	Denney	Francis	Ball	Maxwell			
41		19 CHORLEY	4-1	L	253	Kelly	Verity	James	Bagshaw	Pemberton 2	Edmunds	Hancock	Benn	Denney 1	Maxwell 1	Ball	Freeman			
42		26 Accrington Stanley	1-2	L	738	Kelly	Wilson	Dolby	Marquis	Pemberton	Verity	Hancock 1	Benn	Denney	Maxwell	Ball	Donaldson			
43	Mar	4 WITTON ALBION	2-2	L	395	Kelly	Wilson 1	James	Marquis	Edmunds	Verity	Hancock	Dolby	Pemberton	Maxwell	Ball	Donaldson 1			
44		11 Workington	2-0	L	538	Kelly	Wilson	Dolby 1	Bagshaw	Pemberton	James	Hancock 1	Benn	Denney	Maxwell	Ball	Marquis	Verity		
45		18 NETHERFIELD KENDAL	3-0	L	223	Kelly	Wilson	Dolby	Bagshaw	Pemberton 3	James	Hancock	Benn	Denney	Maxwell	Ball	Marquis	Freeman	Donaldson	
46		22 CONGLETON TOWN	3-2	L	227	Kelly	Wilson	Dolby	Bagshaw 1	Pemberton	James	Hancock	Benn	Denney	Maxwell	Ball	Marquis 1	Blair		1og
47		25 Chorley	1-2	L	264	Kelly	Wilson	Dolby	Bagshaw	James	Pemberton	Marquis	Benn	Denney	Maxwell 1	Ball	Donaldson	Blair	Freeman	
48	Apr	1 ASHTON UNITED	2-3	L	258	Kelly	James	Dolby 1	Bagshaw	Pemberton 1	Marquis	Hancock	Benn	Maxwell	Calcutt	Ball	Denney	Donaldson	Blair	
49		5 EASTWOOD TOWN	1-0	L	151	Kelly	Blair	Dolby	Bagshaw	Marquis	James	Calcutt	Donaldson	Pemberton 1	Maxwell	Ball	Denney	Lee		
50	Feb	15 MATLOCK TOWN	4-3	L	279	Kelly	Blair	Dolby	Bagshaw	Marquis 1	James	Calcutt	Donaldson	Pemberton 1	Denney 1	Ball	Verity	Lee		1og
51		22 Whitley Bay	3-1	L	240	Kelly	Blair	Dolby 2	Freeman	Marquis	James	Calcutt	Donaldson	Pemberton	Denney 1	Ball	Verity	Lee		
52		24 FARSLEY CELTIC	1-1	L	299	Kelly	Blair	Dolby	Bagshaw	Marquis	James	Hancock	Donaldson 1	Pemberton	Denney	Ball	Wilson			
53		29 Gretna	2-1	L	88	Kelly	Blair	Dolby	Bagshaw	Verity	James	Hancock	Donaldson	Pemberton	Maxwell	Calcutt	Denney 1	Freeman	Lee 1	
54	May	1 Ashton United	2-2	L	255	Kelly	Lee	Marquis	Bagshaw	Pemberton	James 2	Hancock	Donaldson	Maxwell	Denney	Ball	Verity			

2000/01

Champions of UniBond League Division One: Promoted

						1	2	3	4	5	6	7	8	9	10	11	12	13	14	
1	Aug	19 CHORLEY	1-1	L	272	Kelly	Verity	Marquis	Bagshaw	James	Thompson 1	Calcutt	Benn	Denney	Maxwell	Ball	Dolnaldson	Dolby		
2		22 Harrogate Town	2-1	L	325	Kelly	Verity	Marquis	Bagshaw	Donaldson	Thompson 1	Calcutt 1	Benn	Maxwell	James	Ball	Dolby	Denney		
3		26 Gretna	1-0	L	92	Kelly	Verity	Marquis	Bagshaw 1	Donaldson	Hancock	Calcutt	Benn	Maxwell	James	Ball	Dolby	Denney		
4		28 WORKINGTON	1-0	L	253	Kelly	Verity	Dolby	Bagshaw	Donaldson	Thompson	Calcutt	Benn	Maxwell 1	James	Ball	Morrow	Marquis	Denney	
5	Sep	2 BRANDON UNITED	1-0	FAC	256	Kelly	Verity	Marquis	Bagshaw	Donaldson	Thompson 1	Calcutt	Benn	Maxwell	James	Ball	Hancock	Denney		
6		9 Vauxhall Motors	0-2	L	134	Kelly	James	Marquis	Bagshaw	Donaldson	Thompson	Calcutt	Benn	Denney	Maxwell	Ball	Dolby	Stratford		
7		16 SALFORD CITY	0-1	FAC	209	Kelly	Donaldson	Stratford	James	Marquis	Thompson	Hancock	Benn	Calcutt	Maxwell	Dolby	Ball	Denney		
8		23 Trafford	3-1	L	183	Kelly	Quinn	Stratford	James	Marquis	Thompson	Hancock 1	Benn	Hayward 2	Maxwell	Dolby	Calcutt			
9		27 EASTWOOD TOWN	4-1	L	158	Kelly	Quinn 1	Stratford	James	Marquis 1	Thompson 1	Hancock 1	Benn	Hayward	Maxwell	Dolby	Verity	Calcutt	Denney	
10		30 North Ferriby United	1-2	L	215	Kelly	Quinn	Stratford	Bagshaw	Marquis	Thompson	Hancock	Benn	Hayward	Maxwell 1	James	Calcutt	Denney		
11	Oct	6 LINCOLN UNITED	2-0	L	205	Kelly	Quinn	Stratford	Bagshaw	Marquis	Thompson	Hancock 1	Benn	Hayward	Maxwell 1	James	Calcutt			
12		10 Ossett Town	1-1	L	192	Kelly	Quinn	Stratford	Bagshaw	Marquis	Calcutt	Hancock	Benn	Hayward	Maxwell	James 1	Verity	Donaldson		
13		14 GUISELEY	3-0	L	340	Kelly	Quinn	Stratford 1	Bagshaw	Marquis 1	Thompson	Hancock	Benn	Hayward	Maxwell	James	Verity	Dolby	Donaldson	1og
14		21 Congleton Town	2-0	L	410	Kelly	Quinn	Stratford	Bagshaw	Marquis	Thompson	Hancock	Benn	Hayward 2	Maxwell	Donaldson	Verity	Dolby	James	
15		23 Ashton United	2-0	L	212	Kelly	Quinn	Stratford	Verity	Marquis 1	Thompson	Hancock	Benn	Hayward 1	Maxwell	Donaldson				
16		28 MATLOCK TOWN	0-2	L	218	Kelly	Quinn	Stratford	Verity	Marquis	Thompson	Hancock	Benn	Hayward	Maxwell	Donaldson	Ball	Dolby	James	
17	Nov	4 Gainsborough Trinity	2-3	FAT	392	Kelly	Quinn 1	Stratford	James	Marquis	Thompson	Hancock	Benn	Hayward	Maxwell 1	Dolby	Calcutt			
18		11 KENDAL TOWN	4-1	L	183	Kelly	Quinn	Stratford	James	Calcutt	Thompson	Hancock 1	Benn	Hayward 1	Maxwell	Dolby	Ball	Donaldson	Verity	2og
19		18 Eastwood Town	1-0	L	170	Kelly	Quinn	Stratford	James	Marquis	Bagshaw	Hancock	Benn	Hayward 1	Maxwell	Dolby				
20		21 Harrogate Town	1-1	LC	139	Kelly	Quinn	Ball	Verity	Marquis	Bagshaw	Lindley	Benn 1	Hayward	Patterson	Dolby	James			
21		25 ASHTON UNITED	1-2	L	274	Kelly	Quinn	Stratford	James	Marquis	Bagshaw	Hancock 1	Benn	Hayward	Maxwell	Dolby	Ball	Calcutt	Thompson	
22		29 EMLEY	3-2	LC	157	Kelly	Verity	Donaldson	Bagshaw	Thompson	Lindley	Valcutt	Quigley	Hayward 1	Maxwell 1	Ball	Quinn	Benn 1	James	
23	Dec	2 Kendal Town	1-0	L	122	Kelly	James 1	Marquis	Bagshaw	Calcutt	Thompson	Hancock	Benn	Hayward	Maxwell	Ball	Quinn			
24		9 WINSFORD UNITED	4-1	L	188	Kelly	James	Marquis	Bagshaw	Calcutt	Thompson	Hancock	Benn 1	Hayward 2	Maxwell 1	Ball	Quinn	Verity	Denney	
25		11 Yorkshire Amateur	2-1	CC	98	Brown	James	Marquis	Bagshaw	Verity	Lindley	Quinn	Benn	Thompson 1	Maxwell 1	Ball	Calcutt			
26		16 Witton Albion	2-5	L	376	Brown	James	Marquis	Bagshaw	Calcutt	Thompson	Hancock 1	Benn	Hayward	Denney 1	Ball	Quinn	Verity		
27		19 Frickley Athletic	3-3	LC	133	Brown	Verity	Marquis	Quinn	Wright	Thompson	Hancock	Benn	Hayward 2	Maxwell 1	Ball	Calcutt	Lindley		
28		23 TRAFFORD	1-0	L	277	Williams	James	Quinn	Bagshaw	Calcutt	Thompson	Hancock	Benn	Hayward 1	Maxwell	Ball	Lindley			
29	Jan	6 VAUXHALL MOTORS	0-1	L	405	Kelly	James	Marquis	Lindley	Lacey	Thompson	Quinn	Benn	Hayward	Maxwell	Ball	Verity	Dolby		
30		13 Chorley	1-2	L	312	Kelly	James	Dolby	Verity	Lacey	Thompson	Hancock	Benn	Hayward	Denney 1	Ball	Quinn	Lindley		
31		24 FARSLEY CELTIC	0-2	LC	112	Kelly	James	Dolby	Donaldson	Verity	Thompson	Quinn	Benn	Hayward	Maxwell	Ball	Hancock	Lindley	O'Brien	
32		27 CONGLETON TOWN	1-2	L	233	Kelly	James	O'Brien	Bagshaw	Calcutt	Thompson	Hancock	Benn	Hayward	Maxwell 1	Ball	Quinn	Lindley		
33		31 HARROGATE TOWN	4-2	L	189	Kelly	James	O'Brien	Lindley	Bagshaw	Thompson	Hancock 1	Benn	Hayward 1	Maxwell 2	Calcutt	Dolby			
34	Feb	3 Belper Town	2-0	L	216	Kelly	James	O'Brien	Lindley	Bagshaw	Thompson	Hancock	Benn	Hayward 2	Maxwell	Calcutt	Quinn			
35		13 Glasshoughton Welfare	2-0	CC	60	Kelly	James	Marquis	Bagshaw	Lacey	Quinn	Calcutt	Wharton	Thompson 2	Hayward	Donaldson	Maxwell	O'Brien		
36		17 Workington	5-2	L	323	Kelly	James	O'Brien	Bagshaw	Lindley	Thompson 1	Wharton	Benn 1	Hayward	Maxwell 2	Calcutt 1	Quinn	Marquis	Lacey	
37		24 Matlock Town	4-1	L	300	Kelly	James	O'Brien	Bagshaw	Lindley	Thompson 1	Hancock	Benn	Hayward	Maxwell 3	Calcutt	Quinn			
38	Mar	10 Stocksbridge PS	3-0	L	291	Kelly	James	O'Brien	Bagshaw	Lindley	Thompson	Hancock 1	Benn	Hayward	Maxwell 1	Quinn 1				
39		14 OSSETT TOWN	0-2	CC	177	Kelly	James	Donaldson	Quinn	Lacey	Marquis	Hancock	Benn	Hayward	Maxwell	Calcutt	O'Brien	Lindley		
40		17 FARSLEY CELTIC	3-0	L	339	Kelly	James	O'Brien	Bagshaw	Lindley	Thompson	Hancock 1	Benn	Hayward 2	Maxwell	Calcutt	Quinn	Marquis	Lacey	
41		24 OSSETT TOWN	3-2	L	286	Kelly	James 1	O'Brien	Bagshaw	Lindley	Thompson	Hancock	Benn	Hayward	Maxwell 2	Calcutt	Lacey			
42		28 BELPER TOWN	2-1	L	174	Kelly	James	O'Brien	Bagshaw	Lindley	Thompson	Hancock	Benn	Hayward 1	Lacey 1	Calcutt	Marquis	Wharton		
43		31 Lincoln United	2-2	L	213	Kelly	James	O'Brien	Bagshaw	Lindley	Thompson	Hancock	Benn	Hayward 1	Lacey	Calcutt 1	Quinn			
44	Apr	4 RADCLIFFE BOROUGH	0-1	L	197	Kelly	James	Marquis	Lacey	Lindley	Thompson	Hancock	Benn	Hayward	Maxwell	Calcutt	Quinn	Wharton		
45		7 STOCKSBRIDGE PS	1-0	L	275	Kelly	James	O'Brien	Wharton	Lacey	Thompson	Hancock	Benn	Hayward	Maxwell 1	Calcutt	Quinn			
46		14 NORTH FERRIBY U	2-1	L	338	Kelly	James	O'Brien	Wharton	Lacey 1	Thompson	Hancock	Benn	Hayward 1	Maxwell	Calcutt	Quinn	Lindley		
47		16 Farsley Celtic	3-0	L	264	Kelly	James	O'Brien 1	Lindley	Lacey	Thompson	Hancock	Benn	Hayward 2	Maxwell	Calcutt	Quinn			
48		21 Winsford United	2-1	L	215	Kelly	James	O'Brien	Bagshaw	Lacey	Thompson	Hancock	Benn	Hayward 1	Lindley	Quinn	Denney	Wharton	Marquis	1og
49		25 WITTON ALBION	4-1	L	386	Kelly	James	O'Brien	Bagshaw	Lacey	Thompson 2	Hancock	Benn	Hayward 1	Lindley 1	Quinn				
50		28 GRETNA	2-2	L	320	Kelly	James	O'Brien	Bagshaw 1	Lacey	Thompson	Hancock 1	Benn	Hayward	Lindley	Quinn	Maxwell	Calcutt	Marquis	
51	May	1 Guiseley	0-0	L	367	Kelly	James	Marquis	Bagshaw	Lacey	Wharton	Lindley	Benn	Denney	Maxwell	Quinn	Hayward	Briggs		
52		5 Radcliffe Borough	2-1	L	269	Kelly	James	Marquis	Bagshaw	Wharton	Thompson	Hancock	Benn	Hayward	Maxwell 2	Quinn	Lindley	Denney	Lacey	

2001/02

10th in the UniBond League Premier Division

			Opponent	Score		Att	1	2	3	4	5	6	7	8	9	10	11	12	13	14	
1	Aug	18	BURTON ALBION	1-4	L	648	Kelly	Bagshaw 1	James	Richards	Lacey	Thompson M	Hancock	Benn	Hayward	Maxwell	Wharton	O'Brien	Lindley	Nunn	
2		22	BURSCOUGH	0-2	L	360	Kelly	Wharton	James	Richards	Bagshaw	Thompson M	Hancock	Benn	Hayward	Maxwell	Calcutt	O'Brien	Lindley		
3		25	Worksop Town	2-3	L	361	Kelly	James 1	O'Brien	Richards	Bagshaw	Thompson M 1	Hancock	Benn	Hayward	Maxwell	Calcutt	Wharton	Lacey		
4		27	Whitby Town	1-1	L	358	Kelly	James	O'Brien	Lindley	Lacey	Richards	Hancock	Benn	Hayward 1	Maxwell	Calcutt	Wharton			
5	Sep	1	BLYTH SPARTANS	2-2	L	337	Kelly	James	O'Brien	Lindley 1	Stansfield	Richards	Hancock 1	Benn	Hayward	Maxwell	Calcutt	Wharton			
6		4	Gainsborough Trinity	1-4	L	398	Kelly	James	O'Brien 1	Lindley	Stansfield	Richards	Hancock	Benn	Hayward	Maxwell	Calcutt	Wharton			
7		8	Altincham	0-1	L	644	Pfannenstiel	James	O'Brien	Lindley	Stansfield	Richards	Hancock	Benn	Hayward	Maxwell	Wharton	Quinn	Thompson M		
8		12	BISHOP AUCKLAND	0-2	L	221	Kelly	James	O'Brien	Richards	Stansfield	Thompson M	Hancock	Benn	Hayward	Maxwell	Wharton	Lindley	Quinn		
9		15	MARINE	2-3	L	308	Kelly	James	O'Brien	Richards	Stansfield	Thompson M	Lindley	Benn	Hayward 1	Maxwell 1	Quinn				
10		18	Droylsden	2-2	L	143	Kelly	James	O'Brien	Richards	Stansfield	Thompson M	Quinn	Benn	Hayward 1	Maxwell 1	Calcutt				
11		22	Bamber Bridge	1-2	L	320	Kelly	Quinn	James	Richards	Stansfield	Thompson M	Nazha	Benn	Hayward	Maxwell 1	Calcutt	Lindley			
12		26	HARROGATE TOWN	3-1	LC	156	Kelly	James	O'Brien	Lindley	Stansfield	Thompson M 1	Hayward	Benn	Maxwell 1	Nazha 1	Calcutt	Quinn			
13		29	DROYLSDEN	3-2	FAC	297	Kelly	Quinn	O'Brien	Richards	Stansfield	Thompson M	Hayward 1	Benn	Maxwell	Nazha	Calcutt 1				1og
14	Oct	2	Hucknall Town	0-1	L	186	Taylor	Quinn	O'Brien	Richards	Stansfield	Thompson M	Hayward	Benn	Maxwell	Nazha	Calcutt				
15		6	FRICKLEY ATHLETIC	3-0	L	325	Dootson	Quinn	O'Brien	James 2	Stansfield	Thompson M	Hayward	Benn	Maxwell	Nazha 1	Calcutt				
16		9	Farsley Celtic	2-0	LC	121	Dootson	Quinn	O'Brien	Lindley	Stansfield	Thompson M	Hayward	Benn	James 1	Nazha	Calcutt 1	Hancock			
17		13	Marine	2-4	FAC	371	Kelly	Quinn	O'Brien	James	Stansfield	Thompson M	Hayward 1	Benn	Maxwell 1	Nazha	Calcutt	Hancock	Lindley		
18		17	EMLEY	2-1	L	391	Dootson	Quinn	O'Brien	Lindley	Stansfield	Thompson M	Hancock	Benn	Hayward	Nazha	Calcutt 2	James	Richards		
19		20	Lancaster City	0-4	L	437	Dootson	James	O'Brien	Lindley	Stansfield	Thompson M	Hancock	Benn	Hayward	Nazha	Calcutt	Richards	Quinn	Maxwell	
20		27	DROYLSDEN	3-1	L	253	Dootson	Bairstow 1	O'Brien	Richards	Stansfield	Thompson M 1	Hayward 1	Benn	Maxwell	Nazha	Calcutt	Lindley	Quinn		
21	Nov	3	Kendal Town	2-3	FAT	199	Dootson	Bairstow	O'Brien	Richards	Stansfield	Quinn	Hayward 1	Benn	Maxwell	Thompson 1	Nazha	Lindley			
22		7	GAINSBOROUGH TRIN.	2-0	L	220	Dootson	Bairstow	O'Brien	Richards	Stansfield	Thompson M	Hayward	Benn	Maxwell 1	Nazha 1	Calcutt	Quinn			
23		10	Colwyn Bay	2-1	L	309	Dootson	Bairstow	O'Brien 1	Richards	Stansfield	Thompson M	Hayward	Benn	Maxwell	Nazha	Calcutt 1	Hancock	Quinn		
24		17	VAUXHALL MOTORS	1-3	L	274	Dootson	Bairstow	O'Brien	Richards	Stansfield	Thompson M	Hancock	Benn	Maxwell	Nazha 1	Hayward	Quinn			
25		21	GATESHEAD	3-5	L	186	Dootson	Bairstow	Quinn	Richards	Stansfield 1	Thompson M 1	Hancock	Benn	Maxwell	Nazha	Hayward 1	Wharton	James		
26		24	Marine	2-1	L	274	Dootson	Bairstow	O'Brien	Richards	Stansfield	Thompson M	Hancock 1	Benn	Maxwell 1	Hayward	Wharton				
27	Dec	1	Guiseley	1-0	LC	225	Dootson	James	O'Brien	Richards	Stansfield	Thompson M	Quinn	Benn	Maxwell 1	Potter	Wharton				
28		8	Accrington Stanley	1-5	L	674	Dootson	Hayward	O'Brien	Richards	Stansfield	Bairstow	Hancock	Benn	Maxwell 1	Chambers	Wharton	Quinn	James	Potter	
29		11	Ossett Albion	6-3	CC	92	Pfannenstiel	James	O'Brien	Bairstow	Stansfield	Quinn	Hancock	Richards	Hayward 4	Maxwell 2	Wharton	Benn			
30		15	HYDE UNITED	3-1	L	323	Montgomery	James	O'Brien 1	Wharton	Stansfield	Thompson M	Hancock	Benn	Maxwell	Chambers	Hayward 2	Richards	Quinn	Lindley	
31		26	Burton Albion	0-3	L	2141	Montgomery	Quinn	O'Brien	Richards	Stansfield	Thompson M	Hancock	Hayward	Chambers	Maxwell	Wharton	Potter	James	Lindley	
32		29	Barrow	3-2	L	1351	Montgomery	Quinn	James	Richards	Stansfield	Thompson M 2	Hancock	Wharton	Maxwell 1	Potter	Calcutt	Benn	Lindley		
33	Jan	9	WHITBY TOWN	5-0	LC	107	Montgomery	Quinn	James	Richards	Stansfield	Wharton	Hancock	Benn	Hayward	Potter 1	Calcutt 3	Lindley	O'Brien	Maxwell 1	
34		19	RUNCORN FC HALTON	3-1	L	304	Montgomery	Hayward 1	James	Wharton	Stansfield 1	Thompson M	Hancock	Richards	Potter	Maxwell 1	Calcutt				
35		23	BAMBER BRIDGE	5-2	L	398	Montgomery	Hayward 1	James 1	Richards	Stansfield	Thompson M	Hancock 1	Benn	Potter 1	Maxwell 1	Calcutt				
36		30	BLYTH SPARTANS	7-1	LC	133	Montgomery	Hayward 4	James	Richards	Stansfield	Thompson M	Hancock	Benn	Potter 1	Maxwell 2	Calcutt	Quinn	Wharton	O'Brien	
37	Feb	2	Blyth Spartans	1-4	L	404	Montgomery	Hayward	O'Brien 1	Richards	Wharton	Thompson M	Hancock	Benn	Potter	Maxwell	Calcutt	Quinn	Bagshaw	Lindley	
38		9	Emley	0-1	L	386	Montgomery	Hayward	James	Richards	Wharton	Thompson M	Hancock	Benn	Potter	Maxwell	Calcutt	Quinn	Bagshaw	Lindley	
39		16	WORKSOP TOWN	1-5	L	438	Montgomery	Hayward 1	James	Richards	Bagshaw	Thompson M	Hancock	Benn	Potter	Maxwell	Wharton	Quinn	O'Brien		
40		23	Burscough	2-0	L	213	Montgomery	Bagshaw	James	Richards	Stansfield	Thompson M	Lindley	Benn	Potter	Maxwell 1	Hayward 1	Quinn			
41		27	Garforth Town	2-1	CC	102	Montgomery	Bagshaw	James 1	Wharton	Lindley	Thompson M	Quinn	Benn	Potter 1	Maxwell	O'Brien	Stansfield	Richards		
42	Mar	2	LANCASTER CITY	1-0	L	285	Montgomery	Bagshaw	James	Lindley	Stansfield	Thompson M	Quinn	Benn	Potter	Maxwell	Hayward 1	Hancock			
43		9	Matlock Town	2-1	LC	443	Montgomery	Quinn	James	Lindley	Stansfield	Thompson M 1	Hayward	Benn	Potter 1	Maxwell	Calcutt	Hancock			
44		12	Farsley Celtic	0-1	CC	122	Montgomery	Wharton	James	Richards	Stansfield	Thompson M	Quinn	O'Brien	Potter	Maxwell	Calcutt	Hayward	Benn	Hancock	
45		16	ACCRINGTON STANLEY	1-2	L	420	Montgomery	Quinn	James	Lindley	Stansfield	Thompson M	Hancock	Benn	Hayward 1	Maxwell	Calcutt	Richards			
46		19	Frickley Athletic	0-0	L	447	Montgomery	Quinn	James	Lindley	Stansfield	Thompson M	Hancock	Benn	Hayward	Maxwell	Calcutt	O'Brien			
47		23	Hyde United	0-2	L	389	Montgomery	Quinn	James	Lindley	Stansfield	Daly	Hancock	Benn	Hayward	Maxwell	Calcutt	O'Brien	Richards		
48		27	HUCKNALL TOWN	0-1	L	213	Montgomery	Bagshaw	James	Richards	Stansfield	Thompson M	Hancock	Quinn	Hayward	Benn	Calcutt	Daly			
49		30	Vauxhall Motors	1-2	L	206	Armstrong	James	O'Brien	Martin	Stansfield	Bagshaw	Hancock	Benn	Hayward	Quinn	Calcutt	Richards	Lindley 1	Daly	
50	Apr	1	ALTRINCHAM	4-1	L	306	Armstrong	Bagshaw	James	Martin 1	Stansfield	Thompson M	Hancock	Benn	Hayward 2	Maxwell 1	Calcutt	Quinn	Lindley		
51		3	Gateshead	7-0	L	130	Armstrong	Bagshaw	James 1	Martin 1	Stansfield	Thompson M	Hancock	Benn	Hayward 2	Maxwell	Calcutt 2	Quinn	Richards 1		
52		6	BARROW	2-0	L	413	Armstrong	Quinn	James	Martin	Stansfield	Bagshaw	Hancock 1	Benn	Hayward 1	Maxwell	Lindley				
53		10	ACCRINGTON STANLEY	1-0	LC	471	Montgomery	Quinn	James 1	Richards	Stansfield	Bagshaw	Hancock	Benn	Hayward	Maxwell	Lindley	Briggs	Wharton		
54		20	Bishop Auckland	4-0	L	452	Armstrong	Quinn	James	Martin 1	Stansfield	Daly	Hancock	Benn	Hayward 1	Maxwell 1	Calcutt 1	Richards	Lindley	Wharton	
55		23	Runcorn FC Halton	2-0	L	269	Armstrong	Quinn	James	Martin	Stansfield	Daly	Hancock	Benn	Hayward 1	Maxwell	Calcutt 1	Richards	Lindley		
56		27	COLWYN BAY	5-0	L	265	Armstrong	Quinn	James	Martin 1	Daly	Thompson M	Hancock	Benn	Hayward	Maxwell 3	Calcutt	Richards	Lindley 1	Wharton	
57		30	Accrington Stanley	0-1	LC	1107	Montgomery	Quinn	James	Richards	Lindley	Thompson M	Hancock	Benn	Hayward	Maxwell	Calcutt	Wharton	Thompson(I)		
58	May	3	WHITBY TOWN	1-1	L	361	Montgomery	Quinn	James	Martin	Daly	Lindley	Hancock	Benn	Hayward	Maxwell 1	Calcutt	Richards			

LC Final second leg April 30 lost 4-5 on penalties a.e.t.

2002/03

7th in Unibond League Premier Division

#	Month	Opponent	Score	Comp	Att	1	2	3	4	5	6	7	8	9	10	11	12	13	14	
1	Aug	17 GATESHEAD	2-0	L	323	Armstrong	Holmes	James	Martin	Stansfield	Mitchell	Quinn	Benn	Hayward 1	Maxwell	Prendergast	Painter	Lindley 1	Atkinson	
2		19 Hyde United	1-3	L	406	Armstrong	Holmes	James	Martin	Stansfield	Mitchell	Quinn	Benn	Hayward 1	Maxwell	Prendergast	Painter	Lindley		
3		24 Runcorn FC Halton	0-2	L	265	Turner	Holmes	James	Martin	Stansfield	Mitchell	Quinn	Benn	Hayward	Painter	Prendergast	Tracey	Lindley		
4		26 MARINE	2-1	L	332	Turner	Daly 1	James	Martin	Stansfield	Mitchell	Quinn	Benn	Hayward 1	Painter	Prendergast	Tracey	Lindley		
5		31 Ashton United	4-1	L	280	Turner	Daly	James	Lindley	Stansfield 1	Mitchell	Quinn	Benn	Hayward	Tracey 1	Prendergast	Painter 2			
6	Sep	4 HUCKNALL TOWN	0-3	L	341	Turner	Daly	Atkinson	Lindley	Stansfield	Mitchell	Quinn	Benn	Hayward	Tracey	Prendergast	Painter	Martin		
7		11 GAINSBOROUGH TRINITY	1-0	L	261	Turner	Daly	James	Lindley	Stansfield	Mitchell 1	Quinn	Benn	Hayward	Maxwell	Prendergast	Painter	Martin		
8		14 BARROW	2-2	L	368	Turner	Daly	James	Lindley	Stansfield	Mitchell 2	Quinn	Benn	Hayward	Maxwell	Prendergast				
9		8 Blyth Spartans	2-1	L	268	Turner	Quinn	James	Martin	Stansfield	Mitchell	Lindley	Benn	Hayward	Maxwell 1	Prendergast 1	Tracey			
10		21 Lancaster City	3-2	L	352	Turner	Quinn	James	Martin	Stansfield	Mitchell	Lindley	Benn	Hayward 2	Maxwell	Prendergast 1	Painter	Tracey		
11		25 WORKSOP TOWN	0-1	L	402	Pfannenstiel	Quinn	James	Martin	Stansfield	Mitchell	Lindley	Benn	Hayward	Maxwell	Prendergast	Painter	Daly		
12		28 Whitby Town	4-0	FAC	517	Pfannenstiel	Daly	Quinn	Martin 1	Stansfield 1	Mitchell	Lindley	Benn	Hayward	Maxwell 1	Prendergast 1	Painter	Tracey	Rouse	
13	Oct	1 Frickley Athletic	3-0	L	236	Pfannenstiel	Daly	Quinn	Martin	Stansfield	Mitchell	Lindley	Benn	Hayward 2	Tracey	Prendergast 1	Painter			
14		5 ACCRINGTON STANLEY	1-1	L	760	Pfannenstiel	Daly	Quinn	Martin	Stansfield	Mitchell	Lindley 1	Benn	Hayward	Maxwell	Prendergast	Tracey			
15		9 HYDE UNITED	5-1	L	301	Pfannenstiel	Daly	Quinn	Martin	Stansfield	Mitchell	Lindley	Benn	Hayward 1	Maxwell 2	Prendergast 2	Painter	Tracey		
16		12 BRIDLINGTON TOWN	3-5	FAC	425	Pfannenstiel	Daly	Quinn	Martin	Stansfield 1	Mitchell	Lindley	Benn	Hayward	Maxwell 2	Prendergast	Painter	Tracey	James	
17		15 Hucknall Town	2-1	L	150	Pfannenstiel	Daly	Quinn	Martin 1	Stansfield	Mitchell	Lindley	Benn	Hayward 1	Maxwell	Prendergast	Painter			
18		19 Wakefield & Emley	0-2	L	449	Pfannenstiel	Daly	Quinn	Martin	Stansfield	Mitchell	Lindley	Painter	Hayward	Maxwell	Prendergast	Tracey	James		
19		26 Gainsborough Trinity	2-2	L	404	Pfannenstiel	Daly	James	Quinn	Stansfield	Mitchell	Lindley	Benn	Hayward	Maxwell 2	Prendergast	Painter			
20		30 COLWYN BAY	4-2	L	234	Pfannenstiel	Daly	James	Quinn	Stansfield 1	Mitchell	Lindley	Benn	Hayward 1	Maxwell	Prendergast 2	Painter	Tracey		
21	Nov	2 RUNCORN FC HALTON	3-2	L	345	Pfannenstiel	Quinn	James	Walsh	Stansfield	Mitchell 1	Painter 1	Benn	Hayward	Maxwell	Prendergast 1				
22		9 DROYLSDEN	3-1	L	314	Pfannenstiel	Quinn	James	Walsh 1	Stansfield	Mitchell	Painter 1	Benn	Hayward	Maxwell	Prendergast	Lindley	Tracey	Atkinson	1og
23		12 Altrincham	0-0	L	495	Pfannenstiel	Daly	James	Walsh	Stansfield	Mitchell	Painter	Benn	Hayward	Maxwell	Prendergast	Tracey			
24		20 SPENNYMOOR UNITED	2-2	LC	165	Pfannenstiel	Reece	James	Walsh	Daly	Mitchell	Lindley	Benn	Tracey 1	Maxwell	Atkinson	Hayward 1	Stansfield		
25		23 WHITBY TOWN	2-3	L	340	Pfannenstiel	Tracey	James	Walsh	Stansfield	Mitchell	Lindley	Benn	Hayward 1	Maxwell	Prendergast 1	Painter			
26		30 ALTRINCHAM	0-1	FAT	437	Pfannenstiel	Tracey	James	Walsh	Stansfield	Mitchell	Painter	Benn	Hayward	Maxwell	Prendergast				
27	Dec	3 Worksop Town	1-7	L	571	Pfannenstiel	Tracey	James	Walsh	Stansfield	Mitchell	Painter	Benn	Hayward	Maxwell	Prendergast	Lindley	Richards	Daly	1og
28		7 LANCASTER CITY	0-1	L	257	Holmshaw	Daly	James	Walsh	Stansfield	Mitchell	Lindley	Benn	Hayward	Maxwell	Tracey	Painter	Bingham		
29		10 Yorkshire Amateur	4-1	CC	56	Holmshaw	Reece	Tracey	Richards	Daly	Mitchell 1	Lindley	Benn	Painter 1	Bingham 1	Prendergast 1	Hayward	Walsh		
30		14 Accrington Stanley	1-3	L	873	Pfannenstiel	Daly 1	Tracey	Walsh	Stansfield	Mitchell	Lindley	Benn	Hayward	Maxwell	Prendergast	Bingham			
31		28 Stalybridge Celtic	2-2	L	847	Holmshaw	Tracey	Atkinson	Collins	Stansfield	Mitchell	Walsh	Benn	Hayward	Painter 1	Wright				1og
32	Jan	22 OSSETT TOWN	4-5	LC	134	Pfannenstiel	Tracey	Atkinson	Walsh	Stansfield	Mitchell 1	Quinn	Benn	Bingham	Painter	Lindley 2	Dunne	Smith	Vickerage 1	aet
33		29 HARROGATE TOWN	1-0	L	437	Holmshaw	Tracey	Quinn	Collins	Stansfield	Mitchell 1	Walsh	Benn	Hayward	Painter	Wright	Lindley	Bingham		
34	Feb	1 Gateshead	1-1	L	266	Holmshaw	Tracey	Quinn	Collins	Stansfield	Mitchell	Walsh	Benn	Hayward 1	Painter	Wright	Lindley	Bingham		
35		8 ASHTON UNITED	1-1	L	271	Holmshaw	Tracey	Quinn	Collins	Stansfield	Mitchell	Walsh	Benn	Hayward	Painter	Wright 1	Maxwell	Atkinson		
36		12 ECCLESHILL UNITED	1-0	CC	130	Holmshaw	Quinn	Atkinson	Collins 1	Stansfield	Mitchell	Walsh	Benn	Hayward	Tracey	Wright	Maxwell	Painter		
37		15 Marine	2-4	L	288	Holmshaw	Quinn	Atkinson	Collins	Stansfield	Mitchell 1	Walsh	Benn	Hayward 1	Maxwell	Tracey	Painter	Wright		
38		22 VAUXHALL MOTORS	1-0	L	253	Holmshaw	Quinn	Wright 1	Collins	Tracey	Mitchell	Walsh	Benn	Hayward	Maxwell	Painter				
39		25 Burscough	1-0	L	145	Holmshaw	Quinn	Atkinson	Collins 1	Donaldson	Mitchell	Walsh	Benn	Hayward	Tracey	Wright	Thompson			
40	Mar	11 Harrogate Town	0-2	CC	312	Storer	Tracey	Quinn	Collins	Painter	Mitchell	Walsh	Benn	Hayward	Maxwell	Wright	Atkinson	Elliott		
41		19 BLYTH SPARTANS	5-1	L	188	Howe	Quinn	Donaldson	Collins 2	Stansfield	Mitchell	Walsh	Benn	Hayward	Maxwell 1	Tracey	Painter	Wright		2ogs
42		22 Vauxhall Motors	1-0	L	251	Howe	Quinn	Donaldson	Collins	Stansfield	Mitchell	Walsh	Benn	Hayward	Maxwell	Tracey 1	Wright			
43		24 FRICKLEY ATHLETIC	2-2	L	294	Howe	Quinn	Painter	Collins 1	Stansfield	Mitchell	Walsh	Benn	Hayward 1	Maxwell	Wright	Elliott			
44		27 Droylsden	0-2	L	176	Howe	Quinn	Atkinson	Painter	Stansfield	Mitchell	Walsh	Benn	Hayward	Maxwell	Wright	Elliott			
45		29 ALTRINCHAM	1-1	L	440	Storer	Quinn	Atkinson	Collins	Stansfield 1	Mitchell	Walsh	Painter	Hayward	Maxwell	Wright	Elliott			
46	Apr	5 Barrow	2-3	L	1022	Howe	Quinn	Atkinson	Collins 1	Stansfield	Mitchell	Walsh 1	Donaldson	Hayward	Maxwell	Wright	Painter	Elliott		
47		9 WAKEFIELD & EMLEY	1-1	L	288	Howe	Quinn	Atkinson	Collins	Stansfield	Mitchell	Walsh 1	Tracey	Hayward	Maxwell	Wright	Painter	Elliott		
48		15 Colwyn Bay	0-2	L	118	Howe	Quinn	Atkinson	Collins	Stansfield	Mitchell	Walsh	Tracey	Hayward	Maxwell	Wright	Painter	Elliott	Holmshaw	
49		19 STALYBRIDGE CELTIC	2-1	L	329	Holmshaw	Tracey	Quinn	Collins 1	Stansfield	Mitchell	Walsh	Donaldson	Hayward 1	Maxwell	Painter	Thompson			
50	Mar	21 Harrogate Town	2-5	L	607	Thompson	Tracey	Quinn	Collins	Stansfield 1	Mitchell	Walsh	Donaldson	Hayward	Maxwell 1	Painter				
51		23 BURSCOUGH	3-2	L	168	Storer	Tracey	Quinn	Collins	Stansfield	Mitchell	Walsh	Donaldson	Hayward 1	Maxwell 1	Painter 1				
52		26 Whitby Town	1-0	L	332	Storer	Quinn	Tracey	Collins	Stansfield	Mitchell	Walsh	Donaldson	Hayward 1	Maxwell	Painter				

Nov 20: won 5-4 on penalties a.e.t.

2003/04

17th in UniBond League Premier Division

#	Month	Date / Opponent	Score	Comp	Att	1	2	3	4	5	6	7	8	9	10	11	12	13	14	
1	Aug	16 HUCKNALL TOWN	1-2	L	297	Boswell	Smith C	Crossley	Donaldson	Stansfield	Wood	Quinn	Walsh D	Vickerage	Tracey 1	Wright	Benn	Serrant	Walsh S	
2		19 Ashton United	2-0	L	210	Boswell	Quinn	Serrant	Collins 1	Stansfield	Crossley	Walsh D 1	Benn	Maxwell	Oleksewycz	Wright	Donaldson	Smith C		
3		23 Runcon FC Halton	2-1	L	271	Boswell	Quinn	Serrant	Collins 2	Stansfield	Smith C	Walsh D	Benn	Hayward	Maxwell	Wright	Oleksewycz			
4		25 RADCLIFFE BOROUGH	1-1	L	347	Boswell	Quinn	Serrant	Collins	Stansfield	Smith C	Walsh D	Benn	Hayward 1	Maxwell	Oleksewycz	Tracey			
5		30 Vauxhall Motors	2-6	L	204	Boswell	Mitchell	Quinn	Collins	Stansfield	Smith C	Walsh D 1	Benn	Hayward 1	Maxwell	Oleksewycz	Wright	Tracey		
6	Sep	3 WORKSOP TOWN	0-1	L	367	Boswell	Mitchell	Serrant	Smith C	Wood	Quinn	Walsh D	Benn	Tracey	Maxwell	Wright	Oleksewycz			
7		6 BARROW	2-2	L	315	Boswell	Mitchell	Serrant	Collins	Stansfield	Wood	Walsh D	Quinn	Hayward 1	Maxwell 1	Wright	Tracey	Smith C	Oleksewycz	
8		9 Spennymoor United	4-2	L	263	Boswell	Quinn	Serrant	Collins 1	Stansfield	Mitchell	Walsh D	Smith C	Hayward 1	Oleksewycz 2	Tracey				
9		13 Alfreton Town	1-1	L	517	Boswell	Quinn	Serrant	Collins	Stansfield	Mitchell	Walsh D 1	Smith C	Hayward	Oleksewycz	Tracey	Wright	Donaldson	Benn	
10		17 WHITBY TOWN	2-3	L	295	Boswell	Quinn	Serrant	Smith C 1	Stansfield	Mitchell	Tracey	Benn	Hayward	Oleksewycz 1	Wright	Donaldson	Crossley	Storer	
11		20 STALYBRIDGE CELTIC	2-3	L	283	Boswell	Mitchell	Crossley	Wood	Stansfield	Smith C	Quinn	Benn	Hayward	Oleksewycz 2	Serrant				
12		23 Blyth Spartans	0-0	L	356	Boswell	Quinn	Serrant	Collins	Stansfield	Wood	Walsh D	Benn	Maxwell	Oleksewycz	Smith C				
13		27 Chester-le-Street Town	2-0	FAC	201	Boswell	Quinn	Serrant	Collins 1	Stansfield	Crossley	Smith C	Benn	Maxwell	Oleksewycz 1	Wright	Mitchell	Walsh D		
14	Oct	4 SOUTHPORT	0-1	L	393	Boswell	Quinn	Serrant	Collins	Stansfield	Crossley	Smith C	Benn	Maxwell	Oleksewycz	Wright	Mitchell			
15		11 VAUXHALL MTRS	1-1	FAC	321	Boswell	Quinn	Serrant	Wood	Stansfield 1	Crossley	Smith C	Benn	Hayward	Maxwell	Oleksewycz				
16		14 Vauxhall Motors	3-1	FAC	278	Boswell	Quinn	Mitchell	Wood	Stansfield	Smith C 1	Oleksewycz 1	Benn	Maxwell	Painter 1	Wright				
17		25 Runcorn FC Halton	1-0	FAC	379	Boswell	Quinn	Mitchell	Wood	Stansfield	Smith C	Oleksewycz	Benn	Hayward 1	Maxwell	Wright	Crossley	Walsh D		
18		28 Burscough	1-1	L	154	Alderson	Quinn	Serrant	Wood	Stansfield	Mitchell 1	Smith C	Benn	Hayward	Painter	Walsh D	Oleksewycz	Tracey		
19	Nov	1 VAUXHALL MTRS	6-2	L	360	Boswell	Quinn	Crossley 1	Collins 1	Stansfield	Mitchell	Oleksewycz 1	Benn	Hayward 2	Maxwell	Wood	Wright	Smith C	Walsh D 1	
20		9 BRISTOL CITY	2-5	FAC	2045	Boswell	Serrant	Crossley	Collins	Stansfield	Mitchell	Oleksewycz	Benn	Hayward 1	Maxwell	Wood	Smith C	Walsh D	Wright	1og
21		12 RUNCORN FC HALTON	1-1	L	266	Boswell	Quinn	Serrant	Collins	Stansfield	Mitchell	Walsh D	Benn	Oleksewycz 1	Maxwell	Smith C	Tracey			
22		15 Marine	0-2	L	328	Boswell	Quinn	Serrant	Smith G	Mitchell	Crossley	Walsh D	Benn	Tracey	Maxwell	Smith C	Hayward	Stansfield		
23		19 BISHOP AUCKLAND	1-6	LC	102	Boswell	Mitchell 1	Quinn	Walsh D	Stansfield	Russell	Tracey	Wright	Oleksewycz	Maxwell	Wood	Pickles	Alderson		
24		22 ALTRINCHAM	1-1	L	320	Boswell	Smith G	Serrant	Quinn	Stansfield	Crossley	Walsh D	Benn	Hayward	Maxwell 1	Oleksewycz	Wright			
25		29 Whitby Town	1-1	FAT	251	Boswell	Quinn	Serrant	Smith C	Stansfield	Crossley	Walsh D	Benn	Hayward 1	Maxwell	Oleksewycz	Collins			
26	Dec	3 WHITBY TOWN	1-0	FAT	229	Alderson	Quinn	Serrant	Collins 1	Stansfield	Smith C	Walsh D	Benn	Hayward	Maxwell	Oleksewycz				
27		6 Wakefield & Emley	1-0	L	319	Alderson	Quinn	Serrant	Collins	Smith G	Crossley	Walsh D	Benn	Hayward 1	Maxwell	Smith C				
28		9 Liversedge	5-1	CC	106	Alderson	Quinn	Serrant	Walsh D	Stansfield	Smith G 1	Smith C	Benn	Oleksewycz 3	Maxwell	Wright 1	Collins	Russell	Helliwell	
29		13 Southport	1-0	L	746	Boswell	Smith G	Serrant	Collins	Stansfield	Crossley	Walsh D	Benn	Hayward	Maxwell	Quinn	Oleksewycz	Smith C 1		
30		20 Barrow	1-3	PC	525	Boswell	Quinn	Heinemann	Smith C	Stansfield	Crossley	Walsh D	Oleksewycz 1	Hayward	Russell	Serrant	Pickles	Helliwell		
31		26 HARROGATE TOWN	2-3	L	530	Boswell	Smith G 1	Serrant	Collins	Stansfield	Crossley	Quinn	Benn	Hayward	Maxwell	Oleksewycz 1	Smith C	Heinemann		
32	Jan	3 Radcliffe Borough	0-2	L	319	Boswell	Smith G	Heinemann	Quinn	Stansfield	Crossley	Serrant	Benn	Hayward	Oleksewycz	Wright	Smith C			
33		10 Hucknall Town	0-1	FAT	573	Boswell	Quinn	Serrant	Walsh D	Stansfield	Crossley	Hayward	Benn	Oleksewycz	Maxwell	Wright	Heinemann			
34		24 Stalybridge Celtic	0-2	L	439	Boswell	Quinn	Heinemann	Walsh D	Stansfield	Crossley	Serrant	Grayston	Hayward	Maxwell	Wright	Oleksewycz			
35	Feb	7 Barrow	0-4	L	1043	Boswell	Jones	Serrant	Quinn	Stansfield	Crossley	Walsh D	Grayston	Hayward	Maxwell	Wright	Oleksewycz	Bullimore		
36		10 Lancaster City	3-1	L	265	Boswell	Quinn	Serrant	Jones	Stansfield	Bullimore	Walsh D	Grayston	Hayward 2	Maxwell 1	Oleksewycz				
37		14 BURSCOUGH	0-2	L	281	Boswell	Quinn	Wright	Jones	Crossley	Bullimore	Walsh D	Grayston	Hayward	Maxwell	Oleksewycz	Smith C			
38		18 HALIFAX TOWN	1-3	CC	382	Alderson	Quinn	Wright	Walsh D	Naylor	Serrant	Helliwell	Grayston	Hayward	Maxwell	Smith C 1	Walsh S			
39		21 FRICKLEY ATH.	0-0	L	288	Boswell	Quinn	Wright	Bullimore	Jones	Crossley	Walsh D	Grayston	Hayward	Maxwell	Serrant	Smith C			
40		23 Droylsden	0-3	L	188	Boswell	Quinn	Serrant	Jones	Walsh S	Crossley	Smith C	Grayston	Hayward	Maxwell	Wright	Alderson			
41		28 Gainsborough Trinity	3-3	L	495	Alderson	Quinn	Serrant	Jones	Smith C	Crossley	Walsh D	Painter	Hayward 1	Maxwell 1	Grayston				1og
42	Mar	3 DROYLSDEN	0-2	L	223	Alderson	Quinn	Serrant	Jones	Walsh D	Crossley	Smith C	Painter	Hayward	Maxwell	Grayston	Helliwell			
43		6 BLYTH SPARTANS	1-1	L	275	Britton	Quinn	Serrant	Jones	Walsh D	Crossley	Smith C	Painter	Maxwell	Hayward 1	Grayston	Helliwell			
44		10 Whitby Town	1-0	L	197	Britton	Quinn	Serrant 1	Grayston	Jones	Crossley	Helliwell	Walsh D	Smith C	Maxwell	Russell	Pickles			
45		13 Altrincham	0-1	L	622	Britton	Quinn	Grayston	Walsh D	Crossley	Serrant	Helliwell	Smith C	Painter	Maxwell	Russell	Greaves	Naylor	Pickles	
46		17 ALFRETON TOWN	0-1	L	240	Britton	Quinn	Serrant	Naylor	Crossley	Walsh D	Helliwell	Smith C	Oleksewycz	Maxwell	Russell				
47		23 Worksop Town	2-1	L	425	Britton	Quinn	Serrant	Jones	Crossley	Walsh D	Helliwell	Smith C 1	Oleksewycz	Maxwell 1	Grayston	Naylor	Greaves	Russell	
48		31 ASHTON UNITED	2-1	L	314	Britton	Quinn	Serrant	Walsh D	Naylor	Crossley	Helliwell	Smith C 1	Oleksewycz 1	Maxwell	Grayston	Painter	Russell		
49	Apr	3 WAKEFIELD & EMLEY	1-2	L	326	Britton	Quinn	Serrant	Walsh D	Naylor	Heinemann	Helliwell	Smith C 1	Oleksewycz	Maxwell	Grayston	Painter			
50		6 Frickley Athletic	1-0	L	287	Britton	Quinn	Serrant	Walsh D	Naylor	Crossley	Helliwell	Smith C	Oleksewycz 1	Maxwell	Heinemann	Painter	Russell		
51		10 SPENNYMOOR U	0-0	L	256	Britton	Quinn	Serrant	Walsh D	Naylor	Crossley	Helliwell	Smith C	Oleksewycz	Maxwell	Heinemann	Russell			
52		12 Harrogate Town	1-0	L	662	Britton	Quinn	Serrant	Walsh D	Naylor	Crossley	Russell	Smith C	Oleksewycz 1	Painter	Heinemann	Maxwell	Grayston	Greaves	
53		17 Hucknall Town	0-0	L	510	Britton	Quinn	Serrant	Walsh D	Naylor	Grayston	Russell	Smith C	Oleksewycz	Painter	Heinemann	Greaves			
54		19 MARINE	1-1	L	226	Britton	Quinn	Heinemann	Walsh D	Naylor	Crossley	Helliwell	Smith C	Oleksewycz 1	Painter	Russell	Greaves			
55		21 GAINSBOROUGH TRIN.	0-0	L	247	Britton	Quinn	Serrant	Walsh D	Naylor	Crossley	Helliwell	Smith C	Oleksewycz	Painter	Heinemann	Greaves	Pickles		
56		24 LANCASTER CITY	0-2	L	306	Britton	Brompton	Serrant	Walsh D	Jones	Crossley	Greaves	Smith C	Oleksewycz	Pickles	Grayston	Heinemann	Quinn		
57		28 SPENNYMOOR U	3-1	PO	303	Britton	Quinn	Serrant	Walsh D	Jones	Crossley	Helliwell	Smith C	Oleksewycz	Painter 1	Heinemann 2	Maxwell	Russell		
58	May	1 Ashton United	2-1	PO	354	Britton	Quinn	Serrant	Walsh D	Jones	Crossley 1	Helliwell 1	Smith C	Maxwell	Painter	Heinemann	Oleksewycz	Russell		
59		3 BURSCOUGH	2-0	PO	870	Britton	Quinn	Serrant	Walsh D	Jones	Crossley	Helliwell	Smith C	Maxwell	Painter	Heinemann	Oleksewycz 1	Grayston	Russell 1	aet

Back; Kenny Wright, Adrian Hall, Paul Sutcliffe, Eddie Hill, Dean Benn, Gary Land, John Margison. Front; Darren Waters, Andy McGregor, Mick Hall (player/manager), Simon Tavernier (capt.), Paul Armitage, Neil Wigglesworth.

2004/05 season. Back; Dave Helliwell (kit), Marc Thompson, Dean Jones (capt.), Gareth Clayton, Karl Colley, Andy Britton, Michael Naylor, Adam Oldham, Paul Helliwell, Allan Pearce, Ian Roscow (ass. mgr). Front; Andy Quinn, Ryan Crossley, Steve Oleksewycz, Dan Sherriffe, Carl Shutt (manager), Danny Walsh, Craig Smith, Ben Jones.